DRAMA
for Students

Advisors

Susan Allison: Head Librarian, Lewiston High School, Lewiston, Maine. Standards Committee Chairperson for Maine School Library (MASL) Programs. Board member, Julia Adams Morse Memorial Library, Greene, Maine. Advisor to Lewiston Public Library Planning Process.

Jennifer Hood: Young Adult/Reference Librarian, Cumberland Public Library, Cumberland, Rhode Island. Certified teacher, Rhode Island. Member of the New England Library Association, Rhode Island Library Association, and the Rhode Island Educational Media Association.

Ann Kearney: Head Librarian and Media Specialist, Christopher Columbus High School, Miami, Florida, 1982–2002. Thirty-two years as Librarian in various educational institutions ranging from grade schools through graduate programs. Library positions at Miami-Dade Community College, the University of Miami's Medical School Library, and Carrollton School in Coconut Grove, Florida. B.A. from University of Detroit, 1967 (magna cum laude); M.L.S., University of Missouri–Columbia, 1974. Volunteer Project Leader for a school in rural Jamaica; volunteer with Adult Literacy programs.

Laurie St. Laurent: Head of Adult and Children's Services, East Lansing Public Library, East Lansing, Michigan, 1994–. M.L.S. from Western Michigan University. Chair of Michigan Library Association's 1998 Michigan Summer Reading Program; Chair of the Children's Services Division in 2000–2001; and Vice-President of the Association in 2002–2003. Board member of several regional early childhood literacy organizations and member of the Library of Michigan Youth Services Advisory Committee.

Heidi Stohs: Instructor in Language Arts, grades 10–12, Solomon High School, Solomon, Kansas. Received B.S. from Kansas State University; M.A. from Fort Hays State University.

DRAMA
for Students

Presenting Analysis, Context, and Criticism on
Commonly Studied Dramas

VOLUME 25

GALE
CENGAGE Learning™

Detroit • New York • San Francisco • New Haven, Conn • Waterville, Maine • London

Drama for Students, Volume 25

Project Editor: Ira Mark Milne

Rights Acquisition and Management: Beth Beaufore, Jocelyne Green, Jacqueline Key, Kelly Quin, Sue Rudolph

Composition: Evi Abou-El-Seoud

Manufacturing: Drew Kalasky

Imaging: Lezlie Light

Product Design: Pamela A. E. Galbreath, Jennifer Wahi

Content Conversion: Civie Green, Katrina Coach

Product Manager: Meggin Condino

For product information and technology assistance, contact us at
Gale Customer Support, 1-800-877-4253.
For permission to use material from this text or product,
submit all requests online at **www.cengage.com/permissions.**
Further permissions questions can be emailed to
permissionrequest@cengage.com

While every effort has been made to ensure the reliability of the information presented in this publication, Gale, a part of Cengage Learning, does not guarantee the accuracy of the data contained herein. Gale accepts no payment for listing; and inclusion in the publication of any organization, agency, institution, publication, service, or individual does not imply endorsement of the editors or publisher. Errors brought to the attention of the publisher and verified to the satisfaction of the publisher will be corrected in future editions.

Gale
27500 Drake Rd.
Farmington Hills, MI, 48331-3535

978-0-7876-8121-0
0-7876-8121-0

ISSN 1094-9232

This title is also available as an e-book.
ISBN-13: 978-1-4144-3802-3
ISBN-10: 1-4144-3802-8
Contact your Gale, a part of Cengage Learning sales representative for ordering information.

Table of Contents

The Study of Drama

We study drama in order to learn what meaning others have made of life, to comprehend what it takes to produce a work of art, and to glean some understanding of ourselves. Drama produces in a separate, aesthetic world, a moment of being for the audience to experience, while maintaining the detachment of a reflective observer.

Drama is a representational art, a visible and audible narrative presenting virtual, fictional characters within a virtual, fictional universe. Dramatic realizations may pretend to approximate reality or else stubbornly defy, distort, and deform reality into an artistic statement. From this separate universe that is obviously not "real life" we expect a valid reflection upon reality, yet drama never is mistaken for reality—the methods of theater are integral to its form and meaning. Theater is art, and art's appeal lies in its ability both to approximate life and to depart from it. For in intruding its distorted version of life into our consciousness, art gives us a new perspective and appreciation of life and reality. Although all aesthetic experiences perform this service, theater does it most effectively by creating a separate, cohesive universe that freely acknowledges its status as an art form.

And what is the purpose of the aesthetic universe of drama? The potential answers to such a question are nearly as many and varied as there are plays written, performed, and enjoyed. Dramatic texts can be problems posed, answers asserted, or moments portrayed. Dramas (tragedies as well as comedies) may serve strictly "to ease the anguish of a torturing hour" (as stated in William Shakespeare's *A Midsummer Night's Dream*)—to divert and entertain–or aspire to move the viewer to action with social issues. Whether to entertain or to instruct, affirm or influence, pacify or shock, dramatic art wraps us in the spell of its imaginary world for the length of the work and then dispenses us back to the real world, entertained, purged, as Aristotle said, of pity and fear, and edified—or at least weary enough to sleep peacefully.

It is commonly thought that theater, being an art of performance, must be experienced—seen—in order to be appreciated fully. However, to view a production of a dramatic text is to be limited to a single interpretation of that text—all other interpretations are for the moment closed off, inaccessible. In the process of producing a play, the director, stage designer, and performers interpret and transform the script into a work of art that always departs in some measure from the author's original conception. Novelist and critic Umberto Eco, in his *The Role of the Reader: Explorations in the Semiotics of Texts* (Indiana University Press, 1979), explained, "In short, we can say that every performance offers us a complete and satisfying version of the work, but at the same time makes it incomplete for us, because it cannot simultaneously give all the other artistic solutions which the work may admit."

Thus Laurence Olivier's coldly formal and neurotic film presentation of Shakespeare's *Hamlet* (in which he played the title character as well as directed) shows marked differences from subsequent adaptations. While Olivier's Hamlet is clearly entangled in a Freudian relationship with his mother Gertrude, he would be incapable of shushing her with the impassioned kiss that Mel Gibson's mercurial Hamlet (in director Franco Zeffirelli's 1990 film) does. Although each of performances rings true to Shakespeare's text, each is also a mutually exclusive work of art. Also important to consider are the time periods in which each of these films was produced: Olivier made his film in 1948, a time in which overt references to sexuality (especially incest) were frowned upon. Gibson and Zeffirelli made their film in a culture more relaxed and comfortable with these issues. Just as actors and directors can influence the presentation of drama, so too can the time period of the production affect what the audience will see.

A play script is an open text from which an infinity of specific realizations may be derived. Dramatic scripts that are more open to interpretive creativity (such as those of Ntozake Shange and Tomson Highway) actually require the creative improvisation of the production troupe in order to complete the text. Even the most prescriptive scripts (those of Neil Simon, Lillian Hellman, and Robert Bolt, for example), can never fully control the actualization of live performance, and circumstantial events, including the attitude and receptivity of the audience, make every performance a unique event. Thus, while it is important to view a production of a dramatic piece, if one wants to understand a drama fully it is equally important to read the original dramatic text.

The reader of a dramatic text or script is not limited by either the specific interpretation of a given production or by the unstoppable action of a moving spectacle. The reader of a dramatic text may discover the nuances of the play's language, structure, and events at their own pace. Yet studied alone, the author's blueprint for artistic production does not tell the whole story of a play's life and significance. One also needs to assess the play's critical reviews to discover how it resonated to cultural themes at the time of its debut and how the shifting tides of cultural interest have revised its interpretation and impact on audiences. And to do this, one needs to know a little about the culture of the times which produced the play as well as the author who penned it.

Drama for Students supplies this material in a useful compendium for the student of dramatic theater. Covering a range of dramatic works that span from 442 BC to the 1990s, this book focuses on significant theatrical works whose themes and form transcend the uncertainty of dramatic fads. These are plays that have proven to be both memorable and teachable. *Drama for Students* seeks to enhance appreciation of these dramatic texts by providing scholarly materials written with the secondary and college/university student in mind. It provides for each play a concise summary of the plot and characters as well as a detailed explanation of its themes. In addition, background material on the historical context of the play, its critical reception, and the author's life help the student to understand the work's position in the chronicle of dramatic history. For each play entry a new work of scholarly criticism is also included, as well as segments of other significant critical works for handy reference. A thorough bibliography provides a starting point for further research.

This series offers comprehensive educational resources for students of drama. *Drama for Students* is a vital book for dramatic interpretation and a valuable addition to any reference library.

Sources
Eco, Umberto, *The Role of the Reader: Explorations in the Semiotics of Texts*, Indiana University Press, 1979.

Carole L. Hamilton
Author and Instructor of English at Cary
Academy, Cary, North Carolina

Introduction

Purpose of the Book

The purpose of *Drama for Students* (*DfS*) is to provide readers with a guide to understanding, enjoying, and studying dramas by giving them easy access to information about the work. Part of Gale's "For Students" literature line, *DfS* is specifically designed to meet the curricular needs of high school and undergraduate college students and their teachers, as well as the interests of general readers and researchers considering specific plays. While each volume contains entries on "classic" dramas frequently studied in classrooms, there are also entries containing hard-to-find information on contemporary plays, including works by multicultural, international, and women playwrights.

The information covered in each entry includes an introduction to the play and the work's author; a plot summary, to help readers unravel and understand the events in a drama; descriptions of important characters, including explanation of a given character's role in the drama as well as discussion about that character's relationship to other characters in the play; analysis of important themes in the drama; and an explanation of important literary techniques and movements as they are demonstrated in the play.

In addition to this material, which helps the readers analyze the play itself, students are also provided with important information on the literary and historical background informing each work. This includes a historical context essay, a box comparing the time or place the drama was written to modern Western culture, a critical essay, and excerpts from critical essays on the play. A unique feature of *DfS* is a specially commissioned critical essay on each drama, targeted toward the student reader.

To further aid the student in studying and enjoying each play, information on media adaptations is provided (if available), as well as reading suggestions for works of fiction and nonfiction on similar themes and topics. Classroom aids include ideas for research papers and lists of critical sources that provide additional material on each drama.

Selection Criteria

The titles for each volume of *DfS* were selected by surveying numerous sources on teaching literature and analyzing course curricula for various school districts. Some of the sources surveyed included: literature anthologies; *Reading Lists for College-Bound Students: The Books Most Recommended by America's Top Colleges*; textbooks on teaching dramas; a College Board survey of plays commonly studied in high schools; a National Council of Teachers of English (NCTE) survey of plays commonly studied in high schools; St. James Press's *International Dictionary of Theatre*; and Arthur Applebee's 1993 study *Literature in the Secondary School: Studies of Curriculum and Instruction in the United States.*

Input was also solicited from our advisory board, as well as from educators from various areas. From these discussions, it was determined that each volume should have a mix of "classic" dramas (those works commonly taught in literature classes) and contemporary dramas for which information is often hard to find. Because of the interest in expanding the canon of literature, an emphasis was also placed on including works by international, multicultural, and women playwrights. Our advisory board members—educational professionals— helped pare down the list for each volume. If a work was not selected for the present volume, it was often noted as a possibility for a future volume. As always, the editor welcomes suggestions for titles to be included in future volumes.

How Each Entry Is Organized

Each entry, or chapter, in *DfS* focuses on one play. Each entry heading lists the full name of the play, the author's name, and the date of the play's publication. The following elements are contained in each entry:

Introduction: a brief overview of the drama which provides information about its first appearance, its literary standing, any controversies surrounding the work, and major conflicts or themes within the work.

Author Biography: this section includes basic facts about the author's life, and focuses on events and times in the author's life that inspired the drama in question.

Plot Summary: a description of the major events in the play. Subheads demarcate the play's various acts or scenes.

Characters: an alphabetical listing of major characters in the play. Each character name is followed by a brief to an extensive description of the character's role in the play, as well as discussion of the character's actions, relationships, and possible motivation.

> Characters are listed alphabetically by last name. If a character is unnamed—for instance, the Stage Manager in *Our Town*—the character is listed as "The Stage Manager" and alphabetized as "Stage Manager." If a character's first name is the only one given, the name will appear alphabetically by the name. Variant names are also included for each character. Thus, the nickname "Babe" would head the listing for a character in *Crimes of the Heart*, but below that listing would be her less-mentioned married name "Rebecca Botrelle."

Themes: a thorough overview of how the major topics, themes, and issues are addressed within the play. Each theme discussed appears in a separate subhead, and is easily accessed through the boldface entries in the Subject/ Theme Index.

Style: this section addresses important style elements of the drama, such as setting, point of view, and narration; important literary devices used, such as imagery, foreshadowing, symbolism; and, if applicable, genres to which the work might have belonged, such as Gothicism or Romanticism. Literary terms are explained within the entry, but can also be found in the Glossary.

Historical Context: this section outlines the social, political, and cultural climate *in which the author lived and the play was created.* This section may include descriptions of related historical events, pertinent aspects of daily life in the culture, and the artistic and literary sensibilities of the time in which the work was written. If the play is a historical work, information regarding the time in which the play is set is also included. Each section is broken down with helpful subheads.

Critical Overview: this section provides background on the critical reputation of the play, including bannings or any other public controversies surrounding the work. For older plays, this section includes a history of how the drama was first received and how perceptions of it may have changed over the years; for more recent plays, direct quotes from early reviews may also be included.

Criticism: an essay commissioned by *DfS* which specifically deals with the play and is written specifically for the student audience, as well as excerpts from previously published criticism on the work (if available).

Sources: an alphabetical list of critical material used in compiling the entry, with full bibliographical information.

Further Reading: an alphabetical list of other critical sources which may prove useful for the student. It includes full bibliographical information and a brief annotation.

In addition, each entry contains the following highlighted sections, set apart from the main text as sidebars:

Media Adaptations: if available, a list of important film and television adaptations of the play, including source information. The list may also include such variations on the work as audio recordings, musical adaptations, and other stage interpretations.

Topics for Further Study: a list of potential study questions or research topics dealing with the play. This section includes questions related to other disciplines the student may be studying, such as American history, world history, science, math, government, business, geography, economics, psychology, etc.

Compare and Contrast: an "at-a-glance" comparison of the cultural and historical differences between the author's time and culture and late twentieth century or early twenty-first century Western culture. This box includes pertinent parallels between the major scientific, political, and cultural movements of the time or place the drama was written, the time or place the play was set (if a historical work), and modern Western culture. Works written after 1990 may not have this box.

What Do I Read Next?: a list of works that might complement the featured play or serve as a contrast to it. This includes works by the same author and others, works of fiction and nonfiction, and works from various genres, cultures, and eras.

Other Features

DfS includes "The Study of Drama," a foreword by Carole Hamilton, an educator and author who specializes in dramatic works. This essay examines the basis for drama in societies and what drives people to study such work. The essay also discusses how *Drama for Students* can help teachers show students how to enrich their own reading/viewing experiences.

A Cumulative Author/Title Index lists the authors and titles covered in each volume of the *DfS* series.

A Cumulative Nationality/Ethnicity Index breaks down the authors and titles covered in each volume of the *DfS* series by nationality and ethnicity.

A Subject/Theme Index, specific to each volume, provides easy reference for users who may be studying a particular subject or theme rather than a single work. Significant subjects from events to broad themes are included, and the entries pointing to the specific theme discussions in each entry are indicated in **boldface**.

Each entry may include illustrations, including photo of the author, stills from stage productions, and stills from film adaptations, if available.

Citing Drama for Students

When writing papers, students who quote directly from any volume of *Drama for Students* may use the following general forms. These examples are based on MLA style; teachers may request that students adhere to a different style, so the following examples may be adapted as needed.

When citing text from *DfS* that is not attributed to a particular author (i.e., the Themes, Style, Historical Context sections, etc.), the following format should be used in the bibliography section:

"*Our Town.*" *Drama for Students.* Eds. David Galens and Lynn Spampinato. Vol. 1. Detroit: Gale, 1998. 227–30.

When quoting the specially commissioned essay from *DfS* (usually the first piece under the "Criticism" subhead), the following format should be used:

Fiero, John. Critical Essay on *Twilight: Los Angeles, 1992.* *Drama for Students.* Eds. David Galens and Lynn Spampinato. Vol. 2. Detroit: Gale, 1998. 247–49.

When quoting a journal or newspaper essay that is reprinted in a volume of *DfS*, the following form may be used:

Rich, Frank. "Theatre: A Mamet Play, *Glengarry Glen Ross.*" *New York Theatre Critics' Review* Vol. 45, No. 4 (March 5, 1984), 5–7; excerpted and reprinted in *Drama for Students*, Vol. 2, eds. David Galens and Lynn Spampinato (Detroit: Gale, 1998), pp. 51–53.

When quoting material reprinted from a book that appears in a volume of *DfS*, the following form may be used:

Kerr, Walter. "*The Miracle Worker,*" in *The Theatre in Spite of Itself.* Simon & Schuster, 1963. 255–57; excerpted and reprinted in *Drama for Students*, Vol. 2, eds. David Galens and Lynn Spampinato (Detroit: Gale, 1998), pp. 123–24.

We Welcome Your Suggestions

The editorial staff of *Drama for Students* welcomes your comments and ideas. Readers who wish to suggest dramas to appear in future volumes, or who have other suggestions, are cordially invited to contact the editor. You may contact the editor via e-mail at: **ForStudents Editors@cengage.com.** Or write to the editor at:

Editor, *Drama for Students*
Gale
27500 Drake Road
Farmington Hills, MI 48331-3535

Literary Chronology

480 B.C.: Euripides is born in Salamis, Greece.

428 B.C.: The version of Euripides's *Hippolytus* that is still performed today is first staged.

406 B.C.: Euripides reportedly dies in Macedonia.

1450: *The Second Shepherds' Play* is written around this time.

1828: Henrik Ibsen is born on March 20 in Skien, Norway.

1882: Henrik Ibsen's play *An Enemy of the People* is written and published.

1906: Henrik Ibsen dies after several strokes on May 23 in Christiana (now called Oslo), Norway.

1909: Eugène Ionesco is born on November 26 in Slatine, Romania.

1911: Max Frisch is born on May 15 in Zurich, Switzerland.

1925: Pam Gems is born on August 1 in Bransgore, Hampshire, England.

1928: Edward Albee is born on March 12 in Washington, DC.

1930: Stephen Sondheim is born on March 22 in New York City.

1930: Maria Irene Fornes is born on May 14 in Havana, Cuba.

1930: Harold Pinter is born on October 10 in London, England.

1938: Caryl Churchill is born on September 3 in London, England.

1947: Bryony Lavery is born on December 21, in Wakefield, Yorkshire, England.

1957: Harold Pinter's *The Dumb Waiter* is written and performed.

1958: Max Frisch's *The Firebugs* is first performed.

1959: Eugène Ionesco's *Rhinoceros* is first staged in Dusseldorf, Germany.

1961: Edward Albee's *The American Dream* is staged for the first time in New York City.

1964: Lynn Nottage is born in New York City.

1967: Edward Albee wins the Pulitzer Prize for Drama.

1975: Edward Albee wins the Pulitzer Prize for Drama.

1977: Maria Irene Fornes's *Fefu and Her Friends* is produced in New York City.

1985: Stephen Sondheim's *Sunday in the Park with George*, written with James Lapine, is awarded the Pulitzer Prize for Drama.

1986: Stephen Sondheim's *Into the Woods*, written with James Lapine, is first produced in San Diego, California.

1987: Caryl Churchill's *Serious Money* premiers in London.

1991: Max Frisch dies of cancer on April 4 in Zurich, Switzerland.

1994: Edward Albee wins the Pulitzer Prize for Drama.

1994: Eugène Ionesco dies on March 28 in Paris.

1996: Pam Gems's *Stanley* is first produced in London, England.

1998: Bryony Lavery's *Frozen* is first produced in Birmingham, England.

2002: Harold Pinter is awarded the Nobel Prize for literature.

2005: Lynn Nottage's *Fabulation; or, The Re-Education of Undine* premiers in New York City.

Acknowledgments

The editors wish to thank the copyright holders of the excerpted criticism included in this volume and the permissions managers of many book and magazine publishing companies for assisting us in securing reproduction rights. We are also grateful to the staffs of the Detroit Public Library, the Library of Congress, the University of Detroit Mercy Library, Wayne State University Purdy/Kresge Library Complex, and the University of Michigan Libraries for making their resources available to us. Following is a list of the copyright holders who have granted us permission to reproduce material in this volume of *DFS*. Every effort has been made to trace copyright, but if omissions have been made, please let us know.

COPYRIGHTED EXCERPTS IN *DFS*, VOLUME 25, WERE REPRODUCED FROM THE FOLLOWING PERIODICALS:

America, v. 175, November 16, 1996. All rights reserved. Reproduced by permission of America Press.—*American Drama*, v. 8, spring 1999. Copyright © 1999 American Drama Institute. Reproduced by permission.—*Early Theatre: A Journal Associated with the Records of Early Drama*, v. 8, 2005. Reproduced by permission.—*Explicator*, v. 55, summer 1997. Copyright © 1997 by Helen Dwight Reid Educational Foundation. Reproduced with permission of the Helen Dwight Reid Educational Foundation, published by Heldref Publications, 1319 18th Street, NW, Washington, DC 20036-1802.—*German Quarterly*, v. 25, November 1952. Copyright © 1952 by the American Association of Teachers of German. Reproduced by permission.—*Guardian*, April 6, 2006. Copyright © 2006 Guardian Newspapers Limited. Reproduced by permission of author.—*Journal of American Drama and Theatre*, v. 3, spring 1991. Reproduced by permission.—*Modern Drama*, v. 33, September 1990; v. 40, winter 1997; v. 44, winter 2001 Copyright © 1990, 1997, 2001 by the University of Toronto, Graduate Centre for Study of Drama. All reproduced by permission.—*New Republic*, v. 198, January 18, 1988. Copyright © 1988 by The New Republic, Inc. Reproduced by permission of *The New Republic*.—*The New Yorker*, v. 80, March 29, 2004. Copyright © 2004 by Hilton Als. All rights reserved. Reprinted with permission of The Wylie Agency.—*Proceedings of the PMR Conference: Annual Publication of the International Patristic, Mediaeval and Renaissance Conference*, vol. 8, 1983. Copyright © 1983 by Villanova University. Reproduced by permission.—*San Francisco Chronicle*, January 18, 2007 for "A Serial Killer Strikes, and Now a Mother Must Wrestle with Forgiveness," by Robert Hurwitt. Reproduced by permission of the author.—*South Central Bulletin*, v. 26, winter, 1966. Copyright © 1966 The Johns Hopkins University Press. Reproduced by permission.—*Theatre Journal*, v. 32, May 1980. The Johns Hopkins University Press. Reproduced by permission.

COPYRIGHTED EXCERPTS IN *DFS*, VOLUME 25, WERE REPRODUCED FROM THE FOLLOWING BOOKS:

Bahr, Ehrhard. From "Max Frisch," in ***Dictionary of Literary Biography, Vol. 124, Twentieth-Century German Dramatists, 1919–1992***. Edited by Wolfgang D. Elfe and James Hardin, Gale Research, 1992. Reproduced by permission of Gale, a part of Cengage Learning.—Gray, Frances. From "Caryl Churchill," in ***Dictionary of Literary Biography, Vol. 310, British and Irish Dramatists Since World War II, Fourth Series***. Edited by John Bull, Gale, 2005. Reproduced by permission of Gale, a part of Cengage Learning.—Lamont, Rosette C. From ***Ionesco's Imperatives: The Politics of Culture***. University of Michigan Press, 1993. Copyright © 1993 by the University of Michigan. All rights reserved. Reproduced by permission.—Lane, Nancy. From ***Understanding Eugène Ionesco***. University of South Carolina Press, 1994. Copyright © 1994 University of South Carolina. Reproduced by permission.—Lucas, F. L. From ***The Drama of Ibsen and Strindberg***. Cassell, 1962. Copyright © 1962 F. L. Lucas. Reproduced by permission of the author.—Mael, Phyllis. From "Maria Irene Fornes," in ***Dictionary of Literary Biography, Vol. 7, Twentieth-Century American Dramatists***. Edited by John MacNicholas, Gale Research, 1981. Reproduced by permission of Gale, a part of Cengage Learning.—Morwood, James. From "Hippolytus," in ***The Plays of Euripides***. Edited by general: John H. Betts; series: Michael Gunningham. Bristol Classical Press, 2002. Copyright © 2002 by James Morwood. All rights reserved. Reproduced by permission of Gerald Duckworth & Co. Ltd.—Roudané, Matthew C. From "A Playwright Speaks: An Interview with Edward Albee," in ***Critical Essays on Edward Albee***. Edited by Philip C. Kolin and J. Madison Davis. G.K. Hall & Co., 1986. Copyright © 1986 by Philip C. Kolin and J. Madison Davis. All rights reserved. Reproduced by permission of the author.—Trussler, Simon. From ***The Plays of Harold Pinter***. Victor Gollancz Ltd., 1973. Copyright © 1973 Simon Trussler. Reproduced by permission.—Worthen, W. B. From ***Modern Drama and the Rhetoric of Theater***. University of California Press, 1992. Copyright © 1992 by The Regents of the University of California. Reproduced by permission.

COPYRIGHTED EXCERPTS IN *DFS*, VOLUME 25, WERE REPRODUCED FROM THE FOLLOWING WEB SITES OR ONLINE SOURCES:

From ***Contemporary Authors Online***. "Bryony Lavery," www.gale.com, Gale, 2007. Reproduced by permission of Gale, a part of Cengage Learning.—From ***Contemporary Authors Online***. "Eugene Ionesco," www.gale.com, Gale, 2007. Reproduced by permission of Gale, a part of Cengage Learning.—From ***Contemporary Authors Online***. "Henrik Ibsen," www.gale.com, Gale, 2007. Reproduced by permission of Gale, a part of Cengage Learning.—From ***Contemporary Authors Online***. "(Iris) Pam(ela) Gems," www.gale.com, Gale, 2002. Reproduced by permission of Gale, a part of Cengage Learning.—From ***Contemporary Authors Online***. "Lynn Nottage," www.gale.com, Gale, 2006. Reproduced by permission of Gale, a part of Cengage Learning.—From ***Contemporary Authors Online***. "Stephen Sondheim," www.gale.com, Gale, 2007. Reproduced by permission of Gale, a part of Cengage Learning.

Contributors

Bryan Aubrey: Aubrey holds a Ph.D. in English. Entries on *Frozen* and *Stanley*. Original essays on *Frozen* and *Stanley*.

Jennifer A. Bussey: Bussey is an independent writer specializing in literature. Entries on *Fabulation; or, The Re-Education of Undine* and *Into the Woods*. Original essays on *Fabulation; or, The Re-Education of Undine* and *Into the Woods*.

Klay Dyer: Dyer holds a Ph.D. in English literature and has published extensively on fiction, poetry, film, and television. He is also a freelance university teacher, writer, and educational consultant. Entries on *The American Dream*, *Hippolytus*, and *Rhinoceros*. Original essays on *The American Dream*, *Hippolytus*, and *Rhinoceros*.

Joyce M. Hart: Hart has degrees in English and creative and is a freelance writer and published author. Entries on *The Firebugs* and *Serious Money*. Original essays on *The Firebugs* and *Serious Money*.

Neil Heims: Heims is a writer and teacher living in Paris. Entries on *An Enemy of the People* and *The Dumb Waiter*. Original essays on *An Enemy of the People* and *The Dumb Waiter*.

Sheri Metzger Karmiol: Karmiol has a doctorate in English Renaissance literature. She teaches literature and drama at the University of New Mexico, where she is a lecturer in the University's Honors Program. Karmiol is also a professional writer and the author of several reference texts on poetry and drama. Entry on *The Second Shepherds' Play*. Original essay on *The Second Shepherds' Play*.

Carol Ullmann: Ullmann is a freelance writer and editor. Entry on *Fefu and Her Friends*. Original essay on *Fefu and Her Friends*.

The American Dream

EDWARD ALBEE

1961

First produced in late January 1961 at the York Playhouse in New York City, *The American Dream* was conceived by Edward Albee as a critique of the culture and social ideals of America in the aftermath of World War II. The world of the play is one of bourgeois (affluent middle class) sensibilities and a seemingly point-less veneer of small talk and dull conversation. On the surface, it is a play about a generation dedicated to getting satisfaction (an important word in Albee's play) without doing any of the hard work necessary to build a satisfying life. More deeply, as Albee himself has stated, *The American Dream* is a play about "the substitu-tion of artificial for real values in this society of ours."

Lingering barely below the seemingly trivial surface of *The American Dream*, moreover, is a destructive and often sadistic world. It is a world in which language is used to bludgeon, to manip-ulate, and to hide rather than illuminate the emotions that come to define a caring and cul-tured world. As the audience is drawn deeper and deeper into the world of the play, Albee pulls back layers of the veneer as a chef might peel an onion. With each exchange, the Dreams that accumulate during the course of the play (of prosperity, of love, and of family, to name but a few) fall away, revealing a world that is on the cusp of slipping forever into a nightmarish cycle of mutilation and destruction.

Edward Albee (AP Images)

Two Plays by Edward Albee: The American Dream and The Zoo Story, Signet, 1961, was released more recently by Plume in 1997.

AUTHOR BIOGRAPHY

Edward Albee was born on March 12, 1928 in Washington, DC. He was adopted in infancy by the millionaire Reed Albee, the son of a famous vaudeville producer, who moved the family back to Larchmont, New York. Brought into a family of great affluence, Albee was never comfortable, clashing frequently with his stepmother, who attempted to keep him away from the theater life and to shape him into what she considered a respectable man of elevated social standing. He attended Rye Country Day School before moving to the Lawrenceville School, from which he was expelled. He entered the Valley Forge Military Academy (Wayne, Pennsylvania) in 1943, graduating in 1945. His education continued at Choate Rosemary Hall (Wallingford, Connecticut) and then at Trinity College (Hartford, Connecticut). He was expelled from Trinity in 1947 for not attending classes and not attending compulsory chapel.

Moving to New York's Greenwich Village, Albee spent ten years trying to establish himself as a playwright. In a pattern that continues to define the careers of many young writers, he held a variety of odd jobs during this period, including office boy, salesman in a record store, and messenger for Western Union. His break came in September 1959 when his play *The Zoo Story* was produced for the first time at the Schiller Theater Werkstatt in West Berlin. (Albee jokes often that he got his start as far off Broadway as any writer could.) Part of a double bill with Samuel Beckett's *Krapp's Last Tape*, *The Zoo Story* is often seen as the beginning of a new wave of American theater, the work of a writer who clearly respected, but also moved forward from, the influences of such predecessors as Eugene O'Neill (1888–1953), Tennessee Williams (1911–1983), and Arthur Miller (1915–2005). In a sense responsible for marking American drama as part of a more cosmopolitan exercise, Albee is more often seen as part of the family of the Theater of the Absurd that includes the Irishman Samuel Beckett (1906–1989), the Romanian

Eugène Ionesco (1909–1994), and the Frenchman Jean Genet (1910–1986).

In a writing career that has spanned decades, Albee has written dozens of plays, beginning with *The Zoo Story* (1958), which was first produced in West Berlin on September 28, 1959. (The first American production of the play was on January 14, 1960 at the Provincetown Playhouse.) *The American Dream* (1961) was Albee's fifth play, and was followed immediately by what is arguably his most well-known work, *Who's Afraid of Virginia Woolf?* (1962). In 2005, a collection of his non-dramatic writings was published under the title *Stretching My Mind: Essays 1960–2005*.

Albee has received three Pulitzer Prizes for Drama: for *A Delicate Balance* (1967), *Seascape* (1975), and *Three Tall Women* (1994). He has also been recognized with a Gold Medal in Drama from the American Academy and Institute of Arts and Letters (1980) as well as both the Kennedy Center Honors (1996) and the National Medal of Arts (1996). His plays have won or been nominated for numerous Tony Awards, and Albee himself was honored with a Special Tony Award for Lifetime Achievement in the Theater in 2005.

Edward Albee still lives near Greenwich Village in New York City.

PLOT SUMMARY

Act 1

The American Dream is a play that is written and designed to be staged in one, uninterrupted scene. It opens with the characters of Mommy and Daddy sitting in their armchairs, which are facing each other across the stage and are arranged diagonally to the audience. Their first words are complaints about the lateness of some expected visitors. Who these visitors are and the exact nature of their visit remains unclear. Before mentioning that she headed out to buy a new hat that day, Mommy concludes that "people think they can get away with anything these days . . . and, of course they can."

Before she begins her story about hat shopping, Mommy playfully chides Daddy to pay attention to her. He promises to listen, and the story tests his promise very strongly. Mommy recounts the story about purchasing a hat that

she thought was beige but that was actually the color of wheat when she walked out of the store. She is made aware of this difference only when she meets the chairman of her women's club on the street just outside the store. Mommy returns to the store, making what she calls "a terrible scene" in order to get the color that she wants. She laughs, but is satisfied, as she tells Daddy how the clerk talked her into buying the same hat again by promising her that a lovely beige hat will remain beige, and not become a new color like wheat. At this point, the word *satisfaction* enters the play.

After complaining once again about the tardiness of their expected visitors, Daddy observes that he has not been satisfied in his attempts to get the leak in their toilet fixed. Mommy notes that the fixed toilet is not for her satisfaction but for Grandma's sake, since she cries every time she visits the bathroom anyway. Mommy and Daddy complain once again about the lateness of the visitors, and agree that Grandma is getting feeble-minded.

Grandma enters the scene, loaded down with boxes of all sizes neatly wrapped. Following Mommy's instructions, Grandma dumps the boxes at Daddy's feet, complaining as she does that he has not yet gotten the toilet repaired. As she turns to get the rest of the boxes that she claims to have piled off stage, Grandma laments how being old means that people talk to her disrespectfully, which leaves her without a sense of dignity. "You got to have a sense of dignity," Grandma notes, concluding that if people let attention to dignity slip then "civilization's doomed."

Changing the subject suddenly, Mommy accuses Grandma of reading her book club selections. Grandma replies angrily that she does because she is old and no one will talk to her anymore with dignity and respect. She exits the room, with the promise of returning with more boxes.

Mommy and Daddy are momentarily sorry for their tone when speaking with Grandma, but their talk soon turns to how nicely she wrapped the boxes scattered around Daddy's chair. Mommy begins a story about her Grandma, poor and struggling after Grandpa died, would wrap up lunches on pretty little boxes for Mommy, who was also poor, to take to school. Although Mommy knew that Grandma would sacrifice her own food for those lunches, she pretended that the box was actually empty. The other school children, raised with a concern for others, would offer her food every day, never knowing that the pretty little boxes contained wonderful lunches.

Daddy responds to the lunch story by calling Mommy "a very deceitful little girl." She explains that she only did it because she was poor, but since she married Daddy she has been very rich. Mommy then reveals that she wants to put Grandma in a nursing home (Daddy refuses to do so) and that she has no qualms about living off of Daddy's money or having him look after Grandma as part of the marriage contract. Dadddy declares his love for Mommy, as Grandma reenters the scene, carrying more boxes.

As though she has heard the conversation that has been unfolding, Grandma continues her treatise on old age by way of expanding her discussion to attack Mommy, calling the younger woman "a tramp and a trollop and a trull." ("Trull" is slang for a woman of very bad reputation, as in a harlot or prostitute.) Grandma continues her attack, pointing out to Mommy that Daddy is no longer interested sexually in his wife.

Daddy responds quietly by saying that he is very sick, and does not even really want to live anymore. Mommy changes the topic abruptly, returning to her complaints over the late visitors. The doorbell rings suddenly, triggering a quick exchange between the three characters that marks Daddy's inability to make decisions recently. Mommy ties this indecisiveness to a decline in what she calls his "masculin[ity]."

Daddy finally moves to open the door, allowing Mrs. Barker to step into the room. After the usual pleasantries, Daddy makes an odd request: "Now that you're here, I don't suppose you could go away and maybe come back some other time." Mrs. Barker takes the odd question in perfect stride, responding "Oh, no; we're much too efficient for that."

After inviting Mrs. Barker to sit down and cross her legs, Daddy asks what exactly she does. She is, in fact, the chairman of Mommy's woman's club, whom Mommy has not recognized. Blaming the artificial light for her confusion, Mommy suddenly asks Mrs. Barker if she would like to take off her dress in order to be more comfortable. Mrs. Barker does, and settles back into her chair wearing only her slip.

Mrs. Barker offers to smoke, an option that Mommy opposes with some force. Mommy then begins to walk through the boxes scattered on the floor, stepping on a number of them despite Grandma's admonitions not to. Mrs. Barker asks if they can assume that that the boxes are for "us," using the plural despite the fact that she had come to the apartment alone. When asked if they are accustomed to receiving boxes, Mrs. Barker replies elliptically that it often depends on why "they" have come to a specific place.

Daddy interrupts, saying that he has "misgivings" and "definite qualms" which, it turns out, are about an operation he had some time earlier during which something was taken out and something else put in. Mommy remarks that Daddy had always wanted to be a Senator, but has recently changed his focus to wanting to be Governor. Mrs. Barker responds with an enthusiastic story about ambition, speaking passionately about her brother who runs a little newspaper called *The Village Idiot*. He is also, she continues, a man who wants everyone to know that he is married and loves his wife intensely.

When Grandma tries to reenter the conversation, she is silenced rudely and abruptly by Mommy, who mimics the older woman. Grandma responds with a brief commentary on the limitations of middle age (meaning Mommy) before acknowledging that the imitation had a good rhythm but really lacked in content. Grandma then sets out to try to explain the mystery of the boxes, but Mommy silences her once again.

The exchange becomes increasingly mean spirited as Mommy pushes Daddy to have Grandma taken away in the van. The apartment is too crowded, Mommy claims, and Grandma adds too much clutter. The two women bicker back and forth about language and upbringing as Daddy and Mrs. Barker watch with interest.

Returning the discussion to the reason for Mrs. Barker's visit, Daddy admits that he had called for the visit. Mrs. Barker responds with a list of committees and activities that she is part of, including the Ladies' Auxiliary Air Raid Committee. She then moves directly to question the family about their opinions on air raids. Mommy and Daddy respond adamantly that they are hostile, to which Mrs. Barker responds that they would be no help to her since "there's too much hostility in the world these days as it is." Grandma leaps in, announcing that according to a recent government study there are too many old people in the world as well. Mommy calls her a liar, orders Daddy to break the older woman's television, and then celebrates her good fortune in finding such a fine man for a husband. She could, she says, have married a poor man or a man confined to a wheelchair.

Mommy feels badly after remembering that Mrs. Barker's husband is physically handicapped. Feeling faint, Mrs. Barker asks for some water, which, after more squabbling, Mommy leaves the room to get. Mrs. Barker immediately begs Grandma to explain to her why she has been invited to the apartment, and what Mommy and Daddy hope to accomplish with this meeting. Grandma, reveling in the power of the moment, toys with Mrs. Barker before offering her a cryptic hint.

The hint takes the form of a story about a couple (very much like Mommy and Daddy) who had lived in an apartment (very similar to the one in which they now stood) some twenty years earlier. The couple, so the story goes, was looking to adopt a baby, and had contacted a woman (very much like Mrs. Barker) to help them satisfy their desire for a child. Problems accumulated once the baby arrived: it did not look like either of its parents, it cried incessantly, and it had eyes only for the adoptive Daddy. Mrs. Barker responds that, given this last item, "any self-respecting woman would have gouged [the baby's] eyes right out of its head." This is exactly what happened, Grandma acknowledges.

When the baby begins to play with its genitals, the couple cuts off its penis and then its hands. Mrs. Barker agrees totally with the decisions. The baby then calls its adoptive Mommy a bad name, which led to the couple cutting out its tongue. Again, Mrs. Barker is in full agreement. Still the baby grew, until one day the couple realized that "it didn't have a head on its shoulders, it had no guts, it was spineless, [and] its feet were made of clay." When the baby finally died, the adoptive parents called the agency and demanded their money back. As Grandma concludes, in an line that echoes those from earlier in the play: "They wanted satisfaction."

Off stage, Mommy and Daddy struggle; he cannot find Grandma's room and she cannot find water in the kitchen. Mommy asks Mrs.

Barker to come into the kitchen with her, which the visitor does hesitantly. Before she leaves the living room, though, Grandma makes her promise not to tell her story to anyone.

As Mrs. Barker leaves the stage, the doorbell rings. Grandma yells for the visitor to come in, which he does. Grandma asks if he is the van man come to take her away, but he is not. She compliments his looks and his physique, commenting that he should try for the movies. He agrees with her, then goes on to describe himself: "Clean-cut, midwest farm boy type, almost insultingly good-looking in a typically American way." She congratulates him on knowing what and who he is, then pronounces him the American dream.

The Young Man goes on to explain that he is looking for work, and wonders to himself if there was money enough in the house to hire a handyman. Grandma tells him how she had just won 25,000 dollars in a baking contest, using the pseudonym Uncle Henry. (Her winning recipe was for something called Day-Old Cake.)

Grandma suddenly says that the Young Man looks familiar. He replies that he is incomplete, which he explains by way of telling the story of his birth and his life as an identical twin separated in childhood from his brother. Since that moment, he tries to explain, he has always been incomplete, searching for a connection that will let him feel whole again. Grandma feels deep pity for him, but their conversation is cut short when Mrs. Barker returns from the kitchen.

Shocked by the new arrival, Mrs. Barker wonders aloud what the Young Man is doing there. Grandma explains that he is the van man who has come to haul her things away. She instructs him to begin carrying her boxes off stage, which he does.

Turning her attention to Mrs. Barker, Grandma explains that there is a dilemma with Mommy and Daddy that must be resolved soon. Grandma whispers a possible solution to Mrs. Barker, who appears slightly shocked but agrees to go along with the plan. As the Young Man finishes clearing away all the boxes, Grandma says goodbye and exits the stage.

Mommy and Daddy return to the stage to find Grandma gone. Beginning to panic, Mommy asks Mrs. Barker where she went, only to be told that the van man came to take her away. Mommy falls into tears, saying that the van man was an invention that had been used to keep Grandma under control. Grandma, off stage, turns to the audience, admitting that she, too, is interested in watching the events unfold onstage. The Young Man is reintroduced into the scene, with Mrs. Barker making the introductions. He is given over to the family as a kind of replacement for what is referred to only as "the other one."

As the conversation on stage begins, Grandma turns to the audience, suggesting that this is the point at which it is the best time to leave. She bids the audience good night, and the curtain closes.

CHARACTERS

Mrs. Barker

A simplified exaggeration of the typical American housewife, with her sense of social responsibility, Mrs. Barker is representative of a society that would place a child (known as the bumble) in a home where it could be mutilated and brutalized. Hiding behind her complicity in the decline of American culture (that is, the death of the Dream), Mrs. Barker remains willfully blinded to the game that unfolds around her despite the fact that, at times, she is transparent in marking her history with the family.

As the back story or history of Mommy and Daddy is pieced together during the play, the connection between Mrs. Barker and the family becomes one of increasingly complex speculation. There are various moments early in the play when family members suggest that they know Mrs. Barker, but are not quite sure about the context of their previous connections. At times, these lapses in memory seem innocent enough, but as the layers of language and story accumulate this innocence gives way to much darker suspicions. Mrs. Barker has been a guest in this household many years earlier, and was instrumental in delivering the original child to the sadistic couple and was, therefore, complicit in the abuse that followed.

Just as Grandma comes to represent the role of the creative artist in the play, Mrs. Barker comes to represent the audience watching *The American Dream* unfold, and disintegrate, on stage before them. An outsider, not always capable of following the verbal barrages that fill the stage, she (like the audience) is responsible for her own role in the drama that is unfolding as well as for the meanness and inhumanity that has taken hold of the world on the stage.

Mrs. Barker's unwillingness to acknowledge the clear parallels between herself and the character in Grandma's story of the Bye Bye Adoption Service is one of the most prominently absurd moments in the play. Her role in the placement of the bumble cannot be denied, despite her attempts to do so, just as the role of the audience in holding on to the American dream despite its obvious limitations in the world of the play and beyond, cannot be ignored.

Daddy

Daddy is a kind of negative presence in *The American Dream*. Once a rich man and a model of the masculine world, Daddy has been reduced both physically (through his operations), sexually (he no longer sleeps with Mommy), and even intellectually (he giggles like a child and cannot make a decision) during the course of his life. During the absurdist moment of social theater when Mrs. Barker is invited to undress, for instance, Daddy giggles childishly as a kind of sexualized infant or, conversely, sexually mature adult reduced to an infantile response. More significantly, Daddy has been reduced verbally to a man who simply follows the lead that is set by Mommy. His words echo those spoken by her; she sets the tone and subject of each conversation; and inevitably she closes the conversations down through her attacks on either Daddy or Grandma.

Whereas Mommy emerges as a tyrannical sadist within the family structure of the play, Daddy is infantilized, turned into a child-like figure in need of discipline and punishment for his actions. Uncomfortably for the audience, Daddy almost seems to invite and at times almost enjoy the rituals of public humiliation. In this sense, Daddy is a masochistic figure who takes pleasure from the pain and humiliation that defines his relationship with Mommy.

Grandma

Stepping outside the scene in the final moments of the play to function as the ironic commentator on the events unfolding, Grandma becomes the director of the play as it moves inexorably to its close. She is also the character in the play most obviously aware of the games that are unfolding and her role in them. She defines her role through a series of typically absurdist strategies, from her feigned deafness and memory lapses to her epigrammatic wordplay and occasional obscenity. These strategies of feigned deafness and ignorance effectively disconnect Grandma from the fatal conversations and debilitating word games that have come to define the household in which she lives. It is this distance that allows her the freedom to escape the walls of the play as the introduction of the Young Man sets in motion a cycle of violence that seems determined to repeat itself. Significantly, Grandma's crossing back and forth from the world of the play to the world of the audience underscores Albee's sense that the two worlds do speak to each other in profound and often disturbing ways.

Grandma is also the character who introduces the finely wrapped gift boxes that come to litter the stage for most of the play. Symbolic of the empty, though alluring, promise of the American dream itself, Grandma's boxes prove evocative reminders of the history connecting Grandma and the much younger Mommy. Their history is one defined in youth, as in older age, by deprivation and deceit. Depriving herself of food in order to send her daughter with a gloriously wrapped lunch, Grandma unwittingly provides her daughter with a prop that allows her to present herself in the image of a terribly deprived child.

Seeing herself as a marginalized figure within the household, Grandma speaks often about the plight of old people in the modern world, a feeling that can be related, too, to the role of the innovative artist within a society increasingly driven toward a celebration of the mediocre and the mass produced. Stepping outside the frame of the play as it nears its final scene, Grandma reveals the true power of her vision, directing the play towards a resolution for the various dilemmas facing the remaining characters. She then interrupts the play to conclude its action, offering the staged reunion as an open-ended moment for the audience to reflect upon. Is this the beginning or the ending of the American dream? Has the Dream itself withered in modern culture or is it still a viable source of inspiration and motivation? How do we reconcile the sadism of Mommy with the promise of a Dream future? These and many

other questions are left unanswered as Grandma bids the audience good night.

Mommy

The stereotypical bad mother, Mommy is the most verbally vicious of the characters. She is a woman who hides her attacks on Grandma and her diminishment of Daddy under the guise of family disciplinarian. Her tongue is persistently sharp, her sarcasm dull edged and exaggerated, and her tone defined by scorn and derision. More disturbing still is the pervasiveness of her sadism. She emasculates Daddy at every chance, and, if one believes Grandma's story of the bumble of joy to be truthful, she mutilates the couple's adopted child as a part of his disciplined upbringing. As part of the dynamic of Albee's play, Mommy's sadism controls the stage, expressing itself in a pattern of physical and verbal violence that is almost entirely unchecked and unchallenged. One of the more disturbing aspects for an audience watching this pattern unfold itself is the discomfort that attaches itself to the experience of bearing witness to the violence and to the final recognition that the world of the play remains firmly under control of Mommy as the stage fades to black.

As one of the more lucid commentaries of Grandma makes clear, Mommy is a manipulative, vicious woman who married Daddy for his money and power, and who cares little (if at all) for the people around her. As the story of the bumble underscores, Mommy is representative of the potential brutality and selfishness lingering barely below the surface of modern American society.

Young Man

A blond with a Midwestern look to him, the Young Man describes himself as a type, a character that is built around a single idea or quality and is presented without a sense of individuality. This self-definition is significant given that Grandma labels him the American dream, the ideal that all other Americans strive to achieve.

But as the Young Man's story underscores, the Dream itself is an illusion, a veneer to cover the hollowness of his own existence. The product of the murder of his lost identical twin (known in Grandma's story as the bumble), he is a Dream that is defined by a progressive loss of all emotion and desire. He carries the emotional scars that parallel the physical mutilations weighed upon the bumble by Mommy some twenty years earlier. As the play ends, the Young Man is brought together with a Mommy and Daddy, forming a family that is left at the end of the play in a kind of limbo. As Grandma offers in her final statement, this is a play in which "everybody's got what he wants...or everybody's got what he thinks he wants."

THEMES

The American Dream

For the generation of characters that populate Albee's *The American Dream*, the decades following World War II were seen initially as a revitalization of the promise of the American dream. Coined in the early 1930s, the term marked a significant break with the imaginative, political, and economic models of the Old World (Europe). Fueled by the emergence of American big business, the completion of a transcontinental railway, and the promise that came with an energized natural resource industry, the celebration of the "rags to riches" story familiar in American lore led to a pervasive belief that any American citizen who had a modicum of talent and worked extremely hard could accumulate financial wealth and political power. Writers have always been drawn to the promise of this Dream ideal, most notably in F. Scott Fitzgerald's *The Great Gatsby* (1925), John Steinbeck's *Of Mice and Men* (1937), and more tragically, Arthur Miller's *Death of a Salesman* (1949).

In the early decades of the twentieth century, the American dream faced some of its stiffest tests. The Great Depression, the growing pressures of racial discrimination, and the hangover of two World Wars left many Americans feeling disenfranchised, cut off from the promise of the Dream. But with the economic prosperity of the postwar period, and with it the rise of suburban America, the Dream regained its energy. Improvements to home comfort and employment stability, combined with a dramatic rise in personal income levels and an expansion of educational options, became the hallmark of the modern version of the Dream.

Although the counterculture politics of the 1960s and subsequent decades saw a waning of the prominence of the American dream as a wholly positive ideal, it has remained prominent in American culture as both a touchstone of hope

TOPICS FOR FURTHER STUDY

- Playbills (posters advertising a theatrical performance) are unique works of art in themselves. Playbills are also designed to give the potential audience member a sense of the themes or focal points of the play. Design an original playbill that you feel captures the themes and ideas explored in Albee's *The American Dream*.

- In her closing statement to the audience, Grandma observes that *The American Dream* is a comedy. Research the history of comedy, and write an essay in which you argue in support of Grandma's statement or raise a challenge to it.

- One of the more interesting aspects of *The American Dream* is the moment near the end of the play when Grandma steps out of the play to become the writer-director of the closing scene. In a thoughtful essay, discuss some of the more important implications of this scenario.

- Research the shifting definitions of family and family life in American culture since the 1950s, both of which are important concepts in many of Albee's plays. Keep a journal in which you note your thoughts about the changing face of families in American culture. How have ideas about family structure changed in the decades since 1950? Is there such a thing as a typical American family? Do you feel that film and television represent families in an honest or truthful way? Write an essay addressing these questions.

and a source of deeply felt frustration. In Albee's *The American Dream*, this fading ideal is represented most obviously by the Young Man, a clean-cut American beauty who appears physically attractive but who is emotionally empty and deeply scarred from the memories of his tragic detachment from his identical twin brother. Without meaning in his life, the Young Man reduces himself to a man who will do anything for money, making him, ironically, the perfect embodiment of the American dream.

In the end, the Young Man as the ideal physical manifestation of the American dream is a mask that hides both the emptiness and the dark undercurrents that have come to redefine the Dream in the modern world.

Language and Violence

As in most of Albee's plays, there is a powerful relationship in *The American Dream* between language and violence, both as language is directed between individuals in the play and how these same individuals do violence to language itself. Grandma's frequent comments about the way that old people are talked to (dismissively and disrespectfully) illustrate that language has a strong impact on the power that the verbally aggressive characters wield upon those characters who are less articulate. Although Grandma can and does hold her own in the battles with Mommy that flare up during the course of the play, she is adamant in her argument that the elderly are disempowered by the language that is attached to them. Similarly, Mommy emasculates Daddy with her mocking words and tone, depriving him of his masculine spirit and making fun of his effectiveness as both a decision maker and sexual partner. Her frequent references to sex take on a mean-spirited and destructive force in this new context.

In this sense, language becomes an active and aggressive component of the play. The word *mutilation*, for instance, is acted out physically and violently in the play, most obviously in the murder of the bumble joy but also in the mutilation of the American dream of prosperity and of the ideals of family. Such words as *love* and *truth* are pushed to the point of deformity as each successive layer of the sadistic games of Mommy and Daddy are exposed.

At other times, Albee turns language into a literal tool of the sadistic Mommy. When she sees that the bumble joy only has eyes for Daddy, for instance, she removes both the child's eyes and the possibility of that phrase ever appearing in such a sentence ever again. It is impossible, Mommy knows, for the child to have eyes only for Daddy if the child has no eyes at all.

Sneakers *from the* From Home *Series by* Christina Richards *(© Christina Richards / Corbis)*

STYLE

Objects as Symbols

Although *The American Dream* is not a play that relies heavily on symbols, the boxes that Grandma brings to the stage early in the play do acquire a symbolic presence as the scenes unfold. Enigmatic in that they serve no real function in the play, the colorfully wrapped boxes are complimented by Mommy and Daddy for their beauty without any concern for their content. Ironically, when Grandma gets close to revealing the contents of the boxes (and by extension, their meaning), she is silenced by Mommy. As they do with the other important issues in their lives (including their faith in the power of the American dream), Mommy and Daddy find satisfaction in attending to surface appearances rather than to exploring the more complex depths. The boxes, in this sense, are a diversion, a jumble of pretty distractions that allow Mommy and Daddy to remain emotionally and intellectually distant from the harsh realities of the world that they have created.

But as the audience comes to understand later in the play, the boxes do contain things. More specifically, they contain the seemingly haphazard collection of items that Grandma has accumulated during her life, including enema bottles and a blind Pekinese. Seen in this light, the boxes become symbolic of Grandma's version of the American dream, the detritus and clutter that mark the failings of her body and the limitations that have pressed in upon her throughout her life. Fueled by her contest win, Grandma packs up her Dreams and moves on in search of a new play and a new stage.

Satire

Satire is a technique that uses irony to undercut misguided behaviors or to censure social and political attitudes. From its origins in the writing and culture of the ancient Greeks, satire has remained a powerful tool of writers, like Albee, determined to engage their art as provocation and social critique. The tone of satiric literature ranges from a kind of detached commentary on proceedings (such as Grandma's comments at the end of the play) to fully expressed anger and vehement contempt for the human conditions (Grandma's brief but pointed comments on the treatment of the elderly). Given that most satire relies heavily on balancing word play with criticism, it is appropriate that irony is one of its chief tools.

The satiric voice in *The American Dream* is put in place through a series of linguistic and performance-based juxtapositions. Mommy attacks Daddy viciously through her use of sarcasm (the dullest form of irony) when mocking his diminished masculinity, while her celebration of her love for him is undercut even more when the audience realizes that she only married him for his money. These juxtapositions take on a much darker tone when the audience hears the story of Mommy's sadistic treatment of the bumble of joy. An earlier joke about Daddy being all ears loses its humor when recontextualized by the blinding of a child because he only has eyes for Daddy.

At its best, satire reveals a sophisticated versatility of speech, a strong moral center through which one might speak to social and cultural improprieties. Put simply, satire is defined, in large part, by many of the same traits that readers can attribute to *The American Dream*.

Epigrams

An epigram is a statement, whether in verse or prose, that is concise, carrying an unmistakable message (often criticism), and witty. In *The American Dream*, Grandma often speaks in epigrams, particularly through her epigrammatic commentaries on the treatment of the elderly. The brevity of her powerful statements underscores neatly the power of language to shape the reality of those to whom it is applied. To Grandma, what defines age is not her biological condition or emotional state, but the way people talk down to her. More specifically, it is the way that Mommy uses language to bludgeon her into submission.

These epigrammatic commentaries position Grandma as an observer of the world at large and, more specifically, of the household in which she lives. Such a position anticipates nicely her transformation at the end of the play from epigrammatic observer to director of the final scene, which allows her, too, to move beyond the world of the play and to relocate herself and her boxes elsewhere. As Nicholas Canaday, Jr. argued most elegantly, it is in this final shift of Grandma from player to director that generates whatever hope the play might have: "In the character of Grandma the play suggests that whatever meaning is possible is achieved through an attitude of courageous realism that can enable man to conduct himself with dignity, through the simple enjoyment of whatever experience can be enjoyed, and through the creative act of the artist."

HISTORICAL CONTEXT

Theater of the Absurd

Theater of the Absurd is a loose name given to a dramatic movement that originated in France during the 1940s and 1950s. Originally coined by the critic Martin Esslin in a book on European-theater from these decades, the term has been linked most often with the works of four major playwrights who rose to prominence during this period: Eugène Ionesco (1909–1994), Samuel Beckett (1906–1989), Jean Genet (1910–1986), and Arthur Adamov (1908–1970). Albee is often cited as the playwright who brought Absurdist theater to the United States.

Although very distinct in terms of their styles and dramatic philosophies, each of these men used his work to explore the absurdity of the human condition in the contemporary world. Influenced variously by such thinkers as Søren Kierkegaard (1813–1855) and Jean-Paul Sartre

COMPARE & CONTRAST

- **1960s:** Albee and other playwrights from this period are drawn to explorations of the dynamics of marriage, which are changing dramatically at this time. As divorce rates begin to increase and feminism begins to find a footing in mainstream American culture, the ideas that form traditional understandings of marriage are increasingly brought into question.

  Today: Plays, films, and television shows continue to focus on the dynamics of marriage, despite the fact that divorce is more common today than it was in the 1960s.

- **1960s:** Ageism, a term referring to stereotyping and prejudice against individuals or groups because of their age, is still a relatively new concept when Albee's play is first produced. The term itself is not formally recognized until 1969, when the gerontologist Robert N. Butler uses it to describe a

  systematic cultural discrimination against the elderly.

  Today: A number of national and international programs are in place to advocate for the civil and human rights of the elderly, making ageism an important political issue.

- **1960s:** Belief in the truthfulness of words and their meanings is still prevalent, carrying over from the modernist traditions of the earlier decades of the century.

  Today: Language as the foundation of reality and truthfulness has increasingly been questioned by theorists and writers. This questioning has come to be known as postmodernism. A key tenet of the postmodernist shift is that language is a powerful tool that can be used to the benefit or the detriment of individuals, institutions, and cultures.

(1905–1980), these Absurdist writers believed that life is without meaning or purpose and that it is only through a conscious and willed commitment to a cause that a life gains meaning. Without this commitment, a life remains defined by purposelessness, by apathy, and, as in the case of *The American Dream*, by an emptiness that turns even the greatest of Dreams into tragedy.

To most of the writers associated with this movement it was important to note that this absurdity could not be explained by logic or any rational structure. In practice, this translated to a break from many longstanding stage conventions. Realistic characters were no longer the focal point of the plays, and consistencies in time and place gave way to openness and fluidity. Meaningless plot shifts, repetitive or even nonsensical dialogue, and dream-like sequences are commonplace in these plays. Not surprisingly, Absurdist plays often focus thematically

on such issues as alienation, the haunting inevitability of death, and the pressures to conform in an increasingly mediocre world. At risk, according to many of these plays, were the powers of love to hold the world together, the bracing strength of the humanities, and the politics of human rights and dignity.

The Nuclear Family

The term nuclear family was developed in the late 1940s to distinguish the family group consisting of parents (usually a father and mother) and their children from what is known as the extended family group, which expands in definition to include grandparents, aunts, uncles, and the full deployment of cousins. Although the nuclear family structure has been around for decades, it underwent a radical rise in prominence during the post-War boom of the 1950s and 1960s.

Urban Paris Landscape with Tree *by Kevin Cruff* (*© Kevin Cruff / Corbis*)

But, as Albee explores often in such plays as *The American Dream* and *Who's Afraid of Virginia Woolf?*, the nuclear family found itself threatened by both external pressures (the sexual revolution, for instance, and the pressures of transition from an extended family structure) as well as a particularly powerful constellation of assumptions and expectations of the ideal family. With a sadistic Mommy and an emasculated and infant-like Daddy, the family of *The American Dream* becomes a tragic parody of the traditional nuclear family, defined as the play's family is by mutilation, manipulation, and verbal savagery.

CRITICAL OVERVIEW

From its opening performances in Berlin through its various stagings and restagings across North America, *The American Dream* has been simultaneously praised and criticized by reviewers. Writing in the *New York Times* in January of 1961, Howard Taubman is a representative case in point. "It is agreed that Edward Albee has talent," he begins. "*The Zoo Story*, still running, established that point. *The American Dream . . .* reinforces it." And while Albee's "style remains elliptical" and his absurdist technique is handled "with a disarmingly child-like and sardonic freshness" there is a brittleness to the play, Taubman argues, that leaves the darkened story burdened by "a kind of bitter comic current of free association." Despite its brilliance, Taubman concludes, *The American Dream* "grows tiresome" and leaves an audience "glad to be quit of it[s]" darkening spirit.

Not surprisingly, this debate carried on in the years following the play's initial appearance in the United States. Writing in the *English Journal* in 1966, Herbert R. Adams, for instance, argues about whether Albee is writing in the Absurdist tradition at all. His conclusion is stated openly: despite the obvious similarities in theme and technique, Albee "doesn't belong in the same ballpark with [the absurdist playwrights] [Eugène] Ionesco, [Jean] Genet, [Samuel] Beckett, or [Harold] Pinter." Writing the same year in the *South Central Bulletin*, Nicholas Canaday, Jr., calls *The American Dream* "a textbook case of the response of the American drama to this existential vacuum [affecting modern life], and at the same time this play of 1961 is perhaps our best example of what has come to be known as the 'theater of the absurd.'" Revisiting the debate in 1978, Foster Hirsch, writing in *Who's Afraid of Edward Albee?*, recognizes *The American Dream* as Albee's "most purely absurdist piece," while C. W. E. Bigsby, writing in *Modern American Drama, 1945–2000*, dismisses the play as "derivative" and "slight."

CRITICISM

Klay Dyer

Dyer holds a Ph.D. in English literature and has published extensively on fiction, poetry, film, and television. He is also a freelance university teacher, writer, and educational consultant. In this essay, he discusses Albee's play as a kind of requiem for the death of the ideals and the hopefulness surrounding the American dream.

Edward Albee's *The American Dream* is specifically about the contours of the American dream as it came to be imagined and reimagined as the United States entered into the second half of the twentieth century. The Dream that Albee alludes to in the title of his fifth play is built on the unquestioned assumption that with the maturation of a post-World War II economy

WHAT DO I READ NEXT?

- Dealing with a body of work as important and diverse as that produced by Edward Albee often makes for difficult choices, but no reading of his work would be complete without time spent exploring what is probably his best-known play, *Who's Afraid of Virginia Woolf?* (1962).

- Insightful for fans and students alike is Albee's collection of essays from 1960 through 2005, *Stretching My Mind* (2005), which collects for the first time ever Albee's writings on theater, literature, and the political and cultural battlegrounds that have defined his career. Many of the selections included in this volume have been drawn from Albee's private papers, and many are published here for the first time.

- Samuel Beckett's *Waiting for Godot* (1952) is a defining play to understand the provocative and groundbreaking work that is most often attributed to the Theater of the Absurd.

- Arthur Miller's *Death of a Salesman* (1949) provides a profound pairing with *The American Dream*. In the tragic tale of Willy Loman, Miller adds his own satiric voice to the legion of writers determined to show that the drive to achieve the much-celebrated American dream through a single-minded emphasis on material gain leads inevitably to disaster.

- Elaine Tyler May's *Homeward Bound: American Families in the Cold War Era* (1990) explores the shifting dynamics of the American family in the wake of two World Wars combined with the cultural pressures that accompanied the 1960s.

and culture, America would emerge into a new environment of sustainable prosperity, social advancement, and cultural maturity. Paradoxically, and despite the achievement of a higher

❝

> UNSATISFIED, GRANDMA TURNS AWAY FROM THE PLAY. INTERRUPTING ITS OBVIOUS AND DISTURBING SLIDE INTO REDUNDANCY, SHE MARKS CLEARLY THAT THERE IS NO NEED TO VENTURE ANY FURTHER INTO THIS NOW-FAMILIAR FUTURE."

standard of living in the post-war era, the much-anticipated *better* life remained an ever-elusive goal for a generation driven forward increasingly by the pressures of what the characters of Mommy and Daddy describe as a deeply held belief in their right to have "satisfaction" in all aspects of their lives.

Defining itself increasingly by the ebb and flow of the Dream itself, post-war American culture became a kind of absurdist desert marked by conformity, emptiness of intellect and spirit, and perceptible disfiguring of language. Ironically, however, the residents of this world rarely, if ever, see their lifestyle as spiritually vacant or overtly homogenous and manufactured. As Albee's enquiry into the shifting counters of the Dream underscores, the modern American lifestyle has come to be increasingly defined by the mass-marketed ideas of middle-class family values and carefully packaged nostalgia. Emerging as the iconic symbol of this spiritually and creatively vacant culture is the Young Man, a physically superior man whose family history has left him vacant, scarred, and unable to see the emptiness of the world into which he so deeply desires to enter.

Having gained recognition in his life due to his Dream-like appearance, the Young Man is, he admits openly, an idealized type, the "clean-cut, midwest farm boy type, almost insultingly good-looking in a typically American way." To the residents of the small apartment, however, he is quickly reimagined as an iconic symbol of the youthful hopefulness of an era gone-by. He is a symbol of a time before the Dream was forced to confront the realities of a failed marriage, declining health, open hypocrisy, and brutal savagery. Partially hidden from view and partially an open secret, these conditions leave a bloody stain across both the play

and an entire generation. The image of the American dream, youthful and physically perfect, becomes for Mommy and Daddy a redefining moment of their lives, a symbol of the opportunity to try again to build a family in such a way that might allow both parents and the Young Man an opportunity for salvation.

Trapped in a post-war world that is, according to the Dream, supposed to nurture and protect them, Albee's characters find themselves imprisoned by the savagery of their shared past. For Mommy and Daddy, it is a past defined by the mutilation and death of their adopted bumble joy, while for the iconic Young Man, the memories are of the tragic loss of his identical twin. Unable and unwilling to move forward into a world that acknowledges the emptiness of his life and the superficiality of his beauty, the Young Man lives in a perpetual state of incompleteness. "I can feel nothing," he repeats over and over, "I can feel nothing. And so... here I am... as you see me." He is, as he admits openly, only a body and a face without a spirit or a soul.

As the final scene of the play unfolds, guided by Grandma (who has transformed herself from character to director), Albee's characters are offered an opportunity to correct the course of the Dream, allowing the Young Man to become a part of the family he so deeply longs to find and for Mommy and Daddy to undo the memory of the savagery of twenty years earlier. Despite the profundity of this opportunity, however, the characters remain static, unchanging. Mommy turns to Mrs. Barker, for instance, and remarks that this Young Man is "much better than the other one," marking this Young Man not as a new beginning but as a continuation of the previously established (and brutally sadistic) pattern. As Grandma (and the audience) look on with growing awareness of what is actually occurring, Mrs. Barker underscores this continuance with her response to Mommy's enquiry as to the name of the Young Man. "Call him whatever you like," Mrs. Barker begins. "He's yours."

With two words (*He's yours*) Mrs. Barker marks a transfer of ownership that reimagines the American dream from an autonomous individual to a newly purchased commodity, much like the beige hat that Mommy buys as the play opens. Indeed, when Mommy tells Mrs. Barker that she does not know how to thank the woman for delivering the Young Man to them, the response is clear and chilling: "Oh, don't worry about that," Mrs. Barker responds almost casually, "I'll send you a bill in the mail."

Reduced to something that can be bought and sold on the open market, the American dream is neither a marker of individual freedom nor of a hopeful new beginning. He is, as Mrs. Barker further underscores when asked what his name is, simply a continuation of what has come before. "Call him what you called the other one," Mrs. Barker answers. It is an answer that is met, tellingly, with puzzled glances and an admission that neither Mommy nor Daddy can remember what "the other one" was called.

In this moment, Albee's characters turn away from the underlying truths about their shared pasts. In the end, even mutilation and sadism fails to illuminate the layering of horrors that has shaped these lives: savagery, erasure of identity, disfigurement of language, and the end of hope. The culture of Albee's play has devolved into a nightmare, fracturing from the moral and humane ideals of the moment and slipping into a much darker ethos of alienation, anomie, and anger. Sequestering themselves in the private spaces of their apartment, and encountering their world only through their visions and revisions of their own sense of power and status, Mommy and Daddy withdraw themselves from the intricacies and questions of their own time, a withdrawal that leads ultimately to decay and to mutilation. Their lives, to be continued now with the training of yet another Young Man, are defined by their own refusal to understand the world around them, a denial that stems from an inability to accept their complicity in the death of the American dream and to see a new path, or imagine a new way. Raising their glasses in celebration, Mommy and Daddy fall back on the ideals that they have been raised to value more than all others: "we'll drink to celebrate," Mommy says as she begins the toast that will seal the fate of the play and of the American dream. "To satisfaction! Who says you can't get satisfaction these days!"

Unsatisfied, Grandma turns away from the play. Interrupting its obvious and disturbing slide into redundancy, she marks clearly that there is no need to venture any further into this now-familiar future. Moving herself into conversation with the audience, she rejects the celebration of past glories and the resurrection of past

dreams that is taking place on the stage. With the integration of the Young Man comes the collapse of the Dream; the play threatens to spiral out of control, losing itself once again in a morass of delusion and pain. In the final moments, it is Grandma who reveals the deepest truth of the play: that being free and clear of this stage, and of the language and the silences that defined her for so long, is her only hope of survival. Ultimately, she reveals to those willing to listen, there are horizons that extend farther than those imagined in the nightmarish world of the American dream.

Source: Klay Dyer, Critical Essay on *The American Dream*, in *Drama for Students*, Gale, Cengage Learning, 2008.

Matthew C. Roudané

In the following interview, given by Roudané, Albee discusses his views on both the artistic and the social role of theatre.

...Albee, like Arthur Miller, is a much-interviewed playwright. And although Lawrence's reminder—that we should never trust the artist but the tale—is important, scholars nonetheless may gain useful insight into a writer's vision by listening to his conversations. Albee's interviews allow scholars to trace parallel developments between his plays and dramatic theories. Albee's once scathing attacks on critics he considered myopic appear less frequently. Albee no longer "defends" his transition from Off-Broadway to the Great White Way; his more experimental pieces; his willingness to take aesthetic risks. This is not to imply, of course, that Albee's rage and anger have diminished. Albee's protests against various crimes of the heart appear as intense as the days when he was labeled the new Angry Young Playwright. But recent interviews reveal a more mature, thoughtful Albee. Now he simply tries to explain, precisely, his convictions...

Q: *Why is it so vital for you to break down the actor / audience barrier during the performance? And on what levels do you wish to engage your audience?*

A: First of all, you have to discover what audience you're talking about. The ideal audience I'd like to reach is the audience that brings to the theater some of the same attention and work that I do when I write a play. The willingness to experience the play, if the play is successful, on its own terms, without predetermining the nature of the

THE SINGLE JOURNEY THROUGH CONSCIOUSNESS SHOULD BE PARTICIPATED IN AS FULLY AS POSSIBLE BY THE INDIVIDUAL, NO MATTER HOW DANGEROUS OR CRUEL OR TERROR-FILLED THAT EXPERIENCE MAY BE."

theatrical experience. Someone who's seeing a play should be seeing the first play he has ever seen. I am referring to a state of innocence in which our theater is most ideally approached; the key is for one to have no preconceptions, as if it's the first theatrical experience that person has ever had. If people approach the theater that way, viewing the spectacle becomes an experience of *wonder* for them rather than saying that, "oh, I can't relate to this" or "the play is 'difficult' and therefore I can't take it!" If one approaches the theater in a state of innocence, sober, without preconceptions, and willing to participate; if they are willing to have the status quo assaulted; if they're willing to have their consciousness raised, their values questioned—or reaffirmed; if they are willing to understand that the theater is a live and dangerous experience—and therefore a *life-giving force*—then perhaps they are approaching the theater in an ideal state and that's the audience I wish I were writing for.

However, that is not the way everybody approaches theater. It's not even the way I approach the theater all the time, although I wish I did. But we should all approach the theater in this state of innocence. But the one thing a playwright can't do is write for an "audience" at all successfully. If you're writing for a group of intellectuals, then you're leaving other people out, proving only how smart you are. If you're trying to reach a larger audience than your work would normally reach, you're probably telling half-truths rather than total Truth; you're probably oversimplifying that which by its very nature is incredibly complex! There are some plays I write that are difficult, some that are easy, some that will reach more people than others, even in that ideal audience. But the basic, the essential thing is to let the play happen on its own terms the way it wants to happen.

And then assume there will be enough people who are willing to let it happen on its own terms. That's about all one can do.

Many people at the colleges I visit ask me over and over again, "Why do you ask such tough questions and why do your plays seem so difficult or depressing?" Or "Why don't you write happy plays?" About what, happy problems? But I keep reminding them that drama is an attempt to make things better. Drama is a mirror held up to them to show the way they do behave and how they don't behave that way any longer. If people are willing to be aided in the search for total consciousness by not only drama but all of the arts—music and painting and all the other arts give a unique sense of order—then art is life-giving. Art gives shape to life; it increases consciousness.

Q: *Death pervades your theater. Why your preoccupation with death?*

A: As opposed to the slaughter in Shakespeare, the tuberculosis and consumption in Chekhov, the death-in-life in Beckett? Is that what you mean? There are only a few significant things to write about: life and death. I am very interested in the cleansing consciousness of death; and the fact that people avoid thinking about death—and about *living*. I think we should always live with the consciousness of death. How else can we possibly participate in living life fully? . . .

Q: *Such playwrights as Arthur Miller or David Mamet explore the myth of the American Dream, the myth embracing the work ethic as a means to material success and so on. Could you comment on this?*

A: I'm quite in favor of hard work, something I do a lot of myself! There's nothing wrong with the notion of making your own way. What is wrong with the myth of the American Dream is the notion that this is all that there is to existence! The myth is merely a part of other things. Becoming wealthy is O.K. I suppose, but it is not a be all to end all. People who think that the acquisition of wealth or property or material things or power; that these are the things in life; the conspicuous consumption of material things is the answer; this creates a problem. The fact that we set arbitrary and artificial goals for ourselves is a problem, not the hard work ethic *per se* . . .

Q: *As a playwright, do you see yourself as a social critic?*

A: Directly or indirectly any playwright is a kind of demonic social critic. I am concerned with altering people's perceptions, altering the status quo. All serious art interests itself in this. The self, the society should be altered by a good play. All plays in their essence are indirectly political in that they make people question the values that move them to make various parochial, social, and political decisions. Our political decisions are really a result of how we view consciousness. Plays should be relentless; the playwright shouldn't let people off the hook. He should examine their lives and keep hammering away at the fact that some people are not fully participating in their lives and therefore they're not participating with great intelligence in politics, in social intercourse, in aesthetics. It's something that I dearly hope runs through all of my plays . . .

Q: *Your vision seems to deal with certain profound crimes of the heart: the individual's inability to deal honestly, or what the existentialists would call authentically, with the self and the other. Is this accurate?*

A: Yes, I suppose it is. After all, what else is there to deal with? The single journey through consciousness should be participated in as fully as possible by the individual, no matter how dangerous or cruel or terror-filled that experience may be. We only go through it once, unless the agnostics are proved wrong, and so we must do it fully conscious. One of the things that art does is to not let people sleep their way through their lives. If the universe makes no sense, well perhaps we, the individual can make sense of the cosmos. We must go on, we must not add to the chaos but deal honestly with the idea of order, whether it is arbitrary or not. As all of my plays suggest, so many people prefer to go through their lives semiconscious and they end up in a terrible panic because they've wasted so much. But being as self-aware, as awake, as open to various experience will produce a better society and a more intelligent self-government . . .

Source: Matthew C. Roudané, "A Playwright Speaks: An Interview with Edward Albee," in *Critical Essays on Edward Albee*, edited by Philip C. Kolin and J. Madison Davis, G. K. Hall, 1986, pp. 193–99.

Nicholas Canaday Jr.

In the following essay, Canaday explores Albee's The American Dream *as a dramatic catalogue of typical responses to the basic assumption that modern life has no meaning. Unlike traditional interpretations of this play, however, Canaday argues that it offers some positive responses to this anxiety.*

The many varieties of probings in and around the center of life in our time—whether sociological, philosophical, religious, or literary—are so well known by now that terms like "anguish" and "estrangement" and "nothingness" have become, if not household words, at least basic to the jargon of the academy. Edward Albee's *The American Dream* is what might be called a textbook case of the response of the American drama to this existential vacuum, and at the same time this play of 1961 is perhaps our best example of what has come to be known as the "theatre of the absurd." Thus *The American Dream* is appearing with increasing frequency in the drama anthologies and the American literature survey texts. By means of caricature and the comic irrelevancy of its language the play mirrors the meaninglessness of American life. The Young Man, who appears on stage near the end of the play, is the symbol of the American Dream, beautiful in appearance but without real substance. He embodies Albee's view of the present extension of this familiar myth. The general critical view that "Edward Albee's plays are ferocious attacks on lethargy and complacency in American society" and "a savage denial that everything is just dandy" is supported by Albee's own remarks in his introduction to the Coward-McCann Contemporary Drama Edition of the play. Thus the void at the center of modern life is the basic assumption upon which this play rests; the action is primarily concerned with typical responses to this existential situation. It is the purpose of this essay to categorize these responses and then to offer the suggestion that in this play there are certain positive values that have thus far been overlooked by critics. It seems to me that such values are implied in the absurd world of *The American Dream*, even though the center has gone out of life, all forms are smashed, and—to coin a cliché—God is dead.

THUS ALBEE'S *THE AMERICAN DREAM* MAKES
THE ASSUMPTION THAT THE DREAM IS HOLLOW AND
SHOWS THE CAUSES AND SYMPTOMS OF A SICK
SOCIETY."

The first type of response is represented in the play by Daddy. His attitude is fatalistic. In his opening speech, as he and Mommy are vaguely awaiting the arrival of "them"—whether Mrs. Barker, the Van Man, or just for something to happen—he answers Mommy's remark that "they" are late: "That's the way things are today, and there's nothing you can do about it." From the very beginning Daddy's tone is resigned, particularly in contrast to the whining, griping qualities in the complaints of Mommy. Even when Daddy goes on to list the needed repairs to icebox, doorbell, and toilet, it is clear that he really does not expect to get anything done about them. "That's the way things are today," he says, "You just can't get satisfaction."

Both ineffectualness and resignation have so reinforced each other in Daddy's character that "Oh dear; oh dear" becomes his typical reaction to whatever happens. The past is meaningless to him; he cannot even recall the name of the son they had adopted some years before. After Mrs. Barker has been present for some time on stage and then leaves, Daddy cannot recall her name; and when Mommy sends him off to break Grandma's television set, he cannot even find her room. His resignation seems to be due to the meaninglessness of his life and to his subjection to the dominating presence of Mommy. His response to this domination, like everything else he does, is characterized by a typical lack of resolution: "I do wish I weren't surrounded by women; I'd like some men around here." His only defense against Mommy is to withdraw into his own empty world, pretending to listen to her and responding just enough to keep her satisfied, which of course is all that she requires. There is nothing in life he wants anymore: "I just want to get it over with."

Mommy represents a second characteristic response to the void of modern life. She is a fanatic, who seeks to manipulate and dominate people in order to get her own "satisfaction." Heedless of the opinions or feelings of others, she is capable of casual cruelty (as when she tells Daddy she has the right to live off him because she married him and is entitled to his money when he dies) or nauseating flattery (as when she praises Daddy's firm masculinity in an attempt to make him get rid of Grandma)—capable of any means to attain her own ends. When she tells of her shopping expedition to purchase a hat, she makes it clear that her method of dealing with people is to create such an unpleasant scene that she finally has her way. By throwing hats around and screaming as loudly as she can she finally manages to get "satisfaction." The rest of the play demonstrates how she practices this method.

Mommy's treatment of everyone is imperious and demanding. Her attacks on Daddy show a ruthless disregard for his personality, and her relationship with Grandma is one long terrible scene of cruel bullying insult. She rages at Grandma, alternately telling her that she has nothing to say or that she is a liar. She threatens to hide Grandma's teeth, break her television, and send her away. This last embarrasses Daddy, who would rather not think about it. But Grandma refuses to be bullied by the woman that Grandma herself had warned Daddy not to marry because she was "a tramp and a trollop and a trull to boot." Grandma regards her as not having improved any with age. Mommy responds angrily that Grandma is *her* mother, not Daddy's, but Mommy fails to break up whatever relationship there is between Grandma and Daddy.

At the end of the play Mommy is quite pleased to have the Young Man waiting on her as a servant might. She sends him to fetch sauterne to celebrate their new family relationship, and he certainly will provide no resistance to her aggressiveness. She orders everyone to take a glass and drink to "satisfaction," which they all do as the play ends.

Mrs. Barker represents a third response to the existential vacuum. Her thoughts and actions are based not upon any principle or principles she holds within herself, for she has none. Instead she is a sensitive weather vane constantly seeking to align herself with the opinions of others and especially sensitive to the ideas (insofar as she knows what they are) of the various groups with which she is associated. Mrs. Barker represents a collectivistic response to absurdity, although not in the political sense. She is rather a kind of caricature of the other-directed person. From the beginning of the play Mrs. Barker is identified as a representative of organizations. She participates in Responsible Citizens Activities, Good Works, the Ladies Auxiliary Air Raid Committee, the Woman's Club, and of course the Bye-Bye Adoption Service, which explains her presence on stage. She announces when she first appears that she is a "professional woman"—that is to say an organization woman—and then reveals that she has been listening outside the door before coming in. This bit of eavesdropping allows her to blend into the conversation as soon as she enters, because she knows who is in the room and the tone of their remarks. In this way she avoids offending anyone. As it happens, Daddy has had a change of heart about sending Grandma away just before Mrs. Barker enters, and since she may be the person coming to get Grandma, he wishes aloud that Mrs. Barker might now just go away. Mrs. Barker's answer is characteristic: "Oh no; we're much too efficient for that." She represents an efficient organization and carefully chooses to have no view on the matter for herself.

Mrs. Barker is a caricature of amiability, ignoring the inconsistencies that arise when she agrees with everyone in turn. She talks enthusiastically about this "jolly family," as she calls it, finds their stories "engrossing" or "gripping," and exclaims several times about the "good idea" or the "nice idea" that someone had. In the end she remarks how glad she is that they are all pleased with the solution to their problem, a solution which has actually been engineered by Grandma. On three separate occasions in the dialogue Mrs. Barker takes contradictory positions on both sides of an argument. In effect, her method is to agree with the last speaker. When she and Mommy are talking about Woman Love in the country, the chief exponent of the movement seems to be Mrs. Barker's dear brother with his dear little wife, and Mrs. Barker agrees that the national tendency to hate women is deplorable. Just after that Daddy makes his complaint about being surrounded by women and wanting the companionship of men, and Mrs. Barker enthusiastically agrees with him. Later the question arises whether Mommy is being polite enough to Mrs. Barker. She allows

Mommy to persuade her of her good will, but as soon as Mommy leaves the room she agrees with Grandma that Mommy is mistreating her as a guest in the house. Finally, when confronted with the Young Man, who may be about to take Grandma away. Mrs. Barker says indignantly: "How dare you cart this poor old woman away!" But when he answers that he is paid to do it, Mrs. Barker says: "Well, you're quite right, of course, and I shouldn't meddle." Such confrontations show Mrs. Barker's shallowness and within her an element of fear that makes her so quick to please.

When she is asked a direct question, even about a simple matter, Mrs. Barker becomes pathetic. After Grandma has arranged for Mrs. Barker to introduce the Young Man into the family, Grandma asks Mrs. Barker if this has helped her accomplish her mission. It has helped, of course, because she has had no idea of what to do or even why she is there. When she accepts the credit for the "happy" ending from Mommy, she does it in the name of "professional women," so in a sense she does not claim to have solved the problem herself. About the usefulness of Grandma's assistance, however, she says: "I can't tell, yet. I'll have to . . . what *is* the word I want? . . . I'll have to relate it . . . that's it . . . I'll have to relate it to certain things that I *know,* and . . . draw . . . conclusions." What Mrs. Barker knows, when she knows anything at all, is the opinion of others, the rules of the various organizations, the collective mind of any group, however small, with which she comes in contact. Without such knowledge she is completely unable to respond even on a trivial subject. It is no wonder that at one point in the play she remarks pathetically: "But . . . I feel so lost . . . not knowing why I'm here." Is it possible that her name characterizes her? Could she be a barker for a cheap show, an amiable front woman who represents those inside the seductive but shaky tent of consensus?

It is to Grandma—the most appealing character in Albee's play—that we must look for a positive response to the existential vacuum. Although there seems to be no solution in the cosmic sense to the absurdity of our world, there is at least a way to make this world bearable. Among the commentators on the play there is general critical agreement that Grandma stands apart from the other characters. One critic writes: "The characters are dehumanized types, played in a mannered, marionette style—except Grandma, who is honest and therefore a real person." Another critic relates her to the American Dream motif: "Grandma is an anachronism: she represents the solid pioneer stock out of which the American Dream might have come had it not been corrupted instead." Having said these things, however, few critics see in Grandma or in the play generally any positive values applicable to the present. According to one writer, Albee "imparts no sense of a cure, the knowledge of paths toward enlargement, not the diminution of life." The observation has also been made that Albee "attempts to satirize a situation which he sees as both painful and irremediable," and thus his work is "largely a negation of the possibility of meaningful human action." Such lack of hope for the future is also reflected in this comment: "Sadly, however, we cannot say that Albee's outlook produces any . . . hope. As he perceives the future, he can see only annihilation, performed by a devouring world." One critic demurs by observing that Albee's "harshly satirical stance presupposes positive sense and meaning." This critic does not spell out precisely what the meaning is, but perhaps there are positive values implicit in this play, and, if so, we must turn to an analysis of the character of Grandma to find them.

The first positive value that Grandma represents is one of attitude. She is realistic; she has a sense of her own freedom and especially of her own dignity. Amid all the whining and sighing her most characteristic speech is cheerful: "How do you like them apples?" Her attitude is tinged with cynicism in her present situation, but this is a necessary antidote to the more than slight nausea we feel about the relationship between Mommy and Daddy. Even in her first comic entrance Grandma maintains her dignity. To Mommy's question about the boxes she is carrying Grandma replies: "That's nobody's damn business." One of her early speeches concerns the sense of dignity that is so important: " . . . that's all that's important . . . a sense of dignity. You got to have a sense of dignity, even if you don't care, 'cause if you don't have that, civilization's doomed." We see dignity in Grandma when she responds to Mommy's threats. "You don't frighten me," she says, "I'm too old to be frightened."

There is value also in Grandma's realistic attitude. She says that she is a "muddleheaded old woman," but the fact is that she sees more clearly than anyone else in the play. Through her the audience learns why Mommy married Daddy and much about their present relationship. Through Grandma we learn about Daddy's disillusionment with Mommy and with marriage, and of course the whole story of their adoption of a son years before is told by Grandma to Mrs. Barker. In three separate speeches Grandma gives a realistic picture of old age, yet manages at the same time to retain her own dignity. She knows about the threat of the Van Man who may take her away—whether he is the keeper of an old folks' home or Death itself—and when Mommy begins to talk about his arrival, Grandma says contemptuously, "I'm way ahead of you." The fact is that she is far ahead of all the other characters in the play.

Still another value is in Grandma's enjoyment of living. She apparently has lived a full and pleasant life, although we are given few details. But the good is enjoying the experience of life, which she has done. The things she has collected in her boxes, "a few images, a little garbled by now," do provide comedy, but the old letters, the blind Pekinese, the television set—even the Sunday teeth—all of which she thinks of sadly, indicate that she did enjoy life in the past. This cannot be said of any of the others. Some of Grandma's old spirit is revealed as she greets with appreciation the Young Man. She is the only one who knows the essential vacuity of the Young Man, but she can still enjoy his handsome, muscular appearance with an honest pleasure unlike that of the simperingly coy Mommy. "My, my, aren't you something!" Grandma says to the Young Man. And later she adds with a characteristic view of herself: "You know, if I were about a hundred and fifty years younger I could go for you."

Most important, however, Grandma is the only one in the play who shows a creative response to life. It is not merely that she makes plans, sees them carried out, and thus significantly exercises a freedom that the others do not. The baking contest represents Grandma's plan by which she intends to escape her dependence on Mommy and Daddy, and its $25,000 prize enables her to do just that at the end of the play. This in itself is significant enough compared to the aimless activities of Mommy, Daddy, and Mrs. Barker. But Grandma also is a kind of creative artist in her own way. Mommy tells how Grandma used to wrap the lunch boxes that Mommy took to school as a little girl, wrap them so nicely, as she puts it, that it would break her heart to open them. Grandma did this in spite of the poverty of the family. There is much comic nonsense in this story as Mommy tells it, but it also points to a creativity only partly suppressed. Certainly Grandma's use of language and her comments about language reveal another creative response to life. In general the comic irrelevance of the language mirrors the meaninglessness of life and demonstrates especially that language as gesture has replaced language as communication. For Grandma, however, language does serve to communicate, and her comments on style are both amusing and significant. Mommy tries to imitate her, but Grandma scornfully points out Mommy's failure to achieve harmony of rhythm and content.

Finally, another kind of creativity is shown in the way Grandma provides the resolution of the play by suggesting to Mrs. Barker what to do about the Young Man and by prompting the Young Man about taking a place in the family. Having arranged all this, Grandma steps outside of the set, addresses herself to the audience, and as a kind of stage manager observes the "happy" ending she has created. It is happy because, as she says, "everybody's got what he thinks he wants." She is satisfied: "Well, I guess that just about wraps it up. I mean, for better or worse, this is a comedy, and I don't think we'd better go any further." Life may have a void at its center, but perhaps how you wrap it up—one recalls the lunch boxes—has in itself a value.

Thus Albee's *The American Dream* makes the assumption that the dream is hollow and shows the causes and symptoms of a sick society. Through comic caricature it reveals three desperate responses to the existential vacuum, and then it goes on to do one thing more. In the character of Grandma the play suggests that whatever meaning is possible is achieved through an attitude of courageous realism that can enable man to conduct himself with dignity, through the simple enjoyment of whatever experience can be enjoyed, and through the creative act of the artist.

Source: Nicholas Canaday Jr., "Albee's *The American Dream* and the Existential Vacuum," in *South Central Bulletin*, Vol. 26, No. 4, Winter 1966, pp. 28–34.

SOURCES

Adams, Herbert R., "Albee, the Absurdists, and High School English?" in the *English Journal*, Vol. 55, No. 8, November 1966, pp.1045–48.

Albee, Edward, *The American Dream*, in *Two Plays by Edward Albee: The American Dream and The Zoo Story*, Signet, 1961, pp. 57–127.

Bigsby, C. W. E., *Modern American Drama, 1945–2000*, Cambridge University Press, 2000, p. 128–29.

Bloom, Harold, ed., *Edward Albee*, Chelsea House Publishers, 1987.

Canaday, Nicholas, Jr., "Albee's *The American Dream* and the Existential Vacuum," in the *South Central Bulletin*, Vol. 26, No. 4, Winter 1966, pp. 28–34.

Edemariam, Aida, "Whistling in the Dark," in the *Guardian*, January 10, 2004, p. 2.

Gussow, Mel, *Edward Albee: A Singular Journey*, Simon & Schuster, 1999.

Hirsch, Foster, *Who's Afraid of Edward Albee?* Creative Arts, 1978, p. 18.

Kolin, Philip C., ed., *Conversations with Edward Albee*, University Press of Mississippi, 1988.

Mayberry, Bob, *Theatre of Discord: Dissonance in Beckett, Albee, and Pinter*, Fairleigh Dickinson University Press, 1989.

Stenz, Anita Maria, *Edward Albee: The Poet of Loss*, Mouton, 1978.

Taubman, Howard, "The Theatre: Albee's *The American Dream*," in the *New York Times*, January 25, 1961, p. 28.

FURTHER READING

Bottoms, Stephen, ed., *The Cambridge Companion to Edward Albee*, Cambridge University Press, 2005.
    An overwhelmingly valuable resource, this volume of scholarly essays and interviews is meticulously researched, comprehensive in its scope, and wide reaching in its grasp of the subtleties and significances of this body of complex work.

Esslin, Martin, *The Theatre of the Absurd*, Vintage, 2004.
    Even four decades after its original publication, Esslin's groundbreaking study still reads as insightfully and provocatively as ever. In many ways this is the book that marked the emergence of a new type of theater whose major figures shattered dramatic conventions and paid little if any attention to psychological realism. In 1961, Esslin coined the phrase "Theatre of the Absurd," giving a name to the phenomenon of plays that dramatize the absurdity at the core of the human condition.

Gottdiener, Mark, *The Theming of America: American Dreams, Media Fantasies, and Themed Environments*, Westview Press, 2001.

> *The Theming of America* takes Albee's thesis from *The American Dream* and extends it into a readable and engaging exploration of the nature of social and cultural change in America since the 1960s. Moving from discussions of Graceland and Dollywood to commentaries on Las Vegas and the local mall, Gottdiener shows how modern Americans cannot escape the profusion of recognizable symbols and signs attached to virtually all aspects of their culture.

Mann, Bruce, *Edward Albee: A Casebook*, Routledge, 2002.

> A relatively short collection of scholarly and critical essays, this volume is remarkable for the consistently high level of writing and the determined innovation that it brings to the discussion of Albee's plays.

The Dumb Waiter

HAROLD PINTER

1957

Harold Pinter's *The Dumb Waiter* (1957) is a two character, one-act play. Set in a claustrophobic basement furnished like a cheap hotel for transients or even a prison cell, it is a study not so much of the two hit men temporarily staying there as they wait for their orders, but of the character of their interaction and of the nature of their condition, and by extension, the nature of the context defining the human condition.

Like cogs in a machine, subject to mysterious directives, bound together but alienated from each other, the hit men follow the orders they are given. They themselves seem to determine nothing. Their entire being is defined by their obedience to invisible, all-powerful, and quietly menacing forces. While the title of the play seems to refer to a small elevator built into the wall, usually used to transport food and trash from one floor in a building to another, Pinter is not referring only to the dumb waiter as a contraption, but to each one of the men as well. Both are waiting; both are dumb; one waits dumbly for the time to carry out an assassination; the other, unknowingly, for his own execution. Indeed, each man is a dumb waiter.

The paramount literary influence on Pinter's play is Samuel Beckett's *Waiting for Godot*, first published in French in 1952 and in Beckett's own English translation in 1954. Essentially, the play is an obscure rendition of two tramps waiting for the arrival of the mysterious Godot, the play

Harold Pinter *(The Library of Congress)*

seems to be a series of grim vaudeville turns by the two. Nothing really seems to happen except for the meaningless passage of time in a world emptied of meaning in which people live devoid of purpose or power. *Waiting for Godot* was a radically influential and transformative play. Indeed, the influence of *Waiting for Godot* on *The Dumb Waiter* is obvious.

A more recent text of *The Dumb Waiter* can be found in *The Bedford Introduction to Drama*, published in 1989 and edited by Lee A. Jacobus.

AUTHOR BIOGRAPHY

Harold Pinter was born to Jewish parents in a working-class neighborhood of East London on October 10, 1930. His father was a tailor. As a child he underwent the terror of being bombed during the Nazi blitzkrieg. The effect was to make an enduring pacifist of him and to embue him with a strong sense of the evil of power and its pervasive menace in human interactions. These issues became the primary concerns of his plays.

In 1948, Pinter entered the Royal Academy of Dramatic Art. But he found the school stulti-fying and left to join a touring repertory theater

that performed extensively throughout England and Ireland. At the same time, he was writing poetry, short stories, and a novel. In 1956, Pinter married Vivien Merchant, an actress, and began writing plays, which sometimes were vehicles for her. Merchant filed for divorce from Pinter in 1975, after he had begun what became a long-standing relationship with the historian Antonia Fraser. Pinter married Fraser after both their divorces were ratified in 1980. With Merchant, Pinter had a son, Daniel, who broke ties with his father after his parents' divorce.

Pinter's first play, *The Room*, was performed in 1957. It flopped. His next play, *The Dumb Waiter*, also written in 1957, was the first in a series of plays, including *The Caretaker* (1959), *The Birthday Party* (1957), and *The Homecoming* (1964). It was this group of plays that brought Pinter to international prominence and placed him in the same league as dramatists like Samuel Beckett and Eugène Ionesco. In the mid-1950s, these playwrights had begun to produce difficult and disturbing dramas that seemed alien to conventional ideas of theater, focusing partic-ularly on the use of language as a dramatic and a symbolic element. Their plays, moreover, pre-sented worlds that were bleak and fearsome, but also ridiculously meaningless or absurd. This type of drama came to be known as the Theater of the Absurd.

In all, Pinter has written twenty-nine plays. In addition to writing for the theater, Pinter began, in the 1960s, to write original screenplays and adaptations of other writers's work for the movies. He wrote a number of them for the London-based, blacklisted American director, Joseph Losey, and Pinter himself acted in a num-ber of films and on stage.

Although Pinter had refused to serve in the British military in 1948, his plays were seen as bleak representations of reality and not recog-nized as political statements. In the 1980s, how-ever, Pinter began to be publicly outspoken about political issues. He was ejected from the American embassy in Turkey at a reception in his honor, after he confronted the ambassador from Turkey regarding the torture of prisoners. Pinter has been a resolute critic of the American invasions of Iraq and of the Israeli occupation of Palestinian territories. In his 2005 speech accept-ing the Nobel Prize, he condemned the United States and the Bush administration for the inva-sion of Iraq and for its imperial and military activities in general. Pinter did not himself attend the ceremonies in Oslo because of the cancer with which he was diagnosed in 2002; he spoke instead by closed-circuit television. Like so many people living with cancer, Pinter has continued to live a productive life.

PLOT SUMMARY

First Encounter

Although *The Dumb Waiter* is a one-act play with no scene divisions, it is unobtrusively divided into a series of encounters between Ben and Gus in what seems to be a dormitory room in the basement of what apparently is or was a restaurant. They seem to be rising from sleep. Gus is tying his shoelaces and Ben, sitting on his bed, is reading the newspaper. Gus walks a few steps and then unties his laces, and takes off his shoes. From within one shoe Gus takes out a flattened, apparently empty box of matches and from the other a flattened pack of cigarettes. Then he puts his shoes back on. As Gus goes through these maneuvers, Ben looks up from his paper and regards him, apparently with disapproval, indicated by a rattling of his newspaper. Once he has put his shoes back on, Gus wanders off the set. Ben follows him with his eyes. Then the sound of a toilet chain being pulled is heard, but it is not followed by the sound of a toilet flushing. When Gus returns, Ben "slams down the paper" and begins talking about a story he has just read in the paper.

An old man who tried to cross a street congested with traffic by crawling under a truck was run over when the truck started to move. The two condemn the inappropriateness of a man of eighty-seven crawling under a truck. When Gus expresses disbelief at the story, twice Ben points out that it must be so because it is written in the paper. The encounter ends when Gus again exits to the lavatory. There is the sound of the chain being pulled but no subsequent sound of the toilet flushing. Gus returns

Second Encounter

Gus tells Ben he wants to ask him a question. Before he can, Ben asks him "What are you doing out there?" Before Gus can answer, Ben shoots another question at him: "What about

MEDIA ADAPTATIONS

- *The Dumb Waiter*, a 1987 film adaptation of the play, was directed by Robert Altman and stars John Travolta as Ben and Tom Conti as Gus. It was broadcast on television in 1989, and was released on VHS by Prism Entertainment.

the tea?" Gus explains he is about to make it. Ben fires back "Well, go on, make it." Instead Gus sits. He begins to describe the crockery. He alludes to someone called "he." "He" has provided "some very nice crockery this time." There is the suggestion of a mysterious superior and that this is not their first "job" for him. What that job is has not been made explicit and never is until the end of the play. Ben asks Gus why he cares about the crockery, ominously adding that he is not going to eat. Gus responds that he has brought a few biscuits. Adding to the sense of foreboding, Ben tells him that he ought to make tea and eat them quickly since there is not much time left.

Third Encounter

Gus does not go to make tea. He takes out his flattened empty cigarette pack and asks Ben if he has any cigarettes. Ben does not look up from his paper or answer and Gus continues, saying he "hope[s] it won't be a long job, this one," indicating that what they are doing is a routine operation. Ben still makes no response and Gus again says, this time as if remembering he has not yet done so: "Oh, I wanted to ask you something." Instead of responding, or possibly as a response to prevent Gus's question, Ben "slams down" his paper and tells Gus another story from the paper, as if distracting him, about an eight-year-old girl who has been accused of killing a cat. They earnestly speculate if it might have been her brother who did it and blamed her. Ben goes back to his paper and Gus rises.

Fourth Encounter

Gus asks: "What time is he getting in touch?" "He" is presumably their boss. Ben says nothing. Gus repeats the question. Ben responds irritably: "What's the matter with you? It could be any time."

Fifth Encounter

Gus says "I was going to ask you something." Ben says "What?" Gus then asks Ben why the toilet takes so long to flush. The "ballcock" in the toilet is broken, Ben explains. Gus says he had not thought of that. The banality of what they are saying suggests that there is something they are not saying, although what that is remains unclear.

Sixth Encounter

Gus says he has not slept well and complains about the quality of the bed and the lack of a second blanket. His attention is diverted by a picture on the wall of a cricket team. He points it out to Ben, who does not know what he is talking about and asks again: "What about that tea." Gus responds that the members of the team "look a bit old" to him.

Seventh Encounter

Gus remarks that he would not like to live in the room they are in. He wishes there were a window to see outside. Ben asks him what he wants a window for. Gus says that he'd like a view, that it helps pass the time. He complains about his job, that he spends the day enclosed in a room and when he leaves at night, it is dark outside. "You get your holidays, don't you?" Ben retorts. Gus complains that they are only for two weeks. Ben chides him for not appreciating how infrequently they have to work. Ben explains his problem is Gus has no interests. Gus says he does so, but when pressed, cannot name any. Ben mentions several of his and how he is always ready for work. Gus responds by asking Ben if he does not "ever get a bit fed up?" Ben does not know what he is talking about.

Eighth Encounter

Gus is out of cigarettes. The toilet finally flushes. Gus complains some more about working conditions. Remembering their last job, he complains that "He doesn't seem to bother about our comfort much these days." Ben rebukes Gus, telling him to "stop jabbering," but Gus goes on. Ben tells him to make the tea already and that they will not have to wait much longer.

Ninth Encounter

Gus takes out a packet of tea and says that he has been meaning to ask Ben something. Ben says "What the hell is it now?" Gus asks Ben why he stopped "the car that morning, in the middle of a road." Ben answers evasively. "We were too early," he says. The answer does not satisfy Gus. He does not understand how they could be too early since they left after they got a call telling them "to start right away." "Who took the call, me or you?" Ben snaps. Gus admits it was Ben and Ben repeats "We were too early." But Gus can not let it go; "Too early for what?" he says. Ben does not answer. Finally, Gus breaks the silence by supposing the answer that Ben withholds. "You mean someone had to get out before we got in?" Ben remains silent and Gus continues trying to figure things out. He says the sheets on the bed did not look fresh and smelled a little. He complains that he does not want to share his sheets with someone else and remarks that the fact that the sheets are not fresh shows that "things [are] going down the drain" because "we've always had clean sheets laid on up till now." Ben points out that Gus has slept in those sheets all day. Gus concedes that it might be his smell on the sheets and perhaps he does not know what he himself smells like.

Tenth Encounter

Ben looks at the newspaper. Finally, he interrupts his silence, exclaiming "Kaw!" about something he has just read. Gus asks what town they are in? He says he has forgotten. Ben tells him Birmingham. Gus suggests that they can go to watch the city's soccer team play. Ben tells him that they are playing away, that there is no time, anyhow. Gus points out that "in the past," they stayed over to watch a game. Ben's response is ominous: "Things have tightened up, mate." Gus says that they have never been to Tottenham or "done a job" there, Ben contradicts him. Gus says that he would remember Tottenham. Ben says "Don't make me laugh, will you?" Gus wonders when "he" is going to get in touch with them. Ben does not respond. Gus shifts the subject back to soccer. They argue about which team is playing where, Ben contradicting whatever Gus says.

Eleventh Encounter

A new force enters the play. "An envelope slides under the door." Gus notices it and points it out to Ben. Ben asks what it is. Gus says he does not know. Ben tells him to pick it up. Gus approaches it slowly and picks it up. Ben continues to direct him. Gus opens it. There are matches inside. He hands Ben the envelope. There is no note included. Ben orders Gus to open the door to see if he can catch whoever slipped the envelope under it. Gus gets his gun, opens the door, but no one is there. Gus puts his gun back under his pillow.

Twelfth Encounter

Gus looks at the matches, comments that they will come in handy, and he and Ben go back and forth about how useful the matches are, how Gus is always running out of matches, and finally, Gus says "I can light the kettle now." He does not move to do that, however, and they talk a little more about the matches until Ben slaps Gus's hand as Gus cleans his ear with one of the matches, telling him not to waste them but to go and "light it." Gus has just said he "can light the kettle now," but he does not know what Ben is referring to. They bandy words back and forth until it is clear that Ben is telling him to make tea. Before he begins to, Gus and Ben argue whether properly speaking one says "light the kettle" or "light the gas." Ben says "Light the Kettle." Gus says, "You mean the gas," even though he himself had just used the expression "light the kettle." Ben responds "What do you mean, I mean the gas," ominously as his eyes, according to the stage directions, narrow. The inane but sinister argument continues for a good twenty lines with Ben attacking and Gus defending himself until a moment of real and senseless violence erupts when Ben grabs Gus "with two hands by the throat, at arm's length," and yells "THE KETTLE, YOU FOOL! " Gus capitulates, saying "All right, all right," but does nothing. Ben asks him what he is waiting for. Gus says he wants to see if the matches light. He strikes one on the box; it does not. He tosses the matches under the bed and retrieves them as Ben stares at him. He strikes a match on his shoe and it lights. Fed up, Ben says "Put on the bloody kettle, for Christ's sake," realizing it is an expression he had derided in the foregoing argument. Gus goes out and then returns, saying "It's going." When Ben says "What?" Gus says "The stove," using the word "stove" instead of "kettle" or "gas."

Thirteenth Encounter

The question Gus has been trying to ask Ben begins to emerge when Gus muses "I wonder who it'll be tonight." He clears his throat and says "I've been wanting to ask you something." Ben expresses annoyance that Gus is "always asking [him] questions." Ben then asks Gus why he is sitting on his [Ben's] bed. He says Gus never used to ask "so many damn questions." He asks him "what's the matter with you?" Gus tries to defend himself by saying— before he even gets to ask the question—"No, I was just wondering." Ben tells him to "stop wondering," to do his job and "shut up." But Gus is not thwarted. He says that was what he was wondering about. Ben responds as if he does not know what Gus is talking about. Gus asks hesitantly "who it's going to be tonight?" Ben refuses to answer, seeming not to know what Gus is talking about, throwing questions like "Who what's going to be? " and "Are you feeling alright?" back at him. And Ben tells him again, "Go and make the tea." Nothing is said, but something sinister is evident.

Fourteenth Encounter

Ben is alone as Gus is offstage making tea. He takes his revolver out from under his pillow and makes sure it is loaded. Inspecting the weapon while Gus is off-stage, suggests that he knows something Gus does not about how the gun will be used.

Gus reenters, not yet having made tea because there is no gas and he does not have a shilling to drop in the gas meter, nor does Ben. Ben says they will have to wait for Wilson for the shilling. But he might not come; "he might just send a message." Wilson never does appear. Waiting for Wilson satirizes the main conceit of Samuel Beckett's *Waiting for Godot*. Ben tells Gus he just might have to wait for his tea until afterwards. As Gus complains that he likes to have his tea beforehand, Ben "holds the revolver up to the light and polishes it," telling Gus "you'd better get ready."

Gus is becoming irritable. He grumbles about the fact that Wilson has not provided gas. When he says that the room they are staying in is Wilson's "place," Ben challenges him, but Gus insists it is. As he speaks he begins to wonder about the other jobs they have done for Wilson, how "nobody ever hears a thing," how Wilson does not always show up at all, how difficult he finds it to talk to him. Ben tells him to be quiet, but Gus persists, wondering "about the last one." Ben acts as if he does not to know what Gus is talking about, and Gus says it is about "that girl."

Fifteenth Encounter

Ben ignores what Gus has just said and angrily goes back to reading the newspaper. Gus, who had been rather compliant, has become frustrated and impatient. He has not had his tea, after all. He asks "How many times have you read that paper?" In anger "Ben slams the paper down," asks Gus what he means, threatens to box him in the ear if he does not watch out, accuses him of taking liberties, and warns him, when Gus tries to explain, to "get on with it, that's all." But Gus has begun to wonder about his past jobs and cannot stop talking. He reverts to the subject of the girl. From what he says, it appears that they killed her. Gus is disturbed, not because they killed her, but because of the messiness involved and wonders who cleans up after them. Ben calls him a fool.

Sixteenth Encounter

They hear a noise inside the wall between the beds and notice that a dumb waiter is built into the wall. Inside the dumb waiter is a note appearing to be an order for food. It reads "Two braised steak and chips. Two sago puddings. Two teas without sugar." Gus comments on the tea, not having been able to have any himself and now apparently being directed to make some for others. Gus is puzzled at the order, but Ben says that the place must have been a café, that it has "change[d] hands," and that where they are had been a kitchen. Gus wonders who owns the place now. "Well, that all depends," Ben says. He is interrupted by the clatter of the dumb waiter. This time the piece of paper reads "Soup of the day. Liver and onions. Jam tart." Do these words signify actual food items as they usually do, or are they codes, perhaps informing Ben about a decision higher-ups have made with regard to the job? The interpretative limits for this text seem to be flexible. Some silent business follows. Ben looks into the dumb waiter but not up the shaft. Gus, behind him, puts his hand on Ben's shoulder and Ben throws it off. Gus then looks into the dumb waiter and *up* the shaft. This gesture alarms Ben who pushes Gus away from the dumb waiter, tosses his gun onto the bed and tells Gus that they had better "send something up." Gus agrees and when he goes to shout something

up the dumb waiter, Ben stops him. They go through a bag of food Gus has with him, noting the items. Ben suggests they send the packet of tea; Gus objects, pointing out it is all the tea they have. Ben reminds him it is useless since they can not turn on the gas. Gus says "Maybe they can send us down" a coin for the gas meter. Ben ignores him and asks what else Gus has in his bag and Gus takes out a sugared pastry called an Eccles cake. Ben scolds Gus for never having told him he had brought one and he scolds him as well for only bringing one and none for him. He adds that they can not "send up" just one Eccles cake but does not answer when Gus asks "Why not?" Instead he tells Gus to get a plate. Gus asks if he cannot keep the cake since "they don't know we've got it." But Ben tells him he can not keep it. Then Ben finds a bag of potato chips in Gus's bag and the same routine is repeated as Ben scolds Gus, telling him he is "playing a dirty game," and "I'll remember this," presumably not just for failing to declare all his food, but for the insubordination that this reflects. Once they have piled up the food they have gathered on a plate and are about to put it in the dumb waiter, before they can, the dumb waiter goes up empty. Ben tells Gus it is his fault for "playing about," that they will have to wait until it comes down again. Ben puts the plate on the bed, puts on his shoulder holster and begins to knot his tie. He tells Gus he ought to get ready.

Seventeenth Encounter

Gus puts on his tie and shoulder holster. He wonders how their room can be a café since the gas stove has only three rings, not allowing for much cooking. Ben answers dryly: "That's why the service is slow." Gus keeps up his inconsequential chatter and Ben does not answer him. The dumb waiter returns. Gus retrieves a note demanding more dishes, the redundantly named "Macaroni Pastitsio" and the exotic "Ormitha Macarounada." He puts the plate of their snacks on the dumb waiter and shouts its contents into the shaft. The dumb waiter goes up and Ben reprimands Gus for having yelled because "it isn't done." He then tells him to get dressed because "It'll be any minute now."

Eighteenth Encounter

Gus continues complaining about the "place," especially about the lack of tea and biscuits. Ben tells him that eating "makes you lazy" and that

Gus is getting lazy. He asks Gus if he has checked his gun and notes that he never polishes it. "Gus rubs his revolver on the sheet." Ben fixes his tie in preparation for the job. Gus continues his chatter. He wonders about the cook and if there is another kitchen and if there are more gas stoves. Ben assures him, with dry condescension, that there are. He asks Gus if he knows "what it takes to make an Ormitha Macarounada." Gus does not. Ben begins to tell him, but cuts himself short before he says anything and tells Gus to be quiet.

Gus puts his revolver in its holster and continues to complain. He wants to get out of the place. He wonders why "he" has not gotten in touch with them yet. He says that he and Ben have always done "reliable" work. He hopes their job is easy. He has a bad headache. The dumb waiter descends again with more food orders and the packet of tea they had sent up. They can not fill the orders and Ben says "urgently" that they "better tell them" so. As he is about to write a note, he discovers a speaking tube he had not seen, in the wall, beside the dumb waiter. Gus first speaks into the tube after they figure out how it works and says "The larder's bare!" Ben takes the tube from him and politely repeats that there is no more food. Someone on the other end seems to be complaining about the inadequacy of each of the items they have sent up. The conversation ends as Ben reports that the voice instructed him to "light the kettle!" suggesting the earlier argument about the correct idiom, but Gus points out "there's no gas." He is annoyed at being instructed to make tea for others when there is none for him. Ben says nothing. Noticing how bad Ben looks, Gus says that he could use an "Alka-Seltzer" himself. Ben says that the time is near.

Nineteenth Encounter
Gus complains that he does not like having to do the job while he is hungry. Ben silences him, saying he must give him his instructions. Gus does not know why since they always do the same thing. Ben repeats "Let me give you your instructions." He states them; Gus repeats them. They never mention the actual deed of killing, only all their moves preceding that. When they finish, Gus "shivers," exits, and the sound of the toilet chain pulled in the lavatory is heard.

Twentieth Encounter
Gus reenters; he is troubled and thoughtful. Why, he asks Ben, did "he" send them matches when "he knew there was no gas." Ben does not answer. Gus repeats the question twice. Ben answers he does not know what Gus is talking about. Gus continues: "Who is it upstairs?" Ben evades the question, commanding Gus to be silent. Gus persists. Ben commands him to "Shut up!" Ben hits him twice on the shoulder "viciously." That does not stop Gus. Nearly hysterical, he cries out "What's he doing it for? We've been through our tests.... What's he playing these games for?" As he is ranting, the dumb waiter returns. Gus "seizes" the note, which is an order for "Scampi." He crumples the note and frantically yells through the tube: "WE'VE GOT NOTHING LEFT! NOTHING! DO YOU UNDERSTAND?" Ben pushes him away, calls him a maniac, screams "That's enough," and replaces the speaking tube.

The dumb waiter ascends, Gus and Ben look each other in the eye. Gus sits on his bed. Ben starts to read the paper, throws it down, exclaims "Kaw!" as he had earlier when other stories caught his attention, and says "Have you ever heard such a thing?" without saying what he is reading. The two of them comment incredulously about the unrecounted story.

Gus leaves, he says, to get a glass of water. The whistle of the speaking tube blows. Ben answers and is told it is time and that the mark will be coming in right away. Ben hangs up the tube, calls to Gus twice, combs his hair, and is ready. The toilet is heard to flush. Gus stumbles in through the door stripped of his jacket, vest, tie, holster, and revolver. He looks at Ben. In silence, "they stare at each other."

CHARACTERS

Ben
Ben is one of the two men waiting in a basement to carry out what appears to be a hired killing. He is the one in charge of the operation. He is rather quiet and does not question his assignments or complain about his working conditions. He spends the time waiting reading the newspaper and is fascinated by odd human interest stories usually involving strange twists of violence, like an old man being killed ducking under a truck or some youngsters killing a cat. He is often evasive

when he speaks. He tells his partner as little as possible about their assignment and often responds to his questions by saying he does not know what he is talking about. His attitude towards his superiors is deferential. He believes in their authority and, in a limited way, has authority himself. After his partner, Gus, shouts into a speaking tube, Ben apologizes to whoever is on the other end. He is capable of violence and lunges at Gus when he cannot contain his rage at Gus's undisciplined behavior. He gives orders to Gus without feeling the need to explain himself. He often demeans Gus and treats him with condescension and disdain. Ben insists that his way of speaking or doing things is the correct way. If the play is seen as the symbolic representation of mankind's powerlessness in the face of a cruel God or cruel fate, Ben can be seen as the agent of that cruelty. If viewed from a psychological standpoint, Ben is tormented by his very role as an agent of torment.

The Dumb Waiter

The dumb waiter—commonly found in a house built for servants—is a small elevator to carry things between floors. Although conventionally a prop, the dumb waiter can be seen as a kind of mechanical character in the play. It is used to convey orders to the two men in the basement from an unidentified character upstairs. The orders it carries seem to be orders for food, but the mysterious context in which they arrive can make them seem like codes or representations of demands made on mankind by higher forces, demands that seem unreasonable or impossible to fulfill either because of mankind's inadequacy or the exotic quality of the demand. Although only a mechanical object, in the play the dumb waiter is given almost metaphysical power. It can signify the confusion in communication that people often experience in their interactions. It can also be seen as the imperfect channel of communication between mankind and an unseen deity or incomprehensible fate.

Gus

Gus is talkative, inquisitive, and even resentful of his superiors. Whereas Ben spends much of the time they are waiting sitting on his bed reading the newspaper, Gus is often in motion, taking off and putting on his shoes, going to the toilet, fooling with matches, or looking at the crockery. He knows nothing about the job they are going to do, and, despite its apparently grim

nature, his chief concern is to have his tea. When he is unable to have tea, it frustrates him greatly. Gus also tries to withhold some of his food when Ben suggests they send it upstairs in an attempt to meet the demands of the person or people sending down orders. His food becomes a sacrificial object to send up, foreshadowing Gus himself as a sacrificial object. But the sacrifice seems meaningless. Gus complains about how he and Ben are treated by the man they are working for. He is bored, objects to the smell of their bed sheets or the lack of a window in the room. Whereas Ben is an executioner, Gus is a victim. At the end of the play, it appears that he is the person they have been assigned to kill. Unlike Ben, Gus has doubts about what they are doing and is full of troubled questions about their situation. He is inefficient and slow in obedience. He is not really tough but rather desperately childlike and confused. He displays a rebellious nature, raging against an authority that is incomprehensible to him. If the play is read as a symbolic representation of mankind's predicament in relation to God or fate, Gus represents the desperation people can feel who sense themselves abandoned in a world without meaning or a loving God. In terms of the play's structure, it is Gus who propels the action by his questions, complaints and outbursts.

The Room

The room Ben and Gus wait in is entirely nondescript except for its two beds and two doors, one on the left, one on the right. It has no windows but it can communicate to a limited world outside, to a bathroom through the doors, and to the upstairs through the dumb waiter and a speaking tube. It is possible to think of the room as signifying a place of testing for both Ben and Gus. Indeed, Gus cries out that they have already been tested and demands to know why they are being tested again. In Jean-Paul Sartre's one-act play, *No Exit* (1944), hell is represented by three people confined to a single room for eternity. In *The Dumb Waiter*, the room Ben and Gus occupy can be thought of as a kind of purgatory through which they are passing, but a purgatory that leads them not to Heaven but to a Hell of coldly uncaring meaninglessness.

Wilson

Wilson is not an on-stage character in *The Dumb Waiter* but is mentioned by Ben and Gus as the man they are working for and who may or may not appear. He is often only referred to as "he," reinforcing his shadowy nature and mysterious presence. Nothing is really known about him. Perhaps he is the person upstairs sending orders down on the dumb waiter. Perhaps it is someone else. It is not clear if Ben and Gus work for one man or for an amorphous organization. Perhaps they, as well as the audience, do not know. As a character who never appears, Wilson is similar to Godot, in Samuel Beckett's *Waiting for Godot*, a play in which two characters interact in a barren landscape as they wait for the mysterious Godot to appear. Why they are waiting and what he will bring them are not revealed. Wilson, like Godot, can be thought of as representing a God who is himself hidden and whose purposes are hidden, a god who makes all of us into dumb waiters—people waiting stupidly or quietly for something and ultimately only finding death.

THEMES

Alienation

While the word alienation is never mentioned in *The Dumb Waiter*, the atmosphere of the play reeks of it. Ben and Gus, long-time partners who have worked closely together, are isolated from each other. Their overt conversation is composed of empty exchanges about articles in the newspaper. The conversation that goes on beneath the surface, which is expressed through their attitude towards each other, shows distance and evasion governing their intercourse. The work they do is also representative of a fundamental alienation in their world. They have no say in where they go or what they do. They seem unsure about the forces for whom they work or exactly what is wanted of them by their superiors, as all the business with the orders coming on the dumb waiter suggests. In addition the work they do, killing people, is a pure example of alienation.

Avoidance

Pinter is often discussed as a playwright whose concern is to show the difficulties or the failures in communication that people experience. More pointedly, in *The Dumb Waiter*, Pinter seems to be showing how people use words to avoid communicating. In *The Dumb Waiter* he seems to be exploring the rhetoric of evasion. Ben repeatedly uses the newspaper to give him things to talk to Gus about, and the two of them become entangled passionately in discussions and arguments about the most trivial things from weird news items such as which soccer team was playing where. Meanwhile, Ben particularly avoids any real contact or conversation with Gus, who does strive for it. Ben's evasion is necessary considering what seems to be the underlying plot of the play, that he is about to kill Gus at a moment that will be determined for him.

Betrayal

The suggestion of betrayal is implicit in *The Dumb Waiter*. No overt reason for the tension between Ben and Gus is ever presented, but there are suggestions that Ben, who is Gus's partner and superior, seems to know something that he is withholding from Gus. What was he thinking about when he stopped their car as he was driving to the job while Gus was asleep in the seat next to him? Gus wants to know, but Ben does not say. Similarly, Ben warns Gus several times throughout the play that he is getting lazy and that his attitude towards his work and his superiors is poor. In their last confrontation, as Gus stumbles disarmed into the room and Ben faces him with a gun, while ambiguity still lingers regarding Ben's previous knowledge that it is Gus whom he was hired to kill, it seems likely that Ben did know it. The ambiguity of the last moments leaves open the question of whether he will complete his betrayal of his partner or, as it were, betray his superiors. Ironically, from the point of view of those superiors who have ordered Gus's extermination, Gus himself is the one having betrayed them by his questioning, resentful, and rebellious attitude. By ordering Ben to kill Gus they are, in addition, forcing him to betray himself, hence his irritability towards Gus. Ben must purge himself of any fellow feeling for Gus.

Obedience and Resistance

The work that Ben and Gus do requires unquestioning obedience to the to forces that direct them but of which they are only peripherally aware. As hired killers, they are expected to surrender moral judgment, human compassion, awareness of the humanity of the Other and replace those traits with unstinting, unquestioning obedience. Their obedience is demanded in seemingly lesser matters, too, as their anxiety to fulfill the food orders that come via the dumb waiter show. The apparent fault that puts Gus in

TOPICS FOR FURTHER STUDY

- Pinter's early plays, like *The Dumb Waiter*, often called "comedies of menace," reflect the spirit of the 1950s, a decade characterized by a number of generalized anxieties about nuclear war, gang violence, economic repression, political witch hunts, and nervous breakdowns. Choose any one of these areas to research. Write an essay on your findings, introducing and exploring the issue, and setting it in historical, political, economic, and cultural contexts. Using your paper as a basis, introduce and explain the issue to your class.

- In addition to *The Dumb Waiter*, read Pinter's plays *The Room*, *The Caretaker*, and *The Homecoming*. Write an essay exploring the ways these plays resemble and differ from each other in terms of plot, characters, themes, dramatic construction, and tone.

- With one other member of your class, perform *The Dumb Waiter* or a selection from it for your class. Prepare a working script of the play in which you note the interpretive choices you have made, such as the way you choose to deliver the lines or the way you

move on stage. Then explain why you have made those choices.

- The characters in *The Dumb Waiter* use speech as a way of avoiding communication. Write a story in which the characters speak with each other, interact, and do things together but never really say what is on their minds. Or, describe a situation in which you avoided saying what you wanted to say and another situation where you spoke to cover up what you meant. How is such speech different (or not different) from lying?

- Write a sequel to *The Dumb Waiter*. What can happen next? If you think that there is not a possible sequel to *The Dumb Waiter*, despite its open ending, write an essay discussing why you feel this way. Be sure to cite examples from the play in support of your argument.

- Lead a class debate based on this question: Is there a hero and a villain in *The Dumb Waiter*? If so, who is the hero, and who is the villain? Why? If not, why not?

danger is the beginning of curiosity, questioning, and self-assertion, feeble as it is, that he displays. Obedience always faces a threat from the opposite that it generates, which is resistance. The traits Gus shows are threats to obedience. Ben, on the other hand, shows himself, until the end of the play, to be perfectly obedient. It is not clear whether his obedience will continue or if something else in him will prevail. It is reasonable to assume that Ben's extreme irritation with Gus throughout the play is a result of a conflict within himself between his obedience to his masters and some sort of fellow-feeling towards his partner, a feeling he must stifle.

STYLE

Interactions Presented as Encounters

The Dumb Waiter is a one-act play performed without interruption. Pinter achieves a sense of structure by setting up a series of encounters between the two characters. These encounters flow one into the next but each one is also complete in itself within the context of the play, the way a scene is. The encounters establish a pattern in the relationship between Ben and Gus and they serve to define the characteristics of each. The encounters have the shape of old vaudeville routines and they mix the comic interaction and timing of those kinds of routines with an underlying quality of menace that is conveyed by the intensity of each character's participation in those routines. The climax of the play, when Ben repeatedly punches Gus in the shoulder, transforms slapstick into anxious rage. The final moments of the play, a second climax, is only a nonverbal encounter in which the ambiguity of the relationship between Ben and Gus hovers unresolved over the play and over the audience, as if removed from the play and given to the audience as a choice. The choice is between the kind of alienated, evasive relationships presented in the play, the kind that must terminate in betrayals of both oneself and other people, or relationships that begin to realize a shared essential something that can connect people to each other. The final encounter in *The Dumb Waiter*, then, is not the climactic encounter between Ben and Gus but an encounter between the play itself and its audience.

Pauses

The word "pause" appears nearly two dozen times as a stage direction in *The Dumb Waiter*, the word "silence" some half a dozen times, and a notation that the two characters stare at each other without saying anything appears frequently, too. The play ends, in fact, with the direction that there is a long silence in which the characters stare at each other. If the spoken words in *The Dumb Waiter* are essential tools of evasion and signify alienation, the pauses, silences, and moments when Ben and Gus stare at each other signify, without being conveyed by verbal props, the essential but buried matter of the play—the mysterious connection and the incipient betrayal that constitutes the relationship between the two characters and the action of the drama. What is hidden by talk is revealed, even if only darkly, by silences. The anxiety, confusion, conflict, and tension governing the interactions between Ben and Gus provoke a sense of some indefinably menacing danger hovering about and defining the texture of the world they inhabit.

HISTORICAL CONTEXT

The Cold War

The sense of indefinable menace and of insecurity that permeates *The Dumb Waiter* reflects the Zeitgeist, or spirit of the time, that pervaded the 1950s because of the Cold War. The Cold War was a conflict between the United States and the Soviet Union, now Russia, and a group of smaller countries, for political, military, and economic control of the globe. In its most menacing form, the Cold War consisted of an arms race between the two super powers, as they were called, to build the most daunting weaponry, particularly in the form of nuclear bombs. The Soviet Union and the United States had been allies against Nazi Germany, Fascist Italy, and Imperial Japan during World War II from 1939–1945. After the war, they slowly became foes, partly because of different political structures.

The war against Japan ended when Harry Truman, then President of the United States, ordered the dropping of atomic bombs on the Japanese cities of Hiroshima, on August 6, 1945, and Nagasaki, on August 9, 1945. In addition to destroying these two Japanese cities, the dropping of the atomic bombs announced to the world, and especially to the Soviet Union's dictator, Joseph Stalin, that the United States was a power to fear. Stalin, after the war, had imperial designs on many of the countries of Europe and indeed managed to subordinate many Eastern European countries to the Soviet Union. In response to the American bombs, the Russians also built nuclear weapons, and each country established bases from which they pointed their weapons at the other country's major cities. This policy of Mutually Assured Destruction both kept the balance of power between the two super states and caused a general malaise among most of the people, as well as resistance in some. There were general, compulsory shelter drills that people, including school children, were forced to participate in. Some, like the philosopher/mathematician Bertram Russell in Britain, protested the building, testing, and deploying of nuclear weapons. The menacing sense of looming danger pervasive in *The Dumb Waiter* reflects this cultural condition.

Gangster Movies

The models for the two hit men, Ben and Gus, are the gangsters in the films Hollywood turned out in the 1940s and 1950s where gangsters were played as suave and debonair, yet disturbing and menacing, characters by actors like Humphrey Bogart, Edward G. Robinson, Farley Granger, George Raft, Yul Brynner, Dan Duryea, and James Cagney. They were often odd mixtures of brutality and delicacy, of charm and cruelty, of

COMPARE & CONTRAST

- **1950s:** An air of fear and menace taints many human interactions and ways of thinking because of the Cold War, which pits countries like Great Britain and the United States on one side against the Soviet Union on the other. Each side has a cause for anxiety because each has the capability to engage in nuclear warfare.

  Today: An air of fear and menace taints many human interactions and ways of thinking because of the "War on Terror," which pits western governments like the United States and Great Britain against several Middle Eastern governments and religious factions who believe themselves to be waging a holy war and who stage terrorist attacks around the world.

- **1950s:** "Organization men" working for large corporations shape their lives to conform to the rules set down by their employers. They seem to be cogs in a great machine rather than spontaneous individuals.

  Today: In the global economy, workers are treated like interchangeable parts of a great machine. Rather than becoming integral parts of a corporation which they serve and which offers them a secure, lifelong career, people experience uncertainty in their jobs and face the possibility of layoffs and corporate downsizing.

- **1950s:** People are distracted from their anxieties and from independent and organized opposition, in Western Europe and the United States, by public relations, entertainment, sports, and advertising.

  Today: People are distracted from their anxieties and from independent and organized opposition, in Western Europe and the United States by public relations, entertainment, sports, advertising, and technological gadgetry.

bravado and cowardice. They were suave and crude, attractive and repellent, narcissistic poseurs without a strong center. Ben tries to maintain an air of cool detachment, reading the paper, stoically doing his job. He makes sure to fix his tie and comb his hair before he goes into action. Not only does Pinter model his thugs on the hero-gangsters of these movies, but the characters themselves, especially Ben, seem to be deliberately modeling themselves on the movie images.

The Holocaust

Between 1933 and 1945, the Nazi German government rounded up some ten million people, among them Jews, Gypsies, homosexuals, and communists, and incarcerated and systematically exterminated them. Without warning, a knock could come at the door and a whole family, or whole towns, could be taken, in minutes, to places known as death camps. The sense of dread this introduced into the world's psyche is reflected in *The Dumb Waiter*.

The Organization Man

The idea of the organization man, a man who worked for, and conformed to, the dictates of a large corporation—which became the source not only of his income but the arbiter of everything about the way he lived his life, raised his family, and comported himself—strongly influenced the mainstream culture of the 1950s. The critical response to that culture by writers and artists trying to make sense of or reform, reshape, and, from their point of view, reinvigorate that culture, became a powerful counter-cultural movement in this decade and the decade that followed. Ben and Gus can be seen as serious parodies of those men and the organization they work for is a shadowy representation of those corporate entities.

The Theater of the Absurd

Theater of the Absurd refers to a kind of play written during the 1940s, 1950s, and 1960s, primarily in Europe, and especially in France. Playwrights

Scene from the 2007 Trafalgar Studios 1 production of The Dumb Waiter, *starring Jason Isaacs as Ben and Lee Evans as Gus (© Donald Cooper | Photostage)*

like Albert Camus, Jean Genet, Jean-Paul Sartre, Samuel Beckett, Fernando Arabal, Edward Albee, Harold Pinter, and Eugène Ionesco wrote dramas that reflected their vision of a world that had lost meaning and purpose. Camus, in *The Myth of Sysiphus* used the term "the absurd" to characterize a philosophy of existence that saw no meaning in the universe and made each individual responsible for the creation of meaning and purpose despite the emptiness of existence. The term "Theater of the Absurd" was invented by the theater critic Martin Esslin in 1962 when he wrote a book of that name exploring the work of these playwrights.

Vaudeville

Pinter's dialogue is often reminiscent of the kind of routines that were perfected in vaudeville by teams of comedians, one being a straight man and the other bouncing off him to deliver the laugh lines. The routines usually worked due to the confusion that existed between the two because each had a different frame of reference from his partner when he spoke. By the 1950s, vaudeville in theaters was pretty much a thing of the past, replaced by movies and, especially, by television. But television, in the 1950s, did not destroy vaudeville. It simply caused it to relocate, leaving the grand movie palaces and lodging on the small home screen. The routines in *The Dumb Waiter* often are reminiscent of the kind of routines performed by the great vaudeville acts like (George) Burns and (Gracie) Allen or Jack Benny—a master of the frozen pause and silent, sidelong glance—and one of his several straightmen, or especially of (Bud) Abbott and (Lou) Costello. All these were popular television performers in the 1950s. One of Abbott and Costello's most famous routines, "Who's on First," seems particularly relevant to *The Dumb Waiter* because of the rhythm of its banter and because of the way it highlights the frustrations of non-communication, especially when words become devoid of meaning.

CRITICAL OVERVIEW

"The drama of Harold Pinter," Katherine H. Burkman wrote in *The Dramatic World of Harold Pinter: Its Basis in Ritual*, "evolves in an atmosphere of mystery." Burkman continues: "While the surfaces of life are realistically detailed, the patterns below the surface are as obscure as the motives of the characters." The mysterious quality that informs *The Dumb Waiter* is specifically a function of Pinter's strategy of removing any information that can set the action of the play or the attitudes of its characters in context. The audience knows nothing about them but what they say in the course of their conversations with each other, which is little indeed. This scarcity of information has been the focus of much critical discussion. R. A. Buck, writing in the *Explicator*, cites Thomas F. Van Laan's observation that readers and critics often fill in "what [Pinter] has supposedly neglected to record." Buck then states that "by 'filling in' an absurdist play, we risk losing sight of the precise language of the text and thus its performing function." Buck proceeds to argue that this "has happened to such an extent in Pinter criticism that discussions of the ending of *The Dumb Waiter* have neglected to emphasize the power of the linguistic ambiguity in the last lines of the play." While he attempts to avoid what he considers an interpretive error by conducting a close reading of the closing stage directions of the play, Buck, too, fills in what might be happening but is not textually indicated, suggesting the possibility that Gus enters through the door on the left and someone else, unspecified, enters as the door on the right is thrown open. Indeed, it is, according to Van Laan, inevitable that readers help construct the events of the play, just because so much is omitted and much of what is included in *The Dumb Waiter* seems to be functioning to avoid rather than to reveal what has happened, what is happening, and what will happen.

Despite the room for filling in that exists in *The Dumb Waiter*, most critics actually do agree on the essentials of the play. "Two men ... are on assignment and wait for the specific details in a basement room," James R. Hollis comments in *Harold Pinter: The Poetics of Silence*. After a straightforward summary of what occurs on the surface, Hollis suggests that it is possible to "allegorize *The Dumb Waiter*," to read the play symbolically. The very bareness of the play invites this; the play is, after all, an attempt to find meaning where meaning as it is generally experienced is absent. Hollis suggests that "the hierarchical power upstairs could be identified as a deity. . . . The little creatures scurry about on their terrestrial plane and try to guess what [he] wants." But Hollis rejects this sort of reading as unnecessary, as do most of Pinter's critics. Rather than theological readings, most critics take a more down to earth tack. Hollis considers that what is represented in *The Dumb Waiter* is "man's suspicion that there is a power that is not so much malevolent as detached and unconcerned." This interpretation stands without identifying that power as supernatural or, for example, corporate or governmental. Hollis sees Gus and Ben as alternative possible responses to the mystery of such a dominant power: one submits and one rebels. Arnold P. Hinchliffe, writing in *Harold Pinter*, presents a more sociological reading, quoting the Yugoslavian critic Istvan Sinko: "When the functionary begins to reflect on the meaning of his job, he must die." Hinchliffe himself refuses to be as specific, concluding a survey of critical responses to *The Dumb Waiter* by observing that "Pinter's exploration of the lower depths has an unmistakable, if indefinable, relevance to life as we live it."

> WHAT KEEPS *THE DUMB WAITER* GOING FOR A READER OR VIEWER IS THE SENSE THAT SOMETHING IS GOING TO HAPPEN. BUT, UNTIL THE LAST MOMENT OF THE PLAY, NOTHING REALLY DOES HAPPEN."

CRITICISM

Neil Heims

Heims is a writer and teacher living in Paris. In this essay, he discusses the nature of the relationship between Ben and Gus.

"I asked you a question," Gus insists towards the end of *The Dumb Waiter*, after Ben has studiously ignored not one, but a series of questions from Gus throughout the play. Ben ignores Gus's questions either by keeping silent, by giving evasive answers, or by refusing to understand what Gus is talking about. But it is not only Gus's questions that Ben ignores. The action of *The Dumb Waiter* is fashioned to present the strategies that one man uses to ignore and discredit another completely. Readers and viewers may surmise that he is, in consequence, significantly ignoring and, in some way, dehumanizing himself, as well.

The first moment of contact between Ben and Gus in the opening of *The Dumb Waiter* is immediately subverted before it can impress itself on them as an experience of contact. It becomes, rather, an instance of evasion. Nothing is spoken.

When *The Dumb Waiter* begins, Ben and Gus are together in a basement room with twin beds and two doorways. Ben is lying on one of the beds, reading the newspaper. Gus, unlike Ben, is fidgety. First, sitting on his bed, Gus ties his shoelaces "with difficulty." Then he stands, yawns, walks to the door on the left, stops, shakes his foot, kneels, unties the shoelace he has just tied, takes off the shoe slowly, and extracts a flattened matchbox from inside the shoe. Ben has lowered his newspaper and watches him. Gus shakes the match box and examines it. At that moment, "their eyes meet."

WHAT DO I READ NEXT?

- Pinter's play *Betrayal* (1978) was made into a film with Ben Kingsley and Jeremy Irons in 1983. It portrays the story of a long adulterous affair in reverse chronological order. As in *The Dumb Waiter*, Pinter works with themes of trust and betrayal in a situation where one character knows of another's disadvantage while the other does not.

- *Dutchman* (1964) is a one-act play by Amiri Baraka, who was then writing under his birth name of LeRoi Jones. The play was made into a film in 1967. The play concerns the menacing and finally violent encounter between a young black man and a young white woman who are alone together in a subway car. As in *The Dumb Waiter*, the play is set in a confined space and the characters have no means of escape.

- Israel Horovitz's play *The Indian Wants the Bronx* opened in 1968 with Al Pacino in the leading role of a street punk who terrorizes an East Indian visitor to New York City who has stopped to ask him for directions. As in *The Dumb Waiter*, the play uses a seemingly everyday situation and transforms it into a life and death confrontation.

- *Our Lady of the Flowers*, by the French poet, novelist, homosexual, and thief, Jean Genet, was written in prison and first appeared in French in 1943. It was published in an English translation by Bernard Fretchman in 1963. It tells the story of a French drag queen and his pimp lover, who betrays him as an act of love. As Pinter does in *The Dumb Waiter*, Genet explores the ambiguity of a relationship between two men, one of whom seems to be dominant and the other submissive. Genet's language, unlike Pinter's minimalism, is richly ornate.

- Samuel Beckett's *Waiting for Godot* was first performed in its original French in 1952 in Paris and in 1955 in London in an English translation made by Beckett himself. It concerns two tramps waiting, for some unspecified reason, in a kind of no man's land for someone, or something, named Godot. It is a true precursor to *The Dumb Waiter*.

Immediately "Ben rattles his paper and reads." Gus proceeds with more of the same kind of stage business as before, putting back the shoe and undoing the other one similarly and extracting a flattened pack of cigarettes to complement the flattened matchbox. Again Ben has lowered his paper and watches Gus until their eyes meet. As before, at that instant, Ben turns away; he "rattles his paper and reads." Gus continues his routine, this time exiting through the door on the left. Alone Ben slams the paper down on the bed and "glares after him."

When eyes meet, in general, something significant is happening between the two people whose eyes they are. Often such meeting signifies an understanding and a connection. As their eyes meet, so do the people. Eyes meeting can also cause embarrassment. Then the revelation of something that such an encounter crystallizes is felt as undesirable. The connection is avoided and immediately repudiated. This happens twice during the first moments of *The Dumb Waiter* for Ben and Gus. Something that is conveyed must not be conveyed, nor can it be acknowledged as known. There can be no connection between them. Their eyes turn away from each other; the moment of contact is denied. Ben and Gus momentarily share something they cannot share. What it is, is unstated. That is the essence of the play; Ben and Gus share something they cannot share. The story *The Dumb Waiter* tells is the anatomy of the pattern of their relationship and not really the murky story of hired killers cooped in a room, tormented by unseen superiors through the mechanism of a dumbwaiter. That story is only a vehicle for this one.

Consequently, the apparent "surprise ending" of *The Dumb Waiter* is not at all surprising. It is not an O'Henry-twist of the plot but the inevitable conclusion or even essence of the plot, which is constituted by an exploration of Ben and Gus's paralyzed relationship with each other.

There is something like contempt for Gus that Ben is showing, something like irritation, something like a feeling of superiority. "Something like," because nothing is sure and definite in *The Dumb Waiter*. The murky surface that the play presents is the inevitable result of a continuous practice of or dedication to avoidance or evasion. With avoidance and evasion as the governing principles of speech and action, nothing can be known for sure. When nothing can be known for sure, the consequence for the human psyche must be anxiety and a sense of the absurd. If meaning is deliberately avoided, meaning, certainty and clarity become impossible. Everything seems, consequently, meaningless.

The Dumb Waiter is a drama of schematic relationship. It presents two varieties of response in a situation of powerlessness and uncertainty. Its focus is the interplay of those responses rather than a psychological study of character. It is not a play intended *by its content* to reflect or comment on the actual world in which the play is being performed or read. Because it is schematic, it does not need direct referents. Its drama is as if distilled from the tone of anxiety, menace, uncertainty, and alienation that characterized the 1950s in Britain as well as the United States. It is not necessary to construct equivalents between the text of the play and the actual world to see how the play reflects the spirit of its time. Just by using the clichéd scenario of a B-grade Hollywood movie for the *mise en scène* and the style of a vaudeville comedy team as the paradigm for his characters' conversations, Pinter liberates himself from plot and dialogue and in their place reflects the era's mood.

When Gus returns from the toilet, after the play's opening pantomime, Ben begins a series of maneuvers designed to avoid contact with him, designed, in a sense, to deny the existence of his presence even while coping with the fact that he is present. Ben's actions constitute a series of feints designed to avoid and evade contact while appearing to make contact. The newspaper, which had been used in the pantomime as the means of turning his eyes away from Gus, now becomes the vehicle for spurious contact. When Gus returns, Ben begins a conversation

with him regarding a story he has just seen in the paper. Dramatically, Ben and Gus use the newspaper story to avoid talking about something while letting off steam. Theatrically, Ben and Gus are performing the first of many vaudeville-type routines. It is a comic dialogue. One performer gets the gag lines and one acts as a straight man, feeding him questions which allow the comic to build the routine. Throughout *The Dumb Waiter* Pinter uses and deepens this old music hall technique in order to show that there is some unstated conflict between the two that is expressed in falsely comic exchanges that make it appear they are in tune. Gus looks interested in Ben's account and even his cries of "Go on!, Get away," and "Incredible," show that his response to the story is the same as Ben's. But in this skit and in the following ones, the content of their exchanges is less important than the tone of the conversations, the mood they create, and what is revealed about the personalities of the speakers by the power dynamics that shape the exchanges. In this trivial instance, Ben is overwhelming Gus.

After this bit of social cementing and reestablishing the order of authority, after they have, perhaps, made a connection with each other, Gus says, "I want to ask you something." It is a humble request. It is the first of many times he will announce this desire. Many of their encounters start this way. In this first one, Ben does not give Gus the time to ask. He answers, instead, with a question and a touch of irritation: "What are you doing out there?" This does not allow Gus either to repeat his question or to answer Ben's. Ben expresses impatience that Gus has not yet made tea for them. Gus says he is about to make the tea, but does not move. This device is repeated throughout the play. Its dramatic effect on viewers and readers is to contribute unobtrusively to the climate of anxiety that defines the play: making tea presents an ongoing unfinished situation.

The unasked question and the undelivered answer even more forcefully represent the anxiety-provoking unfinished situation in the play. Some twenty lines later, after Ben has sidetracked the conversation from Gus's question with the demand he make tea, and a discussion of the crockery in the kitchen, the interlude ends when Gus notes that he hopes the job won't be long. Gus then remembers what he had begun earlier and says "Oh, I wanted to ask you something." Again Ben dodges, not even acknowledging that Gus has spoken. Once again,

Ben slams down the newspaper, apparently not in irritation, but in response to a disturbing story in the paper, and tells Gus about an eight-year-old girl who apparently killed a cat.

For a third time, after they toss the cat story back and forth and Gus again shows impatience, Gus tells Ben he wants to ask a question. This time Ben says, "What?" Gus asks him if has noticed how long it takes for the tank in the lavatory to fill. Undoubtedly, this question is the prelude to another or a way to repress some other question. Viewers or readers may wonder: All that time just to ask a plumbing question? After some back and forth, Ben answers the question: "It's got a deficient ballcock, that's all," and this is apparently to Gus's satisfaction. That is not, however, enough really to satisfy Gus. Immediately after accepting the answer, he begins to complain about not having slept well, about not having enough blankets. He stops abruptly when he notices the picture of a soccer team on the wall. The presence of the picture leads to quite a bit of conversation about soccer, soccer players, and whether Ben and Gus did or did not see a particular game in a particular city, all done in their usual argumentative mode. Interlaced inside this conversation are Gus's complaints about how the work is getting more constricting and Ben's assortment of advice and reproaches.

Most of the conversation throughout the play is trivial. In addition, nothing much really happens, at least not until the dumbwaiter starts acting up. Even then, there really is little on the surface that would catch a viewer's or reader's attention. What keeps *The Dumb Waiter* going for a reader or viewer is the sense that something is going to happen. But, until the last moment of the play, nothing really does happen. Ben and Gus are waiting, killing time, and there is something continually suggested, continually approached, that is not being dealt with. At the last minute, when Gus stumbles in and, as in the opening moment of the play, he "looks at Ben," both now keep their gazes fixed. Yet, whatever is going to happen, does not happen. The play ends as they stare at each other.

It is reasonable to conclude, consequently, that just as the speech and action leading up to this moment are not important in the overall story line, so what happens the moment after the end of the play does not matter, either. What is important is the closing scene that Pinter

EACH OF PINTER'S EARLIEST PLAYS BECOMES MORE TERRIFYING THE MORE ONE IS AWARE THAT, IF ANY ACTION IS INEXORABLE, THIS IS ONLY BECAUSE THE ELEMENT OF FREE-WILL IS *THERE* BUT IS BEING IGNORED."

has imbued with the power to represent a fundamental expression of the human situation, which is the ambiguous relationship between people who are always on the verge of destroying one another or being destroyed.

Source: Neil Heims, Critical Essay on *The Dumb Waiter*, in *Drama for Students*, Gale, Cengage Learning, 2008.

Simon Trussler

In the following excerpt, Trussler describes the personality traits particular to Ben as well as those that are particular to Gus.

... *The Dumb Waiter*, the last of the three plays Pinter wrote during 1957, had to wait another three years for its first performance, in a double-bill with *The Room*. The service-lift of this one-acter's title is a sort of *machina ex deis*, [a machine from God] which operates to and from a basement that was once—perhaps still is—the kitchen of a cafe. Here, Ben and Gus, the play's only characters, are awaiting instructions from the boss of some vague but evidently well-organised underworld gang. And so Pinter's storey-by-storey exploration finally descends from that upper-floor *Room*, by way of the ground-floor lounge of *The Birthday Party*, into the windowless and no doubt damp basement so feared by Rose Hudd.

Goldberg and McCann were reduced to homelier proportions in *The Birthday Party* when caught off the job, and thus off their guard—indeed, the very reference to the terrorising of Stanley Webber as "a job" [31] added its touch of reality. Ben and Gus might almost be instruments of the same anonymous "organisation" as Goldberg and McCann—but, less bright and ready-tongued, and therefore a few rungs down the salary scale, they are only entrusted with the simpler tasks which don't need much initiative. Indeed, the pair don't even know why they've been sent to Birmingham, and don't waste time in surmise. The orders will come in good time.

The play is thus the sum total of the desultory conversational ploys and pauses with which the pair while away the intervening hours, until the sudden, unnerving descent of the dumb waiter into their basement. This makes a beautiful moment in the theatre, poised teetering between terror and bathos, disturbing, as it does, their disputes about whether Gus saw Aston Villa beaten in a cup-tie here years ago, or whether one should properly say "light the kettle" or "light the gas." The orders sent down in the dumb waiter, although they are for meals rather than murders, are treated with great seriousness by Ben and Gus—but with increasing despair as their ad hoc offerings of eccles cakes, potato crisps and bars of chocolate prompt the powers upstairs to make demands for ever more exotic dishes.

At last, the pair having gone over their instructions one last time, the speaking-tube informs Ben that the night's victim is about to enter: he tries to call Gus, who has gone to the lavatory off left—but it is Gus himself who stumbles in from the right-hand entrance "stripped of his jacket, waistcoat, tie, holster and revolver . . . body stooping, his arms at his sides." Ben's revolver is levelled at him, according to his orders: there is a long silence as the two stare at each other, and the curtain falls.

Without a doubt this is Pinter's least complicatedly comic play. Ben's credulous belief in what he reads in his newspaper, his occasional stabs at textbook phraseology, and, most hilarious of all, the pair's frantic theorising about the upstairs cafe, and their attempts to match the variety of its menu—all these ingredients keep the "menace" well below surface most of the time. The play's opening is more assured, as if Pinter were more certain of his power to compel attention without an immediate plunge into dialogue, than in either of the earlier plays. Gus is simply tying up his shoelaces, while Ben, lying reading his paper, becomes increasingly engrossed in his colleague's activities as Gus removes one shoe after the other—to extract first a flattened matchbox, then a flattened cigarette-packet. He shakes the packet and examines it, Pinter directs, and stamps off to the lavatory.

Considerable attention is paid to the whereabouts of this lavatory, as it is also to the layout of the basement and its decoration—right down to an old cricketing photograph on the wall. Gus "wouldn't like to live in this dump."

> I wouldn't mind if you had a window, you could see what it looked like outside . . . I mean, you come into a place when it's still dark, you come into a room you've never seen before, you sleep all day, you do your job, and then you go away in the night again . . . I like to look at the scenery. You never get the chance in this job.

A place, and the purpose of its mysterious visitors: here is a re-statement of that dominant theme of each of Pinter's first three plays. True, his touch is here of the lightest—and faults of over-explicitness, such as Ben's prolonged repetition of the speaking tube's complaints to the management, are few and far between. But behind the chatter about the quality of the china, beyond the search for substitutes for scampi, there is a vein of seriousness that touches and tempers *The Dumb Waiter* at several points.

There are two dumb waiters in the play: the non-speaking service lift, and the bovine Gus, whose business, as Ben has to remind him, is also, unquestioningly, to wait.

Gus: What for?
Ben: For Wilson.
Gus: He might not come. He might just send a message.
He doesn't always come.

This verbal echo of *Godot* is no doubt a deliberate parody, and not to be taken too seriously. What becomes much more serious, for Gus, is his insistence on fnding such niggling fault with the order of things as he finds them. Somewhere there is a boss, who issues orders, which it is Gus's duty to carry out: that is all he knows in Birmingham, and all he needs to know.

Yet he remains dissatisfied—complaining about the bed and the basement itself, wondering who clears up after the job's been done, and, increasingly, bothered about the job itself. "Don't you ever get a bit fed up?" he asks Ben. Ben doesn't: he even takes the injunctions of the dumb waiter in his stride. Not so his companion:

> What's he doing it for? We've been through our tests, haven't we? We got right through our tests, years ago, didn't we? We've proved ourselves before now, haven't we? We've always done our job. What's he doing all this for? What's the idea? What's he playing these games for?

The methodology behind this speech is typical of Pinter. The pervasive mystery becomes more mysterious by being reduced to commonplace terms of tests and qualifications, whilst the particular mystery is also heightened because Gus himself shares the mystification. And it is *because* Gus expresses his doubts so freely that he is being put to the test. He even dares to be inquisitive about who the evening's victim is going to be. The form of the dramatic irony is, as ever, a precise predicate to its content.

Without the hindsight of a first acquaintance with the play Gus's imminent death at the fall of the curtain is pointless—indeed, it amounts to a vulgarisation of the whole action, a cheap device to twist the tail for the sake of twisting the tail. Once again, it is only when one has got the message in its entirety that one can look at it properly line by line—and realise, for example, *why* Ben and Gus are so very different in character. It is *always* Gus who asks the probing questions, *always* Ben who by-passes them, or tells Gus, more or less vehemently, to shut up. Because of this, one gets the feeling that he "knows something"—that he has been entrusted with more information than Gus, precisely because he accepts it, as he accepts everything he is asked to do, without question. (Such an interpretation illuminates Ben's unnaturally quick reassurance of Gus when the dumb waiter first makes its appearance, as it does his roadside halt for no good reason while Gus was asleep on the way: so that whilst Ben doesn't know that Gus is to be his victim until the last moment, he knows that he knows *more* than Gus.)

I wouldn't be so insistent about the difference between the two men, had not most critics talked of Ben and Gus as more or less interchangeable. They are not: if one really looks at what Gus does and says, one could not be at all sure that, if he found himself in Ben's situation as the curtain fell, he would really duly kill his comrade-in-arms. One is in no doubt at all that this is precisely what Ben means to do: and he must do it *because*, in Ben's position, Gus might have disobeyed his orders.

Each of Pinter's earliest plays becomes more terrifying the more one is aware that, if any action is inexorable, this is only because the element of free-will is *there* but is being ignored. Petey *could* have stopped Goldberg and McCann from abducting Stanley. Gus *could* have taken his dissatisfaction one step further, and opted out: or, alternatively, he might have passed his last-chance test and, by accepting the dumb waiter and its orders as readily as Ben, thus have given himself over as completely as his companion to the "organisation."

The racial implications of *The Birthday Party* make it reasonable to think of the "organisation" Goldberg and McCann as a quasi-fascist one: and maybe, just as irony is added to such an interpretation by that play's reversal of racial roles, it's also impossible—indeed, paradigmatically, helpful—to think of the crooks of *The Dumb Waiter* as the tools of some civil or religious establishment that demands absolute obedience. Certainly, the oracular nature of the dumb waiter's injunctions makes a religious interpretation tempting. But *The Dumb Waiter* is much less explicit in this respect than *The Birthday Party*—not in its physical and personal details, which are as rich yet down-to-earth as ever, but in the greater opacity of its theme . . .

Source: Simon Trussler, "Domestic Interiors," in *The Plays of Harold Pinter*, Victor Golancz, 1973, 6 pp.

SOURCES

Buck, R. A., "Pinter's *The Dumb Waiter*," in the *Explicator*, Vol. 56, No.1, Fall 1997, p. 45.

Burkman, Katherine H., *The Dramatic World of Harold Pinter: Its Basis in Ritual*, Ohio State University Press, 1971, p. 3.

Hinchliffe, Arnold P., *Harold Pinter*, Twayne Publishers, 1967, pp. 63, 68.

Hollis, James R., *Harold Pinter: The Poetics of Silence*, Southern Illinois University Press, 1970, pp. 43, 50.

Pinter, Harold, *The Dumb Waiter*, in *The Bedford Introduction to Drama*, edited by Lee A. Jacobus, St. Martin's Press, 1989, pp. 842–54.

FURTHER READING

Billington, Michael, *The Life and Work of Harold Pinter*, Faber and Faber, 1996.
> Billington combines biography and an examination of Pinter's works in the context of the events of his life.

Goodman, Paul, *Growing Up Absurd: Problems of Youth in the Organized System*, Random House, 1960.
> This book is a classic study of the effects of what Goodman calls "the organized society" that began to dominate the working and social lives of young people in the 1950s. *Growing Up Absurd* examines problems of powerlessness, meaninglessness, and capricious authority.

Kerr, Walter, *Harold Pinter*, Columbia University Press, 1967.

    A drama critic for the *New York Herald Tribune* and, after its collapse, for the *New York Times*, Kerr explores Pinter's plays as examples of existential suspense dramas.

Thompson, David T., *Pinter: The Player's Playwright*, Macmillan, 1985.

    Thompson examines the influence of Pinter's early and extensive career as an actor in repertory companies playing everything from classic Greek and Shakespearean dramas to Agatha Christie melodramas and his later career as a playwright.

Whyte, William H., *The Organization Man*, University of Pennsylvania Press, 2002

    Whyte's anatomy of 1950s corporate culture and its pervasive and coercive influence became a classic sociological study that defined much of the phenomena of that decade.

An Enemy of the People

HENRIK IBSEN

1882

An Enemy of the People, published in 1882, is Henrik Ibsen's response to the public reception of, and the critical assault upon, his preceding play, *Ghosts* (1881)—a play about sexual vice, moral corruption, and syphilis. Indeed, *Ghosts* turned Ibsen into a kind of enemy of the people. In Norway, the published edition of the play sold poorly and could find no theater to produce it. *Ghosts* was first performed by a touring company in Chicago and, when *Ghosts* opened in London, according to Peter Watts, writing in the Introduction to the Penguin edition of the play, reviewers called it "putrid" and an "open sewer." A reviewer in the *Daily Telegraph* is cited by George Bernard Shaw in *The Quintessence of Ibsenism* as calling Ibsen "an egotist and a bungler...A crazy cranky being." Thus, Dr. Stockmann, the protagonist of *An Enemy of the People* is a version of Ibsen himself. The playwright who uncovers social disease and corruption is represented as a physician who uncovers diseased water and social corruption, is vilified and yet persists in his mission to expose lies and corruption just as Ibsen continued to write probing dramas.

Although its plot so perfectly parallels Ibsen's own experience as the author of *Ghosts*, the plot of *An Enemy of the People* was actually based on several real and similar events. A Dr. Meissner was the Medical Officer at a health spa at Teplitz in Bohemia, now part of the Czech Republic, in the 1830s. When cholera broke out

Henrik Ibsen (*AP Images*)

there, he issued a public warning and the guests, of course, all left. Rather than drawing praise, his action aroused the wrath of the townspeople. As in *An Enemy of the People*, they threw stones at his house. Meissner left the town. In 1880, a chemist in Norway's capitol, Oslo, then called Christiania, challenged the sanitary conditions of a steam kitchen, causing a public uproar and a meeting like the one in the fourth act of *An Enemy of the People*.

Ironically, unlike *Ghosts*, *An Enemy of the People* was a popular and critical success. *An Enemy of the People* is concerned not only with the problems of corruption and pollution but also with the problem of the relation between the individual and society; the tendency of a democracy to deteriorate into a mobocracy; and the likelihood for moral ideals to be pushed aside by the pressures of self-interest.

While there are several accurate standard translations of *An Enemy of the People*, many are somewhat stilted. In the edition referred to here, the play in a translation by Peter Watts is called *A Public Enemy*. It appears in *Ibsen: Ghosts and Other Plays*, published by Penguin Books in 1964. An adaptation by Arthur Miller can be found in *Arthur Miller: Collected Plays 1944–1961*, published by the Library of America in 2006.

AUTHOR BIOGRAPHY

Norwegian playwright Henrik Johan Ibsen was born on March 20, 1828, in the small port town of Skien, Norway. His father, Knud Ibsen, was a prosperous merchant, his mother, Marichen Altenburg, a painter. The fortunes of the family took a downturn when Ibsen was around eight years old. Thus, Ibsen's childhood was marked by their poverty and the social ostracism they endured. When he was fifteen, Ibsen became a pharmacist's apprentice and began to write plays. At eighteen he fathered a child but abandoned both the woman, ten years his senior, and the child, and moved to Christiania, (now called Oslo) Norway's capitol city, in order to attend the university there. Instead, however, he dedicated himself to playwriting. His first plays appeared in 1850. *Catiline* was published under the pseudonym Brynjolf Bjarme but was not performed. *The Burial Mound*, which also appeared in 1850, was staged unsuccessfully.

Between 1850 and 1865, when his play *Brandt* brought him to prominence, Ibsen wrote a number of plays, but gained no recognition. Of equal, if not more, importance for the education of the playwright, however, was the period of some dozen years beginning in 1851 that Ibsen served as a stage poet and stage manager at several of Norway's theaters. He wrote verse plays, not the realistic prose dramas he has become famous for, and he staged over 100 plays by other dramatists.

In 1858, Ibsen married Susannah Thoresen. Their only child, a son, Sigurd, was born in 1859. In 1864, Ibsen received a grant from the Norwegian government to travel and, with supplemental aid from the Norwegian writer, editor, and theater director Bjørnstjerne Bjørnson (1832–1910), Ibsen left for Italy and remained abroad, living in Rome, Munich, and Dresden over the next twenty-seven years, returning to Norway sporadically.

Ibsen's most significant decision regarding his work occurred when he stopped writing psychological, philosophical, mythological and historical verse plays and began, with *Pillars of Society* (1877), writing prose dramas concerned with contemporary social issues, filled with gender, political and psychological conflicts. *A Doll's House*, a drama about a woman who becomes aware of the self-denial demanded of her—and all women—in the conventional

MEDIA ADAPTATIONS

- A 2005 screen adaptation of *An Enemy of the People* was produced in Norway by Aage Aaberge and Kaare Storemyr and directed by Erik Skjoldbjærg, with a screenplay by Nikolaj Frobenius. It was distributed by Columbia TriStar Nordisk Film.

- *An Enemy of the People* was adapted by Arthur Miller, directed by Jack O'Brien, and produced by David Griffiths for television in 1990.

- *Ganashatru* (1989) is a film adaptation of *An Enemy of the People* that was written and directed by the Indian filmmaker Satyajit Ray and released by the National Film Development Corporation of India.

- *An Enemy of the People* was adapted as a film in 1978, with a screenplay by Alexander Jacobs and Arthur Miller, directed by George Schaefer, and starring Steve McQueen and Bibi Andersson. It was produced by Steve McQueen, distributed by First Artists, and released on video by Warner Brothers.

- *An Enemy of the People* was adapted for television by Arthur Miller and aired in 1966. Directed by Paul Bogart, this version includes James Daly in the starring role.

marriages of the nineteenth century, followed in 1879. *Ghosts* and *An Enemy of the People* were written shortly thereafter in 1881 and 1882, respectively. In 1884, Ibsen wrote *The Wild Duck*. After writing plays calling for dedication to honesty and truth, in *The Wild Duck*, Ibsen explored the problem of too obsessive a dedication to truth and honesty. Ibsen wrote seven more plays after *The Wild Duck*. They include *The Master Builder* (1892), *John Gabriel Borkman* (1896), and one of the classic modern psychological dramas, *Hedda Gabler* (1890). After his last play, *When We Dead Awaken* (1899), a non-realistic meditation on the sacrifices an artist makes for the sake of his art, Ibsen suffered

several strokes. The first impaired his ability to walk. The second, a year later, affected his ability to remember words. Watts recounts that Ibsen said to his son one day "Look what I'm doing," as he struggled with pencil and paper to write letters. "I'm sitting here trying to learn the alphabet—and I was once an author." Ibsen died in Christiania, Norway on May 23, 1906.

PLOT SUMMARY

Act 1

Within the comfort of a prosperous bourgeois household, dinner has been eaten and Dr. Stockmann and his two boys are out for an after-dinner walk. The table has not been cleared. Mrs. Stockmann is serving some cold roast beef to Billing, a reporter for the *People's Herald* who has stopped by. Peter Stockmann, her husband's brother and the mayor of the town, enters. Peter refuses Mrs. Stockmann's invitation to have something to eat. Mr. Hovstad, the editor of the *People's Herald* enters, hoping to discuss an article Dr. Stockmann had written for the paper, concerning the health spa that has just been built and the prosperity it is expected to bring to the town.

Dr. Stockmann returns from his walk with his sons Eylif and Morten, bringing Horster, a good-natured young ship's captain, with him. He greets his brother warmly and invites him to stay for a toddy. The mayor declines, saying he must go. Doctor Stockmann remains impervious to his brother's sourness and talks of the excitement of living in the bustle of a big city, especially after spending so many years in poverty in a small, out-of-the way town in the north. He asks his wife if the mailman has come yet. She says "no."

Peter turns the conversation to the Baths, remarking that Hovstad mentioned he was going to print Dr. Stockmann's piece on them. Dr. Stockmann recalls the essay and says that he would prefer that the piece not be printed yet. Peter accuses Dr. Stockmann of showing insufficient regard for Society and of stubbornly refusing to subordinate himself to Society. They argue and Peter leaves in anger. Mrs. Stockmann mildly rebukes her husband for angering his brother, but the doctor says he did not do anything to him to cause his temper to flare, adding that the mayor should not expect Dr. Stockmann to "give him an account of things before they happen." Mrs. Stockmann asks what there is to give an account of. Dr. Stockmann does not answer but wonders why the postman has not come yet.

Hovstad, Billing, and Captain Horster emerge from the dining room, having finished their meal, and join Dr. Stockmann for conversation, cigars, and toddies. Captain Horster tells them he is sailing to America. Billing remarks that, consequently, he won't be able to vote in the local elections. Horster says he does not follow politics and knows nothing about them. Billing says he ought to vote anyhow because "Society's like a ship—every man must put his hand to the helm." Horster, the seafarer, retorts, "That might be all right on land, but it wouldn't work at sea."

Dr. Stockmann turns the conversation to tomorrow's edition of the *People's Herald* and Hovstad remarks that he intends to print the doctor's piece praising the baths. Stockmann surprises him by telling him he'll have to delay printing it without explaining why. Their conversation is interrupted when Stockmann's grown-up daughter, Petra, enters. Amid greetings and offers of a toddy, Petra hands Dr. Stockmann the letter he is waiting for that she got from the postman as she was leaving that morning. Stockmann takes the letter and goes into his study to read it.

Petra is a teacher who dedicates her life to her work. Her younger brother Morten says that he has no intention of working when he grows up. Rather he will be a Viking. When his brother, Eylif, objects that he would have to be a heathen in that case, Morten agrees and Billing approves, much to Mrs. Stockmann's chagrin. Petra uses the contretemps to argue that their world is full of hypocrisy. "At home you have to hold your tongue, and at school you have to stand up and tell lies." When she says she wishes she had the money to start her own school, Captain Horster offers her the large empty dining room in his house for a school. Hovstad, remarks that she is more likely to be a journalist than a teacher and asks her if she has yet translated the English novel he intends to serialize in the paper. She says she has not, but will.

Emerging from his study Dr. Stockmann waves the letter excitedly and proclaims that he has "news that'll surprise the town." His hunch has turned out to be true. He wishes Peter were there to hear what he has learned. A sample of

the water from the Baths that he sent to the university laboratory to be tested, just as he expected, shows the water is contaminated. That accounts for the several cases of illness that broke out among visitors to the baths last year. Polluted waste water from the tannery just above the Baths seeps into the stream that provides the water for the spa. Mrs. Stockmann says, "What a blessing you've found it out in time!" Stockmann points out that the conduits will have to be re-laid to channel the water to avoid the tannery. He had been silent until he had sure evidence, he explains, because he did not want to cause a panic. Now he feels vindicated by the report because he had argued, against his brother, that the conduits originally ought to have been laid as he now sees they must be. Hovstad promises to print an article in the paper about the discovery. Dr. Stockmann gives his paper arguing that dangerous infusoria contaminate the springs to Petra to have their maid deliver it to his brother. Stockmann is heady with the excitement of being the savior of the town and imagines all the glory that will be his because of his discovery.

Act 2

The next morning Mrs. Stockmann hands her husband a letter from his brother. The mayor writes that he is returning the article and that he is coming over. Mrs. Stockmann is worried about how Peter will take the news of the discovery, fearing he will be jealous that it was Dr. Stockmann and not himself who found out that the water is contaminated. She advises her husband to share the honor of the discovery publicly with his brother. Dr. Stockmann agrees, saying that it does not matter to him, "as long as I can get things put right."

Morten Kiil, Dr. Stockmann's father-in-law, having heard the news about the baths from Petra, stops by. He does not believe that what Dr. Stockmann says about the baths is true, but is delighted, nevertheless, believing that Dr. Stockmann is playing a trick on his brother and the other leading citizens of the town. As Morten Kiil is leaving, Hovstad enters, and Kiil is even more delighted. He thinks that Hovstad is in league with Dr. Stockmann and that Stockmann has the power of the press behind him. For Hovstad, the corruption of the purity of the water is a metaphor for the corrupt politics of the town's governing clique. Hovstad hopes to bring the clique down through the scandal that will ensue regarding the mismanagement of the construction of the baths and help put his own party, the Liberals, in power. Dr. Stockmann defends the governing circle, arguing that the town owes them a lot. Hovstad concedes that, and assures Dr. Stockmann that when he writes against the bureaucrats, he will acknowledge that, but that he is motivated in his campaign by his belief in democracy. Hovstad wishes to help "emancipat[e] the humble, down-trodden Masses!"

Aslaksen, the paper's printer, enters. He has come to offer Dr. Stockmann his support. It will be a good thing, he says, for Dr. Stockmann to have "a solid majority" behind him. Stockmann is grateful but also a little puzzled. He says that redoing the Baths ought to be a routine matter. Aslaksen advises him that the authorities may bristle at taking suggestions from "outsiders" and offers to "arrange a little demonstration." Aslaksen says the small tradesmen support Dr. Stockmann because the Baths are important to the town as the source of its economic prosperity.

When Aslaksen leaves, Hovstad expresses contempt for his moderation and promises that his support will be defined more sharply than Aslaksen's. Hovstad promises to use the paper in case the mayor resists Dr. Stockmann's attempt to re-engineer the baths. Under those conditions, should he face opposition, Dr. Stockmann agrees to let Hovstad print his report about the danger of the baths. Hovstad leaves.

Dr. Stockmann is feeling a sense of security and pleasure at being "in complete agreement with one's fellow-townsmen" and of "doing something of such great practical value." In this spirit he greets Peter. The mayor is not in the same high spirits as his brother. He talks of the expense of reengineering the Baths. The project will take two years. Surrounding towns will use the bad publicity to establish themselves as tourist attractions for those who seek curative waters. Above all, the mayor declares, he is not convinced by Dr. Stockmann's report. The doctor, as usual, Peter asserts, is exaggerating. Rather than painting Dr. Stockmann as a hero, Peter warns his brother that he will be responsible for the ruin of the town. Dr. Stockmann counters that Peter is upset because he is responsible for where the conduits for the baths were laid, having ignored Dr. Stockmann's advice. The mayor concedes there is some truth in that, but quickly reverts to arguing that maintaining

the appearance of his authority is necessary for the good of the town, as is opening the new spa. The mayor accuses his brother of not being motivated by devotion to the truth but by a warped personality. He says that Dr. Stockmann is not able to respect authority, that he is constitutionally rebellious. He warns his brother that pursuing his course will have damaging effects on his wife and children, that he will be dismissed from the board of directors of the Baths and that his reputation as a doctor will be tarnished. He orders Dr. Stockmann not to release his report and demands, since he *has* already released it to the newspaper, that he write another report stating that after further and deeper investigation, he has reached the conclusion that his earlier report was mistaken and that he has full confidence in the board of directors of the Baths to take any steps necessary to deal with whatever minor problems might exist. Dr. Stockmann refuses. The mayor reiterates that there will be terrible consequences for Dr. Stockmann and his family if he continues in his opposition. But the mayor's assertions only harden the doctor's resolve. Petra supports her father wholeheartedly. Mrs. Stockmann, although she knows her husband is right, is frightened, reminds him that the world is full of injustice, that they will again have to live in poverty. But the doctor, citing responsibility to his two boys, says he will not back down.

Act 3

In the newspaper office Billing and Hovstad agree that Dr. Stockmann's report on the danger of the water strengthens their campaign against the mayor and they will keep at it until "the whole of this privileged class comes crashing down." Dr. Stockmann enters and tells them to go ahead and print his report on the danger of the baths. Since his argument with his brother that morning, the issue, although still centered on the baths, has taken on greater scope for him. It has become a matter of overturning corrupt practices and replacing entrenched power with fresh ideas.

The newspaper men's motives in supporting Dr. Stokmann are tainted with self-interest. Aslaksen is afraid of offending the authorities. He limits his criticism to cautious banalities. Billing, despite his rebellious stance, is trying to get a political position for himself. Hovstad is willing to compromise his ideals for the sake of the paper's circulation and to make the paper's politics acceptable to its readers by serializing an English novel with the simplistic attitude that God rewards those who do good and makes the works of evildoers end badly. When Petra returns the book, refusing to translate it because it is reactionary, he defends his duplicity. His support for her father, moreover, is largely motivated by his attraction to her. Petra leaves the newspaper office in anger. Aslaksen comes into Hovstad's office to inform him that the mayor has entered the offices by the back door so as not to be seen and wishes to speak to him.

As it did the last time the mayor appeared, the direction of the play changes. The mayor's confrontation with his brother redefined and sharpened the conflict between them. Now, he will subvert the wills of Dr. Stockmann's allies. He will get them in his power and make an alliance against Dr. Stockmann in order to counter the idea that the baths are contaminated. He explains that it will be expensive to re-engineer the baths, that in order to do it, as mayor, he will "raise a municipal loan" and tax the working people, the shopkeepers, and the small homeowners since the shareholders of the baths refuse to give any more money for the baths. To support Dr. Stockmann's report under those circumstances, the newspaper would have to support raising of taxes. Realizing that reporting that the baths are unhealthy will hurt the town and themselves financially, the three agree that Dr. Stockmann's report may be incorrect and that Dr. Stockmann himself is in the wrong for promoting it. They agree to print the mayor's statement about the safety of the baths rather than Dr. Stockmann's scientific report explaining their toxicity. As the mayor is fishing in his pockets for his statement, Dr. Stockmann returns to the newspaper office as he said he would to read the proofs of his article.

Peter hides in another room, leaving his ceremonial mayor's hat and cane in plain sight in the office. Dr. Stockmann finds that Aslaksen and Hovstad, who had previously been cordial to him, are cold and dismissive. They say they are busy and haven't had the time to set his article yet. He volunteers to come back later, still believing he will be seen as a popular hero when his essay is printed. Before he can leave the office, his wife enters, having come to prevent his article from being printed for fear of the repercussions, but Dr. Stockmann dismisses her concern. About to leave, he notices Peter's mayoral hat and cane.

He understands that Peter has come to sabotage him and win their support. He puts on the hat, and opening the door to the room where Peter is hiding, exposes him. Peter reenters, enraged at being discovered and mocked by his brother. The doctor's triumphant moment is short-lived. Aslaksen and Hovstad explain they will not print his report in the paper, that they do not dare to, no matter what, because it would offend public opinion if they did. Seeing the injustice, Mrs. Stockmann overcomes her anxiety about the consequences to her family and voices support for her husband. He pledges that he is not defeated, that if the paper will not print his essay, he will issue it as a pamphlet, or, better, he will rent a hall in town and read his paper publicly.

Act 4
The setting is a room in Captain Horster's house. Dr. Stockmann is to give a public reading of his report. A group of townspeople have arrived early and gossip, revealing that they already believe Dr. Stockmann is in the wrong, particularly because no one in town except Horster would make a room available to him for the meeting. Slowly the room fills. Billing comes from the paper to cover the meeting, and Dr. Stockmann's whole family is there, too, to support him. The mayor is also present. As Dr. Stockmann begins to mount the platform to begin his reading, Aslaksen interrupts him saying that before they proceed they ought to elect a chairman for the meeting. Dr. Stockmann says there is no need, but Peter says there ought to be a chair, and the consensus is with him. Dr. Stockmann objects, pointing out that he has called the meeting only to read his paper. But the mayor argues that reading the paper "might possibly give rise to differences of opinion." Dr. Stockmann, not yet aware of the extent of the sabotage, capitulates.

Aslaksen is elected chair and then prevents Dr. Stockmann from reading his paper, calling on the mayor, instead, to address the assembly. Peter inflames the crowd, arguing that no one "would consider it desirable that unreliable or exaggerated statements as to the hygienic condition of the Baths and of the town should be spread abroad." He concludes, consequently, that Dr. Stockmann should not be allowed to read the report. He is followed by Hovstad, who repudiates his support for Dr. Stockmann. When Stockmann is finally permitted to speak, it is with the proviso that he say nothing about the condition of the Baths.

In his address, Stockmann does refer to the pollution of the Baths, but only in passing, as a way to move on to what he says he considers a worse problem, namely the opinion of the majority. Dr. Stockmann argues that the majority is never right. The minority of people, those who can see beyond what the mob can see are, in fact, in the right. Public opinion, Dr. Stockmann argues, is a coercive, ignorant, and destructive force. People, he argues, must be educated, must cultivate their reason and intelligence in order for valid democracy to exist. His fundamental condemnation is that his townsmen are willing to build their fortune on the fraud that the baths are safe when they are not. This position angers the crowd and they condemn Dr. Stockmann and censure him as a public enemy or enemy of the people. He is reviled by all, by those like Billing who have enjoyed his hospitality and those like his father-in-law, Morten Kiil, who utters a vague threat to the doctor because Stockmann has revealed that Kiil's tannery is one of the worst sources of pollution. The members of the audience on stage have become a mob and the act ends as they talk about storming Dr. Stockmann's house and breaking his windows.

Act 5

It is the next morning in Dr. Stockmann's study. The windows are smashed. Dr. Stockmann is gathering the stones the mob has lobbed into the house. He will keep the stones and bequeath them to his sons, he tells his wife. The glazier will not come to repair the windows; the landlord sends a notice that the family is being evicted. Stockmann and his wife talk about moving but he says that mobs determine policies everywhere. Unexpectedly Petra returns home from school. She has been fired because the head of her school received three letters of complaint about her and her "advanced opinions." The only person not cutting the family is Captain Horster, who stops by to see how they are and to tell them that because he let Dr. Stockmann use his house for the meeting and saw him safely home afterwards, he has been removed from his position as a ship's captain. One thing common to all the rebuffs that have been suffered is that glazier, landlord, headmistress, and ship owner all said they regretted acting as they did but that they dared not act otherwise because of public opinion or their party affiliation.

As Captain Horster is telling the Stockmanns that he has an idea where they may go should they wish to leave the town, Peter Stockmann knocks at the door and is invited in. The doctor points out with bitter humor that it is chilly in the house and the mayor disingenuously apologizes "that it was not in my power to prevent the excesses of last night" when he was, after all, their architect. As if to prove his insincerity the mayor presents his brother with a notice of termination from the Board of Directors of the Baths and informs him, furthermore, that "the Householders's Association has drawn up a manifesto which they are circulating from door to door, urging all reputable citizens to refuse to employ you." The mayor advises his brother to leave town for six months and then return and tell the townspeople that he has taken time to weigh the matter carefully and wishes to apologize for his error regarding the Baths. Peter admits that would serve him and his cronies well and that he would be able to manipulate fickle public opinion in his brother's favor under those circumstances. Dr. Stockmann refuses to cooperate. The mayor says he has no right to jeopardize his family, but Dr. Stockmann counters that he has no right to participate in dirty and deceitful dealings.

Peter mentions that Mrs. Stockmann's father, Morten Kiil, is a very wealthy man and will be leaving a considerable amount of money to his daughter and grandchildren. Dr. Stockmann says he did not know his father-in-law was that rich but he is glad that his family will be provided for despite his own impoverished circumstances. The mayor tells his brother not to count on Kiil's fortune because he can change his will. Stockmann retorts that that is unlikely to happen since Kiil is delighted that Stockmann has given the directors of the Baths so much trouble. This remark affects Peter more profoundly than Stockmann would have expected. Something makes sense to Peter and he leaves, entirely severing his ties with the doctor. Morten Kiil enters, and it becomes clear what had incensed the mayor.

Since the Baths are said to be dangerous to health rather than curative, their value has collapsed. Morten Kiil has spent the morning buying up the shares in the Baths cheap with the money intended for his daughter and grandchildren. Everyone else has put pressure on Stockmann to recant, and he has resisted. Now it is his father-in-law's turn. Since the polluted water comes mainly from his tannery, Kiil hopes to force the doctor to recant so that his (Morten Kiil's) name will be cleared. If Stockmann persists in his insistence that the Baths are unhealthy, the shares will have no value. If, on the other hand, he recants, the shares will become valuable. Thus the financial future of Dr. Stockmann's wife and children hinge on his decision. Kiil gives Stockmann until two o'clock to decide.

Hovstad and Aslaksen enter. Seeing Kiil, they assume that Dr. Stockmann's condemnation of the Baths was merely part of Kiil's scheme to lower the value of the shares in the Baths. They want a piece of the action. If Dr. Stockmann comes to terms with them and promotes the Baths, they promise to put the newspaper at his disposal and turn public opinion in his favor. Stockmann asks them what is in it for them and they tell him that the paper's financial health is shaky. They want him to subsidize the paper. If he refuses they will continue to vilify him. Enraged, Dr. Stockmann takes up his umbrella and brandishes it at them. His wife comes in, subdues him, and Aslaksen and Hovstad manage to make their escape from the house.

Dr. Stockmann sends a note to Morten Kiil refusing to participate in his scheme. He tells his wife that they will not leave the town, that he will write, using his pen against the corruption he has uncovered. Captain Horster offers to let the Stockmanns live in his house. As for his medical practice, Stockmann points out that he will still have his poor patients, the ones who do not pay and who most need his care. Vigorous with the righteousness of his cause, when his sons are sent home from school because other boys fought with them because of their father, Dr. Stockmann proclaims that they shall not go back, that he will teach them himself. He will grow them into "decent, independent men." He will open a school with Petra in Captain Horster's dining room where the meeting took place, and he will get other students, not from the middle class but from the poor, the street urchins. His wife, although she supports him, is nervous about the future. His daughter, Petra, has nothing but admiration for him. He himself feels unbeatably strong because he is standing alone, true to right principles, not swayed by corrupt self-interest or public pressure.

CHARACTERS

Aslaksen
Aslaksen prints the local newspaper, *People's Herald*. He considers himself to be progressive politically but believes that radicalism must be tempered by moderation in all his opinions and actions. Aslaksen views the matter of the baths as a political issue rather than as a matter of public health, and he frames it as one needing his sober backing against the authorities, whom he believes must be moved to cooperate but must not be offended. He is, above all, however, entirely self-interested; he abandons Dr. Stockmann and supports opening the Baths, and suppressing the evidence of their bacterial infestation, when his self-interest is threatened. He serves as the chairman of the meeting at which Dr. Stockmann is vilified.

Billing
Billing is a reporter for the *People's Herald*. He is first a supporter of Dr. Stockmann but, like his colleagues on the newspaper, turns against Stockmann when his own self-interest is threatened. Billing presents himself as a disinterested outsider politically but he is actually positioning himself to secure a place on the town council.

Captain Horster
Horster is fired from his job as the captain of a ship after he provides Dr. Stockmann with his house to use as a meeting hall. Although he claims to be an unpolitical man, Horster is independent and is guided by a sense of right and wrong. After the Stockmann family is left homeless, he offers to let them live in his house and after Petra is fired as a teacher, he offers to let her use his house as a school.

Hovstad
Hovstad is the editor of the *People's Herald*. At first, he supports Dr. Stockmann, but out of self-interest Hovstad later turns against him. Like the other newspapermen, Hovstad is a hypocrite. Hovstad reveals that he is willing to compromise his ideals for the sake of the paper's circulation and to make the paper's politics acceptable to its readers by serializing an English novel with the simplistic attitude that God rewards those who do good with success and makes the works of evildoers end badly. When Petra Stockmann returns the book, refusing to translate it and showing him its faults, he defends his duplicity.

Hovstad's support for her father is largely motivated by his desire for her.

Morten Kiil

Morten Kiil is Dr. Stockmann's father-in-law. He is the owner of the tannery responsible for polluting the waters. He is a spiteful man who buys up shares in the Baths at discount rates, after Dr. Stockmann's report of their unhealthiness has deflated the value of the Baths's stock. Kiil uses the money that was to be his daughter's inheritance to purchase the shares, and he hopes to force Dr. Stockmann into recanting his opposition in order to clear Kiil's own name and reputation for having been the source of the pollution. His initial delight in Dr. Stockmann's discovery of the pollution was the result of his desire to be revenged on the members of the town council for excluding him from sitting on it. The extent of his depravity is evident from the fact that he initially believes that Stockmann was simply inventing a hoax. Kiil projects his own disreputable character onto others.

The Mayor

See Peter Stockmann

Eylif Stockmann

Eylif is Dr. Stockmann's thirteen-year-old son. He seems to be more conventional than his brother, noting when his brother says he would rather not work and become a Viking, that he would then have to be a heathen.

Mrs. Katherine Stockmann

The doctor's wife, Mrs. Stockmann, is aware that her husband's ethical stand endangers his livelihood and, consequently his family's welfare. Although she tries to restrain him, when the town turns against him, she supports him. She is a generous housekeeper and is accustomed to feeding visitors at her table whenever they stop by.

Morten Stockmann

Morten is Dr. Stockmann's ten year-old son. Both his boys are attacked by other boys because of their father's stand, and both are told to stay away from school for a while until the issue cools off. Morten seems to be more adventurous than his brother; he states that he does not wish to work when he grows up but to become a Viking.

Peter Stockmann

Dr. Stockmann's brother, Peter Stockmann is the mayor of the town and the police chief. He is one of the major supporters of the baths despite their hazard to the patrons' health. He argues that there is no hazard, that his brother is just a crank. Peter is unscrupulous in his actions. He seems to be jealous of his brother. He is puritanical and miserly. Nevertheless, he has given the doctor financial help, but rather than out of the goodness of his heart, it was to keep up the family's appearance. He himself follows a frugal regimen and disapproves of his brother's generosity and the hospitality he provides to others. Although Peter actually sets himself above the good of society and manipulates others in order to achieve his will, he accuses his brother of being unable to subordinate himself to the social good.

Petra Stockmann

Doctor Stockmann's daughter, Petra, is a school teacher. She strongly believes in her father's principles and stands up for him. She is fired from her teaching job for her loyalty to her father. She refuses to translate an English novel she considers reactionary. She seems to have been named after her uncle Peter, but she is unlike him; in contrast, she is steadfast, principled, and virtuous.

Dr. Thomas Stockmann

Dr. Stockmann is branded a public enemy when he discovers that the waters of the baths are polluted and poisonous and then insists that the baths cannot be advertised and reopened for clients. He is a good-spirited and generous man. He is a scientist whose loyalty is to the truth rather than to any political party or ideology. He has been poor and has had to struggle in order to feed his family. When the play opens, he is in a more comfortable position than he had been in in the past. Stockmann lives in town and his idea to build the Baths has given him a salary as a member of the board of directors of the Baths. He also has a good private practice. Despite fierce threats against his family's fortune and safety, he persists in following the path of truth and honor. By nature, he is open, trusting, and ebullient. When Peter disparages his way of living, he returns his grouchiness with cheerful rebuttals. Even in his anger, when he learns Peter has subverted his supporters, he expresses his rage with mockery, putting on Peter's mayoral hat. When the windows of his house are smashed, he makes a joke about the draftiness of the house. Stockmann also can show solid determination. He is strengthened by his ordeal and is dedicated to replacing corrupt ideas with fresh ones. He sees that not only the waters of the town are polluted—so are the ways the townspeople think.

Townsfolk

The townsfolk who appear at the meeting in act 4 can be seen as a character. They represent a mob and mob mentality. Rather than thinking about the issues at hand, they are swayed by the manipulative rhetoric of the mayor and actually become violent.

THEMES

Self-Interest

One thing that all Dr. Stockmann's opponents have in common is a firm dedication to their own self-interest even when it is at the expense of the common good, as it always is. The Mayor, Dr. Stockmann's brother Peter, is not the least bit civic-minded. He is concerned with his own reputation, with his power, and with his sense of his own virtue. The liberal newspapermen, Aslaksen, Billing, and Hovstad are all corrupt. What makes them corruptible is that their devotion to their own interests takes precedence over devotion to truth and concern for others. Morten Kiil attempts to discredit Dr. Stockmann's efforts and attempts to corrupt Dr. Stockmann's honor because he is offended that his good name and his father's good name before him will be besmirched by the news that his tannery is responsible for the water's toxicity.

Social Responsibility

Dr. Stockmann embodies the social responsibility that his opponents have replaced with self-interest. He is in some ways a vain man. He relishes the esteem he believes his discovery that the water is deadly will bring him. But vanity like that is different from self-interest. Dr. Stockmann's allegiance is to truth and right action. His pride is the result of the success he has in making a discovery. His daughter, Petra, is also motivated in all her actions and reactions by an unshakeable sense of social responsibility. Captain Horster's chief characteristic is his generosity. Mrs. Stockmann, fearful about the consequences to her family of her husband's actions,

TOPICS FOR FURTHER STUDY

- In *An Enemy of the People*, the issue that provokes the central conflict in the play is the quality of the water at the Baths. Today, climate change is a major political and ecological issue, and many people disagree with the scientists on this issue. In a paper of at least a thousand words, trace the political and ecological issues involved in the problem of climate change and describe the conflicts that this has provoked. As you do so, compare current issues and responses to those presented in *An Enemy of the People*.

- With several members of your class, organize a debate around the following topic: The majority is always wrong. Cite historical examples and examples from the play.

- At the conclusion of *An Enemy of the People*, following the belief that education will contribute to social improvement, Dr. Stockmann decides to open a school. Focusing either on Western European countries or on the United States, create a timeline tracing the movement to make schooling compulsory and list the philosophies behind that movement.

- Dr. Stockmann is at first blind to the nature of his society. When he realizes its power to condemn him, rather than being weakened by this revelation, he is strengthened. Write a short story or a ballad about a person who is strengthened by adversity.

nevertheless overcomes that fear because of loyalty to her husband, and because he is right.

Honor

The foundation of the conflict in *An Enemy of the People* is the absence of any sense of honor in any of the leaders of the towns. Honor means dedicating oneself to the service of something true, good, or transcendent. That is not the calling of any of Dr. Stockmann's adversaries or of the common people represented in the meeting in act 4. They are shown to be a mob even before the meeting begins, as they talk among themselves when they agree to see how Aslaksen responds to the events.

Conformity

The force that Ibsen identifies as allowing social injustice to thrive is the force of conformism. One after another, Dr. Stockmann's fellow citizens refuse contact with him, they say, not because they wish to but because they "dare" not. The glazier will not fix his windows only because he does not dare not to conform to the general will. Petra's school superintendent, apparently, thinks of herself as progressive as Petra, but she dares not, she says, offend public opinion. Consequently she conforms her beliefs and actions to the low dictates of public opinion, stifling anything that differs from it. Conformity seems to be how the townspeople cope with divided loyalty. That split is caused by a conflict between what is the right thing to do and what social pressure demands. Loyalty to a narrow self-interest, and the wish to avoid ostracism or worse punishment, leads them to conform to policies they do not approve of but fear to oppose.

Democracy

As the plot develops, the value of democracy becomes a central issue before which all the other issues—pollution, corruption, greed, jealousy—fall. Dr. Stockmann, once he is cast as the enemy of the people, begins to question the wisdom of the people or the good of a government by the people. The term Stockmann uses is the majority. The conclusion he reaches is that the majority is always wrong, that the few individuals who can see beyond the majority bear the truth and can indicate the right paths to follow. The two forces that Ibsen shows are able to subvert democracy are cowardice—which leads ordinary people to conform to mass opinion—and those few people, like the mayor, who can manipulate public sentiment. The mayor and others like Aslaksen and Hovstad, do this because of their own corrupt personalities and because of their skill in corrupting others.

STYLE

The Fourth Wall

An Enemy of the People is a realistic play. That means that in it, Ibsen creates the illusion of realism, that what is happening on the stage looks like life as it really happens. The play proceeds as if it were happening in a room in which the fourth wall of the room has been removed and the audience, unknown to the persons of the play, is peering into their private spaces.

Prose Plays

Ibsen thought of himself as a poet and he began his career writing in verse. His first great successes, plays that are still staged, such as *Brand* and *Peer Gynt*, were verse dramas. But with *Pillars of Society* in 1877, Ibsen abandoned verse and wrote plays only in prose, attempting to find the language of the middle-class of his time. Ibsen's poetry, once he began to write in prose, can be found in the rhythms of his plays and the depth of his imagination. Readers of Ibsen's plays in English are seriously disadvantaged since most of the translations of his works can seem stodgy and wordy, artificial and clumsy—problems his original Norwegian-language work does not suffer from.

Reversal and Recognition

The kind of dramatic plot that Aristotle favored in the *Poetics* involves a reversal of fortune and a recognition of something that had until then been hidden but that is of primary importance for the fate of the hero and in the creation of his heroism. Until the moment of the reversal's occurrence, the hero of the drama believes in both his good fortune and his clarity of vision. Once reversal and recognition occur, the hero realizes he has been blind to what really is and that his sense of his own superior fortune was mistaken, was vain, or was a fault that kept him from being able to know something it is essential for him to know. The way he faces that previously-hidden something, not his actions until then, determines his stature.

In *An Enemy of the People*, Dr. Stockmann is at first, although insightful in his hunches, blind to the social truth that is both his undoing and his opportunity to discover his real power. He expects to be rewarded for his discovery that the springs are contaminated. Instead he is reviled. Being reviled, however, illuminates for him the truth of the individual's vision and the spurious value of the majority's adulation. "Bred to a harder thing / Than Triumph," in the words the Irish poet W. B. Yeats, in his poem, "To A Friend Whose Work Has Come To Nothing,"

Dr. Stockmann finds the power of his own individual strength. Being deprived of the opportunity to enjoy social and professional triumph, he emerges as the hero of what is, again in Yeats's words, "most difficult"—standing alone.

The Well-Made Play

Ibsen's realistic plays take the form of the well-made play, the theory of which was developed in France in the first part of the nineteenth century by a prolific playwright, librettist, and man of the theater, Eugene Scribe, 1791–1860. The well-made play is a play in five formally determined acts. Its development is logical. One action inevitably determines the next. It depends, moreover, on standard devices, like letters or documents that pass among the characters. In a well-made play, the first act presents relatively congenial action, but by its conclusion some kind of conflict begins to emerge. That conflict and the tensions it creates are developed in the second act and intensified in the third. The fourth act brings the business to a head in a scene crowded with characters on the stage. In that act, furthermore, the hero is brought to a low point. The fifth act presents the major characters once more in a series of encounters that resolve the conflict. Ibsen took this formal structure—often used for farcical social comedies of misunderstanding and reconciliation—and transformed it, as is obvious in *An Enemy of the People*, by the seriousness not only of his subject matter and his themes but also by the profundity of his dramatic intentions.

HISTORICAL CONTEXT

Reaction to Ghosts

An Enemy of the People was written as Ibsen's response to the acrimony with which *Ghosts* was met. *Ghosts* uses the biblical theme that the sins of the fathers will be visited on the sons to explore issues like sexual immorality and venereal diseases, which were shocking topics in 1881. Beyond that, however, *Ghosts* challenges the predominant *Weltanschauung* or world view prevalent when Ibsen wrote it. As offensive as writing about promiscuity and syphilis, the real offense in *Ghosts* resides in the fact that it is a story in which evil is not overcome and the good do not triumph and endure. The public outcry when *Ghosts* appeared was not merely in regard to the play. Ibsen himself was personally attacked and vilified in the basest terms.

The Emergence of the Era of the "Little Man"

Serious plays, such as the great Greek plays or those by William Shakespeare, were in general about members of the nobility. But Ibsen wrote during the second half of the nineteenth century when the social emphasis had been moved away from the nobility to the people, particularly the bourgeoisie—merchants, entrepreneurs, learned professionals. This shift stemmed from the American and the French Revolutions that occurred at the end of the eighteenth century. Thusly, Ibsen took his heroes and villains from the middle class, from small town burgesses. Aslaksen, who shuns conflict and cowers behind "moderation" notes that he willingly would criticize the national government. It is the local officials he is loathe to criticize. He is not equipped for the drama of such a conflict. But conflict on that local level is the material Ibsen uses as he makes "little people," as opposed to aristocrats and royalty, the vehicles for presenting timeless conflicts. Themes and issues and twists of fate that affect Greek rulers and Shakespearean nobility are reinvented and reinvigorated as they are explored in small-town, middle-class, domestic contexts.

The Development of Science

The danger Dr. Stockmann discovers is the result of microscopic organisms, single cell creatures invisible to the naked eye. The existence of such life forms is hard to believe for people who can only believe what they can see, but lack the sophistication to deduce causes from effects. The 1880s, when *An Enemy of the People* was written, were a time of great advances in science, particularly in the realm of microscopy. In 1880, work with microscopes led to the discovery of the bacillus that is responsible for typhoid and of the parasite responsible for malaria. These discoveries were not universally accepted or acclaimed when they were first made. When Charles-Louis-Alphonse Laveran, for example, presented the findings of his microscope work on malaria to the Academy of Medicine at Paris, many were skeptical. An inability to accept the possibility of science as a way to discover powerful but invisible forces contributes to the general skepticism regarding Dr. Stockmann's discovery. Morten Kiil represents this position openly

COMPARE
&
CONTRAST

- **1880s:** Social observers like Ibsen are concerned about the power that newspapers have to shape public opinion and influence political action.

   Today: The power of the mass media to influence opinion is a recognized fact and a matter of concern to those who see the media as a force that undermines the vitality and efficacy of democracy.

- **1880s:** Pollution occurs following the industrial revolution. Social reformers write about how seriously the air and water are being polluted and how the quality of life and man's relationship with the environment are being compromised.

   Today: The world-wide consumption of fossil fuels is polluting the air and water and, because of climate change, public figures make films warning that the survival of the earth as a habitable environment for living things is threatened.

- **1880s:** Like Dr. Stockmann, who considers leaving Norway, many Norwegians are in fact emigrating. Most move to the United States to find work.

   Today: Norway attracts immigrants because it has one of the highest standards of living in the world, a humanitarian social system, a policy of offering refuge to victims of war and oppression, and good employment rates.

---

when he scoffs at the idea that there could possibly be little animals, as he thinks of the deadly microorganisms, in the water.

CRITICAL OVERVIEW

According to F. L. Lucas in *The Drama of Ibsen and Strindberg*, Luigi Pirandello, the twentieth-century Italian playwright, declared that "after Shakespeare, without hesitation, I put Ibsen first." Richard Gilman, writing in *The Making of Modern Drama: A Study of Büchner, Ibsen, Strindberg, Chekhov, Pirandello, Brecht, Beckett, Handke*, reports that the author James Joyce learned Norwegian just to read Ibsen's plays. Gilman states that Joyce wrote to Ibsen in 1901 to say how much he valued "your willful resolution to wrest the secret of life." But Ibsen was and often is seen, as Gillman characterizes it, as a "narrow, programmatic ... social philosopher," or worse. His characters can appear to be stereotypes used to illustrate an idea or represent one side of a conflict. William Morris, the late nineteenth-century English poet, utopian anarchist, and designer of books, tapestries, and furniture

wrote, Lucas reports, that he "hated" Ibsen's plays. Despite admitting that they were well written, Morris asserted they were "not literature." Lucas also states that the great psychological novelist Henry James called Ibsen "ugly, common, hard, prosaic, bottomlessly bourgeois." But James continued: "And yet of his art he's a master." Lucas goes on to note that what James found in Ibsen was "the presence and the insistence of life." It was not only these preeminent literary figures who found Ibsen troublesome. In 1881, as he was writing *An Enemy of the People*, just after *Ghosts* had appeared, Ibsen had been called "an egotist and a bungler," by an unnamed critic in the London *Daily Telegraph* and "A crazy fanatic" who is "Not only consistently dirty but deplorably dull," in the English magazine *Truth*. The English playwright, George Bernard Shaw, after citing both these and further condemnations of Ibsen and his admirers in his book *The Quintessence of Ibsenism*, goes on to treat *An Enemy of the People* as a drama of ideas developed inside political situations. Shaw reiterates and supports Ibsen's distrust of the majority and his reservations about the value of democracy as

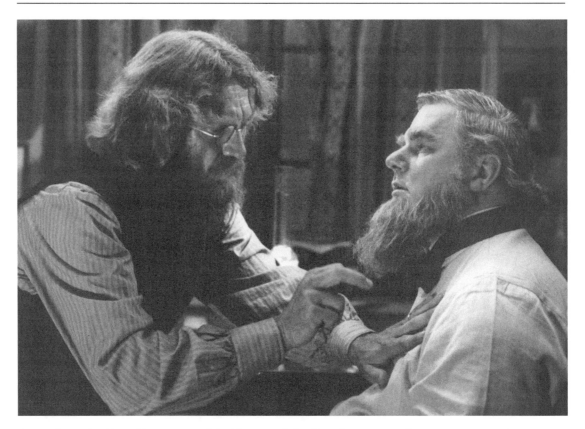

Scene from the 1977 film version of An Enemy of the People, *starring Steve Mcqueen as Doctor Thomas Stockmann and Charles Durning as Peter Stockmann* (Solar | 1st Artists | The Kobal Collection)

an enlightened system of government. The American playwright Arthur Miller, writing in the preface to his 1950 adaptation of *An Enemy of the People*, argues that "Ibsen is really pertinent today," and adds that Ibsen embodies the principle that "the dramatic writer has, and must again demonstrate, the right to entertain with his brains as well as his heart."

The view of Ibsen as, above all else, a social playwright, a dramatist concerned with political and social issues, is indeed influential; but, it is also limiting. There is another view of Ibsen the dramatist, the view that his plays are "poetic fantasies which have a lyrical nuance uncommon in the history of the drama," as Maurice Valency argues in *The Flower and the Castle: An Introduction to Modern Drama*. In Valency's opinion, Ibsen is a romantic writer who uses social issues to engage the great romantic themes: individual liberty, the opposition between the individual and his society, and dedication to truth. In Ibsen's penetration of the varieties and

vicissitudes of the human character, and in his concern for the values that transcend human circumstances, Ibsen defines the poetry of social drama.

CRITICISM

Neil Heims

Heims is a writer and teacher living in Paris. In this essay, he argues that in An Enemy of the People *Ibsen not only wrote a drama concerning social issues but one in which a man becomes a hero through his confrontation with adversity.*

What makes *An Enemy of the People* a great play is its ability to portray several major themes simultaneously. It can be read as a well-made play that is concerned with specific social issues and that explores the larger conflict between morality and greed. It can also be read as a drama of human growth and the destiny that is implicit in character.

WHAT DO I READ NEXT?

- *All My Sons* (1947), by Arthur Miller, is a social drama about a weapons manufacturer who has prospered during World War II by manufacturing sub-standard aircraft that have subsequently caused the death of several pilots.

- Ibsen's *Ghosts* (1881) concerns the bitter consequences of one man's sexual promiscuity: his son inherits syphilis from him and his wife realizes that her self-sacrifice for her husband was in vain.

- *The Cherry Orchard* (1904), Anton Chekhov's last play, presents an old Russian aristocratic family caught helplessly in the midst of historical change.

- *The Iceman Cometh* (1939), by Eugene O'Neill, takes place in a saloon populated by a group of alcoholic men who have lived their lives without integrity.

- *Howards End* (1910), a novel by E. M. Forster, concerns a society in transition and the conflicts that result when individual values and aspirations clash with social values and expectations.

Dr. Stockmann is placed on one side of the social conflict when he asserts that the water for the Baths is contaminated with dangerous bacteria. The mayor, the newspapermen, and the rest of the town are on the other side of the issue, refusing to accept the scientific truth as truth because it threatens their self-interests. Dr. Stockmann's conflict is with them individually and collectively. He represents moral rectitude in his desire to prevent an awful epidemic. They represent what appears to them to be the good of their town, the forces of economic survival, and even prosperity for the town. Their shortsightedness, were it not so dangerous, might appear comic. But since it is deliberate, it can be seen as reprehensible or even evil. Once, after all, the Baths are opened, their deadly nature will

> DR. STOCKMANN'S AWFUL BURDEN IS THAT HE CAN ONLY FIND HIS IDENTITY IN HIS ALLIANCE WITH THE TRUTH. HIS IDENTITY AS A HUMAN BEING DEPENDS, FOR HIM, UPON SERVING WHAT IS RIGHT."

be discovered. But that is something Dr. Stockmann's enemies refuse to consider. This willful blindness is as foolish as it is evil. The financial catastrophe the mayor and, ultimately, the entire town want to avert will come crashing down on them. Essential for the maintenance of their blindness is the vilification of Dr. Stockmann. His enemies can only indulge their self-interest if they can assert that Dr. Stockmann is a malicious troublemaker who ought not to be believed, rather than a concerned scientist and ministering physician. The theme of the townspeople's blindness and also of Dr. Stockmann's blindness, although of a different sort, gives *An Enemy of the People* a dimension beyond the well-made drama of conflicting social interests that the play obviously is.

An Enemy of the People has within it elements that make the great Greek plays of authors like Sophocles and Euripides the marvels that they are. In those plays, their authors describe the existential and psychological condition of men and women whom fate unexpectedly upsets and turns around. Although plays like *Oedipus Rex* or *The Trojan Women* probe the relationship between people and their environments, each play's profundity and depth of seriousness come from its exploration of its protagonist's relationship to his or her own character and actions. The heart of the drama in plays like those resides in the way the hero meets unwanted fate and the transformation the hero consequently undergoes. Usually the paradoxical situation is such that a character achieves transcendental greatness by being brought low. The blindness that a hero like Oedipus first believed to be clear sight comes to be recognized for the blindness it is. Attainment of the awareness of ignorance becomes illumination. The heroism of the hero is the result of the hero's recognition of a former, characteristic blindness and of his or her acceptance of fate, especially accepting his or her complicity in that fate. Such acceptance is the precursor to, and the precondition for, a final transcendence of fate. The hero has the strength to bear the identity he or she discovers to be his or hers and, somehow, to triumph over fate while seeming to succumb to it.

The drama of *An Enemy of the People* transports Dr. Stockmann from one sort of self-confidence to another. At the beginning of the drama, he is sure of his place within his community (mistakenly), of the community's good will towards him (which exists as long as he conforms to its requirements), and of his good will towards the community (which is qualified by his sense of duty to truth). To the extent that *An Enemy of the People* is seen as a play about political corruption, ethical choices, and the dangers of democracy, it is a vigorous and rigorous social drama. Dr. Stockmann, when the play is considered in that way, is an instrument to move forward the plot of the play, a vehicle to carry its issues. He is a catalyst to reveal the pollution in the government of the town as well as in the Baths, and of the pollution in people's natures that derives from opportunism. Fittingly, too, the play dissects how the possibility of democracy can be corrupted through the manipulation of public opinion by instruments of mass media run by people intent on shaping public opinion to their private interests—and thereby subverting democracy. The newspapermen, Aslaksen, Billings, and Hovstad, are contemptible just because they are not true to the highest values of their journalistic profession. They are for sale to the highest bidder. Dr. Stockmann is commendable because he is always true to his calling as scientist and physician. His action is never determined by his desire to serve his own interest. That puts him at odds with the rest of the town. His allegiance is to the truth, which it is his professional duty to discover and to defend. That ought to be the case with the newspapermen, too, but it is not.

Dr. Stockmann's awful burden is that he can only find his identity in his alliance with the truth. His identity as a human being depends, for him, upon serving what is right. That allegiance to the truth and to himself is tested and proven when his expectation that the community will honor his discovery of the plagued water is subverted and he is branded a public enemy

rather than a savior of the community. The twist in the plot, whereby he recognizes that he is an outcast among venal men and that his comfortable status among them is no longer comfortable, and that he has suffered a serious reversal of fortune, despite—or in fact because of—his virtue, brings the play into a different realm from the one it seemed to inhabit. As in the great Greek works and as in Shakespeare, the matter of the play is not (or is not only) social issues and political struggles, but the constitution of the human character. Dr. Stockmann's response to his fall is not to be defeated but to be strengthened. He rises to a level of humanity higher than he had occupied before his fall. His strength comes not from the support of a majority, or from conforming to how things are, but from his own resolve to stand by himself as a herald of how things ought to be. Stockmann's condemnation of majority rule is not petulant or spiteful. Actually, it is not a condemnation of democracy, at all, but a condemnation of ignorance. After his sons are sent home from school because the other boys are picking fights with them because of him, and after his daughter is dismissed from her teaching job because of him, Dr. Stockmann turns those assaults into opportunity. His next step is to make a school of his own in which he will educate street urchins— lower class children whom he will rescue from ignorance and through whom he will create the strength of democracy. That strength, Stockmann maintains, resides in the intelligence of a citizenry able, in consequence of their education, to govern themselves justly and truly.

All Dr. Stockmann's major adversaries, Ibsen shows, are loyal not to the truth but to the advancement of their own projects and, fundamentally, to themselves. In order to be so, they must baffle their vision and become blind to the truth. The newspaper men represent this leaning towards blind self-interest. So does Dr. Stockmann's brother Peter. Peter represents a consciousness of things and values entirely different from his brother's. The newspapermen waver in their allegiance. Peter is steady in his. They are corruptible, ready to support whoever will reward them. Peter is corrupt, ready and quite able to subvert anyone who may block him. Morten Kiil, Dr. Stockmann's proud and unscrupulous father-in-law, is a pure and even diabolical malevolence. He embodies the triumph of opportunity over morality and of self over other. While the newspapermen are weak in virtue, Peter Stockmann and Morten Kiil are strong in vice. *An Enemy of the People* is not only about social issues but about the human beings who shape social issues and conflicts. The play, like the Greek tragedies it has transformed into bourgeois drama, shows how environment, conflict, and even fate are functions of character. The problem of the contaminated water exists, in the first place, because of Peter's willful and jealous insistence that the conduits be laid as they were despite his brother's considered advice to lay them upstream of the tanning factory. Because of his characteristic need to dominate, Peter erred, and his need to seem above criticism and reproach causes him to persist in his error and deepen it.

Even when he appears to be writing a realistic drama about social issues and conflicts, Ibsen is constructing the archetypal roles of human characters. That does not mean that his plays are not concerned with the issues they purport to be about. But they also use those issues to explore the fundamental aspects of character. Dr. Stockmann is not merely the instrument Ibsen uses to deliver a sermon, but a man who realizes his own potential. Dr. Stockmann's major discovery is not the danger lurking in the apparently innocent waters of the Baths or even of the political corruption of the town or the ability of his neighbors to be willingly misled. His discovery is instead the direction of his own disposition. Following that direction (as a teacher and a reformer) in the face of opposition transforms him from the protagonist of a play into the archetype of a hero.

Source: Neil Heims, Critical Essay on *An Enemy of the People*, in *Drama for Students*, Gale, Cengage Learning, 2008.

Gale

In the following excerpt, the critic gives a critical analysis of Ibsen's work.

Hailed as one of the pioneers of modern drama, Henrik Ibsen broke away from the romantic tradition of nineteenth-century theater with his realistic portrayals of individuals, his focus on psychological concerns, and his investigation into the role of the artist in society. While initially utilizing conventions associated with the "well-made play," including exaggerated suspense and mistaken identity, Ibsen later used dialogue, commonplace events, and symbolism to explore the elusiveness of self-knowledge

> *AN ENEMY OF SOCIETY* DEMONSTRATES IBSEN'S CONTEMPT FOR WHAT HE CONSIDERED STAGNANT POLITICAL RHETORIC. AUDIENCES ACCUSTOMED TO THE ROMANTIC SENTIMENTALITY OF THE 'WELL-MADE PLAY' WERE INITIALLY TAKEN ABACK BY SUCH CONTROVERSIAL SUBJECTS. "

and the restrictive nature of traditional morality. Once writing that "I prefer to ask; 'tis not my task to answer," Ibsen did not establish distinct dichotomies between good and evil, but instead provided a context in which to explore the complexities of human behavior and the ambiguities of reality. Martin Esslin explained: "Ibsen can... be seen as one of the principal creators and wellsprings of the whole modern movement in drama, having contributed to the development of all its diverse and often seemingly opposed and contradictory manifestations: the ideological and political theatre, as well as the introspective, introverted trends which tend towards the representation of inner realities and dreams."

Ibsen was born to wealthy parents in Skien, a lumbering town south of Christiania, now Oslo. The family was reduced to poverty when his father's business failed in 1834. After leaving school at age fifteen and working for six years as a pharmacist's assistant, Ibsen went to Christiania hoping to continue his studies at Christiania University. He failed the Greek and mathematics portions of the entrance examinations, however, and was not admitted. During this time, he read and wrote poetry, which he would later say came more easily to him than prose. He wrote his first drama, *Catilina* (*Catiline*), in 1850 and although this work generated little interest and was not produced until several years later, it evidenced Ibsen's emerging concerns with the conflict between guilt and desire. While *Catiline* is a traditional romance written in verse, Ibsen's merging of two female prototypes—one conservative and domestic, the other adventurous and dangerous—foreshadowed the psychological intricacies of his later plays.

Shortly after writing *Catiline*, Ibsen became assistant stage manager at the Norwegian Theater in Bergen. His duties included composing and producing an original drama each year. Ibsen was expected to write about Norway's glorious past, but because Norway had just recently acquired its independence from Denmark after five hundred years, medieval folklore and Viking sagas were his only sources of inspiration. Although these early plays were coldly received and are often considered insignificant, they further indicated the direction Ibsen's drama was to take, especially in their presentation of strong individuals who come in conflict with the oppressive social mores of nineteenth-century Norwegian society. In 1862, verging on a nervous breakdown from overwork, Ibsen began to petition the government for a grant to travel and write. He was given a stipend in 1864, and various scholarships and pensions subsequently followed. For the next twenty-seven years he lived in Italy and Germany, returning to Norway only twice. While critics often cite Ibsen's bitter memories of his father's financial failure and his own lack of success as a theater manager as the causes for his long absence, it is also noted that Ibsen believed that only by distancing himself from his homeland could he obtain the perspective necessary to write truly Norwegian drama. Ibsen explained: "I could never lead a consistent life [in Norway]. I was one man in my work and another outside—and for that reason my work failed in consistency too."

Ibsen's work is generally divided by critics into three phases. The first consists of his early dramas written in verse and modeled after romantic historical tragedy and Norse sagas: *Gildet paa Solhaug* (1856; *The Feast of Solhaug*), *Fru Inger til Ostraat* (1857; *Lady Inger of Ostraat*), *Haermaendene paa Helgeland* (1858; *The Vikings at Helgeland*) and *Kjaerlighedens Komedie* (1862; *Love's Comedy*). These plays are noted primarily for their idiosyncratic Norwegian characters and for their emerging elements of satire and social criticism. In *Love's Comedy*, for example, Ibsen attacked conventional concepts of love and explored the conflict between the artist's mission and his responsibility to others. *Brand* (1866), an epic verse drama, was the first play Ibsen wrote after leaving Norway and was the first of his works to earn both popular and critical attention. The story of a clergyman who makes impossible demands on his congregation, his family, and himself, *Brand* reveals the fanaticism

and inhumanity of uncompromising idealism. While commentators suggest that Brand is a harsh and emotionally inaccessible character, they also recognized that this play reflects Ibsen's doubts and personal anguish over his poverty and lack of success. In comparison to Brand, the protagonist of Ibsen's next drama, *Peer Gynt* (1867), while witty, imaginative, and vigorous, is incapable of self-analysis. Although this play takes on universal significance due to Ibsen's use of fantasy, parable, and symbolism, it is often described as a sociological analysis of the Norwegian people. Harold Beyer explained: "[*Peer Gynt*] is a central work in Norwegian literature, comprising elements from the nationalistic and romantic atmosphere of the preceding period and yet satirizing these elements in a spirit of realism akin to the period that was coming. It has been said that if a Norwegian were to leave his country and could take only one book to express his national culture, [*Peer Gynt*] is the one he would choose."

Ibsen wrote prose dramas concerned with social realism during the second phase of his career. The first of these plays, *De Unges Forbund* (1869; *The League of Youth*), a caustic satire of the condescending attitudes of the Norwegian upper class, introduced idiomatic speech and relied upon dialogue rather than monologue to reveal the thoughts and emotions of the characters. Written, as Ibsen declared, "without a single monologue, or even without a single aside," *The League of Youth* evidenced Ibsen's shift from an emphasis on grandiose plot structures to characterization and interpersonal relationships. During his stay in Munich, when he was becoming increasingly aware of social injustice, Ibsen wrote *Samfundets Stotter* (1877; *The Pillars of Society*). A harsh indictment of the moral corruption and crime resulting from the quest for money and power, this drama provided what Ibsen called a "contrast between ability and desire, between will and possibility." The protagonist, Consul Bernick, while first urging his son to abide by conventional morality and become a "pillar of society," eventually experiences an inner transformation and asserts instead: "You shall be yourself, Olaf, and then the rest will have to take care of itself." Ibsen's next drama, *Et Dukkehjem* (1879; *A Doll's House*), is often considered a masterpiece of realist theater. The account of the collapse of a middle-class marriage, this work, in addition to sparking debate about women's rights and divorce, is also regarded as innovative and daring because of its emphasis on psychological tension rather than external action. This technique required that emotion be conveyed through small, controlled gestures, shifts in inflection, and pauses, and therefore instituted a new style of acting. *Gengangere* (1881; *Ghosts*) and *En Folkefiende* (1882; *An Enemy of Society*) are the last plays included in Ibsen's realist period. In *Ghosts* Ibsen uses a character infected with syphilis to symbolize how stale habits and prejudices can be passed down from generation to generation; *An Enemy of Society* demonstrates Ibsen's contempt for what he considered stagnant political rhetoric. Audiences accustomed to the Romantic sentimentality of the "well-made play" were initially taken aback by such controversial subjects. However, when dramatists Bernard Shaw and George Brandes, among others, defended Ibsen's works, the theater-going public began to accept drama as social commentary and not merely as entertainment.

With *Vildanden* (1884; *The Wild Duck*) and *Hedda Gabler* (1890), Ibsen entered a period of transition during which he continued to deal with modern, realistic themes, but made increasing use of symbolism and metaphor. *The Wild Duck*, regarded as one of Ibsen's greatest tragicomical works, explores the role of illusion and self-deception in everyday life. In this play, Gregers Werle, vehemently believing that everyone must be painstakingly honest, inadvertently causes great harm by meddling in other people's affairs. At the end of *The Wild Duck*, Ibsen's implication that humankind is unable to bear absolute truth is reflected in the words of the character named Relling: "If you rob the average man of his illusion, you are almost certain to rob him of his happiness." *Hedda Gabler* concerns a frustrated aristocratic woman and the vengeance she inflicts on herself and those around her. Taking place entirely in Hedda's sitting room shortly after her marriage, this play has been praised for its subtle investigation into the psyche of a woman who is unable to love others or confront her sexuality.

Ibsen returned to Norway in 1891 and there entered his third and final period with the dramas *Bygmester Solness* (1892; *The Master Builder*), *Lille Eyolf* (1894; *Little Eyolf*), *John Gabriel Borkman* (1896), and *Naar vi dode vaagner* (1899; *When We Dead Awaken*). In these final works, Ibsen dealt with the conflict between art and life

and shifted his focus from the individual in society to the individual alone and isolated. It is speculated that *The Master Builder* was written in response to Norwegian writer Knut Hamson's proclamation that Ibsen should relinquish his influence in the Norwegian theater to the younger generation. Described as a "poetic confession," *The Master Builder* centers around an elderly writer, Solness, who believes he has misused and compromised his art. *Little Eyolf*, the account of a crippled boy who compensates for his handicap through a variety of other accomplishments, explores how self-deception can lead to an empty, meaningless life. The search for personal contentment and self-knowledge is also a primary theme in *John Gabriel Borkman*, a play about a banker whose quest for greatness isolates him from those who love him. In his last play, *When We Dead Awaken*, subtitled "A Dramatic Monologue," Ibsen appears to pass judgement on himself as an artist. Deliberating over such questions as whether his writing would have been more truthful if he had lived a more active life, *When We Dead Awaken* is considered one of Ibsen's most personal and autobiographical works.

After completing *When We Dead Awaken*, Ibsen suffered a series of strokes that left him an invalid for five years until his death in 1906. Although audiences considered Ibsen's dramas highly controversial during his lifetime because of his frank treatment of social problems, present scholars focus on the philosophical and psychological elements of his plays and the ideological debates they have generated. Ibsen's occasional use of theatrical conventions and outmoded subject matter has caused some critics to dismiss his work as obsolete and irrelevant to contemporary society, but others recognize his profound influence on the development of modern drama. Haskell M. Block asserted: "In its seemingly limitless capacity to respond to the changing need and desires of successive generations of audiences, [Ibsen's] work is truly classic, universal in implication and yet capable of endless transformation."

Source: Gale, "Henrik Ibsen," in *Contemporary Authors Online*, Gale, Cengage Learning, 2007.

F. L. Lucas

In the following essay, Lucas considers Ibsen's promotion of individualism and the attacks that his views first encountered.

> IBSEN NEVER WROTE A PROSIER PLAY. BUT THIS IS NOT A CONDEMNATION. COMEDY CAN QUITE WELL DISPENSE, ON OCCASION, WITH POETRY. YET HOW MANY AUTHORS WOULD HAVE DARED WRITE A PLAY ABOUT ANYTHING SO PROSAIC AS—DRAINS?"

Ibsen had been prepared for a storm over *Ghost*. But he was certainly not prepared for the tornado that actually blew up. He was not daunted. But he was very angry. And, like Luther, he found anger inspiring. *An Enemy of the People* was his counter-defiance; and he completed it with what was, for him, unusual speed.

He seems, indeed, to have begun thinking of this play as early as the spring of 1880, provoked by the far milder outcry over *A Doll's House*. That summer, however, he turned to meditating *Ghosts,* published in December 1881. Finally, further exasperated by the abuse of *Ghosts*, he finished *An Enemy of the People* in the following summer of 1882; whereas from 1877 to 1881 and from 1882 to 1896 each new play regularly took him two years. Further, as Gran points out, *An Enemy* does not show any trace of Ibsen's usual recastings and redraftings.

It cannot be doubted that, though the poet assumed an air of icy indifference, the reception of *Ghost* left him really furious. To his friend Hegel he wrote, when he was already thinking over *An Enemy* (16/3/1882):

'All these withered, decrepit figures who have thus fallen upon my work, will one day receive a crushing verdict on themselves in future literary history. People will find out how to identify the anonymous poachers and footpads who have pelted me with filth from their lurking-place in Professor Goos's delicatessen-shop newspaper and other like localities.'

But Ibsen was in no mood to wait for the literary historians of the future. He would vindicate *himself*, here and now. So he sat down and wrote *An Enemy of the People*. He might ironically describe it as 'a peaceful work, that can be read by wholesale-merchants and their wives'. But this description might have left the whole-sale-merchants considerably astonished.

What particularly angered Ibsen was the abuse from the 'liberal' Left. Natural enough that, on the Right, bigoted clerical conservatism should lift up its many heads and bray; but he had not expected this chorus to be so loudly joined even by professed democrats. Accordingly in *An Enemy* he kept some of his sharpest cuts for so-called radical journalists who were anxious, not to civilize public opinion, but merely to trot behind it. 'I am more and more convinced,' he wrote to Brandes, 'that there is something demoralizing in all contact with politics, or adherence to parties. Never, under any circumstances, shall I be able to join any party which has on its side the majority. Bjørnson says the majority is always right. As a practical politician, I suppose he must. But I, on the contrary, feel compelled to say—the minority is always right.'

An Enemy of the People is based, like *A Doll's House*, on episodes of real life. Ibsen had heard of a certain Dr Meissner at Teplitz whose house was stoned in the thirties, because he reported an outbreak of cholera, and so ruined the spa's season. Also a certain Thaulow (1815–81), an apothecary in Christiania, who had a long feud with the Christiania Steam Kitchen, after publishing in 1880 a pamphlet called *The Pillars of Society in Prose,* had been howled down at a meeting in February 1881; and died a fortnight later. Further, Dr Stockmann appears to contain elements of Georg Brandes, Bjørnson, Jonas Lie, and Ibsen himself. The very name Stockmann is taken from the home of Ibsen's childhood at Skien.

The plot is simple. A small Norwegian town sets up as a spa, largely thanks to the energy of a certain Dr Stockmann. But its penny-wise town-council has laid the pipes too cheaply; and Stockmann's analysis confirms his fears that the water now teems with microbes. The patients are less likely to be cured than poisoned. So the pipes must be relaid—at great expense.

Dr Stockmann, being a simpler, much more sanguine and muddle-headed person than Ibsen, expects this vital discovery of his to be hailed by his fellow-townsmen with shouts of gratitude. For he is saving them from a scandal and a disaster that might have cost many lives. Still worse, it might have cost the town itself, in the long run, a lot of money. Little he knows the blinding potency of wishful thinking.

Consequence—a sharp lesson in practical psychology. The Doctor's brother Peter,

Mayor and Chief of Police, is furious. Nothing so horrid can possibly be true. Not a word more of it! The Doctor's rich and cunning old father-in-law, Morten Kiil (whose own tannery is poisoning the Baths) takes the whole story for a clever trick of the Doctor's to discredit his brother the Mayor. Hating the Mayor, old Kiil is delighted. He promises, if the Doctor proves right, a gift of twenty—no, on second thoughts, *ten* pounds—to charity. Hovstad, editor of the local left-wing paper, is equally delighted—for the moment. What a chance to ruin the town-council! But when Hovstad comes to realize also the expense and unpopularity involved, he at once rats to the side of the Mayor.

At a public meeting Dr Stockmann is howled down, and voted a public enemy. His windows are smashed. His post is taken away. His daughter is dismissed from the school where she teaches. His landlord gives him notice. And his father-in-law blackmails him by investing the money that Stockmann's wife and children would inherit, in the condemned Baths. Indeed, if the Doctor will not recant, old Kiil will leave all to charity. (Stockmann's father-in-law is a great fellow for charity!)

Such are the rewards of serving humanity. But Stockmann, like a Voltaire or an Ibsen, remains undaunted. He realizes, at last, what Ibsen himself, in his more resolute and less sceptical moods, so passionately believed:

> 'The strongest man on earth is he who stands most alone.'

Or as Matthew Arnold had put it:

Alone the sun arises, and alone
Spring the great streams.

Ibsen never wrote a prosier play. But this is not a condemnation. Comedy can quite well dispense, on occasion, with poetry. Yet how many authors would have dared write a play about anything so prosaic as—drains? Curiously enough, this prosaic work was immediately followed by one of the pieces where Ibsen most deeply infused his prose with hidden poetry—*The Wild Duck*.

But if Ibsen never wrote a prosier play, he never wrote one more breezy and more boisterous. Perhaps its unusual dash and high spirits were helped by the unusual rapidity with which its author's anger tossed it off. *An Enemy of the People* becomes, in my experience, even more amusing than one might expect, when acted and produced with vigour. For here, as so often,

comedy gains by being seen rather than read; whereas tragedy, unless superlatively staged, is often better read than seen.

The most effective thing in the play is its hero; who seems mainly a mixture of the hopefully pugnacious Bjørnson (who had dared to defend *Ghosts*), and the grimly pugnacious Ibsen. Dr Stockmann, said his creator, 'is in part a grotesque, hare-brained fellow'. But, he also said, 'Dr Stockmann and I get on splendidly; we agree so well in many ways; but the Doctor has more of a muddle-head than I, which may make things more tolerable from his mouth than they would be from mine.' In short, the tight-buttoned Ibsen could here, for once, let himself go; with a freedom that, when he spoke in his own person, his self-critical reason usually (not always) checked and inhibited. Further, the human jackals and crocodiles that the Doctor hunts, are quickened by Ibsen's angry hands into a very grotesque and lively variety of game.

One of the play's main themes may seem trite—'Honesty is the best policy'. Yet it has been objected by one Ibsen-critic (whom it really would be unkind to name), that Stockmann 'brought a calamity on his native place by his awful propensity for blabbing out the truth'. This wisdom seems worthy of Peter Stockmann himself. Would a hundred cases of typhoid have been less of a calamity?

But not all the ideas behind the play are so simple. Ibsen has here travelled a good deal towards the Right since the days of *Catiline*. 'Ha! ha!' cries Hovstad. 'So Dr Stockmann has turned aristocrat since the day before yesterday.' Applied to Ibsen himself, that would be only a half-truth. For he remained a liberal. But he had come to feel that there is no real progress for communities without progress in the individuals composing them. Hence his warning in 1885 to the workers of Trondheim that democratic liberty required, also, an aristocratic element 'of character, of mind and will'. We have not moved much nearer that goal in our age of totalitarian tyrannies, and a world still further plebeianized by mass-standards and over-population.

An Enemy of the People then, has by no means lost its point. Its first audiences seem to have been favourable, but not swept away. A generation later, however, in 1905, on the day of the massacre in Kazansky Square, the play was performed, says Stanislavsky, at the Moscow Art Theatre. At the moment when

Dr Stockmann remarks, 'One must never put on a new coat when one goes to fight for liberty and truth', such a pandemonium of applause burst from the delighted theatre that the performance had to stop. The audience stormed towards the footlights. Hundreds of hands were stretched out to Stanislavsky who was playing the Doctor. And many of the younger, more agile playgoers jumped on the stage to embrace him. Little their Russian exuberance guessed that all their revolutionary ardour was only to exchange the tyranny of Czars for the tyranny of Commissars; that Peter the Great was to be succeeded by a series of Peter Stockmanns.

Norwegians are by nature less effusive than Russians: but Gran similarly tells how in 1915 Dr Stockmann's denunciations of stupid majorities were cheered by a packed Norwegian theatre; long sickened of political claptrap and intrigue.

However, as Dr Stockmann says, truth itself does not stand still. 'Truths are by no means wiry Methusalehs, as some supposed. A normal truth lives, say, as a rule seventeen or eighteen years—twenty at most—seldom longer.' Since then, though 'the damned compact majority' can be stupid and tyrannical as ever, we have come to suffer also from another curse, the damned compact *minority* that makes up for numbers by fanaticism and organization—the Party, Fascist, Nazi, or Communist, which can bludgeon the masses into pseudo-majorities such as Ibsen never dreamed of, where 99.9 per cent. vote the 'Yes' of slaves. Under such régimes the Dr Stockmanns of our age have found, to their cost, that though in civilized societies he may be strongest who stands most alone, that truth holds true no longer under the brutality of police-states. Such men ended in the Lipari Islands, in the Lubianka Prison or Siberia, in Sachsenhausen or Dachau, or in the grave. Fortunate the man who, like Pasternak, was merely gagged, and reviled as, precisely, 'an enemy of the people'. Which suggests that, as one would expect, the Russian propaganda-machine has forgotten Ibsen—or it would hardly have chosen the very phrase which Ibsen's play has left so charged with ridicule.

Small wonder then if Russian Marxist critics like Plekhanov or Lunacharsky had little use for the individualism of *An Enemy of the People*, with what Lunacharsky called its 'laughable tirades'. For even writers who should have retained some traditions of freedom, like Hugo von Hofmannstal, could come in this century to write: 'Our time is unredeemed, and do you know what it wants to be redeemed from?... The individual...Our age groans too heavily under the weight of this child of the sixteenth century which the nineteenth fed to monstrous size.' Ibsen would have smiled pretty grimly.

If we had a National Theatre, it could hardly do better to educate the public than perform *An Enemy of the People* every single year.

Source: F. L. Lucas, "*An Enemy of the People* (1882)," in *The Drama of Ibsen and Strindberg,* Cassell, 1962, pp. 171–77.

SOURCES

Gilman, Richard, *The Making of Modern Drama: A Study of Büchner, Ibsen, Strindberg, Chekhov, Pirandello, Brecht, Beckett, Handke,* Da Capo, 1974, pp. 50–51.

Ibsen, Henrik, *An Enemy of the People,* in *Ghosts and Other Plays,* translated by Peter Watts, Penguin, 1964, pp. 103–220.

Lucas, F. L., *The Drama of Ibsen and Strindberg,* Cassell, 1962, pp. 295, 299.

Miller, Arthur, Preface, in *Arthur Miller: Collected Plays 1944–1961,* Library of America, 2006, p. 261–63.

Shaw, George Bernard, *The Quintessence of Ibsenism,* Hill and Wang, 1913, pp. 92–97.

Valency, Maurice, *The Flower and the Castle: An Introduction to Modern Drama,* Macmillan, 1963, p. 123.

Watts, Peter, ed., Introduction, in *Ghosts and Other Plays,* Penguin, 1964, pp. 11, 16.

Yeats, William Butler, *The Collected Poems of W. B. Yeats,* Macmillan, 1962, p. 107.

FURTHER READING

Adler, Stella, *Stella Adler on Ibsen, Strindberg, and Chekhov,* edited and with a preface by Barry Paris, Alfred A. Knopf, 1999.

> Stella Adler, who died at the age of ninety one, in 1992, was known as one of the great acting teachers of the twentieth century. This book is a collection of her lectures. The five that are devoted to Ibsen consider him as a pioneer of modern theater who tore down and reconstructed the way dramas were created. Adler's lectures focus on Ibsen's plots, his themes, his values, and the demands that his plays make on actors as well as the opportunities they offer.

Beyer, Edvard, *Ibsen: The Man and His Work*, translated by Marie Wells, Condor/Souvenir Press, 1978.

Beyer offers an account of Norway in Ibsen's lifetime and its literary environment. Then the book goes on to trace the development of Ibsen's career, his art, and his thought.

Gosse, Edmund, *Henrik Ibsen*, Charles Scribner's Sons, 1907.

Gosse, 1849–1928, was an English poet and critic who wrote this literary biography shortly after Ibsen's death. Gosse shows how Ibsen's life and work were understood by one of his younger contemporaries.

Sage, Steven F., *Ibsen and Hitler: The Playwright, the Plagiarist, and the Plot for the Third Reich*, Carroll & Graf Publishers, 2006.

Sage asserts that Dr. Stockmann's acts and pronouncements were formative in shaping the Nazi leader Adolf Hitler's ideology and the course of his ascent and rule.

Tennant, P. F. D., *Ibsen's Dramatic Technique*, Bowes & Bowes, 1948.

This is a compact and well-focused study of Ibsen as a dramatist, his approach to constructing stories for the stage, as well as his approaches to presenting stories on the stage, and for methods of creating roles for actors.

Fabulation; or,
The Re-Education of Undine

LYNN NOTTAGE

2004

Lynn Nottage's *Fabulation; or, The Re-Education of Undine* was published by Dramatists Play Service in 2005, the year after it was originally produced in New York City. It is a riches-to-rags story that follows the apparent decline of Undine from her high-profile job in Manhattan back to the projects where she grew up. Although she loses her status, wealth, and pride, she gains wisdom and self-knowledge that would have eluded her in her prior existence. Facing the people from her past, she must come to accept them and herself as she learns that one can never truly outrun the past.

Although the characters are primarily African-American, and the play is often categorized as an African-American play, most of the content is universal. Nottage may be making a statement about the particular importance of African Americans honoring each other in all social strata and taking pride in their past, but the themes are applicable to many backgrounds and experiences. There is nothing, after all, about Undine that is only relevant to African Americans or even women. She is a person who finds herself in a situation faced by many people the world over and in all eras. The result is an accessible play about confronting uncomfortable personal truths.

AUTHOR BIOGRAPHY

Lynn Nottage was born in 1964 in New York City, and grew up in Brooklyn. As of 2007, she

Lynn Nottage *(Paul Hawthorne / Getty Images)*

still lived in New York City. Even as a young girl, she enjoyed writing scripts in her personal journal. When she was a teenager, she attended the High School of Music and Art in New York, and then attended Brown University, from which she graduated with a bachelor's degree in 1986. She then went to the Yale School of Drama, where she completed her Master of Fine Arts degree in 1989. Although she worked as a press officer for Amnesty International after graduating, she later returned to writing. It was a short play entry that reignited her desire to write scripts; that play, *Poof!* won an award. Since then, most of Nottage's career has been in drama. She has worked as an award-winning playwright and as a visiting lecturer in playwriting, and scripts continue to inspire and motivate her creativity. Her plays have been produced worldwide.

After *Poof!*, Nottage turned her attention back to an article she had read about unpaid soldiers in Mozambique who took matters into their own hands by nabbing hostages. The resulting play was her 1997 work, *Mud, River, Stone.*

The year 2004 was a busy one for Nottage. One of her plays to see publication was *Crumbs from the Table of Joy*, which tells the story of a widower and his two daughters who move from Florida to New York to live with family. Set in the 1950s, the African-American family faces personal struggles within the family, along with social struggles in the upheaval of the day. *Intimate Apparel* was also published in 2004, and tells the story of a long-distance relationship and the challenges that come when the couple marries. *Fabulation; or, The Re-Education of Undine*, although published in 2005 by Dramatists Play Service, was first produced in 2004. It is an unusual rags-to-riches-to-rags story of an African-American woman who overcomes her humble beginning, becomes arrogant in her success, and takes a dramatic fall back to where she started. Nottage has received a number of prestigious awards for her playwriting, including a New York Foundation for the Arts fellowship and a Guggenheim Fellowship in 2005.

PLOT SUMMARY

Act 1

SCENE 1

The play opens with Undine in her office on the phone with a client. Undine runs a public relations (PR) firm, and is working on a client project as her assistant (Stephie) is madly trying to find someone fabulous to accompany her to a major event that night. Undine wants someone who will help her make a great entrance, but Stephie is having trouble making it happen. Undine's accountant is waiting to see her, and hits Undine with terrible news. Her account has been emptied, and she should seriously consider filing for bankruptcy. Undine's husband, Herve, has left and apparently had been slowly taking their money. Shocked, Undine continues to treat everyone around her with little respect and speak tersely to them. The accountant continues to try to get through to her, but Undine digs in her heels, insisting that she will not give up her business. When an Federal Bureau of Investigation agent arrives to talk to Undine about her husband's identity fraud, she is even more shocked. The agent also explains that their research has shown no record of an Undine Barnes Calles until fourteen years prior to that day. He says, "you seem to have materialized from ether." At this point,

Undine excuses herself and addresses the audience directly. She explains that she came from a humble background, acquired excellent schooling, and broke from her past to become the owner of a "fierce boutique PR firm catering to the vanity and confusion of the African American nouveau riche." She then explains that she met Herve at a party, and she was swept away by his Latin charm and the fact that "he gave me flair and caché." They married, he got his green card, and they led a glamorous life. Then Undine grabs her chest and yells for Stephie.

SCENE 2

When the next scene opens, Undine is talking to her doctor and learns that she did not have a heart attack, just a severe anxiety attack. She tells him that her husband left her, she is broke, and she is going to have to close her successful business. The doctor tries to cheer her up with the good news that she is pregnant, to which she responds by addressing the audience directly again. She talks more about her relationship with Herve, how exciting it was when they met and fell in love. Although she had been dating a washed-up rapper, Herve was more sophisticated and more in line with the image she was working so hard to establish for herself.

SCENE 3

In the next scene, Undine and a friend, Alison, are talking in Undine's office about the disaster that has befallen Undine. It has already been covered in the paper, and Undine is furious with Herve and humiliated for herself. Alison is the only friend who has not totally abandoned her, and Undine tells the audience that Alison also changed her name when she achieved success and wealth outside of Harlem, where she was reared. When Undine asks if she can stay with Alison, she is subtly turned away with shaky promises of having dinner together soon.

A Yoruba priest arrives in Undine's office, on the advice of the accountant. The priest says that Undine has angered the god Elegba, and he wants her to go home in order to appease him (and give him a thousand dollars and a bottle of rum). Undine decides she has nothing to lose, so she pays the money and makes plans to return to Brooklyn to see her family.

SCENE 4

Undine shows up at her parents' house, to the surprise of everyone. Her mother is welcoming,

but her brother, Flow, mocks her for distancing herself from them when she was so successful in the city. He is clearly bitter. Undine asks him how his epic poem about Brer Rabbit is going, and although he has been working on it for years, he insists that he is still going to finish it. Undine tells the audience that Flow had been successful in the military, but came back from Desert Storm changed. He now works as a security guard at Walgreen's.

Undine tells her mother she does not know how long she will need to be there, and her mother tells her she will have to sleep with her grandmother. Undine is fine with that. Undine tries to talk to her father, who speaks in a distant way about a man in the neighborhood who solved a prize-winning math problem, but was killed before he could collect the money. Undine turns to the audience and tells about her family. Although she told all of her friends in New York City that her family was killed in a fire, her parents actually had wanted to be on the police force, but were not able to pass the exams. So they became security guards at a university. She strikes up chit-chat with her mother, and when Flow asks about the father of Undine's child, Undine gets defensive because she feels like she has become such a negative stereotype as a single African-American mother in the projects.

SCENE 5

Undine goes to the room she will share with her grandmother. Her grandmother talks about how she wishes Undine had not left the family the way she did, and that the tension at home was not as bad as Undine makes it out to be. Then Undine learns that her grandmother has been using heroin to make herself feel better. When Undine asks her mother if she knows, she dismisses the idea. The grandmother convinces Undine to go get more drugs for her, and while Undine is in the middle of the deal, the police arrive. Undine is placed under arrest.

SCENE 6

In jail, Undine meets a harsh woman who tries to start something with her, and another woman who tells Undine just to ignore the other inmate. She then asks Undine if this was her first time as a prostitute, and Undine tells her that is not why she is there at all, that it was just a misunderstanding. The inmate then tells Undine how a guy was looking at her wrong and talking nasty to her, so she attacked him and was arrested. When Undine goes before the judge, she is sentenced to a drug program that she must attend or face a year in prison.

Act 2

SCENE 1

As the second act opens, Undine is sitting in on one of her drug counseling group sessions. The other addicts are talking about their struggles with addiction, and one man, Guy, tries to encourage them to enjoy the peace of being clean. Undine remarks that the irony is that the descriptions of crack by the addicts make her want to try it. When pushed to share her own story, Undine makes up a story of addiction and even manages to cry. Guy encourages her to look at her pregnancy not as a burden, but as an opportunity to learn. Undine is intrigued by him, and accepts his invitation to a date. On the date, he tells her that he is a security guard at a movie theater, but that he wants to be a firefighter. She tells him that she once had a successful PR firm. He tells her how much he respects her for her battle against addiction and her preparing to be a single mom. He wants to see her again, but she says it is not a good idea. He always stays positive, and Undine tells the audience, "His sincerity is sickening," while also admitting that everything that makes him so different from Herve makes him appealing.

SCENE 2

In the courtyard of the projects, Undine runs into two old friends, Rosa and Devora. Although Undine tries to avoid them, they see her and talk briefly about the roads their lives have taken. Rosa is still living in the projects, and Devora has moved into the city after becoming a financial planner. Devora had heard of an Undine who was a PR executive, but does not realize that it was the same Undine. As Devora leaves, Rosa mentions social services, and Undine calls it "the most dreaded part of the system."

SCENE 3

The next scene opens with Undine finally at the front of the line at social services, where she confronts a sarcastic and hostile case worker. They argue over forms and the length of the line until Undine escalates the argument to the point that the case worker has Undine taken by paramedics to a psychiatric hospital. They give her antipsychotic drugs she can not take because

of her pregnancy, and Undine still has to face social services the next day to get the right form.

SCENE 4

Undine eventually makes it through the system and is able to see a doctor. The doctor informs Undine that she is farther along in her pregnancy than she thought. Undine is surprised and also frustrated at the doctor's telling her she should have come in sooner to receive proper prenatal care.

SCENE 5

Undine goes to a drug store in an entirely different neighborhood because it is such a nice store. She runs into Stephie, who is working there while she looks for a better job. Undine is embarrassed to see Stephie. When Stephie leaves, Undine finds her vitamins, shoplifts them, and heads home.

SCENE 6

Back at home, Flow is talking about a shoplifter at his store that he tried to turn around with a moving speech about making better choices to honor the heritage of African Americans. Then he teases Undine about how big she is and her name, and their mother scolds them both for being childish. Undine is frustrated because someone called for her, but neither parent nor the grandmother remembers anything about the call or the caller. Flow recites his partially completed poem, and the family listens. When he is done, they talk about how they saw the article about Undine where she said her family had died in a fire. She claims it was a misunderstanding, but they know better. Undine addresses the audience with general questions about her life, and then announces that the authorities caught up to Herve.

SCENE 7

Undine visits Herve in prison, where he is surprised to find her pregnant. He asks whose baby it is, and she releases her anger on him. She accuses him of being a selfish user, and he accuses her of being closed off to the world.

SCENE 8

In her next group counseling session, Undine learns that Guy was the one who called her home. She and Guy talk during someone else's heart-wrenching discussion of addiction, but their conversation soon becomes the center of attention. He tells her that if she wants him to be there for her delivery, he will. She admits to being confused and angry with the world, and accepts his offer.

SCENE 9

In the next scene, Undine is pushing her baby while Guy coaches her. She is reluctant to bring a child into this world, but when she releases her hesitation, the baby comes out. The last sound in the play is a baby's cry as the lights go down.

CHARACTERS

Undine Barnes Calles

At thirty-seven, Undine owns a successful boutique PR firm in New York City. She is married to an exciting, sophisticated man, and she seems to have completely overcome her humble beginnings in the Brooklyn projects. She has changed her name from Sharona to the more refined Undine, become a mover and shaker, and has even made up a story about her family dying in a fire, but she learns that she cannot truly change the truth of her past. When her husband turns out to be a criminal and a thief who leaves her alone, pregnant, and penniless, Undine returns home to face the family and community she abandoned. Her pride makes her return difficult, and she is defensive and judgmental. But in crisis, she opens her heart and looks at herself more closely. She then grows strong in a way she could not have understood in her former life.

The play is essentially about Undine's personal growth after realizing that she had built her life among selfish, superficial people who knew little of loyalty or compassion. When her business and money are gone, so are her friends and connections. The reader has to wonder if Undine's pride kept her from looking for a job working for someone else rather than leave the city quietly. Regardless, she returns to the safety net of her family, taking her attitude with her. She clearly feels comfortable at home because she settles in quickly, speaking her mind with no concern for other people's feelings. Her preoccupation with herself is clear in how quick she is to criticize those she left behind when she went to start her business in the city. She shows little gratitude, and she does not even apologize to them for telling everyone they were dead. They know she was ashamed of them, yet she is unwilling to see her own arrogance. By the end of the play, she has come to understand herself better as a part of her family, and she will be forced to put her selfishness aside because she will have a baby depending on her. The reader cannot help but think that Undine's welcoming Guy into her life is a sign that she is softening and learning from her many mistakes.

Father

Undine's father is emotionally distant and does not engage on a personal level with the other members of the family. He seems to see the world through pessimistic eyes and has given up on the idea of living his dreams. When he is not at work, he is either sitting in a bar with his friends, or sitting at the table at home drinking beer and occasionally talking to his family. He seems to have a broken spirit, and the world has made him cynical and detached.

Flow

Flow is Undine's brother. He was successful in military school and in his subsequent military service. However, the time he spent in Operation Desert Storm changed him in a profound way. Undine says that he was never able to reconcile his love of freedom with his love of the uniform. Like his parents, Flow works as a security guard, although he insists that he will one day finish his epic poem about Brer Rabbit. The work he puts in on his poem, and his passion in discussing it, reveal an intellectual side of Flow. He analyzes his world, but unlike his father, he is still determined to make whatever changes he can. Evidence of this is not only in the intellectual exercise of the poem, but in his workplace where he tries to turn a young man's life in a better direction after the young man is caught shoplifting. Flow is somewhat hot-tempered (probably a result of his internal anger), and when the young man does not know who Nelson Mandela is, Flow sends him off with the police. When Undine returns, Flow is resentful and sarcastic; he tries to make her feel awkward and unwelcome. He believes she abandoned the family and only thought of herself when she went to New York City to pursue her dreams, and then came back only when she needed help.

Grandmother

Undine's grandmother has lived a life of hard work as a wife and mother. In her old age, she feels unsatisfied and useless with little to look forward to every day. She has become a drug addict, shooting heroin to make the days go by more easily. She is not proud of her drug use, but she does not try to hide it from Undine on Undine's first day back. Undine's grandmother makes her feel guilty and manipulates Undine into going to buy more drugs for her, which lands Undine in jail.

Guy

Guy is a sensitive man Undine meets in her drug counseling group session. He is battling his addiction and respects Undine for being a fighter. He works as a security guard at a movie theater, but he dreams of becoming a firefighter. He is insightful, persistent, and sincere. Undine senses early on that he is trustworthy, and she agrees to have him attend the birth of her baby. Perhaps because of his own struggles, he encourages Undine and tries to help her rebuild her belief in herself. Undine remarks how different he is from Herve, and her attraction to Guy shows the audience that Undine is changing and growing.

Herve

Herve is Undine's soon-to-be-ex husband. Although exciting, sophisticated, and suave, he has little moral fiber. He uses Undine to get a green card, then puts no effort into their relationship, and is finally imprisoned for fraud. His cruelty is apparent in the fact that before he left Undine, he gave her no warning that he was planning to leave her, and he slowly siphoned all of their money out of their account. Undine is left penniless and pregnant, neither of which moves Herve. His only redeeming quality is that he sees Undine for who she has become, and he is not afraid to tell her. In this, he challenges her to look at herself honestly.

Mother

Undine's mother struggles to keep the family together in the face of adversity and broken dreams. She and her husband had hoped to join the police force when they were young, but had to settle for jobs as security guards. Undine's mother finds a level of contentment in her home in the projects by settling into denial about certain things (like her own mother's drug use), and holding onto hope about others (such as her family living harmoniously).

Sharona

See Undine Barnes Calles

Stephie

Stephie is Undine's executive assistant in the first scene of the play. She is young, stylish, and a good worker. While she does not seem to be overly ambitious or career-oriented, she is committed to finding work that will take her somewhere. She seems to have good instincts about the workplace, as she was a valued employee to Undine, and then when she works at the drugstore, she understands the importance of getting along with her coworkers. Unlike Undine, Stephie does not judge people, although this is partly because she is fairly self-absorbed; when Undine comes into her drugstore, Stephie is friendly and inquisitive, but never says anything to make Undine feel embarrassed.

THEMES

Duality

Nottage introduces the theme of duality in *Fabulation; or, The Re-Education of Undine* most obviously through the protagonist, Undine. Nottage reinforces this theme in other ways throughout the play, as well. In Undine, Nottage has created a character who is effectively two people. Her internal struggle comes from the fact that she only wants to be one person—the one she created. Still, she is Sharona (her given name, the one that her family and friends knew her by when she was young), the girl who grew up in the Brooklyn projects, where her family struggled and she saw despair, violence, and hopelessness. She is also Undine, the successful businesswoman in New York City who is powerful, smart, and wealthy. Undine was created by Sharona when Sharona was determined to sever all ties with her former life, even to the extent of inventing a tragic story about her family dying in a fire. In the second to last scene of the play, Undine tells Guy that her old self was killed in order for her new self to exist. She knows that she is two people in one mind and body. What she learns, however, is that the duality of the truth of her life is inescapable. She may have become Undine through hard work and intention, but she will always be the product of Sharona's experiences and roots.

TOPICS FOR FURTHER STUDY

- Read about the Walt Whitman projects (where Undine's family lives in the play) in Brooklyn and see if you can gain insight into the real-life culture of the community there. Imagine the life of one person living there who is in some way similar to you, and write three days' worth of journal entries for this imagined person.

- How would this play be different if it depicted the lives and struggles of people of another racial or ethnic group? Outline the play with the same basic plotline and many of the same themes, but with totally different characters. Pay special attention to how you preserve the intent of the play while applying it to new circumstances. Add a concluding paragraph sharing your insights.

- Undine skips over most of the details of her rise to the top in New York City. Write a one-act prequel that portrays more of Undine's childhood, teenage years, and her young adulthood. Be sure your script is consistent with the information Nottage gives in hers.

- How have business opportunities for African-American women changed in the last ten to twenty years? Research the changes by finding statistical information as well as markers such as major events or examples of women who have been the first to achieve certain milestone accomplishments. Create a timeline presenting the information you have found.

- Undine's self-image changes significantly over the course of the play. Create a work of art in any medium you choose that you believe would be an accurate self-portrait of Undine at the beginning of the play. Create a second one for the end of the play.

Nottage supports the theme in other characters and situations in the play. For example, Flow is a man with a divided nature. He has deep insight into duality in the hearts and reactions of others. It seems to run in the family because when Undine asks her father how he is, he responds, "I is and sometimes I ain't."

The Pitfalls of Attempting to Escape the Past

At the heart of *Fabulation; or, The Re-Education of Undine* is a message about the impossibility of removing oneself from the past. The past is the truth, and so it can not be changed. Undine tries to change her past by reinventing herself and telling lies about her family, but none of that changes the truth of what her past is. Nottage addresses the past on another level, too. While Undine cannot change what the past was, neither can she outrun it. Her circumstances take a dramatic downturn, and she is left with no alternative but to return literally to her past. A grown woman, she must swallow her pride and return to her family's house, depending on them for support. At first, Undine regards her circumstances as somewhat tragic and speaks fatalistically: "I think I'm officially part of the underclass. Penniless. I've returned to my original Negro state, karmic retribution for feeling a bit too pleased with my life." She is ultimately unable to leave the past behind for good; her situation forces her to accept, learn, and grow.

As with the theme of duality, Nottage takes care to reinforce the theme of the past through the words of other characters. When Flow tells his family about the young shoplifter he lectured in an effort to help him see a better way, he says that "there ain't no greater crime than abandoning your history." In a group drug counseling session, one of the addicts talks about the pain of breaking past habits, and he says, "I will no longer inhabit the places of my past." This is the other side of the theme. Where Undine attempted to disconnect from her past for reasons of status and pride, the addict wants a brighter, cleaner future and wants to break from his destructive past. In his case, he is right to turn from his past. But it is critical that he never forget it, which is what he and Undine have in common.

Feminism

While *Fabulation; or, The Re-Education of Undine* is not intended to be an anthem to feminism, it does depict some important feminist truths about

Aerial view of Park Avenue, New York City
(© Stock Connection Distribution / Alamy)

modern society. First, Undine is a strong, independent, successful businesswoman who builds her public relations firm. She does this by her mid-thirties, and is taken seriously in her field. This indicates that a woman (and an African-American woman, at that) has access to opportunities today. Second, the character of Inmate #2 shows that women are no longer willing to be objectified and oppressed by chauvinistic attitudes. This woman is in prison because a man was talking to her and treating her like a demeaned sexual object, and she physically assaulted him to protect not only herself, but to teach him not to treat women like that. Recounting the incident, she tells Undine what she said to him, "I work from 9 to 5 at Metrotech, my man, don't you look at me like a 'ho, don't you talk to me like a 'ho, don't you disrespect me like a video 'ho." She tells Undine, "Now, he gonna think twice 'fore he place a hand on another woman. Believe it." She is not willing to stand for being objectified when she has worked so hard to make a respectable life for herself and her family.

STYLE

Rapid Pace

The pace of *Fabulation; or, The Re-Education of Undine* is rapid and at times dizzying. This is intentional, as Nottage explains in the Author's Note before the play begins. Indeed, she intends the play to move from scene to scene without blackouts. This makes the action of the play move quickly and keeps the audience engaged with little time to process the action and characterization of one scene to the next. Still, the play is tightly written, and the characters' decisions and reactions are consistent with the foundation Nottage lays as the play develops. But where other plays give audience members an opportunity to anticipate outcomes, this play keeps their attention focused on the "present" in the play without having a chance to worry about its "future."

From the perspective of characterization, the rapid pace makes the audience sympathetic to Undine. Just as she is swept away by the rapid, uncontrollable change in her life, so is the audience. They understand better how she must feel, especially since she is in most scenes. The audience sees her go immediately from her office to a doctor's exam room, from a street corner to a jail, and from a group counseling session to the delivery room. It is all happening so fast, that the audience can not help but have a level of understanding as to how Undine must feel being tossed around in the wake of disaster. Seeing her grow into maturity, wisdom, and compassion is then all the more impressive. By the end, the audience is more likely to respect Undine and have hope for her future because of the way she has handled such rapid, unexpected change.

Symbolism

Nottage uses symbolism in a very subtle, natural way in the play. Perhaps the strongest symbol in the play is the job of security guard. Undine's mother, father, brother, and potential boyfriend are all security guards. Sometimes the characters are seen in their uniforms, and sometimes (as with Guy) it is only indicated. This is significant because the two words "security" and "guard" should give her an indication where to place her trust. Security guards come to represent family, love, and acceptance for Undine. These are the people who will stick by her side and encourage her. In her previous life, she would never have hobnobbed with anyone in such a lowly position, but the people she chose in that life abandoned her when it was convenient to do so. The people in the security guard uniforms (sort of a twist on the white cowboy hats that showed who the good guys were in Westerns—where the bad guys wore black hats) are the ones who are actually loyal and true.

Another symbol is Undine's pregnancy itself. Unprepared for motherhood, Undine grapples with her situation. At one point, she talks about how to solve it as a problem rather than how to fold it into her life. At another point, she sees it as something that makes her a stereotypical single, black mother in the projects. Regardless, the pregnancy is what contributes to her return home and what makes her compassionate and understanding to other overwhelmed women. In the waiting room of her doctor's office in Brooklyn, she has compassion for a scared young pregnant woman and takes her hand, admitting that she is also scared. The pregnancy symbolizes Undine's share in humanity. She is joined with other women in a unique way, and she takes part in a universal human experience. She is not better than those she thought she had surpassed; she is part of their community and experience.

Another symbol is Devora's business card. Devora has risen above her past in the projects, but has not cut herself off from her roots. She still visits and maintains relationships from her past. As a successful financial planner, she is actually attempting to help other women in her community instead of denying them altogether, as Undine had done. When Devora gives Undine her card, it gives her a slight paper cut, "just enough to draw blood." That cut from the card shows that Undine's thinking had been misguided, and it also shows that she has fallen so far that she is now on the receiving end of charity from a friend. The card, taken by Undine, symbolizes her newfound humility.

Aside

Nottage uses the theatrical technique of asides as an effective way to fill in the back story to allow the audience access to Undine's private thoughts. Asides are when a character speaks directly to the audience without the other characters hearing it. Like monologues (which are spoken by characters who are alone, as if the character is talking to himself or thinking out loud), asides let the audience know what the character's true thoughts and feelings are. Undine shares with the audience certain chapters from her past, along with her perspectives on them. She also speaks directly to the audience to reveal what she is thinking about another character or what her hidden reaction to something is. It builds trust and intimacy between the character and the audience.

HISTORICAL CONTEXT

Single Motherhood

Since the mid-1990s, the number of single-parent homes has remained steady. Of all households in the United States, about nine percent are headed by single parents; this is almost double what it was in 1970. Most single parents are mothers because of personal and court preferences. Census Bureau statistics for 1995 revealed that almost two-thirds of all African-American family groups with children were headed by single parents, and the numbers of those headed by fathers is extremely low. The story behind the statistics is that there are more than ten million single mothers (of all races) striving to support themselves and their children, all while acting as both mother and father on a day-to-day basis. In fact, there are almost twice as many single mothers as stay-at-home mothers.

The challenges to the single mother can be overwhelming. For low-income families, the possibility of higher education or private schooling is out of the question. Faced with a family to rear and a basic education at best, these single mothers must find the best job (or jobs) they can, work long hours, pay a lot of what they earn to child care, all while providing guidance and nurturing at home. For these reasons, many families rely on grandparents to help bring up the children.

Professional Career Opportunities for African-American Women

African-American women have faced challenges in the workplace because of their race and gender. While women have worked and fought to have access to the same opportunities and pay, so have racial minorities. Gradually, the business world has been opened to African-American women, but some areas are still undergoing growing pains. Part of the problem is education. For many urban areas with large African-American populations, public schooling struggles to keep up with the increasing demands of the modern

Brick apartment buildings in a housing project bordering Myrtle Avenue in Brooklyn (© James Marshall / Corbis)

world. There are often fewer resources, teachers struggling with discipline, and overcrowded class-rooms. As a result, it can be difficult to get a good education, even for motivated students. Further, because of their family situations, many students have to work jobs or care for younger siblings in addition to keeping up with school work.

Besides educational issues, it can be difficult for young African-American women to get their feet in the door in businesses because of a lack of contacts. Networking can be a critical part of a young person's career. Many people network through family connections, fraternities and soror-ities, and internships. As more African-American women are achieving career success, they are mak-ing a focused effort to encourage and support other young women coming into the workplace. There are also scholarships and other programs to help African-American women attend college and even go on to graduate or professional schools. But as of 1996, only 22 percent of African-American women held managerial or professional specialty jobs. The

captains of industry—Donald Trump, Bill Gates, Martha Stewart, and others—are still primarily white, and mostly male.

African-American Women Writers
Just as African-American women are gaining influence and status in other areas of business and society, they are also gaining prominence in American literature. Continuing a tradition that began and was grown through the works of Zora Neale Hurston, Countee Cullen, and Gwendo-lyn Brooks, today's African-American women writers have shown impressive staying power. Writers such as Toni Morrison, Maya Angelou, Nikki Giovanni, and Alice Walker have been writing and lecturing for more than twenty years. In fact, Walker won the Pulitzer Prize in 1983, and Gloria Naylor's *The Women of Brew-ster Place* won the National Book Award the same year. Picking up the baton was Toni Mor-rison, who won the Nobel Prize for Literature in 1993. But Morrison is far from alone at the top of the literary world. Other African-American

women whose voices have gained acclaim in the 1990s and into the 2000s include Edwidge Danticat and Pearl Cleage.

CRITICAL OVERVIEW

The critical reception of *Fabulation; or, The Re-Education of Undine* has been mixed. While some critics praise Nottage's clever, fast-paced look at the futility of trying to escape one's past, other critics feel that the play lacks thematic depth and well-rounded characterization. For instance, Nicholas de Jongh, writing in the *Evening Standard* calls the play a "slick, modern, urban morality" play. *American Theater* critic Randy Gener describes the play as a "surreal fusion of *Absolutely Fabulous*; and a classic trickster tale" before labeling it a "very tall cautionary urban parable." Gener concludes: "Spiritually, *Fabulation* is an American descendant of the West Africa fable, whose animating verve lies in the psychic concept of nyama (energy of action), in which the erotics of laughter convey a moral theme: The past is never truly past."

In *Variety*, reviewer Charles Isherwood criticizes Nottage for not revealing enough about Undine's psyche. He also notes that Nottage does not "dwell at length on her pointed observations about the fragile perches of ambitious black Americans in the social hierarchy." Isherwood further finds characters such as Undine's grandmother a little far-fetched, explaining: "Nottage sometimes stretches a little too far into absurdity to subvert stereotype." Still, he praises the play for not being too heavy-handed in its moralizing and for being stylistically strong. He writes that "the play's snappy pacing and episodic narrative ensure that neither its cartoonish moments nor its sentimental asides drag the play down." Frank Scheck, writing in *Hollywood Reporter*, offers a different view of the play's pacing, describing it as "a series of brief, sketch-like scenes that prove dizzying in their variety and density," and adding that "Nottage's writing is not always quite as sharp as it aspires to be."

But Nottage's critics give *Fabulation; or, The Re-Education of Undine* credit where they see it due. For all the flaws that he sees in the play, Scheck nonetheless praises the play as a whole because "the social messages are imparted with an antic, unpretentious wit and style."

Indeed, Isherwood also observes that "the play settles on a gently satiric tone that allows us to catch glimpses of the complicated human beings shackled to their clichéd roles in American culture."

CRITICISM

Jennifer A. Bussey

Bussey is an independent writer specializing in literature. In the following essay, she delves deeply into the comparisons between Voltaire's Candide *and Nottage's* Fabulation; or, The Re-Education of Undine.

There have been many comparisons made between Lynn Nottage's play *Fabulation; or, The Re-Education of Undine* and Voltaire's classic novel *Candide*. Such a comparison requires looking closely at the protagonists of the two works, the storylines, and the underlying messages in each. Two writers could hardly be more different than Nottage (an African-American woman who was raised in Brooklyn and has come into her own as a modern playwright) and Voltaire (a product of the French Enlightenment who was an intellectual and political rebel known for his sharp wit; the French Enlightenment was an eighteenth-century philosophical movement that exalted the power of human reason and sought greater liberty and rights through social and political reform). Thus, a comparison of their works is an intriguing undertaking.

First, a brief summary of *Candide* is in order for those who have not read it, or have not read it recently. In *Candide*, the main character is a young, naïve man who meets calamity after calamity, all the while spouting the optimistic philosophy of his mentor and companion, Pangloss. According to this philosophy, the world is the best of all worlds, and everything that happens must necessarily be for the best because it takes place in the best of all worlds. Thus, when Candide and Pangloss see another of their companions drown trying to save another man, they do nothing to stop it because Pangloss declares that the sea itself was put there for that very moment. The novel is rich with satire and irony, and the main characters encounter horrible circumstances and wretched people, smiling through it all under the banner of optimism. In the end, Candide buys a farm and abandons Pangloss's philosophy (although Pangloss sticks

WHAT DO I READ NEXT?

- Leith Mullings writes about her own experiences and the findings of her research about African-American women's experiences in *On Our Own Terms: Race, Class, and Gender in the Lives of African-American Women* (1996). Mullings takes a historical view to see how and why the modern experience is what it is in terms of race and gender as it applies to work, family, relationships, and society.

- *Crumbs from the Table of Joy and Other Plays* (2004) contains some of Nottage's best-known plays. This collection includes Nottage's first play and shows her growing interest in African themes and issues.

- Nottage's *Intimate Apparel* (2005) is one of her most-produced plays, and it attracted significant attention to the playwright's work. It is the story of a skilled Jewish undergarment maker in New York, and her romance by mail that grows into a marriage. The couple struggles with getting to know one another while facing the difficulties of being a mixed-race couple in a time before this was accepted.

- In Kathy Perkins's and Roberta Uno's anthology *Contemporary Plays by Women of Color* (1996), the editors demonstrate the diversity of experiences, voices, and styles among a group of talented ethnic women playwrights. Eighteen works are included by African-American, Asian-American, Latin-American, and Native-American writers.

- *The Ground on Which I Stand* (2001) is Pulitzer Prize–winner August Wilson's keynote address to the Theatre Communications Group. In this address, Wilson challenges African-American artists of all kinds to take control of their cultural identity and importance. The speech led to a great deal of discussion and debate about diversity in American theater.

> BOTH CHARACTERS FIND THEMSELVES IN A RAPID DESCENT, ENCOUNTERING DANGEROUS CHARACTERS, BECOMING THE VICTIMS OF MISUNDERSTANDING, AND GOING THROUGH OUTRAGEOUS EXPERIENCES."

to his guns), but merely substitutes the beliefs of another man instead. Candide is ultimately a static character who never takes a stand on his own or learns to think for himself. He is, however, a man of his word. Throughout the story, he is in pursuit of Cunegonde, the woman he loves (although it is really no more than an infatuation). When she becomes ugly and loses all of her charms, his love vanishes. Still, he marries her because that is what he agreed to do when they were both in love.

Like Candide, Undine mismanages her life by adhering to a hollow philosophy. Candide's optimism never did him any good, and only made matters worse. Undine believes that severing ties with her past and reinventing herself will make her the person she has created. This belief does her no good because she ends up face to face with the very past she ran so hard to escape. Both characters delude themselves into thinking the world is what they want it to be, but only Undine learns that there is another truth outside of her delusions. Candide never quite learns this. Candide stays basically selfish and immature, whereas Undine shows signs of personal growth and wisdom. Not only does she allow Guy to become a part of her life despite the fact that he is everything she avoided in her New York City life, but when Undine is in the waiting room with another pregnant woman, she sets aside her bruised ego (at being called old) and reaches out for the young woman's hand to admit that she is just as scared. Undine rejects her selfish impulses so that she can extend humanity and compassion to a young, scared woman.

Undine also shows a capacity to be open and vulnerable in love. Candide is written as a caricature, so it only stands to reason that his story lacks real emotion or personal insight. Candide's experience of love is full-blown infatuation to the point of obsession, which has little to do with genuine emotions. Candide never really knows Cunegonde, he sets her on a pedestal, like Don Quixote does with Dulcinea in Miguel de Cervantes's *Don Quixote*. The romance is much more about the pursuit and the excitement than it is about really knowing a person and loving her based on a substantial relationship. But Candide is so clueless about love that he agrees to go ahead and marry Cunegonde even after he loses interest in her. He has no concept of marriage, and he is too lazy to consider that he might truly fall in love some day with another woman. Undine ditches her washed-up rapper boyfriend when she is swept up in the romance of Herve. He is exotic and sophisticated, and the romance is enough for her. This is akin to Candide's feelings toward Cunegonde. But when Herve turns out to be a thief who abandons Undine, she sees him clearly and opens herself up to another man, Guy. The last scene of the play shows Guy coaching Undine through the delivery of her baby. When the play ends with the baby's cry, Nottage suggests that the three of them will be a family. Undine has been honest with Guy, and he has been honest with her. They have accepted each other and respect each other, so the relationship is based on something abiding. There is hope for Undine that is lacking for Candide.

Another important element to compare is the storylines of the two works. In both cases, the characters start out comfortable, content, and living with wealth and status. In short order, both are thrown from their lifestyles and sent on a journey. Candide is in search of a new life (though he does not know what he is seeking) and Cunegonde, and Undine is searching for a new life (though she does not know what she is seeking, either). Both characters find themselves in a rapid descent, encountering dangerous characters, becoming the victims of misunderstanding, and going through outrageous experiences. And while Candide's misadventures take him all over the world, Undine's misadventures in Brooklyn are so varied and extreme that they seem to be unfolding in a large setting. So both characters are bumped around from misadventure to misadventure, moving toward an undetermined goal. But when Candide lands, he is in a calmer setting, having learned almost nothing,

while Undine is in a more demanding setting, having learned quite a lot. This is an important lesson because it shows how two very different people can go on similar journeys and, based on their personalities and willingness to learn, have completely different outcomes.

The last area to look for comparisons is in the messages, or themes, of each work. *Candide* is designed to show the futility of ridiculous philosophies and the importance of trustworthy authority. The novel shows corrupt or misguided authority in every realm—religious, political, military, and interpersonal. People are misled, given false hope, victimized, and even killed in the wake of unfit authority. While *Candide* and *Fabulation; or, The Re-Education of Undine* both depict the negative outcomes of foolish philosophy, they part ways on the issue of authority. Undine's life has been about removing herself from under the authority of anyone but herself. In her story, there is almost no authority figure with any power over her except for the police to arrest her and the court to enforce a drug rehabilitation requirement. But this depiction of authority is different from Voltaire's because the police in Undine's story are fair and right in their application of the law. In other areas of her life, such as family and business, however, Undine is her own authority. In that sense, the reader might draw a parallel because Undine's authority over her own life has been so lacking. This is so subtle, however, that is unlikely that Nottage is intentionally making a comment about authority. Similarly, Nottage's themes of duality and the past do not readily apply to Voltaire's work.

Deep comparisons between Nottage's *Fabulation; or, The Re-Education of Undine* and Voltaire's *Candide* are difficult to find or seem somewhat contrived. On the surface, however, there are interesting parallels between Nottage's play and Voltaire's fable. They both have larger-than-life protagonists whose lives take a series of twists and turns in their descents. Both portray the trouble that comes from adhering to a misguided and delusional belief system. Both also show the importance of learning from life's lessons and being willing to mature. In these cases, it is valuable to realize that such lessons are so universal that they appear in very different works by very different writers in very different historical contexts.

Source: Jennifer A. Bussey, Critical Essay on *Fabulation; or, The Re-Education of Undine*, in *Drama for Students*, Gale, Cengage Learning, 2008.

Gale

In the following excerpt, the critic gives a critical analysis of Nottage's work.

Lynn Nottage is a playwright whose work is intended to lend a voice to the experience of the African-American woman. As a child growing up in Brooklyn, New York, she began writing plays in her journal. As she recalled in an interview posted on the Kentucky Educational Television Web site, "I think for me the journey begins downstairs at the kitchen table of my house. Down there was a gathering place for so many women. To come home from school, and my grandmother would be sitting at the table, and my mother would be sitting at the table. The woman from across the street would be sitting at the table. And they all had stories to tell. They were nurses, teachers; they were activists; they were artists. And I think that is where I got all of my inspiration as a writer."

Seeking a world beyond Brooklyn, Nottage attended the High School of Music and Art in New York, then went on to Brown University and Yale Drama School. After graduation, she worked as national press officer for Amnesty International and gave up creative writing for some time. Sitting down to work on an entry for a short-play competition, she produced the work *Poof!* in one sitting. The drama, which deals with abuse against women, won an award, and Nottage decided to rededicate herself to writing plays.

Nottage's play *Mud, River, Stone* had its origin in an article the author read about some demobilized soldiers in Mozambique who took hostages because they were never paid for their services. Nottage used the incident as the setting for her drama about an upper-class African-American couple who travel to Africa for a second honeymoon. They want to search for their roots, but instead, they find themselves taken hostage. Symbolically, Nottage sought to portray her own search for Africa and its meaning. *Back Stage* reviewer David Sheward wrote that the play starts out as "clever comedy," but declines into "conventional melodrama." *Variety* reviewer Robert L. Daniels also felt that the play loses focus, but he also had praise for the early scenes, in which "the characters are clearly defined, the landscape picturesque, the dialogue laced with humor." Reflecting on her experience

in creating this play, Nottage told the Kentucky Public Television interviewer: "I most certainly will write more about Africa. I find when I have spare time I read nonfiction books about the Congo. I am fascinated by the Congo, fascinated by the politics of that region and the legacy of colonialism. By the brutality. I think some of that comes out of working at a place like Amnesty International—I studied the abuses of countries. The Congo was one of the most aggressive violators of human rights."

Crumbs from the Table of Joy is set during the 1950s and concerns two teenaged girls whose conservative, widowed father moves with them from Florida to New York City, where they all move in with their free-thinking aunt. To their surprise, their father soon comes home with a new wife—a white, German woman. Nottage explained to the Kentucky Educational Television interviewer that she wrote the play in part to try to understand the extreme changes that were taking place in society at that time: "*Crumbs from the Table of Joy* is about a displaced Southern family smack in the center of New York City, in the 1950s, trying to cope with those changes. Coping with integration, trying to cope with big-city ideals with a small-town sensibility." Reviewing the play for *Back Stage*, William Stevenson called it "at times moving and at times slow-going," but concluded: "the action picks up in the second act, with more conflict and a stirring ending."

In *Intimate Apparel* Nottage portrays a plain, hard-working seamstress who creates deluxe lingerie for her clients. Although the garments she sews are imaginative and erotic, in her personal life the woman is repressed and has few close relationships. She begins a correspondence with a man working on the Panama Canal, and he eventually comes to New York, where they marry. Their real-life relationship turns out to be very different from what either imagined it would be, and the second act of the play deals with their disappointments and the way they cope with them. Reviewing the play for *Hollywood Reporter*, Jay Reiner stated that it is a "seemingly simple and straightforward piece of stagecraft that gradually takes on a life and meaning all but impossible to resist." *National Catholic Reporter* contributor Retta Blaney described it as "simple yet lovely."

Explaining her mission to the interviewer for Kentucky Public Television, Nottage said: "I think that the African-American woman's voice is important because it is part of the American voice. But you would not know that by looking at TV or films. You would think that we do not exist. And part of my mission as a writer is to say, 'I do exist. My mother existed, and my grandmother existed, and my great-grandmother existed, and they had stories that are rich, complicated, funny, that are beautiful and essential.' And the stories have become the myth of America. . . . I want people to know that my story, that of the African-American woman, is also the American story."

Source: Gale, "Lynn Nottage," in *Contemporary Authors Online*, Thomson Gale, 2006.

SOURCES

De Jongh, Nicholas, "Critic's Choice Top Five Plays," in the *Evening Standard*, March 10, 2006, p. 48.

Gener, Randy, "Conjurer of the Worlds: From Richly Imagined Epochs to Unsparing Satires, Lynn Nottage's Roving Imagination Channels History's Discards into Drama," in *American Theatre*, Vol. 22, No. 8, October 2005, pp. 22–26.

Isherwood, Charles, "Downward Spiral for Gotham Diva," in *Variety*, Vol. 395, No. 6, June 21, 2004, p. 45.

Nottage, Lynn, *Fabulation; or, The Re-Education of Undine*, Dramatists Play Service, 2005.

Scheck, Frank, Review of *Fabulation; or, The Re-Education of Undine*, in *Hollywood Reporter*, Vol. 384, No. 31, July 6, 2004, p. 18.

FURTHER READING

Cleage, Pearl, *Flyin' West*, Dramatist's Play Service, 1995.

Cleage is among America's foremost contemporary African-American women writers and playwrights. This play tells the story of African-American women pioneers in the old West and their fight to create a life of fulfillment and freedom.

Curry, Cuthrell, *Making the Gods in New York: The Yoruba Religion in the African American Community*, Routledge, 1997.

Curry reviews the growing presence and influence of Yoruba culture in religion in the United States. In addition to a historical review, Curry informs the reader about Yoruba beliefs and rituals.

Hall, Roger, *Writing Your First Play*, Focal Press, 1998.

Hall is a professor of creative writing. Here, he covers the basics of characterization, plot development, setting, and other important elements, along with examples and writing exercises for students new to the process.

Krasner, David, *American Drama 1945–2000: An Introduction*, Blackwell Publishing, 2006.

Krasner provides an overview of American theater beginning with the conclusion of World War II and finishing at the end of the twentieth century. He covers major plays and playwrights, taking time to discuss major influences and breakthroughs.

Fefu and Her Friends

MARIA IRENE FORNES

1977

Fefu and Her Friends by Maria Irene Fornes was first produced at the Relativity Media Lab (part of the New York Theatre Strategy) on May 5, 1977, and was directed by Fornes herself. It was performed to a wider audience at the Off-Broadway venue, the American Place Theatre, on January 8, 1978. Fornes published the script of her short play in the winter 1978 edition of the *Performing Arts Journal*, or *PAJ*. PAJ Publications published the most recent edition of *Fefu and Her Friends* as a slim book in 1990.

   Fefu and Her Friends is Fornes's fifteenth play. When it was produced, she was an established playwright and director. Nevertheless, it was one of Fornes's most successful plays and it was also an unusual format for the absurdist playwright because it relied more on realism than her earlier plays. Fornes won an Off-Broadway award, or Obie, for *Fefu and Her Friends*. The play's themes of gender roles, sexuality, love between women, and insanity strike chords within a society still coming to terms with the sexual revolution of the 1960s—a revolution some historians claim has actually been going on since the 1920s. *Fefu and Her Friends* is a play that remains raw and relevant today.

AUTHOR BIOGRAPHY

Maria Irene Fornes was born on May 14, 1930 in Havana, Cuba, to Carlos Luis and Carmen Hismenia Fornes. In 1945, when Fornes was only

fifteen, her father died. Later that same year, Fornes, her mother, and her sister immigrated to the United States. Settling in Manhattan, Fornes attended Catholic school but dropped out before graduating so that she could work. Fornes became a naturalized U.S. citizen in 1951.

As a young adult, Fornes wanted to be a painter and spent a lot of time in Greenwich Village and even a few years in Paris. While in Paris, she saw and was struck by the original production of Samuel Beckett's absurdist masterpiece *Waiting for Godot*. The themes in Beckett's play have echoed throughout Fornes work. When she returned to Greenwich Village in 1957, Fornes spent a few more years supporting herself as a custom textile designer before discovering her love of playwriting. Her first professionally produced production, *The Widow*, was staged in 1961. Fornes has gone on to write more than forty plays, directing many of them herself. In 1972, Fornes teamed up with other playwrights to create the New York Theatre Strategy, which opened in 1973. The New York Theatre Strategy was envisioned as a place where playwrights could test out their ideas. *Fefu and Her Friends* was originally staged there in 1977, using the theatre's office and costume shop as part of the set.

In the 1970s, Fornes became deeply involved in Hispanic theater through INTAR, the Hispanic American Arts Center in New York City, where she taught workshops for aspiring Hispanic playwrights. In the 1980s, some of Fornes's works were criticized as being too Hispanic, whereas her 2000 production, *Letters from Cuba* (based in part on correspondence with her only brother who remained in Cuba), was considered to be not Hispanic enough. Fornes is also a feminist playwright although some have criticized her work as not being feminist enough.

Fornes has been honored with numerous awards and grants including nine Obies (Off-Broadway theater awards)—one of them for *Fefu and Her Friends*, two Rockefeller grants, two National Endowment for the Arts grants, and a Guggenheim fellowship. She is still writing and directing plays.

PLOT SUMMARY

Part 1

Fefu and Her Friends is a three-part play. The first part has one scene, the second part has four scenes, and the third part has one scene. The scene in part 1 begins at noon in the living room of Fefu's country home in New England. It is a spring day in 1935 and Fefu has invited her friends over for a meeting. When the play opens, Fefu, Cindy, and Christina are waiting for the others to arrive. Fefu tells the others that her husband married her "to have a constant reminder of how loathsome women are." Cindy is surprised, but Fefu assures her that she agrees with Phillip's assessment. Fefu explains that what she is really interested in is "exciting ideas," giving the impression that she is less invested in what she is saying than in the reaction she gets from others. She tells Cindy and Christina that she likes revulsion: "It's something to grapple with." Fefu illustrates her point by describing the worms and fungus found on the underside of a stone: "It is another life that is parallel to the one we manifest. . . . If you don't recognize it. . . . *(Whispering)* it eats you."

Hearing voices out on the lawn, Fefu picks up her gun and shoots at Phillip, who gamely falls down for a moment and pretends to be dead. It is a strange game between Phillip and his wife. Fefu leaves and Cindy tries to convince Christina that Fefu is not crazy although she has an odd marriage. Cindy assures Christina that the gun is only loaded with blanks. Rattled, Christina asserts, "One can die of fright, you know." They argue over putting the gun away; neither wants to touch it. Fefu returns just as Christina is about to toss a silk shawl over it but, embarrassed, Christina pretends to be dancing instead.

Fefu informs Cindy that she has fixed the toilet in her bathroom and Cindy is surprised that Fefu does her own plumbing. Fefu admits to the other women that Phillip scared her this time, that she thought he might really be hurt because he has threatened to one day put real bullets in the gun. Christina tells Fefu that she is "crazy," "stupid," and depressing but Fefu implores Christina to just laugh at her instead. "I know I'm ridiculous. Come on, laugh." Fefu now tells them that she likes men better than women. She watches her husband, brother-in-law, and gardener outside during her soliloquy. "Women are restless with each other. . . . They are always eager for the men to arrive. When they do, they can put themselves at rest, tranquilized and in a mild stupor."

Fefu leaves to check the toilet and Cindy sings a song to soothe Christina. Julia arrives, wheelchair-bound. She was injured in a hunting accident but Cindy assures Christina that the bullet did not touch Julia. Emma, Paula, and Sue arrive soon thereafter. There is a happy reunion among friends while Christina is introduced around. They discuss lunch and the meeting/rehearsal they will have later, then disperse to different areas of the house. Julia takes up Fefu's rifle, removing the remaining slug and smelling the barrel. She blacks out for a moment, then says, "She's hurting herself." Julia leaves to lay down and Cindy reloads the gun. Cecilia arrives and introduces herself to Cindy and Christina.

Part 2

Fornes wrote and directed this middle part of the play to be performed in four parts simultaneously. The audience is divided into four groups and is moved to each location until they have seen all the scenes. They are reunited again for part 3.

IN THE LAWN

It is afternoon and Fefu and Emma are on the lawn playing croquet and eating apples. Emma tells Fefu that she obsessively thinks about people's genitals all the time; she finds it very strange that people aren't more self-conscious of their genitals. The two friends have an easy rapport. Fefu confides in Emma, "I am in constant pain. . . . It's not physical, and it's not sorrow." She describes her pain as being something spiritual but she cannot adequately express what it is. Fefu abruptly leaves to get lemonade and Emma recites William Shakespeare's "Sonnet 14": "Not from the stars do I my judgment pluck." She is commenting on Fefu's enduring and beautiful spirit. Fefu returns with Paula and Cecilia.

IN THE STUDY

Christina is sitting at the desk in the study reading a French textbook. Cindy sits nearby reading a magazine. They read pieces aloud to each other and languidly philosophize. Cindy asks Christina if she's having a good time and Christina says she is. They talk about Fefu and Christina struggles to identify what it is about Fefu that unsettles her. "Her mind is adventurous." Christina determines that Fefu's adventurousness leads to some measure of disregard for convention and that she, Christina, is probably more of a conformist and therefore threatened by Fefu. Cindy tells Christina about a strange dream she had the night before. In her dream, she was threatened by an angry young doctor and escapes with her sister in a taxi, waking just before he catches her. Neither know what this dream means.

IN THE BEDROOM

Julia's guest room is a converted storage room. She lays in the bed, dressed in a hospital gown, and is hallucinating quietly. In her monologue, Julia describes being abused by unidentified attackers: "They clubbed me. They broke my head. They broke my will. They broke my hands. They tore my eyes out. They took my voice away. They didn't do anything to my heart because I didn't bring my heart with me." She explains that the judges love her and that's why they beat her. "He said that I had to be punished because I was getting too smart." They are also after Fefu and Julia cries out to her judges to spare Fefu "for she's only a joker." Julia says her prayer, declaring man to be human and woman to be, among other things, evil and the source of evil. "The mate for man is woman and that is the cross man must bear." In an echo of Fefu and Emma's conversation on the lawn, Julia says that man's sexuality is physical and therefore pure whereas woman's sexuality is spiritual "and they take those feelings with them to the afterlife where they corrupt the heavens." Julia hallucinates that she is being slapped for not believing her prayer. Sue interrupts her, bringing in a bowl of soup.

IN THE KITCHEN

Paula declares to Sue that she has determined that a love affair lasts exactly "seven years and three months" and goes on to describe the pattern in detail. Paula recommends celibacy to solve the problem of overlapping love affairs, then puzzles over how the mind and body each differently get over a breakup. Sue asks her if something wrong. Paula says no and Sue leaves to take soup to Julia. Cecilia enters the kitchen and it becomes apparent that there was a relationship between her and Paula, which has fizzled out. Cecilia apologizes repeatedly for not calling and Paula shrugs it off. Paula tells Cecilia that she has been examining herself since they were together and is disappointed that she hasn't made more of her life. Paula was the less dominant one in their former relationship and organized herself around Cecilia's happiness. When Cecilia left, Paula's life lost meaning. Fefu interrupts, coming into the kitchen for lemonade. She invites them to croquet and Paula apologizes to Cecilia, "I'm not reproaching you." Cecilia, speaking up for the first time since Paula began pouring out her heart, takes Paula's hand and says, "I know. I've missed you too."

Part 3

The final part of the play takes place in the living room in the evening. The women all enter, moving about their business while Cecilia is telling Sue, "We cannot survive in a vacuum. We must be part of a community." Julia connects this with her isolation as a person who has hallucinations because only other hallucinating people can understand what she is going through. The group prepares for their meeting. They are having a dress rehearsal for an educational fundraising event. Fefu opens the presentation; Paula goes next. Emma is dressed in an exotic costume for her part and she recites from the writings of Emma Sheridan Fry, a children's acting teacher. While they discuss the order of their presentation, Cecilia sits next to Paula and puts her hand on Paula's leg, absentmindedly. When they finish, everyone except Cindy and Julia go to the kitchen to prepare coffee. Christina comes running back into the living room because there's a water fight in the kitchen over who will do the dishes. Emma, Paula, Sue, and Fefu begin chasing each other through the house with pans of water. Christina hides on the couch until the water fight is over.

Cindy tells Julia, "She's been hiding all day." They ask after each other's lives. Cindy has broken up with her boyfriend or husband, Mike, and Julia is too concerned with death to have a love life. "I think of death all the time." Paula, Sue, and Emma, delivering coffee, try to brighten the mood with silly jokes. Everyone except Paula retreats to the kitchen to drink coffee. Cecilia enters from the lawn. She promises Paula again that she will call her but will not be specific about when. Paula stands her ground and tells Cecilia she is not available to be called at just any time. Paula and Cecilia leave the living room in different directions while Fefu sits quietly on the steps. She observes Julia—*walking*—as she briefly comes into the living room, picks up the sugar bowl, puts it back down, and returns to the kitchen. Immediately thereafter, Julia, Sue, Cindy, Christina, Emma, and Cecilia come

into the living room. Julia is back in her wheel-chair. Paula returns from upstairs. Sue reminisces about old friends of theirs who were sent to "the psychiatrist" because they were not conforming to a womanly ideal.

Paula remembers when she was new to the faculty and thought that everyone who was rich was happy. She has changed her mind. "I think we should teach the poor and let the rich take care of themselves." Paula starts crying; Cecilia kisses her and they leave the living room. Sue, Christina, Cindy, and Emma go out to the lawn to look at the stars, leaving Fefu and Julia behind to talk. Fefu asks Julia directly if she can walk and Julia says she cannot. Fefu is frustrated with Julia for not trying. "What is it you see?" Fefu demands of her. "And you're contagious. I'm going mad too," Fefu accuses Julia. Fefu admits to Julia that Phillip hates her; Fefu is devastated by this knowledge. She implores Julia to fight with her, grabbing her and shaking her. Christina comes in on this scene and Fefu is sure the other woman's good opinion of her is totally ruined. She grabs her gun, saying she's going to clean it. Christina tells her not to and Fefu calls her "*silly*." Cecilia enters, ready to leave. Fefu goes onto the lawn. Julia is worried that she told Fefu something about the judges and that now she will be in trouble. A shot rings out and Julia touches her forehead. Just like in the first hunting accident, she is mysteriously bleeding. Then Julia's head falls back and she dies. Fefu enters the living room with a dead rabbit, surprised that she has killed it.

CHARACTERS

Fefu Beckmann

Fefu (pronounced Feh-foo) is the host of this gathering, which is held at her house in the New England countryside. She is friends with everyone except Christina, whom she has just met. Fefu is a well-heeled philanthropist, giving talks and fundraising for education. At her house, she is a thorough and welcoming host and has a playful, fun spirit. There are also glimpses of her dropping under some kind of strain. The audience is introduced to Fefu's strange relationship with her husband Phillip at the very beginning of the play but Fefu's bright behavior glosses over her unhappiness, which only gradually emerges. In part 2, she tells

Emma she is in some sort of spiritual pain. The poem Emma recites, "Not from the stars do I my judgment pluck," is Shakespeare's "Sonnet 14," and the last line, "Thy end is truth's and beauty's doom and date," expresses Emma's deep respect for Fefu's character—she believes in her friend even though Fefu doesn't much believe in herself anymore. Christina, meanwhile, represents how many other people respond to Fefu's brash comments and actions. She is appalled and repulsed, which Fefu sees and tries to mitigate by asking Christina to laugh at her. In part 3, Fefu is sitting on the stairs near the living room, glum, a face she hides from everyone else as she dashes around to get lunch or fetch lemonade or fix a toilet. She fully reveals her unhappiness to Julia at the end of the play: "Phillip can't stand me.... I need him, Julia. I need his touch. I need his kiss. I need the person he is." Her torment is that Phillip does not need or want her. Fefu, a scholar and a feminist, is crippled by her own powerlessness in her marriage.

Phillip Beckmann
Phillip is Fefu's husband. He is offstage on the lawn for the entire play. Phillip and Fefu have a strange relationship—such as Fefu shooting blanks at him and Phillip falling down for a moment, pretending to be hit—but Fefu insists they are happy. At the end of the play she admits to Julia that Phillip can't stand her: "He's left. His body is here but the rest is gone." This line is interesting in light of the fact that Phillip is never actually seen or heard—as if he were indeed gone. Fefu's dead rabbit is also proof that there was a real bullet in the rifle. The question remains: who put it there?

Stephany Beckmann
See Fefu Beckmann

Emma Blake
Emma is boisterous and outgoing, jumping into Julia's lap, kissing one of the women sitting on the couch, and taking part in the water fight. She is wealthy and likes to travel, showing up at Fefu's house wearing an outfit she bought in Turkey. Emma has also brought along an even more outlandish costume to wear for their fund-raiser event. Emma is a performer and likes to recite—her recitation of Emma Sheridan Frye's work is the core performance of their fund-raising event. Emma and Fefu are especially close with each other. Despite her extroverted

behavior, Emma pays close attention to her friends and has keen insight into their personalities; however, her own emotions are not revealed.

Christina
Christina is new to this circle of friends and only knows Cindy and Julia. She is disturbed by Fefu's talk and frightened by the group's outlandish behavior, such as Fefu shooting blanks at her husband and the extensive water fight over who will do the dishes. Christina prefers to conform—to not stand out or be involved in conflict—and she admits to Cindy that Fefu confuses her. "I suppose I do hold back for fear of being disrespectful or destroying something—and I admire those who are not. But I also feel they are dangerous to me." Christina's remark to Fefu at the end of the play, when Fefu picks up her rifle again, is telling of Christina's priorities: "I don't care if you shoot yourself. I just don't like the mess you're making." This concern is domestic to an extreme rather than compassionate.

Cindy
Cindy is a friend of Fefu's and cares for her despite Fefu's wild behavior. She is patient and spends most of the play in company with Christina, who doesn't know this group of friends. Cindy does not express an opinion as to whether she approves of Fefu or not, giving readers the impression that she rides the fence: she mutely goes along with Fefu's ideas but maintains a calm, normal exterior, not talking or behaving like Fefu or Emma. Cindy has a disturbing dream wherein an angry young doctor chases her. Her dream draws on a fear of authority figures: her significant other, Mike; a young male doctor; and secret policemen. In her dream, she is aided only by her sister Meg. For a moment in the dream Cindy commands everyone's respects by yelling, "Stop and listen to me." She has been separated for a few months from Mike and there are hints that she is unhappy, but, except for describing the dream, Cindy never opens up about her feelings.

Paula Cori
Paula, like the other women, is a friend of Fefu's and an educator. She is less well off than her wealthy friends but has come to the conclusion that she is no less happy. Paula and Cecilia had a romantic relationship that has recently fizzled out. Paula tells Cecilia, "I'm not lusting after you," when Cecilia continues to give her mixed

signals. Paula is clearly still drawn to Cecilia but determined to not be the less-dominant figure in any future relationship. When Cecilia repeatedly, emptily promises to call Paula so they can talk, but refuses to commit to a time, Paula refuses to be infinitely available to her. The stronger Paula is, the more Cecilia is attracted to her. But unlike Cecilia, this is not manipulation on Paula's part. She sincerely cares for Cecilia and is willing to walk away from their relationship if Cecilia continues to abuse her emotionally.

Cecilia Johnson

Cecilia is a friend of Fefu's and is Paula's former lover. She and Paula drifted apart although Cecilia's disinterest in the relationship seems to have precipitated the breakup. Throughout the play, Cecilia sends Paula mixed signals, sometimes being cold to her and sometimes affectionate. Cecilia is manipulative, trying to maintain control in their relationship, not inviting Paula to call her but telling Paula that she will call, and then refusing to commit to a time. When Paula shows her strength and refuses to be run over by this manipulation, Cecilia is inexplicably drawn to her ex-lover. In this play, Cecilia's dominating behavior is a masculine foil to Paula's feminist strength.

Julia

Julia is one of the central characters of this play. She is wheelchair-bound following a mysterious hunting accident. She now suffers from petit mal seizures, also known as absent seizures, where the person loses consciousness for a few seconds. Julia may in fact be epileptic and her seizures were brought on by the bang of the hunter's gun rather than a blow to the head. Julia assures everyone that she is adapting well. She matter-of-factly tells Cindy, "I'm very morbid these days. I think of death all the time." There is a lot of tension surrounding Julia's presence in Fefu's house because of the gun Fornes has placed in the living room. At the end of the play, the tension is resolved by Julia's death—another mysterious hunting accident. Fefu is outside shooting rabbit (an irony since Cindy told Christina in part 1 that Fefu doesn't hunt anymore because of her love of animals *and* because the gun is supposedly loaded with blanks) but at the crack of Fefu's gun, Julia slumps over, dead.

In part 2, alone in her room, the audience observes Julia's most private thoughts. She hallucinates freely, wrought with guilt and tormented by imaginary judges. These imaginary judges hold her accountable for deviant thoughts and behavior and the slightest misstep brings further pain. Julia tries to comply with their wishes but knows she will not be free of them until she truly believes, in her heart, what they tell her is fact. The things she is to believe include the fact that she is not smart, that Fefu is not smart, that human beings are men while women are both evil and a gift to men just like oxen for farming. Julia's death may be foreshadowing Fefu's future decline.

Sue

Sue is an educator and a friend of Fefu's. She is helpful: making lunch, serving food and coffee, and washing dishes. She is also the treasurer of their fundraising group. Sue is playful, demonstrating the many uses of ice cubes on a stick as well as taking part in the water fight. She is also sensitive to others' feelings but does not push them when they do not want to talk. Little is known about her life outside this single day at Fefu's house, except that she, like the others there, have been smart enough to not be sent to the psychiatrist like some of their former friends were. Sue is a feminist-in-hiding, breaking out at the appropriate times but generally sticking to the gender role expected of her. Sue is one of the most domestic women in this play—kind and fun to be with, but also bland and forgettable.

THEMES

Relationships between Women

Fefu and Her Friends highlights a multitude of ways in which women relate to each other. Fefu and Emma are close friends and appear to have known each other for a long time. They talk easily and intimately, unlike Fefu and Christina, who are unable to find common ground. Everything Fefu says and does is appalling or discomforting to Christina, who clings to conformity as much as Fefu casts it off. Another type of relationship that Fornes explores is the romantic relationship. Cecilia and Paula are old lovers whose relationship has failed. They are still drawn to each other but it is clear by the end of the play that they will not connect again. Through Fefu, Fornes expresses the idea that women are uncomfortable with each other and seek to be with men or to be like men. Men get along with each other easily, unlike women with

TOPICS FOR FURTHER STUDY

- In small groups of four to eight people, write a one-act play portraying these characters ten years after *Fefu and Her Friends* ends. Take into account historical events and personalities, adding your own creative touch. Perform your play for your class. When all of the class plays have been presented, engage in a round-table discussion to examine the different interpretations.

- Social classes are hierarchical (status-driven) divisions within society that often fall along lines of wealth, race, or religion. Fornes touches lightly on this matter in her play but social class has always been a significant issue. Research social classes as they were organized in the 1930s and write a paper comparing these divisions to social classes today. Has the class divide widened or narrowed over the intervening years?

- Emma recites from Shakespeare and from Emma Sheridan Fry. Choose a poem or passage from a book and memorize it, then recite it with dramatic flair for your class. Do you feel you have a deeper understanding of this piece now that you have it memorized? Why or why not? Write a brief response on your discoveries.

- One question that critics pose about *Fefu and Her Friends* is: Is this a feminist play, an anti-feminist play, or just a play that happens to have an all-female cast? Write an essay in which you address this question, using examples from the play to support your thesis. When all of the class's papers are turned in, take a survey of your classmates to find out what the most common and uncommon conclusions were.

other women. Although the women in this play are all friends, they are each separated by uncertainty, fear, and confusion, and they only open up to one another reluctantly.

Conformity and Insanity

Julia is losing the battle with her inner demons. Her inner judges force her to denounce her intelligence. They beat her. She must recite a "prayer" that encapsulates a decidedly anti-feminist, misogynistic point of view. Julia's grip on reality is shaken when a stray remark from Fefu leads her to believe she has committed a grievous error and accidentally told someone about the judges. Fefu and Julia's fates seem linked. Fefu is the only friend Julia mentions by name in her hallucinations, fearing that the judges will be after her next. Of all the friends meeting that day, Fefu's inner struggles most closely resemble Julia's. Fefu even thinks she has had her own hallucination when she sees Julia walk into the living room and pick up the sugar bowl. While this may have been another absent seizure, because Julia can't remember it happening, Fefu cannot be sure of herself now. Julia is a prisoner in her own mind. even as her body is unable to move. Her death at the end of the play is a merciful release.

One of the ways a person's power over their lives and even themselves, can be undermined is through a diagnosis, or even just a suspicion of insanity. Sue illustrates this when, during part 3, she recalls a couple of women whom they used to know—intelligent, beautiful, young—who were each sent to the psychiatrist because they were *too* beautiful and *too* smart. They are recalled as if they were dead, cut down in their prime, because being sent to the psychiatrist was a kind of societal death. The compromise with society is conformity, as represented in the characters of Sue, Christina, and Cindy. Conformity is safe, a known pattern that nearly everyone can follow. It is also dull in its predictability. Many times conformity also masks societal ills wherein one group has power over another and maintains that power through general acceptance of the situation (such as accepted inequities of gender, race, and religion).

Sexuality, Power, and Gender Roles

The women of *Fefu and Her Friends* are concerned with sexuality and the power it confers. In the first line of dialogue in the play, Fefu says, "My husband married me to have a constant reminder of how loathsome women are." Although Fefu is saying this to excite controversy and conversation, by the end of the play the audience comes to understand the pain Fefu bears because this statement is so *true*. She weeps to Julia that she needs her husband—emotionally and physically—but he dislikes her and will not fill that role for her. Phillip has asserted his dominance in their relationship; he is the one in control. This is a startling conclusion because Fefu otherwise is a strong, intelligent, confident woman. Cecilia tries to use similar tactics of withholding affection to manipulate her former lover, Paula. Paula has grown wise and, although she is still attracted to Cecilia, she stands her ground every time Cecilia tries to belittle her. Paula's strength, in fact, draws Cecilia to her.

Julia allows herself to believe that men's sexuality is pure and women's is not—and that women are evil and are only some tool gifted to men by God. These are deeply ingrained stereotypes that feminists have long struggled to overcome. Fefu and her friends are illustrative of the various forms these struggles can take: Fefu and her failing marriage; Cecilia and Paula fighting for dominance or equality with one another; Cindy, separated from her significant other but closed-mouthed about her pain; Sue, stable and very domestic; Emma, also stable and anything but domestic; Christina and her fear of nonconformity; and Julia, beating herself for daring to be powerful, intelligent, and female.

STYLE

Absurdism

Absurdism is a belief that human existence is chaotic and meaningless. Fornes was strongly influenced by Theater of the Absurd playwrights such as Samuel Beckett, and her early plays reflect this. *Fefu and Her Friends* was a new, more realistic form for Fornes but still has prominent absurdist elements. First, the play has no real plot; it is a presentation of a series of conversations between women with no particular direction or resolution. The conversations that are strung together to form the content of this play are very loosely connected, leaving the meaning of the overall production open to interpretation. Events such as Fefu shooting blanks at her husband, Julia's hunting accidents, and the water fight are also absurdist elements.

Foreshadowing

Foreshadowing is a device whereby the playwright places clues that warn about future events. In *Fefu and Her Friends*, Fornes heavily foreshadows

Julia's death with the inclusion of the rifle, multiple discussions about whether the gun is loaded with real bullets or not, and Julia's frequent talk about death. "I will die . . . for no apparent reason," she prophesizes in part 3. The hunting accident which left Julia paralyzed, combined with the presence of the rifle, leaves the audience to wonder throughout the play what will happen when the rifle is fired while Julia is nearby.

HISTORICAL CONTEXT

Between Two Wars

At the time *Fefu and Her Friends* takes place, the world is recovering from the ravages of the Great War, later known as World War I (1914–1918). The U.S. economy, under the earnest direction of President Franklin D. Roosevelt and his New Deal programs, is recovering from economic depression, which hit the country hard in 1929. Germany, also economically depressed and smarting from the harsh restrictions of the Treaty of Versailles, became a hotbed of resentment. The National Socialist German Workers' Party (Nazi Party) was formed in 1919 and took over the government when its leader, Adolf Hitler, was elected Führer of Germany in 1933. After Hitler came into power, he began to break restrictions established by the Treaty of Versailles—restrictions on actions such as conscripting citizens into military service, building an arsenal, and invading nearby countries. World War II (1939–1945) officially began when Germany invaded Poland on September 1, 1939.

In the United States, many people were averse to becoming involved in problems overseas as they felt the United States had enough of its own problems. Dust storms ravaged many of the agricultural states in the Midwest, while mobsters and criminals (like Bonnie and Clyde) ran rampant across the country. Few, if any, were aware of the inhumane treatment happening at concentration camps and death camps in Europe. The United States held off direct involvement in World War II until December 7, 1941, when the Japanese attacked Pearl Harbor, Hawaii. At Fefu's country house in New England, these problems are far away; Paula is the only one to mention contemporary issues when she worries that they should focus more on teaching the poor. These women are under a different kind of assault, unseen and difficult to overcome, involving sexuality and gender roles.

COMPARE
&
CONTRAST

- **1930s:** The United States is slowly recovering from an economic depression that started with the stock market crash of 1929. Many people were unemployed (25 percent), their lives destroyed by deep poverty, as Paula notes in the play. From 1933–1938, President Franklin D. Roosevelt enacts a number of programs, collectively called the New Deal, designed to stabilize the economy.

  1970s: Soaring energy prices cause people to fear an economic recession. Unemployment is around 6.2 percent. The Organization of Arab Petroleum Exporting Countries (OAPEC) places an embargo on shipping oil to the United States from October 1973 to March 1974, resulting in prices at the pump as high as $6.13 per gallon. It takes a decade for gas prices to return to normal levels.

  Today: Companies are downsizing and laying workers off even as income disparity is becoming more pronounced. Unemployment stands at 4.5 percent. Following Hurricane Katrina in 2005, which destroyed oil refineries in the Gulf of Mexico, the price of gasoline at the pump rises to $3.04 per gallon, the highest price since March 1981.

- **1930s:** Eugene O'Neill, an American playwright known for popularizing realism, wins the Nobel Prize for Literature in 1936. Noncommercial theatres and plays with a social or political message are emerging. Experimental theater (such as absurdist or avant-garde) is in its infancy, primarily in Europe, and will fully flourish after World War II.

  1970s: Both realism and absurdism continue to be popular forms in theater. Musicals like *A Chorus Line* are very popular. Experimental forms such as improvisation and performance art are being explored. Plays about minorities and women also become more numerous, reflecting society's emerging awareness of issues related to gender and race. In addition, more women and minority playwrights see their work produced.

  Today: Plays range from experimental to realistic. Theater, always in competition with cinema and television, is increasingly threatened by other media such as the Internet, DVDs, and iPods. Still, media has never been able to fully replace the experience of live theater.

- **1930s:** The first wave of feminism dies out once women are granted the right to vote in the United States in 1920. The country is in the grips of terrible economic depression and strict gender roles are somewhat loosened as women seek work, earn Social Security rights from President Roosevelt's new law, and vote.

  1970s: The second wave of feminism begins. Women are fighting for the passage of the Equal Rights Amendment and have been doing so ever since gaining the right to vote. The controversial *Roe v. Wade* decision is handed down in 1973, giving women the right to seek an abortion if they so choose.

  Today: More women than ever are political leaders. Nancy Pelosi became the first female U.S. Speaker of the House in January 2007.

Women's Rights

Women played a large role in supporting the U.S. economy during World War I, taking on the jobs men had to leave behind to go fight overseas. When the war was over, women did not readily give up their careers and freedoms. In the United States, the National Women's Party was formed in 1913 to fight for women's rights. Their primary goal was suffrage, or the right to vote. They saw success with their campaign in

1920, when the 19th Amendment to the Constitution was ratified. Icons of this era include Amelia Earhart and Eleanor Roosevelt. Earhart was the first female pilot to fly solo across the Atlantic in 1932 and she inspired many women with her independent spirit. Roosevelt, as First Lady, was very active alongside her husband, President Franklin D. Roosevelt, in promoting the New Deal programs. She was known to be a no-nonsense woman, strong-willed, independent, and a suffragist. Roosevelt was, however, opposed to the Equal Rights Amendment because she believed it would be detrimental for women, and she was not alone in this reasoning. The Equal Rights Amendment was never ratified, although it continues to be proposed into legislation at every Congress. Fefu, like Earhart and Roosevelt, is a strong, independent woman, although she has discovered that strength and independence do not automatically equate with happiness in life.

CRITICAL OVERVIEW

Fefu and Her Friends was well-received when it was first produced in 1977 and again in 1978. Writing for the *New York Times*, Richard Eder describes Fornes's directing as "uneven" and awkward but praises the script as "the dramatic equivalent of a collection of poems." He summarizes: "It is an imperfect evening but a stimulating one; and with moments of genuine splendor in it." Walter Kerr, also writing in the *New York Times* and reviewing the same production, gives *Fefu and Her Friends* a scathing review. He complains that the play is too "philosophical." He does not enjoy the intimacy of part 2 when the audience visits different rooms to see the scenes performed, and he does not see why the women are getting together. Kerr concludes: "If I lasted as long as I did, it was because I kept hoping during my constant journeyings that I *might* find a play in the very next room."

These critics saw the Off-Broadway performance at the American Place Theater in January 1978. Fornes, recalling the question-and-answer sessions she hosted for audiences during that production, writes for the *Performing Arts Journal* in 1983: "I began to notice that a lot of the men looked at the play differently from the women. . . . They insisted on relating to the men in this play, which had no male characters." She

also writes, in response to critics such as Kerr: "The only answer they have is that it is a feminist play. It could be that it is a feminist play but it could be that it is just a play. . . . it is natural for a woman to write a play where the protagonist is a woman. Man is not the center of life."

CRITICISM

Carol Ullmann

Ullmann is a freelance writer and editor. In the following essay, she discusses sickness, madness, depression, and contagion in Fornes's Fefu and Her Friends.

Fefu and Her Friends gives audiences a-day-in-the-life view of eight progressive 1930s New England women who have gathered to discuss the very practical matter of a fundraising event that they are hosting to raise money for education. All of these women are involved in education and have made it their career. Despite their independence, their intelligence, and their playful spirits, gloom touches them all, especially Fefu and Julia.

The idea of madness is tossed around almost carelessly in the beginning of the play when Christina confides to Cindy that she thinks Fefu is "crazy" and Cindy concurs that she is, albeit "a little." On the surface, they are referring to the outrageous things Fefu says and to her shooting blanks at her husband. The gun firing scared them and they are trying to calm their pounding hearts. Cindy explains to Christina about Phillip and Fefu, "They are not crazy really. They drive each other crazy." Christina is unconvinced. As the most timid character in this play, Christina is completely out of her element around Fefu. She tells her so a little later in part 1, "I think you're crazy" and "You depress me." Christina is accusing Fefu of not only being insane but also being contagious because her madness has depressed Christina and depression can be perceived as a first (though not irrevocable) step down the road to insanity. Fefu claims she is sane and implores Christina to not be depressed on her account: "Don't be depressed. Laugh at me if you don't agree with me. . . . I know I'm ridiculous."

Julia is the epicenter of the darkness that runs throughout the play. The victim of a mysterious accident that left her paralyzed, Julia is in the grips of a quiet madness. Julia believes that none are aware of what she is going through

WHAT DO I READ NEXT?

- *Renasence and Other Poems*, by Edna St. Vincent Millay, was published in 1917 to critical acclaim. Millay was self-sufficient and progressive, much like the characters in Fornes's play.

- *Rosencrantz and Guildenstern Are Dead* (1966), by Tom Stoppard, is an absurdist take on the question of fate and free will, a question that could be asked regarding Julia's death.

- *Abingdon Square* (1987), by Marie Irene Fornes, is a play with a strong historical element. The play follows a young woman, Marion, from when she is married at age fifteen to nine years later when she nurses her estranged and dying husband.

- *Latin American Dramatists since 1945* (2003), by Tony Harvell, covers more than 700 playwrights and 7,000 plays. Entries are organized by country and playwright, and contain biographical information as well as extensive bibliographic records for each author.

- "The Yellow Wallpaper" (1892), by Charlotte Perkins Gilman, tells the tragic story of a wife who is locked in her room by her husband on the advice of her doctors. This short story is told in the first-person through entries in the wife's journal.

- *Feminist Theatre Practice: A Handbook* (1999), by Elaine Aston, provides information and exercises to aid in feminist performance. It is divided into three sections.

because she is careful to keep it a secret, although Cindy has overheard her hallucinations. Cindy tells Fefu and Christina, "I fear for her." Her medical condition is perfectly understandable—Julia is epileptic. The details of her accident are unclear such that it is not certain if the hunter's gunshot or the fall and blow to the head brought on Julia's seizure initially. She now suffers from

> JULIA IS THE EPICENTER OF THE DARKNESS THAT RUNS THROUGHOUT THE PLAY."

petit mal seizures, known today as absence seizures, which are characterized by temporary loss of consciousness, with the victim staring off into space for a short period of time. Whether or not Julia understands her medical condition, she is also now in the grips of serious hallucinations wherein she believes herself to be persecuted by a group of nameless judges. Fefu says of Julia, before her accident, "She was afraid of nothing.... She was so young and yet she knew so much." This has been completely undermined; Julia is hardly the same person they once knew. The women are all disturbed and Julia is desperate to convince them that she is fine, lest the judges torment her more.

When she hallucinates, Julia is alternately being beaten by her judges and trying to placate them by reciting what they want to hear, mainly concerning the filthy and evil nature of women and their bodies, and the inherent purity of men. "He said that I had to be punished because I was getting too smart." Julia believes that she was already killed once by the judges but revived when she repented. She is crippled because of her former bad beliefs and behavior. Julia's condition is reminiscent of Fefu's comment about the worms under the rock:

> You see, that which is exposed to the exterior... is smooth and dry and clean. That which is not... underneath, is slimy and filled with fungus and crawling with worms. It is another life that is parallel to the one we manifest.... If you don't recognize it... *(Whispering)* it eats you.

Julia is being destroyed by her madness because she refuses to acknowledge that that is what it is.

The imagined judges who hurt Julia are also interested in Fefu, whose intelligence and forthright behavior is threatening to their misogynist beliefs. Julia tries to claim that Fefu is not smart, perhaps hoping to spare Fefu what she is going through. When Julia first arrives, she unloads Fefu's rifle, noticing the slug is a blank. She says cryptically, "She's hurting herself," then slips into an absent seizure. Even through the filter of Julia's madness, her words ring true.

The meaning of this is made clear as the characters unfold their innermost thoughts and the audience learns of Fefu's depression. The gun is a masculine, violent way for Fefu to release her anguish over her failing marriage. But it is also a temporary relief, perhaps because it is only loaded with blanks.

Fefu's seemingly careless regard for life frightens Christina, who does not feel that this is natural behavior, even for an adventurous woman. She is right, but this conclusion is not puzzling when one is aware that Fefu pines for a husband who despises her, and that Fefu has lost interest in her life's work. "I am in constant pain. I don't want to give in to it. If I do I am afraid I will never recover," Fefu tells Emma in part 2. This is the first direct indication that Fefu is not as strong, nor as happy as she appears. Fefu covers up her depression with domestic concerns. Whenever she is overly aware of the pain she feels, she rushes out of the room to fetch lemonade, fix a toilet, or make lunch.

Fefu accuses Julia (much as Christina did to Fefu earlier, only this time with more insistence), "You're nuts, and willingly so." Julia denies her madness. Fefu continues, "And you're contagious. I'm going mad too." Fefu hallucinated that Julia walked across the living room when no one else was around, so it would appear to be true, that Fefu is also mad. Or was this an absent seizure and Julia does not remember? Madness and depression are not the same things, despite efforts to equate the two for purposes of neutralizing a person's independence. Sue remembers a friend from years ago, who dated twenty-eight men in one semester because she was both beautiful as well as kind to each man who asked her out. She got in trouble with her superiors for dating too many men. "And the worst thing was that after that, she thought there was something wrong with her." As seen with Julia's imagined judges, authority figures have a lot of influence on one's beliefs and self-esteem.

Gloria Schuman, another friend, was sent to a psychiatrist for writing a brilliant paper. "He almost drove her crazy. They just couldn't believe she was so smart." Julia recalls, "Everybody ended going to the psychiatrist." "Ended," not ended up. Those who were sent to the psychiatrist—those who were perceived as having mental problems—were no longer valued because they were marked by madness (real or otherwise). The only identity left to them was that of patient.

"Those were difficult times," Sue remarks. She also notes that most people, herself included, knew better than to report how many men they were dating or to be honest at their medical check-ups. Otherwise they would end up like naïve Susan Austin, who "said she was nervous and she wasn't sleeping well. So she had to see a psychiatrist from then on." Emma assumes Austin was crazy but Sue assures her she was not. This is the stigma of being sent to the psychiatrist.

Repeatedly, Fornes is telling audiences through *Fefu and Her Friends* that the brightest women are brought down by madness, whether actual or implied. This is the fate that Fefu desperately wants to avoid, and she seeks refuge from this by pretending to be fine, by hiding within the domestic sphere. Women like Fefu take care of their houses, prepare food for their families and guests, and otherwise behave in a feminine, subservient manner. Sue and Christina are superior examples of domesticated scholars. Fefu is quite the opposite. She tells Cindy and Christina, "I like being like a man. Thinking like a man. Feeling like a man." Fefu has few avenues for dealing with her problems—a failing marriage and depression—because the world she inhabits prefers to treat women themselves as the problem rather than as human beings who need help. The underlying implication is that "Woman is not a human being. . . . Woman generates the evil herself."

Source: Carol Ullmann, Critical Essay on *Fefu and Her Friends*, in *Drama for Students*, Gale, Cengage Learning, 2008.

Piper Murray

In the following excerpt, Murray interprets Fefu and Her Friends *as an astute examination of how and why women gather together.*

Maria Irene Fornes's *Fefu and Her Friends* leaves us with a vision that is nothing if not ambivalent. Coming as the climax of eight women's efforts to throw off "the stifling conditions" that have brought them together, Julia's sympathetic death—apparently the result of a shot fired by Phillip's unsympathetic gun—shocks and confuses. In an effort to explain this strangely ambiguous ending, many critics have looked to one of its most obvious roots: the conflicted psyches of Fefu and her friends. In such an interpretation, Julia's real and hallucinated struggle, however dramatic, becomes just an extreme example of the pain and paralysis that

IN THE END, OF COURSE, FEFU AND HER FRIENDS CAN HARDLY BE SAID TO BLOW THE WORLD APART, OR EVEN TO LAY THE FOUNDATION FOR A NEW ONE."

all the women experience. All of these women, it would seem, have internalized the kind of judges Julia hallucinates in her Part Two monologue. All of them must strive to create an identity not dependent on men (or "man") for its definition, one that celebrates both the plumbing that women can call their own and the fact that women can do all their "own plumbing." . . .

Fefu and Her Friends introduces us early on to the abject—and to the ambivalence that always characterizes its performance. Perhaps this is nowhere more evident than in Fefu's preoccupation with plumbing. "Plumbing is more important than you think" Fefu tells Christina, and revulsion is exciting:

> that which is exposed to the exterior . . . is smooth and dry and clean. That which is not . . . underneath, is slimy and filled with fungus and crawling with worms. It is another life that is parallel to the one we manifest. It's there. The way worms are underneath the stone. If you don't recognize it . . . (*Whispering.*) it eats you.

Or, in Julia's case, it paralyzes you. As Julia makes clear in her hysterical monologue in Part Two, hers is a constant struggle to forget "the stinking parts of the body," even though "all those parts [that] must be kept clean and put away [. . .] are the important ones: the genitals, the anus, the mouth, the armpit." Men and women both might be accused of "act[ing] as if they don't have genitals," but, as Julia reiterates through her "prayer," it is *woman* who is fundamentally, mythologically, not only condemned to but, in fact, founded on that denial. And we can imagine how exhausting that constant denial must be, considering that "women's entrails are heavier than anything on earth."

Though Julia's may be the most extreme case, to some extent we come to know all of Fefu and her friends as abject identities. In the merry-go-round of Part Two, for example, we encounter in each of

the scenes a kind of hysterical production through which, into all the play and laughter, erupts a pain neither purely physical nor purely emotional: Cindy relates a dream in which she is nearly strangled by a man who rubs her nipples, while Sue sucks on Fefu's ice cubes before returning them to the freezer, declaring "I'm clean." And through it all, despite her frequent testimony that she takes pleasure in what others find disgusting, Fefu seems to spend an awful lot of time wielding a plunger, presumably in order to keep the abject at bay. Despite her tendency to feed (on) the very things that revolt her, that is, Fefu appears unusually preoccupied with ensuring that the "the rubber stopper [. . .] falls right over the hole"—making sure, that is, that the once-abjected will not reproduce itself. Indeed, for the risk-taker Christina takes her to be, it would seem that Fefu takes a remarkable number of precautions when it comes to plumbing.

Why is plumbing—as Fefu and Julia both describe it—so "important"? Why, in a gathering and performance that is supposed to be about educational reform, does the plumbing seem so often and so insistently to come up? At one level, we might say that the power with which Fefu endows her plumbing makes *Fefu* a paradoxical performance from the beginning. For plumbing, especially when it is not performing as it is supposed to, reminds us of the physical fact of the body and its production of waste. At the same time, however, when it is functioning as we expect it to, plumbing is also precisely what enables us to *conceal*, to forget, the fact of our bodily functions. In other words, plumbing is like the perfect performative described by Butler: while it may function as witness to the body and its avenues of abjection, it also functions as a "smooth and dry and clean" denial of that same function. We might also wonder, of course, whether Fefu's prophylactic activity is not meant as a guard against another kind of bodily (re)production, as well. As the Shakespearean sonnet that Emma recites to Fefu in Part Two suggests, Fefu remains childless; she has not yet "convert[ed]" herself "to store" by fulfilling the promise of reproduction. And if Fefu would like to keep it that way, then she must constantly check to make sure that the rubber stopper/diaphragm "falls right over the hole." For we might remember that it is Fefu's husband, and not Fefu, who controls whether the gun shoots blanks or the real thing—no matter whose hands it is in or who it is aimed at.

As Fefu's question to Christina ("What do you do with revulsion?") suggests, the abject always serves a performative function. We learn early on in *Fefu* that so much talk about the abject, along with the revulsion it produces, is never *merely* talk; it is also a production that *does* something, that acts. From the very first line, "[m]y husband married me to have a constant reminder of how loathsome women are," Fornes's play draws us into a world where every utterance does something, enacts some inequality between men and women (and, though this is less frequently noted, between women and women). Julia tells her audience that as soon as she believes the prayer that condemns women as inhuman and spiritually sexual, she "will forget the judges. And when I forget the judges," she goes on, "I will believe the prayer. They say both happen at once. And all women have done it." In other words, if she can forget the performative and (re)productive nature of the female "sex," and simply allow it to "materialize" as if it were "natural" (much like the plumbing), then she will finally have become a woman who can walk with other women. Indeed, it would seem that it is this very act of forgetting that makes "woman" what she is in the first place. Julia's failure to live up to this performative demand will, of course, be fatal. To Emma's offer to stage a dance for her (and we know from Julia's monologue where dancing got Isadora Duncan), Julia happily replies, "I'm game." And so she is: like the deer and the rabbit that are literally hunted, Julia's perception that she is "game" for her persecutors finally becomes a paralyzing and deadly reality, and one that, like any performative utterance, is never clearly either the result or the cause of the act it performs...

In the end, of course, Fefu and her friends can hardly be said to blow the world apart, or even to lay the foundation for a new one. But that the play successfully (if not happily) performs this struggle in all its ambivalence might be evident in the fact that, as Fornes herself has noted, nobody seems to know quite what to do with the sheer number of women in this play. As Helene Keyssar writes of her own experience as an audience member, spectators of both sexes often find themselves "disconcerted, not only by being moved from our stable and familiar positions, but by our proximity to each other to the characters; we are *in* their spaces but not of them. Their world remains separate from ours, and there is nothing we can do to make a difference

in their world" (100; original emphasis). If we are invited to be in their spaces but not of them, made to feel how little difference our presence makes in their world, then what does that say for the status of *Fefu* as a feminist performance? Does *Fefu*, in fact, perform the feminist work we might as critics call on it to do? Or does it allow us to remain just indifferent enough to view the happiness and unhappiness of Fefu and her friends as "mere" performance, regarding them as something between real women and drama queens? Forne's own comments about the play's reception have suggested that many audience members continue to judge how well Fefu and her friends are together through the familiar lens of hom(m)osociality; indeed, many of the post-performance questions about the play often concern neither Fefu nor any of her seven friends, but the few male characters who never even appear. We, too, it would seem, are always waiting for the men to arrive.

Perhaps no other play demonstrates so clearly as *Fefu and Her Friends* the fundamental—and founding—ambivalence that necessarily constitutes female homosocial desire in a culture where the men play outside in the fresh air while the women gather inside, "in the dark." Certainly the complicated struggle of Fefu and her friends to become "well together" seems to imply, with Butler. that "[e]xceeding is not escaping, and the subject exceeds precisely that to which it is bound" (*Psychic Life* 17). In the same way, however, the passionate attachments that Fefu and her friends do develop would also seem to enact the kind of ambivalent hope that Peggy Phelan identifies with feminist critical theory: "What makes feminist criticism performative," she writes, "is not its utopian pitch toward a better future but, rather, the 'intimate dissonance' inspired by the recognition of mutual failure, in the here and now—the failure to enact what one can barely glimpse, can only imagine, and cannot reproduce." In other words, because feminist criticism (and performance) is itself performative, it cannot ever hope to have achieved its end once and for all. Instead, it must find its hope in the very necessity and fragility that repetition has to offer it. Looking at the play in this way, as Fefu and her friends gather around Julia's body in the final scene of Fornes's play, we might ask, not once but many times, just what kinds of passionate attachments *Fefu and Her Friends* makes possible—*between women*.

Source: Piper Murray, "'They Are Well Together. Women Are Not': Productive Ambivalence and Female Hom(m)osociality in *Fefu and Her Friends*," in *Modern Drama*, Vol. 44, No. 4, Winter 2001, pp. 398–415.

Penny Farfan

In lhe following excerpt, Farfan examines Fornes's unusual staging choices in Fefu and Her Friends *as well as how the play's* mise-en-scène *("putting into the scene") drives its feminist message.*

The first time that Maria Irene Fornes attended a rehearsal of one of her plays, she was amazed to be informed by the director that she should not communicate her ideas about staging directly to the actors but should instead make written notes that they would discuss together over coffee after rehearsal. This exclusion of the playwright from the rehearsal process seemed to Fornes "like the most absurd thing in the world." As she later commented,

> It's as if you have a child, your own baby, and you take the baby to school and the baby is crying and the teacher says, "Please I'll take care of it. Make a note: at the end of the day you and I can talk about it." You'd think 'This woman is crazy. I'm not going to leave my kid here with this insane person.'

Since her initial theatrical experience, Fornes has directed many of the first productions of her own work, having resolved that if she did not direct, the "work would not be done" at all. She has "never [seen] any difference between writing and directing" and for this reason she rarely goes into rehearsal with a completed script in hand.

The organic relationship between dramaturgy and *mise-en-scène* in Fornes's work is perhaps nowhere more evident than in her 1977 play *Fefu and Her Friends*, in the middle section of which the audience is divided into quarters, taken out of the main auditorium, and rotated through four intimate playing areas representing rooms in Fefu's house, where the actresses simultaneously repeat interlocking yet distinct scenes four times, once for each section of the audience. Fornes arrived at this unique staging by chance while she was looking for a space in which to present her as-yet-unfinished play:

> I did not like the space I found because it had large columns. But then I was taken backstage to the rooms the audience could not see. I saw the dressing room, and I thought, "How nice. This could be a room in Fefu's house," Then I was taken to the greenroom. I thought that this also could be a room in Fefu's house. Then we went to the business office to discuss terms.

JULIA ALIGNS HERSELF EXPLICITLY WITH FEFU, IMPLYING THAT SHE ALSO IS TOO SMART AND IS THEREFORE IN SIMILAR DANGER OF PUNISHMENT BY THE JUDGES; AND INDEED, OF ALL THE CHARACTERS IN THE PLAY, FEFU IS MOST DIRECTLY INVOLVED IN THE STRUGGLE THAT HAS LEFT JULIA CRIPPLED."

> That office was the study of Fefu's house ... I asked if we could use all of their rooms for the performances, and they agreed.

> I had written Julia's speech in the bedroom already. I had intended to put it on stage and I had not yet arrived at how it would come about. Part of the kitchen scene was written, but I had thought it would be happening in the living room. So I had parts of it already. It was the rooms themselves that modified the scenes which originally I planned to put in the living room.

> People asked me, when the play opened, if I had written those scenes to be done in different rooms and then found the space. No. They were written that way because the space was there.

Yet while Fornes attributes the staging of *Fefu and Her Friends* to chance, she has also stated, "When something happens by accident, I trust that the play is making its own point. I feel something is happening that is very profound and very important." Indeed, as I will argue here, in reconfiguring the conventional performer-spectator relationship, Fornes's *mise-en-scène* in *Fefu and Her Friends* realizes in theatrical terms an alternative model for interaction with the universe external to the self such as that proposed by the metatheatrical actress/educator-character Emma as a means of transforming Fefu's pain. In this respect, *Fefu and Her Friends* posits postmodern feminist theatre practice as a constructive response to the psychic dilemmas of the play's female characters. As Emma says, "Life is theatre. Theatre is life. If we're showing what life is, can be, we must do theatre."

Set in New England in 1935, *Fefu and Her Friends* involves eight women who seem to share a common educational background and who gather at Fefu's house to prepare for what seems to be a fundraising project relating to education. One of these women, Julia, suffers from a mysterious and apparently psychosomatic illness that became evident a year earlier when she collapsed after a hunter shot a deer. She has not walked since and still occasionally blanks out. Alone in her bedroom in Part Two, Julia undergoes a long hallucination punctuated by threats and blows from invisible "judges" who seem to epitomize patriarchal authority. During the course of her hallucination, she reveals that the onset of her illness was a punishment for having got "too smart" and that the conditions of her survival were to become crippled and to remain silent about what she knows. Even now, however, though she attempts to appease the judges by reciting a creed of the central tenets of patriarchal ideology, Julia remains covertly but essentially defiant and unindoctrinated, challenging conventional wisdom relating to women and attempting to get the judges off the trail of her friend Fefu, who is also considered to be "too smart." Thus, in the 1930s context in which the play is set, Julia's physical symptoms both express and suppress her resistance to women's subordination within patriarchal society, as did those of the "smart" female hysterics treated by Sigmund Freud, Josef Breuer, and others around the turn of the century.

Described by Fornes as "the mind of the play—the seer, the visionary," Julia herself implies \that her insights into the patriarchal construction of female inferiority are repressed common knowledge when she states at the end of her Part Two monologue, "They say when I believe the prayer I will forget the judges. And when I forget the judges I will believe the prayer. They say both happen at once. *And all women have done it.* Why can't I?" (emphasis added). Julia's connection to the other characters in the play is borne out by the simultaneous staging of Part Two, when, at the same time that she is in the bedroom reciting the patriarchal creed under threat of violence from invisible tormentors, Paula is in the kitchen describing the pain of breaking up with her lover Cecilia, Cindy is in the study recounting a nightmare about an abusive male doctor, and Emma and Fefu are on the lawn discussing Emma's obsession with genitals and Fefu's "constant pain." Fornes's sense of the appropriateness of a certain amount of sound-spill between the various playing areas in Part Two suggests that Julia's forbidden knowledge functions as the intermittently or partially audible subtext

underlying all the characters' interactions, which have been described by W. B. Worthen as "transformations of Julia's more explicit subjection."

The connection between Julia and the other characters is confirmed in Part Three of *Fefu and Her Friends* when the women reminisce about their college days in terms that resonate with and confirm the reality of her hallucinations: female intelligence is associated in these recollections with madness, while college professors and doctors are represented as actual versions of Julia's hallucinated judges and are referred to similarly, by means of the pronoun they." Elaine Showalter has written that "hysteria and feminism ... exist on a kind of continuum" and that "[i]f we see the hysterical woman as one end of the spectrum of a female avant-garde struggling to redefine women's place in the social order, then we can also see feminism as the other end of the spectrum, the alternative to hysterical silence, and the determination to speak and act for women in the public world." The common educational background of the women in *Fefu and Her Friends* signifies their shared experience of the pressure to become indoctrinated into the system of beliefs outlined in Julia's prayer. At the same time, the reunion of these women on the basis of their ongoing commitment to education may suggest a fundamental concern on Fornes's part with representing characters engaged in the project of researching alternative modes of response to the knowledge articulated by the hysteric Julia as "the mind of the play." In this sense, the term *Lehrstück* or "learning play" that Bonnie Marranca has used to describe Fornes's 1987 work *Abingdon Square* is applicable to *Fefu and Her Friends* as well.

Julia aligns herself explicitly with Fefu, implying that she also is too smart and is therefore in similar danger of punishment by the judges; and indeed, of all the characters in the play, Fefu is most directly involved in the struggle that has left Julia crippled. Fefu is married to a man she claims to need and desire, but who has told her that he "[married her] to have a constant reminder of how loathsome women are" and who engages her in a terrible "game" whereby he falls to the ground after she shoots at him with a rifle that has thus far been loaded with blanks but that he has threatened one day to load with a real bullet. Fefu's interest in the male-associated activities of shooting and plumbing and her assertions that she "like[s] men better than women" and that she "like[s] being...thinking...[f]eeling like a man" indicate that her strategy for coping with the pain of her marriage is male-identification, but this mode of response is problematized by the presence of female friends who cause her to confront the patriarchal construction of female inferiority. In the opening scene, for example, Cindy forces Fefu to acknowledge a discrepancy between what her husband Phillip says about women being "loathsome" and what she herself knows of women based on her own personal experience. This invalidation of her posture of male-identification makes being around women a dangerous situation for Fefu. As she states in Part One,

> Women are restless with each other. They are like live wires...either chattering to keep themselves from making contact, or else, if they don't chatter, they avert their eyes...like Orpheus...as if a god once said "and if they shall recognize each other, the world will be blown apart." They are always eager for the men to arrive. When they do, they can put themselves at rest. tranquilized and in a mild stupor. With the men they feel safe. The danger is gone. That's the closest they can be to feeling wholesome. Men are muscle that cover the raw nerve. They are the insulators. The danger is gone, but the price is the mind and the spirit... High price.—I've never understood it. Why?— What is feared?—Hmmm. Well...—Do you know? Perhaps the heavens would fall.

The devastating recognition scene that this speech anticipates occurs near the end of the play when, in a moment that may support Julia's assertion that "[h]allucinations are real," Fefu "sees" Julia walking and understands that her illness is a psychosomatic response to an insight that she will not or cannot communicate except through the hysterical paralysis of her body. Unaccepting of what she perceives as Julia's passive and voluntary submission, Fefu tries to force her to her feet to fight and then takes action herself, exiting to the lawn with the now-loaded rifle. Like the hunter who shot a deer and mysteriously injured Julia, Fefu now shoots a rabbit and Julia once more suffers the wound, which this time may be fatal.

Beverley Byers Pevitts has argued that the death of Julia signifies the symbolic killing off of woman as created by the dominant culture in order to enable the emergence of a new self-determined female identity, yet Fornes's assertion that her characters should not be seen as symbolic or representative figures makes Pevitts's positive interpretation of the ambiguous ending of *Fefu*

and Her Friends problematic. With regard to this question of the play's ending, Fornes's starting premises for her work on *Fefu* may perhaps be instructive. By her own account, she began writing the play with two " fantasy" images in mind. The first image was of a "woman...who was talking to some friends [and then] took her rifle and shot her husband"; the second was a joke involving "two Mexicans speaking at a bullfight. One says to the other, 'She is pretty, that one over there.' The other one says, 'Which one?' So the first one takes his rifle and shoots her. He says, 'That one, the one that falls.'" In the completed play, Fornes has brought these two starting premises together so that, however indirectly, Fefu shoots Julia rather than her husband Phillip and, in doing so, takes the place of the men in the "joke" who objectify women to the point of annihilation. Notably, in Part One of the play, Julia remarks of Fefu's use of the gun, "She's hurting herself"; inasmuch as taking up the gun is a male-associated strategy of domination, Julia's observation is correct. In this *Lehrstück*, then, Fefu's male-identification is ultimately as self-destructive and ineffectual a strategy of resistance to women's subordination within patriarchal culture as Julia's hysteria.

Source: Penny Farfan, "Feminism, Metatheatricality, and Mise-en-scène in Maria Irene Fornes's *Fefu and Her Friends*," in *Modern Drama*, Vol. 40, No. 4, Winter 1997, pp. 181–93.

W. B. Worthen

In the following excerpt, Worthen discusses Fornes's political, feminist approach in Fefu and Her Friends, *particularly how she challenges the audience's inherently uncomfortable response to the play itself.*

...Fornes's most assured play, *Fefu and Her Friends*, brings the gendering of the realistic spectator fully into view, revealing "his" covert control of the women of the stage. The play opens at a country house in 1935. Fefu has invited a group of women to her home to rehearse a brief series of skits for a charity benefit to raise money for a newly founded organization. In the first scene, the women arrive and are introduced. Many seem to have been college friends, two seem to be lovers, or ex-lovers. Much of the action of the scene centers on Julia, who is confined to a wheelchair as the result of a mysterious hunting accident: although the bullet missed her, she is paralyzed from the waist down. In part 2, Fornes breaks the audience into four groups, who tour Fefu's home—garden, study, bedroom, and kitchen: "These scenes are performed simultaneously. When the scenes are completed the audience moves to the next space and the scenes are performed again. This is repeated four times until each group has seen all four scenes." In part 3, the audience is returned to the auditorium. The women rehearse and decide the order of their program, Fefu goes outside to clean her gun, and suddenly a shot rings out; Julia falls dead, bleeding, though again the bullet seems to have gone elsewhere.

The play examines the theatrical poetics of the feminine not only as theme, but in the visible protocols of the spectacle as well, by unseating the invisible spectator of realism and by dramatizing "his" authority over the construction of stage gender. Early in the play, for instance, Fefu looks offstage and sees her husband approaching: "*FEFU reaches for the gun, aims and shoots. CHRISTINA hides behind the couch. She and CINDY scream... FEFU smiles proudly. She blows on the mouth of the barrel. She puts down the gun and looks out again.*" As Fefu explains once Phillip has regained his feet, "It's a game we play. I shoot and he falls. Whenever he hears the blast he falls. No matter where he is, he falls." Although Phillip is never seen in the play, his attitudes constantly intrude on the action—"My husband married me to have a constant reminder of how loathsome women are"—and mark the presence of a powerful, masculine, destructive authority lurking just offstage. The shells may be live or only blanks ("I'm never sure," says Fefu), but it hardly matters. The exchange of power takes place through the "sighting" of the other.

The power of the absent male is everywhere evident in *Fefu*, and particularly imaged in Julia's paralysis. As Cindy suggests when she describes the accident, Julia's malady is a version of Fefu's "game": "I thought the bullet hit her, but it didn't... the hunter aimed... at the deer. He shot":

> Julia and the deer fell... I screamed for help and the hunter came and examined Julia. He said, "She is not hurt." Julia's forehead was bleeding. He said, "It is a surface wound. I didn't hurt her." I know it wasn't he who hurt her. It was someone else... Apparently there was a spinal nerve injury but the doctors are puzzled because it doesn't seem her spine was hurt when she fell. She hit her head and she suffered a concussion but that would not affect the spinal nerve. So there seems to be no reason for the paralysis. She blanks out and that is

caused by the blow on the head. It's a scar in the brain.

The women of *Fefu and Her Friends* share Julia's invisible "scar," the mark of their paralyzing subjection to a patriarchy that operates on the "imaginary," ideological plane. The hunter is kin to Julia's hallucinatory "voices" in part 2, the "judges" who enforce her psychic dismemberment: "They clubbed me. They broke my head. They broke my will. They broke my hands. They tore my eyes out. They took away my voice." Julia's bodily identification is broken down and reordered according to the "aesthetic" canons prescribed by the male voice, the silent voice that characterizes women as "loathsome." This internalized "guardian" rewrites Julia's identity at the interface of the body itself, where the masculine voice materializes itself in the woman's flesh. The subliminal voice infiltrates the deepest levels of psychological and physiological identification, enforcing a crippling gesture of submission:

> (*Her head moves as if slapped.*)
> Julia: Don't hit me. Didn't I just say my prayer?
> (*A smaller slap.*)
> Julia: I believe it.

The gun business derives from a joke, as Fornes reports in "Notes": "There are two Mexicans in sombreros sitting at a bullfight and one says to the other, 'Isn't she beautiful, the one in yellow?' and he points to a woman on the other side of the arena crowded with people. The other one says, 'Which one?' and the first takes his gun and shoots her and says, 'The one that falls.' In the first draft of the play Fefu explains that she started playing this game with her husband as a joke. But in rewriting the play I took out this explanation." It's notable that the gun business dates from Fornes's original work on the play in 1964, as Fornes suggests in "Interview." For a fuller reading of Fornes's theater, see Worthen, "*Still playing games.*"

As Fornes remarked to Gayle Austin, "Julia is really not mad at all. She's telling the truth. The only madness is, instead of saying her experience was 'as if' there was a court that condemned her, she says that they did" (Austin 80).

Fornes suggests that "Julia is the mind of the play," and Julia's scene articulates the shaping vision of *Fefu* as a whole, as well as organizing the dramatic structure of part 2 ("Notes"). The action of *Fefu and Her Friends* takes place under watchful eyes of Phillip, of the hunter, of Julia's "guardians," a gaze that constructs, enables, and thwarts the women of the stage: "Our sight is a form they take. That is why we take pleasure in seeing things." In the theater, of course, there is another invisible voyeur, whose performance is both powerful and "imaginary." *Fefu and Her Friends* extends the function of the spectator beyond the metaphorical register, by decentering "his" implicit ordering of the theatricality of the feminine. First performed by the New York Theater Strategy in a SoHo loft, the play originally invited the spectators to explore the space of Fefu's home. In the American Place Theater production, the spectators were invited, row by row, to different areas of the theater—a backstage kitchen, an upstairs bedroom, the garden and the study sets—before being returned to the auditorium, but not to their original seats. At first glance, Fornes's staging may seem simply a gimmick, a formalist exercise in multiple perspective something like Alan Ayckbourn's *The Norman Conquests* (1973). yet Ayckbourn's trilogy—each play takes a different set of soundings from the events of a single weekend—implies that there could be, in some mammoth play, a single ordering of events, one "drama" expressed by a single plot and visible from a single perspective. *Fefu and Her Friends*, though, bears little confidence in the adequacy or authority of the single viewing subject characteristic of both film and of fourth-wall realism, and more closely approximates the decentering disorientation of environmental theater. Different spectators see the drama in a different sequence and in fact see different plays, as variations invariably enter into the actors' performances. Fornes not only draws the audience into the performance space, violating the privacy of the stage, she actively challenges and suspends the epistemological priorities of realistic vision

and its privileged, private subject: the invisible, singular, motionless, masculine "I." By reordering the audience's function in the theatrical process, *Fefu* reorders its relation to, and interpretation of, the dramatic process it shapes.

As Cecilia says at the opening of part 3, after we have returned to the living room, "we each have our own system of receiving information, placing it, responding to it. That system can function with such a bias that it could take any situation and translate it into one formula." In performance, *Fefu and Her Friends* dramatizes and displaces the theatrical system that renders woman visible: the predication of feminine identity on the sight of the spectator, a "judge" multiplied from the singular "he" into an audience of "them." In this sense, Fornes's theatrical strategy works to replace the "objective" and objectifying relations of realistic vision with the more "fluid boundaries" sometimes said to describe women's experience of themselves and others. Writing the play, Fornes sought to avoid "writing in a linear manner, moving forward," and instead undertook a series of centrifugal experiments, exploring characterization by writing a series of improvisational, extraneous scenes (Cummings 53). Perhaps as a result, the staging of *Fefu* challenge the institutional "objectivity," the controlling partitions of realistic vision. The play not only realizes Julia's absent voices, it reshapes the audience's relation to the drama, requiring an interpretive activity that subordinates "plot" to "atmosphere" or "environment," one that refuses recourse to a single, external point of view.

Stanley Kauffman's reading of the play's filmic texture is at once shrewd and, in this sense, misapplied: "I doubt very much that Fornes thought of this four-part walk-around as a gimmick. Probably it signified for her an explanation of simultaneity (since all four scenes are done simultaneously four times for the four groups), a union of play and audience through kinetics, some adoption by the theater of cinematic flexibility and montage. But since the small content in these scenes would in no way be damaged by traditional serial construction, since this insistence on reminding us that people actually have related/unrelated conversations simultaneously in different rooms of the same house is banal, we are left with the *feeling* of gimmick."

It should be noted that Fornes also remarks, "I don't mean linear in terms of what the feminists claim about the way the male mind works." For the phrase, "fluid boundaries," and for much of my understanding of feminist psychoanalytic theory, I am indebted to my late colleague Joan Lidoff. Patrocinio Schweickart argues, referring to the work of Nancy Chodorow and Carol Gilligan, that "men define themselves through individuation and separation from others, while women have more flexible ego boundaries and define and experience themselves in terms of their affiliations and relationships with others."

In *Fefu and Her Friends*, vision is achieved only through displacement, by standing outside the theatrical formula of realism. The play undertakes to dramatize both the results of realistic bias—in the various deformations suffered by Julia, Fefu, and their friends—and to enact the "other" formula that has been suppressed, the formula that becomes the audience's mode of vision in the theater. To see *Fefu* is not to imagine an ideal order, a single, causal "plot" constituted specifically by our absence from the performance; not only are there several "plots," but we have shared the space in which they have been enacted. *Fefu* sharply illustrates how a "subversive text" can open up theatrical rhetoric, exposing "the negotiation of meanings to contradictions, circularity, multiple viewpoints" (Forte 117). *Fefu and Her Friends* decenters the absent "spectator" as the site of authentic interpretation, replacing "him" with a self-evidently theatricalized body, an "audience," a community sharing irreconcilable yet interdependent experiences. In *Fefu*, Fornes provides what Glaspell could not discover in *Trifles*: a means of politicizing our interpretive activity as spectators. The environmental design of the play invokes the realistic ideal of verisimilitude even as it renders any sense of spectatorial "objectivity" impossible. The perspective offered by the realistic box appears to construct a community of witnesses but is in fact grounded in the sight of a single observer: the realistic audience sees with a single eye. *Fefu* challenges the "theory" of realistic theater at its source, by dramatizing—and displacing—the covert authority of the constitutive *theoros* of realism and the social order it reproduces: the offstage man. In this regard, Fornes's theater shares its rhetoric with the theater of Brenton, Barnes, Churchill, Osborne, Kennedy, and many others who work to stage our performance as a political act. The genius of *Fefu and Her Friends* lies in the way that Fornes renders the relations of visibility palpable, dramatizing their

coercive force and the gender bias they inscribe within our own performance of the play.

See Jane Gallop's description of the oculocentrism of theory "from the Greek *theoria*, from *theoros*, 'spectator,' from *thea*, 'a viewing.'" It should be noted that theater of this kind is, in the careful sense developed by Benjamin Bennett, anti-Fascist, in that it not only opposes the imagined uniformity of response latent in the single perspective of realism and the single "personality" produced by poetic theater, but it also forces the audience to negotiate its own variety of responses as part of the play's condition of meaning. See *Theater as Problem* chapter 4, esp. 159–63.

Source: W. B. Worthen, "Framing Gender: *Cloud Nine* and *Fefu and Her Friends*," in *Modern Drama and the Rhetoric Theater*, University of California Press, 1992, pp. 182–93.

Phyllis Mael

In the following excerpt, Mael gives a critical analysis of Fornes's life and work.

"Innocence, tenderness, a sense of humor, a special kind of joy"—these are the ingredients María Irene Fornés wants in her plays. Structure or form makes these ingredients cohere. According to Fornés, structure is not necessarily words or plot but what takes the audience from one thing to another. "Structure is a personal and idiosyncratic sense of order which is abstract and instinctive." She compares structure in drama to form in abstract painting: "When looking at an abstract painting, we see the elements basic to painting. When looking at a figurative or representational painting, we are not as aware of the abstract elements of composition which must be [present] in order for the painting to be good. Structure refers to the basic elements of playwriting which must be there regardless of content."

Her experimental plays have earned her recognition and critical support. Author and critic Phillip Lopate has written that Fornés "helped clear a way through the claustrophobic landscape of Broadway vapidity and Off-Broadway ponderous symbolism, by making theater that was fresh, adventurous, casual, fantastic, perceptive and musical." Like that of many other recent avant-garde playwrights, Fornés's work has earned both recognition and financial support from several universities and philanthropic foundations. For her work in the theatre she has received awards from the Whitney Foundation

> *FEFU AND HER FRIENDS* IS FORNÉS'S MOST
> SUCCESSFUL PLAY TO DATE. SIMILAR TO SOME OF
> HER OTHER PLAYS IN USING CINEMATIC ELEMENTS
> AND DEMONSTRATING A TENDERNESS TOWARD THE
> CHARACTERS, *FEFU AND HER FRIENDS* DIFFERS IN
> BEING MORE REALISTIC, DEVELOPING CHARACTERS
> MORE FULLY, AND CONTAINING DECIDEDLY
> FEMINIST CONTENT."

(1961), the University of Minnesota (1965), Cintas Foundation (1967), Yale University (1967-1968), Boston University (1968), the Rockefeller Foundation (1971), the Guggenheim Foundation (1972), the National Endowment for the Arts (1973), and the New York State Council on the Arts (1976). These awards testify to her continuing search for new forms to express a personal idiom for theatre.

Fornés emigrated from her native Cuba to the United States in 1945 with her mother and sister. In 1954 she went to Europe and spent three years painting, returning in 1957 to New York, where she worked as a textile designer. In 1960 she began writing plays and had her first production in 1961. She has also directed plays, principally her own. Since 1973 she has been president of the New York Theatre Strategy, an organization that produces the work of experimental American playwrights. In addition to writing plays in English, she has written in Spanish such plays as *Cap-a-Pie* (1975) and *Lolita in the Garden* (1977)—both important contributions to INTAR, a New York native Spanish theatre.

Although some might consider her works too abstract, too concerned with form and texture, Fornés insists a strong message is present in most of her plays. But she distinguishes between political thinking and art. In her plays she is "teaching something that is, that exists, but is not telling what to do about it. To indicate what the next step should be, what to do next is political action and not the function of art at all. The function of art is to reveal."

Tango Palace (1964), her first important play, is about the power struggle between Isidore, "an androgynous clown," and Leopold, "an earnest youth." Their struggle is as stylized as the tango Isidore ostensibly attempts to teach Leopold and as deadly as the bullfight in which they engage, a fight which culminates in an embrace as Leopold kills Isidore.

Isidore and Leopold represent the twin poles of an archetypal battle (father-son, teacher-student). As the play opens, Isidore is resting in a shrine, occasionally emerging to toss cards at Leopold. According to Isidore, the cards "contain wisdom" which Leopold must memorize, such as "All is fair in love and war." But Leopold protests this socialization process, wishing instead to learn in his own way, listening to his inner voice. *There! You Died* (1963), the original title, refers to a line that exemplifies Isidore's desire to be omnipotent. Attempting to convince Leopold that all knowledge emanates from him, Isidore tells Leopold he will die should he burn the cards containing Isidore's words of wisdom. When Leopold asserts himself by setting fire to a card, Isidore trips him and shouts: "There! You died." But Leopold springs to his feet insisting that he only tripped, thus rebelling against Isidore's authority.

The Successful Life of 3 (1965) exhibits, according to Richard Gilman, Fornés's "occupation of a domain strategically removed from our own not by extravagant fantasy but by a simplicity and matter-of-factness that are much more mysterious." He goes on to suggest that the correct style for staging the play would be "doing it as though it were a movie...with the film's freedom precisely from the oppressions of finite time and space...eliminating all the integuments, the texture of verisimilitude and logical connection which...Fornés had excluded as part of her principle of writing."

A vivid example of the cinematic influence in *The Successful Life of 3* is the use of "freeze" shots of the characters. Three people assume characteristic expressions at certain moments in the play: He ("handsome young man") "looks disdainful"; She ("sexy young lady") "thinks with a stupid expression"; 3 ("plump, middle-aged man") "looks with intense curiosity." The three stereotyped characters form an absurd triangle which both replicates and undermines conventional romantic notions. The illogical use of time and space and the parodies of masculine rivalry, financial success, justice, and roles of women all serve to subvert conventional theatrical and ethical values.

Fornés's next play, the musical *Promenade* (1965), is her greatest critical success prior to *Fefu and Her Friends* (1977). The play mixes wit and compassion, humor and tenderness, zaniness and social satire as prisoners named 105 and 106 journey from prison out into the world and back again. Fornés's lyrics (aided by the music of Rev. Al Carmine) comment on unrequited love, the abuse of power, the injustice of those who are supposed to uphold the law, and the illogical and random nature of life. The play questions the nature of truth as the mother sings: "I have to live with my own truth / Whether you like it or not . . . I know everything. / Half of it I really know, / The rest I make up." Social criticism is evident but attenuated by the absurdity of its presentation. "Costumes / Change the course of life," as 105 and 106 discover when they place their prisoners' jackets on an injured man who is then taken away by the jailer. Although 105 and 106 have escaped into the world to "discover the appearance of sin," having been "unacquainted with evil," they soon learn to steal from the poor as well as the rich. In the last scene of the play they sing "When I was born I opened my eyes, / And when I looked around I closed them; / And when I saw how people get kicked in the head, / And kicked in the belly, and kicked in the groin, / I closed them. / My eyes are closed but I'm carefree." For *Promenade* and *The Successful Life of 3* Fornés received the Obie award for distinguished playwriting in 1965.

A *Vietnamese Wedding* (1967) was one of Fornés's two plays written to protest American involvement in Vietnam. (The other is *The Red Burning Light*, 1968.) *A Vietnamese Wedding*, originally performed as a part of the week-long protest called Angry Arts Week, is not a play, according to Fornés. She says, "Rehearsals would serve the sole purpose of getting the readers acquainted with the text and the actions of the piece. The four people conducting the piece are hosts to the members of the audience who will enact the wedding, and their behavior should be casual, gracious and unobtrusive." During the performance ten people are selected from the audience to participate in the wedding, during which the tradition of matchmaking and the symbolic objects used in the ceremony are explained.

The entire audience participates in the celebration that follows the wedding.

Dr. Kheal, first produced in 1968 at the Judson Poets' Theater, New York, is one of Fornés's most frequently performed plays. The playwright, who states she is a teacher by nature, empathizes with the eccentric Dr. Kheal, who is "very wise and wonderful in his madness." Denying that Dr. Kheal is related to fascistic teachers such as the teacher in Ionesco's *The Lesson* or Miss Margarida in *Miss Margarida's Way*, Fornés says "Dr. Kheal insults people because he is desperate, because people are so stupid. He is saying something and gets angry and frustrated because people don't understand what he says." Dr. Kheal (like Isidore in *Tango Palace*) insists he is always right because he is the master and proceeds to lecture on the elusiveness of truth, the impossibility of understanding beauty, and the mathematics of love. Alone onstage with his lectern, blackboard, and charts, Dr. Kheal, according to Gilman, offers "a wholly new epistemology, logical, convincing, aggressive, farseeing . . . and entirely unreal."

Molly's Dream (1968) illustrates the influence of cinema on people's dreams of romance. The play, in fact, ironically examines how fantasies are nourished by the movies. Molly, a waitress in a saloon, falls asleep and dreams of Jim, "endowed with sublime sex appeal . . . dressed in glittering lace, looking like a prince in a fairy tale." The fairy-tale atmosphere is strengthened by the appearance in her dream of John (modeled after John Wayne) and Alberta (modeled after Shirley Temple). By giving themselves to a passion, the filmic prototypes are completely transformed (John to Dracula then Superman, Alberta to Hedy Lamarr). Molly and Jim observe the transformations of John and Alberta but are too proud to fully engage in the intense passion required to establish a relationship. Molly becomes merely a silly imitation of Marlene Dietrich, which only further alienates her from Jim.

Although Jim and Molly sing "If we had met some other time perhaps / Perhaps we'll meet again some other time," the end of the play suggests that Molly has not learned from the dream. While she sleeps with her head on a table, the young man who played Jim in her dream enters and leaves the saloon. Molly awakens alone.

Fefu and Her Friends is Fornés's most successful play to date. Similar to some of her other plays in using cinematic elements and demonstrating a tenderness toward the characters, *Fefu and Her Friends* differs in being more realistic, developing characters more fully, and containing decidedly feminist content.

In the opening scene, Fefu says she envies men because "they are well together. Women are not." The play contradicts Fefu's statement by showing women laughing, relaxing, playing, and caring for one another. Eight women gather at Fefu's house ostensibly to discuss plans for a fund raising activity. Through their interaction, women relate in a way that is relatively new in theatre, and an emerging feminist consciousness is acknowledged: "Women can be wonderful with each other.... All women need to do is recognize each other and like each other and give strength to each other and respect their own minds." The dominant mood of the play is the joy of female friendship.

During the second part of the play, the audience is divided into four parts and invited into Fefu's home. These close-ups (another example of Fornés's use of cinematic style) enable members of the audience to experience the women's relationships in a more intimate manner than would be possible on a proscenium stage. In the kitchen Sue prepares chicken soup. Fornés sees the literal nourishment related to the psychological nourishment the women provide for each other. Paula sits at the kitchen table and tallies up mathematically the sum of a love affair. In the study Christina and Cindy relax in a gentle scene Fornés includes for its texture and the loveliness of the experience.

Pain and fear, however, are also depicted. Julia's paralysis reflects the suffering that strong, intelligent women can experience. Her paralysis may be caused by her identification with nature, suffering at the hands of man the hunter; she refuses to accept the patriarchal view that women are generically different from men. Fefu's hallucination toward the end of the play suggests her growing participation in Julia's vision. Christina, a conformist willing to accept the dominant patriarchal view, finds women such as Fefu frightening. Concerned with a more conventional sense of order, Christina admits that some of her way of life is endangered by Fefu's way of thinking.

Fefu and Her Friends is a feminist play presenting intelligent women who understand the distortion of women's personalities that can occur in a patriarchal world in which women are strangers about whom horrendous myths are perpetrated. "The human being is of the masculine gender," Julia recites in the prayer the Judges would have her (and all women) believe. The play counters that view by inviting the audience into a woman's home to share the pains and joys of female friendship.

Fefu and Her Friends was a critical success. Fornés received Obie awards for both her playwriting and her directing. Michael Feingold in the *Village Voice* described the play as "the only essential thing the New York theatre has added to our cultural life in the past year." Rob Baker in *After Dark* stated: "Once or twice a decade, I suppose, a play or book or song comes along and so changes the way you look at the world that theater or literature or music will never be quite the same again. *Fefu and Her Friends* is just such an experience."

Through her playful imagination, graceful sense of humor, tender concern for humanity, and exquisite understanding of dramatic structure, Fornés has created a variety of plays which provide both enjoyment and enrichment.

Source: Phyllis Mael, "Maria Irene Fornes," in *Dictionary of Literary Biography*, Vol. 7, *Twentieth-Century American Dramatists*, edited by John MacNicholas, Gale Research, 1981, pp. 188–91.

Jules Aaron

In the following review, Aaron praises Fornés's production of her own play, concluding "Fefu and Her Friends challenges our preconceptions about life and the theatre through boldly drawn women."

In the introduction to her feminist play *The Mod Donna*, Myrna Lamb characterizes woman's entrapment in traditional roles as preventing the "conception of truth, of a true feeling, a true relationship, a true intensity, a true hatred, even." In the plays of such disparate writers as Lamb, Susan Miller, Edward Bond, Wendy Wasserstein, Jack Heifner, and Maria Irene Fornes, the complex needs and relationships of women are pointedly explored. Currently, Fornes's *Fefu and Her Friends*, in its West Coast premiere in Pasadena, California, indicates a theatrical breakthrough in creating important plays about women's relationships.

Fefu and Her Friends concerns the exhilirating, constant pain of women defining their roles in the "logical world of men." In 1935, Fefu, a bright, outrageous woman, meets with seven friends in her New England country home to prepare a group presentation about education. Among the women are Julia, confined to a wheelchair with a mysterious spinal injury after witnessing the shooting of a deer, two ex-lovers, Celia and Pauline, and an educator, Emma, whose conference presentation is based on the early twentieth-century writings of acting teacher Emma Sheridan Frye. The psychological and historical details only provide the audience with tangible reference points for approaching the startling, inexplicable events of the play.

Fornes's own direction of *Fefu* is a study of space and time, logic and intuition, reality and hallucination. As Emma says, "Environment knocks on the gateway of the senses." While exploring this women's world temporarily without men, Fornes probes the audience's psychological and theatrical senses as well. In the production at the Greenhouse Theatre, the play is divided into three acts without intermission. The first and third acts take place in Fefu's living room; in the second, the audience physically moves through the bedroom, kitchen, study, and garden of Fefu's house in four audience groups (the scenes are played through four times), as interludes of the ballad "Ramona" drift over the speakers placed throughout the grounds. The opening act thus becomes a distant theatrical viewing of the situation; in the second act, "real" time is intimately and somewhat uncomfortably shared in the four spaces; and in the third act, the action drifts in surreal time between the real world of the theatre and the hallucinatory workings of the characters' minds.

The theatrical, mystical tone of the play is set by the game that Fefu plays with her husband. Within the first few minutes of the play, she picks up a rifle and "shoots" him across the lawn. He falls and plays dead. Fornes's universe is arbitrary; mundane questions of plumbing have equal validity with questions of sanity. Fefu's life and the play itself are filled with both ordinary and symbolic tasks; activities like fixing the toilet, water fights, and reunions with old lovers fill the women's lives, bringing them together. Yet, though in the last moments of the play, Fefu sees Julia walk, a moment later she is again in her wheelchair. Fefu picks up a rifle and walks out on the lawn. We hear a gun shot. As Fefu brings a dead rabbit into the room, blood inexplicably trickles down Julia's forehead.

Fornes's production, which was first performed at Padua Hills Playwright's Festival last summer, works dynamically in the cavernous main theatre, annex buildings, and grounds of the Greenhouse Theatre. The multiple realities of the play are suggested by Nora Chavooshian's finely detailed settings (combining artificial outside grounds off the living room with the natural sounds of crickets). Fornes's direction elicits fine ensemble work from the eight actresses and strong emotional responses from the audience. Fornes began as a painter and her work unfolds with bold brush strokes: as in a Munch painting, we surround Julia's bed in the claustrophobic room and uncomfortably share the horror of her hallucinations; or, evoking a Renoir landscape, we watch Fefu drift across the lawn eating an apple after a croquet game with Emma. Like remembered photographs, it is haunting and disorienting to pass other groups moving into new rooms and to catch glimpses of empty spaces which we have previously visited. The momentary connections of the women illuminate the dark hallucinatory landscapes of the characters' minds.

Fefu and Her Friends challenges our preconceptions about life and the theatre through boldly drawn women, temporarily divorced from relationships, trying to sort out the ambiguities of their lives. Julia's wound in *Fefu* is our own. Fornes provides no answers, but her women make startling strides in confronting the oppressive environment of prescribed relationships in art as well as in life.

Source: Jules Aaron, Review of *Fefu and Her Friends*, in *Theatre Journal*, Vol. 32, No. 2, May 1980, pp. 266–67.

SOURCES

Austin, Gayle, Colette Brooks, Anne Cattaneo, Marie Irene Fornes, Marjorie Bradley Kellogg, Karen Malpede, Julia Miles, Joan Schenkar, Roberta Sklar, and Elizabeth Wray, "Backtalk: The 'Woman' Playwright Issue," in the *Performing Arts Journal*, Vol. 7, No. 3, 1983, pp. 90–91.

Eder, Richard, "Fefu Takes Friends to American Place," in the *New York Times*, January 14, 1978, p. 10.

Fornes, Marie Irene, *Fefu and Her Friends*, in the *Performing Arts Journal*, Vol. 2, No. 3, Winter 1978, pp. 112–40.

Kerr, Walter, "Stage View: Two Plays Swamped by Metaphors," in the *New York Times*, January 22, 1978, p. D3.

FURTHER READING

Armstrong, Ann Elizabeth, and Kathleen Juhl, eds., *Radical Acts: Theatre and Feminist Pedagogies of Change*, Aunt Lute Books, 2007.

> This book is a collection of essays about teaching feminist theatre and includes essays by the feminist playwrights Ellen Margolis and Cherrie Moraga.

Delgado, Maria M., and Caridad Svich, eds., *Conducting a Life: Reflections on the Theatre of Marie Irene Fornes*, Smith and Kraus, 1999.

> This book is a collection of tributes and reminiscences from the wide array of people Fornes has worked with over her forty-year career. Contributors include the critic Susan Sontag and the playwright Caryl Churchill.

Esslin, Martin, *The Theatre of the Absurd*, Vintage, 2004.

> First published in 1962, Esslin's book coined the term "Theatre of the Absurd" and defined a tradition that, Esslin argues, emerged from the work of European playwrights in the 1940s.

Giard, Robert, *Particular Voices: Portraits of Gay and Lesbian Writers*, MIT Press, 1997.

> Photographer Giard published almost 200 photographs that he took of gay and lesbian writers in the 1980s. Giard captures not just playwrights but also poets, critics, historians, novelists, and activists.

Kent, Assunta Bartolomucci, *Maria Irene Fornes and Her Critics*, Greenwood Press, 1996.

> Kent's was the first full-length book dedicated to Fornes's work. The critic closely examines Fornes's writings in their historical, theoretical, and production-based contexts.

The Firebugs

MAX FRISCH

1958

Max Frisch's *The Firebugs* (first published in German as *Herr Biedermann und die Brandstifter*, and sometimes translated in English as *Biedermann and the Firebugs*), is one of the playwright's most enduring plays. It was first conceived of in a short entry in one of Frisch's diaries (*Tagebuch, 1946–1949*; Diary, 1946–1949). The original concept was similar to the final play—a parody about middle-class people who pride themselves on their generosity and open-mindedness to the point of being blind to the dangers that are threatening them. Frisch revised the diary entry into a radio play in 1951. The radio play turned out to be popular, so Frisch reworked it for the stage. The play was performed on stage for the first time in 1958.

Although the plot of the play is predictable, the clever dialogue has maintained the play's popularity. As a parable exposing the threat of Nazism, the play is also meant to lead audience members into questioning their own moral characters. The exchanges between the firebugs (two homeless arsonists who have intimidated Biedermann into allowing them to spend the night in his attic) and Biedermann are especially funny, as well as very revealing of Biedermann's attempts to hide his real feelings. The firebugs talk their way into Biedermann's home and then manipulate their host to the point that they are given beds, generous meals, the best wine and cigars, and finally the match that will bring the firebugs' arsonist plans to fruition. Biedermann

Max Frisch (AP Images)

is so blind to the firebugs' intentions that his inability to deal with them reveals Biedermann to be a man who is having a moral crisis. He must not turn away a homeless person from his home on a rainy night, must not deny a hungry person food, and must not believe that strangers will do him harm without first giving them a chance to prove themselves otherwise. Of course, the firebugs do prove that Biedermann's initial suspicions are correct, but by the time Biedermann discovers this, it is too late. He is so preoccupied by his own fear of the arsonists that he can no longer take any action except to appease the firebugs.

An English-language edition of the play was printed by Hill and Wang in 1963.

AUTHOR BIOGRAPHY

Max Frisch was a Swiss architect by training but gave up this profession when he became a successful author. He was a prolific writer throughout his life, producing plays, novels, and diaries. Many of his plays continue to be performed around the world, including his one-act drama, *The Firebugs*.

Frisch was born on May 15, 1911, in Zurich, Switzerland. His father, Franz Bruno Frisch, was Austrian. His mother, Karolina Wildermuth, was German. At college, Frisch took classes in German literature and philosophy. But after his

father died in 1932, he had to drop out of school to support his mother. He turned to journalism for his first job. This gave him the opportunity not only to hone his skills as a writer but also to travel around Europe. However, after attempting to produce literary works, he became dissatisfied with the results and gave up his dream of becoming a writer. Later, with the support of a generous family friend, he returned to school and majored in architecture, which had been his father's profession.

In 1942, Frisch opened an architect office and married Constanze von Meyenburg. They lived together for twelve years, during which time they had three children. The couple separated and then officially divorced in 1959. By this time, Frisch had written several novels, but it was his work in drama that brought him the most critical attention. His first play, *Santa Cruz* (1944), involved a journey through a dreamscape. But with his next plays, such as *Now They Are Singing Again: Attempt at a Requiem* (1945), *The Chinese Wall* (1947), *When War Was Finished* (1949), as well as *The Firebugs* (1958), Frisch began to focus more on problems he saw in the world around him, especially the effects of war. As his skill in drama improved, he had a chance to gain the acquaintance of Bertolt Brecht, famed German playwright, whose work Frisch had studied in school. Brecht's work would highly influence Frisch's writing as the playwright matured.

Frisch's success with drama gave him confidence to return to his novel writing. He wrote three major novels in the next ten years: *Stiller* (1954; I'm Not Stiller), *Homo Faber. Ein Bericht* (1957; Homo Faber: A Report), and *Mein Name sei Gantenbein* (1964; A Wilderness of Mirrors). However, it was Frisch's plays that brought him the most international fame. In 1958, he won the prestigious Georg-Buchner Prize, the greatest honor given for German-language literature. In the 1960s, Frisch's work was translated for English-speaking audiences as his *Firebugs* and his other more famous play *Andorra* (1961), a play about racial prejudice, were staged in London and in the United States for the first time. In 1985, he was given the Common Wealth Award for distinguished work in literature for his life's work.

In 1987, Frisch was invited to attend the Moscow Peace Congress, where he delivered a speech about working toward world peace. He died of cancer on April 4, 1991. He was living in Zurich at the time.

PLOT SUMMARY

Scene 1

Frishch's *The Firebugs* is a one-act play divided into eight scenes. All scenes take place in the main character's (Gottlieb Biedermann's) house. The play opens with a dark stage. Then a match is lit. All the audience can see is Biedermann's face in the flame of the match. Biedermann lights a cigar. Then the stage lights come on, and the audience can see that Biedermann is surrounded by firemen wearing helmets. Biedermann complains that no one, nowadays, can even light a cigar without thinking of the possibility that their houses might burn down. He throws away the lighted cigar, disgustedly, and leaves the stage.

The firemen act as a chorus (an old drama technique from ancient Greek tragedies in which a group of actors fill in the background of a play by reciting lines, often in poetic stanzas). The firemen explain that they are there to watch and listen. They are looking for dangers that others might not see. There have been many fires in the recent past, and not all of them were a matter of fate. Some fires occur because of stupidity.

Scene 2

The setting is now in the living room of the Biedermann house, where Biedermann is reading the newspaper. He complains about a report he has just read about another fire. "They ought to hang them!" he shouts. The story is about a peddler, who somehow gets himself invited into a person's home, where he is invited to spend the night in the attic. Anna, his maid, tells him that someone is waiting to talk to him. Anna refers to this person as "the peddler." Biedermann tells Anna he does not want to talk to him. He asks Anna what the peddler wants. Anna says the peddler wants kindness and humanity. Biedermann says he will throw the man out himself. But then he recounts. He is not, after all, inhuman.

Before Anna can leave, Schmitz (the peddler) enters the room. He is athletic and dressed in an outfit reminiscent of a prison uniform. Schmitz tells Biedermann not to worry. He is not a peddler. Rather, he is an unemployed wrestler. He came inside the Biedermann's house to

get out of the rain. He then apologizes for intruding.

Biedermann slowly changes his tone of voice. He offers Schmitz a cigar and some food. As Schmitz waits for Anna to bring the food, he tells Biedermann that he saw him the night before at the pub. He says that Biedermann was right to believe that all the firebugs should be hanged. He says Biedermann is the old-fashioned kind of citizen, who has a conscience. Then Schmitz asks if Biedermann has an empty bed he could spare. But before Biedermann can answer, Schmitz laughs and says he does not really need a bed. He is used to sleeping on the floor. Schmitz changes the topic, mentioning how everyone, nowadays, is so suspicious of each other. But not Biedermann, Schmitz insinuates. Biedermann still believes in people. Any one else might give him some food but then would secretly call the police to have him taken away. But not Biedermann, Schmitz says.

Anna enters the room and announces that a Mr. Knechtling is there and would like to speak to Biedermann. Knechtling is a man who used to work for Biedermann. Knechtling invented the formula for Biedermann's hair tonic. Biedermann has fired him. Knechtling has a sick wife and three kids that he has to feed, but Biedermann has no sympathy for him. Biedermann tells Anna to tell Knechtling to get a lawyer if he wants anything from him. Biedermann hears his wife coming in, and he invites Schmitz up to the attic. His wife has a heart condition, and he does not want her to be concerned about seeing Schmitz in the house.

In the attic, Biedermann shows Schmitz where he can sleep. Before Biedermann leaves, he asks Schmitz to assure him that he is not a firebug. Schmitz laughs. Downstairs, Babette hears a noise in the attic, then tells the audience that she is so proud of her husband because he faithfully checks the attic each night to make sure there are no firebugs up there.

The chorus closes the scene by reminding the audience they are always watching what is happening.

Scene 3

Biedermann and Babette are discussing Schmitz while Biedermann is preparing to leave for the office. Biedermann tries to reassure his wife that Schmitz is not a firebug. When Babette questions her husband about how he knows this, Biedermann says he asked Schmitz "point blank." He says she should not be so suspicious. Babette tells her husband he is too good. But she promises to give Schmitz breakfast before she tells him to leave.

Babette offers Schmitz breakfast. Babette tries to bring up the subject of Schmitz leaving, but Schmitz cleverly guides the conversation so that Babette begins to feel sorry for him. He tells her that she still thinks he is a firebug. Babette denies this. Schmitz then brings up a story about his childhood, during a time when he was in an orphanage. Schmitz then tells Babette that he will leave. He will go out in the rain. Then he mentions his friend Willi. Willi has told him that no one is willing to offer charity these days. Schmitz says Willi would really be surprised to see how nice Babette and her husband have been treating him. And just then the doorbell rings, and Schmitz announces that it is probably his friend Willi.

The chorus ends the scene with the statement that there are now two firebugs in the house. They talk about cowardice and fear and how blind weak people can become. They know there is evil about them, but they secretly hope they will somehow avoid it. The weak are defenseless, so that in fact, they welcome evil with open arms.

Scene 4

Schmitz and Willi Eisenring are in the attic. They are rolling big barrels into the attic. They remind each other to keep quiet, for Schmitz fears Biedermann may call the police. Eisenring does not think so. He says Biedermann is just as guilty as they are. The reason is that Biedermann makes too much money.

Biedermann bangs on the door. When the door is opened, Biedermann tells Schmitz to leave immediately or his wife will call the police. Biedermann is angry because of all the noise. When Biedermann sees Eisenring, he is taken aback. When he asks why there are now two of them, Eisenring turns to Schmitz and says "Didn't I tell you? Didn't I say it's no way to act." Schmitz hangs his head in shame. The more Biedermann chastises the men for taking advantage of him, the more Eisenring berates Schmitz, as if Eisenring is taking Biedermann's side.

Biedermann notices the barrels and asks where they came from. Eisenring reads a label and says they were imported. When Biedermann complains that the whole attic is filled with the barrels, Eisenring blames Schmitz for his poor calculations. He claims that Schmitz thought the attic was much bigger. When Biedermann asks what is in the barrels, Eisenring tells him, gasoline. Biedermann thinks this is a joke, until he smells it.

A policeman appears and says Knechtling has committed suicide. When the policeman asks what is in the barrels, Biedermann lies, saying it is hair tonic.

As Biedermann attempts to leave the house, the chorus blocks his way. They try to warn him about the gasoline. Biedermann says it is not their business. He asks them why they must always imagine the worst. He tells them that he is free to think whatever he wants to think, even if that means he does not want to think at all. All he is doing is trying to be good hearted. When the chorus asks if he smells the gasoline, Biedermann replies that he smells nothing. The chorus comments on how quickly he has become used to the smell.

Scene 5

Biedermann tells Babette to fix a goose for dinner. Then he says if he reports Schmitz and Eisenring to the police he will make the two men his enemies, and then all it would take would be one match and the house would go up in flames. So he decides to invite them to dinner. Biedermann goes to the attic, where he finds Eisenring stringing a cord. Eisenring asks Biedermann if he has seen the detonator cap. Biedermann takes it as a joke. He tells Eisenring he has a sense of humor, but does not like his idea of a joke. Eisenring replies that he has learned that a joke acts as a camouflage. It is either a joke or sentiment that works best. Eisenring finds the detonator, and when Biedermann asks, Eisenring tells him the cord in his hand is the fuse. Biedermann again takes it as a joke and tells Eisenring that he cannot scare him. But he warns Eisenring to be careful, because not everyone has a sense of humor like his.

There is a brief encounter with a man who is called the Professor. Eisenring talks to him, but the Professor does not respond. The scene ends with Babette telling the Professor that she understands what he has to say is urgent, but she is busy fixing the dinner. The chorus then concludes by saying that the Professor sees no barrels and does not smell the gasoline because he deals only in abstractions, until it all explodes.

Scene 6

Biedermann is in the living room with Mrs. Knechtling, telling her he has no time to think about the dead. The widow leaves. Biedermann tells Anna to make the table setting simple—no table cloth, no silver, and no candles.

Scene 7

Biedermann walks to the front of the stage and addresses the audience, telling them that they can think what they want, but he knows that as long as the two men are well fed and are kept laughing, he is safe. He then says the idea that Schmitz and Eisenring are arsonists came on him slowly, although he was suspicious from the start.

Scene 8

Biedermann jokes with Schmitz and Eisenring at the dinner table and tells Babette that she has no sense of humor when he tells her that he helped Eisenring measure out the fuse. He laughs and says the next thing they probably will do is to ask him for some matches. Eisenring and Schmitz ask Biedermann if he has a table cloth and silverware. Biedermann tells Anna to bring out all the silver. Anna comes in with a card from the Professor, telling Biedermann that he wants to see him. Anna says the Professor says he is waiting because he wants to expose something.

Schmitz says he was once an actor, before the theater burnt to the ground. Schmitz had two lines in a play: "Who calleth?" and "EVERYMAN! EVERYMAN!" Then Schmitz calls out Biedermann's name and continues repeating it. When Biedermann asks who they are, Schmitz answers that he is the ghost of Knechtling. Eisenring reprimands Schmitz, telling him that he is making Biedermann shake. Eisenring says Biedermann is a good man. After all, he employed Knechtling for fourteen years.

Sirens are heard outside. Babette calls out "Firebugs! Firebugs!" Biedermann says he is glad the fire is not at their house. Eisenring explains that that is how they do it. They distract the fire department with one fire, so they can set another one. Biedermann asks them to stop joking. Eisenring says he is not joking. They are firebugs. They chose his house because it is situated close to the gas works. Biedermann refuses to admit that he believes they are firebugs. Instead, he thinks of them as his friends. The men say they must leave. Biedermann thinks

they are leaving because they do not believe him, and he wants to know what he can do to get them to believe him. Eisenring tells him that he can give him some matches. Biedermann does. The men leave, and the Professor enters. In very academic language that is hard to understand, the Professor reads a statement, then hands the paper to Biedermann. He says he wanted to improve the world. He watched Eisenring and Schmitz and knows exactly what they are doing. What he just recently discovered, though, is that they are doing it for the pure joy of it. The Professor then walks off the stage and sits in the audience.

Babette and Anna quiz cannot believe Biedermann gave them matches. Biedermann says that if they were firebugs, they would have had their own matches.

The play ends with the chorus. They say the story is useless because arson does not accomplish anything.

CHARACTERS

Anna

Anna is the maid in the Biedermann household. She does what she is told, whether it makes sense or not. Anna is probably a bridge between the Biedermann couple, with all their wealth, and the firebugs, who do not even have a place to live. Anna lives in the house but is not of the same social ranking as the Biedermanns, but she is better off than the firebugs who roam from one house to another in search of shelter and food. She is an objective observer of what goes on in the house; but like the Biedermanns, Anna does nothing to stop the firebugs.

Babette Biedermann

Babette is the wife of Gottlieb Biedermann. She is not easily persuaded to trust the two homeless men. However, she is completely devoted to her husband and will go along with whatever he says. Thus, she too is caught up in the trap that Schmitz and Eisenring are setting.

Schmitz, one of the firebugs, easily lures Babette into accepting his presence in her house by telling her about his difficult childhood. Babette, who was, at first, on guard of this stranger, gives in to Schmitz because he has touched her heart. However, whereas her husband thinks that the firebugs are just joking around about setting fires, Babette sees no humor in the firebugs' statements. She is more level-headed than her husband, but in spite of this, she takes no action against the firebugs. Although she may be more honest and more instinctual in her responses to the firebugs than her husband, she submits to her husband's authority, denying her own instincts.

Gottlieb Biedermann

Gottlieb Biedermann (referred to as Biedermann for most of the play), is the central character. Biedermann is a successful businessman, living a very comfortable life. It is in Biedermann's house that the play takes place.

Biedermann represents the middle-class citizen who, according to this play, tends to turn away from imposing danger because he is torn between wanting to look like an ideal citizen who maintains a sense of humanity in spite his wealth, and his own natural suspicions that something happening around him might be terribly wrong. He wants to appear to be good-hearted but only when his interests are at stake. On the one hand, Biedermann feels he has a right to dismiss a long-time employee because he believes the man is being greedy. The situation with the homeless men, however, becomes more personal. Charity, Biedermann believes, is a good trait; but his focus is narrow.

Because Biedermann does not want to appear to lack understanding when it comes to the homeless, he denies to himself what he instinctively knows to be happening right in front of him. He does not want to be called cold-hearted, at least not by either of the firebugs. He wants to be seen as someone who does not jump to conclusions when considering the poor. Biedermann represents the middle-class citizen who is comfortable in his life and therefore does not want to put himself out of his comfort zone by standing up for any kind of social injustice.

Chorus

The Chorus is a group of men dressed as firemen. Their role is to set the background of what is happening in the play, to fill in missing details, and to summon up a conclusion of what has already happened. As firemen, they fail, as it is assumed that the Biedermann house does burn. The Chorus might represent government officials who fail to stop the spread of Nazism in Europe.

Willi Eisenring

Willi Eisenring is the second firebug to show up at Biedermann's home. Eisenring's manner of manipulation of the Biedermanns differs from Schmitz's. Eisenring is more direct, using truth, which he states is the best camouflage. When, for instance, Biedermann asks what Eisenring is looking for in the attic, Eisenring tells him he is looking for a detonator cap. Eisenring's dead-serious answers to Biedermann's questions make Biedermann think the man must be joking. Eisenring also manipulates Biedermann by siding with him when Biedermann criticizes Schmitz. For example, when Biedermann says Schmitz has gone too far by inviting Eisenring to also stay in the attic, Eisenring agrees with Biedermann, criticizing Schmitz's manners. Eisenring might stand for the atrocities that were committed by the Nazis, such as the killing of millions of Jewish people. These actions were so out of the scope of ordinary citizens, they had difficulty believing the stories they heard, just as Biedermann had trouble believing Eisenring.

Mr. Knechtling

Mr. Knechtling is the employee of Mr. Biedermann's who invented the hair tonic that Biedermann sells. Knechtling asks for a percentage of the profits and he gets fired for doing so. Knechtling commits suicide by sticking his head into a gas oven. Knechtling could represent the Jewish population that was gassed in the concentration camps in Germany under Nazi rule. At the end of the play, Schmitz pulls the table cloth over his head and pretends that he is the ghost of Knechtling who has come back to haunt Biedermann.

Mrs. Knechtling

Mrs. Knechtling appears briefly in the play to talk to Biedermann after her husband has killed himself. Biedermann tells Mrs. Knechtling he has no time to talk about the dead.

Ph.D.

See The Professor

The Professor

The professor appears in the attic to watch the firebugs, as if he were studying them. Before the play ends, however, the professor declares that he wants to be disassociated from the firebugs because they are setting fires and destroying lives just for the fun of it. The professor is a satirical representation of those who live in an academic setting and study theories without fully engaging in the real world.

Sepp Schmitz

Although his friend Eisenring sometimes calls him Sepp, throughout this play he is referred to as Schmitz. Schmitz is the first to knock on the door of the Biedermann's house, asking if they have an extra bed. He is a very clever man, who mocks Biedermann without Biedermann knowing it. Schmitz also weasels his way into the house by making Biedermann feel guilty for all that he has accumulated. Schmitz tells stories about hardship in his youth. He does this to work on the Biedermann's empathy. When the Biedermanns are close to throwing Schmitz out or calling the police, Schmitz compliments them. In particular, when Schmitz first starts talking to Biedermann, he even compliments the man for saying that all the firebugs should be hanged. He tells Biedermann that he has done "exactly the right thing." Then Schmitz adds, "You're the old-time type of solid citizen." Schmitz also tells Biedermann that he is the kind of man with a conscience. Schmitz, along with his friend Eisenring, are the firebugs, the metaphor for Nazism. They represent evil, chaos, and ruin of society for pure self pleasure.

THEMES

Self-Deception

The theme of self-deception is played out through Biedermann, the main character of *The Firebugs*. Biedermann wants to believe certain things about himself that are not necessarily true. Biedermann reportedly shouts out in a pub that all firebugs should be hanged, and then later he reads a story in the newspaper about another fire in the city and repeats his sentiments about hanging any arsonist. When Schmitz later reminds Biedermann of these statements, Biedermann weakly tries to explain himself, especially when Schmitz agrees with Biedermann that all firebugs should be hanged. Of course, Schmitz is playing with Biedermann and even goes so far as to compliment Biedermann, saying that he is one of the few men left who still have a conscience. Biedermann is so flattered by Schmitz that he offers the man breakfast. He goes along with Schmitz's idealized vision of him, even though he has recently fired a loyal employee who merely asked for a bonus.

TOPICS FOR FURTHER STUDY

- Research Swiss involvement with the Nazis during World War II. Did Swiss businessmen, particularly Swiss bankers, in any way aid the Nazis? Did the Swiss government have a relationship with Germany's Nazi government? Write a paper reflecting on your findings and present the information to your class.

- Frisch won awards for his work as an architect. Find out, by researching Frisch's life, what these awards were and what they were for. Copy pictures of the buildings he designed and present them to your class, along with any other interesting details about Frisch's architecture.

- Frisch's play has been produced in every decade since it was first staged. In each decade, there have been different reasons that this play was pertinent to the audience. How do you think audiences would relate to the play today? Lead a discussion in your class on this topic. Be sure to address the following questions: What issues do you think the firebugs would symbolize in your culture today? What unaddressed dangers are currently threatening society?

- In Frisch's play, there are no scenes that are only between Schmitz and Eisenring. Create a scene between the firebugs. Stay true to their personalities but expand on what they might be thinking. Keep their sharp wit as they discuss why they are arsonists, how they expect to get away with the crime, and what they plan to do next. You might even add an introduction and conclusion by a chorus. When the scene is complete, ask a classmate to join you in delivering the lines to your class.

Instead, Biedermann begins to believe he is this rare man with a conscience, even though he shows no concern when Knechtling commits suicide over the loss of his job. Neither is there a sign of a conscience in Biedermann when Knechtling's widow comes to the house. Biedermann's only words for her then is that he has no time to talk about the dead. And yet, Biedermann continues to insist that he is a man with great humanity. Humanity is the reason Biedermann gives to his wife for allowing both Schmitz and Eisenring to stay in their house.

In order to keep himself self-deceived and to justify his assumptions about himself, Biedermann refuses to see what is happening right in front of him. When he finally admits that maybe Schmitz and Eisenring are arsonists, he is so strung up in wanting them to think he is a compassionate man, he convinces himself that if he makes friends with them, they will spare his house. Biedermann's ridiculous self-deception goes so far that he gives the firebugs a match. He cannot deny them the match because if he did, or so he believes, they will think he does not trust them, which he does not. Biedermann is easy to manipulate because he is so filled with his own self-deception.

Apathy

The theme of apathy is also played out through Biedermann but with a little help from the chorus of firemen and the Professor. One definition of the word *apathy* is a lack of concern. Actually the professor, despite his small role in this play, may be the most apathetic character. He studies the firebugs on an abstract level. They make an interesting subject. He wants to observe them to figure out why they do what they do. In other words, he tries to define them, which requires that he take an objective stance. But when cities are burning down around him, it would seem that he might want to come forward and show some concern. However, he does not. The only concern he demonstrates is for his own benefit, at the end, when he jumps off the stage. He has discovered that the firebugs act for no better reason than for their own enjoyment, which offends the professor. His subjects no longer interest him after this discovery, and he signs a statement to make it clear that he does not want to have anything more to do with them. But he does not try to stop their actions.

The chorus of firemen do not take action either, although they warn Biedermann to watch out because danger is lurking around him. They know what Schmitz and Eisenring are doing in the attic and yet they do not stop them. A chorus is not usually directly involved in the actions of a play, but this chorus is made up of firemen, which was done for some specific purpose. If they are firemen, why do they not stop the arsonists? This may be due to the fact that Frisch wanted to use the firemen as another example of apathy.

Biedermann, Babette, and Anna are also apathetic. Anna does merely as she is told, though she senses the firebugs are up to no good. Babette, though seemingly more suspicious than her husband, allows her husband to soothe her into a state of apathy. And Biedermann, who is even more fully aware of what is going on, convinces himself that the best thing to do is to do nothing at all. A policeman comes into the attic, for example, and still Biedermann does not take action. He could have easily turned Schmitz and Eisenring over to the authorities then. But he does not. Biedermann hopes that in doing nothing, his life will remain undisturbed.

Need for Approval

Biedermann also demonstrates a need for approval. He works very hard to make Schmitz and Eisenring his friends by laughing at what he thinks are their jokes (even though the firebugs are telling Biedermann very important truths, Biedermann cannot believe them and thus thinks they are joking with him). Though the humor comes at Biedermann's expense, Biedermann dismisses his own sense of danger and laughs at the arsonists' insistence that they are indeed planning to burn down Biedermann's house. Biedermann also removes all signs of affluence, such as table cloths and silverware from the dinner table, believing that this will make the men (who are used to prison meals) feel more comfortable. When the men ask for the luxuries, Biedermann jumps up and complies with their wishes. It appears that Biedermann will do almost anything for the men so they will think of him as their friend, even giving them the matches to set his house ablaze.

Guilt

It is Biedermann through which another theme is played out. This time the theme is that of guilt. Although Biedermann is guilty of many things, most of which he does not acknowledge, there are two specific instances in which he clearly demonstrates that he feels guilty. The first is when the policeman shows up in Biedermann's attic. At this point, Schmitz and Eisenring have stacked several barrels of gasoline in the attic and are setting a fuse.

Prior to the policeman's appearance in the attic, Biedermann had been having a conversation with the firebugs, asking them what was in the barrels. Although he smells the gasoline and senses that that is what the barrels hold, when the policeman notices the barrels and asks Biedermann what is in them, Biedermann lies. He tells the policeman that the barrels are filled with hair tonic. Why does he do this? It is because he feels guilty. He wants to believe that Schmitz and Eisenring are innocent, that they merely need a place to sleep and to find food. But he cannot fully accept this, even though he tries to laugh at the men, as well as at his own foolishness. But when the policeman appears, Biedermann is awakened to the truth. He is force to fully realize the truth. But he cannot turn the firebugs over to the police. By allowing Schmitz and Eisenring to stay in his house and for turning a blind eye toward their activities, Biedermann has become an accomplice to their arson. That is why he feels guilty. Why had he not called the police earlier? How could he have allowed the men to carry all those barrels to his attic? How could he not have known what they were doing? Circumstantial evidence makes Biedermann look like an accomplice, and he knows this.

Another time that Biedermann exhibits guilt is when he strips the table of all luxuries. He has Anna set the table for dinner without the refinements, such as silver knife rests. Who but a wealthy man could afford a silver knife rest? So all the silver candle sticks and linen table cloths and napkins are stored away. All signs of Biedermann's wealth are hidden before he invites Schmitz and Eisenring to the dinner table. There are various reasons for this. Biedermann might have wanted the men to feel welcome, believing that the men were not used to having such a finely set table. However, Biedermann might have done this because he felt guilty for possessing so much wealth, so much more than the homeless men own. Biedermann wanted, in as many ways as possible, to prove that he and the firebugs were on equal ground. That was Biedermann's definition of humanity.

Manipulation

The theme of manipulation is played mostly through the firebugs. They manipulate both Biedermann and Babette throughout the play. They do this through different techniques, depending on the situation and the conversation that is taking place. Schmitz is especially good at manipulation. He begins his first conversation with Biedermann insinuating that Biedermann might be afraid of him because of his build. He tells Biedermann that he is a wrestler. In other words, Schmitz is telling Biedermann that he should not even think of throwing him out. This is very direct manipulation by intimidation. Then when Biedermann offers Schmitz some bread, Schmitz asks if that is all Biedermann has. This is slightly less direct manipulation, but nonetheless it makes Biedermann feel foolish. Of course he has more, but he had not intended on offering it. However, after being asked such a direct question, how can Biedermann lie? When the bread is offered, Schmitz asks if he can also have some cheese, meat, and tomatoes, then adds: "If it's no trouble." Of course it is no trouble, so his request is honored.

Schmitz also manipulates Biedermann by complimenting him, making Biedermann confused, not knowing if he should acknowledge the compliment or refute it. Schmitz knows that Biedermann will accept it, and thus Schmitz will get his way again. For example, when Biedermann threatens to put Schmitz out of his house, Schmitz plays on Biedermann's inflated sense of self-importance, telling Biedermann that he is a good-hearted man, one of the few that know how to be generous with strangers. Through this tactic, Schmitz manipulates Biedermann by daring Biedermann to admit that he is, in fact, not good hearted, which Biedermann cannot do. As the play nears the end, Schmitz's manipulation gains strength. It begins to grow a bit more sinister. With a table cloth draped over his head, Schmitz pretends to be Knechtling, Biedermann's former employee who committed suicide. Schmitz insinuates either that Knechtling has come to haunt Biedermann or else that Knechtling is the Angel of Death, come to claim Biedermann's life. It is at this point that Schmitz is about to leave so he really no longer needs to persuade Biedermann, so the manipulation becomes more intimidating.

Elsa Gabriele passes by the battle ruins of Berlin in October 1945 as she accompanies her family to school. The boys carry their shoes to save on wear and tear. (*Fred Ramage | Keystone Features | Getty Images*)

STYLE

The Use of a Chorus

The use of a chorus (a group of actors, or an individual, on stage who often speak in unison) in drama dates back to the ancient Greek tragedies from around the fifth century B.C.E. In the Greek plays, most of the action took place offstage, and thus the chorus was used to fill the audience in on details of what supposedly was happening away from the stage. In ancient times, the chorus did not consist of trained actors but rather singers and dancers. That is one reason why the lines for the chorus are written in a specific meter, or beat. Seldom if ever did the chorus enter into the actions of the play, although the chorus did empathize with what was going on. Rather, the chorus represented a kind of general voice of humanity. A chorus can

also been seen as a narrator, such as readers find in a novel, a voice but not a character in the story. Sometimes a chorus might also provide an analysis of what is going on in the drama. In Greek tragedy, it was customary to have twelve to fifteen members in the chorus. However, in Shakespearean plays of the sixteenth century, the usual form of a chorus was a single actor narrating the lines. Bertolt Brecht, a playwright of the twentieth century and a man who heavily influenced Frisch, also used a chorus in some of his plays. Brecht believed drama was to be used to educate audiences, and his chorus was used to make the message of his play very clear. The chorus was also used to interrupt the action of the play, to purposefully remind the audience that the play was not intended as an escape from reality, but rather to think about real issues that were occurring in ordinary life outside of the theater.

Epic Theater

Bertolt Brecht influenced Frisch's form of drama in many ways. One of these was through Brecht's use of Epic Theater, which Frisch sometimes emulated. In traditional dramatic theater, the audience sits back and is basically entertained by the play. However, in Epic Theater, the audience is drawn into the play. Frisch did this in different ways. He has his characters talk to the audience directly on several occasions. This would not usually be done in traditional drama, where the illusion of an invisible wall (sometimes called the Fourth Wall) between the audience and the stage is assumed. In a traditional staging, it is as if the audience is eavesdropping on private conversations. Not so in Epic Theater. Toward the end of Frisch's play, for example, one of the characters (the professor) actually jumps into the audience, which serves to break the imaginary dividing line between the audience and the players on the stage.

Another difference between the two forms of theater is that traditional dramatic theater tends to appeal to the emotions, whereas in Epic Theater, the emphasis is on appealing to the audience's intellect. In other words, the play's purpose is to make the audience think. Rather than identifying emotionally with the characters, in Epic Theater, the playwright wants the audience to reflect on their own lives and how their lives are affecting society. Although Epic Theater does entertain—there are humorous moments in Frisch's play, for example—the driving force behind the play is to teach the audience lessons that might cause social change. Epic Theater entails setting up the stage and performing in such a way that the audience is constantly aware that the drama is a re-enactment of reality, not reality itself. This is supposed to encourage the audience to be more critical about the material that is being presented. Very few, if any, props are used. Very bright lights flood the stage. And choruses, or cards with messages, are displayed and are often employed to interrupt the flow of dialogue and to emphasize the play's message.

Satire

Ever since the theater of the ancient Greeks, satire has been used in drama to cleverly (and openly) criticize certain aspects of society. Today, political satire is quite evident on stage, on the radio, and on television (for example the political satire of the *The Daily Show*). In Frisch's play, the satire is social, aimed at the playwright's (in particular that of Europe and the United States) middle-class societies who were very slow to take action against the Nazi agenda of genocide. Satire used in this play is aimed at correcting a lack of morality—or as the character Biedermann often refers to it—a lack of humanity. Satire is a tool that the playwright uses to open the eyes and minds of his audience. Satire can use comedy, but the message underneath is often biting—a sharply pointed criticism. Satire can be used as a form of education, as the playwright presents mockingly humorous situations that nonetheless hit home, causing the audience to leave the performance still laughing but hopefully changed in the pattern of their thoughts. Besides including clever dialogue and humor, satire often uses exaggeration to make a point. For instance, Biedermann's character is an exaggeration of how people tend to look away from some event they do not want to think about. Biedermann comes across as a buffoon in the process. This is done on purpose because the playwright wants to make sure that his satirical criticism is not missed.

HISTORICAL CONTEXT

Switzerland's Neutrality

Switzerland is a centrally located country in Europe (approximately 16,000 square miles in size) that comes under the cultural influences of the countries that border it, namely, Germany, Italy, France, Austria, and Liechtenstein. The land surface is made up of mostly mountain ranges and valleys, and the country has few natural resources. Politically, Switzerland is divided into twenty-six cantons (similar to states) and is governed by what is referred to as a direct democracy (voters have the right to present the government with referendums to void laws they do not agree with). Although there are many languages and dialects spoken in the country, there are only four officially recognized languages: German, French, Italian, and Romansh. As of 2007, Switzerland, which is considered an isolationist country by tradition, had not joined the European Union.

Historically, Switzerland did not have a unified government until the French took control in

COMPARE & CONTRAST

- **1950s:** The world is recovering from the damage caused by the spread of Nazism, its planned genocide of non-Aryan people, and World War II.

  Today: Although outlawed in many European countries, Neo-Nazi groups still exist on the fringe of society, and they continue to recruit new members, mostly in Europe and in the United States. Websites, music bands, and other media produced by Neo-Nazis reflect the philosophy of anti-Semitism, racism, and homophobia.

- **1950s:** Frisch's play *Firebugs* is staged in Europe and the United States as a statement against the social pressure to go along with the war policies of the Nazi regime. The

  play is influenced by the atrocities of World War II.

  Today: Tim Robbins, a famous actor and playwright, is loudly criticized after his play *Embedded* opens in Los Angeles. The play is meant to raise the audience's consciousness about, and be a protest against, the war in Iraq.

- **1950s:** Switzerland creates a five-year plan to build its military in order to defend its right to neutrality.

  Today: Swiss voters attempt to abolish the Swiss militia entirely. The bill does not pass. However, the number of active members in the militia, as well as the military budget, is significantly reduced.

1798 and created a constitution that brought the governance of the country together and dissolved the cantons. This proved very unpopular, as the citizens of this region relied heavily on tradition, which the French government was trying to destroy. In the next decades, there were civil uprisings as well as invasions from Russia and Austria. However, through the Congress of Vienna in 1815, Switzerland regained its independence and was declared by the then-European powers a permanently neutral territory. One more small war broke out in the Swiss territory, this time a civil uprising between the Catholics and Protestants. This uprising lasted only one month, and at the end, in 1849, the leaders of both sides created a new constitution. That was the last battle that was ever fought on Swiss soil.

During World War I and World War II, Switzerland proclaimed neutrality. Although Swiss armies guarded the borders and may have been the determining factor for German forces not entering the country during World War II, the Swiss soldiers were not involved in any battles. However, there have been allegations that

the Swiss neutrality might have been compromised in that they banked money stolen from the German Jewish population by the Nazis. Also interesting to note, Switzerland housed many Allied officials who spied on Germany, which some have claimed aided in the defeat of Nazi Germany.

Switzerland is one of the more affluent countries in Europe and enjoys one of the lowest rates of unemployment. Banking is a large industry in Switzerland, and because of its nondisclosure agreement (people can deposit money in Swiss banks without fear that their finances will be disclosed to government authorities), large sums of money are deposited in Swiss banks, sometimes for reasons that are not legal, such as money laundering in the drug trade or tax evasion by wealthy foreigners. Also, because the Swiss have to import much of their food and other products, it has been inferred that in the past, one reason Switzerland may not have become involved in trying to stop the spread of Nazism during the 1940s was because their largest trade partner was (and still is) Germany.

View across the Limmat River and the old town of Zürich from the top of Grossmünster church (© Eric Nathan | Alamy)

Nazism and Adolph Hitler

Nazism generally refers to National Socialism, or the ideology held by the National Socialist German Workers' Party, for which Adolph Hitler (1889–1945) was appointed the chancellor, in 1933, and was given dictatorial rights. Nazis reigned in Germany from 1933 to 1945, when the Allies outlawed the Nazi party after the defeat of Germany at the end of World War II. Nazism was a totalitarian form of government under which everything was controlled by the governing body. Nazism has its roots in various ideologies, but one of the major beliefs is of a pure Aryan race made up of people of Nordic ancestry. Nazis attempted to purge the German population of people who were not of Nordic heritage, thus purifying the German society. Nazis believed that the Aryan race was superior to all other ethnicities. Hitler worried that if Germans were allowed to marry people of other ethnicities, the Aryan race would be polluted. Hitler's ideas were recorded in a publication called *Mein Kempf* (1925–1926). In this book, Hitler claimed that there was a Jewish conspiracy to take over the world. Hitler was intent on stopping this from happening. Hitler was very much opposed to democracy and believed that a successful government was best run by one wise leader. Other groups that Hitler did not approve of included people of African descent, the Romani tribes, homosexuals, and people with physical impairments or illnesses.

On September 1, 1939, Nazi Germany invaded Poland. Two days later, the United Kingdom and France declared war on Germany, and World War II had begun. Germany pressed on to invade Norway and Denmark. France was Germany's next conquest. Germany also heavily bombed England and gained land in northern Africa and Yugoslavia. In 1941, German troops entered the Soviet Union (Russia). There seemed no chance of stopping the Nazis. Only a few European countries remained clear of the German threat, and this included Switzerland, Sweden, Portugal, and Spain. After the United States declared war on Japan as a result of the bombing of Pearl Harbor in December of 1941, Hitler declared war on the United States. As the countries in Europe came under the control of the Nazis, the Nazi policy of ethnic cleansing began in each newly-overrun country. The persecution, especially of Jews, in all conquered countries, was pointedly pursued.

Bertolt Brecht (1898–1956)

Bertolt Brecht, one of Germany's most famous playwrights and poets, was a strong influence on Frisch's dramatic writing. Threatened by the rise of Nazism, which caused strict censorship of his work, Brecht went into self-exile, living in Denmark, in Sweden, and in the United States during World War II, a time during which he wrote most of his successful plays. Brecht developed his own theories for drama, including his Epic Theatre concept. Brecht also believed in what he called the alienation effect (*Verfremdungseffekt* in German), through which he constantly kept his audiences distracted so they would not become emotionally involved in the plays. For example, actors might change characters right in front of the audience in the middle of a scene. Brecht wanted his audiences to remain detached emotionally so they would be able to critically analyze the messages his dramas were portraying. Some of Brecht's plays that are translated into English include *The Three Penny Opera* (1928); *Life of Galileo* (1938); and *Mother Courage and Her Children* (1939). Some of Brecht's influences in drama included the Japanese form of drama called Noh and Greek tragedy, both of which use choruses to put forward a narrative on stage.

CRITICAL OVERVIEW

Frisch's satirical drama *The Firebugs* is often referred to as a commentary on the spread of Nazism across Europe during the 1930s and 1940s and the willingness of some middle-class citizens (especially the Swiss middle class, of which the author was a part) to ignore the dangers inherent in this political philosophy. Although not widely reviewed, the play has also been called an absurd comedy about moral depravity and self-deception. Other comments that are often repeated in regards to this play concern the play's ability to remain relevant in contemporary society, fifty years after it was first staged.

The first U.S. production of Frisch's play was reviewed by Howard Taubman, writing for the *New York Times*. The play was produced off-Broadway, which means it was not staged in a major theater. The response to the play was mixed at this time, some reviewers, such as Taubman, remark on the fact that some of the effects of the play, such as the Chorus, might be a little too European for U.S. audiences. However, Taubman praises the play, which he finds to be "so broad that it often resembles a burlesqued charade." However, Taubman adds that "the subject is no laughing matter. Mr. Frisch's lightest banter is dusted with ironic fallout."

Vincent Canby, also writing in the *New York Times*, states that the play "is not so much a conventional play as an eight-scene climax, a dramatized convulsion that cannot be stopped any more easily than can a sneeze once started." Canby was reviewing an Americanized version of Frisch's play, in which the firebugs are black and the Biedermanns are white, thus adding the theme of racism to the drama. Canby finds the racial issues in this version to be "quite valid."

There was also a German-language production of Frisch's play in the United States in the late 1960s, a time when the country was deeply involved in the Vietnam War. Henry Raymont, writing for the *New York Times*, quotes Maria Becker, the leading actress of this production, as saying that in previous years, the play may not have been as pertinent to people in the United States, but "the dehumanization of the Vietnam war, has changed all this." Raymont describes the play as one that "probes piercingly into the subject of individual responsibility for social and political condition."

Bruce Weber, writing for the *New York Times*, states that Frisch's play is "an acrid comic parable about the lily-livered middle class." Weber continues his description by referring to the play as "Frisch's condemnation of Swiss neutrality during the rise of Nazism," further commenting that it "decries the complacency of comfortable citizens in threatening times." Weber says that despite the fact that the audience immediately understands who the bad guys are, the play is not a simple one. On the contrary, Weber claims that Frisch was not afraid of dealing with ambiguities. His characters are both scorned for their ignorance and empathized with for their misguided actions.

WHAT DO I READ NEXT?

- Frisch's novel *I'm Not Stiller* was originally published in 1954. The story is about Anatol Stiller, a wanted man who disappears from his home town in Switzerland and then apparently reappears seven years later. Police question the protagonist of this novel, who denies that he is the man they are looking for. Readers come to their own conclusions as to whether or not this man is, or is not, Stiller. The story is full of angst and psychological depth.

- Friedrich Dürrenmatt was a contemporary of Frisch's and is often mentioned along with Frisch as one of Switzerland's most famous playwrights. Dürrenmatt's *Physicists* (1962) is a play about three men living in a mental institution who claim to be famous scientists. The play is centered on the role of science and its potential to destroy the world, a theme that is just as current today as when the play was first conceived.

- Switzerland's neutrality during World War II and its influence on the literature and society of this small country is examined in a series of essays in *Switzerland and War* (2000), edited by Joy Charnley and Malcolm Pender. Although Switzerland remained neutral during the war, the country was affected by the war around them, and continues to defend itself against accusations that the Swiss government aided Nazi Germany's war efforts.

- Frisch published two sketchbooks (*Sketchbook: 1946–1949* [1950] and *Sketchbook: 1966–1971* [1972]). These are collections that Frisch kept of his reflections on economics, politics, and society. Also included are interviews and ideas for future stories and plays. They provide an inside look at how the playwright thought and felt.

- Bertolt Brecht was a mentor of Frisch's and also a very celebrated dramatist. One of Brecht's plays that has been popular in the United States is *The Caucasian Circle*, first produced in 1947. The play was adapted from a thirteenth-century Chinese drama in which two communities fight over a piece of land.

The "themes of denial and self-justification," in the play still "have resonance today."

CRITICISM

Joyce M. Hart

Hart has degrees in English and creative writing and is a freelance writer and published author. In this essay, she examines how Frisch uses satire in his drama, bringing humor, wit, sarcasm, and tragedy together to deliver his message.

Frisch uses satire in his play *The Firebugs* to deliver his commentary on middle-class society, and to waken audiences to the problems he saw in relationship to the lack of action made toward abating the rise of Nazism. Indeed, the purpose of satire is not to entertain. Rather, satire is most often meant to bring about social or political change. In Frisch's play, humor, sarcasm, irony, and tragedy are employed as a means to communicate a moral lesson.

In scene 5 of *The Firebugs*, just as Eisenring is laying out the fuse that will light the barrels of gasoline in Biedermann's attic, Biedermann questions Eisenring about why he continually tells jokes. Eisenring responds: "That's something we've learned." When Biedermann asks for more information, Eisenring adds: "A joke is good camouflage." Indeed, this is also the approach that Frisch has taken as a dramatist.

> BY RIDICULING BIEDERMANN, THE STAND-IN FOR THE MIDDLE-CLASS, FRISCH USES HUMOR TO CAMOUFLAGE HIS MESSAGE THAT COMPLACENCY IS A DANGEROUS STANCE THAT WILL ULTIMATELY LEAD TO TRAGEDY."

The object, or victim, of much of the play's humor is Biedermann, who, in this case, stands for middle-class society, those who are comfortable with life. Their basic needs are met, and they can afford small luxuries. Because of this, they may forget about those who do not live as they do; nor are they compelled to political action in the same way as people whose basic needs are not being met. By ridiculing Biedermann, the stand-in for the middle-class, Frisch uses humor to camouflage his message that complacency is a dangerous stance that will ultimately lead to tragedy.

Biedermann is a man without a backbone. He makes grand statements, such as his opening remarks that all arsonists should be hung. But as soon as Schmitz begins questioning Biedermann's sense of humanity, Biedermann capitulates. Schmitz does this by using wit. First he agrees with Biedermann for believing that arsonists should be put to death. Then he praises Biedermann for saying so. Whereas Biedermann felt righteous in making his statements at first, now that he hears Schmitz agree with him, Biedermann begins to question himself. Schmitz continues by stating that Biedermann has a conscience. But Frisch cleverly switches this statement from meaning something positive to becoming insulting. As soon as Schmitz makes the comment that Biedermann might be one of the last men with a conscience, he adds a story about the circus owner he used to work for. The owner reportedly said "If anybody has a conscience, you can bet it's a bad one." This statement makes Biedermann a bit uneasy and the comment that the circus owner died in a fire makes Biedermann change the subject.

Just a few lines later in the same scene, Schmitz ridicules Biedermann, quite subtly and quite effectively. He relates that Anna has told him that there is not an empty bed in the house. It is obvious to Schmitz that this is not the truth. He probably had been watching the house for several days and knew that there were only three people living in the large home. So Schmitz tells Biedermann that that is what everyone says. So Schmitz turns the tables on Biedermann again, by telling him that it does not matter. Schmitz is used to sleeping on the floor. In doing this, Schmitz has stolen Biedermann's excuse for turning him out. Saying that there are no empty beds is an easy (and supposedly gentle or at least non-confrontational) way of turning homeless people away. In case Biedermann is still thinking of getting rid of Schmitz, the firebug mentions that he was brought up poor. Everyone in the audience probably recognizes Schmitz's tactic of using pity to get his way, but not Biedermann. Biedermann is upright and proud of himself. He will not allow himself to be considered one of those people who mistrust poor people. Schmitz is both making fun of Biedermann and manipulating him at the same time. Schmitz is taking full advantage, through his wit, of Biedermann's inflated self-image, and, slowly but surely, he is exposing Biedermann as the fool that he is.

Sarcasm comes into play when Biedermann discusses Mr. Knechtling, the employee he has recently fired. Knechtling tries to speak with Biedermann, but Biedermann tells Anna that Knechtling can "stick his head in the gas stove or get a lawyer!" Biedermann becomes self-conscious when he remembers that Schmitz is sitting in the room with him. And Schmitz jumps right on the opportunity. He immediately asks, "Who'd have thought you could still find it, these days?" When Biedermann asks what he is talking about, Schmitz replies, "Humanity!" Of course, Schmitz pretends to be referring to the fact that Biedermann has not yet thrown him out of his house and has graciously offered him food. However, Schmitz is also being sarcastic. No one with any sense of humanity would tell a depressed person to stick their head in a gas stove. Schmitz also adds the phrase, "God will reward you!" Schmitz is sarcastically referred to the fact that he is planning on burning down Biedermann's house. Biedermann tries to collect himself, telling Schmitz that he should not think of him as being inhuman, especially after his obvious comment about Knechtling. And once again, Schmitz uses Biedermann's concern to his advantage. Schmitz challenges Biedermann,

BIEDERMANN UND DIE BRANDSTIFTER, SUBTITLED *EIN LEHRSTÜCK OHNE LEHRE* (A DIDACTIC PLAY WITHOUT A LESSON), IS THE FIRST OF FRISCH'S PARABLE PLAYS. BIEDERMANN IS NOT AN INDIVIDUAL BUT A TYPE: THE BUSINESSMAN WHO COMBINES PLEASANT BEHAVIOR WITH RUTHLESS BRUTALITY IN ORDER TO SUCCEED IN THE CAPITALIST WORLD; HE IS AN OPPORTUNIST AND A COWARD."

again using sarcasm, by stating what has not yet been proven to be true. Schmitz says: "Would you be giving me a place to sleep tonight if you were inhuman?—Ridiculous!"

Irony is used when Babette enters the play. She hears a noise in the attic and is at first frightened (as she should be). But then she remembers her husband, and his attentiveness (or so she thinks) to the problem of the firebugs. She comments to the audience that ever since the threat of arson has become so widespread, her husband vigilantly checks the attic every night to assure her that their house is safe. She is very thankful for this. He does this so she can sleep well at night. Babette's fault is her innocence and her complete trust in her husband. Rather than trusting her own intuitions, she relieves herself of any responsibility for her own safety. Instead, she relies on her husband's good sense, which the audience already knows does not exist.

The tragedy of the play is not that Biedermann's house will be burnt down, but rather than he does nothing to stop it. He takes no action, not because he is incapable of doing so or does not know what is going on, but because of his own tragic flaw: weakness. He has built himself up on the labor and wit of others. When it comes time for him to truly face a situation, he is not able to react. Biedermann is manipulated by people who are smarter than he is; people who understand the flaws in his character. Biedermann has constructed his sense of self in a manner that does not reflect his true personality. He has lied to himself, and Schmitz and Eisenring, the firebugs, can see right

through him. In some part, Biedermann understands this, and he does not want the firebugs to expose him to anyone else. It is bad enough that they know that he is a fake. And so the house will burn. Biedermann, Babette, and Anna may die, as might the community around them, all because of Biedermann's tragic flaw.

Source: Joyce M. Hart, Critical Essay on *The Firebugs*, in *Drama for Students*, Gale, Cengage Learning, 2008.

Ehrhard Bahr

In the following excerpt, Bahr gives a critical analysis of Frisch's life and work.

German drama during the 1950s would be unthinkable without the works of Max Frisch and Friedrich Dürrenmatt; the lack of postwar drama in West Germany was made up for by these two Swiss playwrights between 1945 and 1960. They were the best qualified to fill this vacuum because they were writing in German and were so close to the situation in postwar Germany, yet they were not politically compromised by previous accommodation with the Nazi regime. Furthermore, they had stayed in close contact with the development of modernist drama—in particular German exile drama, which had found a haven at the Zurich Schauspielhaus (Playhouse). Plays by exiled dramatists such as Bertolt Brecht, Ferdinand Bruckner, Ödön von Horvàth, Friedrich Wolf, and Carl Zuckmayer had been produced there during the 1930s and 1940s, and some of the best German actors and directors had found employment in Zurich after 1933. The Zurich Schauspielhaus was thus an ideal place for young dramatists to learn their trade. Dürrenmatt and Frisch made use of the opportunity offered to them in the 1940s, and they found inspiration for their own works from the plays produced at the Schauspielhaus. By the 1960s Frisch and Dürrenmatt were internationally recognized dramatists whose plays were translated into many languages and performed in many countries. Although Frisch became increasingly disappointed with the inertia of the technical apparatus of the theater and neglected drama in the 1970s and 1980s in favor of prose, he never abandoned it.

Frisch was born in Zurich on 15 May 1911 to Franz Frisch, an archictect, and Lina Wildermuth Frisch. His mother's family had immigrated to Switzerland from Württemberg, Germany. Frisch studied German literature at the University of Zurich from 1931 until his father died in 1933; he then left school and became a freelance journalist, writing mainly for the *Neue Zürcher Zeitung* (New Zurich Newspaper). In 1936 he took up the study of architecture at the Eidgenössische Technische Hochschule (Federal Institute of Technology) in Zurich. After receiving his degree in 1941 he opened an architectural office. He married Gertrud Anna Constance von Meyenburg in 1942; they had three children. In 1944 Frisch was invited to assist at rehearsals and write for the Schauspielhaus. After World War II, in which he served as a gunner on the Swiss border, Frisch won an architectural competition for a public outdoor swimming pool in Zurich, the Freibad Letzigraben, which was built from 1947 to 1949. The first play he wrote, *Santa Cruz*, was performed in 1946 and was published in 1947; his first play to be performed and published was *Nun singen sie wieder* (performed, 1945; published, 1946; translated as *Now They Sing Again*, 1972). They were followed by *Die chinesische Mauer* (performed, 1946; published, 1947; translated as *The Chinese Wall*, 1961).

Santa Cruz is a dream play. Santa Cruz is not a geographical place but a realm of dreams and self-fulfillment. Its opposite is a castle in a wintry European landscape that stands for reality, marriage, and renunciation. Past and present are synchronized in the dream action of the play. An adventurer and a cavalry officer court the same woman; she opts for marriage and reality but cannot give up her dreams. Neither can her husband, whose alter ego is the adventurer. Only when the adventurer within him dies can the officer and his wife find peace in their life in the castle. Frisch's first play shows the influence of Hugo von Hofmannsthal and Paul Claudel.

Nun singen sie wieder, subtitled *Versuch eines Requiems* (Attempt at a Requiem), deals with war crimes and the vain hope of a moral change. After ordering the shooting of twenty-one hostages, Karl deserts from the army and hangs himself. His wife and child perish in an air raid. The members of the enemy air force are killed in action. The dead celebrate their symbolic requiem with bread and wine. They are committed to a change in spirit, but the survivors do not hear their message. Their deaths will have been in vain unless the audience listens to the song of the hostages, who died singing. Frisch's stage directions specified that scenery was to be present only to the extent that the actors needed it; in no case was it to simulate reality. The impression of a play on a stage was to be preserved throughout. Showing the influence of Thornton Wilder's *Our Town* (1938), the play fails as a Zeitstück (play dealing with current events) because neither time nor place is defined.

Die chinesische Mauer, revised in 1955, 1965, and 1972, is a farce. Its subject is the endless cycle of human self-destruction. The construction of the Great Wall of China around 200 B.C. is an allegory for the atomic bomb. Anachronism is the main principle of the play; the characters include "Der Heutige" (Today's Man), Romeo and Juliet, Napoleon Bonaparte, Christopher Columbus, Don Juan, Pontius Pilate, Brutus, Philip of Spain, Cleopatra, Emile Zola, and Ivan the Terrible. Instead of traditional dramatic conflict, there is a constant exchange of quotations, referring to events of the past. Even with his knowledge of history, Der Heutige cannot stop the cycle.

In 1948 Frisch met Brecht, whose theory of the epic or anti-Aristotelian theater would continue to exercise considerable influence on Frisch's dramatic production until the early 1960s. Frisch's fourth play, *Als der Krieg zu Ende war* (When the War was Over, 1949), is set after the fall of Berlin in 1945. Agnes, a German woman, plans to kill a Soviet colonel while her German husband hides in the cellar. Although neither understands the language of the other, the colonel and Agnes overcome prejudice and fall in love. When the colonel learns that Agnes's husband had participated in the massacre of Jews in the Warsaw Ghetto in 1943, he leaves rather than arresting her husband as a war criminal. Brecht wanted Frisch to take a stand in favor of the Soviet "liberation" of Germany, but Frisch considered the conflict between humanity and inhumanity the main theme of the play.

Frisch spent 1951 and 1952 in the United States and Mexico on a Rockefeller grant. His next two plays were *Graf Öderland* (1951; translated as *Count Oederland*, 1962) and *Don Juan oder Die Liebe zur Geometrie* (1953; translated as *Don Juan; or, The Love of Geometry*, 1967). *Biedermann und die Brandstifter* (1958; translated as *The Fire Raisers*, 1962), first written as a radio drama, is one of Frisch's most provocative plays.

Graf Öderland, which underwent two revisions after its premiere in 1951, was a failure because it does not provide convincing motivation for the protagonist's actions. An ambitious state prosecutor changes into an ax murderer with romantically anarchistic notions. But as he overthrows power in order to be free, he is taking over the opposite of freedom: power. Finally the revolutionary takes over as dictator of a new government. At the end Öderland desperately wants to wake up from the nightmare of murder and anarchy he has created. Frisch expressly rejected an interpretation of the play as an allegory about Adolf Hitler or a critique of modern democracy.

In *Don Juan oder Die Liebe zur Geometrie* Don Juan is an intellectual in search of his identity. He tries to escape his destined role as a seducer by loving geometry more than women, but the power of the myth catches up with him. He stages his death and descent into hell so as to escape to his first love, geometry. This escape is denied to him, but he experiences his own hell after he marries Miranda, a former prostitute. He becomes a prisoner in his own castle: he cannot leave the castle because he would then have to live as Don Juan again. He ends up as a henpecked husband and father, reading about his own legend in the 1630 version by Tirso de Molina.

Biedermann und die Brandstifter, subtitled *Ein Lehrstück ohne Lehre* (A Didactic Play without a Lesson), is the first of Frisch's parable plays. Biedermann is not an individual but a type: the businessman who combines pleasant behavior with ruthless brutality in order to succeed in the capitalist world; he is an opportunist and a coward. Because of lack of courage Biedermann allows two suspicious vagrants to camp in his attic, even though there have been newspaper reports about arsonists disguised as peddlers asking for a place to sleep. The vagrants store gasoline barrels in Biedermann's attic and openly handle detonators and fuses in front of him. He cooperates because he does not want to make them his enemies. On the other hand, he has no scruples about driving his employee Knechtling to suicide, because he has nothing to fear from Knechtling. Concerned only with saving himself and his house, Biedermann serves the arsonists a sumptuous dinner; in the end he provides them with the matches they use to set his house on fire. Biedermann and his wife perish in the flames. A chorus of firemen provides commentary in a parody of Greek tragedy. In 1959 Frisch added a "Nachspiel" (epilogue) showing Biedermann and his wife in hell, unchanged and as foolish as ever. Frisch rejected any political interpretation of his "didactic play" as an

allegory of the Nazi burning of the Reichstag in 1933 or the Communist takeover of Czechoslovakia in 1948. Unlike Brecht, who wanted to change the world with his theater, Frisch did not believe in the revolutionizing effect of the stage. Also, in spite of the absurd aspects of the plot, Frisch did not want his play to be understood as theater of the absurd. Denouncing Eugène Ionesco and his followers, Frisch declared in 1964 that a public that finds satisfaction in absurdity would be a dictator's delight.

Die große Wut des Philipp Hotz (The Great Madness of Philipp Hotz, published, 1958) is a "Schwank" (slapstick farce) that premiered together with *Biedermann und die Brandstifter* in 1958. The conventional stereotype of the intellectual who is unable to act, Philipp Hotz attempts to break out of the prison of his daily life by locking his wife in a closet, destroying the furniture that symbolizes the bourgeois existence from which he wants to escape, and enlisting in the French foreign legion. Hotz even fabricates an adultery that he has not committed. All his efforts to be taken seriously end in failure. Rejected by the foreign legion because he is nearsighted, he returns to his wife and home and the routines of his daily life.

In 1958 Frisch was awarded the Georg Büchner Prize by the German Academy of Literature in Darmstadt, the Literature Prize of the City of Zurich, and the Veillon Prize of Lausanne. In 1959 he was divorced from his first wife. In 1961 he moved to Rome. That year he had his greatest success on the stage with *Andorra* (published, 1961; translated, 1964). The twelve scenes of *Andorra* are linked by statements made by various characters as they step out of the action of the play to give accounts of their deeds and motivations from a witness box in the foreground of the stage. With the exceptions of Andri and Barblin, the characters are mere types without names. Andri is a young man who is thought to be a Jew who was rescued from persecution by the Schwarzen (Blacks) across the frontier and adopted by the local teacher. Andri is, however, the teacher's illegitimate son by the Señora, a woman from across the border. Although he is not Jewish, the prejudices of his social environment impress on Andri the supposedly Jewish characteristics that he finally accepts, even after he learns of his non-Jewish origin. When he falls in love with Barblin, who—unknown to him—is his half sister, Andri believes that his foster father objects to the affair because he is Jewish. Andri perishes as a Jew when the Schwarzen invade Andorra and take him away, while Barblin's head is shaved because she is considered the Judenhure (Jew's whore). Nobody offers any resistance to the invasion by the Schwarzen. Everybody is guilty, including the teacher, who invented the pious lie of adopting a Jewish child instead of confessing to his illegitimate son; he hangs himself in the schoolroom. The Andorra of this play has nothing to do with the actual state of this name; Frisch said in his notes to the play that Andorra is the prototype of a society ruled by prejudice and fear. There are unmistakable allusions to Switzerland and its relationship to Nazi Germany, even though Frisch stressed in his stage directions that, for example, in the uniform of the Schwarzen any resemblance to the uniforms of the past should be avoided. *Andorra* was criticized for "obscuring rather than analyzing the aberration of anti-Semitism" and of minimizing the Holocaust.

In 1965 Frisch moved to the Ticino, in southern Switzerland. That same year he received the Schiller Prize of Baden-Württemberg. His comedy *Biografie: Ein Spiel* (published, 1967; translated as *Biography: A Game*, 1969) was first produced in 1968. The play, whose subtitle means both "A Play" and "A Game," is introduced by a "Registrator" (chronicler), who reads the stage directions at a lectern. Kürmann, a professor of psychology, wants to start his life over again, like an actor repeating a scene during a rehearsal. He is convinced that he knows exactly what he would do differently. The Registrator and Kürmann's wife Antoinette agree to let him repeat the scene, but it leads to the same result. All other attempts to change the outcome of his life also fail: he is invariably confronted by death from cancer within seven years. Kümann is limited by his own identity; any particular scene of his life could have been different, but Kürmann cannot adopt a different personality. As Frisch said in his notes to the play, the theater grants an opportunity that reality denies: to repeat, to rehearse, to change.

In 1969 Frisch married Marianne Oellers; the marriage ended in divorce a few years later. After traveling to Japan he was a guest lecturer at Columbia University in New York in 1970-1971. In 1974 he received the Great Schiller Prize

of the Swiss Schiller Foundation and became an honorary member of the American Academy of Arts and Letters and the National Institute of Arts and Letters. In 1975 he traveled to China. He received the Peace Prize of the German Book Trade in 1976. His *Triptychon: Drei szenische Bilder* (translated as *Triptych: Three Scenic Panels*, 1981) was published in 1978 and premiered in 1979. *Triptychon* consists of three loosely connected scenes dealing with a common theme, that of death. The first scene deals with the embarrassment caused by the death of a seventy-year-old man; the second is a conversation among the dead, who find eternity banal; the last scene deals with the insoluble relationship between a man and his dead lover.

In November 1989 there was to be a referendum on the abolition of the military. Frisch had been a critic of the Swiss army and its ideology since 1974, when he attacked the Swiss arms industry, Swiss resistance to the immigration of political refugees, and the concept of defense by withdrawal behind an Alpine Maginot Line in his *Dienstbüchlein* (Service Booklet). His extended dialogue *Jonas und sein Veteran* (Jonas and His Veteran), which premiered in 1989, and his pamphlet *Schweiz ohne Armee? Ein Palaver* (Switzerland without an Army? A Palaver), published the same year, were Frisch's contribution to the debate on the future of the Swiss army. *Jonas und sein Veteran* consists of a ninety-minute conversation between a Swiss army veteran of 1918 and his grandson Jonas, who faces the alternatives of army service or civil disobedience and emigration. Neither alternative appeals to the young man, who is more interested in a career in computer science. His grandfather is of no help, because his advice consists of historical reminders of Swiss failures and sarcastic analyses of the army as part of Swiss folklore, as an elite unit to protect Swiss capitalism, or as a prop to shore up Swiss national identity. The dramatic dialogue discusses alternatives but does not provide a conclusion. Passages from Frisch's *Dienstbüchlein* are quoted at great length by the grandfather. The proposal to abolish the military was defeated; but it was supported by 35.6 percent of the voters, forcing the army to consider reforms.

In 1989 Frisch was awarded the Heinrich Heine Prize of the City of Düsseldorf. He died in Zurich on 4 April 1991. Although he wrote

FRISCH PROBES VARIOUS HUMAN
RELATIONSHIPS TO DISCOVER HOW GENUINE AND
HONEST THEY ARE."

extensive notes and suggestions for staging his plays, Frisch never provided a comprehensive theory of drama. He questioned the didactic effectiveness of Brecht's epic theater, doubting that anyone would ever change his or her viewpoint as a result of a stage performance. What Frisch had in common with Brecht was his rejection of attempts to imitate reality; the audience is never supposed to forget that what is happening on the stage is make-believe. Throughout his career Frisch was concerned with reminding his audience that his plays were not representations of the world but of our consciousness of the world.

Source: Ehrhard Bahr, "Max Frisch," in *Dictionary of Literary Biography*, Vol. 124, *Twentieth-Century German Dramatists, 1919–1992*, edited by Wolfgang D. Elfe and James Hardin, Gale Research, 1992, pp. 138–47.

Walter E. Glaettli

In the following excerpt, written in 1952, Glaettli discusses Frisch as an emerging playwright. This review explores the very themes in Frisch's earlier works that would later reappear in The Firebugs, *thus providing further insight on the play.*

... One of the outstanding representatives of modern German drama whose reputation as a playwright is becoming increasingly widespread is Max Frisch, a native of Zurich who has thus far written five plays, *Santa Cruz, Nun singen sie wieder, Die chinesische Mauer, Als der Krieg zu Ende war* and *Graf Oderland*. We may somewhat discount Frisch's Swiss citizenship as a factor in his career as a writer, since none of his works has its setting in Switzerland. It has, on the other hand, no doubt proved an advantage by giving him, in contrast to young authors in Germany, the opportunity of observing and keeping in touch with the trends of literature in the West. An architect by profession, Fisch [sic] began his experiments in playwrighting during the war, and so he gained a lead which made it at least difficult, if not impossible, for his fellow-

playwrights in Germany to overtake him in the years immediately following it.

I have used the term "experiment" deliberately, not to imply that Frisch concerns himself principally with technical devices, but rather to indicate that he attempts in each of his plays to find *the* form of expression that will affect the reader or spectator most deeply. He is aware that the present-day author who does have something to say can fail utterly to reach his public when he uses conventional dramatic forms. What Max Frisch has to say is not new; his message is the eternal one of truth and humanity. Precisely because he is imbued with great seriousness of purpose, he has resorted to surrealistic, expressionistic, and other such techniques to express his ideas.

Die chinesische Mauer, Frisch's third play (first performed in Zurich in 1946) could, like his first, *Santa Cruz* be labeled a "dream play." He himself calls it a comedy, but what he presents is a tragedy thinly disguised as a masquerade—a peculiar combination of profound thought and light, playful outward form. The setting is the court of the Chinese emperor Hwang Ti, who is giving a garden party at which there is much talk both of the completion of the Great Wall and of a glorious victory in battle. Among the Emperor's guests are such historic and fictitious celebrities as Columbus, Cleopatra, Don Juan, Napoleon, and Romeo and Juliet, and one can scarcely help noticing that the Emperor's speech about the unequaled heroism of his army has the empty ring of Hitler's ravings.

The setting of the play is thus in actuality the entire world; the time is all times, past and present.

... Though *Die chinesische Mauer* is not a problem play, the innumerable anachronisms perform somewhat the same function. The fusion of all times and places is used to show that man remains essentially the same irrespective of when and where he lives. Frisch's characters are, however, by no means stripped of their personal characteristics and reduced to mere "existences." They are completely portrayed people whose rich variety gives the play its comedy-like atmosphere. The apparently gay mood is heightened still further by the visors worn by the participants. These masks are the visible symbols of the spiritual mask that each of us wears. The mask motif and the concept that "All the world's a stage and all the men and women merely players" may be derivative, but for Frisch no divine being assigns roles in the drama of life; man himself dons his mask and wears it well enough to deceive even himself. Upon occasion Frisch lifts the veil for a moment: the "actor" falls out of his role to reveal not a hidden divine order but a bare, meaningless *Nichts*. Just as the mask is the symbol of man's self-deception, so the great Chinese Wall is the symbol of all false illusions fettering mankind. But one character in the play wears no mask: the poet Min Ko, *ein junger Mann von heute*. He alone is aware of the falsehood and delusion entangling man and—to return to the plot—writes revolutionary songs in an attempt to arouse the nation against the despot who built the Great Wall and hence is responsible for the general deception. Yet he too fails at the crucial moment. The tyrannised masses finally rise and storm the Emperor's palace, but the revolution achieves only the completion of the fateful cycle: the hero of the people comes to power as the new dictator, and one may well prophesy the replacement of the Great Wall with a bigger and better one.

Als der Krieg zu Ende war (1948) is a more realistic drama. It takes place in 1945, immediately after the war, in the living room and cellar of a partially bombed house in Berlin. The living room is occupied by a group of Russian officers and soldiers; the cellar is the hiding place of the previous owners of the house, Captain Anders, a *Heimkehrer*, and his wife Agnes. Discovered by the Russians, Agnes, in order to save her husband, sacrifices herself by consenting to visit the Russian colonel each day on the condition that the cellar is not to be entered. In contrast to the other Russians, of whom we hear only acts of cruelty and bestiality, Colonel Stepan Iwanow proves to be a man of noble mind. In the course of time Agnes' feelings toward him develop into true love. One day Captain Anders, leaving his hiding place, is caught and identified by a Jewish Russian soldier as a war criminal of the worst sort. Stepan Iwanow, believing that Agnes has merely trifled with his love to protect her husband, leaves the house without speaking to her. She, on her part, has no full understanding of what has occurred. The import of the tragedy is apparent when Anders forgives Agnes her love affair on the grounds that her action was conditioned by the war situation and justifies his own responsibility for the slaughter of thousands of Jews in Warsaw on the same grounds. The fact that her husband can so casually equate these two very differently motivated actions is sufficient to drive Agnes to despair and suicide.

While Frisch's previous plays were slow in gaining recognition, *Als der Krieg zu Ende war* rapidly conquered the stages of Germany and was performed in New York in the winter of 1950–51. Its success in Germany can be accounted for on the basis of topical interest. Its lack of equal success on the American stage may be due, in part, to the lack of subjective experience of the conditions described and to the time that had elapsed since the conclusion of the war.

The play is generally understood to report a tragic incident of the chaotic conditions of the early post-war months and appears, at first glance, to have little in common with *Die chinesische Mauer*. On closer inspection, however, we find the basic problem to be the same. The relationship of truth and falsehood, poetically but vaguely expressed in the bewildering chaos of *Die chinesische Mauer*, becomes a far more clearly defined issue in *Als der Krieg zu Ende war*. Frisch probes various human relationships to discover how genuine and honest they are. He reveals the falsehood of conventional social life, man's inability or unwillingness to perceive his own or another's guilt, and his tendency to belittle or even disregard the horrible. The strongest and most dangerous opponent of truth is the man with convictions.

... In this apparently more realistic work Frisch has the heroine deliver a monologue in which she gives expression to a consciousness transcending that of the individual—one elucidating the plot and breaking through its surface like that of the chorus of Greek tragedy. Thus, in spite of all obvious differences, both plays are typical expressions of Frisch's dramatic work. Both deal with the same fundamental problem; both reveal the author's profound pessimism; both embody outstanding experimental techniques. Moreover, both have similar defects. *Die chinesische Mauer* has virtually no coherent plot, and the net of questions in which the author becomes entangled bewilders the spectator. In *Als der Krieg zu Ende war* the basic question is clearly stated and satisfactorily solved but Frisch appears to have been so completely occupied with it that he has either overlooked or purposely neglected the questions arising in the reader's mind about the motivation of Agnes' deceit of her husband and about the extent to which her love for Stepan is more than physical desire. Such unanswered questions weaken the effectiveness of the drama. This same weakness appears in all of Frisch's works; all suffer from a certain lack of clarity because the basic problems are overshadowed by vaguely defined secondary problems which the author fails to solve satisfactorily ...

Source: Walter E. Glaettli, "Max Frisch, a New German Playwright," in *German Quarterly*, Vol. 25, No. 4, November 1952, pp. 248–54.

SOURCES

Barnes, Clive, "Cocteau Repertory Does Max Frisch's *Firebugs*," in the *New York Times*, March 27, 1975, p. 32.

Canby, Vincent, "Theater: A Transformed *Firebugs*," in the *New York Times*, July 2, 1968, p. 36.

Frisch, Max, *The Firebugs*, Hill and Wang, 1963, pp. 4, 7, 9–10, 13–14, 21, 33, 49, 76, 79.

Raymont, Henry, "Theater: *The Firebugs* Gives Lesson," in the *New York Times*, November 27, 1969, p. 52.

Taubman, Howard, "*The Firebugs* Opens Off Broadway," in the *New York Times*, February 13, 1963, p. 7.

Weber, Bruce, "An Acrid Comic Parable about Nazis," in the *New York Times*, June 18, 2002, p. E3.

FURTHER READING

Bessel, Richard, *Nazism and War*, Modern Library, 2006.
    Bessel, a noted historian, presents an in-depth look into Nazism in Germany and its effects on the world, providing a detailed perspective on the political, economic, and social environment that helped to foster the overwhelming sweep of Nazism across Europe.

Brecht, Bertolt, *Brecht on Theatre: The Development of An Aesthetic*, translated by John Willett, Hill and Wang, 1977.
    Brecht revolutionized theater just as Frisch began bringing his plays to the stage. Brecht's influence was very strong not only in Germany but all over the Western world. Brecht's concepts of theater are fully explained in this collection of essays.

Lichtenstein, Claude, *Playfully Rigid: Swiss Architecture, Graphic Design, Product Design, 1950–2006*, Lars Müller Publishers, 2006.
    Frisch was an architect in Switzerland (as was his father) before he became a full-time writer. This book provides a perspective of what architecture looked like in Frisch's time as well as how it has changed over the decades.

Wistrich, Robert S., *Hitler and the Holocaust*, Modern Library, 2003.
    Wistrich argues that the indifference of many European societies aided Hitler in his determination to exterminate the Jews. In this book, Wistrich explores a 2,000-year history of anti-Semitism leading to the rise and fall of the Third Reich in Germany. In the process, Wistrich attempts to answer why the Holocaust happened and how it differs from other forms of twentieth-century genocide.

Frozen

BRYONY LAVERY

1998

Frozen, by British playwright Bryony Lavery, was first produced in 1998, by the Birmingham Repertory Theatre, in Birmingham, England. It is available in an edition published by Faber and Faber in 2002. *Frozen* is about the murder of a ten-year-old girl by a child-molesting serial killer and the crime's aftermath. There are three main characters, whose stories begin separately but then gradually converge. Agnetha, a psychiatrist from New York, presents evidence that violent criminals are brain damaged and not responsible for what they do. Nancy, the mother of the victim, is eventually able to forgive the murderer, Ralph, who for his part finally learns to feel remorse.

Frozen raises issues of great importance for criminal justice. Is the murderer evil or is his crime only the symptom of an illness? The play also explores the act of forgiveness. How can it be possible for a mother to forgive a man who has sexually molested and murdered her young daughter? With its powerful emotional impact, *Frozen* has been an international success. In recent years it has been one of the most produced plays in the United States and has also been produced around the world in cities such as Dublin, Amsterdam, Madrid, and Paris. The play also became the subject of controversy when Lavery was accused of plagiarizing the work of an American psychiatrist, Dorothy Otnow Lewis, whose life and work closely resembled that of the character Agnetha in the play.

Bryony Lavery *(Thos Robinson / Getty Images)*

AUTHOR BIOGRAPHY

British playwright and director Bryony Lavery was born on December 21, 1947, in Wakefield, Yorkshire, England. Her father was the principal of a nurse training college; her mother stayed at home raising their four children. In an interview with the *Observer* newspaper, Lavery described her childhood as "very happy and very poor." Lavery attended the University of London, where she first began writing plays, three of which were produced while she was still a student. She graduated with a Bachelor of Arts degree in 1969.

In the 1970s, while working as a theater administrator, she began to make a name for herself in Britain's emerging alternative theater movement. She was especially concerned with writing plays that had prominent roles for women. Her play, *Sharing*, which she also directed, was produced in London in 1976. With a friend, Gerard

Bell, Lavery then formed a collective group, Les Oeufs Malades, which performed her plays in small venues. During the 1970s and 1980s, Lavery was artistic director for a number of small theater groups in London, including Extraordinary Productions, Female Trouble, and Gay Sweatshop.

Lavery has written over fifty plays. Some of the most notable include *Origin of the Species* (1984), *Her Aching Heart* (1990), *Kitchen Matters* (1990), *More Light* (1996) and *Goliath* (1997), the latter a one-woman show in which the actress plays all the characters. In 1991, she cowrote *Peter Pan* (based on the book by J. M. Barrie), and played the role of Tinkerbell herself.

In 1998, *Frozen*, Lavery's most well-known play, was produced. It won TMA Best Play 1998 and Eileen Anderson Central Television Award for Best Regional Play 1998. When *Frozen* moved to Broadway in 2004, it was nominated for a Tony Award. The play became controversial when Lavery was accused of plagiarizing some of her material from an article in the *New Yorker* about a psychiatrist who had studied serial killers.

Lavery's most recent plays are *A Wedding Story* (2000), *The Magic Toyshop* (2001; adapted from the novel by Angela Carter), *Illyria* (2002), and *Last Easter*, which was produced in New York at the Lucille Lortel Theatre in 2004.

Lavery has also written television and radio plays, and is the author of a biography of the actress Tallulah Bankhead. She taught playwriting at Birmingham University from 1989 to 1992. She is an honorary doctor of arts at De Montfort University and a fellow of the Royal Society of Literature.

PLOT SUMMARY

Act 1

Act 1 of *Frozen* begins in New York, where psychiatrist Agnetha Gottmundsdottir is about to leave her apartment and catch a plane to London. As she leaves she bursts into tears and screams into her carry-on bag. She recovers her composure and leaves for the airport.

In scene 2, Nancy is at home in her back garden in the evening, nipping some buds off her flowers. Her monologue gives insight into her family situation. It appears that her relationship with Bob, her husband, has become difficult. She has two daughters, Ingrid and Rhona, who are always quarreling. Nancy recalls that she wanted Ingrid, who is the older of the two, to take pruning shears to her grandmother's house, but Ingrid protested. Nancy then let Ingrid go out somewhere else and told Rhona to take the shears to Grandma. Rhona has not yet returned.

In scene 3, Ralph washes his hands in the sink. He says it is one of those days when he just knows he is going to do it, although he does not specify what he means. He then describes how he goes out in his van and tries to entice a young girl on the street to get in the van with him. He keeps cushions and a sleeping bag in the van, and it does not take him long to tempt the girl to step inside.

Scene 4 is in Rhona's bedroom, seven months later. Rhona is still missing. Nancy says she has lost two stone (twenty-eight pounds), and started smoking again. She has left Rhona's room exactly as it was, and she believes that Rhona is still alive.

In scene 5, Ralph brings a suitcase into his room. He has been questioned by the police about an incident in Scotland, which he denies having anything to do with. The police found nothing incriminating in his room, but his landlady has asked him to leave anyway. He packs some pornographic videotapes involving children in his case. He has all the titles written down in his notebook and is proud of the fact that the tapes cost a lot of money and he had to get them from abroad.

On board the flight to England in scene 6, Agnetha works on her laptop, referring to the title of her academic thesis, "Serial Killing . . . a forgivable act?" Scared of flying, she writes an angry email to her collaborator Dr. David Nabkus. She cannot get the stewardess to bring her the brandy she thinks she needs.

Scene 7 takes place four years later. Nancy has joined an organization called FLAME, which publicizes cases of missing children. She has just returned from addressing a parent/teachers meeting in which she tells the story of Rhona, who is still missing, on her fifteenth birthday. Nancy believes Rhona is still alive. She recounts the story of how FLAME found another child who had been missing for nine years. Nancy's activities with FLAME have brought her closer to her husband, who had been having an affair, but she does not have much understanding of how

her daughter Ingrid is coping with her sister's disappearance.

Twenty years later (scene 8), Ralph sits on a bench. He has just had a tattoo of the Grim Reaper done on his ankle. He shows other tattoos, on his arms. He remembers exactly where he got each tattoo, and how long it took the tattooist to do it. Then he sees a young girl somewhere and hears her laughing. He pays close attention and is obviously beginning to plan another abduction.

In scene 9, three or four days later, Nancy is walking in the sun. She says that the police have arrested a man for an unsuccessful abduction, and they have found the remains of other children in the earth floor of a lock-up shed. The man has named Rhona as one of the children. Nancy reflects that all the time she thought Rhona was alive, her daughter was actually buried in the shed.

In his cell in scene 10, Ralph describes the way he was interrogated by police, who have tried to tie him to the areas in which the crimes were committed by questioning him about where he got each tattoo. When he discovered they had found his shed and his collection of videos, he confessed to the crimes. This did not stop the police from threatening him with violence.

In scene 11, Nancy reflects on the fact that the shed where Rhona was buried was close by. She has passed it many times. Her thoughts oppress her like a heavy weight.

Agnetha addresses an academic audience in a large hall in London (scene 12), beginning to explain her research on the brains of criminals. She has also examined Ralph, who is now serving a life sentence without parole for the murders of seven young girls over a period of twenty-one years. The scene switches to the prison, with Agnetha talking to Ralph, measuring the circumference of his head and doing various tests. After one test, in which she taps him on the bridge of the nose, his rapid blinking suggests that he has damage to the frontal lobe of the brain. The frontal lobes are part of the cortex and allow people to make rational judgments and adapt to the rules of everyday life.

In scene 13, Nancy is in her house, smoking. She is thinking that she would like to see Ralph die and watch him suffer like Rhona suffered. She has seen on a videotape showing that in America, the family of the victim is allowed to attend the execution of the criminal. She quotes an eighty-year-old grandmother whose grandson was murdered, as saying that she could forgive but not forget. Nancy thinks that forgiveness must take guts. Her mother will not forgive the killer and neither will her husband. Nancy then reveals that Ingrid has decided to travel in Asia. Nancy does not understand her daughter's motivation and has little sympathy for her.

Agnetha meets Ralph again in prison (scene 14). The scene alternates between the questions she asks him for word-fluency and other structured tests and the explanation she gives to her academic audience, in which she says she believes she can show that Ralph's responses are abnormal (due to brain damage).

In scene 15, Nancy reports how she watched as the shed where the crimes were committed was razed to the ground. She is grief-stricken and calls out for her daughters.

Agnetha continues her examination of Ralph in scene 16, noting that he has a limp. She asks him where he got a scar on his forehead, and he gives two explanations, first that he fell off a roof when he was drunk, second, that he was in a car crash when he was sixteen. He also says he blacked out after falling down a mine shaft, and that his mother threw him into the sink when he was little.

Nancy hangs out her washing in the garden (scene 17). She has received postcards from Ingrid in Tibet, and gifts including prayer flags that, according to Ingrid, help to spread compassion. Nancy is not impressed. She cannot sleep and feels barely alive. The authorities will not even let her have her daughter's remains for burial. She pegs out the flags and they wave in the wind. Ingrid returns.

Agnetha concludes her address in scene 18. She explains research showing that toddlers who have been abused respond to a classmate in distress differently from children who have not been abused. They show no concern for the welfare of the distressed child but lash out with anger and physical assaults. To illustrate this, Agnetha and Ralph are shown together; she cries because her colleague David recently died, but he responds aggressively. Agnetha continues her lecture by saying that severely abused children also suffer brain damage. Such brain damage means that they are unable to form strong connections with other human beings.

In scene 19, Nancy says that she has just returned from the chapel of rest, where she and Ingrid viewed Rhona's remains that are collected in two cardboard boxes. Nancy held her daughter's skull and said it was beautiful. She placed Rhona's toy, Leo the Lion, in the coffin with the remains. When they return, Ingrid tells her she must let go of her anger, visit Ralph and forgive him. Nancy says if she visited him, she would kill him. She cannot forgive.

Act 2

In scene 20, Agnetha calls Mary, the wife of her deceased colleague, David. She is worried that Mary may have read the email she sent to David from the airplane. Mary has not. Agnetha tells her that she misses David.

In scene 21, Nancy tells Agnetha that she wants to meet Ralph. She wants him to know how she feels, and why he picked Rhona. She has tackled all the bureaucratic red tape and was told that a recommendation from Agnetha could speed up the process of getting permission.

Ralph explains to Agnetha (scene 22) how methodical he is and how furious he is that the authorities have destroyed his video collection. Agnetha asks him if he feels any remorse, and explains to him the meaning of the word. Ralph says no. He tells Agnetha about his childhood. Agnetha decides not to recommend Nancy for a visit.

In scene 23, Nancy is determined to get permission to visit. Her marriage has broken up, and her family, except for Ingrid, oppose her desire to visit Ralph.

Agnetha concludes her address in scene 24. She says that serial murderers are not evil because they have no control over what they do. Their actions are only symptoms of their illness.

Nancy visits Ralph in prison in scene 25. She says she forgives him. After a long pause, he thanks her. She says she wants him to know she does not hate him, and that she has brought some photographs of Rhona. She shows them to him. He claims he did not hurt her and she was not frightened. Nancy disputes both statements. She asks him about his family, and he tells of beatings received from his father. Only then does he see, as Nancy points it out to him, that Rhona must have been as hurt and frightened by what he was doing to her as he was by his father's actions. He starts to cry and tells Nancy not to come again.

In scene 26, Agnetha sings happily to herself. It appears that she has regained her joy in life. In the next scene, Ralph struggles to write a letter to Nancy in which he says he is sorry for what he did. He seals the letter but then tears it up.

In scene 28, Nancy is drinking her morning tea and talking about a date she had with a man the previous evening. They spent the night together. She is not sure what is going on in her life but Ingrid is encouraging her.

Agnetha and Ralph meet again (scene 29). Ralph says he is sick; he has a pain in his heart, but the doctor says there is nothing wrong with it. He says the pain began the night after Nancy came to see him. Agnetha says that what he is feeling may be psychological; it may be remorse. As she leaves him, she gives him a kiss on the cheek. In the next scene, Agnetha is about to leave London and is elated.

In his cell, Ralph is working out (scene 31). He thinks he has cancer, and to beat the disease, he fashions a belt into a noose, stands on a chair, kicks the chair away and hangs himself.

In the final scene, Agnetha and Nancy meet in a memorial garden after attending Ralph's funeral. Nancy asks Agnetha if she thinks Ralph committed suicide because of her visit, and Agnetha replies yes. Agnetha is in mourning for David, who died six months ago in a traffic accident. She reveals that two days before he died, she slept with him. She asks Nancy whether she should tell his wife. Nancy says no, she should just live with it. The sun breaks through and music plays. Nancy smiles at Agnetha.

CHARACTERS

Bob

Bob is Nancy Shirley's husband at the time Rhona is killed. He does not appear directly in the play. He has an affair with another woman, and eventually he and Nancy get divorced.

Agnetha Gottmundsdottir

Agnetha Gottmundsdottir is an American psychiatrist from the New York School of Medicine who flies to London to present her research findings in a lecture to an academic audience. For ten years, Agnetha and her collaborator, Dr. David Nabkus, a neurologist, have been conducting psychological and neurological research into the criminal brain. They have studied two hundred and fifty dangerous criminals, including fifteen on Death Row. When Agnetha examines Ralph, she is convinced that, like the other criminals she has studied, he suffered brain damage as a child and is therefore not responsible for what he did. This enables her to have some empathy for him as an individual, and she even hugs him and kisses him on the cheek when she says goodbye. Like Nancy, Agnetha is also suffering from grief following the death of a loved one. In her case, it is the recent death of her colleague David. They had a long association. She worked with David every day for ten years, and just two days before he died, she slept with him for the first time. His senseless death has shattered her belief in the beneficence of life, and she must learn to forgive him for leaving her so abruptly. When she first appears in act 1, scene 1, she is clearly upset, and gives in to a crying fit. On the airplane from New York to London, she is furious with David for getting himself killed, because his death shows her that there is no justice in the world. She must also learn to deal with her own guilt, since David was a married man and Agnetha is good friends with his wife. Like Nancy, Agnetha is frozen up inside, and must find a way to embrace life again.

Dr. David Nabkus

Dr. David Nabkus, a neurologist, was Agnetha Gottmundsdottir's colleague. He was killed in a road accident six months before the play begins. However, his voice is heard in the play in act 1, scene 18, when Agnetha plays an audiotape of David speaking about his research. He gives a description of the behavior of an abused boy toward a classmate in distress.

Ingrid Shirley

Ingrid Shirley is Nancy's elder daughter. She does not appear directly in the play but her words are reported by Nancy. At the beginning of the play she is an adolescent and quarrels with her mother. She thinks Nancy gives too much attention to Rhona. Later, Ingrid learns how to deal with her grief by traveling to Asia and exploring Eastern systems of thought that promote compassion and forgiveness. Even though her mother shows little understanding of what she is trying to do, it is Ingrid who paves the way for Nancy to forgive Ralph. Ingrid is able to let go of the pain of her loss.

Nancy Shirley

Nancy Shirley is the mother of Rhona, the ten-year-old girl who was murdered. She has another daughter, Ingrid. Her husband, Bob, has an affair with another woman and eventually leaves her. Nancy deals with her grief by keeping alive the hope that Rhona is alive and one day will return home. She also finds consolation in joining FLAME, an organization that publicizes cases of missing children; she speaks publicly about Rhona's case as well as those of other children. It is clear from act 1, scene 7, when she talks about the speeches she gives for FLAME, that she enjoys her work and prides herself on the dramatic effect she has as the mother of a victim. She says that she finds such work on behalf of missing children easy and that she was born to do it, but the audience guesses that she is using this work to cover up her pain.

When Nancy learns what actually happened to Rhona, she has a new level of grief to deal with. In act 1, scene 12, for example, when she learns the details of the crime, she goes over her actions on that day, wishing that she had done something differently that might have saved Rhona's life. She urges FLAME to expand its mission to include lobbying for pedophile identification laws. She wants the authorities to inform local communities when convicted pedophiles move into their neighborhoods.

In dealing with her grief, Nancy at first feels only anger toward the killer. She thinks he deserves to be executed. She also feels that her heart has been torn out of her chest and she is unable to feel anything. But encouraged by Ingrid, she eventually learns how to forgive Ralph, and her life starts to move forward again.

Rhona Shirley

Rhona Shirley does not appear directly in the play. She is the daughter of Nancy Shirley, and she is abducted, sexually assaulted, and killed by Ralph Wantage. Her body is not found for several years.

Ralph Wantage

Ralph Wantage is the man who killed Rhona Shirley. He abducted, sexually assaulted, and killed seven young girls over a period of twenty-one years and has been sentenced to life in prison without parole. Ralph was abused as a child by his father and was also in several accidents in which he received head injuries that may have severely damaged his brain. He prides himself on his competence and the efficiency with which he carries out the abduction and murder of young girls. He confines his crimes to an eighty-mile radius of what he calls his "centre of operations," by which he means the lock-up shed in which he keeps his video collection of child pornography and where he also buries his victims. Ralph is extremely methodical and is obsessed with controlling his environment. He makes lists and keeps a notebook in which he records the titles of his porn videos. He plans everything very carefully, and has a high opinion of his own intelligence: "You've got to wake up very early to get ahead of me!" He remembers exactly where he got his tattoos, how long each one took, and even the advertising slogans of the tattoo parlors. Eventually, after Nancy visits him in prison, Ralph appears to feel something approaching remorse for what he did, and he writes a letter to Nancy saying he is sorry. Fearing that he has lung cancer and hoping to avoid a slow death, he commits suicide by hanging himself in his cell.

THEMES

Criminal Culpability

With its focus on issues of criminal justice, the play questions the extent to which violent criminals such as child killers can be held responsible for their acts. The view forcefully presented is that many men who commit the most heinous of crimes show significant brain damage that prevents them, at least in the eyes of the research team of Agnetha Gottmundsdottir and David Nabkus, from forming normal human relationships. The research shows that such criminals often have damage to the frontal lobes of the brain, the function of which, as Agnetha explains, is "to provide judgement, / to organise behaviour / and decision-making / to learn to stick to / rules of everyday life." Such individuals also have a smaller hippocampus, part of the brain that organizes and shapes memories. The result of this kind of damage is that the wiring within the brain that is involved in creating emotional bonds is less dense, less complex, than in normal people, which means that individuals suffering from such brain damage cannot connect well with others. In addition, Agnetha's research reveals that in most cases, including that of Ralph, such individuals suffered from abuse in childhood.

TOPICS FOR FURTHER STUDY

- Describe an occasion when you forgave someone who had wronged you. What made you decide to forgive them? What benefit did you derive from your decision? Write a letter in which you forgive someone for doing something that hurt or offended you. The letter should explain your understanding of why the person behaved as he or she did, preferably in a way that does not express a negative judgment of them.

- Research serial killers. Is there a typical profile of a serial killer? Do serial killers have certain personality traits in common with each other? In an essay, briefly describe two serial killers and how they fit or do not fit the typical profile of such individuals.

- Bearing in mind that Ralph possesses a large collection of child pornography, research the link, if any, between pornography and violent crimes committed by men against women or girls. If pornography is shown to be connected to violence against women, should all pornography be banned, or just pornography involving children, or pornography that contains sexual violence? Would the banning of pornography violate the constitutional right to free speech? Conduct a debate on these topics with your classmates.

- On the issue of crime and punishment, conservatives often insist on the importance of personal responsibility, however deprived a criminal's background might be. However, liberals are more likely to argue that adverse personal and social circumstances mitigate a person's culpability. Which side of the debate are you on? Do you agree with Agnetha in the play that killers are not born but made, or are some people simply evil? Write an essay in which you explain both sides of the argument but note your favor of one or the other.

It is on this basis that Agnetha distinguishes between what she calls "crimes of evil and crimes of illness;" in the former, the perpetrator of the crime has a choice about whether to do it or not; in the latter, he does not, since his illness predisposes him to such conduct. He is driven by forces beyond his control. It is for this reason that Agnetha is able to show compassion to Ralph. "It's not your fault. You can't help it," she tells him.

The view presented in the play is a radical one; according to the law, Ralph, who has not been declared insane, is considered responsible for his actions. The play is weighted heavily towards Agnetha's point of view; it does not address the obvious question that of all the children who are abused, only a few go on to become child killers, which would suggest that there is more to be considered than the criminal's early background.

Revenge and Forgiveness

At first, Nancy's only desire is for revenge against Ralph. She would like to watch him suffer and die; she is clearly in favor of capital punishment. "An eye for an eye / tooth for a tooth," she says. The theme of forgiveness is introduced for the first time shortly afterwards, when Nancy refers to a videotape she has seen in which an American grandmother whose grandson was murdered says she can forgive the murderer. At that point, Nancy cannot even entertain such a notion. She gets no closer to it when Ingrid sends her prayer flags from Tibet with spiritual blessings on them. According to Ingrid, when the flags are hung up and wave in the wind, they spread healing and compassion. But Nancy is not yet ready to hear the message. Later, Ingrid says directly to Nancy that she should forgive Ralph; Nancy resists, still angry and possessed by thoughts of revenge and retribution. When she finally conceives a desire to visit Ralph to find out more about why he did what he did, the burden she has been carrying for so many years begins to ease. She repaints Rhona's room and removes the kiddie furniture. She realizes it is time for her to admit new feelings into her life rather than continue the same old response to the tragedy she suffered; then she will be free once more. When she visits Ralph, she tells him that she forgives him. Her forgiveness, and her ability to listen to Ralph's story with empathy, enables him to feel some remorse for his actions. In forgiving him, she is able to lead him to some limited measure of understanding of the gravity of the crime he committed. Anger (on Nancy's part) and callous indifference (on Ralph's part) give way to more constructive feelings. After this cathartic event, Nancy is able to begin a new relationship with a man, following the break-up of her marriage; her life has started moving forward again. To use the play's central metaphor; she has unfrozen and can live once more in the flow of life.

STYLE

Recurring Metaphor

The metaphor of ice is used many times to indicate a person whose mind has become rigid and inflexible, rendering them incapable of connecting to others and responding adequately to life's demands for change and growth. It is notable that each character speaks frequently in long monologues rather than in dialogue with others.

The ice metaphor first occurs when Nancy reports Ingrid's dream that she was in the frozen Arctic and had lost somebody. The body was under the ice but there was no hole that would enable her to reach it. Later, when Rhona's remains are found, Nancy feels "something heavy / block of ice / burning ice / pressing on my lungs." Agnetha also uses the ice metaphor. She tells her academic audience that her ancestors came from Iceland and uses this as a bridge to inform her audience that she is an explorer in "the Arctic frozen sea that is . . . / the criminal brain." When she explains that the kind of brain damage often seen in criminals makes them inflexible, unable to adapt to new situations, she says, "There's a certain rigidity there / like the person is ice-bound / in a kinda Arctic midwinter."

When Nancy is in distress following the destruction of the shed in which the crimes were committed, the stage direction reads "A sound of splintering ice floes," which suggests that a process of healing may have begun. Two further sound effects occur during Agnetha's explanation of the brain damage suffered by many violent criminals: "somewhere, some liquid starts dripping slowly" and "A sound of something breaking." Both are suggestive of melting ice and convey the idea that knowing the truth about brain damage opens the possibility of understanding and forgiveness on the part of the victims.

Monologue

Much of the play is presented in the form of monologues. A monologue is a lengthy speech given by one character in which the character expresses his or her thoughts aloud. In *Frozen*, entire scenes are given over to monologues. Presenting the play in this form allows the dramatist to underline one of the themes of the play, that each character is frozen in his or her own world, unable to communicate or interact with others or to participate fully in life. A good example of a monologue is in act 1, scene 2, in which Nancy speaks about the events of the day, as well as her family life, touching upon her difficulties with her husband and daughters. Act 1, scene 3 is also a monologue, this time spoken by Ralph, who explains what was going on in his mind when he abducted Rhona. Most of act 1 is in the form of monologues. Act 1, scene 12, in which Agnetha and Ralph appear together is the first scene in which there is any dialogue. Agnetha and Ralph engage in dialogue again in scenes 15, 16, and 18; while in intervening scenes Nancy continues her monologues. It is not until act 2, scene 21 (in the latter third of the play), that Nancy is shown with another character (Agnetha) in dialogue. This is the prelude to scene 25 when Nancy meets Ralph and engages in conversation with him.

HISTORICAL CONTEXT

Serial Killers Frederick and Rosemary West

While Lavery was conceiving and writing *Frozen*, the British public was learning the horrifying details of serial killings carried out by Frederick West and his wife Rosemary. With his wife as an accomplice, West murdered at least twelve young women at the couple's home in Gloucestershire, England. The victims were young women who came as lodgers or to care for the Wests' two young children. They were sexually assaulted, tortured, killed, and dismembered. Their bodies were disposed of under a cellar floor. The first victim was murdered in 1973, and most of the crimes were committed during the remainder of the decade. The murders went unsolved for over twenty years, before Frederick West was arrested in 1994 after police excavated the garden and found human remains. West was charged with eleven murders and confessed to ten of them. Before the case could come to trial, in January 1995 West committed suicide in his cell at Birmingham's Winson Green Prison by hanging himself. In 1995, Rosemary West was convicted of ten murders.

The Wests' third victim was Lucy Partington, a twenty-one-year-old woman who may have been abducted at a bus stop. It is likely that Partington was tortured and kept alive for a week before being murdered in early January, 1974. Some years after the arrest of West and the identification of Lucy's remains, Lucy's sister, Marian Partington, began to speak publicly about her own feelings regarding Lucy's murder. Marian Partington's story influenced Lavery in her writing of *Frozen*. Partington wrote of the fact that the family was not allowed to have Lucy's bones back because they were being kept as exhibits by West's defense lawyers. But Partington, like Nancy in *Frozen*, went to the mortuary and performed a ceremony: As she wrote in the Buddhist magazine *Dharma Life*:

> I decided to place special items in the coffin, and something to represent the elements: a sprig of heather (earth), rescue remedy (water), a candle (fire) and some incense (air).
>
> I gasped at the sight of her skull—it was so beautiful, like burnished gold. Holding her skull was very intense: for a moment I 'knew' a deep reality, and felt that what I was doing was not just for Lucy but for everyone who had suffered a violent death. I wrapped Lucy's skull in her soft brown blanket, while her friend placed some cherished childhood possessions inside to guard her bones.

Readers will recognize the similarity in this description to what happens when Nancy and Ingrid visit the chapel of rest in act 1, scene 19. Partington wrote also about the long path she took that eventually resulted in her being able to forgive. She discovered Tibetan prayer flags, which symbolize compassion, and hung them outside her kitchen window (an idea borrowed by Lavery in the play). Partington also sought a meeting in prison with Rosemary West, who showed no interest in such a meeting, never having acknowledged her guilt.

Restorative Justice

During the 1990s, the approach to crime known as restorative justice was increasingly widespread, both in the United Kingdom, other parts of Europe and the United States. In restorative justice, the victim plays an active role and

Scene from the 2002 Cottesloe Theatre/National Theatre, London production of Frozen, *starring Anita Dobson as Nancy and Tom Georgeson as Ralph (© Donald Cooper / Photostage)*

receives some type of restitution from the offender. Victims will often meet directly with offenders, and such programs are known as Victim-Offender Reconciliation Programs (VORPS) or Victim-Offender Mediation (VOM). The idea is to allow victims to express the impact the crime has had on their lives and to seek answers from the offender about the crime. It also allows offenders to tell their story about why they acted as they did. The theory behind restorative justice is that it helps offenders to face up to what they have done. Research has confirmed that VORPS not only help offenders to come to a better understanding of the effects of their actions on others but also help to reduce a victim's desire for violent revenge. Victims also report that through participating in VORPS they are better able to recover from the stress induced by the crime committed against them (just as Nancy discovers in *Frozen*).

CRITICAL OVERVIEW

Frozen was for the most part well received on both sides of the Atlantic. Writing in *New Statesman* about a production at London's National Theatre, Katherine Duncan Jones comments that one of the distressing aspects of the play is that Rhona's murder "divides the survivors, rather than drawing them closer." For Jones, it is Ralph rather than either of the women who is "the most fascinating character." Jones's conclusion captures the feeling that many reviewers expressed in various ways: "to my amazement this profoundly upsetting play is also strangely uplifting. There are some particularly moving touches in the closing dialogue between the two women."

For Ben Brantley, writing in the *New York Times* and reviewing a production of the play at the East 13th Street Theater, New York, *Frozen* is a "humane and intelligent drama." He comments that it carefully avoids sensationalism. The characters "don't so much vent their intense emotions as betray them through involuntary eruptions that they quickly stifle." The characters also demonstrate the ability to "channel and compartmentalize their most violent and troublesome feelings so that they can lead their everyday lives." Brantley describes the final confrontation between Nancy and Ralph as "unforgettable. Cool heat, in this instance, melts the heart more effectively than any raging fire could."

One dissenting voice to the general chorus of praise for *Frozen* came from Charles Isherwood, reviewing the play for *Variety*. Isherwood questions the play's plausibility, especially the scenes that show the interactions between Agnetha and Ralph, and Nancy and Ralph: "Much of this seems stagy or false—Agnetha's clinical methodologies are laughably simplistic and overly personal...And Nancy's cordial, solicitous attitude to her daughter's killer is not entirely credible, either." Isherwood also comments that Ralph's emotional breakthrough following Nancy's visit is unconvincing, and that in general, "the playwright tends to simplify ideas that are difficult and complex."

CRITICISM

Bryan Aubrey

Aubrey holds a Ph.D. in English. In this essay, he discusses the play in the context of psychological

WHAT DO I READ NEXT?

- *The Susan Smith Blackburn Prize: Six Important New Plays By Women from the 25th Anniversary Year* (2004), edited by Emilie de Mun Smith Kilgore, includes plays by British and American dramatists Dael Orlandersmith, Rinne Groff, Kate Fodor, Helen Cooper, and Charlotte Eilenberg, as well as Lavery's *Frozen*.

- The Forgiveness Project at www.theforgivenessproject.com includes dozens of first-person stories about how victims of crime learned how to forgive those who had wronged them. The Forgiveness Project is a charitable organization that documents and promotes forgiveness, reconciliation, and conflict resolution. It works in prisons, schools, faith communities, and with any group that wants to explore the nature of forgiveness.

- *Lavery Plays 1* (1998) contains four of Lavery's plays: *Origin of the Species*, about an anthropologist who digs up a living woman-like creature; *Two Marias*, which explores family identity, love, and death; *Her Aching Heart*, a parody of historical Gothic romance; and *Nothing Compares to You*, which sheds light on people's need to love and be loved. There is also an introduction by Lavery included in the volume.

- In Steven A. Eggar's *The Killers among Us: Examination of Serial Murder and Its Investigations* (2nd ed., 2001), a noted criminologist and former homicide investigator provides a detailed account of seven up-to-date cases, the myths surrounding serial murderers and the reasons why they continue to kill, the major problems of investigating a serial murder, and an analysis of the different law enforcement agencies that respond to a serial murder. The second edition includes an essay on victimology and an expanded chapter on the victims of serial killers.

> YET NANCY, HAVING BEEN TUTORED BY HER DAUGHTER INGRID ABOUT THE NECESSITY OF FORGIVENESS, IS ABLE TO BRING HERSELF NOT ONLY TO MEET RALPH BUT TO TALK TO HIM CALMLY, WITHOUT ACCUSATION, ANGER, OR JUDGMENT."

and neurological research that has been conducted on violent criminals.

Frozen is not an easy play to read or to watch. The murder of their young child is any mother's worst nightmare, and it is hard, for those who have not suffered such a loss, to imagine how it might be borne, let alone conceive how the parent might eventually bring herself to forgive the man responsible.

In her searching examination of the abduction, molestation, and killing of the fictional Rhona Shirley, and the twenty painful years that her mother Nancy subsequently endures, Lavery makes no concessions to sentimentality. Act 1, scene 2, somewhat ironically titled "Family Life," shows Nancy on the evening of the day Rhona is abducted, not yet realizing that anything is wrong. It is hardly an idealized family portrait: Nancy is exasperated by her mother, complaining that she puts necessary tasks off to the last minute and then wants them done immediately; she is baffled by her husband, who has suddenly starting going to a gym (Nancy will later discover that he is having an affair with the Nautilus instructor); her relations with her elder daughter Ingrid are strained, and she refers to the high-spirited girl as Attila the Hun; Ingrid and Rhona are always fighting, and Nancy relates how she teased Rhona (rather cruelly, the audience might think) that very day, when Rhona tried on some mascara she had taken from Ingrid's room. All in all, Nancy comes across as a mother under pressure, trying to hold her family together but subject to all the stresses and strains of modern family life. When Rhona, who was only sent to her grandmother's because Ingrid refused to go, fails to return, Nancy is plunged into an abyss of pain and uncertainty. For years she convinces herself that the girl is alive, but when that proves not to be the case, she must face the grief, anger, and feelings of emptiness that will be her lot for many years. The road she travels is a hard one, and it seems at one point that she is stuck in a rut, her life having come almost to a halt.

Parallel to Nancy's story is the story of Agnetha. It is the information that Agnetha presents about the criminal brain that enables the audience to grasp how Nancy becomes able to forgive what might seem to be unforgivable. Agnetha, a psychiatrist from New York, is suffering a grief of her own—the death of her colleague—but her main function in the play is to provide hard scientific evidence that violent criminals often suffer from brain damage and are therefore less responsible for their actions than they might at first appear to be. It was this aspect of the play that landed the playwright in trouble, forcing her to deal with accusations of plagiarism. It turned out that the character of Agnetha was heavily based on a real person, Dr. Dorothy Otnow Lewis. Lewis, a psychiatrist, is the author of a book, *Guilty By Reason of Insanity*, in which she describes the many years she has spent studying the most violent of criminals in psychiatric wards, maximum security prisons, and on death row. Lewis and her colleague, the neurologist Jonathan Pincus (who was the basis for Agnetha's colleague Dr. David Nabkus in the play) concluded, based on extensive psychiatric and medical histories of these criminals, that certain functions of their brain had been damaged by childhood abuse and other forms of physical injury. Lewis's work was profiled in a *New Yorker* article by Malcolm Gladwell in February, 1997, and Lewis was later outraged to learn that Lavery had taken so many details of her life and work and put them in the play with no acknowledgement or request for permission. Just to give two examples: first, in the play, Agnetha kisses Ralph on the cheek; Lewis describes how she once kissed the notorious serial killer Ted Bundy on the cheek (in response to a similar kiss he had given her). Second, Ralph's remark to Agnetha that the only thing he regrets is that "Killing girls" (act 2, scene 22) is not legal is an exact echo of a comment made to Lewis by the serial killer Joseph Franklin that he regretted only that "Killing Jews" was not legal. There are many other examples of direct borrowing by Lavery of the exact details of the work done by Lewis and Pincus. These include Agnetha's examinations of Ralph, such as when she taps him several times on the bridge of the nose and concludes from the fact that he blinks more than three times that he may have damage to the frontal lobes of his brain. Armed with a list of the offending passages, Lewis sued Lavery for plagiarism, and although the case never came to court, it did bring some attention to Lewis's remarkable work.

Guilty By Reason of Insanity makes compelling, uncomfortable reading. Lewis interviewed some of the most notorious of serial killers and other murderers in the United States, while Pincus conducted the neurological examinations. They found evidence again and again that these individuals had often suffered childhood abuse on an almost unimaginable scale, involving long histories of beatings by parents and others, and forced participation in unnatural sexual acts, some even involving animals. Some of the details are so horrifying that the reader feels as if he has stepped into some kind of alternative universe in which such things are allowed to happen. Lewis describes these case histories as "bizarre" and "grotesque," and yet there is no reason to believe the offenders were making anything up.

The researchers found that brain damage was equally common. A case in point was that of Arthur Shawcross, who killed ten women, and performed such acts as cutting out the vagina of one of his victims and eating it. Lewis and Pincus discovered that Shawcross, who suffered from amnesia, hallucinations, and blackouts, had scars in his frontal lobes and a cyst on his temporal lobes, which would have adversely affected the functioning of his brain, making him liable to seizures. Lewis commented that "If someone wanted to create a killer brain, that's probably the way to do it." In her epilogue, Lewis explained further that primitive human responses such as fear and aggression spring from the limbic system—brain structures which have links to other parts of the brain and are controlled by the frontal lobes. If the connections between the limbic system and the frontal lobes are disrupted, "we no longer have good control of our urges." In such cases, she asks, "how responsible are we for flying off the handle? It's a hard call. How responsible is a truck driver for a crash if the brakes are worn?" Her point, made persuasively many times, is that serial killers are not born but made, a comment that is echoed in Agnetha's words in *Frozen*: "I just don's believe people are born evil."

In *Frozen*, Ralph is a composite portrait of the wretched, disturbed, violent criminals who inhabit the pages of *Guilty By Reason of Insanity*. The story he tells Agnetha includes numerous incidents—violent abuse by both parents, a car accident that left him temporarily blinded in one eye, a fall down a mine shaft that produced an hours-long blackout—any one of which, according to Lewis, might be enough to create the kind of brain damage that would predispose him to violence. In fact, in comparison to some of the cases recorded in Lewis's book, Ralph's background seems relatively mild. Nevertheless, because of Agnetha's research (which Nancy has read, as she reveals at the end of the play), the two women are able to see Ralph not as a monster but as a human being. That is not as difficult for Agnetha, who has not suffered personally as a result of Ralph's crimes, as it is for Nancy, the mother of a murdered girl. Yet Nancy, having been tutored by her daughter Ingrid about the necessity of forgiveness, is able to bring herself not only to meet Ralph but to talk to him calmly, without accusation, anger, or judgment. By simply asking him questions, she gets him to talk about his childhood, and she listens to what he says. When he describes the pain and humiliation he suffered at the hands of a brutal father, she simply reflects back to him what he has said: "Frightening bugger." Ralph nods. "Hurt you a lot." Has Ralph, the audience may wonder, ever had anyone listen to him in a non-judgmental way? It is because Nancy is able to empathize with him that he breaks down and cries. It is her empathy that creates the first stirring of remorse in him, the first time, it would appear, that he has ever become aware that his actions hurt another human being. Forgiveness achieves what punishment could not, and it is forgiveness, not revenge, that ultimately liberates Nancy.

Source: Bryan Aubrey, Critical Essay on *Frozen*, in *Drama for Students*, Gale, Cengage Learning, 2008.

Robert Hurwitt

In the following review of a 2007 Marin Theatre Company production of Frozen, *Hurwitt praises the production, but criticizes the play. Hurwitt finds that the play is overlong and schematic, and that the emotional climaxes are placed too early in the play.*

Stacy Ross' Agnetha stands in her New York apartment, tense, dressed for travel, checking and rechecking her bags and tickets. Suddenly her jaw starts to quiver. Her eyes widen in panic and recognition. Sobs, then wails shake her so violently that any impulse to laugh quickly gives way to sympathy and curiosity.

It's a very tough scene to play, but the entire, interlocking-monologues structure of Bryony Lavery's *Frozen* is difficult. Director Amy Glazer and three brilliant actors—Lorri Holt, Rod Gnapp and Ross—not only make it work, and make it look easy, but invest the drama with great clarity and deeply moving power in the Marin Theatre Company local premiere that opened Tuesday.

Agnetha's opening, unexpected panic attack sets the tone for the next two, increasingly unsettling quick monologues. Nancy (Holt) is a weary but chirpy Englishwoman, tending her garden and worrying over warring young daughters. There's a lovingly comic air to her familiar frustration, but we already know not to trust the obvious as she talks about getting her youngest, Rhona, to run an errand to Grandma's house.

When Gnapp's creepily obsessive Ralph, meticulously washing his hands, begins to talk about his careful planning and conveniently placed van, the horror starts to seep in. Gnapp's predatory focus and frighteningly neutral tone as he moves toward an unseen child is chilling. The amplified sound of a van door sliding shut reflects back on Nancy's monologue—and the van heard pulling away nearby as she speaks—with a sudden terrible certainty.

Frozen, a hit in London in 2002 and on Broadway two years later, isn't easy. It's a dramatic exploration of the sociopathic mind and the power of forgiveness, taking a worst-case scenario.

Ralph is a serial killer and rapist who preys on children. Nancy is the mother of one of his victims. Agnetha is an American psychiatrist who studies "the Arctic frozen sea that is the criminal brain." Her thesis, developed with her late collaborator, is that the abuse suffered by children who grow up to become serial killers has physiologically altered their brains in ways that make them incapable of normal empathy or remorse.

Lavery based *Frozen* in part on the writings of Marian Partington, the sister of a victim of serial killers and founder of England's Forgiveness Project (whose work she carefully credited), and the psychological research of Dorothy Lewis and Jonathan Pincus (which she didn't

credit). A resulting plagiarism controversy somewhat tarnished the play's success and has been cited as one reason it hasn't appeared here before.

The play's inherent difficulties may be more to blame. It isn't just the use of separate monologues, with limited—if tense and fraught—interactions. The play is a bit overlong and schematic. The emotional arc peaks too soon, since our inherent sympathy for Nancy's loss is stronger than our likely empathy with her second-act struggle to forgive. The added loss and guilt with which Agnetha struggles can seem like an artificial device to inject personal drama into her scenes.

Glazer, her actors and designers overcome most of these problems in a near-perfect production. Erik Flatmo's stark, sterile set—an anonymous-looking shed within tall, squared concrete frames—swiftly turns into everything from Agnetha's apartment and Nancy's garden to Ralph's cell with the help of Kurt Landisman's transformative lights and Steve Schoenbeck's apt ambient sound effects. Fumiko Bielefeldt's smart costumes convey character and the passage of time.

Holt makes Nancy's emotional journey as riveting as it is deeply affecting. With magnetic humanity and unerring nuance, she takes us from frazzled motherhood through determined false hope and heartbreaking grief into a fierce desire for vengeance and a luminously liberating struggle to forgive. Ross plays Agnetha's repressed grief and academic arguments in beautiful counterpoint, her arguments about the criminal brain perfectly illustrated by her tense interactions with Ralph.

Gnapp's performance is the revelation at the heart of *Frozen*. Intense, single-minded, defensive and arrogant, he's both an inhuman monster and a despicable yet eloquent argument against capital punishment. The terrifying image of parental abuse that bursts through his facade should provoke some lively debate at the discussions the company has scheduled after each performance.

Source: Robert Hurwitt, "A Serial Killer Strikes, and Now a Mother Must Wrestle with Forgiveness," in *San Francisco Chronicle*, January 18, 2007, p. E-1.

Gale

In the following excerpt, the critic gives a critical analysis of Lavery's work.

Bryony Lavery began her career working in the British alternative theater, both as a playwright and director known for her comedic touch. She also worked extensively in children's theater and with several theater groups. According to a contributor to *Contemporary Dramatists*, "by drawing on this wide range of experience, Lavery developed a voice quite unique in British theater and a style that reaches beyond the typical middle-class forms of farce and drawing-room humor."

One of Lavery's best-known early plays, *Origin of the Species*, was first produced in England in 1984 and tells the story of an anthropologist who digs up a living woman-creature. In *Her Aching Heart*, first produced in London, England, in 1990, Lavery tells the story of two women who are reading the same historical romance and begin to develop a love affair parallel to the story in the novel. The *Contemporary Dramatists* contributor noted, "That the two lovers are both women is important, but it is not the key to the play's politics. Rather, the interweaving of the modern and the 'historical,' the real and the fictional, and the serious and the silly results in a delightful and complicated play."

Lavery's plays also often address contemporary social issues, such as *Kitchen Matters*, which she wrote for the Gay Sweatshop feminist theater company and is about the company's struggle to survive economically. Lavery based her play *Goliath*, first produced in London in 1997, on the book by Bea Campbell about working-class England and the class and race conflicts that abound in this part of English society. *Goliath* was produced as a one-woman show, with the actor playing all of the characters. As noted in *Contemporary Dramatists*, "the play makes serious political points, but it conveys its messages through emotion and through the vision (and the visionary quality of writing) of a set of characters trapped in time and place. Lavery allows the characters the freedom to strive for means of change, yet she does not offer any easy solutions."

Although best known in London theater circles, Lavery debuted on Broadway in 2004 with her play *Frozen*, which received a Tony Award nomination for best play and greatly increased the public's awareness of her in the United States. The play's primary characters are a social activist named Nancy, whose daughter has been murdered; the pedophile and serial killer who murdered her; and a psychiatrist

studying the killer. The ten-year-old daughter of Nancy disappeared while going to visit her grandmother, but her remains are not discovered until two decades later buried on the property of the convicted pedophile, Ralph, who seems to feel no guilt for his deeds. Writing in *Variety*, Charles Isherwood pointed out that "the drama, set in the U.K., unfolds over the course of more than two decades, and is initially structured as three separate monologues woven together." In one monologue, Nancy describes the day her daughter disappeared and her own evolution into an activist who finds a group that searches for missing children. In another monologue, Ralph describes how he lured Nancy's daughter into his van, how he is upset with how the police exhumed the bodies he has buried, and how he is outraged over the destruction of his child pornography collection. Dr. Agnetha Gottmundsdottir is the psychiatrist-researcher who provides her own perspective of Ralph in the third monologue.

In his review in *Variety*, Isherwood found that Lavery produces "few revelations" in her play and thought that many in the audience "may come away with questions large and small about this play's plausibility." He also noted, however, that "the characters are, for the most part, drawn in convincing detail." In a review of the 2002 London performance of the play, *New Statesman* contributor Katherine Duncan Jones commented that "Lavery's tragedy...is less concerned with telling the grisly tale than with exploring the complex and changing responses of its three characters." Jones went on to note, "Bryony Lavery believes that 'theatre should be cathartic', and to my amazement this profoundly upsetting play is also strangely uplifting. There are some particularly moving touches in the closing dialogue between the two women." Hilton Als, writing in the *New Yorker*, called the play "extremely well-crafted."

In an interview with Matt Wolf for the *New York Times*, Lavery commented on her approach to playwriting, noting that "there always must be hope at the end of a play," which she believes is not easy to achieve. She told Wolf, "Hopelessness is a much safer place. You don't have to work quite as hard if everything is hopeless. You can just despair." As an example, she told Wolf that in *Frozen* she wanted to emphasize "the notion of forgiveness, which I wanted the play to explore." The play also generated controversy for Lavery when a psychiatrist, Dorothy Otnow

Lewis, and *New Yorker* writer Malcolm Glad-well accused her of plagiarizing passages from a 1997 article by Gladwell and a 1998 book by Lewis.

Lavery's play *Last Easter* tells the story of how a group of theater people help one of their friends and colleagues deal with her impending death from cancer. The group makes a pilgrim-age to Lourdes but is so uncomfortable with what they find there that they began to make wisecracks and sing show tunes. "I think it's a play about how miraculous life is," Lavery told Erik Piepenburg for an article in the *New York Times*. "I wanted to let the characters delight us in all their inconsistencies and their bravery as well. They're such an unlikely bunch of saints because they do, in my view, great things for their friends. They're so loving."

In addition to her plays, Lavery is also the author of *Tallulah Bankhead*, a biography of the actress who became a star and, as noted by Hugh Massingberd in the *Spectator*, was the "stylish embodiment of the Twenties." The biography was written as part of Absolute Press's "Out-lines" series, which focuses on the lives of les-bians and gay men. Writing in the *Lambda Book Report*, Bill Greaves commented that Lavery provides a portrait that includes "what report-edly happened in Tallulah's life" bolstered with "but-what-really-probably-happened insights." Greaves also noted that the "writing has the shine and snap of good repartee," adding, Lavery "brings to *Tallulah* a great affection for 'bad girls.'" In his review in the *Spectator*, Massing-berd was less than enamored with Lavery's writ-ing style and said it "might be categorised as Sapphic Solipsism." However, he also noted that "if one can ignore the embarrassing non-sense and the Sapphic special pleading, some-how there is a perceptive study struggling to escape from underneath the persiflage. The bio-graphical material is handled with deceptive deftness."

Source: Gale, "Bryony Lavery," in *Contemporary Authors Online*, Gale, Cengage Learning, 2007.

Lyn Gardner

In the following interview with Gardner, Lavery discusses the plagiarism controversy surrounding Frozen *and how she managed to overcome it and continue writing.*

Bryony Lavery has never been busier. This week, her second new play of the year, *Yikes!*,

> UNTIL *FROZEN*, I WAS ALWAYS CONFIDENT THAT I ENTERTAINED PEOPLE, BUT IT WAS WITH THAT PLAY I FELT THAT I HAD BEEN ABLE TO GO SOMEWHERE DEEPER AND DARKER, BECAUSE AT LAST I HAD THE REAL TOOLS THAT I NEEDED AS A WRITER."

opens at the new Unicorn Theatre in London, hot on the heels of *Smoke*, a romantic comedy with a nasty twist, which has just finished runs in Trent and Scarborough. She's also working on an adaptation of Angela Carter's *Wise Children* for the National Theatre, and is just finishing another new play, called *The Thing with Feath-ers*, for the McCarter Theatre in Princeton—the first of two high-profile US commissions. Lavery isn't just at that satisfying point in her career where she can pick and choose the projects that really interest her: she seems to have the world at her feet.

And yet just over a year ago it looked as if her career was in ruins. Lavery had been accused of plagiarism. Her play *Frozen*, first seen in Britain at Birmingham Rep in 1998 and subsequently at the National Theatre, had transferred to Broad-way, where it was a hit. A harrowing, strangely beautiful and cathartic three-hander, *Frozen* focuses on Agnetha, a criminal psychologist studying the difference between crimes of evil and crimes due to brain abnormality, and her relationships with Ralph, a convicted paedophile and serial killer, and Nancy, whose young daugh-ter was one of Ralph's many victims. Dorothy Lewis, an eminent US criminal psychiatrist who has studied many notorious serial killers, read and later saw the play and claimed that Lavery had "lifted my life", arguing that *Frozen* plagiar-ised passages from a long article about her life and work written by Malcolm Gladwell in the *New Yorker* in 1997.

Sitting in the National Theatre cafe, Lavery is eager to look forward, not back. "As far as I'm concerned, it's all sorted and I really want to move on." She pauses. "What I hate," she says fiercely, "what I'd really hate is if I was always just known as that playwright who was accused of plagiarism. But I'll probably have to live with it." She shrugs sadly and her hands twist nervously together. "News, particularly bad news, travels fast—and in my case it travelled right around the world."

A large, comfy woman in her 50s, Lavery looks as if should have spent her life outdoors on the lacrosse field, not indoors in front of a word processor. And, indeed, she was a late developer. Although prolific—she began writing plays in the mid-1970s and by the time she wrote *Frozen* had already churned out almost 40 plays—her career never looked as if it would set the world alight or win her any prizes. She worked primarily for the Cinderella sectors of theatre, writing for women, children and the radio and specialising in warm, witty feminist subversions of well-known stories (Lavery is an openly lesbian writer, after an early marriage ended in divorce). The glee in these plays was enormously appealing, but her writing seemed to lack a darker edge. It was as if she wouldn't allow herself to be serious.

With her 1997 play *Goliath*, however, something changed. An adaptation of Beatrix Campbell's book about the 1991 riots that set sink estates across Britain ablaze, the play painted a memorable picture of the misery of lives lived on the margins. Being able to draw on someone else's words seemed to free Lavery up as a writer. At around the same time, her mother died, following a mistake on the operating table; a year later her father died, too. Lavery poured her grief and pain into *Frozen*—a story about forgiving those who have hurt us most and finding a way to thaw our frozen hearts.

With that play, Lavery herself recognised that something changed. "After 30 years of writing, I thought I was getting better as a writer. You have to get better. *Frozen* seemed to me to be the proof that I had. Until *Frozen*, I was always confident that I entertained people, but it was with that play I felt that I had been able to go somewhere deeper and darker, because at last I had the real tools that I needed as a writer. All writers have a chasm of doubt about what they do: good writing is always on that dial between absolute doubt in your own abilities and absolute certainty. As you write, you move up and down the dial."

Frozen ignited Lavery's career—only for her to be accused of plagiarism. What's perhaps surprising is that the ensuing furore did nothing to dent that career; in fact, this season *Frozen* will be one of the most produced plays in the US, adding to the growing number of productions around the world. It's certainly helped that the case has never come to court, but it is also a sign of how much the artistic community has rallied behind her.

"I've had a huge amount of support from other writers, particularly from those in the US," she says. "John Guare, who was sued over *Six Degrees of Separation*, rang me up out of the blue one day and cheered me up by telling me how, when it was all going on, he sat on the subway one day, looked around at everybody and thought: 'There's nobody else in this carriage who is being sued for a million dollars.'"

But perhaps her most unlikely ally was Malcolm Gladwell himself. In an extraordinary thoughtful and generous article for the *New Yorker*, Gladwell argued that although Lavery had indeed used his words without his permission, she had transformed them, giving them an artistic life of their own. "Instead of feeling that my words had been taken from me, I felt they had become part of some grander cause," he wrote, later adding: "Isn't that the way creativity is supposed to work? Old words in the service of a new idea."

Inevitably, the experience has left Lavery feeling bruised and battered. "When all the business over *Frozen* broke I moved entirely into an area of doubt," she says. "I felt so guilty—and I still do—that I hadn't taken care of other people's words well enough." Yet while this might have paralysed many writers, Lavery saw her only salvation in continuing to write and channelling the pain and guilt into her work.

"The only thing to do was to write my way through the dark times. And I discovered a joy in it. I had always taken a pleasure in writing, but the joy became deeper, perhaps because what had happened had made me more serious and more rigorous and made me realise just how important every word is." She laughs. "I suppose you could say that I drew on the pain creatively." She raises an eyebrow. "That's writers for you. We use everything."

Not, however, other people's words. "I have changed the way I write. I make sure that I've left any research that I've done a very long way behind," she says. "What happened has made me much more careful and that's a good thing.

I think, writing *Frozen*, I was immensely naive and very stupid. *Frozen*'s subject matter was so thorny I wanted it to be completely accurate, but that meant I wasn't as careful as I should have been. It is typical of me: if I was going to make a mistake, it was going to be a big one."

Yet out of the bad has come good, a whole new raft of work and a new confidence. Lavery may never entirely forgive herself over *Frozen*—but we should. After all, isn't *Frozen* an astonishing play about just that? As Anthony Powell, director of a current Denver production, said, when asked about the controversy around *Frozen*: "The play itself is its own redemption."

Source: Lyn Gardner, "'I Was Naive and Stupid,'" in *Guardian*, April 6, 2006, 2 pp.

Hilton Als

In the following excerpt, taken from a review of a 2004 M.C.C. Theater production of Frozen, *Als praises the play for being well constructed, describing it as a series of monologues that shed light on the self-enclosed inner lives of the characters. Als also further explores the internal conflicts of the characters.*

There is probably no greater horror than that of a child being abducted from his mother and having his barely formed life cut short. And there is probably no actress with greater skill at conveying wounded gentility and moral confusion than Swoosie Kurtz. As Nancy in Bryony Lavery's extremely well-crafted play *Frozen* (at the M.C.C.), Kurtz plays a mother who walks about in a stunned silence brought on by the kidnapping and murder of her little girl by a pedophile named Ralph (the brilliant Brian F. O'Byrne).

It makes no difference that Nancy's daughter was killed twenty years before the action of the play: Nancy is defined by mourning. She is—as the title of the play suggests—frozen by grief. And if to add color to the gray absence at the center of her life she chatters endlessly about the mundane—cocktail parties and the like—so be it. She likes the sound of her own voice; it's like the radio, distracting her from the sound of her daughter's cries, which echo in her imagination, like the sorrow songs.

Set in present-day England, *Frozen* is essentially a series of monologues describing the locked-in lives of three characters. In addition to Nancy and Ralph—who, at the time of the play, has been arrested for a new spate of child-abuse crimes—we have Agnetha (Laila Robins), a slightly younger than middle-aged criminologist who has travelled from the United States to deliver a group of lectures on the physical and emotional characteristics of the criminal mind. Although Agnetha is giving the lectures on her own, her work is a joint effort between her and her late lover, David. When, during the lectures, Agnetha wants to make a point that belongs to David, she rolls tape, and we hear his deep, sonorous voice. It's measured, steady, authoritative—a dream lover's voice. For Agnetha, it is the saddest of lullabies; her eyes fill with tears, as her body, which can't distinguish between public presentation and private pain, remains rigid.

Agnetha is just as paralyzed as Nancy, but, because she is a scientist, she must feign disinterest at all times, especially when she meets and interviews Ralph. As she sits in Ralph's cell, measuring his cranium and describing the criminal personality to the audience—instructing, she attempts to retain some measure of control—we can see her grief begin to seep through. Like the love and the despair that Agnetha will forever try to keep at bay, Ralph and his murky, cruel inner workings remain at a mysterious distance.

Agnetha tries hard to keep it together (and her demeanor can be annoying), but there's a braveness, a vulnerable pluck to her character, especially as it is played by Robins. Her thin frame cuts across the nearly bare stage; she has a deadpan focus and a passion for acting, but she's no showoff. While she is entirely convincing during her various monologues, you can tell that she prefers the relatively brief exchanges that take place when her character interviews Nancy about the crime and when she examines Ralph.

Ralph's repetition compulsion—to sexualize little girls and then silence his guilt about his fetish by dispensing of the victims—is the gravitas that makes the play deeper, and more troubling, than the first act leads you to expect. Lavery does little to explain Ralph's compulsion, except to have him reveal, during one of his unbearably intense monologues, that his father beat him when he was a child. Killing is a supreme act of revenge. By murdering Nancy's daughter, and others like her, Ralph, we glean, is killing the boy he was. This means everything and nothing. We may know the facts, but not the heart bent by and propelled toward destruction. Toward the play's close, when Nancy visits Ralph in jail to say that she at last forgives him, Ralph apologizes, but the sentiment is so far removed from his soul— what there is of it—that it's like watching a blind person trying to read the subtlest of expressions.

It's a great scene because of what Kurtz and O'Byrne do with it. Kurtz has always had one of those faces that belong to another era—that of the silent screen. She's aware (as Lillian Gish was) of what to do with her large eyes and her sweetheart of a mouth. She can say nothing and speak volumes by shifting slightly in her seat (her body is small and strong, like an osprey's). O'Byrne, on the other hand, is all physicality, alternately timid and intimidating, with slicked-back hair exposing a flat white forehead, and his tight, lithe frame encased in a snug wife-beater. The fusillade of words he unleashes barely express his damage, to say nothing of his pathetic attempts at damage control. You get the feeling that if you extended your hand to comfort him he'd gnaw it off, and still not satisfy his bloodlust. You get the feeling, too, that the three characters in *Frozen* are people who have always been attuned to tragedy—that tragedy seems to answer something in each of them. Which is not to say that Nancy wanted her daughter to be taken from her, but that her struggle has always been to find a balance between melancholy and order. The play's crimes come to seem like foregone conclusions, but before that possibility can be further expanded the performance ends, leaving us to our thoughts, and to the Pandora's box that Lavery has opened...

Source: Hilton Als, "Stuck," in *New Yorker*, Vol. 80, No. 6, March 29, 2004, p. 100.

SOURCES

Brantley, Ben, "Cold Murder of a Girl Thaws Feelings Locked in Ice," in the *New York Times*, March 19, 2004.

Gladwell, Malcolm, "Damaged," in the *New Yorker*, Vol. LXXIII, No. 2, February 24, 1997, p. 132.

Isherwood, Charles, Review of *Frozen*, in *Variety*, Vol. 394, No. 6, March 22, 2004, p. 49.

Jones, Katherine Duncan, "Cold Comfort: Katherine Duncan Jones Is Moved by a Mother's Chilling Plight," in the *New Statesman*, July 22, 2002, pp. 40–41.

Kellaway, Kate, "Comedy of Terrors," in the *Observer*, June 23, 2002, http://observer.guardian.co.uk/print/0,,4446565-102280,00.html (accessed August 3, 2007).

Lavery, Bryony, *Frozen*, Faber and Faber, 2002.

Lewis, Dorothy Otnow, *Guilty by Reason of Insanity: A Psychiatrist Explores the Minds of Killers*, Ivy Books, 1998, pp. 248, 288, 324–26.

Partington, Marian, "The Agony and the Empathy," in *Dharma Life*, No. 22, Spring 2004, http://www.dharma-life.com/issue22/agony.html (accessed August 3, 2007).

FURTHER READING

Goodman, Lizbeth, *Feminist Stages: Interviews with Women in Contemporary British Theatre*, Harwood Academic Publishers, 1996, pp. 40–46, 303–307.
   In this interview, Lavery discusses her use of language, her gift for comedy, some of her early plays, and the nature of her feminist viewpoint. She also contributes an Afterword to this volume in which she comments on feminism in British theater.

Innes, Christopher, *Modern British Drama: The Twentieth Century*, Cambridge University Press, 2002, pp. 233–38.
   Innes discusses the feminist alternative in British theater from the late 1950s to the present. He surveys many of the small theater groups to which Lavery contributed, such as Gay Sweatshop, and the frequent practice of communal script creation, which has produced extremely creative work that nonetheless has some theatrical limitations.

Keppel, Robert D., and William J. Birnes, *The Psychology of Serial Killer Investigations: The Grisly Business Unit*, Academic Press, 2003.
   This book examines the underlying psychology of serial killers and why they are often able to remain at large for many years. The book goes inside the operations of serial killer task forces and includes case reviews of some of the most baffling serial killer cases in the United States and Britain.

Schmid, David, *Natural Born Celebrities: Serial Killers in American Culture*, University of Chicago Press, 2006.
   Schmid analyzes what he calls the serial killer industry that has become such a prominent part of American popular culture since the 1970s, making celebrities out of such figures as Ted Bundy, John Wayne Gacy, and Jeffrey Dahmer.

Hippolytus

EURIPIDES

428 B.C.E.

Euripides's *Hippolytus* (428 B.C.E.) is, first and foremost, a play about suffering. Every character in the play suffers to some degree. Indeed, it is their suffering that serves, on one level at least, to create a community that is organized as a kind of counterpoint to the other community in the play—that of the gods who weigh in upon the lives of the characters. Significantly, it is the intersection of these two communities that proves problematic in the play, as the supernatural figure of Aphrodite, in particular, steps forward as a force that must be appeased in her desire for followers.

At another level, though, *Hippolytus* is a play that speaks directly to the cultural and philosophic concerns of more modern times. The play asks many of the tough questions that philosophers and writers have struggled with for millennia. Is there a higher power ordering this world as a kind of transcendent guide to a right and good life? Is there such a thing as a just world or truthful world? What are the powers and limitations of reason and intelligence in dealing with this world? And finally, is it possible to live an ethical or moral life given these questions? If so, how? As Robert Bagg's 1973 translation (titled *Hippolytos*) underscores, these questions are offered and answered with a deep and respectful sense of the power of language.

Euripides (© *Visual Arts Library (London) / Alamy*)

AUTHOR BIOGRAPHY

As is often the case for classical writers, the details surrounding the birth of Euripides are open to debate. The consensus is that Euripides was born on September 23, 480 B.C.E. in Salamis, though it is speculated by some that his birth date was closer to 485 B.C.E.. Mnesarchus or Mnesarchides was his father's name, and Euripides's mother was believed to be named Cleito. Although few solid details of his childhood survive, there is evidence that Euripides was greatly influenced in his youthful reading by such writers as Protagoras (c. 490 B.C.E.–420 B.C.E.) and Socrates (c. 470 B.C.E.–399 B.C.E.).

Euripides was reportedly married twice, once to a woman named Choerile and also to a woman named Melito, though it is unclear which woman was his first wife and which woman was his second. Very little is known of his life beyond his work as a tragedian (writer of tragedies). He is considered the last of the three great tragedians of classical Athens, along with Aeschylus (524 B.C.E.–456 B.C.E.) and Sophocles (495 B.C.E.–406 B.C.E.). Euripides entered a play in the Dionysia (the most famous of Athenian drama festivals) for the first time in 455 B.C.E.,

MEDIA ADAPTATIONS

- The Department of Classics at the University of Otago in New Zealand produced a video version of the traditional Greek staging of *Hippolytus* in 1996.

and placed third in the competition that year. He continued to compete in the festival regularly, winning prizes four times during his lifetime. *Hippolytus* took first prize in 428 B.C.E., having been revised from an earlier version of the play that was not particularly successful with audiences. Euripides was also awarded one posthumous victory for his play *The Bacchae*. Given that Aeschylus reportedly won more than a dozen of these competitions, and Sophocles carried off eighteen victories, it is understandable that Euripides might have become disheartened in defeat. Whatever the reason, Eurpides left Athens in either 407 B.C.E. or 408 B.C.E., when the king of Macedon urged him to come live and write in that country.

Euripides reportedly died in Macedonia during the winter of 406 B.C.E.. Many of his plays were freely revised by Seneca (c. 4 B.C.E.–65 A.D.), the Roman tragedian who was drawn to the rhetoric and violence that were found in the plays of his Greek antecedent.

PLOT SUMMARY

Ancient manuscripts of the Greek plays do not supply stage directions in the sense that modern readers have come to expect them. References in this plot summary are derived from comments by ancient writers, who often provided relevant information about the staging of the plays, as well as from more recent scholarly inferences about Greek theatrical conventions. Accordingly, mention of stage directions in the Plot Summary has been kept to a minimum.

Prologue

The play opens in front of the palace of Theseus in Troizen, with the statues of Artemis (goddess of the hunt) and Aphrodite (goddess of love, lust, and beauty) placed on opposing sides of the stage. The living goddess Aphrodite appears, and in the prologue to the main action declares her intention to punish Hippolytus, the chaste son of Theseus, who chooses to worship Artemis rather than Aphrodite.

Aphrodite's plan has already been put into action as the play opens. She has placed a love for Hippolytus into the heart of Phaidra, the wife of Theseus and stepmother of Hippolytus. Her hope is that Theseus, upon discovery of this love, will kill his son using one of the three fatal wishes that he has been granted by Poseidon (god of the sea and of earthquakes).

Act 1

Hippolytus enters the stage with his entourage of huntsmen leading dogs and carrying weapons from the hunt. He praises the statue of Artemis, placing a garland upon her head as a tribute to her. A servant suggests that Hippolytus might want to honor Aphrodite in the same manner, but the young hunter ignores the advice, thereby completing his insult of the powerful goddess.

The Chorus of townswomen enters, telling the story of the love-sick Phaidra. They wonder at the cause of her illness, positing that she might have gone mad or is responding to some slight from her husband. Or, the chorus suggests, perhaps her sickness is simply evidence of the weakness of woman's nature.

The love-sick Phaidra enters the stage, accompanied by numerous servants and her own Nurse. The Nurse initially talks her queen into confessing to the chorus both the source of her sickness and her resolve to die rather than to continue suffering. The Nurse then turns to comforting the suffering queen, suggesting that Phaidra act on her love rather than allowing herself to be consumed slowly and painfully. Finally, the Nurse promises to assist Phaidra by concocting a special medicine that is strong enough to change the course of love. What she needs in order to complete this antidote, the Nurse explains, is a piece of hair or clothing from Hippolytus. As Phaidra contemplates her decision, she also implores the Nurse never to reveal the truth behind her sickness to Hippolytus.

As the Nurse leaves the stage to secure the token that she needs, she whispers a prayer to Aphrodite, betraying herself as a supporter of the goddess's plan to punish Hippolytus. As Phaidra listens at the door, she hears a commotion within, telling her that the Nurse has betrayed her secret to her stepson. Hippolytus bursts onto the stage, with loud declarations of his horror and dismay at the revelation.

Venting his anger, Hippolytus goes into an extended tirade against the weaknesses of women, calling them "a huge natural calamity" among many other slights, most of which focus on their sexual appetites and what Hippolytus derides generally as their lewdness.

Phaidra raises little defense to these charges, though she does claim that all women "are violated by destiny," creating a hurt that "never leaves." Turning on the Nurse, Phaidra attacks her verbally for her inability to keep a secret and for her lack of loyalty to a queen that has treated her so well. Exhausted and suffering, Phaidra resolves once again to die. As Phaidra exits the stage, the Chorus recounts in detail how Aphrodite has assisted the queen in fulfilling her wish for death. Phaidra hangs herself off stage.

As the townswomen talk about the hanging, Theseus enters the stage, crowned with flowers and demanding to know what event has brought his palace into such an uproar. Informed that his wife is dead, he mourns openly at the suicide as the Chorus announces that the palace has been doomed by these recent events. Examining the corpse of his wife, Theseus sees a tablet "gripped tensely" in her hand. Taking the tablet from her hand, he explodes in horror as he reads the words it holds: that Phaidra was raped by Hippolytus. Theseus calls the god Poseidon, who owes the king "three mortal curses," to murder his son for the crime that has been reported in the tablet. Despite the pleadings of Koryphaios, the leader of the Chorus, Theseus persists in his wish for the murder of Hippolytus.

Hippolytus arrives, drawn by the uproar of his father. The exchange between the two men is powerful drama as the father at first attacks his son verbally before explaining to him the source of his rage. Theseus sentences Hippolytus to exile without trial: "I would drive you beyond the confines of the known world—the Black Sea, the Pillars of Herakles—if I had power enough, my son, I hate you so much." The men exchange angry words, as Hippolytus attempts to argue for his innocence, an effort that proves futile. Turning to the statue of Artemis, Hippolytus departs into exile.

The Chorus intervenes briefly before a messenger arrives with the news that Hippolytus has been trampled to death by his horses, which had been panicked by monstrous geysers and a mammoth bull sent by Neptune at the solicitation of Aphrodite. Theseus iterates his hatred of his son, noting that the story of Hippolytus's suffering has filled him with satisfaction but not pleasure in any form. The messenger asks Theseus of his orders for Hippolytus's body. Theseus orders the body brought to him so he can see the evidence of the death and of his own power in dealing with his transgressive son.

The Chorus speaks briefly, chastising Aphrodite for her role in this tragedy. Artemis appears suddenly, revealing the entire story of Aphrodite's plan to Theseus and criticizes the King for calling the curse of Poseidon upon the head of pure Hippolytus. As Theseus hears the story, he begs with Artemis to let him die in shame.

Koryphaios announces that Hippolytus, still alive but tragically bloodied and disfigured, is being carried to his father on the arms of his friends. He converses with Artemis, who consoles him with the promise that she will avenge his death by killing one of Aphrodite's favorites. The goddess exits the stage, explaining to Hippolytus that she cannot stay to witness his death. Gods and goddesses must "not be touched with the pollution of last agonies and gaspings," she explains.

Theseus and Hippolytus embrace as the son dies, and the King closes the play with a rejection of the influence of Aphrodite: "I have no heart for your graces. I remember forever only your savagery."

CHARACTERS

Aphrodite

Aphrodite is the Greek goddess of love, sometimes referred to in the play as Cypris (the island of her birth, now known as Cyprus). She represents sexual love, which is seen often in Greek drama as an uncontrollable, destructive force that tends to overwhelm the decorum of rational, moral conduct. Contrasted in the opening scene of the play with the influence of Artemis,

Aphrodite is proud and vengeful, especially in her dealings with the chaste Hippolytus, who turns away from sexual relationships in order to live his life, he believes, free from such base desires.

Aphrodite is the catalyst for the deaths of both Phaidra and Hippolytus, placing each of them in a situation that is beyond both the moral and legal powers of their mortal culture to deal with justly and fairly.

Artemis

Artemis is the daughter of Zeus and Leto, and she is primarily understood as the goddess of the hunt and of wild animals. Artemis is associated with the moon, as her twin brother Apollo is associated with the sun. Artemis stands in direct contrast to Aphrodite, the goddess of sexual love, as Artemis was often called the virgin goddess, and many of her followers took vows of chastity. She is the primary guide in the life of the young Hippolytus. Although she shows it only in her final promise to Hippolytus to wreck vengeance on Aphrodite, Artemis is known, too, for her willingness to inflict punishment on mortals who offend her.

Chorus

The Chorus is comprised of women from the town of Troizen, where the play is set. The Chorus offers a variety of background or summary information to help the audience follow the performance, commenting on main themes, and guiding the audience to react in an ideal way to the play as it is being staged. The Chorus expresses the fears or secrets that the main characters cannot, or will not, speak aloud in the play.

Hippolytus

Hippolytus is the son of Theseus by the Amazon queen Hippolyte. He opens the play marking his devotion to a statue of Artemis, the virgin goddess of the hunt. Ignoring a servant's suggestion to show equal respect for Aphrodite (his first mistake in the play), Hippolytus angers the goddess of sexual love to the point that she vows revenge, setting in motion the tragic sequence of events that leads to the deaths of Phaidra and her stepson.

Charged with the rape of his stepmother Phaidra, Hippolytus argues his innocence repeatedly, but is forced into exile by his father Theseus. Thought dead by an accident at sea, Hippolytus turns out to be only fatally injured. After being brought back to his father's palace, Hippolytus lives long enough to forgive his father. Hippolytus ends the play, however, reaffirming his devotion to Artemis, remaining unaware of the connection between his unwavering (and unbalanced) attachment to the cult of chastity and his own death.

In the character of Hippolytus, Euripides creates a deeply flawed tragic figure. A victim of both Aphrodite's vengeful spirit and Theseus's misguided abuse of his power as king, Hippolytus himself is not without complicity in the tragedy of the play. Unsympathetically puritan in his opening rejection of Artemis's suggestion to balance his life somewhere between her influence and that of Aphrodite, Hippolytus is also openly misogynistic (exhibiting a deep hatred of women) in his verbal attacks on his stepmother Phaidra.

Koryphaios
Koryphaios is the leader of the Chorus and serves throughout the play as a commentator on the action that occurs throughout the play.

Messenger
The Messenger is one of the more eloquent rhetorical figures in the play, who carries to Theseus the story of Hippolytus's death at sea as well as the conditions of his exile.

Nurse
The Nurse serves Phaidra; she is a figure whose key reversal in the early stages of the play sets the series of events into motion. At the opening of the play she is dedicated to the well being of her queen, but she later tells Hippolytus of the lustful thoughts of his stepmother. It is this sudden change in loyalty that leads to the suicide of Phaidra.

Phaidra
Phaidra is the wife of Theseus and stepmother to Hippolytus. She is targeted by Aphrodite as part of the revenge for her stepson's rejection of the cult of sexual love in favor of a life lived in chastity. Made sick with a lust for her stepson, Phaidra initially seeks the assistance of her trusted Nurse, who ignores the queen's admonition to keep the secret of the unnatural desires. Phaidra's admission to her Nurse, though a trivial mistake, has disproportionately serious consequences, for when the Nurse undergoes a significant reversal (telling Hippolytus of his stepmother's desires), Phaidra is targeted by Hippolytus in his verbal attacks. Rather than face her husband and deal with the disgrace that will weigh in upon her, Phaidra turns Hippolytus's loathing and her own self-hatred inwards, launching into a tirade of her own about the weakness and vanity of women. Without hope, and destroyed by her own words, Phaidra hangs herself.

In Phaidra, Euripides successfully creates a tragic contrast to the unsympathetic and misguided male characters of the play. She is a sympathetic character seen as struggling honorably against overwhelming odds (put in place by the vengeful goddess Aphrodite) to do the right thing for the good of herself and the benefit of her community. Despite her best effort to act and think prudently, Phaidra finds her spirit (though not her body) yielding to her physical passion, and it is in her ravings about finding freedom in nature (which serve only to intensify her sense of shame and guilt) that audiences come to recognize the depth of her struggles. She is, quite literally, a woman trapped, unable to act out her passions and unable to contain them in socially acceptable ways.

Servant
Hippolytus's servant appears throughout the play.

Theseus
Theseus is the king of Athens, famous in Greek mythology for killing the minotaur. A powerful but gullible man, he believes without question the story that surfaces concerning Hippolytus's alleged rape of Phaidra. Ignoring his son's plea for a due and just process, Theseus rules single-handedly to exile the accused. He also calls on Poseidon to deliver a fatal curse to Hippolytus to punish him. Later in the play, Theseus learns of the error of his judgment, and begs Hippolytus for forgiveness, which his son grants him.

THEMES

The Psychology of Suffering
Euripides was innovative in his deeply held and complex interest in the effects of repeated injustice or continued suffering on his characters. Whereas Sophocles often uses his plays to

TOPICS FOR FURTHER STUDY

- The characters in *Hippolytus* enter into debates regularly in the play. Are the rhetorical skills necessary in these debates represented as positive or negative in the world of the play? Put another way, are these skills liberating or dangerous in the life of the individual? Write an essay that addresses these topics.

- Research the conventions of classic Greek tragedy, making a checklist of what can be expected when approaching a play such as *Hippolytus*. Present your checklist to the class, noting in what ways *Hippolytus* does or does not meet the items on your list.

- One of the most interesting conventions of classical Greek tragedy is the role of the Chorus as a source of supplemental and analytical comments on the events of the play. Imagine a conversation that you might overhear on an average day (between friends, in a store, at school) and write a supplemental commentary in the tradition of a classic Greek chorus.

- Research Greek culture at the time that Euripides was alive. What did the architecture look like? What was the average family structure? What type of government was in power? Find anything and everything you can on ancient Greece and give a class presentation, with visual aids, summarizing your discoveries.

explore the lives of aggressive heroes, who meet their fates as the result of asserting the power of their individual will, Euripides tends to present passive victims, who suffer not because of what they do but because they are trapped in a world that is out of their control. Often, as in the case of Phaidra, these victims will only act when they find themselves pushed to a point of disaster, at which point they react badly or misguidedly, often with tragic results. Instead of more typical portrayals of larger-than-life heroes of Greek tragedy (Sophocles's Oedipus, for example), Euripides focuses upon the weakness of human nature and the tragedy inherent in the human condition.

Other tragedies focus on the relationship between mortals and gods, the nature of human knowledge, and the question of human freedom, but *Hippolytus* explores the suffering of a woman overwhelmed by an incestuous love for her stepson. The tragic suffering of the play has been internalized (rather than played out communally or nationally) and made a matter of psychology rather than of politics. Phaidra's struggle illustrates a division between the intellectual and the emotional woman, the woman who knows what to do in her situation but has no idea how to take the actions necessary. She is trapped, in the language of her time, between the forces of *nomos* (the knowledge that her desire is morally wrong) and *physis* (the physical drive to act on her desires). Her plight suggests that the source of human suffering is not a constellation of force brought to bear by some external force but an intensely powerful division within each individual.

Morality and Knowledge

Stripped of the conventions of traditional tragedy (particularly the traditional mythological explanations of human suffering), Euripides shows an innovative interest in the relationship between the question of moral behavior that concerns itself with sound-mindedness or implied intelligence. The vocabulary of ancient Greece was influenced deeply by the radical ideas of Plato's writings about Socrates (c. 469 B.C.E.–399 B.C.E.). These works put forward a series of propositions (known as the Socratic Paradoxes) that argue that the ancient concept of virtue is aligned powerfully with knowledge, and that no individual ever commits a morally wrong act knowingly. Socrates, as described by Plato, went on to make the striking statement that he would rather suffer a wrong at someone else's hands than commit one himself, which was seen by his contemporaries as the talk of a coward.

Pushing contemporary thought in new directions, though, Plato explains Socrates's paradoxes by expounding a doctrine of the soul as an immortal entity that is harmed by immoral action and that suffers in the next life for crimes committed in this one. (Recall Artemis's exit at the end of the play in order to avoid being polluted by the death of Hippolytus.) According to this paradox, the souls of villainous individuals suffer a form of eternal damnation, while the souls of average people are sentenced to another life on earth. Returning to earth, these people find themselves in a social position that suits their behavior in their previous life. The souls of the virtuous, however, eventually are sufficiently purified to escape the cycle of rebirth and enjoy eternal blessedness in the other world. It was thus maintained that any person who understood the true nature of his life would avoid immoral behavior, subordinating their suffering to the greater concern, which was the health of their souls. Thus, anyone who committed a wrong did so, ultimately, out of ignorance, not understanding that the long term consequences of such an act were far more dire than any immediate loss or humiliation that they might suffer. According to this philosophy, all human behavior is governed by conscious choice and rational decision. A person's behavior is determined, in large part, by the intelligence of the choices made.

Moderation

An important theme in *Hippolytus* is that of moderation as a guiding principle of a good and balanced life. (In Greek, the term *sophrosyne* was often used to signal this state of balance.) In political terms, the idea was used in support of a pattern of deferral, iterating the need to know and understand one's right and proper place in the social structure of the day. (Tragedy is filled with characters who try to rise above their station, thereby disrupting the social order.) In the context of the morality of the day, moderation applied most obviously to a belief in such ideals as chastity or abstinence (for the unmarried) or to monogamy (limiting sexual relationship to only one's husband or wife) for a married person.

This last understanding of moderation proves particularly relevant within Euripides's play. It is Hippolytus's exclusion of sexual love from his worldview, despite Artemis's suggestion, that insults Aphrodite and leads to her revenge. Ironically, Hippolytus remains unwavering in his own immoderate behavior even as the events unfold around him. His diatribe against the wanton ways of women, for instance, is replete with references to the inability of women to contain their lustful ways. Later, in both his passionate defense before Theseus and his final death scene,

Hippolytus repeatedly asserts his chastity and his purity as the most powerful proof of his innocence. "There is one practice that I have never touched," he explains to his father, "though it's exactly what you attack me for: physical love. Until now I've never been to bed with a woman. All I know of sex is what I hear, or find in pictures."

At the same time as he reveals Hippolytus's passionate devotion to chastity and purity, Euripides shows in Phaidra a woman of more balanced demeanor who is suddenly and tragically vulnerable to charges of immoderate behavior. In her desire to suppress her passion for her stepson, Phaidra is, indeed, a woman of chaste mind and body, despite the best efforts of Aphrodite. Phaidra has no desire to break the codes of *sophrosyne* or to be a hypocrite who abides to the ideal only when it is convenient. "I hate those women," she says, "who speak with chaste discretion while reckless lechery warms their secret lives." Indeed, she is praised by the Chorus early in the play for her virtue and her attention to the necessities of the social good.

The dilemma facing Phaidra, though, is that regardless how chaste she remains, it will never be enough to appease the gods (Aphrodite) or the men (Hippolytus and Theseus) who dominate the world in which she lives. By even admitting her unnatural thoughts to her Nurse, Phaidra gives in to the emotional forces at work within her. Breaching the decorum of moderation in her thoughts is enough to set the world of the play into chaos, as Hippolytus's immoderate response (most notably, his diatribe against women) and Theseus's immoderate ruling (exile without appeal to evidence) make clear.

As Euripides makes clear, the ideals associated with *sophrosyne* are without problems for those attempting to live their lives to such high standards. Does Hippolytus excel at moderation or is he narrow minded in his approach to life? Is Phaidra a weak immoderate, or a virtuous woman trapped in a world she cannot control? For all his purity there is something tragically immoderate about Hippolytus and the world he stands for. His is a one-sided life that is, to his own mind at least, being lived in terms of higher ideals and values than those around him.

As *Hippolytus* underscores, the cult of Artemis, like that of Aphrodite, can be at once a positive and a negative influence on the world of human beings. To attach oneself wholly to one is as dangerous as attaching oneself uncritically to the other, rendering the world a place of extremes rather than a balanced system in which justice and civil order can find fertile ground to set root. In the end, Euripides suggests, Hippolytus has denied himself an important element of what it means to be human, and in that conscious decision lies, arguably, the deepest tragedy of this play.

STYLE

Reversal

A common convention in Greek tragedy is the role of reversal, or a change in direction taken by one or more characters during the course of the play. The most obvious case in *Hippolytus* is the reversal of Phaidra's Nurse, who begins the play iterating her devotion to saving Phaidra's life but whose announcement to Hippolytus of his stepmother's desire all but guarantees Phaidra's death. In this sense, a reversal is not so much tied to the change in fortune that defines tragedy as it is to the continuation of a chain of events that unfold across the course of the play.

Very often in Greek tragedy, the reversal is linked intimately to a character's recognition or sudden enlightenment surrounding one of the key issues of the play. Theseus's reversal at the end of the play (asking his son for forgiveness) would be an example of one such moment. Often overlooked is the fact that this late reversal is paralleled much earlier in the play when Theseus, arriving home garlanded for celebration and expecting a great welcome, is greeted with the news of his son's alleged rape and the sight of his wife's corpse.

Rhetoric

Rhetoric, or the art of persuasion through the use of spoken language, was a primary concern of the Greek tragedians, including Euripides, who were fascinated with the means and devices a speaker would bring into play in order to persuade a listener of his or her ideas. In the broadest sense, then, rhetoric can be understood as the exploration of the persuasive effects of language and the means by which those effects are accomplished by a speaker.

Taking their cues from Aristotle's *Poetics*, classical writers were particularly interested in three components of persuasive speech: invention (the finding of arguments), disposition (the arrangement of arguments), and style (the choice of words and use of figurative language). Rhetoricians from this period also designated three classes of persuasion, which they called deliberative (to persuade an audience to approve or disprove of public policy), forensic (to condemn or approve of an individual or individual's behavior), and epideictic (used for ceremony or ceremonial occasions).

Hippolytus is remarkable for its blend of all three classes of rhetoric as a means of providing both thematic content (the story) and meaningful juxtapositions of that content. The Chorus of townswomen, for instance, enter the stage to provide a rhetorically ornate song, the theme of which is the gossip that has been overheard while doing laundry. Similarly impressive rhetorical moments occur in the speeches of the messenger and in the debate between Hippolytus and Theseus over the nature of crime, punishment, and justice.

HISTORICAL CONTEXT

Women and Sexuality

Of the great tragedians, Euripides is particularly interested in issues regarding women. Ironically, he was represented by many of his contemporaries as being a misogynist (a man with a deep hatred of women), but his representations of women and the pressures weighing upon them in Athenian society seem to counter this claim. In *Hippolytus*, Euripides explores the almost casual contempt that Greek men have for the women in Athenian society as well as the intense and often contradictory pressures placed upon respectable women within this culture, especially as such pressure weighs in on issues pertaining to sexual conduct and attitudes.

Hippolytus's vehement attacks on women expose the extremism that informed Greek culture, marking women variously as "insatiably lewd," "a huge natural calamity," and, as Phaidra herself states, "contemptible... vicious, brainless." The crux of these denunciations, as this play makes clear, is the threat of female sexuality, which is seen as a powerful force in Greek society that was at once recognized and feared. As *Hippolytus* underscores, the lustfulness of a woman is uncontrollable or at best barely

COMPARE & CONTRAST

- **428 B.C.E.:** Ancient Greek culture was polytheistic, a term that came from the Greek compound *poly* (many) and *theoi* (gods). Greeks believed in multiple gods and deities, each of which was linked to at least one natural element or event, each with personal traits and individual skills, needs, desires, and complex histories.

  Today: Although polytheistic cultures do exist, most of the world has shifted to a monotheistic belief system, in that many of the major world religions are characterized by belief in a single deity or God.

- **428 B.C.E.:** Ancient Greek culture was defined by openly misogynistic attitudes that would often erupt, as it did in Hippolytus's verbal attacks on Phaidra, around issues of sexual behavior, moral codes, and political power.

  Today: While overt misogyny does still occur in the contemporary world, such attitudes are no longer considered the norm but are seen as aberrations from more inclusive and democratic standards of conduct.

- **428 B.C.E.:** Although there are many stories of incestuous relationships (between family members) in Greek mythology, such tales are focused primarily on establishing rules and beliefs that make such relationships unacceptable. As Phaidra is quick to establish, her lustful feelings for her stepson Hippolytus are never to be acted upon despite her desire to do so.

  Today: In most of the Western world, while incestuous relationships are generally forbidden by custom and/or law, there are still some variations as to the level of acceptance. Within the United States, for instance, marriage between first cousins is illegal in some states, but not in others.

---

controllable (Phaidra knows that she should not give in to her desire, but is in constant struggle not to act upon it) and intensely destructive if released or acted upon. Accordingly, tragedy presents female sexuality as a potent threat to the social order, an energy that needs to be understood and contained for peace and good government to prevail. Any breach in the decorum of the day would end, inevitably, in chaos (at least) or more likely in tragedy.

Tragedy

The term tragedy as it came to be applied to Greek drama arose from a form of theatre defined by Aristotle as being characterized by a serious tone, a sense of dignity, and involving a great person who experiences a dramatic and often fatal turn of fortune. Although Aristotle does allow for such a turn to mark a movement from bad to good, he does argue that the fall from good to bad (as in *Hippolytus*) is preferable for the tragedian because it evokes a deeply felt sense of pity and fear within the audience. This reversal of fortune must be caused, Aristotle also argued, by the tragic figure's crucial mistake (called a *hamaratia*), which might or might not be related to some deeply rooted character flaw. Technically, this turn of fortune must be brought into the protagonist's own decision making rather than the direct influence of a higher power.

To Aristotle, well-written tragedy was used to bring about a catharsis (or purgation or cleansing) for the audience. He believed that most tragic performances left the audience feeling relieved rather than depressed or frightened. Watching tragedy, Artistotle theorized, is a kind of emotional and cultural corrective, that allowed an audience to feel these powerful emotions at proper levels and at safe distances.

1824 engraving illustrating Act 3, Scene 5, of Phaedre, *by Jean Racine, showing Phaedra, Theseus, and Hippolytus* (© Visual Arts Library (London) / Alamy)

Although such later playwrights as William Shakespeare (1564–1616) would build many of his most powerful tragedies on this Greek model, more contemporary theater recognizes a much less precise definition of the term itself. The most fundamental change has been the idea that great tragedy must focus on protagonists who begin the play with power and high status. Such seminal plays as Henrik Ibsen's *A Doll's House* (1879), Arthur Miller's *Death of a Salesman* (1949), and Tennessee Williams's *The Night of the Iguana* (1961) all focus on what might be considered the tragic circumstances haunting middle-class people and relationships.

With this shift in focus from powerful to more ordinary characters came a shift, too, from an emphasis on the classic concept of *hamaratia* to a focus on more modern ideas of self-control, individual freedom, and the pressures of oppressive institutions or attitudes on the lives of free-spirited (and often creative) individuals.

CRITICAL OVERVIEW

As Gary S. Meltzer suggests in *Euripides and the Poetics of Nostalgia*, "critics from ancient to contemporary times have generally considered Euripides a partisan of the intellectual revolution" that was moving through Greece during his lifetime. In his famous comedy *Frogs*, for instance, Aristophanes includes characters representing Aeschylus and Euripides as playwrights vying for recognition as poet laureate of the underworld.

As Ann Norris Michelini summarizes in *Euripides and the Tragic Tradition*, critics have been of two voices in dealing with the plays of Euripides, with opinions oscillating between those who see in the playwright the genesis of a new generation of dramatic tragedy and those who mark in his plays the end of Greek tragedy as it had come to maturity with the words of Sophocles and Aeschylus. Despite such reservations, *Hippolytus* has consistently been recognized as an exemplary play within the Euripidean tradition. Michelini explains that the play has long "impressed critics as being 'richer' in language play than other works by Euripides" and by extension is rich in the rhetoric of drama and tragedy that marks only the best of Greek drama. At the same time, James Morwood has argued more recently in *The Plays of Euripides*, that *Hippolytus* is also a play that "offers a devastating exposition of the fallibility of words." So profound is the failure of language in this play, Morwood notes in a representative argument, that characters collapse in all attempts to communicate with each other. In the end, these characters are driven "into a state of isolation, or arrested development" that ends tragically in a silent, darkened stage.

CRITICISM

Klay Dyer

Dyer holds a Ph.D. in English literature and has published extensively on fiction, poetry, film, and television. He is also a freelance university teacher, writer, and educational consultant. In this essay on Hippolytus, *he discusses the play as a tragic reflection of the faltering ideals of justice and truth in a world that is increasingly defined by political and personal tension as well as damaging self-interest.*

WHAT DO I READ NEXT?

- Of the eighteen surviving plays written by Euripides, the *Bacchae* (c. 405 B.C.E.) is most often discussed as a natural pairing with *Hippolytus*.

- For readers interested in other forms of tragic drama, Shakespeare's *Othello* (first published in 1622) is an essential addition to any reading list. Focusing on sexual politics, obsessive jealousy, and the power of language to alter the optics of reality, *Othello* has interesting parallels with plays from the classic Greek tragedians.

- Aristotle's *Poetics* (c. 350 B.C.E.) is essential background for readers interested in the classical, and still influential, writings on poetry and drama.

- T. P. Wiseman's *Classics in Progress: Essays on Ancient Greece and Rome* (2002) is a provocative and rewarding review and revitalization of many of the ideas that came from ancient Greece and that continue to shape the contemporary world.

- Given that many of the great Greek tragedies explored the spectacle of justice as it was enacted hundreds of years ago, Marilyn Church and Lou Young's *Art of Justice: An Eyewitness View of Thirty Infamous Trials* (2006) offers a unique perspective on the theater of justice as it plays out in real courtrooms across the United States.

One of the defining themes in Euripidean tragedy is a deeply felt political and philosophic longing for the appearance or reappearance of the voice of balanced justice in a world clearly in decay. *Hippolytus* delivers a message that is clear and unflinching: in a world ruled by passion it is the dynamic of self-interest (looking after one's own interest over the common good) that regularly prevails over the high-minded concepts of truth and justice. While all of the leading characters of the play express a belief, and to some

AS THE STAGE FALLS INTO SILENCE, THE IDEALS OF JUSTICE AND TRUTHFULNESS ARE LEFT PERPETUALLY CLOUDED, DETACHED FROM THE PHILOSOPHY OF THE NEW WORLD THAT EURIPIDES IMAGINES AND FROM THE POLITICAL REALITIES OF A SOCIAL STRUCTURE IN TRANSITION."

degree a trust, in the ideals of truth and justice, the play itself casts serious doubt on whether these ideals can find fertile soil in the culture in which Euripides sets his play.

As most viewers of *Hippolytus* will recognize immediately, it is Theseus, the most powerful political figure in the play, who is the embodiment of this tension. A powerful yet gullible man, he opens the play as a man wrongly convinced that his wife has been raped by his son. Trapped in his rage, Theseus confronts Hippolytus, wishing openly for a means of assessing clearly the truthfulness of what has happened, what his son says, and the reports that he has been hearing from those around him: "Ahh, if only we men had command of an infallible instrument," he laments, "and with it could probe our dearest friends' sincerity!" His longing is deep and heartfelt, as he acknowledges to himself, his people, and his audience that humans "need a perfect path into the heart, [so] that one could tell, as clear as a heartbeat, a faithful loving friend from one who is false." Theseus knows that justice and truth are intimately linked, and that without a stable and reliable measure of truth there will never be a stable and reliable source of justice.

The irony of Theseus's opening struggle is significant, given that he has already ignored justice in order to judge Hippolytus guilty of the crime of rape and arranged for Hippolytus's exile from the kingdom. Theseus's decision is hasty and ill-judged but passionately firm: "I banish him beyond our borders... [and] this land will never see him again, as he drifts, begging his way into an alien existence." Significantly, Theseus delivers his punishment without respect for the traditional means of measuring guilt or innocence. He relies instead, as Hippolytus points out, on a "rough justice" that ignores the very ideals of justice and balance that the King longs for. As Hippolytus asks, upon hearing of his father's decision: "You will throw me out? Without a trial? Without looking hard at my oath, without waiting to hear advice from shrewd and farsighted men?" As Hippolytus iterates, his future is, ideally, not to be decided in silence but in an open and transparent debate of the evidence as it is brought forward: "Your decision, I can see, is sealed," Hippolytus laments. "The worst has come, and yet I am blocked from speaking truth."

Theseus's references to just words and worlds resonate throughout the play, establishing *Hippolytus* as a sustained debate about the possibility of justice, about the power of truthfulness, and about the clarity of reason in an unreasonable world. Despite Hippolytus's pleading for his father to allow him "time [to] lay the facts" out in defense of the charges, Theseus casts aside the precepts of justice and the right of an individual to have his voice heard. "We have a born wizard on our hands," Theseus states accusingly, "whose magic would whisk away" the horrors of the crimes of which he has been accused.

In Theseus's view, the evidence carried on Phaidra's tablet when combined with the sight of her dead body convincingly outweighs any defense that Hippolytus might raise. Indeed, Theseus dismisses his son's verbal defense as "oracular ambiquity." Asking that his words be weighed and measured, as justice demands, Hippolytus is dismissed with charges of duplicity, hypocrisy, and self-worship. Rather than listening and assessing the words of his son, Theseus chooses instead to privilege silence (the body, the tablet) over the powers of rhetoric and oral evidence, which are the traditional values of Greek culture. "Why should I grapple with any of your arguments?" Theseus demands of his son. "Her corpse disposes of them all, and drives home your guilt each time my eyes touch her body." The voice of justice, in other words, is tragically inverted in the play, removed from the world of communal, living language of rhetoric and debate, and replaced by the interpretive skills of a single, powerful man whose own limitations are all too clearly underscored with each decision that he makes.

As the play moves towards its close, Theseus comes to regret condemning his son to exile and to death. Confessing the error of his interpretation, Theseus sets the stage for Hippolytus to forgive his father in a dramatic exchange that seems, on the surface at least, to recover the integrity of a just ideal in the play. But this recovery is, at best, tinged by tragic irony, for it is only on his deathbed that Hippolytus finally shows to his father the power of his innocence and the depth of his nobility. As Hippolytus dies, his voice is silenced in perpetuity, recoverable only through memory and lament.

At the same time, the dying gesture of forgiveness does little to lift Hippolytus's misguided loyalty to Artemis. Even as he lays dying, he remains loyal to Artemis as the source of order and meaningfulness in his world, which ironically iterates the reason for his punishment by Aphrodite. The lessons of the play are left unlearned.

Relying on the fallible tools of his own intellect, Theseus turns away from the ideals of justice that have guided him to this point, most notably the processes of balanced deliberation and rational enquiry. Allowing himself to slip towards a skepticism that proves, in the end, tragically unworkable in the practical world of the play, Theseus underscores the paradoxical position of the Euripidean world. For those individuals who believe faithfully in the truthfulness of the signs delivered from the gods is to open the world to manipulation from above, as is the case in Aphrodite's revenge against the young Hippolytus. To believe in the power of intellect and reason is, as Theseus reveals, to allow self-interest and petty politics to hold sway.

Instead of reaffirming the possibility of a just voice returning the world of the play to a thoughtful and just balance, the return of Hippolytus from his wrongful exile does little to right the tragic wrongs of the play. In the end, the play denies any promise of a balanced and thoughtful justice. In the mortal world, the aristocratic potentials of Hippolytus and Phaidra have been silenced by death, and the powerful Theseus has proven himself at once tragically gullible and irresponsibly self-interested. In the higher-order world of the gods, deep tensions offer little reassurance of a return to peace or even of a flash of progressive insight. As the play ends, Artemis exits the stage, unable to witness the death of Hippolytus, but with a promise to revenge his mistreatment by Aphrodite with another death. Even in the mythic world of gods and goddesses, the mechanisms of justice have been replaced by a simple promise of retribution and revenge.

The great tragedy of *Hippolytus*, then, is that the play demonstrates the impossibility of a just voice finding a place in the new world imagined by Euripides. Justice as both philosophic ideal and political practice cannot correct the mistakes and limitations of the play. Justice is left exposed in the final scene, forever vulnerable to deception, manipulation, and the all-too-familiar quest for personal glory and power.

More tragic still is the recognition that the play offers no clear or practical means of bridging this space between a world of idealized justice and one of misguided passion and politics. The innocent Hippolytus dies, the victim of a silencing father (the figure of mortal justice) and a vengeful Aphrodite (the judge from the mythic world). Gone are the days of justice being dispensed by an all-knowing Zeus, and yet to come are the promises of a fully realized democracy in which the power of one man is mediated by the collective will and wisdoms of the many. *Hippolytus* is not a play of restoration or reaffirmation; it is a play of darkening realities and a play of deep divisions, of tragic miscommunications that challenge the belief in a just and ordered world. It is a play, more tellingly, in which the ideals of truth and justice have been reduced to a metaphoric construct open to both thoughtful interpretation but also to tragic manipulation. As the stage falls into silence, the ideals of justice and truthfulness are left perpetually clouded, detached from the philosophy of the new world that Euripides imagines and from the political realities of a social structure in transition.

Source: Klay Dyer, Critical Essay on *Hippolytus*, in *Drama for Students*, Gale, Cengage Learning, 2008.

James Morwood

In the following chapter, Morwood argues that Hippolytus *is a profound exploration of how words cannot adequately shape a stable political state or contain the chaos that perpetually threatens a society.*

In drama as in life, words are inescapably the main means of communication, and in *Hippolytus* it is not only the leading characters who pour them out. Phaedra's tablet, with its false evidence against Hippolytus, signifies, fawns, speaks, shouts, sings, accuses. A corpse is the clearest of witnesses. Phaedra imagines the beams of a house giving voice; Hippolytus wishes that the palace might speak out as a witness. At the story's climactic moment, the whole land sounds

> YET THE PLAY OFFERS A DEVASTATING EXPOSITION OF THE FALLIBILITY OF WORDS. THE CHARACTERS' MOST CONFIDENT SPEECHES ARE SET IN A CONTEXT WHICH REVEALS THE LIMITATIONS OF WHAT THEY ARE SAYING."

forth a terrifying noise as it echoes the voice of the bull.

Yet the play offers a devastating exposition of the fallibility of words. The characters' most confident speeches are set in a context which reveals the limitations of what they are saying. Hippolytus' opening monologue conveys the beauty of the huntsman's life he has chosen but also, and here we have been prompted by Cypris' (i.e. Aphrodite's) prologue, its priggish incompleteness. Determined to stay silent, Phaedra places no trust in words, yet when she does speak, she sounds eminently reasonable as she charts the course of her disastrous passion; even so it can be hard to pin down what she means and a certain sense of hysteria hints at the volcano that seethes beneath. The speech of the Nurse which follows is supremely assured and plausible, yet profoundly corrupting, and her speaking to Hippolytus, which she confidently expects will solve the situation, leads to disaster. It also reduces Phaedra to the humiliating and passive status of an eavesdropper. Later, Theseus' great public pronouncement against Hippolytus is based on false information and delivered in an evil passion. He speaks for the tragedy as a whole when he cries out for a way to tell whether a voice is speaking what is just or not:

> All humans should have two voices, an honest voice and the one they would have had anyway so that the one that speaks dishonest thoughts might be convicted by the honest one—and then we should not be deceived.

For all the good that words do the characters, we can sympathise with Phaedra's magnificent injunction: 'Stop talking!'

If plain words prove a catastrophic medium for communication between the tragic figures, what are the alternatives? To add authority to words through oaths proves ineffective. Blinded by his rage, Theseus brushes aside Hippolytus' compelling imprecations; and the vows of the chorus of women of Trozen and of Hippolytus to keep silent about Phaedra's passion rule out any chance of persuading Theseus that he is wrong to trust Phaedra's words. If oaths are found to be damaging, what about writing? (This, by the way, is the only complete Greek tragedy that talks about spelling.) But Phaedra's tablets make it clear that the authority added by writing only increases the danger inherent in words which are merely spoken. The audience will surely respond with sympathy to the sentiment, so splendidly dismissive of the written word, with which the Messenger concludes his great speech. He says he wouldn't believe Theseus' allegation against Hippolytus even if someone filled all the pinewood on Mount Ida full of writing.

If words and writing are found disastrously wanting, can silence prove a viable refuge, as Hippolytus appears to envisage when he states his view that only voiceless beasts should wait upon women and that this would block the channels of evil communication? The theme of silence is clearly fundamental to the play. In his first version of *Hippolytus*, now lost (we have the second version which won first prize in 428), Phaedra, it seems, openly declared her love for her stepson. Now it is the Nurse who tells Hippolytus of it off-stage as the visible Phaedra listens appalled. Yet her silence in the second version will have no less disastrous an outcome than her speaking in the first; and Hippolytus' silence about the true situation seals his doom while the dead and therefore silent Phaedra is the most devastating of witnesses. Silence proves as inadequate as speech when confronted with the tragic world of *Hippolytus*.

The failure of language to enable the characters to communicate with each other drives them into a state of isolation, or arrested development in the case of Hippolytus, frozen as he is in his adolescent companionship of young huntsmen and his verbal, though not visual communion with the goddess of chastity. Unable to relate to each other in a mature way, the protagonists attempt to define their identities, but even as they insist on their personal integrity, they undermine it. Phaedra's almost obsessive concern with her nobility and her good name is irretrievably subverted by the shameful vindictiveness with which she tries to preserve them in her death by laying her charge against Hippolytus. Theseus sees himself as the decisive man of action and there can be no doubt that he does care about his kingdom, but he is destroyed by his impulsive violence. The worldly-wise old Nurse, impelled by love to help her mistress, causes disaster because that love is linked with a fatal arrogance which makes her believe that she can solve any problem through any means, however morally depraved. Arguing that Phaedra would be sensible to give in to her love for Hippolytus, she counsels against unreal perfectionism:

> You would not make a totally precise and finished job of the roof with which you cover your house.

Yet interestingly enough, the sculptures for the pediments of the recently completed Parthenon were perfectly finished. The craftsmanship of the areas which it was thought would never be seen is in no way inferior to what was visible. The Nurse's corrupting moral relativism is exposed by a building only a stone's throw from the theatre of Dionysus.

As for Hippolytus himself, there is something self-regarding and narcissistic about his stance as a good man. Lines 1078–9 are revealing here:

> If only I could stand facing myself and look at myself, so that I could have wept for the ills I am suffering.

Good he undoubtedly is, but the emphasis with which he insists on this is unappealingly self-righteous. In addition, he gives us a disconcerting hint that he would be prepared to abandon his moral high ground if he felt that it would be of any practical use to do so.

Thus these four deeply flawed characters flounder in a quicksands of non-communication. It is not surprising that they long to escape, Hippolytus to his woods, Phaedra to join him there or on the sands, or to find refuge in death. Even the morally adaptable Nurse says that she will kill herself because of Phaedra's love, and Artemis addresses Theseus in particularly revealing lines:

> Why do you not hide your body in the depths of Tartarus in your shame, or change to a bird and fly upwards and soar above this woe?

The chorus hauntingly encapsulate this poignant theme of escape in some of their finest lyrics.

But the play insists remorselessly that there is no escape. The chorus find themselves reduced to a naked rage against the gods, a feeling echoed by Hippolytus. This tragedy is unique in the way that it is framed by two different gods. At the start Cypris chillingly lays bare her vindictive plans, while at the end Artemis can offer Hippolytus only the consolation that she will exact vengeance for his fate upon a human loved by Cypris, and she proves unable to be close to her favourite at his death. The gods are cruel indeed. And the elemental forces of earth, air and the sun upon which the characters so repeatedly cry prove of no avail to them. The fourth element, water, tends to be viewed by the play—and by Hippolytus—as an escape, as something apart from human torment. Yet the great sea-god Poseidon proves the agent of unjust human vengeance. From the sea comes the bull. The characters inhabit a dark and comfortless world in which the horror represented by that bull is the fundamental reality.

Summing up recent approaches to characterisation in Euripides in 1981, C. Collard suggested that this poet had 'a unique, precocious ability to project personality and its workings in ways which anticipate modern psychoanalysis'. Looking back to Phaedra's recollection of her mother's monstrous love for the bull that fathered the Minotaur, the bull from the sea seems particularly Freudian in its significance, and its symbolic evocation of rampant male fertility suggests that Hippolytus is being destroyed by the very force which he has so determinedly repressed. In this sense it can surely be viewed as something inside Hippolytus as well as an external force. After the Messenger's tremendous speech, the chorus sing an ode not to Poseidon, the god who sent the bull, but to Cypris, the goddess of love. This is surely more than a simple recognition that that goddess has controlled the action. Hippolytus' denial of physical love imposes a terrible violence on his nature and rouses a correspondingly terrible force within him.

So, despite the appearances of the gods at the beginning and end of the play, we are presented with what is essentially a human action in which flawed and isolated human beings attempt to shape their lives at the mercy of forces which they cannot comprehend and act from no rational motivation but rather from a disastrous impulsiveness. The Nurse crazily misunderstands Hippolytus' essential nature as she gambles all on telling him of Phaedra's love. Phaedra fails to

grasp his deep sense of honour when, despite his oath of silence, she aims to undermine any allegations he may make against her by accusing him of rape. Theseus at times seems hardly to know him, scornfully denouncing this mass meat-killer and -consumer as a vegetarian. And Hippolytus loses contact with rational human discourse not only when he contemplates breaking his oath but more significantly in his hysterical rant against women.

Operating 'in a mist' (the phrase is from John Webster's *Duchess of Malfi*), the characters encompass their own and each other's destruction, and—ironically enough—their thoughtless rashness causes the fulfilment of Cypris' determined plan. Yet, despite its profound pessimism about the human condition, the tragedy focuses at its conclusion on the love of a son and father for each other. A goddess' love is evanescent— 'How easily you take leave of our long companionship,' says Hippolytus to Artemis—but amid the shipwreck of their lives Theseus and his dying son are united in a profound love. Euripides had denied them stichomythia (in which the characters speak in single lines) in their terrible scene of confrontation, reserving it for the play's end where it sounds with a deeply moving intimacy. As father and son at last find the words through which they can speak the truth to each other, they finally communicate, and they communicate in words of love. In this tragedy above all, that represents a triumph of the human spirit.

Source: James Morwood, "*Hippolytus*," in *The Plays of Euripides*, Classical World Series, Bristol Classical Press, 2002, pp. 20–24.

Sten G. Flygt

In the following excerpt, Flygt compares the characters of Hippolytus and Phaedra as they are portrayed in the Hippolytus *of the Greek Euripides and the* Phaedra *of the Roman Seneca. Flygt finds that the differences reveal a fundamental split between the worldview of the Greeks and that of the Romans, and that* Hippolytus *may be a more compelling play as a result.*

Although it is generally accepted that Euripides' dramatic writings do not exhibit the mystic grandeur and universality to be found in the plays of Aeschylus and Sophocles, a comparison of a play by Euripides with the corresponding play by Seneca leads to the conclusion that Euripides had not lost the tragic spirit that was Greek. I believe that the basic difference between

"

BUT HIPPOLYTUS IS NOT A THOROUGHLY ATTRACTIVE CHARACTER, FOR HE IS TOO CONSCIOUS OF HIS DEVOTION TO HIS IDEALS OF VIRTUE AND OF HIS OWN PERFECT CHASTITY."

Euripides' *Hippolytus* and Seneca's play on the same subject lies in a differing conception of the tragic. The tragic spirit of the two men makes itself felt in style, structure, and character portrayal, but it is particularly in the conception of character that it allows itself to be detected and examined. If, then we compare... the... main characters in Euripides' *Hippolytus* with the corresponding character in Seneca's *Phaedra*, we may be able to discover and analyze a difference that is fundamental and typical for the two playwrights.

I think there can be no doubt that in Hippolytus Euripides wished to portray a type of genuine devotion to the ideal of chastity. It would be a misconception to believe that Hippolytus' horror of the nurse's proposal is affectation and that his misogyny is a pose concealing lewdness; for the speech of Artemis in the epilogue would alone be sufficient evidence for the sincerity of Hippolytus' feelings, even were this not apparent from his speech and action. But Hippolytus is not a thoroughly attractive character, for he is too conscious of his devotion to his ideals of virtue and of his own perfect chastity. When he offers the wreath to Artemis he cannot refrain from expressing pride and satisfaction in the unique privileges which are his because of his virtue. When Theseus is reviling him and falsely accusing him, this habit of self-consciousness causes him to wish that he might see himself with his own eyes in order to bewail the sorrows that he is enduring. This wish brings from Theseus the just reproach that it is his nature to honor himself more than his parents. Even in the midst of the greatest danger and pain he cannot forget that he is not as other men are; for the messenger reports that while the frightened horses were dragging him along the shore he exclaimed that they were destroying the best of men, and with his dying breath he calls Zeus to witness that a man who

surpassed all others in purity is about to perish. This extreme self-consciousness indicates that he is a fanatical ascetic on the points of sex and honor. He has allowed his ideals to control him to such an extent that he has fallen a prey to them and his mind has become diseased. It is for this reason that he bursts into such violent expressions of horror at the suggestions of the nurse, and it is for this reason that he inveighs so bitterly and blindly against all women. With Euripides' Hippolytus chastity is a mania.

Seneca's Hippolytus is also genuinely chaste, but the roots of his chastity are not diseased as is the case with his prototype. He is far less self-conscious, and his praise of himself is not at all conspicuous. He finds it only natural that he should adhere to the ideal of chastity, for it has probably never occurred to him to do otherwise. He is a man of much simpler mind with slight habits of meditation...

But it is perhaps in the conception of Phaedra that the fundamental difference in viewpoint between the two dramatists is most clearly shown. Each of the characters in the Roman tragedy has been only a degraded parallel of the corresponding character in the Greek play; but the transformation suffered by Phaedra at the hands of Seneca reveals a divergent view of life.

I believe it is safe to say that Euripides' heroine is a study of a conflict in character. Phaedra is naturally and normally a woman of unquestionable chastity and self-control. She tells how, when the madness seized her, she made repeated efforts to quell her passion, but to no avail, until she was forced into a resolution to die rather than dishonor herself. In character she is as chaste... as Hippolytus himself; but it is chastity of a different sort. Hippolytus is driven by an obsession; but in Phaedra's usual self there is none of the psychopathic, as is evidenced by her married life with Theseus, which we can only assume to have been normal and happy. To this fundamental chastity is added an overwhelming and guilty passion. Here it must carefully be noted that it is a fated madness brought upon her by the goddess Aphrodite, who uses the woman as a tool in her scheme to destroy Hippolytus. Euripides has portrayed for us the spectacle of a normally pure-minded woman suddenly and unaccountably smitten with forbidden love. This fated passion is so powerful that it can break her control. The madness has been suppressed and checked by her will and reason, and utterance has not been given to it; but despite suppression or through suppression it has grown so strong that it commences to overthrow her reason. Phaedra raves and utters hints concerning her malady, but an unconsciously exercised check prevents self-betrayal. She recovers her senses, and now, worn out by the dreadful struggles, is attacked by the searching questions of the nurse. At the mention of the name Hippolytus, the name that has been resounding in her mind until it has driven her frantic, she gives an involuntary start. The opening once made, her pent-up feelings begin to break through, at first gradually and then with force increasing to violence. Her natural reason and will have been exhausted by the long effort; they can no longer maintain concealment of her secret. Her fated madness has so far prevailed over her that she faintly hopes—at the same time that she fears—that the nurse will intervene successfully. But once the declaration has been made to Hippolytus and once he has repulsed her, sanity returns and the madness nearly vanishes. There is now no possibility for the woman of chaste soul to live on with this blot upon her. Death is the only course possible and herein does chastity triumph. But her fatal madness also celebrates a triumph, for her violent love has been transformed into as violent a desire to ruin Hippolytus. The power of the Cyprian works through death.

Whereas Euripides portrays a good woman who is ruined by circumstances over which she has no control, Seneca portrays a woman whose lust brings destruction upon others and finally upon herself. We have seen that the Greek Phaedra is a study of conflict in character; the Roman Phaedra is a study in baseness...

It might be said that Euripides' play violates the unity of character by a shift in interest from Phaedra to Hippolytus and that Seneca's play, since interest is patently centered in Phaedra, exhibits a closer adherence to this unity. But I believe that the foregoing character analysis will help to show that the apparent shift in interest in Euripides' play was made necessary by the author's conception of the characters, and that it is therefore indicative of artistry in maintaining the unity of Phaedra as a consistent character. In his play Euripides is interested equally in Phaedra and in Hippolytus as contrasting in their attitudes toward sex. They exhibit different types of sex-madness: Hippolytus, fanatical

chastity, and Phaedra, overwhelming passion. If they did not have opposite attitudes toward the same question, no tragedy would be possible. But it must be admitted that, of the two characters, Phaedra is the more interesting to us, since she is the more complex. Two forces struggle within her soul; Hippolytus is dominated by a single obsession. Now I think it can be said that, since Euripides' interest in the two characters seems to have been about equal, there is no real violation of the unity of character, even though Phaedra physically leaves the action early in the play; for they represent conflicting aspects of the same problem. From the point of view of plot Hippolytus is the main character, since the play is concerned with the exposition of how Aphrodite takes vengeance upon him, and Phaedra is only the tool of the goddess. But from the viewpoint of character, the man and the woman are of equal importance. The development of interest in these characters follows a peculiar path. Hippolytus, offering a garland to Artemis and ignoring the goddess of love, is introduced as the object of Aphrodite's wrath. But interest is then concentrated upon Phaedra as the means of Hippolytus' downfall and as a fresh and different aspect of the sex problem. It is a brilliant study in a short space. But for reasons of consistency in character it becomes necessary that Phaedra be removed from the stage. Smitten by a fatal and fated passion, Phaedra, by nature as chaste as Hippolytus himself, cannot remain alive after the revelation of her secret. To live is for her a moral impossibility. That is, she cannot continue to live and be the same Phaedra. But although she cannot live, her very death directs the course of the subsequent action. The dead Phaedra is as much the tool of Aphrodite as the living Phaedra, and if our criterion of reality is the ability to produce effects, the dead Phaedra is just as real to Euripides as ever was the living Phaedra. It is Phaedra's death, the very event that causes the apparent shift in interest, that maintains the unity of character and the unity of action.

In general, Seneca has very largely taken the play out of the realm of the mystic and exalted. He shows a shift toward realism in the treatment of his characters, but he does not display great skill in subtle psychological analysis. There are, to be sure, shrewd strokes of penetration, as when Phaedra faints in Hippolytus' arms; but they are rather broad and obvious. I think it may be said that, although Seneca's characters approximate realistic standards in portraying more common types of people from daily life, they give an impression of shallowness. They are individuals, lacking in significance beyond themselves. Seneca's world is one of free will, moral responsibility, and guilt. The men and women in it, through flaws of character and lack of self-control, directly involve themselves and others in the consequences of their transgressions. Euripides' world, in the *Hippolytus*, is one where guilt and moral responsibility do not *really* exist, because man's life is not in his own control. Things happen to human beings that are out of all proportion to their deserts, and humanity is at the mercy of whatever forces control the universe. Their desires, their efforts, their merits are of no significance in the cosmic scheme. This is what Euripides seems to be saying in this play, for his characters are not so much individuals as universals, sublimated types of helpless, suffering humanity . . .

Source: Sten G. Flygt, "Treatment of Character in Euripides and Seneca: The *Hippolytus*," in *Classical Journal*, Vol. 29, No. 7, April 1934, pp. 507–16.

SOURCES

Croally, N. T., *Euripidean Polemic: The Trojan Women and the Function of Tragedy*, Cambridge University Press, 1994.

Euripides, *Hippolytos*, translated by Robert Bagg, Oxford University Press, 1973, pp. 37, 47–48, 59, 61, 63–70, 84–85.

Gregory, Justina, *Euripides and the Instruction of the Athenians*, University of Michigan Press, 1991.

McClure, Laura, *Spoken like a Woman: Speech and Gender in Athenian Drama*, Princeton University Press, 1999.

Meltzer, Gary S., *Euripides and the Poetics of Nostalgia*, Cambridge University Press, 2006, p. 11.

Michelini, Ann Norris, *Euripides and the Tragic Tradition*, University of Wisconsin Press, 1987, pp. 277–320.

Morwood, James, *The Plays of Euripides*, Bristol Classical Press, 2002, pp. 20–21.

Powell, Anton, ed., *Euripides, Women, and Sexuality*, Routledge, 1990.

Sommerstein, Alan H., *Greek Drama and Dramatists*, Routledge, 2002.

Webster, T. B. L., *The Tragedies of Euripides*, Methuen, 1967.

FURTHER READING

Mossman, Judith, ed., *Oxford Readings in Euripides*, Oxford University Press, 2003.

A diverse collection of essays from a range of scholarly approaches dealing with the eighteen known plays by Euripides. An invaluable resource for all levels of students.

Pomeroy, Sarah B., Stanley M. Burstein, Walter Donlan, and Jennifer Tolbert, *Ancient Greece: A Political, Social and Cultural History*, Oxford University Press, 2007.

A sophisticated yet accessible introduction for students with little or no knowledge of Greece, this book is enhanced by text boxes featuring excerpts from ancient documents, an extensive glossary, and a timeline and general introduction that provide an overview of Greek history.

Segal, Erich, ed., *Euripides: A Collection of Critical Essays*, Prentice-Hall, 1968.

This comprehensive collection of critical essays on Euripides and his work provides a great introduction for interested students.

Wallace, Jennifer, *The Cambridge Introduction to Tragedy*, Cambridge University Press, 2007.

This very readable introduction explores the relationship between tragic experience and tragic representation. After giving an overview of the tragic theatre canon, including a chapter on the Greek tradition of tragedy, Wallace looks at the contribution that philosophers have brought to this subject, before ranging across other art-forms and areas of debate.

Into the Woods

STEPHEN SONDHEIM AND JAMES LAPINE

1986

Into the Woods, published in 1986, is a collaborative work by Stephen Sondheim (music and lyrics) and James Lapine (story). It was the product of a workshop at Playwrights Horizon in New York City, and was first produced in San Diego in 1986. Less than a year later, the play appeared on Broadway, where it ran for well over a year. In fact, Lapine himself directed it.

Combining the traditional fairy tales of Rapunzel, Jack and the Beanstalk, Cinderella, Little Red Ridinghood, and a childless baker couple plagued by a witch, *Into the Woods* offers an intriguing retelling of these tales as if they are really all part of one big storyline. Sondheim and Lapine introduce humor, mystery, emotion, and action to their imaginative drama. Readers and audience members find themselves at once familiar with the characters and also surprised at the new plot twists and interactions that Sondheim and Lapine have written. The play, a musical, visits themes of longing, pursuit, selfishness, and fantasy. The pace is quick, and the characters remain fairly static as the audience watches how their personalities play out rather than how they develop.

Since its first run, *Into the Woods* has been revived numerous times, with such cast members as Bernadette Peters and Vanessa Williams. The costumes, sets, and overdrawn characters give the play a heightened sense of theater. In 1988, the play won three Antoinette Perry (Tony) Awards. In a

Stephen Sondheim *(Fred R. Conrad | New York Times Co. | Getty Images)*

career marked by famous and beloved plays, Sondheim has added *Into the Woods* to the list of those plays for which he is best known. It is included in many drama anthologies and collections of Sondheim's work, and has even been illustrated for a children's book. Theatre Communications Group continues to publish a paperback of the play; its fourteenth printing was published in 2006, complete with photos from an earlier production.

AUTHOR BIOGRAPHY

It seems fitting that Stephen Sondheim, the respected composer and lyricist, was born in New York City, where he lives today. On March 22, 1930, Sondheim was born to Herbert and Janet Sondheim, a well-to-do couple who were both in the fashion business. Sondheim was an only child. His parents divorced when he was ten, and he and

his mother lived in rural Pennsylvania during Sondheim's teenage years. A family who lived nearby, the Hammersteins, became close friends. Oscar Hammerstein II (who famously co-wrote songs with Richard Rodgers) became a father figure to young Sondheim. It was he who first introduced the young boy to musical theater, and he became a mentor to Sondheim. Sondheim attended Williams College, where he received his bachelor's degree in 1950, before pursuing his interest in music with graduate study in composition and theory. He went to New York City, where he began studying under Milton Babbitt.

Sondheim's first musical, *Saturday Night* was never performed, but it gave him a portfolio to show what he could do. As a result, he landed a job working with Leonard Bernstein on the lyrics for *West Side Story*, which was his first big break. After working with Jule Styne on *Gypsy*, Sondheim's mentoring was complete. He partnered with script writers Burt Shevelove and Larry Gelbart on *A Funny Thing Happened on the Way to the Forum*, and thus proved his ability to write music and lyrics on his own. After a few "concept musicals," Sondheim's *A Little Night Music* showed his ability to marry conventions of musical theater with modern tastes. Subsequent productions, such as *Sweeney Todd* showed the same style.

In 1984, Sondheim collaborated with writer James Lapine for *Sunday in the Park with George*, a work that won the 1985 Pulitzer Prize for Drama. Although this was another "concept musical," the two collaborated again for *Into the Woods* (1986), a more plot-driven and fanciful musical than their first effort. The play was a commercial and career success, further strengthening Sondheim and Lapine's reputations and garnering three Tony Awards.

Sondheim's career has been successful by all measures; he is well known, his work is praised by audiences and critics alike, and he has won prestigious awards for his work in theater. He is a multiple Tony Award winner, receiving the award for the following: in 1963 for *A Funny Thing Happened on the Way to the Forum*; in 1971 for *Company*; in 1972 for *Follies*; in 1979 for *A Little Night Music*; in 1979 for *Sweeney Todd: The Demon Barber of Fleet Street*; in 1988 for best score for *Into the Woods*; in 1994 for *Passion*; and again in 2002 for best revival of a musical for *Into the Woods*. In addition, Sondheim has been nominated numerous times for the Tony for his work on such musicals as *West Side Story* and *Gypsy*. Sondheim's work on *Into the Woods* also won him an *Evening Standard* Drama Award for Best Musical in 1989, a Drama Desk Award for lyrics and outstanding musical in 1988, a New York Drama Critics' Circle Award in 1988, Los Angeles Drama Critics' Circle Award in 1989, and a Grammy Award in 1988. Sondheim also won an Academy Award in 1990 for a song he wrote for the movie *Dick Tracy*.

In 1993, Sondheim was chosen to receive a Lifetime Achievement Award from the Kennedy Center in Washington, DC. His work in musical theater has earned him a reputation as an influential force in American drama. His musicals offer a variety of musical styles and a sharper wit than much musical drama that preceded it. Although his sense of humor is among his best tools, Sondheim's works lack the doe-eyed romanticism of past musicals.

MEDIA ADAPTATIONS

- The 2002 Broadway revival cast recording was released in 2002 by Nonesuch.
- The 1991 original London cast recording was released in 1991 by RCA Victor Broadway.
- The 1991 Broadway performance was released on DVD in 1997 by Image Entertainment.
- *Into the Woods* was adapted as an illustrated children's book in 1988 by Hudson Talbott and published by Crown.
- The 1987 original Broadway cast recording was released in 1990 by RCA.

PLOT SUMMARY

Act 1

Hard-working Cinderella desperately wants to attend the King's Festival, but her wicked stepmother and stepsisters, Florinda and Lucinda, make fun of her. The stepmother throws a pot of lentils into the fireplace ashes, telling Cinderella she may only go if she gets all of them cleaned out in time. Meanwhile, a poor young man named Jack tries to milk his beloved cow, Milky White, who has stopped producing milk. In another cottage, the Baker and his Wife long for a child they seem fated never to have. A Narrator tells the audience about the characters and their desires. Little Red Ridinghood is preparing to visit her sick grandmother, and begs the Baker and his Wife for some bread and treats to take. They give her some things for her basket. After she leaves, a Witch visits the Baker and his Wife, explaining that they are childless because of a curse she placed on the family. It seems that many years ago, the Baker's father stole food from the Witch's garden to feed his insatiable, pregnant wife. Among the things he stole were some magic beans. Enraged, the Witch demanded the baby that was to be born to them and put a curse on the family that they would be barren. When the Witch collected the baby, she put her (Rapunzel) in a locked tower. The Baker never even knew he had a sister. The Witch tells them

that if they want to lift the curse, they must bring her four things for a potion: a cow as white as milk, a cape as red as blood, hair as yellow as corn, and a slipper as pure as gold. She must have these ingredients in three days' time. The Baker is stubborn with his wife, insisting that since it is his family on whom the curse was placed, he should be the one to break it. Nevertheless, his wife follows along and tries to help. Before leaving, the Baker discovers an old coat of his father's that has some beans in it. He wonders if they are the magic beans stolen from the Witch.

All of the characters head into the woods. Little Red Ridinghood is off to see her Granny; the Baker and his Wife are off to find the ingredients; Cinderella, with the help of some birds, has cleaned out the fireplace (but was still left behind by the others) and goes to the woods to visit her mother's grave; and Jack's mother has sent him to market to sell Milky White for at least five pounds.

Cinderella visits her mother's grave beneath a tree, and her mother's spirit answers her. Cinderella wishes to go to the King's Festival, and a beautiful silver gown and gold slippers fall from the tree. After a visit from the Mysterious Man who tells him he would be lucky to get a sack of beans for his cow, Jack trades his cow to the Baker for some "magic" beans. Although the Baker feels guilty for tricking the boy, he sends his Wife home with the cow. Little Red Ridinghood is stalked by a hungry and conniving Wolf, who finds out where the Granny lives so he can eat Granny and wait for the girl. The Baker steals Little Red Ridinghood's cape, but his guilt is too much, and he returns it to her. When she arrives at Granny's cottage, she finds the wolf dressed as Granny, but it is too late; the Wolf eats her just as he did Granny. The Witch visits Rapunzel in the tower by having her lower her extremely long hair to use as a ladder up the side of the tower. A Prince sees all of this and is taken by Rapunzel's beauty.

The Baker comes to Granny's cottage and finds the Wolf. When he kills the Wolf by cutting open his belly, Little Red Ridinghood and Granny emerge. Grateful, Little Red Ridinghood gives the Baker the cape he wanted. Back at Jack's cottage, Jack's mother is mad that Jack made such a foolish trade and tosses the beans out the window. Cinderella has been to the festival and is now running through the woods to escape the Prince and his Steward. The Baker's Wife, walking back home with the cow, sees her gold slippers but is confused about why she is running from such a handsome prince. Milky White escapes, and the Wife chases him. Jack has returned from climbing up the beanstalk that grew magically to the clouds from the tossed beans. He has brought back lots of gold and hopes to buy back Milky White.

The Princes long for their loves, Cinderella and Rapunzel. Having overheard the Princes, the Baker's Wife tricks Rapunzel into lowering her hair, and she pulls part of it out for the potion. The Baker is delighted and realizes that he really does need her help. The Mysterious Man has captured Milky White and returns him to the Baker. But when Jack arrives with a hen that lays golden eggs to pay for Milky White, they all learn that the cow has died. Back at the tower, the Witch has discovered that Rapunzel has been lowering her hair for others, so she cuts it all off and sends Rapunzel to the desert. Her Prince pursues her, but when he runs through a thicket to escape the Witch, he is blinded by the thorns.

On a dare from Little Red Ridinghood (who is now wearing a cape made of wolfskin), Jack decides to return up the beanstalk to get a magic harp. Cinderella's Prince plans to capture his love by hosting another festival and spreading pitch on the steps. Cinderella is not caught, but one of her shoes is. The Baker's Wife offers to

trade her the last magic bean for her last slipper, but Cinderella is more interested in trading shoes (so she will have a pair instead of just one) than in having a so-called magic bean. She tosses the bean aside in her rush. When the Baker returns, his Wife has the gold slipper, and they have everything they need.

Things take a turn for the worse when a dead giant falls from the beanstalk after Jack cut it down to get away from the Giant. Moreover, the Witch's potion does not work when it is discovered that the replacement cow is not really white, but is only covered with flour. The Witch brings Milky White back to life, feeds her the other ingredients and drinks the milk she produces. The potion still does not work because Rapunzel's hair had been tainted by the Witch's touch. The Mysterious Man suggests using the corn silk used to compare the hair color, and then the potion works. The curse against the Baker is broken, and the Witch becomes young and beautiful, but at the cost of her ability to do magic.

Cinderella's Prince is running around trying to find the girl whose foot fits the slipper he caught in the pitch. Cinderella's stepsisters destroy their feet trying to make the slipper fit, but Cinderella arrives and the slipper fits perfectly. She becomes the Prince's bride. Meanwhile, the Witch tells the Baker that the Mysterious Man is his father, but he dies before the Baker can go talk to him. Far away, Rapunzel finds her blind prince and heals his eyes with her tears. As a counterpoint, Florinda and Lucinda are blinded by pigeons as punishment for their cruelty. All seems well until a second, ominous beanstalk grows.

Act 2

For the most part, the characters are doing well. The Baker and his Wife have a baby; Cinderella lives in the castle as a princess; and Jack and his mother live more comfortably, and Milky White is back home with them. The Princes have lost interest in Cinderella and Rapunzel and are now interested in Sleeping Beauty and Snow White. To the dismay of all of the characters, the Giant's widow (the Giantess) has descended the beanstalk to find Jack and avenge her husband's death. Her tromping around has destroyed the Baker's house and Little Red Ridinghood's house. Birds have alerted Cinderella that something is happening in the woods, and she goes to check on her mother's grave. When the Steward, Cinderella and the royal family, and the Witch meet the Giantess face-to-face, they try to satisfy her by giving her the narrator. He tells them that if he dies, they will have to work out their stories on their own. Still, the Witch throws him to the Giantess. When Jack's mother enters and will not stop aggravating the Giantess, the Steward hits her over the head and accidentally kills her. The Giantess stomps Rapunzel to death. The Witch mourns Rapunzel and vows to find Jack and let the Giantess have him.

While everyone looks for Jack, the Baker's Wife and Cinderella's Prince have a tryst. The Wife then feels guilty and gets lost looking for the Baker. When the Giantess gets close, she panics and is crushed by falling branches. Jack is found and he relates that the Baker's Wife is dead. The Witch is ready to hand him over to the Giantess, but the others argue against it, all looking to blame someone else in the group. The Baker leaves the baby with Cinderella, and his father's spirit visits him and tells him to be a man and face his responsibilities. So he goes back and helps plan how to kill the Giantess. While the others go about setting the plan in motion, Cinderella looks after the Baker's baby son. Her Prince enters, and Cinderella berates him for betraying her and tells him she cannot stay with him. He leaves. Little Red Ridinghood delivers the news that Granny has been killed, and elsewhere the Baker tells Jack that his mother has been killed. Together, the group kills the Giant's widow, and all of the characters who died return to share the lessons they learned. The play ends with Cinderella repeating her opening statement: "I wish."

CHARACTERS

Baker

The Baker is cursed with childlessness because of his parents, who lived in the same cottage where he and his wife now live. He is hardworking and determined, but he is also stubborn and reluctant to do things that violate his moral standards. He initially tells his wife that he alone will collect the potion ingredients, but he later realizes that he needs her help. The Baker is a dynamic character who grows over the course of the drama, especially after a visit from his father's ghost. Widowed and feeling unable to go on alone, his father advises him to be a better man than he was and face his responsibilities instead if running away from them. The Baker chooses to be a brave man and a good father.

Baker's Wife

The Baker's Wife is energetic, pushy, and unwavering in her mission to break the spell that has left her and her husband childless. Her moral limits are softer than her husband's, and she pushes him to trick Jack out of the cow they need. She also tricks Rapunzel into lowering her hair, and tries to trick Cinderella out of her slipper. When the spell is broken, and she becomes a mother, she is busy but content. However, she allows herself to be swept away in a romantic moment with Cinderella's Prince, but immediately regrets it. Unfortunately, she does not get the chance to clear her conscience because she is killed when the Giantess stomps through the forest.

Cinderella

Cinderella begins and ends the play with the words: "I wish." In the beginning, she wants to be free of her subservient life and go to the King's Festival. With the help of her mother, she goes, but when she attracts the attention of the Prince, she is not sure she wants him. Eventually, he finds her and they wed, and she has the pleasure of seeing the tables turn on her wicked stepmother and stepsisters. But Cinderella's heart remains with her mother because, when she hears that there is trouble in the woods, she goes to check on her mother's grave. Although Cinderella's life has been difficult, she is not needy or desperate. When her husband, the Prince, cheats on her, she rejects him and everything life in the castle offers. In the end, she is the mother figure, but she is still not satisfied or content.

Cinderella's Mother

Cinderella's Mother appears as a spirit in the tree over her grave. The tree has been watered with Cinderella's tears, and it is the place where Cinderella goes to connect with her mother, the only source of love she has ever known. Her mother is compassionate and becomes a sort of fairy godmother, who grants her daughter's wish to go to the King's Festival. She provides a ball gown and slippers for Cinderella to wear, and the slippers figure largely in Cinderella's future as well as in the Baker's family's future.

Cinderella's Prince

Cinderella's Prince is fickle, immature, and driven by his lustful appetite. He claims to love Cinderella, and he is determined to find her. The harder she is to find and capture, the stronger is his desire for her. But when he finally finds her, he loses interest and becomes infatuated with Sleeping Beauty. Moreover, when he encounters the Baker's Wife in the woods, he seduces her. In many productions, the actor who plays Cinderella's Prince also plays the Wolf, which is fitting since both are motivated by insatiable appetites.

Florinda

Florinda is one of Cinderella's stepsisters. She enjoys making fun of Cinderella in the beginning, and she tries to trick the Prince into thinking she is the one he is seeking to be his wife. But when Cinderella marries the prince and becomes part of the royal family, the tables turn. Worse, Florinda and her sister Lucinda are blinded by pigeons.

The Giants

Jack goes back up the beanstalk to steal the Giant's golden harp. But the Giant chases him down the beanstalk, and Jack chops it down to escape the Giant's wrath. The Giant is killed, and his widow, also called the Giant (but who is, in essence, the Giantess), goes down another beanstalk to find and kill Jack for revenge. She is terrifying, clumsy, bent on revenge, and bloodthirsty. Although the other characters give her the Narrator, she discovers that it is not Jack, and continues to demand Jack. In her rage (and inability to see very well), she inadvertently destroys homes and kills other characters, including Rapunzel and the Baker's Wife.

Granny

Granny is Little Red Ridinghood's grandmother. In the beginning, she is sick and waiting for a visit from her granddaughter when the Wolf comes and eats her. But the Baker rescues Granny and Little Red Ridinghood. Granny later joins forces with the others to kill the Giantess and restore safety and order.

Jack

Jack is led by his emotions and is easily swayed. He has bonded with his "pet" cow, Milky White, and is desperate for her to start giving milk. He does not want the milk because he is hungry, but because he does not want his mother to get rid of the cow. When he goes to sell Milky White, Jack is manipulated by the Mysterious Man who easily sets Jack up to trade the cow for magic beans. When Jack finds giants and treasures at the top of the beanstalk, his main concern is having enough money to buy back his cow. He does not care about wealth or treasures, just having his friend back. Then, when Little Red Ridinghood goads him to go back up the beanstalk for the golden harp, he of course does it, much to the peril of the entire community. Even at the end, Jack has not grown much and is still not a particularly independent-minded young man.

Jack's Mother

Jack's mother is domineering, selfish, and unfeeling. She does not care about Jack's feelings, but does not hesitate to tell him what to do or call him names for being foolish. When he brings treasures back from the Giants, she is happy to have the wealth. Her bossy ways eventually bring about her own demise, however; she insists on arguing with the Giantess (she is trying to protect Jack) and the Steward kills her while trying to keep her quiet.

Little Red Ridinghood

Little Red Ridinghood is young and somewhat naïve, although she knows enough to be wary of the Wolf. Still, the Wolf is able to lead her off the path in pursuit of flowers. Little Red Ridinghood is one of the play's dynamic characters; she shows growth and learning when she emerges from the Wolf's belly and sings a song about knowing more. She has learned from her experiences.

Lucinda

Lucinda is Cinderella's other cruel stepsister. Like Florinda, she initially revels in mocking Cinderella, but gets her comeuppance later in the play.

Mysterious Man

The Mysterious Man appears sporadically throughout the first part of the play, popping in on the other characters in the woods, giving them things or advice they need to move their actions closer to the breaking of the curse. He prompts Jack to make the trade of the cow for the beans, and he returns Milky White to the Baker and his Wife. The Witch later reveals that he is actually the Baker's father, who brought the curse on the family. He did not die, as the Baker thought, but ran out on his family. Toward the end of the play, he encourages his son to make better choices, thus acting like the father figure the Baker always needed.

Narrator

The Narrator serves the simple function of explaining the characters' histories and feelings to the audience. He does not really interact with the characters until they offer him to the Giantess in an effort to appease her. They tell him they do not like the way he tells their stories, and although he tells them they are better off with him than without, the Witch gives him to the Giantess and he is killed. Through this character, Sondheim and Lapine not only provide a traditional narrator befitting a fairy tale story, but they also comment on fiction and reality, while adding humor.

Rapunzel

Little is known about Rapunzel as a person, although her history is revealed to the audience as it is revealed to the Baker. Rapunzel is the Baker's sister that he never knew he had. The Witch took her as part of the Bakers' parents' punishment for stealing from her garden. The Witch has kept Rapunzel to herself by locking her in a tall tower that is only accessible by Rapunzel's very long hair. Rapunzel wishes to have other companions, and she begins allowing the Prince to climb up her hair. When she is banished from the tower by the Witch, Rapunzel finds her blinded Prince and heals his eyes with her tears. She is a tender and honest person with sincere feelings, although her life has left her naïve about the world and relationships. When her Prince rejects her for Snow White, she goes mad and is later crushed by the Giantess.

Rapunzel's Prince

Like Cinderella's Prince, Rapunzel's Prince is passionate about the object of his affection until he gets her. Although he sneaks into Rapunzel's tower and then endures being blinded by thorns for her, by act 2, he is bored with her and has his heart set on Snow White. He is ultimately fickle and immature.

Stepmother

The stereotypical wicked stepmother of fairy tale lore, Cinderella's Stepmother is cruel, mocking, arrogant, and ambitious. After giving Cinderella a seemingly impossible task to complete before going to the Festival, she unceremoniously leaves the poor girl behind while she, her daughters, and Cinderella's Father all leave for the Festival themselves. When Cinderella ends up on the throne, the Stepmother and her daughters are obsequious in their treatment of Cinderella, which is a complete turnaround that is wholly unbelievable.

The Steward

The Steward helps the Prince catch Cinderella. When the Giantess is trying to find the golden harp that Jack stole, the Steward hits Jack's Mother over the head to keep her from further aggravating the Giantess. The Steward's blow kills Jack's Mother.

The Witch

The character of the Witch is known for being the only character in the play who tells the truth. She is the most worldly and clever of the group. While she is not virtuous or selfless, she is honest and forthcoming. For example, she does not try to trick Jack into thinking he is safe, she makes it known that she intends to find him and hand him over to the Giantess. She is also oddly disappointed when the curse is reversed, making her young and beautiful but powerless. She misses her magical powers.

The Wolf

The Wolf is a creature of appetite, and he connives his way into finding out where Little Red Ridinghood's Granny lives so he can lay a trap for her. In his interaction with Little Red Ridinghood, he makes her feel uncomfortable even as he tempts her to break the rules her mother gave her. Of course, the rules are meant to keep her safe, and the Wolf has an altogether different agenda. Everything about him smacks of hunger and desire, and even the Baker (who is hiding, but watching) realizes the danger that the girl could face. The Wolf eats Granny and then tricks Little Red Ridinghood into coming close enough for him to eat her too. But the Baker finds the Wolf, cuts him open, and uses his skin to make Little Red Ridinghood a new cape.

THEMES

Consequences and Lost Innocence

Into the Woods is a retelling of the stories of several classic fairy tales. Those stories are already dark, but in Sondheim's and Lapine's hands, they go a shade darker. Little Red Ridinghood learns within the first act about trust, intuition, and the importance of obeying rules. Prior to learning these lessons, she was naïve and expected everything to be all right despite a devious Wolf lurking about tempting her to break rules and tricking her into giving him information. Because of her innocence, Little Red Ridinghood and her Granny are eaten by the Wolf—serious consequences. Their rescue is a grisly and bloody one, and the girl walks away a little less innocent and a little more wise than before.

Cinderella begins the story with a simple longing to go to the King's Festival, hoping for a temporary escape from her humdrum life of hard work. But her presence at the Festival sets in motion events that turn her world, and that of the Prince's and her entire family's, upside-down. Although her initial impulse is to avoid the Prince, she marries him with the expectation that she will enjoy her "happily ever after." However, the Prince is not the man she thought he was, and his eye soon wanders. In the end, Cinderella's dream is shattered, and although she retains her dignity, she is still filled with longing. Similarly, Rapunzel is the very picture of naïvetée, having been sequestered from the world for her entire life. When she finally escapes her tower and finds what she believes is true love, her heart is set up for heartbreak. The Prince she loves does not love her anymore, and his sights are set on another woman. The turn of events drives her to madness, and she is later crushed under the Giantess's foot.

The Baker and his Wife begin the story as fairly naïve characters, willing to say "yes" outright to any plan that will help them have a child. What they do not know is that their pursuit of the potion to reverse the curse will cost them—and others in their community—heavily. In the end, the Baker is a widower with a baby to raise, and he has lost many of his friends. What began innocently enough ends in tragedy. Jack, although he grows very little in the play, also loses the one person who is most important to him—his mother. Like the Baker, he is emotionally abandoned in the end.

TOPICS FOR FURTHER STUDY

- Choose two other Sondheim musicals, and look for similarities to and differences from *Into the Woods*. Can you see elements that characterize Sondheim's style? You may need to watch video recordings of the performances or listen to recordings of the songs to help get the feel for his particular approach to musical theater. Create a film or a slideshow to teach young actors and directors about Sondheim's style. Your piece should explain each element in detail and provide at least two examples from the works you have explored.

- Because the characters are fairy tale characters, they possess certain universal traits. Choose the character to whom you most relate and the one to whom you least relate, and find two more examples of these kinds of characters in literature. What is it that makes you most or least like them? Prepare a personality profile of the six characters you have selected.

- What is the psychological meaning of the woods? They appear in many fairy tales and other works of fiction, and they carry a great deal of symbolic meaning. After conducting research on various psychological theories on the subject, write your own essay exploring these ideas.

- Fairy tales are not always light-hearted fare. Who were the Brothers Grimm, and how did their names become synonymous with fairy tales? What was the original purpose of such tales, and why did they seek to preserve them? Prepare a short lecture on this topic and present it to your class.

- Find one other fairy tale and determine how you would fit it into the action and plot twists of *Into the Woods*. Outline your addition to the story, and choose one scene into which you will insert your new characters.

Parent-Child Relationships

Throughout *Into the Woods*, parent-child relationships are depicted in various lights. Cinderella is for all practical purposes an orphan. Her mother is dead, and her father has no relationship with her and will not protect her from her wicked stepfamily. Cinderella ultimately learns that, as bad as it is has been having no mother and a disconnected father, it is just as bad to have a husband who is unfaithful. The castle and her position in it are no substitute for true love and respect. Jack and his Mother represent the quintessential dysfunctional family. With a harsh mother, Jack has transferred all of his loving feelings to a cow, who is able to offer him as much warmth and understanding as his mother. He is simple and emotional, his mother is domineering and judgmental, and his father is gone. Consequently, Jack is never taught how to be independent or how to take his place as a man in the world.

The Baker believed all his life that his parents died in a baking accident, but later learns that his father left the family. This is a difficult position for the Baker because he did not have the benefit of growing up with his parents to guide and love him, and then he has to face his resentment toward his father when he learns the truth. But his father returns to him as a spirit to offer much-needed advice at an important point in the Baker's life. It becomes a turning point that enables the Baker to be a good father to his own son—like the father that he so desperately wanted himself.

Rapunzel has been separated from her real parents since her birth, when she was handed over to the Witch. Since then, the Witch has been Rapunzel's entire family and a sort of surrogate mother. But the Witch acts towards Rapunzel completely out of selfishness and possessiveness. She does not want to be alone, so she does not want to share Rapunzel with the world. However, the Witch is unable to see how she is crippling Rapunzel, who needs more than just the Witch in her life, and it ultimately drives Rapunzel away from her.

The Individual in Society

The characters' stories in *Into the Woods* are so interrelated that every decision seems to affect the entire community. This illustrates the importance of the individual's responsibility to his or her society as a whole. When the Baker and his Wife set about collecting the ingredients for the potion, they give little thought to how their tasks will affect others. The Baker senses that Little Red Ridinghood is in danger when he overhears her talking to the Wolf. He is only there because he needs her cape, and the Witch convinces him to forget about protecting the girl and just get the cape. Consequently, Little Red Ridinghood and her Granny are in serious trouble. While the Baker is the one who rescues them, it is only because he sees the cape in the Wolf's mouth, and he wants it. His selfish pursuit brings major consequences on others, just as when he gets Jack in trouble with his mother when he coerces Jack to trade the cow for beans (that the Baker does not believe are really magic). As a result of the trade with the beans, the beanstalk to the Giants' land grows, bringing both treasure and tragedy.

Similarly, if Jack's Mother had been more understanding with Jack, she may not have carelessly tossed the beans out the window in the first place. Her personal reaction brought serious consequences (including death) to members of the community as a whole. But Jack is not completely off the hook, either. If he had listened to his mother instead of making a rash trade for the beans, he would not have ended up with a beanstalk in his yard that would take him to the treacherous Giants' realm. And if he had been able to stand up to Little Red Ridinghood, he would not have gone back up the beanstalk one time too many. These decisions cost his community dearly, as homes are destroyed, friends and family are killed, and two innocent giants also perish. Jack's selfish decisions not only impacted his society, but also affected the lives of the two giants outside of his society.

STYLE

Musical

Sondheim wrote music and lyrics for Lapine's story so that *Into the Woods* would be a musical. The songs in the play accomplish two things. First, Sondheim uses the lyrics to full effect so that they provide background information and character insight, rather than being meant as pure entertainment. In some songs, multiple characters are singing at once, either individually or together, which helps the audience better understand how all the storylines tie together. The songs in *Into the Woods* are as important to the plot as the spoken segments. Second, the play being a musical suits its content and style. It is a fairy tale written to be blatantly fictional escapism. That characters burst into song throughout the play underscores that it is a fantasy, while fueling the play's high level of energy.

Frenetic Pace

Once the characters and their basic situations are introduced, the play takes on a frenetic pace. Although the action of the story is tied together by the Baker and his Wife looking for the ingredients for the potion, the other characters all have their own side stories going on simultaneously. Because they are all on some kind of mission (taking treats to Granny, selling the cow, etc.), there is a lot going on onstage at all times. That the characters are all interrelated only makes the action more complicated.

Throughout the play, there are times when several plots are being advanced at the same time, and the characters alternate lines that are about their own missions and also about a broader theme of the play. This back-and-forth style of delivering lines, especially by actors who are moving on- and offstage through the woods, gives the play an energetic pace. There are only a few times in the entire play (the beginning and end of each act) when the characters are being still and reflective. The high-energy pace of the play underscores the theme of pursuit and the characters's determination to reach their goals.

Fairy Tale

Sondheim and Lapine imbue *Into the Woods* with fairy tale references, characters, and language. The first lines spoken in the play, by the Narrator, are "Once upon a time," and later in the first scene, the Witch says, "I thought. . . . we all might live happily ever after." These are lines that people associate specifically with fairy tales. Scene 2 opens in the woods, which figure largely in the tradition of fairy tales. Little Red Ridinghood, Snow White, Sleeping Beauty, and Hansel and Gretel all take place in the woods. Sondheim and Lapine also make a point of depicting their characters in the exact ways the audience and reader remember them from the classic fairy tales. For example, when Little Red Ridinghood encounters the Wolf in disguise as Granny at the cottage, they exchange the famous lines that audience members and readers know so well (i.e., "What big eyes you have!" "The better to see you with," and so on).

Introducing so many familiar fairy tale elements makes it easy for the audience or reader to surrender to the idea that this is a fairy tale fully in the tradition of the familiar childhood stories. In doing so, the reader understands that the story is a complete fantasy, but that it is also intended to illustrate a lesson.

HISTORICAL CONTEXT

History of Fairy Tales

Myths, fairy tales, and fables have been around since the earliest civilizations. They are a subset of folk tales, differentiated by their inclusion of supernatural elements (magic, talking animals, spells, goblins, and so on) structured around a lesson. The tradition of fairy tales, however, emerged from folk tales and their oral tradition. Tales from ancient Egypt depicted supernatural occurrences as this world and the divine world met. They also depicted a clear separation between good and bad. Because less than one percent of the ancient Egyptians were literate, the oral tradition was critical in preserving and passing down these stories. In fact, some of the Egyptian stories were actually preserved by Greek writers like Herodotus (fifth century B.C.E.). In ancient Rome and Greece, mythologies surrounding the gods were central to classical cultures. Because the stories about the gods depicted them as having human characteristics and flaws, and because the stories involved their interactions with and manipulations of humans, early people were careful to respect the gods and goddesses. The myths not only explained natural phenomena (such as the echo), but they also provided lessons in the form of cautionary tales. Aesop's famous fables (sixth century B.C.E.) were written specifically to teach important lessons in a way that was easy for people and children to understand. In the New Testament, Jesus uses parables in the same way, although without supernatural elements.

In Europe, the fairy tale tradition emerged as more of a social than a religious construct. The most famous writers and preservers of fairy tales are Hans Christian Andersen (1805–1875; Denmark) and Jacob and Wilhelm Grimm, known as the Brothers Grimm (1785–1863 and 1786–1859, respectively; Germany). Their writings provide the basis for such well-known stories as Little Red Riding Hood, Sleeping Beauty, and Thumbelina. Perhaps because of the efforts

COMPARE
&
CONTRAST

- **1986:** Sondheim and Lapine complete *Into the Woods*, and the following year it opens on Broadway. The original Broadway production will run 764 performances, and garner numerous Tony Award nominations with two wins for the writing and music, and one for the acting.

  Today: Another musical based on well-known fairy tale figures, *Wicked* by Stephen Schwartz and Winnie Holzman, has met with the same popularity as *Into the Woods*. It is about the background of the witches from L. Frank Baum's classic novel, *The Wizard of Oz*. The musical opened on Broadway in October 2003. In its first year it was nominated for ten Tony Awards, with three wins for acting, costume, and scene design.

- **1986:** When fairy tales were first told, the best that most women could hope for was a good marriage, which explains the prevalence of stories about young girls who find themselves happily betrothed to princes. By 1986, however, women have several other options to choose from. Indeed, the median age for a woman's first marriage is 23, and according to the U.S. Census Bureau, in 1980, 39 percent of

  American adults are unmarried. This number slowly rises to 41 percent by the end of the decade, indicating an increasing willingness to wait for, or forego, marriage, and an increased social acceptance of that decision.

  Today: The trend of women who marry later in life or not at all continues. In 2005, the median age for a woman's first marriage is 25.5, and 44 percent of Americans over the age of fifteen are unmarried.

- **1986:** Although written between 1937 and 1955, J. R. R. Tolkien's *Lord of the Rings* series remains very popular among young adult readers, as does C. S. Lewis's *The Chronicles of Narnia* series, written between 1949 and 1954. These are the modern fairy tales that have somewhat eclipsed the tales of the Brothers Grimm.

  Today: The overwhelming popularity of J. K. Rowling's *Harry Potter* series has further added to the canon of modern fairy tales. Published between 1997 and 2007, the seven-volume series contains such fairy tale elements as magic, spells, good versus evil, magic animals, and elves.

---

of these writers, fairy tales grew in popularity in Europe toward the end of the seventeenth century. In modern culture, many of the evil and frightening elements have been made more palatable for young children, and the stories have found their way into the mainstream through movies, books, and toys. Despite the sometimes extensive editing that has taken place over time, the main lessons remain intact, thus preserving the original purpose of the stories. More modern renditions of the fairy tale include George Orwell's *Animal Farm* and J. R. R. Tolkien's *Lord of the Rings* series.

Musicals

Musical theater has its roots in the over-the-top burlesques and vaudevilles of the early twentieth

century. Over time, musical theater matured into a form that entertained while moving the hearts of the audience, teaching about life, and commenting on life and society. Theater historians generally agree that the modern musical underwent significant growth between the 1920s and the 1950s. The 1970s had seen a lot of energy and change in musical productions. While there were new conventional musicals (with traditional story structure, clearly good characters versus clearly bad characters, and catchy, family-friendly music) and revivals of classics like *My Fair Lady, Man of La Mancha*, and *The King and I*, there were new styles too. Musicals like *The Wiz* and *Grease* brought rock and roll music to the stage, and "rock operas" like *Jesus Christ, Superstar* and

Scene from the 2007 The Royal Opera ROH2 Linbury Theatre/Covent Garden London production of Into the Woods, *starring Suzanne Toase as Little Red Riding Hood and Nicholas Garrett as Wolf*

(© Donald Cooper / Photostage)

Godspell were also groundbreaking. "Concept musicals," which are built around an idea instead of a storyline, like *A Little Night Music* and *A Chorus Line* brought a more abstract style to musicals and showed that the boundaries of theater could still be pushed.

In the wake of these changes in the 1970s, the musicals in the 1980s were open to further development, and audiences were open-minded about what producers had to offer. Traditionally-styled musicals still had a place, as evidenced by the success of *42nd Street* and *Big Rover*. The quirky *Little Shop of Horrors* appealed to audiences with a dark sense of humor and an appreciation for B-movie plot lines. And the all-time longest running show, *Cats*, first premiered in 1982 and ran for two decades. Less plot-driven, and more like a revue, *Cats* created so much interest that numerous productions were launched all over the world. Another unconventional musical was Sondheim's and Lapine's Pulitzer Prize winner, *Sunday in the Park with George* (1985).

CRITICAL OVERVIEW

Critics tend to embrace *Into the Woods* for its wit, sophistication, and clever retelling of familiar stories. Reviewers note how Sondheim and Lapine bring modern themes and challenges into a setting as old-fashioned as fairy tale woods. David Van Leer writes in *Raritan* that audiences who go to the musical for a dose of Sondheim's usual cynicism "will be surprised by both the fidelity of the treatment and the emphasis on the social, not psychological implications of the stories." Robert L. McLaughlin notes in the *Journal of American Drama and Theatre* that the play:

> explores individual responses to dehumanizing societal forces. Society continues to have a debilitating effect on individuals and couples, but this effect becomes deadly: the entire second act is played out under the threat of imminent total destruction analogous to the threat of nuclear-tipped ICBMs [intercontinental ballistic missiles] we live under every day.

The characters in the play are familiar, but characterized in new ways. In an article for the *Explicator*, Brian Sutton draws parallels between Sondheim's characters and a study about the phases of maturation for college students. He notes that "it is not surprising that the characters, like many incoming college students, at first view the world with a childlike, simplistic dualism that prevents the woods from seeming dark and tangled." He explains that the characters initially see things in terms of black-and-white, right-and-wrong, or dangerous-and-safe, with little understanding of anything in between. Indeed, as Brad Leithauser observes in the *New York Review of Books*: "The 'happily ever after' refrain closes the first but not the final act. Still to come are knives, wandering blind women, murders, and betrayals. It's a disenchanted tale of enchantment." In the *Cambridge Companion to the Musical*, Jim Lovensheimer notes that such familiar characters as Cinderella, Jack, Rapunzel, and Snow White all have personal challenges, but work together "to solve bigger problems." He further notes that the play as a whole is about outsiders, and that the song "'No One Is Alone' is a benevolent anthem to outsiders—people are never completely disconnected from others in their thoughts and actions." McLaughlin remarks on how the characters grow over the course of the play: "To bring order to these chaotic familial relationships, each character must not only achieve his or her quest but also mature psychologically." He adds that when the characters work together to defeat the Giantess, they grow collectively and individually. He explains that "as individuals they are helpless. They need to connect with others and understand how their actions affect others in the human community in order to accomplish anything."

WHAT DO I READ NEXT?

- *The Complete Grimm's Fairy Tales* (1974), by the Brothers Grimm, includes all of the Grimm stories, including the most famous ("Little Red Cap," "Cinderella," "Rapunzel," and others) as well as less well-known stories. This edition is praised by critics for its thoroughness, its excellent translation, and its beautiful illustrations.

- Mark Eden Horowitz's *Sondheim on Music: Minor Details and Major Decisions* (2003) is a collection of interviews and conversations with Sondheim about his writing process. He shares his wisdom about themes, motifs, characterization, rhythm, and mood.

- Stuart A. Kallen's *A Cultural History of the United States through the Decades: The 1980s* (1998) covers the important events and trends of the political scene in the 1980s in America. The book also includes cultural and historical overviews of the decade.

- Meryle Secrest's *Stephen Sondheim: A Life* (1998) gives students of Sondheim's work a biographical overview along with summaries and discussion of his major works.

- *Four by Sondheim* (2000) is a single volume that includes some of Sondheim's best-loved works, written with Hugh Wheeler, James Lapine, Larry Gelbart and Burt Shevelove, respectively. This anthology includes *A Little Night Music*, *Sweeney Todd*, *Sunday in the Park with George* (his first collaboration with Lapine), and *A Funny Thing Happened on the Way to the Forum*.

CRITICISM

Jennifer A. Bussey

Bussey is an independent writer specializing in literature. In the following essay, she explores the theme of pursuit, the portrayal of women, and the presence of external danger to demonstrate how Into the Woods *is clearly a product of the 1980s.*

Published and produced in 1986, *Into the Woods* bears many of the hallmarks of having been written in the 1980s. The setting, the music, and the language is timeless, and the content is applicable to the commonalities of human experience, but the play does bear the subtle fingerprint of that decade. The theme of pursuit, the

> IT IS A TESTAMENT TO SONDHEIM AND LAPINE THAT A PLAY WITH SUCH CLEAR TIES TO THE DECADE IN WHICH IT WAS WRITTEN IS ABLE TO TRANSCEND TRENDS AND TOPICALITY TO BE UNIVERSALLY ENTERTAINING AND RELEVANT."

portrayal of women, and the response to a serious external threat are all portrayed in a way that is consistent with American thought and culture in the 1980s.

The frantic pace and the characters' motivations are all fueled by pursuit and, in some cases, greed. None of the characters are truly content with their current lots in life, and they are in active pursuit of something more. The Baker and his wife drop everything to go after the four ingredients needed to make the potion that will break the curse that has rendered them childless. They are not content with one another, and they forgo all ethics to get the things they need for the potion. Lying (they think) to Jack to get the cow, stealing Little Red Ridinghood's cape outright, trying to swindle Cinderella out of her slipper, and tricking Rapunzel into lowering her much-needed hair—all of these decisions are somehow justified in their minds because their pursuit is more important to them than treating other people fairly.

Cinderella is understandably discontent with her situation, living with a family that does not love her or care about her. Even her own father stands idly by while her stepfamily mistreats her and uses her as a servant. She is as objectified by them as she later is by the Prince. But readers can certainly understand why she would pursue her desire to go to the King's Festival; she wants to have fun and feel like a vibrant young woman, at least for a little while. What is less clear is why, when she catches the Prince's eye, she runs away from him and hides. At that point, it is the Prince who is in pursuit of the thing he wants and that is out of reach. He is relentless in his pursuit, bringing along his Steward and layering pitch on the steps to try to catch Cinderella. His motivation is rooted in immaturity and stubbornness—the more elusive Cinderella is, the more he is determined to have her. His brother,

Rapunzel's Prince, is no better. He sees Rapunzel and is determined to have her, pursuing her up the tower and beyond. But he also loses interest in his lady love after he catches her, and his eye turns to another who he then pursues. The Princes are only interested in pursuit for its own sake.

The Wolf is also in pursuit, but his pursuit of Little Red Ridinghood and Granny is different from the other characters' pursuit of what they want. Where they chase, he plots. He tricks the girl into revealing where Granny's cottage is so he can get there first, eat Granny, then disguise himself and wait for the girl. He gets what he wants, but he soon finds that this leads to his demise.

Jack and his Mother are also pursuing things, but they have very different goals. Jack has to give up Milky White, so he is single-minded in his plans to get her back. His Mother, on the other hand, wants wealth and material comforts. Although all of these characters reflect the emerging consumer culture of the 1980s, perhaps Jack's Mother is the most literal representation. In the 1980s, the pursuit of monetary success and material goods characterized the culture. Indeed, the prevailing culture in America during the 1980s was to do what it took to be successful and to be able to buy nice things. People were encouraged to be dissatisfied with what they had, and this lack of contentment drove people to work long hours and make great sacrifices for the sake of a career and financial success. Surely, audiences in this time period would readily identify with the frantic pursuits of the characters depicted in *Into the Woods*. The question then becomes whether or not they would learn from Jack, who found that once he had taken risks to pursue adventure and excitement, he missed the simple life he left behind.

The 1980s were also a time of greater opportunity and independence for women. This was the result of the activism and growing feminist movement of the 1960s and 1970s, and women in the 1980s were educated and ambitious. Not only did they seize opportunities the women before them had worked hard to make available, but they were outspoken in their fight to receive equal pay and respect in the workplace. At home, more women were willing to wait longer to get married, while others were less fixated on getting married at all. More women became career-oriented, deriving their self-worth and identity from the workplace rather than from running a home or from romantic relationships.

In *Into the Woods*, the Baker's Wife is more assertive and independent than her husband, and it is she who sometimes keeps pushing him toward their mutual goal. Despite living in an oppressive home where she is merely a servant, Cinderella is not desperate to get married. Her self-esteem remains firmly intact, and when her Prince cheats on her, she does not hesitate to leave him. Unlike the traditional Cinderella, this one is not waiting passively for a prince to ride in and rescue her. Finally, the Witch is more interested in power than beauty. When the curse on her is reversed, her youthful beauty is restored but at the cost of her power. She laments the loss of her previous life. All three of these women reflect the changing status and attitudes of women in the 1980s.

Another reflection of the times in *Into the Woods* is the presence of and reaction to a serious external threat. All is well in the woods until the end of act 1, when another beanstalk grows. In act 2, the threat of the new beanstalk is revealed when the widow of the Giant Jack killed climbs down to seek revenge for her husband's death. The Giantess is bigger, stronger, and madder than they are, and because she is a foreign creature, she is mysterious and frightening. Only the Witch seems to know how to handle a giant. The group of characters responds first by blaming one another for bringing this danger into their midst, before they ultimately organize themselves to work together to defeat her.

The Giantess is reminiscent of the Cold War between the United States and the Soviet Union, which was still a prominent issue in the 1980s. President Ronald Reagan and Soviet leader Mikhail Gorbachev were at odds, but fearful of provoking each other because each country possessed nuclear weapons and war could lead to "mutually assured destruction." For Americans, the threat of nuclear war was a serious threat, and the Soviets were perceived as a mysterious enemy (just as the Giantess was in the play). The solution in the play is the same as it is in foreign affairs; the nation (or community) must join together and take action. In the play, while the characters bicker about whose fault it is that the Giantess is there, she roams freely and destructively through the woods. Once they join together, however, the threat is eliminated.

It is a testament to Sondheim and Lapine that a play with such clear ties to the decade in which it was written is able to transcend trends and topicality to be universally entertaining and relevant. Perhaps it is the timeless setting, or the depth of characterization, or the clear cause-and-effect in the action of the play that captures the attention of audiences today.

Source: Jennifer A. Bussey, Critical Essay on *Into the Woods*, in *Drama for Students*, Gale, Cengage Learning, 2008.

Gale

In the following excerpt, the critic gives a critical analysis of Sondheim's work.

Stephen Sondheim's contributions to twentieth-century musical theater have been so significant that the *Dramatists Guild Literary Quarterly* designated its first ten years as the "Sondheim decade." "There can hardly have been an issue since," the editors commented, "when a work by Stephen Sondheim...wasn't a major attraction on the Broadway scene, and often more than one." Sondheim has indeed been instrumental in revolutionizing the stage musical. The composer's ability to incorporate a variety of musical styles into his scores caused T. E. Kalem of *Time* to claim after seeing a Sondheim production that the "entire score is an incredible display of musical virtuosity." Using music, Sondheim creates an attitude for the dramatic situation so that individual songs may push the drama along. Sometimes, unlike most of his predecessors, the composer strays from the traditional rhyming structure. Too, his lyrical cynicism and satire have moved musical comedy from the lighter and simpler shows of Rodgers and Hammerstein to what is termed "conceptual musicals."

Instead of escapism, Sondheim's conceptual musicals present serious concerns and dramatic subtexts. Each of the composer's works depends on one fundamental concept to act as a framework. One of the creators of the new, unromantic musical production, Sondheim has helped to place the musical on a more serious level than that of the traditional Broadway show. When Sondheim composes, it is a cooperative effort. "I go about starting a song first with the collaborators," he once divulged, "sometimes just with the book writer, sometimes with the director. We have long discussions and I take notes, just general notes, and then we decide what the song should be about, and I try to make a title." The composer, according to Sondheim, must stage numbers or draw "blueprints" so that the director or the choreographer may see the uses of a song.

> ESSENTIALLY ABOUT THE LOSS OF INNOCENCE, THE PLAY EXPLORES THE 'GRIM' IN THE BROTHERS GRIMM AND IN OTHER TELLERS OF CHILDREN'S TALES. TURNING FAIRYTALES LIKE *CINDERELLA* AND *LITTLE RED RIDING HOOD* ON THEIR HEADS, THE TWO ACTS OF *INTO THE WOODS* MOVE FROM THE HAPPILY TO THE UNHAPPILY EVER AFTER. "

For Sondheim, collaboration usually begins with the book and book writer from whom "you should steal." Since a good production sounds as though one writer is responsible for both the book and the score, the book writer and composer must work together if a play is to have texture. "Any book writer I work with knows what I'm going to do," explained Sondheim, "and I try to help him out wherever I can; that's the only way you make a piece, make a texture." "I keep hearing about people," he continued, "who write books and then give them to composers or composers who write scores and then get a book writer. I don't understand how that works."

Sondheim's first Broadway collaboration! has an unusual history. At the age of twenty-five, the composer completed the music and lyrics for *Saturday Night*, a musical that never saw the Broadway stage owing to the death of its producer Lemuel Ayers. But *Saturday Night* still served Sondheim well. "It was my portfolio," he once explained, "and as a result of it I got *West Side Story*." The story of the ugly life on a city street, with only glimpses of beauty and love, *West Side Story* is considered one of the masterpieces of the American theater. Beginning its first run in New York in 1957, *West Side Story* ran for 734 performances on Broadway. After an extended tour of the United States, the play began a second Broadway run of 249 performances. In 1961 *West Side Story* was adapted into a motion picture that captured ten Academy Awards and became one of the greatest screen musicals in terms of commercial success.

Many critics have attributed much of *West Side Story*'s popularity to its musical score. In *The Complete Book of the American Musical Theatre*, David A. Ewen named the score as "one of the most powerful assets to this grim tragedy." Ewen cited "Maria," "I Feel Pretty," and "Somewhere" as "unforgettable lyrical episodes." Sondheim's comic songs, such as "America" and "Gee, Officer Krupke!," have also been applauded for their wittiness and their roles as satirical commentaries.

Sondheim's next production was *Gypsy*, a musical based on the autobiography of burlesque star Gypsy Rose Lee. Initially, Sondheim was contracted to write both the music and the lyrics for this show, but actress Ethel Merman felt uneasy with a little-known composer. So Jule Styne composed *Gypsy*'s music while Sondheim wrote the lyrics. Although the play is entertaining in the tradition of Broadway musicals, it is on a deeper level the story of universal human needs. One song from *Gypsy*, "Some People," is considered by several critics to be one of the best ever written.

An old-fashioned burlesque, *A Funny Thing Happened on the Way to the Forum*, followed *Gypsy*. Sondheim and playwrights Burt Shevelove and Larry Gelbart adapted *Forum* from the comedies of Plautus, a classical Roman playwright. The play is bawdy, rough-and-tumble, and fun. A low comedy of lechers and courtesans done in a combination of ancient Roman and American vaudeville techniques, *Forum* is paced with ambiguous meanings, risque connotations, and not-so-subtle innuendos. For instance, a slave carrying a piece of statuary is told by a matron: "Carry my bust with pride." Typically Sondheim, the score is saturated with humor. Some critics have cited "Everybody Ought to Have a Maid" as particularly amusing while "Lovely" has been suspected, at least by one critic, of being Sondheim's satire of his own song "Tonight." For *Forum*, unlike most of his previous plays, Sondheim wrote both the lyrics and the music. "With *Forum*," a *Time* reviewer noted, "Sondheim finally proved that he, like Noel Coward, could indeed go it alone." *Forum* received a Tony Award as the season's best musical and in 1966 adapted for film and released by United Artists as a motion picture starring Zero Mostel, Jack Gilford, Phil Silvers, and Buster Keaton.

During 1970 and 1971 Sondheim produced two works in collaboration with Hal Prince and

Michael Bennett that were considered to be "concept musicals." *Company* (1970) has no plot, but is a montage of observations about the institution of marriage. It depicts five married couples who hold a birthday party for a bachelor friend. As the play progresses, the observer realizes the amount of disharmony present within the marital relationships. *Company* garnered the New York Drama Critics Award and six Tony Awards, and completed a run of 690 performances.

1970's *Follies* focuses upon a reunion of two former showgirls from the fictional Weismann Follies who are about to witness the end of an era signified by the demolition of a once-renowned theater building. The play received seven Tony Awards and the Drama Critics Circle Award for best musical.

In 1973, when several critics worried that the Broadway musical had degenerated to an embarrassing state of high camp and rock music, Sondheim's *A Little Night Music* appeared, restoring faith in musical theater. Critics recognized *A Little Night Music* to be as spectacular as the great musicals that had gone before it, but also recognized its serious vein. Sondheim composed all the musical's songs in three-quarter time or multiples of that meter; this served as the play's concept and tied it together. Three-quarter time was the foundation to which the composer added a Greek chorus, canons, and fuguetos. Subtexts were injected into almost every song—most notably in "Every Day a Little Death," which allows a countess to express her feelings of loneliness as a philanderer's wife. In addition, Sondheim devoted himself to the "inner monologue song," which is a song, a *Time* critic explained, "in which characters sing of their deepest thoughts, but almost never to each other."

Though *A Little Night Music* addresses the standard musical-comedy subject—love—it "is a masquelike affair, tailor-made to fit Sondheim's flair for depicting confused people experiencing ambivalent thoughts and feelings," the *Time* reviewer assessed. Many of the songs illustrate ambivalence because Sondheim likes neurotic people. He once revealed: "I like troubled people. Not that I don't like squared-away people, but I *prefer* neurotic people. I like to hear rumblings beneath the surface." The show's cast of confused characters includes the giddy child-bride whose middle-aged husband takes up with his ex-mistress while his adolescent son has a crush on his new stepmother. Of course, the above-mentioned countess laments the sadness

of her marriage to a straying husband, and a lusty chambermaid salutes carnal love through the play. Critically, *A Little Night Music* was a triumph. Many reviewers agreed that the strongest element in the play is Sondheim's score, which was compared to the work of musical greats such as Cole Porter and Lorenz Hart.

In 1976 Sondheim again collaborated with Hal Prince in the production of *Pacific Overtures*, a show that encompasses 120 years of Japanese history from 1856 to modern times. *Pacific Overtures* was performed by an entirely Asian, male cast and in order to achieve the correct sound, Sondheim used many Asian instruments in the orchestration. He also utilized elements of Japanese Kabuki theater, Haiku poetry, and Japanese pentatonic musical scales. *New York Times* reviewer Clive Barnes considered *Pacific Overtures* to be "very, very different."

Sondheim once again made his presence known on Broadway with *Sweeney Todd: The Demon Barber of Fleet Street*. He became interested in the play in 1973, related Mel Gussow of the *New York Times*, "when he saw a production of the melodrama at the Stratford East Theatre in England. He was captivated by it, although, as he said, 'I found it much more passionate and serious than the audience did.'" Composed as if it were an opera, *Sweeney Todd* is the story of a murderous barber who sends his victims downstairs to a pie shop where they become the secret ingredients in Mrs. Lovett's meat pies. By Sondheim's own admission, the play "has a creepy atmosphere." The main character, Todd, is out for revenge. Judge Turpin, who desired Todd's wife and daughter, shipped the barber off to Australia as punishment for a crime that he did not commit. Todd escapes and returns seeking vengeance. His attempt to kill the judge fails, causing his revenge to snowball into mass murder. In the end, Todd kills Turpin, but by then the barber, too, is doomed.

Sweeney Todd is about revenge. Harold Prince's production, however, mirrors the industrial age, its influences, and its effects. The play received numerous Drama Desk Awards and Tony Awards in 1979, including best score of a musical. In the opinion of director Harold Prince, the play's music is "the most melodic and romantic score that Steve has ever written. The music is soaring." Nearly eighty percent of the show is music, and musical motifs recur throughout the score to maintain the audience's emotional level. Sondheim even incorporated a musical clue, a theme associated with a character, into the score.

In 1984 Sondheim teamed up with artist-turned-dramatist James Lapine to create the musical *Sunday in the Park with George.* For Lapine and Sondheim, their first collaboration was a remarkable success, garnering the 1985 Pulitzer Prize for drama. Their feat was made even more unusual by the fact that *Sunday in the Park with George* is centered around an idea Clive Barnes deemed "audaciously ambitious" in the *New York Post.* "It is to show us the creation of a work of art, the formulation of an artistic style based on scientific principles, and to reveal, in passing, the struggles of an artist for recognition," Barnes explained.

"I write generally experimental, unexpected work," Sondheim told Samuel G. Freedman in the *New York Times;* he made that truth perhaps nowhere more evident than in *Sunday in the Park with George.* Conceptual rather than plot-driven, the play structures itself around two vignettes that are performed as two separate acts. The first follows French pointillist Georges Seurat in the evolution of his renowned painting *A Sunday Afternoon on the Island of La Grande Jatte.* The second is centered upon the artistic struggles of the American great-grandson of the artist, the "George" of the play's title, who pays homage to his ancestor's work through modern laser artistry.

Critical response to *Sunday in the Park with George* was divided. Many felt that the play confirmed the belief that the creative process is inherently undramatic. David Sterritt, in a review for the *Christian Science Monitor,* pointed to a conflict between the desire to depict art and the desire to depict an artist as the source for the play's failure. *Sunday in the Park with George,* he wrote, "hovers between the formal elegance of *La Grande Jatte* and the living, breathing, potentially fascinating life of Seurat himself—but partakes fully of neither." Other critics took exception to what they saw as the autobiographical note sounded by the play's theme: in the depiction of Seurat's rejection by art critics of his time, many felt, was Sondheim's venting of his frustration at his own critical reception. "It is easy to see why Stephen Sondheim should have been attracted to the idea of creating a musical about Georges Seurat, whose career is a way of discussing some of the dilemmas that confront the contemporary artist," Howard Kissel observed in *Women's Wear Daily.* Kissel went on to object to

what he saw as the "defensive" stance Sondheim reveals in songs like "Lesson #8," and to dismiss the notion that the play is avant garde. Instead, the critic expressed the opinion that *Sunday in the Park with George* is merely contrived.

Yet many critics were compelled by the play's premise and convinced of its status as a breakthrough for theater. "To say that this show breaks new ground is not enough; it also breaks new sky, new water, new flesh and new spirit," Jack Kroll proclaimed in *Newsweek.* Kroll not only approved of the material, but he celebrated the pairing of Lapine and Sondheim, declaring that over the course of the musical its creators "take us full circle, implying that there's still hope for vision in a high-tech world and that art and love may be two forms of the same energy . . . , in this show of beauty, wit, nobility and ardor, [that idea] makes this Sondheim's best work since . . . his classic collaborations with Harold Prince."

Not surprisingly, Lapine and Sondheim went on to collaborate on the 1986 musical *Into the Woods.* Again, their collaboration was richly rewarding. Winner of Tony awards for lyrics and outstanding musical, the play was a greater commercial success than *Sunday in the Park with George.* Essentially about the loss of innocence, the play explores the "grim" in the Brothers Grimm and in other tellers of children's tales. Turning fairytales like *Cinderella* and *Little Red Riding Hood* on their heads, the two acts of *Into the Woods* move from the happily to the unhappily ever after. Yet the musical ends on the surprisingly upbeat notes of the song "No One Is Alone," prompting some critics to complain that Sondheim had sold out to public demand for lighter material. Others, however, found the musical wholly appealing. "It is that joyous rarity," wrote Elizabeth L. Bland and William A. Henry III in a *Time* review, "a work of sophisticated artistic ambition and deep political purpose that affords nonstop pleasure."

In 1990 Sondheim earned his first Academy Award for the song "Sooner or Later (I Always Get My Man)," composed for the movie *Dick Tracy* and sung by Madonna. From there, Sondheim went on to create a uniquely American show, *Assassins,* which showcases the assassins and would-be assassins of presidents of the United States. With characters such as John Wilkes Booth and Lynette "Squeaky" Fromme, the musical quickly earned the reputation of being Sondheim's darkest work to date. Undaunted, theater-goers lined up in droves for its sold-out run in 1991.

Two years later Sondheim received a prestigious lifetime achievement award from the Kennedy Center in Washington, D.C. In 1994 he answered with another award-winning musical, *Passion*. Based on an obscure Italian movie, the work features a love triangle between Fosca, an ugly, frail woman; Giorgio, a handsome Italian army officer; and Clara, Giorgio's beautiful mistress. After being assigned to a regiment in Parma, Italy, Giorgio meets the tormented Fosca. The two develop a rapport based on their mutual interest in literature, but their friendship quickly takes a new turn when Fosca declares her obsession and love for Giorgio. Repulsed by Fosca, Giorgio is nonetheless unable to rid her from his mind. Fosca pursues Giorgio relentlessly; when Giorgio finally admits that he too is in love with her, the two consummate their love. Fosca dies shortly thereafter, while Giorgio, on the verge of a nervous breakdown, is admitted to a hospital.

Audiences and critics alike had mixed reactions to *Passion*. *Nation* critic David Kaufman remarked, "A dark tale of an obsessive love that is cut short after it finally finds its perfect object, *Passion* is archetypal Sondheim in its content." Calling the work "passionless," Kaufman concluded that it "emerges as more of an elegant chamber piece than a full-scale musical." Similarly, Ben Brantley in the *New York Times* noted that *Passion* "isn't perfect. . . . There's an inhibited quality here that asks to be exploded and never is." But Robert Brustein of the *New Republic* declared the musical "Sondheim's deepest, most powerful work. . . . *Passion* is a triumph of rare and complex sensibility, fully imagined, fully realized." Despite its mixed reception, the show won several Tony awards, including best musical and, for Sondheim, best original music score.

In 2000, upon the occasion of his seventieth birthday, Sondheim granted an interview to *New York Times* magazine writer Frank Rich. When asked to critique his own work, Sondheim said: "Verbosity is the thing I have to fight most in the lyrics department. . . . 'Less is more' is a lesson learned with a difficulty." He later added: "I'm accused so often of not having melodic gifts, but I like the music I write. Harmony gives music its life, its emotional color, more than rhythm."

Source: Gale, "Stephen Sondheim," in *Contemporary Authors Online*, Gale, Cengage Learning, 2007.

> THE MOST DISTURBING AND UNSETTLING DISPLACEMENT OF CERTAINTY OCCURS WITH THE LOSS OF THE NARRATIVE/DIDACTIC FRAME, PERSONIFIED IN THE DEATH OF THE NARRATOR."

Mark K. Fulk

In the following essay, Fulk defines Into the Woods *as postmodern, further noting that the characters are driven by desire. The adultery that occurs in the play, Fulk claims, is used as a vehicle to explore gender issues.*

The Baker's Wife falls victim to confusion and punishment in the woods in Stephen Sondheim and James Lapine's 1986 musical *Into the Woods*. Like the other characters, she is led into the woods by her desire. Initially, the characters of *Into the Woods* are shaping and controlling their own desires. The chorus of "I wish" that opens the play shows that desire is the motivating factor for entering the woods. At the end of Act I, the wishes of the cast are achieved, and their euphoria is reflected as they reemerge, singing, "Into the Woods, / Then out of the woods . . . — and happy ever after." Although desire again propels some into the woods in Act II, their desires are transformed (or even malformed), and the society they once knew, and which authorized their desires, now exists in chaos and dislocation: the giant Jack slew becomes the locus of desire for the giant's widow, who comes seeking revenge. Narrative control symbolically dies as the narrator is crushed. Jack's Mother and the Baker's Wife also die. The humor, so much a part of Act I, disappears, as even Little Red Ridinghood becomes more mature and sober.

My project explores adultery in Sondheim's plays as a site to chart his gender politics. *Into the Woods* provides the fullest treatment of this topic in Sondheim's corpus, but I will also refer to other works as they become relevant. The Baker's Wife and her tragedy represent one piece in a pattern of gender inequality evident throughout Sondheim's work, an inequality that both reflects and perpetuates the gender inequities in American society of the 1980s and 1990s. In the final analysis, who killed the Baker's Wife? Sondheim and we, the audience.

To fully understand Sondheim's *Into the Woods* and the issues surrounding the demise of the Baker's Wife, one must explore the relationship this play has with postmodernism. As a philosophical and artistic movement, postmodernism embraces certain tenets. While any definitional framework will itself present obstacles, it becomes singularly necessary to have one so as to critique *Into the Woods*'s interactions with it. Sondheim embraces many of the aspects of postmodernity, and in so doing, both represents this form and furthers its multiple and contradictory ends.

Although all definitions of postmodernism are provisional, and open to charges of totalizing or simplifying, I have found Jane Flax's framework the most useful. In her book *Thinking Fragments: Psychoanalysis, Feminism, and Postmodernism in the Contemporary West*, Flax states that postmodernist discourse rests on three premises: the death of man, or the death of the subject; the death of history, or the death of totalizing Enlightenment narratives; and the death of metaphysics, or the death of transcendent, nondiscursive truth. Postmodernist art forms embrace these ideas in a number of creative and often contradictory ways. As we encounter each of these ideas in *Into the Woods*, I will explain them in more detail.

The Sondheim and Lapine musical opens with the assertion of narrative control by the narrator, as well as the all-encompassing desire of the various other cast members. Centered around children's fairy tales, which as a musical tradition have "amounted to a not very cohesive legacy," according to Stephen Banfield, the musical begins with the longing of each of the characters for change or to complete some mission, however that may be conceived, kept safely at a distance from the audience by the overarching and moralizing framework provided by our male narrator. Cinderella explains that these desires are beyond all bounds: "I wish...More than anything... More than life." The excessive nature of this desire further reveals itself when Jack's mother (one of the first to die later) rattles off a series of five "I wish" statements. In fact, excessive desire that demands containment or punishment comes to be symbolized in the music by the rap beat that accompanies the witch's story about the pillaging of her garden, which she symbolizes as both robbery and rape.

At heart, the desire expressed by the characters is positivist. We do not have in Act I merely the desire to survive, except perhaps in the case of Jack's Mother. Rather, the desire focuses on obtaining some goal that will unproblematically improve life. Thus, when Little Red Ridinghood introduces the main motif of the title song, her statement of desire is simple and pure: "Into the Woods—/ It's time, and so / I must begin my journey...Into the Woods / And through the trees / To where I am / Expected, ma'am, / Into the Woods / to Grandmother's house—." Indeed, the purpose and clarity of the mission is so great that it leads Little Red Ridinghood to moralize, moving from self-assurance to directing others: "The way is clear, / The light is good, / I have no fear / Nor no one should." The desires are, in this narrative, to meet their happy ending where good is rewarded and bad is punished. In fact, the woods, which represents the locus and fulfillment of these desires, becomes a place where one can safely journey and seemingly be "home before dark."

The audience thus puts faith not only in the direction of the desires themselves, but the outcome that is known from the familiarity of these childhood tales, and in the friendly older male narrator. The narrator offers himself as a figure of stability and guidance, shaping the narrative and, in apparent detachment, giving the audience the framework they need to understand. In fact, the narrator alone keeps this part of the play from becoming multivocal, a heterogeny of postmodern collage.

Although there are moments in Little Red Ridinghood's portion of the narrative that suggest things may not be as good as her light-heartedness suggests, it is not until the appearance of Cinderella's Mother that the problems of wishing itself are raised. Cinderella's Mother asks, when Cinderella begins with a rather unfocused statement of desire:

> Do you know what you wish?
> Are you certain what you wish
> Is what you want?
> If you know what you want,
> Then make a wish.

Cinderella's Mother suggests that there is the possibility that Cinderella (and the others) really do not know what it is they wish for, nor consider the ramifications of those desires.

Little Red Ridinghood continues as a sort of microcosm of the narrative, as she is led astray by her own desires, tempted by the wolf from the path she chose. Her confusion, however, is not merely a desire for flowers, but also for adventure and romance. The temptation that works, indeed, is not when the wolf tells her of the beauty that lies off the path, but that there are many paths with many destinations:

Little Red Ridinghood:

Mother said,
"Come what may
Follow the path
And never stray."

Just so, little girl—
Any path.
So many worth exploring.
Just one would be so boring.

Temptation here comes in the form of multiplicity, in the possibility that there are numerous paths, perhaps all with the same ultimate outcome. The wolf, who is later destroyed, comes to represent the purveyor of heterogeneous ways, evil only because he uses them as a trap to catch his victim. Little Red Ridinghood, in repeating "Mother said" four times to the wolf, shows her naiveté as well as her vulnerability, and the vulnerability of a child's morality learned only by rote from her parents. Little Red Ridinghood never, for instance, seems to know from her mother, or anyone but the wolf, what lies off the path, both its pleasures and dangers. Indeed, we see the weakness of Little Red Ridinghood's inherited faith when she tells the audience that she has put her faith thus far in "a cape and a hood" that have failed. The wolf is able to use her desire, and prey on her weak faith, to construct a narrative of many paths that seems tempting and convincing, but in the end leads to death.

The night that was to end the journey into the woods elapses, and yet the characters are still caught in their desires as well as their "master" narratives. The end of Act I, Scene ii, shows the characters still after their one desire, and moralizing their failures in ways that do not call the basic thrust of their narratives of progress and improvement into question. From the simple "Never wear mauve at a ball," to the enigmatic "No knot unties itself," to the sententious "Opportunity is not a lengthy visitor," this moment and the one like it in Act I, Scene iv, still embrace the idea of objectivity, the idea that "man" can stand

apart and moralize from a stance that is not implicated in the drama itself. Yet, the play calls this very idea of a totalizing, objective viewpoint into question. Sondheim thus embraces what Flax explains as the death of man and the death of history. While postmodernism rejects both the detached subject and the idea of a positivist, progressive narrative of history (or, I would assume, its stark opposite, the idea of history as one long, continuous descent), the desire for both of these resides in our indebtedness to the Enlightenment. The "birth" of these ideas stretches back to the paradigms constructed during the Enlightenment. And, as Flax notes, "Postmodernists share at least one common object of attack—the Enlightenment—but they approach this object from many different points of view and attack it with various methods for diverse purposes." For Act I of *Into the Woods*, Sondheim's characters all embrace this narrative of progress. Truly, the climax of Act I, with the rebirths of Little Red Ridinghood, the Mysterious Man, and the Witch, embraces this "happy ever after" ending.

However, the end of Act I, while idyllic, also shows the limitations of such an ideal. The idea of progress towards happiness is stopped as the narrative closes with happiness and misery aptly, poetically bestowed. Yet, the Witch's and Cinderella's stepsisters' doom to be perpetually "unhappy" interrupts the overflow of positive feelings in the rest of the cast. Beyond this, however, two more events lead the audience to suspect that all is not ideally settled: the growth of another beanstalk, and the narrator's "To be continued." Still, Act I gives the readers the complete fairy tale closure of most children's stories, and thus, when Act II begins, literally out of the darkness, the audience realizes that the narrative itself (its progress, rewards and punishments) becomes the subject of the less unified, more disjointed, "postmodern" story of Act II.

Act II begins by literally and physically deconstructing the happy outcome of Act I. In a time "later," we see the improvements achieved in Act I: the homes of Cinderella and Jack have materially improved, and the Baker and his wife have their baby. However, the self-congratulatory nature of the opening "wishes" of Act II is rudely set back as desire plummets from wishing "to sponsor a Festival" to the hope to just survive when the female Giant, the distraught wife of the giant that Jack kills, comes seeking revenge. Thus, the utopia of the happy (or miserable) ever after stasis of Act I crumbles into chaos and death in Act II. The demise of utopia follows what political theorist Seyla Benhabib identifies as a key element of postmodern, post-communist political thought. Benhabib argues that postmodernism has led, at least in feminist theory, away from the idea of utopia because of utopia's basis in Enlightenment notions of reason, and because of the practical failure of many such engineered societies ("Feminism and Postmodernism" 29). Following (and developing) the writings of Jean-François Lyotard, Benhabib argues that utopian thinking has normally led, at least since the Enlightenment, to "the crassest instrumentalism ... [in that] the coming utopia exempts the undemocratic and authoritarian practices of the present from critique" ("Feminism and Postmodernism" 30). While Benhabib supports some milder forms of utopian thinking, she rejects utopia because it ultimately leads to unsettling and problematic practices in an attempt to achieve it.

Into the Woods in Act I achieves a kind of utopia, but there are two central problems with that achievement. First, the idea of its perpetuity. This utopia, as conceived in the closing number of Act I, is continual, unchanging and static. Life, however, remains in flux, not simply a static "happy ever after." Secondly, the achievement of this utopia was accomplished by employing the kinds of immoral acts that Benhabib deplores as means to an end. The Giant, when she comes on in Act II, recasts Jack's actions into moral terms that call the initial fairy tale into question: "That boy asked for shelter, and then he stole our gold, our hen, and our harp. Then he killed my husband." By domesticating and moralizing what Jack did, the audience is left to ponder not only the ends of the utopia achieved by Act I, but also the problematic means used to obtain these results.

Act II of *Into the Woods* makes the destruction of utopia real and tangible, and this pain echoes through a plethora of aural sounds, culminating in the "boom," "Squish," "Splat" of the song "The Last Midnight." Indeed, the audience initially becomes uncertain whether they are part of the catastrophe, because the very first effects of the Giant's visit are staged in such a manner that the audience "should be momentarily uncertain as to whether there has truly been an accident on stage." Like the conclusion of *Assassins*, where the assassins may be staged to take aim at the audience, the audience of *Into the Woods* becomes fully (if only momentarily) immersed

in the action of the play. The audience quickly realizes that the safe "fourth-wall" world of Act I is shattering, and even their position as detached spectators may be threatened. This erosion of audience expectation and safety continues from the staged "accident" through the following events: the discounting of faith in the royal family, and thus the safety of established hierarchy; the contradiction of platitudes, so much a part of Act I, characterized in Act II by the assertion of Jack's Mother just before the destruction of the town, that "Giants never strike the same house twice"; and finally the brutal clubbing death of Jack's Mother and the death of the Baker's Wife, which symbolically enacts the destruction of the family.

The most disturbing and unsettling displacement of certainty occurs with the loss of the narrative/didactic frame, personified in the death of the narrator. A full comprehension of this crushing death of the narrator comes when we understand the discussion and debate that informed this pivotal moment in the play. Lapine and Sondheim planned the role of narrator to be a recognizable and stabilizing presence. Lapine told writer Craig Zadan that among their choices to play the role were men not even associated with the theatre, such as Walter Cronkite, Edwin Newman and Tip O'Neill. In fact, in the early run of the play, the narrator was not killed, but actually became both the father and the son of the Baker (Zadan 343–44). However beautiful, this ending was scrapped by the end of the second week of the New York run of the play, and the narrator was finally killed. Sondheim told Zadan that the plot really called for this development:

> The plot, as well as the theme, of the second act is about the chaos that the characters face when dreadful events occur and the controlling force (the Narrator) of the story is removed. To paraphrase something Mike Nichols said when he came to a preview, "We all tend to live our lives as if there were a script." Well, there isn't.

Before his death, the narrator becomes even more didactic and complacent in his assertions, believing himself to be comfortably "not a part of it." Ironically, what he becomes particularly strong about is the very lack of certainty for the cast. Staged here, then, is a moment where theory stands outside, assuredly critiquing theory's lack of knowledge. The narrator tells the audience that the cast was not "familiar with making choices" and that "their past experiences in the woods had in no way prepared them to deal with a force this great." In fact, before proudly rebuffing the group standing behind him, he begins a comment on the "moral issue" of the "finality of stories such as these." In his own defense, he relies on his prescribed and thus knowable role as detached and "objective" spectator, the stance of the Enlightenment philosopher who claims "there must always be someone on the outside" to "pass the story along." Finally, as the rest of the cast organizes against him, he asserts that they will "never know how the story ends," and be "lost" in a "world of chaos." Thus, he echoes the supposed threat of leaving an Enlightenment paradigm of universal truths accessed by detached reason.

The loss of the narrator symbolizes one of the distinguishing and crowning achievements of postmodernism, demonstrating not only the potential of postmodernism but also the anxiety of the loss of a central logos and ethos, even if it were merely a construct. In a rather standard metaphor of detachment, Jack in his song "There Are Giants in the Sky" represents the claim of the Enlightenment that man can stand above, and look down:

> When you're way up high
> And you look below
> At the world you've left
> And the things you know
> Little more than a glance
> Is enough to show
> You just how small you are.

Jack further asserts that, once above, "Exploring things you'd never dare / 'Cause you don't care," the detached observer comes to "know things now that you never knew before, / Not till the sky." Jack foreshadows the attitude of the narrator who finally does not care except when threatened, and who acts as if knowledge is certain and incontestable. Thus, the narrator in the sky achieves a sense of power and unconcern, and the ability to claim to "know," a claim reified in Little Red Ridinghood's earlier song "I Know Things Now." Even Jack, a boy not known for brilliance or even intelligence, ultimately decides to leave this beanstalk pedestal and return to the land below, thus becoming smarter than the narrator, who still insists that he is separate, distinct, and uninvolved with the action transpiring around him

The fear of the unknown and the unknowable after the demise of the narrator translates fairly swiftly into tentative and uncertain action. However, the certainty of knowledge, of fairy-tale endings, still continues to haunt members of the cast, culminating in the "punishment" of the Baker's Wife. Of all these deaths, that of the Baker's Wife becomes most compelling. Her affair with Cinderella's Prince frees her from the desire for the romance of having a prince. She comes to see returning to her husband and their baby as a choice which is now invested with significance because of the affair. As she sings, "Now I understand— . . . And it's time to leave the woods." The Baker's Wife asserts that she has come to understand and is thus liberated, as expressed in her song "Moments in the Woods":

> Just remembering you've had an "and,"
> When you're back to "or"
> Makes the "or" mean more
> Than it did before.
> Now I understand— . . .
> And it's time to leave the woods.

Yet, her understanding is problematic. The woods, which were so easy (in comparison) to enter and return from, with one's desires achieved, have now become, with the destruction of the town, the only place one can reside. The Baker's Wife thus cannot leave the woods. As she tries to retrace her steps, she falls to her death. When her ghost returns in the conclusion of Act II, she is devoid of sexual desire, a disembodied spirit that authorizes the Baker's maternal instinct and, ironically, her own story as a cautionary tale: "Look, tell him the story / Of how it all happened / Be father and mother." Yet, what story can be told and what knowledge can be imparted seems ambiguous. Will the story be the sad and tragic but simple narrative of the giant's arrival and a mother's "innocent" death? Or will it be the story of desire, of contested meanings, and of fulfillment and lack that have characterized the experiences of the surviving cast of Act II?

Thus, the adulterous wife and her death bridges the desire that opens the play and the closure reached in the most famous song from the musical, "Children Will Listen." She becomes the center of desire, a desire that must be contained and rendered powerless through death and idealized motherhood. She also represents postmodernism's (and Sondheim's?) own ambivalence to female empowerment. Her speech must be silenced because she as adulterous wife, even though she decides to return, becomes a destabilizing influence. *Into the Woods* offers another place where these problems can be examined.

Even though the plays are vastly different, some of the same tropes surface concerning women and their sexuality. The adulterous wife becomes the locus where Sondheim chooses to chart these anxieties. Sondheim lets Cinderella's Prince escape his adulterous action, even allowing him to bond with his brother, Rapunzel's Prince, in plotting other possible adulteries in their duet "Agony." Although the Prince is stunned when Cinderella leaves him, he escapes the woods unscathed and perhaps even relieved. This escape becomes possible because the sexual contract of a husband is perceived differently than that of a wife in this play. Laurie Shrage writes that a "husband's adultery may be more 'understandable' and tolerated, while the adulterous wife is forbidden to have (or at least exercise) such desires." If she does, she "may still be held uniquely blamable for the adultery" in ways her married male counterpart will not. She embodies the betrayal of "the family religion" and "the invitation to passion, death, and the destruction of society" (Armstrong 12). Her self-actualization represents "an essential disparity, disequilibrium, and even discord between the two sexes" and the fearful prospect of "a matriarchal society."

Therefore, the Baker's Wife's enacting of her desire, and then her equally bold statement of knowledge (and the power to leave the woods) becomes a challenge to the deeper story of postmodernism itself. Postmodernism claims that there are no knowable, uncontested arenas from which to act. The Baker's Wife, even after the death of the narrator, claims that there are, and further that she has achieved knowledge of them, and can now leave the realms of desire to return unscathed to the world of the family. As her song "Moments in the Woods" argues, she thinks she has the choice to live time as if it is full of individual moments that do not impact other moments; or that she can return to her life, always knowing (and perhaps cherishing) her "moment" in the woods. As her fate tells, neither is truly possible.

The Baker's Wife's death also marks the darkest point of the postmodernist deconstruction this play offers of fairy-tale certainty. The cast is left with ruins, with little hope of ever building a certain (even if fictive) foundation again. The cast, however, cannot live in nihilism, having accepted ruin. To do so would be to die, and there clearly are still goals to reach and lives to live, even without overarching certainty. The

reconstruction, and the move to continue forth with purpose, even if it is tentative, comes in the most famous song of the play, entitled "Children Will Listen." This song offers finally what postmodernism offers: tentative starts towards new narratives, but narratives that are embedded in time and praxis, not detached and objective.

"Children Will Listen" begins with the cautionary. The word "Careful," now the most prominent word, appears six times in this song. This repetition displaces, but only momentarily, the other important repetition that opens both acts of "I wish." The song builds from the truths gained from the experiences of the woods. Thus, the narrative it offers is embedded in the stories that have preceded it, in the experience of the woods and desire itself. It is offered tentatively, softly not in the grand finale, but in the moments before. Zadan relates a disagreement that occurred between Sondheim and Lapine over the placement of this song. Lapine told Zadan that he "wanted the song . . . to build into an incredible anthem that would end the show . . . but Steve didn't agree," worried that "it would become sentimental." "Children Will Listen" remains tentative and quiet because postmodernism can only offer narratives that are embedded, in flux, and experiential. The characters now admit that desire will return, that "every now and then" one has to go into the woods again, but they can go with an awareness of the past and a "mind [toward] the future." The reprisal of the title song afterwards adds to this tentative start at building a better tomorrow: a reaffirmation of the experience as well as the continuation of desire itself in Cinderella's last call of "I wish." Although the characters once more embrace the idea of "happy ever after," it is now more problematic, less binary, and more receptive to the possibility of another opening for desire, for another trip into the woods.

Unlike Sondheim and Lapine's musical, and as a literary critic, I add a third act. It is a tentative move, even characterized by the more postmodern idea(l) of "Reflections" instead of the more monolithic, hegemonic idea of "Conclusion." The triumph of *Into the Woods* is the way it embodies both the wonder and the trouble of postmodernism, both its potentials and its pitfalls. *Into the Woods* offers the move from the Enlightenment fairy-tale of knowability and detachment (Act I) to the enmeshed struggle for survival of postmodernism (Act II). This move is, like

Sondheim's reading of his own conclusion (Zadan 353), tentatively hopeful. Gone are the days of certainty, replaced with the days of possibility, of multiple and possibly contradictory roles and ideas co-existing. Truly, one may even hope that postmodernism as seen in this musical could offer the potential of a "nonviolent relationship to the Other and to otherness in the widest possible sense" that Drucilla Cornell labels as the goal of the "ethical."

Yet, within the hegemony of multiplicity that is postmodernism, Sondheim's play also shows the danger and violence inherent in postmodernism's rejection of liberation. The Baker's Wife comes to represent the limits of postmodern potential. Because there are multiple and controvertible narratives and teleologies possible, the categories of knowledge and liberation become contestable and entangled, even impossible. The volume of essays entitled *Feminist Contentions: A Philosophical Exchange*, from which I have extensively quoted, shies away from any kind of full embracing or engagement with postmodernism for these very reasons. Steven Garber's book *The Fabric of Faithfulness* does the same thing, but for very different moral (and religious) reasons. This unlikely pairing of radical feminism and conservative Christianity becomes united in their rejection of any kind of full acceptance of postmodernism because of the reasons exposed in *Into the Woods*. There are many other examples of this contingent and tentative discussion of postmodernism from all sides of the social and political spectrum. *Into the Woods* deserves reading, hearing, and reiteration because it joins these various discourses in exposing both postmodernism's promises and potentials, as well as its perils and problems.

Source: Mark K. Fulk, "Who Killed the Baker's Wife? Sondheim and Postmodernism," in *American Drama*, Vol. 8, No. 2, Spring 1999, pp. 42–60.

Brian Sutton

In the following essay, Sutton traces the character development in Into the Woods. *Sutton comments that it is this aspect of the play that appeals most to college students.*

A major source of textual pleasure is being able to identify with a character as that character matures. That is one reason that Stephen Sondheim and James Lapine's Tony award winning play *Into the Woods* works well in a college classroom. Even though the characters in the play are

> BY NOW, THE CHARACTERS ARE LITERALLY AND FIGURATIVELY LOST IN THE WOODS. WHEN THE BEWILDERED LITTLE REDRIDINGHOOD SAYS, 'THE PATH IS STRAIGHT,' BAKER REPLIES, 'WAS STRAIGHT. NOW THERE IS NO PATH.'"

drawn from fairy tales, their intellectual and ethical development precisely mirrors the stages described in the most widely cited study of the maturing processes of college students, William G. Perry Jr.'s *Forms of Intellectual and Ethical Development in the College Years*.

Perry describes three main stages in college students' development: viewing the world dualistically and relying on authority to provide the right answers; accepting relativism in a world with no easy answers; and recognizing that even in a relativistic world, one must still form commitments. Although Perry acknowledges that students may be deflected by escapism or similar behaviors, he states that students generally move from dualism, through relativism, and on toward commitment.

Given that *Into the Woods* starts out with the narrator's words "Once upon a time," it is not surprising that the characters, like many incoming college students, at first view the world with a childlike, simplistic dualism that prevents the woods from seeming dark and tangled. In the opening number, the cast sings, "The way is clear / The light is good, / I have no fear, / Nor no one should. / The woods are just trees, / The trees are just wood."

The characters also fit Perry's definition of dualistic thinkers in their faith that authority will provide right answers. Authority may be parental, as when Little Redridinghood and Jack (of "beanstalk" fame) begin their journeys because their mothers tell them to, or when Cinderella reacts to a crisis by seeking advice from her mother's ghost. It may be matrimonial, as when the baker acknowledges that he depends on his wife "for everything." It may be communal, as when each character states a nugget of

folk wisdom that seems to guide his or her conduct, or when Baker, after his home has been
partially destroyed by the giant, is reassured that
"Giants never strike the same house twice." Or it
may be royal, as when the kingdom is threatened
by a giant and the characters' first instinct is to
tell the royal family because "the prince will see
to it that the giant is rid from our land." The way
is clear; the light is good.

But these characters, like Perry's college students, must discover the complexity inherent in
life's journey. Confronted by Wolf, Little Redridinghood simplistically sings, "Mother said, /
'Come what may, / Follow the path / And never
stray.'" But the wolf a wonderful symbol for the
excitement and danger of increased sophistication—replies, "Just so, little girl—/ Any path. /
So many worth exploring. / Just one would be so
boring. / And look what you're ignoring . . . " Little Redridinghood is being led toward the
labyrinth of relativism. Throughout the first
act, the other major characters undergo similar
metamorphoses.

But relativism is not an end in itself. Many
students in Perry's study went through a stage in
which lack of certainty made it difficult for them
to accept responsibility and take a stand. Similarly, near the end of act 1, Cinderella sings
about her ambivalence regarding being pursued
by the prince; "And then out of the blue / And
without any guide, / You know what your decision is, / Which is not to decide." Whereas Perry
states that the students with the most "advanced"
positions tended to use existentialist terminology
to describe their views, Cinderella's attitude at
this point would make an existentialist cringe.
She and the other characters still have a lot to
learn.

Besides supporting inaction, relativism can
also justify ethically questionable actions. When
Baker and Wife desperately need Jack's cow but
have no money to pay for it, the wife argues that
they should pretend their beans are magic and offer
to trade them for the cow: "There are rights and
wrongs / And in-betweens /. . . Everyone tells tiny
lies— / What's important, really, is the size. /. . . If
the end is right, / It justifies / The beans!"

Later, the characters must face the consequences of their actions, as a giant, enraged at
Jack's having stolen her harp and killed her husband by chopping down the beanstalk, ravages
the land. The giant will leave the others alone
only if they let her kill Jack. The characters'

moral dilemma is heightened by the legitimacy
of the giant's outrage, the complexity of Jack's
ethical situation (he was motivated by extreme
poverty to steal, and having stolen, was arguably
acting in self-defense when he killed the pursuing
giant), and the fact that all of them have committed unethical or unwise acts (the fraudulent
selling of the beans, for instance), acts which
have contributed to their current crisis. The situation demands immediate, decisive action. But
instead, having passed beyond simplistic dualism,
each character uses his or her relativistic viewpoint to argue, plausibly but spitefully, that
another character is to blame for the crisis.

By now, the characters are literally and figu-
ratively lost in the woods. When the bewildered
Little Redridinghood says, "The path is straight,"
Baker replies, "Was straight. Now there is no
path." The landmarks of authority have disappeared: Jack's mother, Redridinghood's mother
and grandmother, and the baker's wife have all
been killed; the enchanted place where Cinderella
received advice from her mother's ghost has been
destroyed; the giant has attacked the baker's
house twice, destroying both the house and the
comforting security of folk sayings; the royal family has proved unworthy of trust, both in crisis
facing a giant and, as Cinderella has learned, in
marriage. And the ultimate guardian of order in a
fairy tale, Narrator, has been killed by the giant,
just after warning the others that without a narrator "You'll never know how your story ends.
You'll be lost. . . in a world of chaos." The characters are now terrifyingly free to make their own
decisions, create their own endings.

Perry states that when students lose the comfort of dualistic certainty, they ask such questions
as, "And my enemies? Are they not wholly in the
wrong? . . . Will no one tell me if I am right? Can I
never be sure? Am I alone?" He also states that
some students attempt to "escape. . . to deny
responsibility through passive or opportunistic
alienation." Similarly, many of the minor characters in the play desert the others during the
crisis, saying, "I'm going to hide. Everything
will work out fine in the end." Even Baker, the
character with whom the audience is most likely
to identify, voices a similar urge, in words with
which any college student can identify: "No more
questions. / Please. / No more tests. / Comes the
day you say, 'What for?' / Please—no more."
Later, confronted by Jack's queries about the

world's injustice, the baker angrily says, "Stop asking me questions I can't answer."

Yet finally, Baker and the other major characters reject escapism and seek what Perry calls commitment. First, in a world of chaos, they commit to each other. Consoling the bereft Redridinghood, Cinderella sings, "Mother cannot guide you. / Now you're on your own. / Only me beside you. / Still, you're not alone. / No one is alone." While Cinderella's words could be criticized as sentimentalism, as the song continues, the idea that "no one is alone" takes on a more profound meaning: that our actions affect others. Baker and Cinderella sing, "You move just a finger / Say the slightest word, / Something's bound to linger, / Be heard," and the baker adds, "No one acts alone. / Careful, / No one is alone." Thus the characters, like Perry's most "advanced" students, express their commitment in terms that echo existentialism and its insistence that although each individual bears responsibility for his or her decisions, each decision affects everyone on earth (Sartre 19–21).

Besides committing to each other, the four central characters also commit to a course of action-and they do so without simplistically demonizing the enemy. Even as they prepare a trap to kill the giant and save themselves, the baker and Cinderella sing, "Witches can be right, / Giants can be good." And although their plan succeeds, they remain uncertain of anything beyond the need for responsibility and commitment.

As the play ends, the characters view the woods much differently, singing, "The way is dark, / The light is dim, / But now there's you, / Me, her and him." And just as Perry acknowledges that even the most advanced students still have room for further growth, so the characters acknowledge that their personal journeys are recursive: "Into the woods, each time you go, / There's more to learn of what you know."

If Perry's study accurately captures the process of intellectual and ethical growth for college students, as is widely claimed, then despite the fairy tale background, the situations in *Into the Woods* should prove powerfully recognizable to those students.

Source: Brian Sutton, "*Into the Woods*," in *Explicator*, Vol. 55, No. 4, Summer 1997, 3 pp.

> THE GIANT CAN BE SEEN AS SYMBOLIC OF ANY TYPE OF SOCIETAL CRISIS THAT INTRUDES ON THE PRIVATE LIVES OF PEOPLE AND FORCES THEM TO RESPOND IN SOME WAY TO SAVE THEIR WAY OF LIFE. FACED WITH THIS CRISIS, THE CHARACTERS BICKER AND DIVIDE THEMSELVES."

Robert L. McLaughlin

In the following excerpt, McLaughlin compares the themes in Into the Woods *to similar themes that can be found in several other works by Sondheim. McLaughlin finds that* Into the Woods *explores the often contradictory dynamics between love and society.*

...*Into the Woods,* Sondheim's 1987 musical based on traditional fairy tales, also explores individual responses to dehumanizing societal forces. Society continues to have a debilitating effect on individuals and couples, but this effect has become deadly: the entire second act is played out under the threat of imminent total destruction analogous to the threat of nuclear-tipped ICBMs we live under every day. Change is imperative and just possible if individuals can reestablish human contact, understanding, and sympathy.

Act One of *Into the Woods* presents the psychological growth of several fairy tale characters to the point where they can achieve love relationships. The play begins with the characters going into the woods on quests to solve certain problems caused for the most part by disjointed families. Cinderella is abused by her father's new family; her quest is to go to the king's festival. Jack (of Beanstalk fame) and his Mother are poor because his father has left them; Jack's quest is to get money by selling his best friend, his cow. The Baker and his Wife are unable to have children; their quest is to obtain the items for the Witch's potion and remove the spell. The Witch is an old and ugly mother to her adopted (seized?) daughter Rapunzel; her quest is to drink the potion that will make her young and beautiful. To bring order to these chaotic familial relationships, each character must not only achieve his or her quest but also mature psychologically. Two of the Act One quests present challenges in love relationships similar to ones in *Company*. Cinderella gets her wish to go to the festival but confronts there a new dilemma: the undivided attention of the Prince. Considering her cruel treatment at home and the potential wealth and luxury that come with being a Princess, we, the Prince, and even Cinderella have a hard time understanding why she runs away from him each night. Like Robert (and more significantly from a feminist point of view), she sees commitment as limiting since any definite decision destroys all other possibilities. Running away from the Prince, she thinks that her best course of action is to go home: "You'll be better off there / Where there's nothing to choose, / So there's nothing to lose." In addition, she fears that the Prince would not want her if he knew who she really is and that the Prince, in pursuing her like an animal in a hunt, is objectifying her just as her family does. In leaving him the clue of her shoe in the pitch, she tests his commitment in two ways: first, to see if he will use the slipper to try to find her; and second, to see if, once he sees her in ash-coated rags, he will still want and love her. Of course, the Prince passes both tests and Cinderella answers with her own commitment. She agrees to marry him, giving up all other possibilities with the hope she will be happy in this one. The Baker and his Wife begin the play like the couples in *Company*: they are together but each bristles at lost independence. The Baker, relishing his autonomy, at first refuses to let his Wife help in the quest: "The spell is on *my* house. / Only I can lift the spell . . . " The Baker's Wife longs for the more handsome, wealthy, and glamorous Prince. But in the woods the Baker and his Wife learn a new interdependence. In "It Takes Two" they realize that their marriage demands a loss of independence, but in return they gain the positive qualities and love of the other person. The Baker sings, "I thought one was enough, / It's not true: / It takes two of us" and his Wife describes him the way she had previously described the Prince: "You're passionate, charming, considerate, clever—." The Baker sums up their new interdependence, " . . . I'm becoming / Aware of us / As a pair of us, / Each accepting a share / Of what's there." Cinderella and the Baker and his Wife, then, face the problems the characters in *Company* couldn't resolve and through their learning experiences in the woods become part, at least temporarily, of interdependent love relationships.

However, after Act One shows that such love relationships are possible, Act Two, like *West Side Story,* asks if they can survive in their societal context. The widow of the giant Jack killed comes down from the sky to seek revenge. The giant can be seen as symbolic of any type of societal crisis that intrudes on the private lives of people and forces them to respond in some way to save their way of life. Faced with this crisis, the characters bicker and divide themselves. The wealthy royal family flees the country, leaving behind the lower class characters. Those remaining can't agree on a plan to deal with the giant, and while they bicker, more and more of them are crushed. The futility of their divisiveness climaxes in "Your Fault," where they desperately try to blame each other for the calamity. The Witch leaves them at this low point, when they are isolated and dehumanized: "Separate and alone, / Everybody down on all fours." Eventually, however, the remaining characters, the Baker, Cinderella, Jack, and Little Red Ridinghood, are able to transcend their pettiness through two important steps. First, each loses the person on whom he or she was dependent. Cinderella loses the guiding spirit of her mother when the giant crushes the tree in which she resided. Little Red Ridinghood loses her mother and grandmother when the giant steps on their houses. Jack loses his mother when the Prince's steward kills her to keep her from provoking the giant. And the Baker loses his Wife when the giant crushes her after her dalliance with the Prince. Although this seems to be another instance of outside forces destroying love relationships, these characters must lose the people who support them so that they can continue to grow psychologically. They need to become independent so that they can come to understand their interdependence on a wide range of people, not just one person. This is the second step to their eventual triumph. Although the outside forces encourage division and isolation, to accept such isolation is a mistake. When the Baker abandons the others after the death of his Wife, he meets the Mysterious Man, his father, who years before had abandoned him after the death of his mother. In "No More" the Mysterious Man counsels the Baker that such isolation, while physically possible, is mentally impossible and spiritually damaging: "Trouble is, son, / The farther you run, / The more you feel undefined / For what you have left undone / And, more, what you've left behind."

When the Baker returns to the others, they pool their ideas and their abilities to defeat the giant, and as they put their plan into action, they sing, in "No One Is Alone" what they've learned: that as individuals they are helpless. They need to connect with others and understand how their actions affect others in the human community in order to accomplish anything. They dismiss their previous divisions and isolation: "People make mistakes, / Holding to their own, / Thinking they're alone." Instead, one's actions touch many others: "You move just a finger, / Say the slightest word, / Something's bound to linger, / Be heard. / No one acts alone."

The play's finale, the last reprise of "Into the Woods," is an antithesis to the end of *Sweeney Todd*. There we saw a vision of people thrust apart by their own hate and greed. Here, all the characters return in a final dance, not divided, as the Act One finale was, by class lines, but homogeneous and joyous. And instead of singling us out as Sweeneys, the cast points out our interdependence: "The way is dark, / The light is dim, / But now there's you, / Me, her and him." Our awareness of and willingness to act on this interdependence is necessary for the creation of the kind of society where love relationships, like Tony's and Maria's and the Baker's and the Baker's Wife's, can flourish.

Source: Robert L. McLaughlin, "'No One Is Alone': Society and Love in the Musicals of Stephen Sondheim," in *Journal of American Drama and Theatre*, Vol. 3, No. 2, Spring 1991, pp. 27–41.

SOURCES

Harmon, William, and Hugh Holman, "Fairy Tale," in *A Handbook to Literature*, Prentice Hall, 2003, pp. 203–204.

Leithauser, Brad, "A Funny Thing Happened on the Way to Broadway," in *New York Review of Books*, February 10, 2000, pp. 35–49.

Lovensheimer, Jim, "Stephen Sondheim and the Musical of the Outsider," in *Cambridge Companion to the Musical*, Cambridge University Press, 2002, pp. 181–96.

McLaughlin, Robert L., "'No One Is Alone': Society and Love in the Musicals of Stephen Sondheim," in *Journal of American Drama and Theatre*, Vol. 3, No. 2, Spring 1991, pp. 27–41.

Sondheim, Stephen, and James Lapine, *Into the Woods*, Theatre Communications Group, 1987.

Sutton, Brian, "Sondheim and Lapine's *Into the Woods*," in the *Explicator*, Vol. 55, No. 4, Summer 1997, pp. 233–36.

"Tales of Magic and Wonder from Ancient Egypt," in *Civilizations of the Ancient Near East*, Charles Scribner's Sons, 1995.

Van Leer, David, "Putting It Together: Sondheim and the Broadway Musical," in *Raritan*, Vol. 7, No. 2, Fall 1987, pp. 113–28.

FURTHER READING

Banfield, Stephen O., *Sondheim's Broadway Musicals*, University of Michigan Press, 1995.

> Along with an overview of Sondheim's personal and professional background, Banfield turns to a more detailed discussion of each of Sondheim's Broadway musicals. His examination includes all of Sondheim's works from *West Side Story* to *Into the Woods*.

Maguire, Gregory, *Wicked: The Life and Times of the Wicked Witch of the West (Musical Tie-in Edition)*, Harper Paperbacks, 2004.

> This musical builds on the well-known story of *The Wizard of Oz*, in which the reader learns about the early life of the Wicked Witch of the West. This book was adapted for the musical stage to great success.

Tatar, Maria M., *The Classic Fairy Tales: Texts, Criticism*, W. W. Norton, 1999.

> Divided into six types of fairy tales, the numerous stories collected in this book are drawn from cultures all over the world and throughout history. Each story is preceded by an introduction and includes annotations. Critical essays by a wide range of scholars put fairy tales in a broader literary and historical perspective.

Zipes, Jack, *Happily Ever After: Fairy Tales, Children, and the Culture Industry*, Routledge, 1997.

> Zipes reviews the history and cultural relevance of fairy tales from ancient days to modern times. He pays special attention to how (and why) fairy tales have evolved over time, and what cultures and businesses have done to use fairy tales for their own purposes.

Rhinoceros

EUGÈNE IONESCO

1959

In considering the entire body of Eugène Ionesco's writing, his full-length play *Rhinoceros* (1959) is recognized as the most fully articulated expression of his disgust with the tide of institutional and personal conformism that he saw as a rising force in the twentieth century. Adapted from a short story of the same name, the play was first staged in Dusseldorf in October, 1959, and it is also the play that brought Ionesco's work to a global audience, premiering in Paris in 1960 and at the Royal Court in London later the same year. (The first English production of *Rhinoceros* was directed by Orson Welles and starred Laurence Olivier.) But it was the 1961 Broadway production that starred Eli Wallach as Berenger and Zero Mostel as Jean that launched Ionesco to previously unimagined celebrity. With its warning of how anyone might possibly fall victim to the pressures of conformity, the play has sparked varied and passionate reactions. Some audiences have embraced the implications of the powerful social message while others have balked at what they see as the overt didacticism of the play.

A recent edition of *Rhinoceros* was published by Penguin in 2000.

AUTHOR BIOGRAPHY

Eugène Ionesco was born Eugen Ionescu on November 26, 1909, in Slatina, Romania, to a Romanian father and a mother of French and

Greek-Romanian heritage. Baptized as a Romanian Orthodox, Ionesco spent most of his childhood in France, living in Paris while his father continued his studies. Ionesco returned to Romania with his father in 1925 following his parents' divorce. He went on to study French Literature at the University of Bucharest (1928–1933).

Ionesco married Rodica Burileanu in July 1936, and the two had a daughter, Marie-France, in August 1944. Returning to France in 1938 in order to complete his doctoral thesis, Ionesco and his family remained in Marseille during World War II. They returned to Paris in the mid-1940s, where Ionesco worked in publishing. His work during this period also included translating the works of Urmoz (1883–1923), a Romanian poet who is often considered an influential figure in surrealism and the literature of the absurd.

Ionesco came to the theater relatively late in life, not writing his first play until 1948 (*La Cantatrice chauve*; translated as *The Bald Soprano*), which was first performed in 1950. Recognized as one of the foremost practitioners of the Theater of the Absurd, he quickly produced an impressive series of one-act nonsense plays, including *The Lesson* (1951), *The Chairs* (1952), and *Jack, or: The Submission* (1955). He turned to full-length plays in 1954 with *Amédée, or How to Get Rid of It*, *The Killer* (1958), and *Rhinoceros* (1959). It was during this period, too, that Ionesco was forced into a very public debate over this vision of theater with the famous English critic Kenneth Tynan.

Ionesco's career spanned four decades and included novels, stories, operatic adaptations, as well as essays and theoretical writings. Ionesco received numerous awards and recognitions, including the Tours Festival Prize for film (1959), the Prix Italia (1963), the Society of Authors Theater Prize (1966), the Monaco Grand Prix (1969), the Grand Prix National for Theater (1969), the Austrian State Prize for European Literature (1970), and the Jerusalem Prize (1973). Ionesco was admitted into L'Académie Française in 1970. He was also awarded a number of honorary doctorates during his lifetime, from the University of Leuven, the University of Warwick, the University of Tel Aviv and from New York University. On March 28, 1994, Ionesco died in his residence in Paris, at the age of 84. He is buried in Montparnasse Cemetery in Paris.

MEDIA ADAPTATIONS

- Ionesco's play was first delivered in radio format under the same title in 1959 by the British Broadcasting Corporation (BBC).

- Noted Polish director Jan Lenica made an animated film based on Ionesco's play in 1964.

- *Rhinoceros* was adapted into a film of the same name in 1974, which was directed by Tom O'Horgan. Names of characters were changed from Berenger to John (played by Zero Mostel) and from Jean to Stanley (Gene Wilder), and Karen Black was cast in the role of Daisy. The advertising tagline for the film was somewhat misleading given the dark tone of the original play: "The comedy that proves people are still the funniest animals."

- The Firlefanz Gallery in Albany, New York, produced a puppet version of the play under the same title in January 2006. The puppet show was directed by Ed Atkeson.

PLOT SUMMARY

Act 1
The setting for the play is a provincial town square after church on a Sunday afternoon. Arguments over often trivial details of bourgeois (middle-class) life erupt around the stage. At the center of the loudest of the arguments are Jean, a highly strung self-proclaimed intellectual, and his friend Berenger, an apathetic man who dulls himself with alcohol and seems wholly disengaged from life. Messy in his appearance, Berenger justifies his drinking as a necessary escape from the boredom of the world as he knows it. He is especially bored with his work, which he sees as meaningless. "There are so few distractions in this town," Berenger laments openly to Jean, "I get so bored. I'm not made for the work I'm doing.... every day at the office, eight hours a day."

Jean responds to Berenger's feeble rationalizations with forceful assertions about the strength of his will power, which he stresses is the mark of his superiority: "I'm just as good as you are," he observes. "I think with all due modesty I may say I'm better. The superior man." Jean's reasoning his simple: "The superior man is the man who fulfils his duty."

Their conversation is interrupted by the sound of distant trumpets, which signals the arrival (off stage) of a raging rhinoceros. Its appearance leaves all the characters, with the exception of Berenger, in total amazement. Berenger stands, as though in a stupor, watching the chaos unfold off stage.

As the sounds of the rhinoceros fade into the distance, Berenger orders another round of drinks for Jean and himself. Whereas Jean wants to talk about the dramatic appearance of the rhinoceros in town, Berenger cares little for the discussion and even less about the absurdity of the moment. Overheard from a nearby table is The Logician attempting to explain to an Old Gentleman what a syllogism is (a logical statement constructed from a major premise, a minor premise, and a conclusion). The implications of this conversation are clear: there must be a logical explanation for the appearance of the rhinoceros.

Pressed by Jean to have an opinion on the rhinoceros, Berenger at first attempts to quell the conversation with his suggestion that the animal probably escaped from the zoo. When this fails, he comes up with a number of lame explanations, each of which is challenged and eventually mocked by Jean. Increasingly disinterested in the topic, Berenger accepts Jean's opinions about the rhinoceros, and even agrees, half-heartedly, to curb his drinking. Life, Berenger admits, is too dull and too heavy for him to manage without alcohol.

Having acquiesced to the will of Jean, Berenger is further berated by his friend, at first for giving in so easily to the pressure of Jean's argument and then for his unwillingness to devote his time to cultural and intellectual endeavors. It is through such self-improvement, Jean argues, that Berenger might catch the eye of Daisy, an attractive typist that Berenger is drawn to.

Another rhinoceros rushes by off stage, leaving in its wake a path of destruction (including a dead cat) and a turmoil of words and arguments. A debate erupts about whether it was the same rhinoceros as the first, and whether it was

an Asiatic or an African species. In an important challenge, Berenger suggests that concerning themselves with such distinctions is nonsense. Jean and Berenger argue, and Jean storms away, dismissing Berenger as an alcoholic.

Daisy joins the conversation, which makes the previously disinterested Berenger obviously nervous. She convinces him to make amends with Jean, but he slides once again towards drink rather than moving towards reconciliation. Meanwhile, The Logician follows his earlier long-winded, and obviously illogical, syllogism focusing on cats and paws with even more confusing discussion of rhinoceros horns. The Housewife leads a funeral procession for the dead cat, and the various townspeople vow, with empty emotion, to fight the aggression of the rhinoceroses. The opening act closes with Berenger turning away from the community in order to return to his brandy.

Act 2

Shifting locations to Berenger's office, act 2 opens with the office workers Dudard and Papillon in an argument with Botard, an older man who is intensely skeptical about the news of the rhinoceroses. He believes, in fact, that they are a figment of the journalist's sensationalizing attempts to bolster newspaper sales. A believer in the hard logic of science, Botard discredits all reports as "a lot of made-up nonsense."

Berenger arrives late for work, but Daisy helps him get around the rules of the time sheet. Once in the office, he is asked about his opinion of the rhinoceroses. When he claims to have witnessed the arrival of the rhinos, Berenger is immediately insulted and bullied by Botard, who claims that all the sightings are "a hoax" and "propaganda." on the part of some "furtive underground organization." With Botard's argument complete, the workers return to their work of proofreading law proposals.

The attention of the office turns suddenly to Mr. Boeuf, who has not turned up for work that day. His wife suddenly appears with a telegram from her husband saying that he will be back in town in a few more days. More dramatically, she reports having been chased to the building by a rhinoceros, which is trying to climb the stairs to the office. As Botard is forced to acknowledge, albeit grudgingly, that the rhinoceroses do exist, Mrs. Boeuf has a sudden and surprising revelation: the office rhino is her husband. The responses to his rhino presence ranges from Daisy calling for rescue to recommendations that Mrs. Boeuf collect insurance and file for divorce. Mrs. Boeuf, however, remains deeply devoted to her husband despite his new shape. Leaving the stage, she climbs aboard his back and the couple ride off together.

With this change of events, Papillon, the office manager, begins to calculate Mr. Boeuf's transformation as an office expense that he must find a way to account for. As more rhinoceroses are reported in the town, Botard attempts to explain how he actually never doubted their existence in the first place, though he continues to forward a conspiracy theory as to their origins. As the firemen arrive to save them from the building that has been ravaged by the transformed Mr. Boeuf, Botard vows that he will solve the mystery of the rhinoceroses. Berenger and Dudard, rivals for the affection of Daisy, make dramatic and over-polite gestures to each other as they leave the building.

The action shifts to Jean's apartment. Jean is in bed, coughing, when a knock at his door brings him to greet Berenger, who has come to visit. When the door opens, both men voice similar questions, which show the uniformity of thought as increasingly powerful in this world. Berenger apologizes for the previous day, much of which Jean has already forgotten.

Berenger notices that Jean's voice is getting hoarse and weak, but Jean insists it is Berenger's voice that has changed. The two discuss the pain in Jean's forehead and the bump on his nose. Berenger comes to realize that Jean is changing into a rhinoceros before his eyes, and suggests that the two men head to a doctor immediately. Jean grows increasingly quarrelsome, claiming that all doctors are frauds, that people disgust him, and that he will literally run over anyone who gets in his way.

Pacing his apartment like a caged animal, Jean listens as Berenger tells him the story of Mr. and Mrs. Boeuf, then goes into a long discussion of both Mr. Boeuf and the rhinoceroses. Mr. Boeuf, he claims, had a secret side to his character that came out in the transformation. Rhinos have a right to live, he argues, and society would benefit from a return to the laws of nature. As he paces in and out of the bathroom, Jean is gradually transformed completely; he then remains off stage, threatening Berenger, who is forced to flee the apartment.

As Berenger runs through the apartment building warning the residents of the presence of a rhinoceros, he realizes suddenly that the streets and the apartment building are full of marching rhinoceroses. The act ends with Berenger running out into the street shouting "Rhinoceros! Rhinoceros!"

Act 3

The final act opens with Berenger in the midst of a nightmare of his own transformation. As he awakens, two important things happen: he realizes that he is still human, and he begins to think seriously about the negative effects of his drinking.

Dudard arrives at Berenger's apartment, and the two enter into a long discussion of the epidemic that seems to be sweeping the town. Berenger, increasingly paranoid that he is transforming, demands Dudard to provide an explanation, which the latter must admit he cannot. Dudard does suggest, though, that Jean was transformed because of some personality trait or flaw. Berenger, wanting more and more to remain himself, finds great solace in this theory, and states that he will do whatever he can to remain immune to the change. (He rationalizes his drinking, for instance, by thinking that it keeps him safe.) Dudard, in contrast, begins to theorize that the change might, in fact, be beneficial.

As the conversation continues, the two men argue about the control each has over his future, and how much responsibility each must take for the epidemic itself. Dudard settles on a kind of fatalistic acceptance of whatever reason there might be for the sudden appearance of the rhinos. He also reassures Berenger that he will never be transformed, only because he is not naturally inclined to towards such a bestial condition.

Dudard also reveals to Berenger that their office manager, Papillon, has resigned and turned into a rhinoceros. Whereas Dudard finds this story humorous, Berenger is visibly upset and wonders why Papillon would give himself over to the herd when he was a man of some intelligence and social prominence. Berenger comes to the conclusion that this transformation, unlike most of the others, must have been involuntary. Dudard continues to find the transformations natural, while Berenger increasingly thinks of them as abnormal and troubling. Thinking that his questions will be best answered by the supreme intellect of The Logician, Berenger is especially troubled when he sees The Logician's hat on a rhinoceros passing with a chaotic herd. Despite the fact that even The Logician is not immune to the pressures of herd-like conformity, Berenger vows again to never allow himself to slip into a transformation.

Spending some minutes watching the swarming herds pass in the streets below his window, Berenger is brought back into the moment when Dudard opens the apartment door for Daisy. Dudard is, at first, taken back by her arrival, assuming that it is for a romantic interlude, but he calms when she says that she is just friends with Berenger. She has come at this time, she says, to inform them that Botard has already been transformed into a rhino. The three characters begin another discussion, focusing this time on the social problems that will be caused by the epidemic. Daisy and Botard suggest that getting used to the new state of affairs is the best solution, but Berenger commits himself to resisting acquiescence at all costs. Gradually he is coming to acknowledge to himself that his "duty is to oppose them, with a firm, clear mind."

They start to have lunch, but are interrupted suddenly by the crash of a wall. As the dust settles, they notice that the local fire hall has been destroyed, and that the firemen (now rhinoceroses) are marching as an organized regiment through the town. As Berenger doubts more and more in his ability to withstand the epidemic, Dudard excuses himself politely from the table, declaring that he is heading into the street to join "the great universal family" that he is convinced is taking shape in the streets. Berenger watches as he, too, makes the transformation from rational human to rhinoceros.

Stage directions note that at this point, projections of stylized rhinoceros heads appear on the wall of Berenger's apartment, becoming more and more beautiful with each new wave of images. Similarly, the sounds of the stampede slowly move from chaotic discord to an almost musical accompaniment to the play. Against this backdrop, Berenger declares his love for Daisy. She responds by saying that she loves him, too, and pours him some brandy in celebration. He, in turn, promises to defend her, but she insists that no one intends to do them any harm.

As Berenger begins to feel more and more responsible for the transformations of Jean, Papillon, and Dudard, Daisy advises him to release himself from the guilt and to take advantage of this opportunity to enjoy a happy life. He initially agrees with her, rationalizing that it was probably guilt that caused a lot of people to transform in the first place. As rhinos stampede around them, and their trumpeting is heard over the telephone and the radio, Berenger and Daisy realize that they are the last two people in a town now occupied by rhinoceroses. Daisy weakens, arguing that they should give themselves over to the transformation, while Berenger becomes even more resolved to resist. At first, he suggests that Daisy join with him to become a new Adam and Eve, but when she announces that she intends to allow herself to be swept into the new order, he denounces her as stupid.

Left alone, Berenger begins to question his own existence, his role in driving Daisy to the rhinos, and if it might be possible to convert the rhinos back into humans given time and the power of his own will. Drawn momentarily to the seductive power of the rhinoceroses, and increasingly repulsed by the ugliness of the human world, Berenger finds himself at the brink of desperation. In the powerful final moments of the play, he decides to make his stand as the last bastion of humanity. "I'll take on the whole of them!" he cries. "I'll put up a fight against the lot of them, the whole lot of them! I'm the last man left, and I'm staying that way until the end. I'm not capitulating!"

CHARACTERS

Berenger

Berenger appears in a number of Ionesco's plays, and is the protagonist of *Rhinoceros*. He is a semi-autobiographical figure who represents the condition of the modern man whose life is defined by the meaningless toil of work, by the shallowness of his personal relationships, and by the alcohol that he uses to escape from a world that he can never understand.

His transformation is the central movement in the play. While the other characters literally turn into rhinoceroses, Berenger undergoes a change that is more moral than physical, and that leaves him a completely changed man from the beginning of the play. Entering the stage as an alienated man who obviously drinks too much, he is a man who finds little if any meaning in his work or his personal life, except for his fascination with the beauty of a co-worker named Daisy. Exacerbating this sense of meaninglessness is the fact that Berenger is also too lazy to add culture to his life and is lost in his own musings about the nature of life.

At the same time, Berenger does have flashes of a deeper humanity during the course of the play. His love for Daisy, for instance, does reveal a willingness, and even desire for an emotional contact with another human being. And although Berenger opens the play as a man indifferent to his own passivity, he gradually comes to recognize the absurdity of his own life, which in turn prompts him to make a decision. Does he change his character or does he allow the rhinoceroses to redefine his life for him?

In the powerful closing lines of the play, Berenger makes his decision very clear, announcing to the world and to himself that he will rouse himself from the absurdity of his world and will resist with all his strength the encroaching pressures of the rhinoceroses. Most importantly, Berenger shows himself willing to take responsibility for himself but to expand his sense of responsibility to include those around him as well. "I'm the last man left," Berenger declares with a newfound passion, "and I'm staying that way until the end. I'm not capitulating!"

Mr. Boeuf
Mr. Boeuf is a co-worker of Berenger's who appears off stage as a rhinoceros.

Mrs. Boeuf
Mrs. Boeuf is the wife of Mr. Boeuf, and is a woman who remains devoted to her husband despite the fact that he has been transformed into a rhinoceros.

Botard
Botard is a senior member of the company that Berenger works for. Cynical and jealous of Dudard's increasing status within the firm, he remains skeptical of the presence of the rhinoceroses, looking instead for a rational explanation for their attitudes and behavior.

The Café Proprietor
The Café Proprietor is one of the numerous characters that appear in the first act of the play, and is characterized for the most part by a narrowness of intellect. More significant is his inability and unwillingness to confront the encroaching threat of the rhinoceroses.

Daisy
Daisy is Berenger's love interest, and an important motivation for him to move beyond indifference into an engaged, emotional world. Although she does have more emotion than other members of the community, she is accepting of the presence of the rhinoceroses, and, in fact, continually urges Berenger to get used to the presence of the rhinoceroses and not to feel guilty for his decision not to resist them. Never really willing to commit to an idea or moral framework, Daisy is seduced by the power and the beauty of the rhinoceroses, and sees in them a promise for a pleasure that she believes to be greater than that associated with human love.

Dudard
Dudard works with Berenger in his office and is the most direct rival for the attention (and affections) of Daisy. Like Botard, he believes almost arrogantly in the power of his own intellect to make sense of the absurdities of the world.

The Grocer
The Grocer is one of the numerous characters that appears in the first act of the play, and is characterized for the most part by a narrowness of intellect. More significant is his inability and unwillingness to confront the encroaching threat of the rhinoceroses.

The Grocer's Wife
The Grocer's Wife is another of the many characters that appears in the beginning of the play; she is likewise characterized by a narrowness of intellect. Also like her husband, she is unwilling, or possibly unable, to confront the encroaching threat of the rhinoceroses.

The Housewife
The Housewife is still another character that appears early in the play. She is similar to the Grocer and his Wife in that the Housewife has a somewhat limited intellect. She is also not able nor willing to confront the reality of the rhinoceroses.

Jean
Jean is a representative of a kind of philosophic "super-man" who sees himself as above the morality and ethical beliefs of his own community. Arrogant in his belief in his own intellect and open in his contempt for those he considers the common man (such as Berenger), he is as at the

same time a character riddled with hypocrisy. He believes in education and culture, for instance, but reduces both to a thin veneer of public image rather than seeing them as the means to explore the depths of his own being.

Jean is also the most complex and powerful character in the play to be transformed into a rhinoceros. In some ways, his transformation signals the power of facism, the seduction of conformity, and the very real presence of the absurd in the everyday world. His transformation also underscores the almost bestial nature of humanity. Audiences soon come to understand, in other words, that Jean as a rhinoceros is not really that different in terms of his morality and ethics than Jean the man was.

The Little Old Man
The Little Old Man appears early in the play and is another character who is unwilling to take action against the rhinoceroses due to a lack of understanding.

The Little Old Man's Wife
The Little Old Man's Wife also acts as a supporting character. With her husband, she takes no action against the rhinoceroses, but instead joins the herd.

The Logician
Appearing only in the first act, The Logician is, as his impersonal name suggests, a representative of the rationalism that defines a number of the characters, including Jean, Botard, and Dudard. Moreover, his presence in the play underscores one of the underlying themes of the play: that logic, reason, and the human intellect cannot explain all things in the world. During the course of the play, The Logician is ridiculed, quite appropriately, for his circular logic and his inability to see questions as clearly or as accurately as a man of such powerful intellect should. Through his manipulation of The Logician, Ionesco iterates his belief that the world is an illogical place, at times even an absurd one, and the first step to understanding the world in a meaningful way is to admit the absurdity of the human condition.

The Old Gentleman
The Old Gentleman is yet another character who goes along with the herd.

Mr. Papillon
Papillon is the head of Berenger's office, and a representative of people who place corporate or business agendas above the well being of people and humanist ideals.

The Rhinoceroses
Although the Rhinoceroses are not human characters and they never appear fully formed on stage, they are a collective presence that dominates the play. Most simply, the rhinoceroses represent the human capacity for violence that can erupt, on occasion, into savagery. More subtly, they represent the safety that is found when individuals gather into groups and the dangerous slippage towards a herd mentality that resembles, in more than one way, the totalitarian politics of the Nazi regime.

Despite the fact that the rhinoceroses form a kind of faceless mass, they do take on individual characteristics. When Mr. Boeuf turns into a rhinoceros, for instance, he approaches his wife with some tenderness, which allows her to recognize her husband despite his transformation. In the end, the type of human a person was before his or her transformation influences the type of rhinoceros that is created through the change. In some instances, Ionesco has the rhinos become more beautiful than the humans themselves, underscoring emphatically the ugliness of the human condition. Ionesco uses the characters of the rhinoceroses to underscore how even the obvious savagery of a powerful group can prove seductive within a culture based on passivity and the will to conform.

The Waitress
The Waitress is another character that appears early in the play and is transformed into a rhinoceros with little resistance.

THEMES

The Pitfalls of Fascism
During his lifetime, Ionesco was an open critic of inhumanities associated with Nazism and fascism, both in their pre-War configuration and during World War II. But to read *Rhinoceros* as an attack on fascist politics is simple enough. But more deeply, Ionesco is determined to explore

TOPICS FOR FURTHER STUDY

- Although no fully formed rhinoceroses ever appear on the stage during Ionesco's play, numerous stylized rhino heads do figure prominently. Using whatever supplies you have handy, create a stylized rhino head to represent the power of conformity and the pressures of group thought in the play. Present your creation to the class citing examples from the play that inspired you.

- Research the emergence and development of the movement known as Theater of the Absurd, and create a timeline on which you mark the dates, places, and titles that figure prominently in the movement. If possible, find images of the original playbills or posters to include as visual aids on your project. Look, too, for film or animation adaptations of the major plays.

- *Rhinoceros* and other plays of this sort have a long history of being adapted into a variety of media, from film to puppet plays to animation. Select one episode from the play and translate it into a five or six panel comic-book style representation (also known as graphic storytelling).

- Research fascism and all instances of its appearance throughout history. Based on your findings, write an essay defining fascism from its inception as a concept to its evolution into practice. Does fascism still exist in the world today? Cite specific examples in your argument.

the psychology and mentality of those who succumb with little resistance to Nazism, allowing their individual ideals and free will to be subsumed into a violent group consciousness. In *Rhinoceros*, characters repeat words and ideas that other characters have said earlier in the play, or look for guidance to authority figures that are being assimilated into the power structure of the rhinoceroses.

Constructing the rhinoceroses as a universal family, Ionesco underscores how malleable or impressionable individuals could be seduced by the ranks of a powerful group consciousness such as Nazism. Ionesco's position is made clear through the course of the play: to acquiesce passively to the pressures of the rhinoceroses, either through turning a blind eye to their rise to power or by joining their ranks, is often as harmful as the direct violence that such groups initiate.

Existentialism and Free Will

Rhinoceros hinges on Berenger's gradual realization of the power of his own will to transform him from an alcohol riddled, apathetic man into a self-proclaimed savior of humanity. His struggle to attain this level of self-knowledge is a classic existential one: how to take the meaningless of a life lived in a world of absurdity and make it meaningful through a conscious act of the individual will.

Emphasizing the freedom of each of the characters to actively choose their own path of action (as in the case of Dudard), this play argues against the primary definitions of humans as rational, logical beings (these opinions are expressed through Botard and The Logician). This is not a play, in other words, about the logical construction of meaning, but about the personal discoveries of meaning amidst the swirl and chaos of possible options. Not surprisingly, an individual's movement along such a path is very often fraught with anxiety and, at times, fear. To become aware of the possibilities associated with such a deep personal freedom, as Dudard reveals to Berenger, is also to be aware of the possibilities of choosing to give that freedom over to an outside power (to follow the herd) or, in the most extreme cases, to choose death over life. To live in a rational world, this play asserts, is to live without such profound choices, but to move beyond the rational as such characters as Dudard and Daisy do, is to open oneself into the world that extends beyond the pressures of the ordinary and the everyday.

While other characters, most notably those of a rationalist leaning, fail the ultimate test of will power (giving themselves over to the rhinoceroses), Berenger gains a sense of power as the play unfolds from act 1 (when Berenger is lost in daydreams and alcohol) through to act 3 when

Nazi Germany dictator Adolf Hitler addresses members of the Hitler Youth Movement at Nuremberg on September 12, 1938 (Topical Press Agency / Getty Images)

he emerges as a man who can feel a sense of love and responsibility for all of those around him, including people who have shunned him previously. In the terms of existential philosophy, Berenger becomes the figure of the superman, gathering together the powers of his will to reinforce his love for those around him and to take responsibility for his own role in sustaining humanity.

The Limits of Logic and Rationalism

As is a common theme among dramatists working within the traditions of the Theater of the Absurd, Ionesco makes a sustained effort in *Rhinoceros* to expose the limitations of logic and reason in a world increasingly defined by the illogical and the absurd. He is quick to point out, for instance, that such self-proclaimed rationalists as The Logician and Jean struggle openly in the world of the play, either talking themselves into

circular arguments or rationalizing their acquiescence to the pressures of the rhinoceroses.

To Ionesco, a world in which the savagery of fascism can find fertile soil is a world of absurdity and nonsense. Put another way, it is a world in which logic and rationalism clearly have no power. In the opening act of the play, in particular, Ionesco devotes significant detail to disparaging both the intellect and the rationalizing language of The Logician, the most obvious representative of the rationalist world. In the end, The Logician's view of the world is proven to be illogical and inapplicable to the real world of the play.

To the character of Berenger, especially as the play opens, logic leads only to a deepening doubt about the nature of reality and the condition of the world. Rationality itself, in other words, is never enough to give meaningfulness to the world. What is needed in order to make a life meaningful, both Berenger and Ionesco argue, is the initiative to make a commitment to life and to take responsibility for something significant outside of an individual sense of pleasure or happiness. However illogical it might seem, a meaningful life, Berenger argues, is a life of emotion, dreams, and full (and often frustrating) engagement with the world in all its complexities.

As Ionesco observes in an interview with *The Tulane Drama Review*, one of the keys to the play is to recognize the failure of both logic and language to make sense of the world. "Berenger destroys his own clichés as he speaks. And so, he sees beyond them. His questions no longer have easy answers. Perhaps he arrives in this way at fundamental questions which lie beyond false answers."

STYLE

Off-Stage Appearances

Given that the transformation of humans into rhinoceroses is central to the play, Ionesco must manage both the transformation itself and the philosophic implications of this shift with great care. He does so masterfully by having the rhinoceroses appear off stage, which allows the sounds of the rhinoceroses rather than their appearances to be used to mark threat and destruction. Increasing the volume of the offstage chaos increases the sense of threat as well as capturing the audience's emotional attention. To reveal the animals would, in this sense, lessen their impact, and diminish the sense of destruction that they bring to the town.

Leaving the rhinoceroses off stage also leaves the possibility of their existence in question, which is important in a play that focuses on the psychology of conformity as much as it does on the physical pressures towards conformity. By never allowing the audience to actually see the rhinoceroses in the fullness of their physicality, Ionesco allows for a number of very powerful questions to circulate through the play. Are the townspeople being forced to transform or are they seduced by the idea of becoming one with the herd? What is the relationship between physical strength and political strength in the modern world? And if the rhinoceroses exist only in the collective imagination of the townspeople, is it really possible for one man to resist, and to turn the tide of conformity and violence?

Overlapping Dialogue

Two strategies that Ionesco uses with great impact are overlapping or simultaneous dialogue. At various moments in the play, especially in act 1, characters often say the same words at either exactly or nearly the same time, which underscores the collective thinking that is taking place in the play. The more people that begin to agree with the conforming pressures of the rhinoceroses, the more they take on the same words and same sayings. As the conformity of the play intensifies, the diversity of language diminishes.

At other times in the play, Ionesco has parallel conversations developing (Jean-Berenger, The Logician-The Old Gentleman) that focus on the same ideas and use similar (and often identical) language. Again, Ionesco's goal is to show how quickly a kind of communal thought can take hold of a culture, reducing debate and constructive oppositions to a point of sameness and stagnancy. With the exception of Berenger, the world of the play becomes a world of almost oppressive similarities and shared ideas.

HISTORICAL CONTEXT

Theater of the Absurd

Theater of the Absurd refers to a theatrical movement that began in the 1940s and 1950s. Plays written in the Theater of the Absurd tradition generally revolve around concepts such as the isolation of the individual in society, and the sad nature of the human condition. Such plays, like *Rhinoceros*, generally exaggerate or distort certain aspects of society in order to communicate this. This tendency towards exaggeration or distortion led to a dramatic structure that no longer followed the dictates of presenting a sensible plot or believable character development, which in turn led to a change in the way plays were staged altogether.

Other playwrights who are categorized as writing in the tradition of the Theater of the Absurd are Edward Albee and Samuel Beckett

The Rise of Fascism

Written in part as a response to the politics and ideas that arose in the years leading towards and during World War II, *Rhinoceros* is often seen as a powerful commentary on the rise of fascism

COMPARE
&
CONTRAST

- **1959:** Countries are still recovering from the aftermath of two World Wars, and from the devastating inhumanities of the Holocaust. During this period the brutalities that humans are capable of are underscored in tragic ways.

  Today: War and genocide still exist, though the names, places, and politics of conflict change regularly. Despite the atrocities associated with the previous world wars, little has been learned, it seems, to help nations avoid war.

- **1959:** Fascism wanes following the world wars, though it still holds a place in global politics.

- **Today:** Although still recognized as a part of the political landscape, fascism is no longer the ideological force it was in the middle of the twentieth century.

- **1959:** Plays in the Absurdist tradition are popular and they dominate the critical discussion of theater at this time.

  Today: Absurdist plays, while not as popular as they once were, continue to be studied and performed. Elements of the Theater of the Absurd, however, can still be traced in contemporary plays.

and fascist politics during this period (most obviously in the form of German Nazism.) Generally defined as an authoritarian political ideal that makes individual desires and needs subordinate to the needs of the state and some form of national unity, fascism is usually considered the antithesis of liberal freedoms.

Originally, the term fascism was used by the Italian dictator Benito Mussolini (1883–1945) to define the political movement that controlled Italy from 1922 through 1945. The term became quickly diversified, though, and was attached to a number of political movements that erupted across Europe from 1920 onward, most notably Nazism in Germany. Across its history, as Ionesco points out, fascism has attracted political support from a diverse cross section of the population, from corporate big business through to the working class and impoverished peasants.

CRITICAL OVERVIEW

As Allan Lewis notes in his book *Eugene Ionesco*, the playwright was surprised by the immediate and international success of *Rhinoceros*,

though he always wondered whether audiences were aware of the political implications of the play's multilayered subtexts. Regardless, Lewis continues, critics have consistently seen that play as "a magnificent theatrical demonstration of the ways in which the mind of man can be captured and enslaved by specific and transient doctrines." Writing in 1960, in the *Tulane Drama Review*, Wallace Fowlie holds an opinion that is representative of most reviewers. He sees the play as a work that "will doubtless reach a far wider public than his previous plays." Put simply, as Fowlie suggests: "For the first time in his career, Ionesco has conquered a large public easily and quickly."

The reason for the initial and continued success of the play is, Matei Calinescu argues in *East European Politics and Societies*, due to "its dramatic qualities, its comic language, its rhythm, its original combination of wild farce and anxiety-ridden nightmare." Despite its dark themes and powerful images of violence and degradation, the play continues to find a place in contemporary theater, speaking to the longevity of Ionesco's vision of the dangers confronting the world in the wake of powerful ideologies.

A white rhino from Hluhluwe-iMfolozi Park in Natal Province, South Africa (*Per-Anders Pettersson / Getty Images*)

CRITICISM

Klay Dyer

Dyer holds a Ph.D. in English literature and has published extensively on fiction, poetry, film, and television. He is also a freelance university teacher, writer, and educational consultant. In this essay, he discusses Berenger's famous defense of humanity in the closing lines of the play as an extension of the illogic and meaninglessness of the world portrayed in the play, rather than a heroic escape from its deadening pressures.

That Eugène Ionesco's *Rhinoceros* is a multifaceted look at the human condition is obvious to even the most casual reader. Good is pitted against evil, Berenger is positioned as an outsider in the world, and individuals succumb with various degrees of resistance or compliance to a force that is at once conformist and totalitarian. As the play itself develops, it is also increasingly obvious that the audience is supposed to side with the character of Berenger, the man who stands alone against the epidemic of rhinoceroses that sweep through the town in which he lives. Berenger is treated as a sympathetic or even heroic figure who overcomes his obvious limitations to announce himself in the final lines of the play as the unyielding defender of humanity.

But a close reading of the play reveals some interesting questions about what it is exactly that Berenger sets out to defend. Is he standing in support of a humanity that resists fascism as a political practice? Or is his nemesis the stultifying effects of commerce? And the more one considers these questions, the longer the list of possible challenges grows: Berenger as a defender against violence and absurdity, or Berenger as a defender of language and emotion. Or perhaps, as this essay will suggest, Berenger is a man whose defensive posturing at the end of the play is itself a position in need of clarification. Perhaps the most important question that remains at the end of the play is one that remains open: if a man does not know what it is he wants to defend how is it possible to defend anything at all? Perhaps, in the

WHAT DO I READ NEXT?

- Readers more interested in the life and ideas of Ionesco himself will find his *Present Past Past Present: A Personal Memoir* (reprinted in 1998) a very rewarding addition to their reading list.

- The London playwright Harold Pinter wrote *The Caretaker* (first staged in April 1960), which is a provocative complement to reading the plays of Ionesco.

- Stanley G. Payne's *A History of Fascism* (1996) is a fascinating and readily accessible study of the ideas that so heavily influenced the first half of the twentieth century.

- Along with the plays of Ionesco, Samuel Beckett's *Waiting for Godot* (1952) is a defining work to aid in understanding the provocative and groundbreaking work of the Absurdists.

> IT IS ONLY AFTER A SERIES OF PROFOUNDLY DISCONNECTED RAMBLINGS THAT BERENGER MOVES TOWARDS HIS FINAL WORDS, A FAMOUS STATEMENT THAT APPEARS SUDDENLY AND WITH A SERIES OF EXCLAMATION MARKS ATTACHED."

end, Berenger's passionate promise to himself and to the world is more an act of passionate absurdity than it is moral growth.

As the play opens, there is little to suggest that Berenger has a life or a sense of humanity that is worth defending. The opening act becomes a veritable catalogue of the apathy and the disconnectedness from humanity that has overwhelmed his life. He confesses to his friend Jean, for instance, that he is bored with his work and cut off from a sense of community or belonging. He drinks, he explains, in order to inoculate himself against the pain of the boredom he feels, to dull the pain that Berenger associates with the monotony of the world in which he lives. Alcohol allows him to forget the futility of his work, to deal with the humility that he senses is inevitable in his pursuit of Daisy, and to essentially isolate himself from the greater community around him. "I feel out of place in life, among people," he acknowledges openly to Jean, "and so I take to drink. That calms me down and relaxes me so I can forget."

In this sense, alcohol becomes Berenger's means of shedding the weight of his humanity, enabling him to create an illusion of self-identity that will hold at bay the sense of humanity that will force him to feel connected to the world. As the play opens, Berenger cannot manage a meager whimper of protest when the first rhinoceroses appear, opting instead to sit with his drink disinterestedly, feeling too exhausted "to drag the weight of [his] own body about" while others react with fear, confusion, and even anger.

This is not to suggest that other characters in the play are any more successful than Berenger at establishing a definition of humanity worth defending. Jean claims to have a strong moral fiber and a will power that allows him to connect with the world in a meaningful way, but Jean is hampered by his own thinking, which is often circular and self-contradictory. He pushes Berenger to acquire culture as a means of fighting the alcohol-induced heaviness, but later Jean turns down an invitation to attend the theater because it might bring him in contact with too many people. Similarly, The Logician, a master of false syllogisms, moves forward through the opening act of the play in a muddle of arrogance and rhetorical wrong-headedness matched only by his sense of superiority.

Perhaps the most telling example of this failure to negotiate a sustaining (and therefore defensible) definition of humanity is captured in the character of Botard. Rejecting outright the presence of rhinoceroses in town (despite obvious proof to the contrary), he denounces his fellow townspeople as buffoons, hypocrites, or liars. More significantly, his paranoia leaves him seeing conspiracy everywhere and trusting no one. His whole purpose in life, as he announces repeatedly, is to learn "the names of the traitors" and to uncover "the purpose and the meaning of [the] whole plot."

One might argue, too, that a sign of Berenger's disconnection from a defensible understanding of humanity is the fact that he is deeply impressed by what he sees as the distinguished intellects of both Botard and The Logician. Appropriately, Berenger falls into the flawed logic of believing what these men represent when, near the end of the play, he sees a rhinoceros with a straw hat on his horn identical to that previously worn by The Logician. Berenger makes a logical leap reminiscent of The Logician himself, a man fixated with syllogisms. The thinking unfolds as follows: The Logician wears a straw hat. Later a rhinoceros is seen wearing an identical hat, which leads Berenger to conclude that the rhinoceros is The Logician transformed. Following the lead of Botard and The Logician, Berenger overlooks obvious alternative explanations that might also explain the pairing of rhino and straw hat (there are two straw hats in town, for instance) in order to explain the world according to his already established world view.

Despite his propensity for self-delusion and faulty logic, Berenger is positioned as both an intellectual resistance fighter and the defender of humanity in the famous long speech that concludes the play. But before he reaches this final moment of the play, Berenger wanders through a series of other possible options for dealing with the rhinoceros epidemic. Is it possible for him to talk with the rhinos, and if so what language will he have to use? Can language itself even serve any purpose in this new world? Are the rhinoceroses truly beautiful and are humans as ugly as he has come to believe them to be? As he moves towards his moment of enlightenment, Berenger piles question upon question: questions about his identity, about his physical attributes, and about the nature of being a rhinoceros.

It is only after a series of profoundly disconnected ramblings that Berenger moves towards his final words, a famous statement that appears suddenly and with a series of exclamation marks attached. And it is in the context of these openly ambivalent thoughts that readers are invited to reconsider his sudden determination to never give in to the pressures of conformity. Given this new context, these final words are less heroic and magical and, once again, logically flawed. How is one man planning to resist a hoard of rhinoceroses that has already exhibited a willingness to use violence (they kill a cat in the opening act, for instance) and is, despite Berenger's exclamatory challenges, an intensely seductive presence in the changing world? And what will the future hold for a man who imagines himself as the new Adam? In the moments leading to his declaration, audiences must remember, Berenger is still debating the relative beauty of humans when compared to the green-skinned invaders.

Seen in this new context, Berenger's famous defense of humanity resonates as a tragic commentary on the emptiness of language in the imperfect world of Ionesco's play. The promise of the last man to stand and fight ultimately rings hollow in a play that slides inexorably towards the mindlessness of the herd.

Source: Klay Dyer, Critical Essay on *Rhinoceros*, in *Drama for Students*, Gale, Cengage Learning, 2008.

Nancy Lane

In the following excerpt, Lane argues that Rhinoceros *is a powerful play, and she suggests that it articulates an aversion to politics, both as a practice and as an idea.*

AN ALLEGORY OF NAZISM?

. . . It is well known and widely noted that *Rhinoceros* was inspired by Ionesco's own bewilderment and horror at seeing nearly all his colleagues and compatriots in Bucharest succumb to fascism between 1934 and 1938. "Imagine that one fine morning you discover that rhinoceroses have taken power," he wrote in his private journal around 1940 (*PP* 67). In the play, the rhinoceros is a symbol for the fascist Iron Guards whose rise to power in Romania paralleled the rise of Nazism in Germany. Jean's transformation into a rhinoceros dramatizes Ionesco's own experience of seeing a colleague turn into a fascist: "I spoke to him. He was still a man. Suddenly, beneath my very eyes, I saw his skin get hard and thicken in a terrifying way. His gloves, his shoes, became hoofs; his hands became paws, a horn began to grow out of his forehead, he became ferocious, he attacked furiously. He was no longer intelligent, he could no longer talk. He had become a rhinoceros" (*PP* 80).

Certainly the analogies between the Nazis and the rhinoceroses of the play are obvious. As Jean makes clear in justifying his decision to join the rhinoceroses, the rhinoceros mentality glorifies nature and dismisses outdated moral standards: "Nature has its own laws. Morality's against Nature." When Bérenger asks him if he is

> "A SIMILAR TENSION BETWEEN INTERIOR AND EXTERIOR SPACE UNDERLIES THE PLAY. AS THE RHINOCEROSES TAKE OVER THE EXTERIOR SPACE, THE HUMANS ARE DRIVEN INSIDE BY THE DUST THEY RAISE, THE NOISE THEY MAKE, AND THE DANGER OF BEING TRAMPLED."

suggesting that we replace our moral laws by the law of the jungle, Jean answers, "It would suit me, suit me fine... We've got to build our life on new foundations. We must get back to primeval integrity." Like the Nazis, these are brutal beasts who glory in their strength and trample the weak—the cat, for instance—under foot. They are bullies who rampage through the streets and destroy civilization.

Each of the characters who contracts rhinoceritis has a reason that echoes the rationales or excuses of various groups who became fascists. Jean is a zealous conformist who speaks and thinks only in platitudes. He is an overbearing bully, and therefore it is not surprising that he is among the first to convert. He is, moreover, a racist; when Bérenger maintains during their argument in the first act that "Asiatics are people the same as everyone else," Jean becomes livid and screams, "They're yellow!" Botard is also an ideologue, a left-wing activist who sees conspiracies everywhere and claims to know the secret behind the sudden appearance of the rhinoceroses. As Dudard points out, Botard's passionate and overly simplified attitudes are "entirely dictated by hatred of his superiors." Despite his early opposition to the rhinoceroses, he converts in order to "move with the times." Dudard, on the other hand, represents the type of intellectual for whom "to understand is to justify": "My dear Bérenger, one must always make an effort to understand. And in order to understand a phenomenon and its effects you need to work back to the initial causes, by honest intellectual effort." Dudard's transformation parallels the conversion of Ionesco's antifascist friends to fascism "because in the beginning they gave in on one little detail." "This is the way they all begin.

They admit certain things, with complete objectivity. You must discuss things with them reasonably and objectively. In reality they give in a little, to the right, to the left, without realizing it" (*PP* 79–80). Dudard is a tolerant relativist who maintains in his discussion with Bérenger that as mere humans we are not competent to judge what is normal or abnormal: "Who can say where the normal stops and the abnormal begins? Can you personally define these conceptions of normality and abnormality? Nobody has solved this problem yet, either medically or philosophically." Other characters (Daisy and M. Papillon, for example) are ordinary, otherwise decent citizens who go along with the rhinoceroses because everyone else is doing it or because they are afraid...

REASON VERSUS "LOGIC"

When the play premiered, critics attacked Ionesco for failing to provide a rational defense against rhinoceritis, for mocking the human capacity to reason. Yet the true object of the play's satire is not reason so much as the perversion of reason wherein a system (logic) supplants reality. Bérenger is like the *raisonneur* in Molière's comedies—the one character who speaks with the voice of common sense; he is the only one to point out the basic truth that it is normal to be human and absolutely abnormal to become a rhinoceros. His aversion to the rhinoceroses is founded in his essential humanity and not in some dogma. The dogmatists—Jean, Botard, the Logician—succumb to a system because they cannot exist outside a system. It is dogma that reverses the terms, making the irrational "logical" and perverting reason into irrational rationalizing.

The character of the Logician is the prime example of this kind of antilogic. During the first act, he gives the Old Gentleman a lesson in logic, warning ironically that logic is a very beautiful thing "as long as it's not abused." He then undertakes to teach the old man what a syllogism is, but he makes an elementary error, reversing the last two terms: "The cat has four paws. Isidore and Fricot both have four paws. Therefore Isidore and Fricot are cats"; "All cats die. Socrates is dead. Therefore Socrates is a cat." The Logician's antilogic, founded on a rigid system of false syllogisms, leads him to deny the obvious and lose contact with reality:

Old Gentleman: So then logically speaking, my dog must be a cat?

Logician: Logically, yes . . .

Old Gentleman: So Socrates was a cat, was he?

Logician: Logic has just revealed the fact to us.

Certainly the Logician is an object of satire, like the learned Doctors in *Improvisation*; like them, he is a fool and a pseudointellectual. The fact that he is honored as an intellectual authority satirizes a society so easily duped; this does not mean, however, that the play condemns the human intellect and its capacity to reason. On the contrary, it is the perversion of human reasoning that leads to disaster. When the Logician says that "there are no limits to logic," he is issuing an implicit warning about the danger of allowing any mechanical system to take precedence over obvious truths. As Ionesco told Claude Bonnefoy, "Obviously, logic is external to life. Logic, dialectics, systematologies contain all possible mechanisms, all possible forms of madness. Everyone knows that systematologies lose touch with reality" (*ENT* 121).

DREAMS AND NIGHTMARES

In the same interview cited above, Ionesco opposes the natural logic of dreams to the madness of so-called logical systems: "Dreams are natural, they're not mad." Like so many of Ionesco's protagonists, Bérenger is a dreamer; as he tells Jean, "I do dream. Life is a dream." At the beginning of the play he is nearly somnolent, hung over, apathetic. His contact with waking life is tenuous and painful at best—"Solitude seems to oppress me. And so does the company of other people"; "I sometimes wonder if I exist myself." He feels "out of place in life, among people" and uses alcohol to "forget." So wrapped up is he in his own anxieties and musings that he hardly notices the first passage of the rhinoceros. While all the other characters exclaim and react with surprise and indignation, he merely yawns. As the play becomes more and more like a bad dream, however, Bérenger "wakes up," so that the initial situation is reversed by the end of the play. Asleep in a "normal" world, Bérenger wakes up as the world becomes a nightmare. By the end he is as much out of place as he was in the beginning, but the normal-abnormal polarity has been reversed.

The nightmarish proliferation of rhinoceroses, progressing geometrically at an increasingly frenzied pace, echoes the proliferation of matter (chairs, eggs, furniture, mushrooms, coffee cups, the growing corpse) in other Ionesco plays that

have the quality of a bad dream. Metamorphosis of a human being into an animal is reminiscent of Kafka, an even more disturbing invasion of the human domain than the proliferation of objects because animals are living beings, like humans. As the animal becomes the norm and the human the aberration, the scale of values is reversed. The rhinoceros norm becomes attractive, even to Bérenger, who in a penultimate reversal of attitude tries but fails to become a rhinoceros himself.

SPACE AND DECOR

Like *The Killer*, *Rhinoceros* opens in a brightly lit exterior setting. Whereas the bright light in the earlier play was the objective correlative of the protagonist's euphoric emotional state, however, the light in the later play has no effect on Bérenger's psyche, mired as he is in his own darkness. Moreover, the sets of the first two scenes in *Rhinoceros* are realistic, crowded with scenery, characters and props—quite a departure from what audiences might have expected from Ionesco. For the first time in Ionesco's theater, the main character is shown working in a public office with others, solidly placed within the larger context of society; both the light and the decor of the first two scenes reflect human activity and the normal bustle of daily life. As rhinoceritis spreads in the last two scenes, however, the lighting becomes gloomier, reflecting Bérenger's increasing distress and isolation, and the set returns to the claustrated interior room found in so many earlier plays.

The set also becomes progressively more stylized and less realistic as the human domain (the "normal") is displaced by rhinoceroses (the "abnormal"). Beginning with Jean's physical transformation near the end of act 2, rhinoceros horns and then rhinoceros heads appear on stage. By the end of the last act, rhinoceros silhouettes surround the stage, and the entire upstage wall is covered with stylized rhinoceros heads that, "in spite of their monstrous appearance, seem to become more and more beautiful." After Daisy leaves, Bérenger takes some pictures of human beings out of a cupboard and hangs them on a wall in an effort to find a reflection of his own human image, but "the ugliness of these pictures is in contrast to the rhinoceros heads which have become very beautiful."

Sound effects also have a major role in representing the displacement of the human realm by the rhinoceroses. In the first two scenes, the rhinoceroses are represented primarily by the deafening roar of their hooves as they run by, the sound of which momentarily drowns out human conversation. The roaring and trumpeting of the beasts punctuate the third act, signifying the rapid spread of the epidemic. Only annoying and intermittent in the beginning, they become increasingly intrusive; toward the end, their sounds invade the room through both the telephone and the radio. As the stylized heads became more beautiful, so the noises become more musical and melodious as the rhinoceroses become the norm: "Powerful noises of moving rhinoceroses are heard, but somehow it is a musical sound"; "all these disquieting sounds are nevertheless somehow rhythmical, making a kind of music." It is this music, in fact, that finally seduces Daisy to join the rhinoceroses:

> Daisy: Listen, they're singing!
> Bérenger: They're not singing, they're roaring.
> Daisy: They're singing . . .
> Bérenger: You can't have a very musical ear, then.
> Daisy: You don't know the first thing about music, poor dear—and look, they're playing as well, and dancing . . . They're beautiful . . . They're like gods.

The organization of space, both onstage and offstage, reflects the tension and conflict between human and animal realms. The appearance of the rhinoceroses divides space vertically, with the rhinoceroses occupying the lower level (the street) and the humans occupying second-story rooms. It is only in the first act that human beings appear at street level. The death of the housewife's pet cat is a signal that the street belongs to the rhinoceroses. Staircases—the link between upper and lower levels—figure prominently in the last three scenes. In the second scene, M. Boeuf destroys the stairs leading up to the office, trapping Bérenger and his colleagues. In the last two scenes, the staircases outside Jean's and Bérenger's apartments are visible to the audience. When a character (Bérenger, Dudard, Daisy) mounts them, it symbolizes that character's humanity. Inversely, descending the staircase signifies becoming a rhinoceros; all the characters who become rhinoceroses run down the stairs to join the others on the ground. While the location of the human domain on the upper level signifies human superiority, it also leads to isolation as the rhinoceroses take over the entire ground level and cut off all avenues of escape.

A similar tension between interior and exterior space underlies the play. As the rhinoceroses take over the exterior space, the humans are driven inside by the dust they raise, the noise they make, and the danger of being trampled. While the rhinoceroses are confined to the offstage exterior space in the first two scenes, they invade the onstage space in the last two. Interiors function as both prison and shelter. The humans are trapped in the office in the second act, and Bérenger feels trapped inside Jean's room when Jean becomes a rhinoceros and rhinoceroses block the exits. At the end of act 2 Bérenger is desperate to escape from Jean's room, while in act 3 he is barricaded inside his room, trying to keep the rhinoceroses outside. The barriers that separate inside from outside are easily penetrated, however; the rhinoceroses call Bérenger on the phone, their sounds enter the room over the radio as well as through the walls and windows, the dust they raise fills the room, and their stylized heads eventually cover the entire back wall. The shelter afforded by Bérenger's room is precarious at best, for the rhinoceroses are quite capable of knocking down any wall—Bérenger, Dudard, and Daisy report seeing them demolish the walls of the fire station.

An innovation in organization of space is the extension of the offstage space into the auditorium. In both Jean's and Bérenger's rooms an empty window frame faces the audience in the foreground. Part of the invisible wall that separates the stage from the auditorium, the frame serves both to emphasize Bérenger's isolation from the human world and to involve the audience implicitly in the growing mass hysteria. Jean tries at one point to escape through this window in the second act, but his way is blocked by "a large number of rhinoceros heads" "crossing the orchestra pit at great speed." On several occasions in the third act, Bérenger, Dudard, and Daisy look out through the empty frame into the auditorium, gesturing toward the audience as they describe the rhinoceroses whose heads can be seen passing underneath the window; Bérenger exclaims, for example that, "a lot of them started like that!" while pointing to the audience.

A TRAGIC FARCE

Although *Rhinoceros* has no subtitle, the term tragic farce would be equally appropriate for this play as for *The Chairs*. Ionesco disliked the American production because it turned the play into a silly comedy. "I have read the American critics on the play and noticed that everyone agreed the play was funny. Well, it isn't. Although it is a farce, it is above all a tragedy" (*NCN 208*).

The grimness of the play's basic theme is thrown into relief by use of farcical elements, in keeping with Ionesco's conviction that the comic should be submerged in the tragic and vice versa. The first act in particular is broadly farcical. The contrast between the physical appearance of the two principal characters (Jean is large, pompous, and immaculately groomed, and he is wearing yellow shoes; Bérenger is slim, groggy, disheveled, and rumpled) is an immediate source of humor; they are in this regard reminiscent of Laurel and Hardy. Slapstick and physical humor are prominent: Bérenger spills his drink on Jean, Jean knocks the Old Gentleman into the Logician's arms while flapping his arms like a bird, and the waitress drops a full tray of glasses when she is startled by the passage of the second rhinoceros. While the succeeding scenes become somewhat less farcical as the rhinoceroses become more threatening, physical humor persists throughout the play, from the large Mme Boeuf's leap onto the back of her rhinoceros husband to Jean's transformation into a rhinoceros, as comic as it is terrifying, to Bérenger's constant checking under a bandage he wears on his forehead for any trace of a horn. This broad slap-stick humor is probably the primary explanation for the wide-spread appeal and popularity of the play among mass audiences throughout the world.

Although the outrageous nonsense of the earlier plays is absent, verbal humor is another important source of comedy in *Rhinoceros*. The Logician's idiotic false syllogisms and his lengthy explanation to the Old Gentleman about what happens when you take legs away from cats are very funny, as is the silly argument about which variety of rhinoceros has one horn and which has two. Equally amusing is the contrapuntal dialogue of the first act, in which two simultaneous conversations—one between Jean and Bérenger and the other between the Logician and the Old Gentleman—overlap so that each pair occasionally repeats the words of the other. The rapid-fire repetition of certain exclamations and the accelerated pace of the dialogue add considerably to the comic effect. The twisted logic of Jean's and

Dudard's rationalizing explanations of the rhinoceroses is as funny as it is distressing. Even in the last act, comic touches remain. Daisy and Bérenger fall in love, quarrel, and part in a very short space of time; as Bérenger says, "Oh dear! In the space of a few minutes we've gone through twenty-five years of married life."

Other touches of Ionesco's wit appear as well. When Dudard looks in the paper to find out what really happened the day before, for example, he consults the "dead cats column." As is so often the case, Ionesco does not resist a small reference to himself. When Jean urges Bérenger to improve his mind, he recommends seeing an interesting play—one by Ionesco: "There's one playing now. Take advantage of it."

It is the play's humor that saves it from pathos and sentimentality. Bérenger is a derisory antihero; a well-meaning but inept weakling with a drinking problem, he cannot explain his own resistance to the rhinoceroses. He even tries at the last minute to join them, unsuccessfully. As Ionesco said about the type of character he prefers, "He must be as comic as he is moving, as distressing as he is ridiculous...One has to be able to regard [him] with a lucidity that is not malevolent but ironical" (*NCN 123*). The one unbreakable rule for writing comedy, he said, was that "one must not allow oneself to get bogged down in sentimentality. One needs to be somehow cruel and sardonic with oneself" (*NCN 123*). It is exactly this irony, this sardonic twist, that makes the play a tragedy of derision rather than of grandeur. Read in this light, Bérenger's final words—"I'm the last man left, and I'm staying that way until the end. I'm not capitulating!"—are not heroic so much as they are desperate.

Source: Nancy Lane, "*Rhinoceros*," in *Understanding Eugène Ionesco*, University of South Carolina Press, 1994, pp. 110–23.

Gale

In the following excerpt, the critic gives a critical analysis of Ionesco's work.

Romanian-born French playwright Eugene Ionesco was one of the prominent voices of what is known as the Theatre of the Absurd, a movement of the 1950s and 1960s that blended surrealism with existential thought and vaudevillian clowning. Although he persistently discredited

WHEN WE REALIZE THAT THE INSPIRATION FOR THIS PLAY CAME FROM IONESCO'S REACTION, AS NOTED IN HIS DIARY OF 1940, TO AN ANTIFASCIST FRIEND'S GRADUAL ACCEPTANCE OF AND ULTIMATE CONVERSION TO NAZI FASCISM, THE PLAY TAKES ON A MUCH DEEPER, POLITICAL MEANING."

the label—preferring instead "theatre of derision"—Ionesco, along with fellow absurdists Samuel Beckett, Jean Genet, Arthur Adamov, and Edward Albee, wrote plays that were highly experimental for their time in which traditional plots, structures, and language were replaced with more fragmented, contradictory, and oftentimes nonsensical dialogue, images, and situations. His repeated use of black humor to capture the absurd essence of the human condition and its alienation, its inability to communicate, and its struggle to overcome modern society's destructive forces mark a distinctive trait in Ionesco's early plays, which are often considered his best.

Although labeled an absurdist, Ionesco considered himself a proponent of pataphysics—the science of imaginary solutions popularized by French playwright Alfred Jarry in his *Ubu Roi*. In the pataphysical universe, "every event determines a law, a *particular* law," which, as Richard N. Coe asserted in *Ionesco: A Study of His Plays*, "is the same as saying there is no law, neither scientific, nor moral, nor aesthetic." Therefore, all things become equal, the sensical and the nonsensical alike. Man finds the nonsensical more preferable of the two because it allows him more freedom to think. This, then, is why Ionesco's plays appear to be nonsensical and absurd: in a world where there are no absolutes save truth, humans must invent such things as love, God, and goodness. The result for a playwright like Ionesco is to create the bizarre, the illogical, the nonrealistic because that is what humans find easiest to accept when they cannot agree to accept anything at all.

Though comic and seemingly without surface meaning, Ionesco's early plays often carry a biting social and political commentary, notwithstanding

his repeated claims to be apolitical. Nowhere is this better exhibited than in his first two plays, *The Bald Soprano* and *The Lesson*, where his central theme is the absurdity of language and both its inability to provide us with competent tools for communication and its manipulative qualities which can turn it from a tool to a weapon. In *The Bald Soprano*, which Ionesco reportedly wrote because he wanted to learn English, viewers meet two couples: Mr. and Mrs. Smith, who speak in clichés and platitudes, and Mr. and Mrs. Martin, who appear at first as strangers at the Smiths' home but realize later that they share the same child and the same home. The dialogue among these four characters gradually disintegrates into nonsensical gibberish and finally into meaningless sounds, and the only change comes when in the end the two couples swap identities, and the play begins again where it started. Ionesco saw the play as an attack against the bourgeois and conformity.

In *The Lesson* a professor tutors his young female student in subjects ranging from basic math to complex philology. As the lesson progresses and the student, complaining of a toothache, fails to comprehend the professor's lengthy—and ultimately meaningless—diatribe on the functioning of language, he becomes increasingly agitated. The play reaches its climax when the professor, repeating the word "knife," stabs the girl to death. We soon discover she was the fortieth student he killed that day. Like *The Bald Soprano*, *The Lesson* ends where it begins, and the forty-first student is brought into the professor's chamber, presumably to face the same fate.

The cyclical endings of these early plays reflect a sense of hopelessness and a pessimistic view of the fate of humankind: history will always repeat itself no matter how horrible the event, no matter how widespread public disapproval is. Part of that hopelessness comes from the impotency of language, the most significant attribute/invention of human beings. How can we share thoughts, ideas, love, etc. if we ultimately cannot communicate with one another? Moreover, since language is so imprecise, it can also be misinterpreted and misused, especially upon those who take words at their face value alone. In *The Lesson*, for instance, when the maid discovers the professor has killed his fortieth student for the day, she tells him to wear a Nazi swastika armband so that no one will question what he has done. It is through this one action that the play takes on strong political overtones, marking the first of many criticisms Ionesco would level against the Nazis and the totalitarian regimes of his native Romania.

Ionesco's next two plays, *Jack; or, The Submission* and *The Chairs*, are complementary in that the first play leads up to the beginning of a marriage and the second describes, in part, the ending of one. Again, both plays exploit the impotency of language to effectively communicate and the alienation of modern society. The title character of *Jack* is being coerced by his family—all members of which bear names that are variations of Jack—in finding a wife. They want offspring so that their race will be preserved. In the end, after a courtship that ends with a frenzied discussion where every noun is renamed "cat," Jack chooses Roberte II, a woman with three noses and nine fingers on one hand. Conversely, the Old Man and the Old Woman in *The Chairs* reflect the disintegration of a marriage. Throughout the play they bring in chairs for their several guests who will be attending a speech given by an Orator—a speech the Old Man has prepared as his final commentary on humanity. Gradually, they greet the invisible guests as they arrive, and the chairs—like many objects in Ionesco's plays—proliferate and begin to crowd the now-claustrophobic stage. At the end of *The Chairs*, the Orator, whom the Old Man has entrusted to deliver his message to the people, is able only to utter "the guttural sounds of a mute"; oral language has failed. When the Orator next attempts to communicate by writing an obscure word on the blackboard, its letters finally formulate the word "Adieu"—French for "good bye." Rosette C. Lamont, writing in *Ionesco's Imperatives: The Politics of Culture*, noted that *The Chairs* "is a twentieth-century morality play which does not preach. The message of the play is an anti-message: speech, art, communication of any sort, are the illusions man needs while there is breath."

Ionesco gives many of his characters nondescript names, doing so to show how nonconformists are always at odds with a society that will repeatedly take the easiest path and conform. Ionesco does not focus on individual differences but rather on the basic identity of most people. Nowhere is this better illustrated than in a series of four plays Ionesco began

writing in the late 1950s. Here he pursued his literary attack on the Nazis and the totalitarian regimes George Orwell criticized so well in *Animal Farm* and *1984*. These plays center on a man named Berenger, a modern-day Everyman, though Berenger is not the same character in each of the four plays. The first of these plays is *The Killer*, a Kafka-esque play where Berenger seeks out the Killer who is terrorizing the Radiant City because everyone, including the police and the city's totalitarian Architect/Doctor/ Chief of Police proves incompetent. When Berenger confronts the Killer, he attempts to reason with him, but fails to offer any cogent argument as to why the Killer should not indiscriminately kill people. "The more he talks," Lamont contended, "the more reasons he finds for killing, or rather being killed. Though he is armed, Berenger knows that he, a humanist, will not be able to bring himself to shoot even an enemy who means to destroy him." He learns all too late that the Killer kills without reason. To rationalize with the irrational, Ionesco suggests here, is to fight a losing battle.

The second and certainly most famous of the Berenger plays is *Rhinoceros*, first produced in 1959. As the play opens, Berenger is conversing with his friend Jean when a rhinoceros charges by. Though dismissed at first as an oddity of nature, everyone gradually accepts the animals' presence and, by the play's end, even decides to become one themselves, leaving Berenger to contemplate whether he too should join the herd or not. In the final act, Berenger must fight not only rhinoceritis but his desire to join the herd with his fellows. When he decides in the end to fight them, he becomes a singular hero who challenges the mob mentality and mindless conformity. When we realize that the inspiration for this play came from Ionesco's reaction, as noted in his diary of 1940, to an antifascist friend's gradual acceptance of and ultimate conversion to Nazi fascism, the play takes on a much deeper, political meaning.

Although the next Berenger play, *A Stroll in the Air*, continues the attack against totalitarian regimes, Ionesco moves on to greater philosophical heights with the final Berenger play, *Exit the King*. This play addresses humankind's need to understand its own existence, its own mortality. Like King Lear or Hamlet in Shakespeare's great tragedies, Berenger asks, "Why was I born if it wasn't for ever?" Such metaphysics echo the existential musings of Jean-Paul Sartre and Albert Camus: the questioning of the meaning—or meaninglessness—of life. Having lived for over 500 years, and in that time invented steel, balloons, airplanes, the telephone, built Rome, New York, Paris, and Moscow, and wrote *The Iliad, The Odyssey*, and all of Shakespeare's tragedies, King Berenger is Everyman: his death is the death of all humanity; in his acceptance of his mortality are the seeds of our own metaphysical grapplings with life's inherent meaninglessness.

Ionesco wrote other successful plays in the 1950s and 1960s, including the 1952 radio play *Motor Show*, *Maid to Marry*, *The Leader*, and *Victim of Duty*, the last another play about ruthless authoritarianism. Considered one of his best plays of this period is his first full-length play, *Amedée*. Drawn from a line in T. S. Eliot's poem *The Waste Land*, the play is about a couple's inability to confront their marital problems and to work through their pasts. In fact, Amedée and Madeleine have such difficulty in burying their troubled pasts—Madeleine's infidelity and Amedée's guilt for not having saved a drowning woman—that they remain at the forefront of the couple's present. Ionesco manifests this latent guilt in them by having the couple share their home with the corpse of Madeleine's lover, whom Amedée killed years before but never buried. Now, the couple work effortlessly to keep people and the police from entering their home, no easy task since the corpse is growing larger and larger each day until its physical presence literally fills the entire house. The corpse as metaphor for the growing distance between Amedée and Madeleine is an appropriate one for Ionesco, who relates the corpse to original sin and its growth to the passage of time. The dead body is a constant reminder of the couple's mutual sins, and its unabated growth reflects the mounting guilt they both must contend with for not having loved each other and for having tried to bury, instead of confront, their pasts.

Whether discouraged by the lack of *cause celebre* his later plays received, or feeling he had said in dramatic voice all he needed to say, Ionesco turned later in life to collecting and publishing nonfiction essays, lectures, addresses, criticism, and memoirs. *Fragments of a Journal* and *Present Past, Past Present*, his 1967 and 1968 autobiographies, confirmed his commitment to battle social and political oppression. *Antidotes*, a collection of essays that focus on the corruption of the so-called civilized world, appeared in 1977. The playwright's daughter, Marie-France Ionesco, translated her father's 1934 work *No*, a series of essays on Romanian culture, the demolition of Romanian literary idols, and the role of literature in life. A year later *Hugoliad* appeared, his youthful and scurrilous attack on French literary giant Victor Hugo, which Ionesco had also written during the 1930s. *The Intermittent Quest* is an eloquent and passionate tribute to the two women in Ionesco's life: his wife, Rodica, and his daughter, Marie-France. He devoted most of his remaining years to painting and exhibiting his artwork and lithographs, and died in 1994.

Although Ionesco's plays were once considered avant garde, they have since been reviewed in a less-revolutionary light. However, many of his plays, especially *Rhinoceros*, are still performed and still hold relevance for postmodern audiences. As A. J. Esta noted in a theatre review of a 2002 performance of *Rhinoceros*, Ionesco's "vision of the futility of maintaining one's individuality in the face of conformity is as pertinent as today's headlines."

Source: Gale, "Eugene Ionesco," in *Contemporary Authors Online*, Gale, Cengage Learning, 2007.

Rosette C. Lamont

In the following excerpt, Lamont provides a critical explication of Rhinoceros, *focusing predominantly on Berenger.*

. . . Ionesco's apprehension is not that of a Western European. In many ways it is closer to Buddhism. A Western education does not favor this state of passive resistance, of stubborn endurance: One is taught to improve oneself by doing. A very important and overlooked aspect of *Rhinoceros* is the opposition between two fundamental attitudes, the Eastern and the Western. They are embodied in two characters, Jean and Bérenger.

Jean is a so-called responsible citizen. He feels superior to his friend Bérenger because he has a well-organized existence. He is punctual and hard working. In fact, he takes pride in the minute-by-minute program he has put together to guide him through the days, and he urges his lackadaisical friend to follow it:

Get yourself up to the mark.
Dress yourself properly, shave every day,
    put on a clean shirt.

TRUE HEROISM FOR IONESCO IS A QUALITY OF THE HEART RATHER THAN OF THE MIND. IT IS THE REACTION OF A MODEST MAN WHO WISHES TO REMAIN TRUE TO HIMSELF."

Keep abreast of the cultural and literary events.

Don't let yourself drift.

Work eight hours a day ... but not on Sundays, or evenings, or for three weeks in the summer.

Spend your free time constructively ... by visiting museums, reading literary periodicals, going to lectures.

The end result of this self-improvement will be: "In four weeks you'll be a cultured man."

Bérenger is not in the least tempted by Jean's plan to refashion him into the ideal social being. It is clear from the start that the self-righteous Jean, so proud of his appearance—hat, tie, well-cut suit, polished shoes—is rhinoceros material, whereas the timid loner, Bérenger, a dreamer, is a flawed but endearing human being. He confesses to one fault: he enjoys the occasional lift he gets from a drink. As presented by Ionesco, it is a comic defect, one that testifies to the character's modest humanity. Although Jean is going off to a cocktail party, he maintains that, unlike his friend, he is not a drunkard because "there's moderation in all things," and he is "a moderate person." This statement wall soon be contradicted by his behavior after the first rhinoceros crosses the small public square.

Early in act 1 there is a very amusing scene of slapstick comedy when Jean orders Bérenger to set his glass back on the table without drinking, while he, himself, takes a gulp from his own *pastis*. Bérenger, made nervous by the scolding tone and the arrival of Daisy, the pretty office secretary on whom he has a crush, spills the contents of his full glass upon Jean's trousers. Jean grows enraged. This bit of stage business is in perfect keeping with the farcical mode of the play, but it also serves to emphasize the Chekhovian helplessness, clumsiness, and timidity of the protagonist.

As Bérenger attempts to explain to his domineering friend that he does not drink because he likes the taste of alcoholic beverages, but in order to lighten the burden of everyday existence, Jean grows impatient and scornful.

... It is of course a waste of time to take into his confidence a third-rate conformist who poses as a well-meaning friend. However, what Bérenger describes goes to the very core of the dual feelings the dramatist considers central to his work: heaviness and lightness, air and matter. The important aspect of Bérenger's minor fault—as it is presented by Ionesco, one not foreign to this kind of indulgence—is that this tippling may be a way of momentarily escaping from the existential condition, yet at no time would Ionesco's antiheroic hero exchange his vulnerable human skin for the heavy hide of a beast. Unlike his dreamer of a friend, Jean is embedded in the here and now, and takes pride in being "normal." This assumption is the Achilles' heel of the future rhino who, unlike the sensitive, intelligent Bérenger, does not realize that life "is an abnormal business."

The "abnormal business" that the town will be faced with is the appearance of one rhinoceros, then another (or could it be one and the same, escaped from a nearby zoo?). Excited, slightly frightened, people begin to debate whether the creatures had the same number of horns. Jean, who views himself as a cultured man endowed with a disciplined mind—all Germanic traits—states unhesitatingly: "No, it was not the same rhinoceros. The one that went by first had two horns on its nose, it was an Asiatic rhinoceros; this one had only one, it was an African rhinoceros." Bérenger calls Jean "a pedant who's not certain of his facts because ... it's the Asiatic rhinoceros with only one horn on its nose, and it's the African with two ... " Scientific definitions turn to pure venom as the two friends come close to blows.

Jean: I'm not betting with you. If anybody's got two it's you! You Asiatic Mongol!

Bérenger: I've got no horns. And I never will have ... I'm not Asiatic either. And in any case, Asiatics are people, the same as everyone else ...

Jean: They're yellow! Bright yellow!

Bérenger: Whatever they are, you're bright red!

If every French person knows that a reference to "horns" means that a man is being labelled a cuckold (*le cocu* is traditionally a farcical type), calling a man an "Asiatic Mongol" is both redundant and redolent of racism. Yet, during the German occupation of France, a Romanian refugee might well have been the butt of such an insult. Seen in this light, the farcical attack acquires a deeply sinister coloring, reminding those who lived through that period of the clichéd image of Jews as horned men, subhumans in the image of the Devil. The mild Bérenger bristles at these words. When he shouts that he will never have horns, he may also point out a basic difference between himself and the potential rhinoceros. The latter is a racist through and through, one who judges people by their color. However, in so doing, he has turned "bright red" with rage. Finally, he storms off, shouting that he will not see his friend again: "I'm not wasting my time with a fool like you."

If Jean's propensity to conform, together with his choleric nature, make him the perfect would-be rhinoceros, intellectualism is no guarantee against catching the fatal disease. On the contrary, the intellectual and the middlebrow, convinced as they are of being superior people, are best equipped to rationalize their metamorphoses: neither Botard, the former school teacher, nor Dudard, the deputy-head of the firm in which Bérenger is employed, will escape turning into beasts.

Act 2 begins in the office of a publishing company specializing in law books (much like Durieu where Ionesco was employed between 1948 and 1955). The employees are discussing the latest headlines about the town being overrun by herds of rhinos. Botard is vehement in his rejection of the facts. He will not even yield to the testimony of an eyewitness, Daisy. This rigid man, as proud as Jean of his methodical mind, lives by clichés, albeit liberal ones. He fulminates against the church; his temple is the union. When his colleague Mr. Boeuf (the word means "ox" in French) returns to the office's foyer in the shape of a rhinoceros, Botard's principal concern is that he not be denied the support of the organization. However, faced with this creature, who is even recognized by his wife, Botard can no longer deny the obvious. He proclaims that a conspiracy must be afoot, suspecting Dudard, his superior, of being a traitor. He must expose the deputy-head in order to "get to the bottom of this fake mystery." Ionesco shows in this scene the pattern of "patriotic" denunciations basic to

the mechanism of dictatorships; that is, spying on one's friends, business associates, and even members of one's own family.

This is a masterful caricature of the rancor of semieducated masses, lashing out at phantoms of their making, but refusing to recognize present danger. They are dangerous because they are supremely convinced that reason is on their side. Since they have spent a lifetime grazing on platitudes, it is easy to force feed them. Nor are bovine creatures necessarily peaceful; they trample the unwary. Thus, it is the most natural of transitions for a Mr. Boeuf to turn into a rhinoceros. As to Botard, he is a Boeuf to the *n*th degree.

As act 2 unfolds, the audience witnesses the process of the metamorphosis so eloquently described by Ionesco in his journal. It takes place before our very eyes on the occasion of Bérenger calling on his sick friend Jean.

Bérenger has come to apologize, although the quarrel showed that Jean was in the wrong. It is a mark of the protagonist's generosity that he is willing to forgive and always doubts himself. As he enters Jean's small studio apartment, he finds his erstwhile friend in bed. The man's pulse is regular, but he is suffering from a ravenous appetite. His complexion is turning green (not a sickly pallor, but the greenish-gray of a rhinoceros hide), and a strange bump is rising in the center of his forehead, right above the nose. With every trip the man makes to the bathroom, the bump grows larger, looking at last like a horn. As Bérenger informs the ailing man of Boeuf's transformation, Jean begins to utter hoarse, nasal cries, huffing and puffing from the heat. In an unrecognizable growl, he exclaims: "Well, whether he changes into a rhinoceros on purpose or against his will, he's probably all the better for it."

Ionesco insists that masks are essential to the production. In Barrault's staging, Jean became gradually more and more like a rhinoceros with the addition of certain elements to his face. He seemed to wear a shamanic mask that allowed him to coincide with a savage deity. No doubt Ionesco must have discussed this scene with his lifetime friend Mircea Eliade, the author of *Shamanism, Archaic Techniques of Ecstasy*. In this study Eliade discusses "the shamanic imitation of the actions and voices of animals," or rather the shaman's "taking possession of his helping spirits." Eliade concludes: "Each time a shaman succeeds in sharing in the animal mode of being, he in a manner re-establishes the situation that existed *in illo tempore*, in mythical times, when the divorce between man and the animal world had not yet occurred." Thus, Jean's metamorphosis may be grotesque, even laughable, but it also has a mythical dimension.

. . . The second metamorphosis we witness is both more subtle and more frightening since it takes place on a moral plane. The gradual shift of Dudard's attitude in act 3, when he comes to visit Bérenger, suggests the pernicious infiltration of the virus, its hold upon a fine intelligence.

Dudard begins by voicing his doubts as to what constitutes good and evil. The trained jurist, the impeccable employee is hardly the man to question the fundamental codes of civilized society, yet he wonders: "Evil! That's just a question of personal preference." He is obviously afflicted with the intellectual's malaise: bad faith. In drawing this portrait, Ionesco had in mind a man he admired in many ways, with the exception of his politics, Jean-Paul Sartre. "Dudard is Sartre," he said in New York in the course of a private conversation. For Ionesco, Sartre's failure to denounce the existence of the gulags smacked of rhinoceritis of the Left. As recently as on April 19, 1990, in an article written for *Le Figaro* entitled "When 'they' suddenly discover Havel," the dramatist accuses Sartre of having corrupted the French intelligentsia. He goes on with profound bitterness, and a sense of having at last been justified: "These Leftists were well aware of the immense misdeeds of the Stalinists. They had been warned by men such as Arthur Koestler, Raymond Aron, Jean-François Revel, and myself. We were right, but they vilified us, calling us despicable fascists, cowards, scoundrels." Surrounded by former Communists, Maoists, Castro supporters, assembled at the Ministry of Culture to greet Czechoslovakia's new president, Ionesco reports that he was nevertheless able to raise two fingers in sign of victory.

In *Rhinoceros* Ionesco demystifies the cult of rationalism, Descartes's legacy to Western culture. He shows that this philosophy can serve as blinders at a time of murderous violence. In the scene between Dudard and Bérenger, the latter may appear as hypochondriacal, even cowardly, but his anguish is a positive reaction to the germ of rhinoceritis. This angst is a symptom, like fever, suggestive of the fact that the sick body's struggle must begin before recuperation can

occur. On the contrary, Dudard's superior attitude covers a wavering, ailing conscience.

True heroism for Ionesco is a quality of the heart rather than of the mind. It is the reaction of a modest man who wishes to remain true to himself. While the intellectual wavers, weighing abstract good against abstract evil, and letting real evil overtake him, the intuitive man rejects intuitively what he senses as destructive. Some intellectuals, such as Vaclav Havel, have been able to combine the qualities of the spirit with those of the mind. Despite polar conditions of life, neither Havel nor Ionesco have ever deviated from their path.

The final pages of *Rhinoceros* allow the reader and the audience to follow the tracing of this path. The penultimate scene is that between Bérenger and Daisy. The pretty secretary enters her colleague's room, a basket on her arm. She has brought him lunch. However, this innocent has witnessed a general panic in the office and the streets. M. Papillon (Mr. Butterfly), the head of the department, has joined the herd. Names from one of Ionesco's time capsules are added to that of the flitting creature: Cardinal de Retz, Mazarin, Saint-Simon. "All our great names!" exclaims Bérenger, who seems to have forgotten that they are those of political plotters, dishonest ministers, and literary gossips.

Bérenger and Daisy will also be caught in a time capsule. We are invited to travel through a telescoped future. The couple's conversation goes from a declaration of love to planning a family. However, the presence of rhino heads all around them is oppressive. Ionesco and his bride, Rodica Burileanu, must have felt much the same way in July, 1936, when they were married. Unlike Rodica, however, Daisy is not a true companion in days of misfortune. She wonders whether the rhinoceros world might not be in the right. As her fiancé speaks of their love, she exclaims: "I feel a bit ashamed of what you call love—this morbid feeling, this male weakness. And female too. It just doesn't compare with the ardour and tremendous energy emanating from all these creatures around us." Incensed, Bérenger slaps her face. They have come to the parting of ways. As Daisy says: "In a space of a few minutes we've gone through twenty-five years of married life." The life of the couple has been poisoned by the surrounding climate of opinion. As Daisy makes her escape to join the beastly mob, Bérenger remains alone, defiant yet terrified. He is the last human left on the face of this planet.

What makes Ionesco's protagonist fully human is the fact that he is racked by self-doubt. There is a moment in his soliloquy when he experiences a profound revulsion in regard to his weak body, pallid skin, hairy limbs, smooth brow. He cries out: "Oh, I'd love to have a hard skin in that wonderful dull green colour." The latter is a reminder of the Nazi uniforms.

No one who has seen the Nazi armored vehicles forging forward overrunning the nations they were determined to subjugate, will ever forget it. They seemed undefeatable, a Master Race, Wagnerian demigods. Their propaganda machine rolled in with their tanks, telling the conquered nations that they were weak, corrupt, sinful, and had brought this misfortune upon themselves. Many, like Bérenger, felt a kind of servile admiration for the discipline of people intent only on maintaining their well-oiled war machine. In the death camps, they took superhuman strides, in their greenish uniforms, shiny black boots, always accompanied by sleek attack dogs. The lice-covered, shivering prisoners were faced at every moment with the image of their inferior condition. Yet, those who came to doubt their right to exist were done for; they would not survive the camps.

Nor was there a way of communicating with these automatons. They shouted orders in a language many did not know, and if these orders were not instantly obeyed their whips spoke eloquently. Listening to their "Heils!" and military music, Bérenger wonders whether their raucous song may not have charm. He even tries to bellow as they do, but realizes he is incapable of learning their tongue. But what is the protagonist's language? What is he saying since he is the last creature to utter these sounds? He even wonders whether he understands what he is saying.

It is in this reflection that we may find a key to Ionesco's problematics of style and expression. Following this experience, it was no longer possible for Ionesco to entertain easy relations with the common tongue. As Elie Wiesel said at one of his public lectures: "Words in camp did not mean what they mean outside: 'hunger,' 'thirst,' 'bread.'" When Ionesco denies being an avant-garde writer, it is his way of saying that he does not experiment for the sake of experimentation. However, he is unable to take language for granted. The returning deportee, or exile, sees the once familiar world with the eyes of a stranger. Only then, when we come back among the living

having visited the kingdom of the dying and the dead, do we have a chance to exist again.

The last man is much like the first. Alone among rhinoceroses, Bérenger is as grotesque as Adam among the animals of the newly fashioned planet. "I'm a monster, just a monster!" he shouts. Yet, there is no going back. The protagonist states defiantly:

> I'll take on the whole of them! I'll put up a fight against the lot of them, the whole lot of them! I'm the last man left, and I'm staying that way until the end. I'm not capitulating!

These last words have a Churchillian ring.

Bérenger, the shy dreamer given to fits of exaltation and spasms of anger, a fearful and yet audacious man, ineffectual at work, ill-adapted to society, often dependent on the small comfort of drink, flabby, paunchy, pallid, essentially kind and well-meaning, turns out to be our only champion. Unlikely as it seems—Ionesco wishes us to be aware of the paradox—when this man opposes evil, his act of defiance constitutes the triumph of each and every one of us. We are able to identify with this "man for our time," who has kept his decency among the mob of monsters. He is the emblem of our troubled epoch, an antihero who is a true hero, because he must.

Source: Rosette C. Lamont, "Bérenger: Birth of an Antihero," in *Ionesco's Imperatives: The Politics of Culture*, University of Michigan Press, 1993, 7 pp.

SOURCES

Calinescu, Matei, "Ionesco and *Rhinoceros*: Personal and Political Backgrounds," in *East European Politics and Societies*, Vol. 9, No. 3, Fall 1995, pp. 393–432.

Fowlie, Wallace, "New Plays of Ionesco and Genet," in the *Tulane Drama Review*, Vol. 5, No. 1, September 1960, pp. 43–48.

Ionesco, Eugène, *Rhinoceros*, in *Rhinoceros and Other Plays*, Grove Press, 1960, pp. 1–107.

Ionesco, Eugène, and Emmanuel Jacquart, "Interview: Eugène Ionesco," in *Diacritics*, Vol. 3, No. 2, Summer 1973, pp. 45–48.

Ionesco, Eugène, Richard Schechner, and Leonard C. Pronko, "An Interview with Ionesco," in the *Tulane Drama Review*, Vol. 7, No. 3, Spring 1963, pp. 161–68.

Lewis, Allan, *Ionesco*, Twain Publishers, 1972, pp. 72–73.

Malkin, Jeanette R., *Verbal Violence in Contemporary Drama*, Cambridge University Press, 1992.

Murray, Jack, "Ionesco and the Mechanics of Memory," in *Yale French Studies*, No. 29, 1962, pp. 82–87.

FURTHER READING

Esslin, Martin, *The Theatre of the Absurd*, Vintage, 2004.
Esslin coined the phrase "Theatre of the Absurd," in 1961 before first publishing his corresponding treatise in 1962. This book is essential reading for any student interested in the Absurdist movement.

Kluback, William, and Michael Finkenthal, *The Clown in the Agora: Conversations About Eugène Ionesco*, Peter Lang Publishing, 1998.
An engaging book of imagined conversations, encounters, and interviews based on the poetical and philosophical ideas of Ionesco.

Lamont, Rosette C., *Ionesco's Imperatives: The Politics of Culture*, University of Michigan, 1993.
In this detailed and provocative study, Rosette Lamont rereads the body of Ionesco's work as influenced deeply by the politics and cultural tensions shaping Europe during his lifetime.

She identifies Ionesco's challenge of fascism as a foundation upon which he builds a deeply philosophic critique of language.

Lane, Nancy, *Understanding Eugène Ionesco*, University of South Carolina Press, 1994.
Nancy Lane charts three major phases through which Ionesco's career evolved—from the early absurdist short plays through the humanism of the Berenger plays. Across these phases, Lane argues, Ionesco developed an ongoing exploration of the limitations of language, the metaphysics of mortality, and the struggles for individual freedom.

Payne, Stanley G., *Fascism: Comparison and Definition*, University of Wisconsin Press, 1983.
More scholarly than Payne's other books on this topic, this volume remains one of the key texts for situating the ideas and the ideologies of fascism in the modern world.

The Second Shepherds' Play

ANONYMOUS

c. 1450

The Second Shepherds' Play is part of the Wakefield mystery play cycle. It is play number thirteen of thirty-two contained in the only surviving manuscript, currently held at the Huntington Library in San Marino, California. *The Second Shepherds' Play* dates from the latter half of the fifteenth century. No exact date can be determined, but studies in handwriting analysis of the manuscript suggest an approximate date of mid to late fifteenth century as a composition date. The play was written in Middle English, which is the vernacular (everyday) language that was used in England between about 1100 and 1500. The ascendancy of King Henry VII to the throne marks the end of the medieval period and generally signifies the shift from Middle English to Modern English (the basic predecessor of English as we know it today). Authorship of *The Second Shepherds' Play* is unknown, and the play is simply attributed to the Wakefield Master, whose real identity was also unknown, although a local cleric or monk was probably the author. *The Second Shepherds' Play* is included in *The Norton Anthology of English Literature*, Volume 1 (1993) and in *The Towneley Plays* (2001), Volume 1, edited by Martin Stevens and A. C. Cawley.

The title refers not to a second shepherd but to the fact that this play was the second of two plays that dealt with the biblical Nativity story. Mystery plays, which are so named because they refer to the spiritual mystery of Christ's birth

and death, combine comic elements with biblical stories. For example, in *The Second Shepherds' Play*, the author combines the shepherds' story of stolen sheep and a swindle involving the birth of a nonexistent infant with the biblical story of Jesus' birth in Bethlehem. The dual plot is designed to remind the audience of the two-fold nature of man's existence—the real world on earth and the spiritual world of the afterlife. The play, itself, contains no divisions of act or scene, but there are three distinct scenes: the shepherds' soliloquies in which they lament their poverty, the oppressive natures of their lives, and the terrible weather; the scene with Mak and Gil in which they try to disguise the stolen lamb as their newborn child; and the adoration of the Christ-child in Bethlehem. The text shifts both time and place, referring to Christian saints and to the birth of Christ, although these things and events would have been separated by hundreds of years and reversed in time. Additionally, while the first half of the play takes place in Medieval England, the shepherds are easily able to walk to Bethlehem in a matter of hours, where events occurred fourteen centuries earlier. The audience, however, would have had no concern about such details, since *The Second Shepherds' Play* easily mixes symbolism and realism with entertainment and biblical lessons.

AUTHOR BIOGRAPHY

The series of plays attributed to the Wakefield master are likely the work of many authors over a vast period of years, perhaps as much as a hundred years. There is significant variation in stanza and verse forms, which suggests multiple authors. All of the authors associated with this cycle of plays remain anonymous. Scholars have long since concluded that the authorship of *The Second Shepherds' Play* cannot be determined. The exact date it was written is also unknown, though it is believed to have been composed around the mid to late fifteenth century.

PLOT SUMMARY

The Three Shepherds

Although there are no divisions of scene or act in *The Second Shepherds' Play*, the play falls easily into three distinct parts. The first section

MEDIA ADAPTATIONS

- A dramatic recording of *The Second Shepherds' Play* was directed by Howard O. Sackler and released as a twelve-inch record by Caedmon Records in 1962. As of 2007, the album is unavailable for purchase.

- In 1965, *The Second Shepherds' Play* was filmed by Rediffusion Productions and directed by Charles Warren. The film is titled *Mysteries and Miracles: The Second Shepherd's Play*, with the apostrophe placed incorrectly. As of 2007, the film was not available for purchase.

- A 1975 Films for the Humanities produc-tion of the *The Second Shepherds' Play* is one of three plays staged in *Early English Drama: Quem Quaeritis, Abraham and Isaac, The Second Shepherds' Play*. This film, directed by Harold Mantell, includes additional histori-cal commentary. As of 2007, it was not avail-able for purchase.

- *The Second Shepherds' Play* was filmed for a third time in 1998, and was produced and directed by Eric Peterson. As of 2007, the film was not available for purchase.

- A 2000 production of the *The Second Shepherds' Play* was produced by Films for the Humanities. *Medieval Drama: From Sanctuary to Stage* is available in either VHS or DVD format from Films for the Humanities. This film traces the development of medieval drama, including excerpts from several morality plays.

contains the three shepherds' soliloquies. The play's first speaker is Coll, who begins his soliloquy complaining of the cold weather. He is "ill happed" (badly covered) no matter the weather, since whether "in storms and tempest" he must still tend to his flock. He also complains about his poverty, which he blames on the rich land-owners, "these gentlery-men," who keep him "so hammed, / Fortaxed, and rammed" (hamstrung or confined, overtaxed, and beaten down) that he cannot escape poverty. Coll continues his list of complaints, which he then directs to the rich landowner's overseer, who interferes with the work on the farm. Coll uses the word "husbands" at line 33, not to mean a spouse, but in the archaic use of the word, as one who takes care of the land. Coll does not own the land on which he shepherds the sheep, and he feels himself oppressed by the wealthy. He is brought near to "miscarry" or ruin and thus will never be in a position to work his own land. Coll continues to lament his lack of power and that he dare not complain to anyone about how he is treated, since the landowner's servant has too much power. Coll concludes his soliloquy with the more cheerful expectation that he will soon meet with other shepherds who also share his lonely life.

Gib soon enters the stage. He does not initially see Coll and begins to grumble about the terrible weather. It is cold and the wind so fierce that his eyes water from the misery. Between the snow and sleet, his shoes have frozen to his feet, and he laments that life "is not all easy." Gib also whines that his wife nags him. According to Gib, "she cackles" and thus "Woe is him" since "he is in the shackles," imprisoned in marriage. The rest of Gib's soliloquy continues to articulate his argument that men would be better off forgoing marriage. Men have no will after marriage, says Gib, because their wives control them, whether "in bower nor in bed." Gil has learned his lesson about marrying, but he does note that some men marry a second time, some even a third time. At this point, Gil offers a warning and tells young men that there is little point in later saying, "Had I wist" (wished), since that serves no purpose. It is best for young men to "be well ware of wedding." Gil describes his wife as one who has brows like a pig's bristle and a bitter look on her face. She also has a loud voice and is as "great as a whale." Had he known that she has so much "gall" he would have run until "I lost her" before marrying. At this point in Gib's complaining, Coll finally speaks up and asks that God watch over the audience, who have had to endure Gib's increasingly vicious harangue about his wife and marriage, in general. When Gib realizes that he is not alone he asks if Coll has seen the third shepherd, Daw.

Daw enters and does not see Coll and Gib. Like the others, he begins his soliloquy with a complaint about the miserable weather. The rain and wind is so fierce that Daw compares it to Noah's flood. Daw, though, has faith that God will "turn all to good!" The floods afflict everyone, those in town and those who watch over the sheep and cattle in the fields. The weather creates equality among all men. When Daw greets Coll and Gib they tell him that they have already eaten and since he is late, he has missed the evening meal. His reply is that he will work as little as he is paid. This section of the play ends with Coll, Gib, and Daw singing together to cheer themselves.

Mak, Gill, and Their Baby

The second part of the play is the longest section. Mak enters the stage in disguise, with his head covered and using a southern accent. He is a thief and does not want the shepherds to be on guard. In his first few lines before his identity is discovered, Mak states that his children weep continually. Gib quickly recognizes Mak, though, and warns the others to watch their belongings so that Mak does not steal them. Although Mak pretends to be a yeoman and to have important business, the three shepherds do not believe him. Mak complains that he does not feel well and that he is hungry. When asked about his wife, Mak says that she is lazy, that she drinks, and that every year she produces another child and sometimes two. He says that he wishes her dead. After his complaints, the three shepherds lie down to sleep and insist that Mak lie between them so that they will know if he tries to steal a sheep during the night.

As soon as the shepherds are asleep, Mak arises. He casts a spell over the three shepherds so that they remain sleeping and then steals a sheep from the flock. He immediately takes the sheep to his cottage where his wife, Gill, worries that he will likely hang for being a thief. She comes up with a plan in case their cottage is searched. Gill will hide the ram in the cradle and she will take to her bed as if having just given birth. Mak returns to the shepherds and pretends to have been asleep with them all night. When they awaken, Daw tells of a dream in which a sheep was stolen. Mak responds with his own dream in which his wife gave birth to another baby. Before he leaves, Mak offers to let the shepherds search him for any stolen goods. When Mak gets home, his wife continues to worry that he will hang for stealing the sheep. She immediately swaddles the sheep like a baby and places it in the cradle. After she climbs into bed, Gill begins to moan with pain, as if having just given birth.

The shepherds quickly discover that a sheep is missing and immediately suspect Mak. After the shepherds arrive at Mak's cottage they confront him with their suspicions and are invited to search his house. They find nothing amiss in the house, although Daw does suggest that the newborn baby smells as badly as their missing sheep. As the shepherds begin to leave Mak's cottage, Daw decides to give Mak some money so that his new baby will not starve. Daw insists on seeing the new baby and soon the ruse is discovered. Even though the trick has been discovered, Mak still makes an attempt to deny that his "baby" is the missing sheep, while Gill claims that her baby was stolen by an elf or fairy and this "changeling" was left in its stead. The shepherds toss Mak in a blanket and return to their flock. Although this is not the usual punishment of death for stealing sheep, the story of Jesus's birth that follows in the final section of the play reminds the audience that forgiveness is the focus of New Testament teaching.

The Adoration of the Christ Child

In this final part of the play, the shepherds lie down to rest and an angel appears to them and announces the birth of the Christ child. The humor and absurdity of the previous scene disappears and the shepherds are in awe of the angel and the message that they have received. For those few moments the shepherds forget the cold weather, their poverty, wives, and all of their other complaints. They know they must go to Bethlehem to see the child, even though they "be wet and weary." Gib recalls the prophecy that they have been taught that a savior would be born to relieve them of their sins and all three agree to go and see the baby. The stage directions state that "they go to Bethlehem and enter the stable," but there is no mention of time passing or a lengthy journey undertaken. Each shepherd has brought a gift. Coll offers cherries and Gib offers a bird, while Daw brings a ball for the child. Each gift is symbolic in some way. The cherries are red and symbolize humanity and remind the audience that Jesus will be called upon to shed blood for mankind. The bird symbolizes the dove, the Christian emblem of peace and divinity. The ball (or orb) is the symbol of majesty and power. At this point, Mary briefly recounts how she conceived the infant and tells the shepherds to remember the child. The play ends with the shepherds singing the child's praises.

CHARACTERS

Coll

Coll is the first shepherd to speak. Like the two shepherds who accompany him, Coll is a Yorkshire shepherd and thus familiar to the audience, since they are all from Yorkshire. His complaints are more political than those of the other two shepherds. Coll recognizes the inequities of the world and he relates them to himself. His complaints about the weather focus on the weather as it affects him personally. He is a tenant farmer, who must work the land to survive, but the landowners are letting the flat farmland lie fallow and are instead using the land for sheep. This forces the farmers to work as shepherds, rather than working the land. The sheep must be watched constantly to keep them safe. Coll gets no rest and those like him, who want to care for or husband the land, cannot do so. He feels powerless to fight his oppressors, and explains that "Dare no man reprieve" his master. The inability to even protest his lot adds to Coll's bitterness. His soliloquy is the longest at seventy-eight lines, and so presumably, he is the oldest and most experienced, since he also speaks first. When Mak is confirmed as the thief who stole their sheep, it is Coll who affixes the punishment of tossing Mak in a blanket. Since hanging was the usual punishment for stealing livestock, Coll is more compassionate than might be expected of most shepherds, whose livestock have been stolen. He understands the New Testament and Jesus' teaching about forgiveness.

Daw

Daw is a boy who works for Coll and Gib. He has a very brief soliloquy that only laments the awful weather but which he links to Noah's flood. Because of his youth, he is not angry at the injustices of a life that leaves him working as a shepherd; nor is he disillusioned about women. He is also not a fool. When the shepherds discover that a sheep is missing, it is Daw who immediately exclaims that "Either Mak or Gill" is responsible. After the shepherds search Mak's cottage and leave, it is Daw who is worried that Mak has no money or food for the new baby. It is Daw who discovers the stolen sheep after he tries to give money for the new baby that must be fed. Daw assumes the voice of authority when he orders the two older shepherds to rest after they have recovered their sheep.

Gib

Gib is the second shepherd to enter the stage. Like Coll, he feels oppressed and powerless, but one difference is in how each shepherd begins by complaining about the weather. Where Coll personalized the weather, Gib discusses the weather as an effect upon the world. The remainder of his soliloquy, which is almost as long as Coll's, focuses on marriage and his general unhappiness with his wife and all wives, in general. He is also older and specifically refers to being "late in our lives." Gib's primary complaint is that men have no control over their lives. Unlike Coll, who lays blame for his unhappiness on the unfair division of land and money, Gib sees women, specifically wives, as the oppressors. According to Gib, women must be in control and men "must abide." Gib describes his wife in negative language, comparing her brows to those of a pig and her size to that of a whale. He also directly addresses the audience with such vehemence, that Coll interjects, saying "God look over the raw!" Coll calls on God to protect the audience from being harangued any further.

Gill

Gill is Mak's wife. Mak has told the shepherds that his wife gives birth to a new child every year and in some years two. The audience's first glimpse of Gill is of her spinning wool as a way to earn extra money. Since she is engaged in working late at night and the children are all asleep, her work suggests that she takes an active role in helping to support the household. With her husband, she plots to hide the lamb that Mak has stolen. She is the one who devises the plot to pretend to have just given birth as a way to hide the sheep. She swaddles the sheep and places it in the cradle. Stealing sheep is a hanging offense, and she reminds Mak of this possibility several times, but the play's content does not suggest that she joins Mak solely to protect him. When the shepherds arrive to search for their sheep, she easily hides the sheep and explains that "if it were a greater sleight, / Yet could I help till." Even if she were asked to do more, she would willingly help. Gill enjoys the deception and enjoys being part of the effort to hide the sheep. Her actions suggest that Gill is a good match for Mak.

Mak

Mak is the thief who, after the shepherds are asleep, steals one of their sheep. He is the trickster figure. The trickster is a common figure in Native American stories, but the trickster is also common in many other cultures, as Mak's character illustrates. His role is to play tricks on other characters and sometimes to be the object of other characters' tricks. Mak casts a spell over the shepherds to keep them asleep and steals one of their sheep, but there is no suggestion that Mak is a witch or that he is evil. He is only described within the context of his being a thief. So that his thievery will not be discovered, the sheep is disguised as an infant and swaddled and placed in a cradle. Mak is accustomed to lying. He enters the stage pretending to be what he is not, disguising his voice with a southern accent and his person with a cloak to hide his face. Mak explains to the shepherds that his wife has a baby every year and in some years two babies. He absolves himself of any responsibility for all these children. He is apparently not a good provider, since they are starving, but he does not see this failing. Instead, he explains to his wife that "in a strait I can get / More than they that swink and sweat / All the long day." Thus Mak can do a better job of supporting his family by stealing than men who work for an honest wage. When the stolen sheep is discovered, Mak continues to deny that his "baby" is a sheep and instead claims that his baby was only bewitched to look like a sheep. Like his wife, Mak provides a good deal of comedy in the play.

THEMES

Absurdity

Much of the action and most of the dialogue in the middle section of *The Second Shepherds' Play* is absurd, filled with nonsense and humor. Mak steals a ram and his wife, Gill, is easily able to swaddle the ram in blankets, as a newborn infant is swaddled. Gill takes to her bed and begins moaning so loudly that Mak tells her that all the noise is harming his brain. For her part, Gill embraces her deception so thoroughly that she tells the shepherds "If ever I you beguiled, / That I eat this child / That lies in this cradill." The child in the cradle is the stolen ram, of course, and she has every intention of eating him when the opportunity presents itself. The audience would have enjoyed the humor of Daw's comments that the new baby smelled like a sheep and no doubt laughed heartily when Gill proclaimed her new baby a "pretty child" and a

TOPICS FOR FURTHER STUDY

- Research peasant clothing from the late medieval period in England. After you have several ideas about costuming, consider how, if you were staging this play, you would costume the characters. Would traditional medieval costuming work best? Would you consider modern dress as an alternative? Create a poster that illustrates the kinds of costumes that you would use. Be prepared to defend your choices and explain their importance to increasing the audience's understanding of the play.

- Mak's wife warns him several times that stealing sheep is a hanging offence. Research the fifteenth-century English justice system. Your research should also include information about medieval prisons in England. Choose several of the crimes most often committed by the peasant class and the punishments that these crimes received. Present your findings to the class.

- With small groups of your classmates, prepare a series of posters that recreate the staging of this play. Include drawings of the stage wagons and the placement of scen-ery, including Mak's cottage, the manger scene in Bethlehem, and the pasture where the three shepherds meet and sleep.

- It is thought that drama reflects the values and ideology of the society in which it is written. After a careful study of this play, write an essay in which you consider the following question: What values and beliefs can be drawn from studying *The Second Shepherds' Play*? Be sure to use quotations from the play as supporting material for your argument.

- In fifteenth-century England there was an enormous increase in the number of outlaws and corresponding outlaw legends. In part this was caused by the dire economic plight of the peasant class, who looked to Robin Hood–like figures to rescue them from miserly landlords. Research and read several of these legends and then write your own outlaw legend. Your legend should be historically accurate, in that the events that you are depicting are compatible with this period and location.

"dillydown" (darling). Mak and Gill also try to pass off their new baby's sheep-like appearance as the work of fairies. This whole section is so humorous that the usual punishment of hanging is ignored, although the audience is reminded several times by Gill that stealing sheep is an offense where the punishment is death.

Class Conflict

Coll's opening speech focuses on the inequities of class. By the mid fifteenth century, peasant life in England was undergoing a change. Land-owners had discovered that they could make more money with sheep than by farming, and so farmland was allowed to lie fallow and become pasture for sheep. Tenant farmers, who rented their land from the larger landowners, lost their land, homes, and incomes. To make more pasture for sheep, whole villages were destroyed and those who lived in the villages displaced and made homeless. Coll refers to the economic realities of his world when he says that "husbands" are "nearhands / Out of the door" (nearly homeless). The wealthy landowners have created terrible poverty, but those most affected cannot complain. Coll explains that "Woe is him that him grieve." Even the landowners' servants have authority over the tenants and can use force ("What mastery he maes") to seize any property that belongs to the tenants ("He can make purveyance"). The former tenant farmer must make his living by caring for the sheep. Rather than sleeping inside his warm home at night, the shepherd

Adoration of the Shepherds triptych from late 15th/early 16th century (© *The Print Collector / Alamy*)

sleeps in the fields and guards the sheep. Mak tells Gill that he can provide more support for his family by stealing than by working. But when the shepherds search his cottage all they note are the "two tome platters." There is no meat, either fresh or salted and only empty plates. If Mak can provide more money through stealing than working as a shepherd there cannot be much money to be made as a shepherd. The irony is that Mak is forced to steal a sheep to support his family and yet it is the sheep who created his poverty.

Religious Belief

The third section of the play turns the audience's focus back to the lesson the play is meant to teach. Although much of the play has focused on the misery of the shepherds and their lack of food, religion takes over in the final part of the play and negates the shepherds' misery. All three shepherds are exhausted after the search at Mak's cottage. Coll complains that he is "sore,"

and Gib that the sheep weighed "seven score," or about 140 pounds. Since he complains of the sheep's weight, Gib must have carried the ram from Mak's cottage back to the pasture. Coll and Gib are so exhausted that Daw must get angry in order to force the two of them to stop and rest. However, after the angel appears and sings of the birth of the promised savior, theshepherds awaken and no longer complain of cold, fatigue, or hunger. Religious belief has helped them forget their misery, at least for a short time. The men only recall the beauty of the angel's voice. The three men also realize that they are important, since "so poor as we are / That he would appear, / First find and declare / By his messenger." The angel appeared to them first, not to the wealthy landowners. The play ends with them recognizing that their souls have been redeemed, and they leave the stage singing. The play began with the shepherd's misery, but it ends with their having achieved a sense of worth and purpose. Religious belief is depicted as having provided this change.

STYLE

Educating the Audience

When *The Second Shepherds' Play* was first performed, the audience was likely made up by illiterate townspeople, who would not have been able to read the Bible. Thus, the mystery plays would have been the best way for audiences to learn biblical lessons. The author, then, would be writing to teach religious and moral lessons and educate the audience about biblical scripture and, in some cases, the life of Jesus. The lesson in *The Second Shepherds' Play* is that the misery of poverty and of earthly life will eventually be erased through belief in God and the afterlife.

Mystery Plays

The Second Shepherds' Play is a dramatic presentation that incorporates comedy and liturgy (public worship and ritual) into a theatrical staging. In some cases these plays might also be described as religious pageants, especially when several of the plays are performed as part of a cycle.

Indeed, mystery plays were medieval dramas that explored the so-called mystery of religious scripture. Mystery plays were generally performed from wagons and were part of a cycle of plays exploring both Old Testament and New Testament events. Although mystery plays developed from liturgical drama (a play acted in or around the church that portrays Bible stories or saints' lives) and were initially performed in Latin, they soon began to be performed in the vernacular language of the audience. Mystery plays were designed as a way to teach biblical stories to the uneducated, and almost always illiterate, medieval townspeople. *The Second Shepherds' Play* is the best known and most celebrated of the mystery plays.

Discrepancy and Anachronism

The location for *The Second Shepherds' Play* covers both medieval England and biblical Bethlehem. The two locations and historical periods are discordant, but the audience would not have cared. Other inconsistencies also occur between historical periods, and this is known as anachronism. There are references to Christian saints and to Christ's birth, but saints did not appear until hundreds of years after Christ's birth. However, once again, the audience would not have minded this, since the audience also accepted that religious belief often presents inconsistencies and mysteries that ordinary men cannot understand. The audience simply accepted what was presented on stage without questioning the lack of logic or the inconsistencies too closely. Theater has always relied upon the audience's ability and desire to suspend disbelief; this was as true in the Middle Ages as it is today in modern theater and film.

Soliloquy

The soliloquy is a common dramatic device that offers a way for the playwright to divulge a character's inner thoughts. The soliloquy requires that the character must think that he is alone on stage, as he reveals before the audience exactly what he is thinking. The shepherds use the soliloquy as a way to divulge their misery. Notably, a soliloquy is different from a monologue, in which a character speaks his thoughts aloud, but with the knowledge that other characters are present. In the opening scene of this play, the soliloquy is used by each of the three shepherds to relate important information about their lives to the audience.

Stanzaic Form

Although often associated with poetry, some dramas are also written in stanzas. Formal stanzas should be consistent in terms of meter, length, and rhyme scheme, and each formal stanza should repeat the same structure. *The Second Shepherds' Play* uses a thirteen line stanza with an internal rhyme (ab / ab / ab / ab / cdddc). There are eight long lines with a short ninth line, followed by three lines with a single rhyme. The concluding line rhymes with the ninth line. This form of stanza is a variation of the rondel (a French verse form). The purpose of the recurring rhyme is to create unity between the stanzas.

Religious Symbolism

Symbolism is common in medieval drama. In *The Second Shepherds' Play* the scene with Mak and his wife and their sheep/infant has its own comic meaning, but it is also meant to be symbolic of the more serious nativity scene that ends the play. Mak and Gill's lamb/infant symbolizes the birth of Jesus, the Lamb of God. Symbolism is also obvious in the gifts that the shepherds present to the Christ child. Coll's gift of red cherries symbolizes humanity and blood, which reminds the audience of the crucifixion. Gib gives a bird, which symbolizes the dove, the

COMPARE
&
CONTRAST

- **1400s:** English Landowners gain a monopoly in the grain market when a statute is passed that prohibits the import of grain. Food prices begin to increase while wages remain low (a trend that will continue for the next two hundred years), thus increasing poverty and hunger.

  Today: In 2005, a British newspaper revealed that wealthy landowners were receiving substantial taxpayer-provided subsidies to agricultural farmers. Small farmers do not receive these subsidies.

- **1400s:** Most art and plays are religious in theme and content. Indeed, most of the art produced during this period is commissioned directly by the Church and is intended for the Church.

  Today: Although religious art is still made, most art and plays are produced independently of the church, and their themes and content are not necessarily religious. Rather, most art is today is concerned with political, racial, or sexual themes.

- **1400s:** Bubonic plague, known as The Black Death, continues to claim lives, although not as many as during the 1300s, when one third of Europe's population died. Still, thousands continue to die from plague, creating a significant labor shortage.

  Today: Bubonic plague is almost nonexistent in England, although it still exists in some areas of the world. Even the American Southwest records deaths from bubonic plague each year.

- **1400s:** The first English paper mills open in 1494. This, combined with the new moveable type presses, which were first established in England in 1476 by William Caxton, means that more books can be printed and at less expense. The movement toward literacy in England has begun.

  Today: Although it was sometimes claimed that computers and the Internet would mean the end of printed materials, books, magazines, and newspapers continue to enjoy a huge audience.

Christian emblem of peace and divinity. Daw presents the child with a ball, or orb, the symbol of majesty and power. Kings are often painted with an orb, symbolizing the world, in their hands, suggesting their power over their subjects. Many medieval audiences were much better educated about religious symbols than modern audiences and would have easily understood what each gift was meant to represent.

HISTORICAL CONTEXT

Church Influence and the Creation of Medieval Drama

Although the author is unknown, *The Second Shepherds' Play* provides content, themes, and ideology that reflect the teachings of Catholic Europe, which suggests that the writer might have been a cleric or friar. The use of Christianity as a topic and a force behind theater reflects a significant change from Christian opposition to early theater. Traditionally, the Catholic Church opposed drama because it frequently included nudity, fights with wild beasts, and because the sacrifice of Christians was often included as a part of pagan spectacle in ancient Rome. An additional reason for church opposition was the use of falsehood. In drama, an actor pretends to be someone else. Although modern audiences accept this as "acting," it was interpreted by the early church to be lying.

In the ninth century, musical elaboration of the Latin liturgy began to appear as part of certain feasts. Their purpose was to heighten

Mystery play in the middle ages (© *Lebrecht Music and Arts Photo Library* / *Alamy*)

and enhance the religious experience of the worshippers, and by the 10th century, brief enactments of biblical episodes were practiced at monasteries and abbeys. The most famous was an Easter morning reenactment of the three Marys asking for Jesus at his grave. Clerics dressed for the parts and sang the piece as dialogue, answering one another. These tropes, as they were called, were not plays exactly, but contained all the elements of drama. They had progressive plots, brief development of character, conflict, resolution, and visual spectacle. Over a period of 100 years, tropes became more

elaborate and more complicated. The topics were usually biblical and the actors were clerics, monks, and choirboys. But the language was Latin rather than vernacular languages, and the audiences were almost exclusively limited to those living in monastic communities. By the tenth century, drama would again become acceptable to clergy when it was reborn as liturgical drama. The earliest liturgical dramas were included as a part of the church service and were often simply a dialogue, frequently sung, between two clerics. Eventually this exchange began to include additional participants and by the thirteenth century, these dramas became a means to educate an illiterate congregation. Widespread deaths from plague changed the nature of medieval drama and opened the way for another type of performance. When labor became scarce and expensive, people moved into the cities, which became centers of economic and cultural growth. More elaborate staging of plays began to be included in feast day celebrations, and these performances eventually moved from the church to the town square, which accommodated a larger audience. Eventually plays were sponsored by various guilds or trades, and they became known as miracle or mystery plays.

The Guilds: From Liturgy to Theater

The guild system evolved in the later medieval period, as more people began to move into small towns. The guilds functioned much like a modern union. They provided some protection for merchants, and they helped to maintain standards for goods and services, which benefited both merchants and townspeople. Eventually, the guilds became very powerful. In many villages, the guilds were associated with the Catholic Church and often even had a patron saint assigned. The guilds eventually became a part of every aspect of village life. In addition to the merchants and craftsmen who originated the guild system, there were guilds for fellowship, including drinking, and religious guilds. Although eventually the guild system became too powerful politically and perhaps can be credited with hampering free commerce, the guild system did accomplish a lot of good. Better standards for goods helped to eliminate poor quality and fraud, and guilds helped to train artists and artisans, who became more skilled in their trade. The guilds can be credited with helping to develop better village government and better products and services, and they also helped to provide social venues for townspeople, in large part through their sponsorship of early medieval drama. Cycle or mystery plays evolved in towns and cities and were sanctioned by the church. Vast productions that taught Christian history and values were produced in the towns with lay people as actors and as a part of feast day celebrations. Each guild was assigned a story, from Creation to Judgment, and each guild produced a pageant that best fit the guild's purpose. A great many of the townspeople participated as stage crew, actors, managers, and supporting cast. The audiences were large, drawn from

everyone within traveling distance. Eventually, morality plays grew out of this beginning. The morality plays differed from mystery plays, in that they used allegorical figures to represent mankind's struggle between good and evil. However, with the coming of the great Elizabethan theater, morality plays disappeared as a more modern society demanded greater complexity and more elaborate entertainments. The guilds also began to lose their power and disappear during the Elizabethan age, when Queen Elizabeth's parliament instituted strong laws to govern the guilds.

CRITICAL OVERVIEW

Given the time period in which the play was first written and performed, it was not initially subjected to what we now see as traditional criticism. Indeed, its initial reception and waxing and waning popularity was caused mostly by religious controversies between church and state. *The Second Shepherds' Play* is part of the Wakefield play cycle and was traditionally performed during the feast of Corpus Christi, which celebrated the Catholic Church's teaching that the body of Christ was present in the Holy Eucharist. (The word Eucharist is derived from the Greek and means thanksgiving. Roman Catholics believe that when they participate in the Eucharist, which many Christians call communion, they are partaking of Jesus' body and blood.) The whole play cycle would be performed beginning at dawn and continuing until dusk on that feast day. It has been estimated that it would take fourteen to fifteen hours to perform the entire cycle, and so, in some cases, the cycle might be performed over a period of two days. After Henry VIII established himself as the supreme head of the Church of England in 1534, he moved to eliminate the influence of the Pope and the Roman Catholic Church in all aspects of English life. In many communities, this meant that religious plays were performed less frequently. In some cases, the manuscript was edited to remove content thought to be too heavy in Roman Catholic ideology, but in other cases, the play was removed completely for government review and never returned. In 1540, King Henry issued a decree banning the printing or performance of all plays that did not conform to official Church of England doctrine. In the years that followed the 1540 edict, there were a number of local attempts to ban performances of religious drama, but the plays generated a lot of money for communities, so local officials often ignored the ban. However, in 1576, the Diocesan Court of High Commission completely banned any performances of the Wakefield cycle. None of the plays were performed again until the twentieth century.

The Second Shepherds' Play is the only play from the cycle to still be performed regularly, which suggests that the play provides an entertainment that transcends the nearly 600-year gap between when it was first written and today. In *Medieval English Drama: Essays Critical and Contextual*, Lawrence J. Ross calls *The Second Shepherds' Play* "the finest single achievement of the English cycle drama." Ross argues that the play requires an "appreciation of the brilliant farcical action, realistic characterization, and pungent social protest of its 'secular' part rather than on judgments of the play as a whole." Maynard Mack, Jr., in his essay in *PMLA*, is even more complimentary, stating that the play is one "of radiant simplicity." But even more, it is also "a play of rare sophistication and even artistic daring." Mack praises *The Second Shepherds' Play* for its "skillful modulation" with which the play moves from the shepherds' laments to low comedy to the final revelation of the nativity scene. Almost every anthology of British literature that contains a section on medieval literature includes the text of *The Second Shepherds' Play* as an example of medieval theater.

While it is true that the Wakefield plays were not performed for several centuries after 1576, *The Second Shepherds' Play* has undergone a resurgence in the past hundred years and is often performed as a Christmas play. When the play was presented as children's theater in 1981, Carole Corbeil, writing in the *Globe and Mail* called it "uncloying, unsentimental, uncommercial, funny, warm, and mercifully short." Corbeil also notes in her review that "you don't even have to be a kid to like it." Occasionally *The Second Shepherds' Play* is also titled as *The Shepherds' Play* or *The Shepherds' Christmas*. Because *The Second Shepherds' Play* has been recently limited to performances during holiday entertainment, the play is returning to its medieval roots as it is reincorporated into a religious observance.

> A MORE POSITIVE WAY TO LOOK AT GILL IS TO THINK OF HER AS A PREDECESSOR FOR SHAKESPEARE'S UNRULY WOMEN."

CRITICISM

Sheri Metzger Karmiol

Karmiol has a doctorate in English Renaissance literature. She teaches literature and drama at the University of New Mexico, where she is a lecturer in the University's Honors Program. Karmiol is also a professional writer and the author of several reference texts on poetry and drama. In this essay, Karmiol discusses the play's renderings of women's lives and how the traditional church view of women colors medieval drama.

While the author of *The Second Shepherds' Play* is unknown, the play was likely written by a man, or men. Indeed, there is only one known female author of morality plays written at this time. When literature is written by men, women are seen through male eyes. Because sexual roles can be so embedded in a society that they are unseen by most observers (and sometimes by writers), the way females are portrayed by men is of note. Comedy can help to mitigate these portrayals, in large part because both males and females become the object of humor. This is what happens in *The Second Shepherds' Play*. There are two depictions of marriage in this play and neither should be understood only at face value. In the first portrayal, Gib presents a soliloquy that is so negative toward women and so filled with exaggeration that the audience immediately understands that Gib is a stock comic character—the henpecked husband. His wife makes him so miserable that he condemns all wives and all marriages, since marriage puts men "in the shackles." The second image of marriage is provided by Mak and Gill. The audience sees this marriage twice. In the first instance, the audience sees the marriage only through Mak's eyes as he describes his wife in unflattering terms, although still not as filled with disapproval as the description provided by Gib. Later the audience meets Gill and sees her interaction with her husband, and a completely

WHAT DO I READ NEXT?

- In his essay "The Magi and Modes of Meaning: *The Second Shepherds' Play* as an Index of the Criticism of Medieval Drama" (in *Early Drama to 1600*, Acta, Vol. XIII, 1995, pp. 107–120), David Lampe traces the scholarly criticism of the play as a way to study the political and religious reception of medieval drama from the Elizabethan period to the present.

- *The Chester Pageant of Noah's Flood* is another early English mystery play. It dates from the mid-fifteenth century and was so popular that it was still being performed late in the sixteenth century. This play is available in *Medieval and Tudor Drama: Twenty-Four Plays*, edited by John Gassner, 2000.

- *The Cambridge Companion to Medieval English Theatre* (1994), by Richard Beadle, is directed at students who want to learn more about medieval drama. The book contains a series of essays that provide extensive information about plays, theater, and performance in the medieval period.

- Michael Rose's edition of *The Wakefield Mystery Plays: The Complete Cycle of Thirty-Two Plays* (1961) contains all thirty-two plays, in modern translation. This is an easy-to-read edition rendered in modern English.

- Gail McMurray Gibson's *The Theater of Devotion: East Anglican Drama and Society in the Late Middle Ages* (1995) is an interdisciplinary examination of how drama and art were influenced by religious life in the medieval period.

- *Anthology of Medieval Music* and *Medieval Music* (both 1978), by Richard H. Hoppin, are meant to be used together. When combined, these two texts provide a rich history of medieval music, including both religious and secular music. Since this play also includes several areas in which the shepherds sing, knowledge of the music of the period can further add to a student's enjoyment and understanding of this play.

- *A New History of Early English Drama* (1998), edited by John D. Cox and David Scott Kastan and with a Foreward by Stephen J. Greenblatt, is a historical look at how society influenced the production of medieval theater.

- *A Source Book in Theatrical History* (1959), by A. M. Nagler, is a comprehensive examination on the history of theater throughout the world. There is information about acting, rehearsals, audiences, and many photos and illustrations.

---

different depiction is offered. Instead of the kind of wife that Gib earlier described so negatively that he wished he had never been married ("I would I had run [till] I lost her"), Mak has a wife who is more than his equal.

When men tell women's stories, what do they tell? Women are empty vessels, only understood or seen through their household roles. Women are seen in relationship to children, as mothers, or through their husband's eyes, as wives, but they are not seen solely as women. They are not individuals. In some cases, women are nags, witches, or worse; they are rarely seen as having their own unmet needs. In *The Second Shepherds' Play*, the women are described in negative terms, but it is in describing them that men diminish women. For instance, Mak describes his wife as lazy, as one who "Lies waltering, by the rood, / By the fire," and as one who "drinks well." Besides being a drunk, she is also gluttonous and "Eats as fast as she can." In Gib's soliloquy, women are described as nags or scolds, leaving men "not all their will." According to Gib, "men are led / Full hard and full ill." In the case of Gib's absent wife, women are so controlling that her husband fears for all men who marry. Since the audience never meets Gib's wife, it is impossible to judge the degree of truth in his words. In contrast, Gill is present in the play and is able to refute both her husband's words and those of Gib, who paints all women as equally bad.

Mak complains of his wife's laziness, yet when the audience first sees Gill she is spinning wool. This was not perceived as hard work, however. For a feudal serf, spinning was an obligation of women, who had to spin and weave material for the lord of the manor. Tenant farmers' wives could also earn money from spinning. Indeed, this was the only source of cash income in Mak's household. Since Mak is clearly not a good provider—the search by the three shepherds reveals that there is no food in the house—Gill spins to earn money to provide food for her children. Mak's idea of providing for his family is to steal, and even Gill warns her husband that he is at risk of hanging as a thief. When Mak arrives home with his stolen sheep, Gill is spinning. It is late at night, since the shepherds have already gone to sleep. Since none of the many children that Mak claims to have fathered are in sight, the audience assumes they are also sleeping. This evidence counters Mak's complaints of Gill's laziness. Mak grouses that his wife produces a child every year and in some years two, and so she must be either constantly pregnant or just recovering from childbirth. Rather than lazy, she must be exhausted from constant pregnancy, childbirth, and childcare. More importantly, the audience would have recognized that Gill was not what Mak had claimed her to be; as a result, he is further cast as a comic figure, the traditional stock character of the henpecked husband, who on closer examination is not henpecked at all. Instead, it is his wife who deserves the audience's sympathy.

Despite Mak's complaints about his wife's laziness, research suggests that during the medieval period, women living in rural areas, especially poor peasant women, had hard lives, working every waking hour. In their book, *Women in the Middle Ages*, Frances and Joseph Gies point out that a peasant wife "fully shared her husband's day-in, day-out drudgery." In addition to all the work that women did inside the home, the cleaning, cooking, sewing, and childcare, she also did all of the outside work. While the husband left to work the fields, or in the case of Gib to watch the flock, the wife "milked the cows; soaked, beat, and combed out the flax; fed the chickens, ducks, and geese; sheered the sheep; made the cheese and butter; and cultivated the family vegetable patch." According to the Gies, wives might also work with their husbands—"sowing, reaping, gleaning, binding, threshing, raking, winnowing, thatching." Some wives "even helped with the plowing." Since Mak's family was destitute, Gill likely did not have outside animals for which she was responsible, since it takes some financial means to buy farm animals. Instead, she was likely one of the wives that the Gies suggest "spun and wove to eke out a cash income." The Gies describe the peasants who were "poor cottagers" as living at the bottom of the economic scale. Technically the villeins—the lowest economic level of serfs—lived in small cottages on the manor estate and worked the land. In England many villeins were free, but the Gies note that "freedom, without land, was worth little." The Wakefield Master provides no real information about Mak and his wife, other than their absolute poverty, but given that they are not homeless, as Coll suggests is the case for many peasants, it is likely that their small cottage is on property that they do not own.

Since the historical and social evidence suggests that Gill would have had a hard life, one that would have required that she spend her entire married life performing tedious and often labor-intensive work, it is worth considering why her depiction in this religious drama is so negative. Katie Normington, writing in *College Literature*, explores some of the reasons for the often negative portrayals of women in medieval dramas. Normington writes that "One of the central issues which restricts women characters is that God is placed in absolute authority, and, thus, a strong hierarchical model is at work within the cycles." The early leaders of the Christian church were men, from Paul and Peter, to Philo, to Jerome, to Chrysostom, and Augustine. These men have in common their belief in God and their belief in a world created for and governed by men. Their authority as church leaders and their reliance upon the story of man's fall in Genesis 3 created a dogma of male supremacy that lies at the heart of church doctrine and the tradition of church-based patriarchy that governed society during the Middle Ages. After Adam and Eve fall and they are confronted by God, Adam places the blame on

Eve and complains that the fault lies with the "woman whom you gave to be with me." Adam's words prove to be prophetic, for they define a tradition of affixing the blame for man's fall upon the woman. As punishment for their actions, Adam and Eve are expelled from Paradise, and Eve is told that henceforth she will be subject to man's rule. Early interpretations of Genesis 3, especially those of Paul, Philo Judaeus, Jerome, Augustine, and Chrysostom, provided the foundation upon which the family, church, and society was established. And so with the assistance of the church, the story of Eve became a dominant force in the establishment of a patriarchal society, which resulted in a hierarchy that placed women in a subordinate, silent, and obedient role.

God's punishment to Eve is that her "desire shall be for your husband, and he shall rule over you." While Genesis 3 provides the source for what was to follow, the biblical text does not bear the sole responsibility for the fate of women. Those who interpreted and commented upon its content bear the greatest blame for the church's reliance upon Eve's story as a means to chastise and control women. One of the first commentators to use Eve in this manner was Paul. In his epistle to the Ephesians, Paul tells wives to "be subject to your husbands" and "the husband is the head of the wife." This hierarchy is again reinforced in verse 24: "Just as the church is subject to Christ, so also wives ought to be, in everything, to their husbands." This repeats what Paul says in chapter eleven of his epistle to the Corinthians. In a section that emphasizes the desired behavior and appearance of women, Paul begins by stating that "But I want you to understand that Christ is the head of every man, and the husband is the head of his wife." Paul again mentions the status and role of women in his epistle to Titus. Paul tells women "to be self-controlled, chaste, good managers of the household, kind, being submissive to their husbands, that the word of God may not be discredited." Thus, according to Paul, if women fail to assume their role and the standard of behavior that he has just provided, they are guilty of discrediting God. They are guilty of denying God's decree, which is blasphemous. This is a serious charge, since blasphemy was interpreted as a denial of God's providence or being. Paul's authority is God and Genesis: God made Adam first and then Eve. Therefore, God created the hierarchy, and Paul is only serving as God's mouthpiece.

But perhaps the most damage is derived from the verse that follows. Of the fall, Paul notes that "Adam was not deceived, but the woman was deceived and became a transgressor." No blame for the fall is attached to Adam; the fall is Eve's fault. Yet Paul ignores his own text: Adam was not deceived and Eve was. He knowingly sinned, and yet Paul places no blame on Adam. In ignoring Adam's sin here, he presents a sexist model for the church. Men were not the innocent victims of female deception, and women were not simply flawed copies of the original perfect man. In *Redeeming Eve: Women Writers of the English Renaissance*, Elaine Beilin declares that "the image of a disobedient and talkative Eve reaching for the apple had threatened all women." Unfortunately, and for a thousand years after Paul, many members of the clergy accept and adopt Paul's writings about women as the governing rules for the relationship between wives and husbands. This damaging coloring of women's lives is heavily invested in medieval drama, where just in one drama, *The Second Shepherds' Play*, women are either Gib's definition of fat, loud, and angry, or they are Mak's wife—lazy indiscriminate breeders of countless children. The only remaining option for women is the very brief idealistic Virgin Mary who appears in the final nativity scene. Clearly, though, she is not the model the author had in mind when he created Gib's wife and Gill.

A more positive way to look at Gill is to think of her as a predecessor for Shakespeare's unruly women. Gill is a woman with the kind of humor and courage that Shakespeare will use to define Kate in *The Taming of the Shrew*. Gill is a woman who challenges traditional views of women who manipulate or trick their husbands. Instead of tricking him, Gill is more than willing to help her husband hide the stolen sheep and she does so not just because they are hungry and she needs to feed her children. She willingly engages in Mak's deception because she enjoys it and she enjoys the partnership with her husband. She even expresses a willingness to do more, saying "If it were a greater sleight, / Yet could I help till." She is fully capable of doing more, of being her husband's peer. In helping him, she becomes his equal. And in helping to protect him, she escapes her traditional role of a subservient woman in need of protection. Gill's portrayal on stage might even suggest to the women in the audience that there is another way to circumvent their role as subservient wife. The suggestion is not to engage in committing crimes with her husband. Rather Gill suggests that women can be equal partners with their husbands. They can even help to protect their husbands, when called upon to do so. As a model for medieval women, Gill presents a more fluid paradigm of possibilities. Her portrayal suggests equality, even if true equality is far in the future.

Source: Sheri Metzger Karmiol, Critical Essay on *The Second Shepherds' Play*, in *Drama for Students*, Gale, Cengage Learning, 2008.

Michelle Ann Abate

In the following excerpt, Abate argues that the second shepherd, Gyb, is not merely an echo of the first shepherd, Coll. Instead, Abate claims, Gyb foreshadows the events that are to come later in the play.

As numerous past and present critics have noted, *Secunda Pastorum* is the most widely recognized, anthologized, and analyzed pageant of a mystery cycle, Towneley or otherwise. In the words of David Lampe, 'The Towneley (Wakefield) *The Second Shepherds' Play* is clearly the single most popular piece of medieval English drama, appearing in every anthology of English literature that devotes space to the medieval period'. Given, its popularity, criticism about *The Second Shepherds' Play* has been both numerous and diverse. In addition to examining the pageant from its original cultural and religious contexts, studies have considered it from a wide range of thematic, symbolic, and even theoretical perspectives. Such sentiments pervade current analyses as well.

In spite of all the past and present attention *Secunda Pastorum* has received, none of these studies has focused exclusively on the shepherds in general or Gyb in particular. Although Coll, Gyb, and Daw make important individual contributions to the drama, most critics agree that they are best viewed not as independent characters but as an interdependent unit or whole. Jeffrey Helterman, for instance, argues that Coll, Gyb, and Daw have an ensemble effect that is more important than the contributions made by their individual characters. Similarly, F. P. Manion outlines the benefits of seeing the shepherds not as discrete entities but as a type of chorus working in unison with both each other and the plot. As a result of such sentiments, no articles to date are exclusively devoted to Gyb or the role he occupies in the text. Instead, he is

> INSTEAD OF MERELY SHADOWING HIS COMPANIONS, HE FORESHADOWS KEY EVENTS AND CENTRAL THEMES OF THE PAGEANT. FOR THESE REASONS, GYB IS NOT SIMPLY ONE OF THE CHARACTERS IN *SECUNDA PASTORUM*, BUT A CENTRAL ONE."

commonly considered a mere echo or extension of his cohorts, Coll and Daw. Exemplifying this belief, John Gardner asserts that the vast majority of the second shepherd's speeches do not introduce new information or announce fresh themes in the pageant. On the contrary, they merely 'pick up on Coll's tone'. Such sentiments pervade present analyses as well. Recent essays by Lee Templeton and Ken Hiltner echo or at least fail to challenge these previously established views of the shepherds. Examining the carnivalesque atmosphere within the pageant and its use of punning and political parody respectively, they tend to view Coll, Gyb, and Daw as a unit and lock them into fixed positions.

Although the tendency to emphasize the interconnected nature of the three-shepherds may enhance the overall unity or coherence of *Secunda Pastorum*, it forecloses the possibility that the trio may occupy positions outside this role. More than simply echoing the comments made by the first shepherd or providing a segue to those of the third shepherd, Gyb plays an important and previously overlooked role in *Secunda Pastorum*. Instead of merely shadowing his companions, he foreshadows key events and central themes of the pageant. For these reasons, Gyb is not simply one of the characters in *Secunda Pastorum*, but a central one.

John Gardner articulates what he considers the controlling metaphor of the drama: 'The Second Shepherds' Play* is in a sense an exploration of the Christian significance of the number three: the play focuses on three shepherds; it begins with three soliloquies which open the first of three distinct movements; it treats three motifs appropriate to the Nativity story—law, charity and wonder—and associates them with the Holy Trinity; it closes with the three adorations of the Christ child and the giving of three symbolic gifts'. Given the predominance of this number throughout *Secunda Pastorum*, Gardner concludes that 'threes are by no means simply graceful embellishment. They are the heart of the matter'. While Gardner's observation about the importance of numerology in the pageant is apt, it may be time to alter or modify its focus. After several decades of focusing on the significance of threes in *Secunda Pastorum*, the insight made possible by the bibliographic oversight suggest that the time has come to consider the importance of another digit in the drama: the number two.

Not simply a mere echo or shadow of the first shepherd, Gyb's role as a foreshadower of key events emerges from his opening speech in the play. When Gyb first appears on stage, he remarks, 'Bensté and Dominus.' A mock blessing that would have been understood as comical by even lower-class members of the audience, the second shepherd's invocation establishes one of the central features of *Secunda Pastorum*: the farcical blending of secular and sacred. Although the first shepherd laments the harsh conditions on earth and wonders why God would allow them to exist, he never transforms this disillusionment into heretical comments about the divine. Instead, Coll's discussion of man's cruel state only confirms his belief in a saviour. After articulating the ways in which he is both tortured by the weather and exploited by wealthy landowners, Coll closes with the suggestive lines, 'For I trowe, perdé, / Trew men if thay be, We gett more compané / Or it be noyne.' Although ostensibly foreshadowing the arrival of his companions, Coll's remarks also allude to the arrival of the Christ child in the close of the drama. As Mack Maynard asserts, 'What better introduction could there be to a world in need of redemption, to a story that will end with Christmas?'

Although Gyb reiterates many of Coll's grievances, his opening speech takes a dramatically different tone. Rather than begin with a complaint, Gyb begins with a mock blessing. In addition to deviating from the worldview of his companion, the second shepherd's remark announces the primary comedic element on which the drama is based: the mixing of the pious with the parodic. As numerous past and present critics have pointed out, the vast majority of *Secunda Pastorum* is concerned with the

comic parody of the Nativity rather than the devout retelling of it. But the blend of secular and sacred contributes to its role as a comedy of instruction. According to Rose Zimbardo's definition of the 'comic mockery of the sacred' in *Secunda Pastorum*, the humorous annunciation and adoration scenes in the opening half of the pageant simultaneously foreshadow as they reinforce the sacred and more serious ones that are to come in the final segment. Phrased in a more vernacular (and metaphoric) way, they are the 'spoonful of sugar' that first captures the audience's attention and then helps make the sacred lesson that they are about to receive both more palatable and memorable. Gyb, with his own invocation of the sacred and profane, participates in or contributes to this phenomenon. The mock blessing that he utters in his opening speech is reiterated in a more serious and sacred form later in the pageant when Gyb first sees the Christ child: 'Hayll, sufferan sauyoure, for thou has vs soght!' In this way, the second shepherd has not only helped prepare audience members for the pageant's account of the biblical story, but also assumed an important role in the actual telling of it.

Coupled with alluding to the recurring tension between farce and worship in *Secunda Pastorum*, Gyb's mock blessing also foreshadows transitional speeches by subsequent characters. For instance, when the three shepherds wake from their slumber later in the narrative, the first shehperd makes a proclamation that similarly traffics in mock religiosity: '*Resurrex a mortuus!* . . . / *Iudas carnas dominus!*' Echoing this passage, Mak engages in heretical mockery of sacred invocations at several points in the drama. When preparing to steal a sheep from the unsuspecting Coll, Gyb and Daw, for example, the trickster figure does not ask for the blessing or assistance of God. Instead, he utters, '*Manus tuas commendo, / Poncio Pilato.*' Like Gyb in his opening remarks, Mak forgoes the pious for the parodic. Significantly, because he casts the spell on the shepherds soon after uttering his mock-piety, many critics read Mak as a demonic figure. Dabbling in the supernatural and calling on the assistance of the man who presided over the crucifixion of Christ, the comic trickster has been deemed the Antichrist.

The way in which Gyb's opening speech announces central themes and important events in *Secunda Pastorum* continues into the second stanza. In this section, Gyb shifts his lament from the harsh condition of making of living by animal husbandry to the harsh condition of being a husband. In what has become an oft-quoted passage, the second shepherd launches into an extended harangue about the enfeebling effects of marriage and the emasculating nature of women: 'These men that ar wed haue not all thare wyll; / When they ar full hard sted, thay sygh full styll. / God wayte thay ar led full hard and full yll; / In bowere nor in bed thay say noght thertyll.' In light of this unflattering portrait of wedlock, Gyb admonishes the men of marriageable age in the audience to avoid or at least be cautious about matrimony: 'Bot, yong men, of wowying, for God that you boght, / Be well war of wedying.'

While critics have rightly condemned Gyb's misogyny in this passage, their focus on reprimand has caused them to overlook an important facet of his speech. More than simply announcing the second shepherd as a hen-pecked and embittered husband, his remarks also prefigure the personality of Mak's wife. As Gardner aptly notes, 'Mak's Gill is a living emblem of all Gyb complained about earlier.' Recalling Gyb's unflattering portrait of his spouse, Gill is described 'As sharp as a thystyll, as rugh as a brere.' In addition, the portly and hard-drinking woman is characterized as being 'as greatt as a whall' and frequently having 'wett hyr whystyll.' Echoing Gyb's description of his wife, therefore, Gill has both a literal and figurative 'galon of gall.' In light of Gill's tough demeanour and copious fertility, it comes as no surprise when Mak gives voice to Gyb's closing wish: 'I wald I had ryn to I had lost hir!'.

In addition to foreshadowing Gill's crude personality, Gyb's misogynistic view of women and unfavorable portrait of wedlock anticipates another central event in *Secunda Pastorum*: the couple's comic concealment of the sheep. When the pair hides the stolen animal in a cradle and attempts to pass it off as their newborn infant, Gill makes noises similar to those that Gyb associates with his wife: feigning the pains of childbirth, she not only 'kakyls' but begins 'to crok, / To goyne or to clok.'

Throughout the remainder of *Secunda Pastorum*, Gyb makes additional remarks that teem with future textual resonance. Soon after Mak joins the shepherds, for instance, Gyb identifies him as someone who has the look 'Of stelying... shepe.' In addition to setting the stage for the central secular event of the drama, Gyb's comment alludes to the manner in which the ruse is detected. Interestingly, Mak's criminal potential is not rooted in his generally distrustful nature or prior deviant behavior. Instead, the second shepherd makes his judgment on this character's appearance. Soon after seeing Mak, Gyb observes, 'An thou has an yll noys / Of stelyng of shepe.' Although the word 'noys' is commonly translated as 'noise', it can also be read as 'nose.' Both the *Oxford English Dictionary* and Fernand Mossé's *A Handbook of Middle English*, in fact, list 'noys' as an archaic spelling of 'nose' while the *Middle English Dictionary* includes 'noyse' in its entries for both 'noise' and 'nose.' Putting this knowledge into practice, Marital Rose's modernized translation of *Secunda Pastorum* uses the word 'nose' rather than 'noise' for this line in Gyb's speech.

Awareness that the term 'noys' can be read as 'nose' instead of or in addition to 'noise' adds another facet to his role as a foreshadower. Echoing Gyb's observation that Mak has an 'yll noys' for stealing sheep, the attempt by the comic trickster and his wife several scenes later to conceal the stolen sheep is foiled by the shape of the animal's nose. When Daw removes the blanket covering the couple's supposed newborn infant, he is shocked by its visage: 'What the dewill is this? He has a long snowte!' Upon hearing this exclamation, Coll and Gyb return to the college to investigate and, significantly, the second shepherd unveils the fraud. After seeing the woolly four-footed infant, he proclaims, 'Ill-spon weft, iwys, ay commys foull owte. / Ay so! He is lyke to our shepe!'

In spite of the important individual contributions Gyb makes in *Secunda Pastorum*, he has never been identified as a central or even important character in the pageant. On the contrary, this distinction has consistently gone to the trickster Mak. Wallace H. Johnson, for instance, argues that the drama has received so much critical attention because of 'the appeal of its leading character, the sheep-stealing Mak.' Similarly, Richard Axton asserts that the pageant's primary 'provision of "entertainment" is concentrated in the shape-shifting Mak'. Finally, a recent article by Rick Bowers argues that the trickster figure is the locus for the pageant's comedy and, as a result, the catalyst for its carnivalesque atmosphere.

The way in which the second shepherd hints at key plot developments and announces central themes throughout *Secunda Pastorum* calls this critical tendency into question. Gyb's numerous allusions call for a reconsideration of his importance in the drama. In many ways, these elements allow the second shepherd to equal or even eclipse Mak as the character of import in *Secunda Pastorum*. Accordingly, the misspelling of the *Second Shepherds' Play* as the *Second Shepherd's Play* forms something more than the bibliographic 'myshappe' or disjunction first believed. Rather, it provides a new and previously overlooked interpretive strategy through which to approach and examine this important pageant.

Source: Michelle Ann Abate, "From Shadower to Foreshadower: Taking a Second Look at the Second Shepherd," in *Early Theatre: A Journal Associated with the Records of Early Drama*, Vol. 8, No. 1, 2005, pp. 95–108.

J. W. Robinson

In the following excerpt, Robinson discusses the importance of numerology in The Second Shepherds' Play. *The elaborate use of numerology is representative of early fifteenth-century texts and reveals a complex composition that transforms the traditional nativity story.*

. . . In the *Second Shepherds' Play* a rule is that the three shepherds speak in turn throughout the play. In many mystery plays, groups of three and four characters—soldiers and shepherds, for example—speak in rotation for some of the time, but in the *Second Shepherds' Play* the system is complete. With four exceptions, the second shepherd always speaks after the first, and the third after the second; and when they are all present, all three always speak. As a consequence of this constant rotation of speeches, the first shepherd begins the play and the third ends it. Further, the same number of whole stanzas is alloted to each of them. Each of their opening complaints consists of six stanzas, although young Daw's six are interrupted by an exchange with his two self-righteous elders; their references to the prophets occupy one stanza each; and their praise for the baby Jesus also one stanza each. This symmetry is harmonious, and suggests truth and perfection as well as politeness and graceful behavior. Paradoxically, when the symmetry is broken, it is broken by young Daw only in his eagerness to get at the truth. He is an impatient and clumsy youth, given to flinging himself about and jumping into the middle of

> IN SUMMARY: THE *SECOND SHEPHERDS' PLAY*, WHICH MAY WELL HAVE BEEN INTENDED TO BE STAGED AND ACTED WITH GUSTO, IS GOVERNED BY PATTERNS AND NUMBERS, AND AT THE SAME TIME GIVES A LIVELY APPEARANCE OF SPONTANEITY."

things; he understands better than the two older shepherds what is happening, and interrupts the orderly rotation of the speeches to blurt out the truth, to inflict some cheerful sarcasm on old Nicholas, the first shepherd, and to provide him with some much-needed guidance. It is, appropriately, Daw who ends the play, both because of his insights and because he is third. Since it is his impetuosity which brings the shepherds to the truth, it is tempting to see his interruptions, natural to his character, as produced by organic rather than symmetrical form, but they may also be thought of as playful, and compared to the way in which in Gothic art a figure will extrude slightly from the frame to the enhancement of the whole design . . .

The *Second Shepherds' Play* is composed numerically, perhaps more thoroughly than the other plays by the Wakefield Master, who, it seems, habitually uses numbers within his plots to distinguish the human from the divine, in connection with his practice of elaborating the worldly or evil contrasts to divine truth found in many of the mystery plays, and turning them into foolish *lazzi* which carry a burden of horror with them, or into comic or horrifyingly wrong adumbrations of Salvation. He develops his comic routines along the lines of those already established in the mystery plays (his plays, for example, perform the familiar feat of trying to imitate the angel's song); a difference between his plays and most other mystery plays is that he so plots divine history that the human shadows of salvation swell and multiply and occupy larger proportions of the plays than is usual. The effect is thought-provoking, although his general meaning is hardly more hidden or obscure than the typology found in many of the plays, or than the point of the pagan imitations (which appear in the earliest vernacular plays) of Christian language—"By the grace of Mahound"—from which it had long been necessary for audiences to draw the proper inferences. In fact the playwright makes a point of plainly demonstrating what he is doing by repeating—in a way perhaps characteristic of medieval literature—his jokes. In his play of Noah, for example, Noah has two rounds of fisticuffs with his wife, instead of the usual one round. In the *First Shepherds' Play* the playwright produces not one but five stumbling versions of the sacramental bread and wine. In the *Second Shepherds' Play* he shows his audience what he is up to by providing them with a bold clue (first noticed in modern times by William Empson) in the form of Mak's melodramatic asseveration, spoken as he points to the cradle with the sheep wrapped up in a baby's blanket in it,

> As I am true and lele, to God here I pray
> That this be the fyrst mele that I shall ete this
> day!

...In the *First Shepherds' Play*, the shepherds are busy hopelessly chasing invisible sheep, wasting good flour, and drunkenly addressing the bottle until the angel appears to them and the play takes on a new direction. This play contains 502 lines, divided into 56 stanzas. The angel appears exactly between the end of the first three-fifths of the play and the beginning of the final two-fifths, speaking the whole stanza 34, and the tumult and confusion cease as the first three-fifths of the play come to a halt with the words,

> That chyld is borne
> At Bethelem this morne.

It is in stanza 33 of this play that Jesus Christ is mentioned as the third shepherd crosses himself, in symbolic reference, perhaps, to Christ's human life-span; Sir Gawain crosses himself finally in stanza 33 of *Sir Gawain and the Green Knight*, a thoroughly, "numerous" work...

Many readers have formed the impression that this play is somehow a comprehensive work, and perhaps the most obvious explanation of the significance in it of the number 6 (other than its circular nature and its pythagorean and Christian perfection) is that it has reference to the ages of the world as they are commonly explained in the Middle Ages, in the *Golden Legend*, for example, which varies from St. Augustine in stating that the six ages of the world are the ages of

Adam, Noah, Abraham, Moses, David, and Jesus. As the play opens, the audience sees an old man rising up out of the mud; old Nicholas rises falteringly to his feet, like Adam when God breathed into him (Genesis 2.7), an episode dramatised in all three northern English mystery play cycles. Nicholas is shortly joined by Gilbert, who brings with him the story of his cackling wife, his Eve. The first sixth of the play is in this way reminiscent of the first of the world, the age of Adam. Daw begins his complaint by referring to the impermanence of this world; when he comes to speak the first line of the second sixth of the play he makes a direct reference to Noah— "Was neuer syn Noe floode sich floodys seyn"— as if he is ushering in the second age of the world, the age of Noah. The fifth sixth can clearly be associated with the fifth age of the world, the age of David. It is in this part of the play that the youthful Daw, a diminutive of "David" ("a young one, who keepeth the sheep," 1 Kings 16.11), comes into his own, leading the way to the discovery of the lost sheep, teaching his angry elders to show mercy, and preparing them for the angel's announcement. The beginning of the final sixth of the play plainly inaugurates the sixth age, the age of Christ, the present age.

At the same time, apart from this and other intellectual schemes and symmetrical patterns that may be found in the plot, it is also true that the *Second Shepherds' Play* proceeds at a farce-like pace, with powerful contrasts, climaxes, surprises, theatrical tricks, broad humor, and clowning. The playwright's interest in entertaining and amusing his audience is strong but not exclusive. It is reconciled with an equally strong interest in significant proportions and numbers. In both ways he happily demonstrates the wonder of the Incarnation...

In summary: the *Second Shepherds' Play*, which may well have been intended to be staged and acted with gusto, is governed by patterns and numbers, and at the same time gives a lively appearance of spontaneity. The sequence of the speeches follows a set pattern, yet allows young David to bounce his way through the play. The plot is divided intellectually by numbers, yet is full of suspense and surprises. The stanzaic form is rigidly adhered to, yet the characters seem to be uttering their thoughts as they occur to them. The language is a chronically rhyming mosaic of high and low (mostly low) formulas and idiomatic phrases, and yet the impression given is one of colloquial vigor.

Art such as this, with an extremely rich surface texture, crowded narrative, technical virtuosity, and partially obscure meaning and design is characteristic of the first two-thirds of the fifteenth century in England, towards the end of which period the Wakefield Master most probably worked. His cleverness seems to be never-ending. He has worked up the traditional nativity play into a formal, and highly elaborate and ornamented, representation of this world before and after the Incarnation.

Source: J. W. Robinson, "Form in *The Second Shepherds' Play*," in *Proceedings of the PMR Conference: Annual Publication of the International Patristic, Mediaeval and Renaissance Conference*, Vol. 8, 1983, pp. 71–78.

SOURCES

Abrams, M. H., ed., *The Second Shepherds' Play*, in *The Norton Anthology of English Literature*, 6th edition, Vol. 1, W. W. Norton, 1993, pp. 319–44.

Beilin, Elaine V., *Redeeming Eve: Women Writers of the English Renaissance*, Princeton University Press, 1987, p. 270.

Best, Michael, *Shakespeare's Life and Times*, Internet Shakespeare Editions, University of Victoria, 2001–2005, http://ise.uvic.ca/Library/SLT/intro/introcite.html (accessed August 1, 2007).

Coogan, Michael D., ed, *The New Oxford Annotated Bible*, 3rd edition, Oxford University Press, 2001.

Corbeil, Carole, Review of *The Second Shepherds' Play*, in the *Globe and Mail*, December 11, 1981.

Gies, Frances, and Joseph Gies, *Women in the Middle Ages*, Barnes & Noble, 1978, pp. 146–47.

Harris, John W., *Medieval Theatre in Context: An Introduction*, Routledge, 1992, pp. 192–93.

Hencke, David, and Rob Evans, "Royal Farms Get 1M Pounds from Taxpayers," in the *Guardian*, March 23, 2005.

Mack, Maynard, Jr., "*The Second Shepherds' Play*: A Reconsideration," in *PMLA*, Vol. 93, No. 1, January 1978, pp. 78–85.

Normington, Katie, "Giving Voice to Women: Teaching Feminist Approaches to the Mystery Plays," in *College Literature*, Vol. 28, No. 2, Spring 2001, p. 130.

Ross, Lawrence J., "Symbol and Structure in the *Secunda Pastorum*," in *Medieval English Drama: Essays Critical and Contextual*, edited by Jerome Taylor and Alan H. Nelson, University of Chicago Press, 1972, p. 177.

FURTHER READING

Dyer, Christopher, *Making a Living in the Middle Ages: The People of Britain 850–1520*, Yale University Press, 2002.

This text provides an economic history of England during the Middle Ages. Dyer discusses the economic life of the peasant class, which helps readers of this play better understand the first shepherd's complaints about economic injustice.

Finucane, Ronald C., *Miracles and Pilgrims: Popular Beliefs in Medieval England*, Palgrave Macmillan, 1995.

In this text, the author studies popular belief in miracles, saints, and the importance in believing in some sort of religious intervention for those whose lives were in need of help. The author's study suggests that the lower classes were particularly influenced by this sort of belief.

Fleming, Peter, *Family and Household in Medieval England*, Palgrave Macmillan, 2001.

This book provides a history of family life in the middle ages that relies upon both primary and secondary documents. Fleming provides information about marriage, childbirth, divorce and widowhood. This text provides an interesting examination of the topic that Gib focuses on in his soliloquy.

Hanawalt, Barbara A., *The Ties That Bound: Peasant Families in Medieval England*, Oxford University Press, 1986.

This book provides one of the few texts that explores the lives of English peasants in the medieval period. The author uses court records and coroner reports to examine the economic and family lives of the peasant class.

Rowling, Marjorie, *Life in Medieval Times*, Perigee, 1973.

Rowling's text offers a social history of medieval life that includes information about religious, family, and economic life. The author includes information about both peasants and the nobility.

Schofield, Phillipp R., *Peasant and Community in Medieval England, 1200–1500*, Palgrave Macmillan, 2002.

This book offers an overview of the world of the English peasant. In addition to focusing on family life and the relationship between tenant and lord, the author includes a broader look at how the peasants fit into the legal, economic, and religious life of the medieval world.

Serious Money

CARYL CHURCHILL

1987

Caryl Churchill's play *Serious Money* was first staged in 1987 at London's Royal Court Theatre and was published by Methuen that very year. With hostile corporate takeovers making the news and a growing awareness of the greed of the so-called new market makers (financiers who attempted to make as much money as possible regardless of ethics and laws) both in England and the United States, the play opened at a time when audiences were ready to fully embrace it. Stories about buy-outs, insider trading, and people making huge profits, regardless of the damages they caused, were headline stories. Some of the culprits were jailed, others were still filling their bank accounts, but Churchill's play gave audiences a chance to find some humor in the situation.

Although not everyone is aware of the terminology of stockbrokers, bankers, traders, and other people involved in international finance dealings—which can make following the action a bit difficult at times—the play offers recognizable human traits in its characters. Money, as this play demonstrates, can bring out the best and, more often, the worst in people. Churchill provides a satirical glimpse into the world of finance. *Serious Money* is a comedy, a mystery, and social commentary. It is fast paced and has a unique format featuring overlapping dialogue.

Serious Money won the 1987–1988 Obie Award for best new play, the best comedy of

Caryl Churchill *(Gemma Levine / Hulton Archive / Getty Images)*

the year award from the London *Evening Standard* in 1987, the 1987 Susan Smith Blackburn Prize, and the 1987 Laurence Olivier/BBC Award for best new play. The play continues to fascinate audiences around the world.

AUTHOR BIOGRAPHY

Caryl Churchill was born in London on September 3, 1938. When she was ten, she moved with her family to Montreal, where she spent her childhood. Her writing, which often exposes weaknesses and problems in the social structure, may well have been influenced by her father, Robert, who was a political cartoonist. When it was time for college, Churchill was accepted at Lady Margaret Hall, a part of Oxford University in England, where she majored in English. Before graduating, Churchill had written her first play, *Downstairs*, which won Churchill the first of many awards.

As Churchill was developing her style, the BBC (British Broadcasting Company) took an interest in the aspiring playwright and produced some of her works as radio plays. These included

Ants (1962), *Lovesick* (1967), and *Abortive* (1971). Churchill also wrote plays for television around this same time, including *The Judge's Wife* (1972), *The After Dinner Joke* (1978), and *Crimes* (1982).

Churchill's first professionally staged play occurred in 1972. It was *Owners*, which focuses on the ills of capitalism, hinting at Churchill's leanings toward socialism (which favors communal ownership rather than the capitalist concept of individual ownership). One of her earlier plays that gained much attention was the satirical *Cloud Nine* (1979), which is about the effects of colonization. In 1981, Churchill won an Obie Award for this drama. Then in 1982, *Top Girls* won Churchill her second Obie. Churchill centers on a feminist theme in this play, a theme that often finds its way into many of her plays. The 1987 play *Serious Money* (which also won an Obie) marked Churchill's career, critics believe, as one of Britain's major dramatists of the twentieth century. More recently, Churchill has produced the play *Drunk Enough to Say I Love You?* (2006), which criticizes Britain's willingness to support U.S. war policies in Iraq.

Churchill is often praised for her philosophical insights and her willingness to be innovative in form. Her play *Serious Money* is a great example of how she pushes the traditional form of drama as her dialogue is fast and overlapping, with several characters interrupting one another, other characters switching roles, lines written in a rhyming, lyrical scheme, and songs at the end of each act, though the play is not a musical.

PLOT SUMMARY

Act 1

Serious Money is staged in two acts with no designated scene breaks, although the scenes do have informal names that are quoted throughout this summary.

"A SCENE FROM *THE VOLUNTEERS* OR *THE STOCKJOBBERS* BY THOMAS SHADWELL"

The play begins with a scene from a seventeenth-century play, *The Volunteers* by Thomas Shadwell, first produced in 1693. Mr. Hackwell, Mrs. Hackwell, and two jobbers (traders) are discussing investments. The scene represents the beginning of stock markets. Hackwell and his wife are asking the jobbers if there are any new patents available to invest in. As the four people discuss these possible investments, Mrs. Hackwell wonders if any of them will actually work. Mr. Hackwell says that it does not really matter. They just want to get people interested so they will invest. Once interest grows in the product, so too will the value of the Hackwell's stocks.

"THREE DIFFERENT DEALING ROOMS SIMULTANEOUSLY"

The play moves to contemporary times. There are three rooms shown. In the first is Greville, who is talking on the phone to a potential investor. He offers details of what the deal is worth and how much it will cost. He also predicts how much profit the deal will make in one year.

In another room is Grimes and Scilla, a female trader. Scilla is on two phones. As they talk on the phones, Grimes and Scilla also call out to other traders who keep track of stock prices. Grimes and Scilla also interject personal comments to one another. Grimes asks Scilla what she is doing after work, suggesting they meet at a bar.

In the third room are Jake, Scilla's brother, two salespeople and a dealer. They talk to one another interspersed with conversations on the phones. They talk fast, trying to make deals, as they sense there is about to be a power failure, which there is. All the screens go blank and the phones go dead. There is a loud outcry.

"LIFFE CHAMPAGNE BAR"

Scilla is here with her brother, Jake, and Grimes. They are discussing how much money they are making and how much more they could make. Jake says he has no intention of working after thirty. To accomplish this, he might have to "fight dirty." They mention Zackerman, someone of influence. Jake was supposed to take Zackerman (called Zac) to his father's home on the weekend, but Jake will be out of town. So he asks Scilla to take Zac there.

Zac enters. He is an American. Zac tells the audience that he teaches jobbers and brokers to be "new market makers." Then he tells a story about Merrison and Durkfeld, who are bankers. The bankers appear. Durkfeld suggests to Merrison that he should resign. Durkfeld wants to run the business by himself. Merrison is shocked. Durkfeld tells Merrison to go.

Zac says that it is not the bankers but the traders who have taken over the world of investments. These new traders are hungrier. He is talking about the business in New York. Then he talks about London. When the British Empire was at the height of its power, the British made easy profits on anything. That has changed, Zac says. "The empire's gone but the City of London keeps / On running like a cartoon cat off a cliff— bang. / That's your Big Bang."

"THE MEET OF A HUNT"

Zac is with Greville, Scilla, Mrs. Carruthers, Lady Vere, Major, Farmer, and Frosby. All are on horses.

Many of the lines here are repeated, making the dialogue come across like a song. Frosby, a retired jobber, recites a monologue, stating he is going to cause trouble that involves Scilla and Jake.

"ZAC PHONES TK AND MARYLOU BAINES IN NEW YORK"

Zac calls Marylou Baines, an arbitrageur (a person who makes profits from buying stocks in one market such as the United States and selling them in another market like Japan). TK is Marylou's personal assistant. When Marylou comes to the phone, Zac announces that Jake is dead, an apparent suicide. Then a chain reaction of phone calls occurs as the news of Jake's death runs through a network of people who are all connected by their involvement in the stock markets. The audience learns the D.T.I. (Britain's government regulatory agency, the Department of Trade and Industry) had been investigating Jake's trading practices. Everyone is concerned Jake might have mentioned their names.

There is a flashback with Zac and Scilla at the morgue, identifying Jake's body. Scilla says the day before his death, Jake told her he was concerned something might happen to him. Scilla insists that Jake was murdered. Jake gave her his diary. Scilla is going to investigate all the names in it to see who might have a motive for killing her brother.

"SCILLA AND GREVILLE AT GREVILLE'S HOUSE"

Scilla confronts her father. She asks if he knew why Jake was being investigated and if he had anything to do with Jake's death.

"CORMAN, A CORPORATE RAIDER, BROWN AND SMITH, INDUSTRIAL SPIES, ZAC AND MRS. ETHERINGTON, A STOCKBROKER"

Zac is working with Corman, who is planning a hostile takeover of Albion. A hostile takeover occurs when a company's stock is lower in value than the company's assets. Someone like Corman buys up a majority of the stocks, takes over the company, and makes his profit by selling the assets. Corman asks Zac what the chances are for the takeover. Corman tells Etherington, a stockbroker, to buy up as much stock as she can without drawing attention.

"MARYLOU BAINES AND TK IN NEW YORK"

In a flashback, TK tells Marylou that Jake has left a message about buying stocks in Albion. It is an insider tip, and TK and Marylou jump on it. Marylou teases TK that he will soon be in business on his own because he is doing so well.

"DUCKETT, CHAIRMAN OF ALBION, AND MS. BIDDULPH, A WHITE KNIGHT."

Ms. Biddulph is a white knight, a term for a person (or company) who comes to the rescue of the target of a hostile takeover. Biddulph suggests that she will make a deal with Corman so that Duckett's job, no matter what happens, will be safe.

"CORMAN, ZAC, ETHERINGTON AND OTHERS OF CORMAN'S TEAM"

Corman knows that Biddulph is acting as white knight. Corman is not concerned. Corman tells his people they must get Albion shares bought up, and Corman does not care how they do it. Zac learns that Marylou is working with Biddulph. Corman calls Marylou to confirm this. As he tries to make a deal with her, Scilla walks into the office and accuses Corman of killing her brother. Zac tells her that Jake was offering Marylou insider information for which she paid him a lot of money.

"LIFFE CANTEEN"

Scilla decides to drop the investigation of her brother's death and goes back to work. She talks with two women who are just starting out. They discuss how hard it is to be a woman in their profession. There is a long series of rather derogatory comments from male co-workers until the trading heats up and they become completely involved in their work. Then they sing a song about what they are doing, and the first act closes.

Act 2

"JACINTA CONDOR FLYING FIRST CLASS"

Jacinta is a Peruvian businesswomen. She has a long monologue, which conveys her financial status and her unwillingness to invest her money in her country because Peru is unstable. She prefers to keep her money in European and American banks.

"MEANWHILE THE LONDON METAL EXCHANGE STARTS QUIETLY TRADING COPPER"

Zac talks with Jake in flashback. Jake tells Zac that the D.T.I. has interviewed him. Zac wants to know if Jake mentioned him. Jake says he could not lie about knowing Zac. Then Jake asks Zac what he should do. Zac asks if Jake wants to live in greed or live in fear. Jake chooses greed.

Jacinta joins them. She tells them she has sold her mines. She has invested in coca (cocaine plants) instead. She introduces them to Nigel Ajibala, a cocoa (chocolate plant) importer from Africa. Nigel says he now lives in London, "so one's operation / Is on the right side of exploitation." He insinuates that big European and American companies rip off smaller countries by keeping them in extreme debt. As Nigel puts it: "One thing one learned from one's colonial masters, / One makes money from other people's disasters."

When Nigel and Jacinta are alone, Jacinta praises Nigel for accomplishing an undisclosed plan.

"ZAC JOINS CORMAN AND ETHERINGTON IN CORMAN'S OFFICE"

Nigel, Jacinta, and Jake join the others in Corman's office. Nigel does not have enough money to buy stock in Albion, so Corman lends Nigel two million pounds. Corman promises to set up a franchise for Jacinta to give her more profits. Later, Nigel tells Jacinta and Jake that he does not intend to invest in Albion. He wants Jake to invest in something that will give him a better profit. Jake agrees.

"DUCKETT AND BIDDULPH"

Biddulph is working on a media promotion to make Duckett look good. Biddulph tells Duckett not to worry. Jacinta walks in and asks Biddulph to give her a loan. In return, Jacinta will support Duckett.

"MERRISON AND MARYLOU BAINES AT MARYLOU'S OFFICE IN NEW YORK"

Merrison, who was forced to retire, is angry. He talks to Marylou about getting revenge on Durkfeld. Durkfeld has invested in Corman's business, so Marylou suggests that Merrison do a hostile takeover of Corman's company.

"SCILLA AND GRIMES PLAYING PASS THE PIGS"

While unwinding after work, Grimes and Scilla decide to go to Greville to try to make him talk about Jake.

"GREVILLE AND FROSBY AT GREVILLE'S HOUSE"

Greville is still mourning, drinking with Frosby, when Scilla and Grimes come in. Greville swears he does not know anything about Jake's death or his money. After Scilla and Grimes leave, Frosby confesses that he was the one who turned the D.T.I. on Jake.

"ZAC AND SCILLA OUTSIDE CORMAN'S OFFICE"

Zac is distracted. He knows Jacinta is supporting Biddulph and Nigel may run with the money Corman gave him. Meanwhile, Scilla pretends to be a model and sneaks into Corman's office.

"CORMAN AND DOLCIE STARR"

Dolcie Starr is waiting to take pictures of Corman with a woman. News has leaked out that Corman is trying to take over Albion. Public opinion is against it. Starr thinks she can counter with a fake sex scandal. She takes pictures of Scilla (who is supposed to be a rented model) and Corman while Scilla forces information out of Corman about Jake's past. In payment for the details on Jake, Scilla tells Corman that Jacinta and Nigel have betrayed him.

Zac comes in with Nigel. While Corman is quizzing Nigel about the two million pounds, an agent from the D.T.I., Grevett, walks in. Everyone denies anything illegal is going on, and Corman gives Grevett his business records. Scilla tells Zac to call Marylou to say she is coming to see her. Scilla thinks Marylou might know what happened to Jake and where all Jake's money is. At this point in the play it is becoming apparent that Scilla is more intent on finding Jake's money than his murderer.

"MERRISON AND SOAT, PRESIDENT OF MISSOURI GUMBALLS, AT A DRUGSTORE IN MISSOURI"

Merrison pressures Soat, president of a small gumball company, to do a hostile takeover of Corman's company. Merrison provides the money. Soat agrees.

"CORMAN, GLEASON, A CABINET MINISTER, IN THE INTERVAL AT THE NATIONAL THEATRE"

Gleason, a member of parliament, tells Corman to drop his bid for Albion. He threatens that if Corman does not do as he says, Corman could end up like Jake. Gleason tells Corman that after the upcoming elections, he can go back to what he is doing.

"ZAC AND JACINTA, EXHAUSTED, IN THE FOYER OF THE SAVOY"

Zac and Jacinta declare their attraction for one another before they go to bed together.

"SCILLA AT MARYLOU BAINES' OFFICE IN NEW YORK"

Scilla threatens to expose Marylou. Marylou likes Scilla's drive and offers her TK's job as Marylou's personal assistant.

Zac announces that Scilla never finds out who killed her brother. He figures it must have been a government job. Another scandal would have hurt British elections.

The play closes with a song about how the stock industry has five more years to enjoy, because that is how long it is to the next election.

CHARACTERS

Nigel Ajibala

Nigel is from Africa and deals in cocoa beans. He is posing as a person with a lot of money, though he is living on a very basic budget. Nigel represents a man who is willing to go against his own country's needs and benefits to make a profit. Nigel declares he learned how to be greedy from the colonial powers that once ruled his country.

Marylou Baines

Marylou is an American who runs a very powerful network of wealthy people. Marylou pays Jake for his insider tips and is one of the main players in the money game. She is cold-hearted and immoral. She represents the American version of greed, which is the model for Jake and Scilla.

Ms. Biddulph

Ms. Biddulph is called a white knight because she comes to Duckett's aid. She creates a promotional campaign for Duckett by having media

stories broadcast all the good deeds that Duckett is doing for the community. The stories are mostly false, but the promotion gets the public to stand behind Duckett and stop the hostile takeover.

Jacinta Condor

Jacinta is a very wealthy woman from Peru. She once owned mines in her country but now makes money from the coca trade. She represents a person who takes wealth out of her country and places it in another, more stable country's economy. She is not only greedy, Jacinta is deceitful and promises anything in order to make a good deal for herself. She blackmails people to get them to do as she wants.

Billy Corman

Corman is extremely wealthy, powerful, and greedy. He is always on the lookout for companies to buy out and will do whatever it takes to get them. Corman initiates the takeover bid on Albion, which he has to relinquish after community pressure causes members of the parliament to call the deal off. Corman represents British corporate greed. It is through him that the play looks at how politics and business work hand in hand.

Duckett

Duckett is the head of Albion, the company that Corman wants to take over. Duckett represents the traditional form of business in England, which makes him an easy mark for Corman. When Biddulph comes to rescue Duckett by creating a fantastic media image of him, Duckett does not claim the stories are untrue. He merely goes along with Biddulph. In the end, Duckett's job and company are saved, but not by anything he has done.

Durkfeld

Not much is known about Durkfeld, except that he asks Merrison to retire early. Durkfeld is co-chief of the bank where he and Merrison once worked.

Mrs. Etherington

Mrs. Etherington is a stockbroker and is involved with Corman's takeover bid. Etherington claims she has ethics, so when Corman says something about illegal actions, she pretends not to hear. However, she does whatever Corman tells her to do.

Frosby

Frosby was a stock trader but was asked to retire. Now he holds a grudge against Greville and his children. Frosby thinks Grevill and his children are the reason he was forced out. They represent a new trend that Frosby despises. So he turns Jake over to the D.T.I. for insider trading. Later Frosby regrets this action.

Gleason

Gleason is a member of parliament and represents politicians. He insists Corman call off the takeover bid. Gleason is worried the deal might cause a scandal, which could hurt his party's bid in the upcoming elections. Gleason threatens to do to Corman what was done to Jake. Gleason tells Corman that, as soon as the elections are over, Corman can go on doing as he pleases.

Grevett

Grevett represents the D.T.I., the regulatory government service that watches over financial transactions in the United Kingdom. Although Grevett is curious about what he has overheard in Corman's office, he does not investigate very deeply. Corman keeps Grevett busy reading huge reports. Grevett does not appear to be someone motivated enough to clean up the illegal practices.

Grimes

Grimes is a dealer and works with Scilla. His role is minor. He offends Greville and Frosby when he goes home with Scilla to ask Greville about Jake's death. Grimes has a foul mouth. Grimes represents the non-gentlemanly role of the modern British stock dealer.

Merrison

Merrison was the co-chief executive of a large bank. He was asked to retire early and holds a grudge against Durkfeld, the man who asked Merrison to leave. Merrison decides to do a hostile takeover on Corman's business as revenge.

Soat

Soat is the owner of a small gumball manufacturing company in the States. Merrison threatens to take over Soat's company if he does not comply with Merrison's plan to take over Corman's business. Soat does as he is told.

Dolcie Starr

Dolcie Starr attempts to create a promotional scheme to help save Corman. She decides the best plan is to make Corman look like the devil

that he is. The plan falls apart, however, when Scilla shows up as the model with whom Corman is supposedly having sex. Corman explains that Scilla is Jake's sister, which could implicate Corman in the D.T.I.'s investigations. So the plan does not work.

T.K.

T.K. is Marylou's personal assistant. He has studied under Marylou. When Scilla flies to New York to confront Marylou, Marylou replaces T.K. with Scilla. T.K. (as well as Scilla and Jake) represent the next generation of illegal traders.

Greville Todd

Greville is Jake and Scilla's father. He represents the old time stock trader who was in power before the Big Bang. Greville has made the transition better than some of the other older men in the business, but he cannot adjust to all the changes. He especially does not like women in the field. Scilla accuses her father of favoring Jake. She also accuses Greville of being responsible for Jake's death, which is never proved. Greville denies both.

Jake Todd

Jake is a very ambitious stock trader. He becomes involved with Marylou and makes a lot of money. He passes insider information to Marylou, an illegal activity, for which he gets caught. Jake tells his sister, the night before his death, that he is worried about something. He does not give her details. Jake represents the young, up and coming dealer, who wants money more than anything. Money is equated to power; and Jake is hungry enough to do whatever it takes to bring in the big money.

Scilla Todd

Scilla is Jake's sister and the daughter of Greville. She represents one of the first women to work in the stock market. She feels she is discriminated against because the men do not let her in on some of their deals or tell her how to play the market. When she discovers that her brother is dead, she first tries to figure out who killed him. The more she investigates his death, the more she realizes that Jake was a lot more powerful and had a lot more money than she realized. Soon her search for his murderer turns into a search for where he has stashed his money. Her search leads her to Marylou. Marylou sees how determined

Scilla is and decides that Scilla will make an excellent personal assistant, so she hires her at the end of the play, thus turning Scilla into another Jake.

Zac Zackerman

Zac is in banking. He is one of the few Americans who also works in the United Kingdom in association with the big stock brokers and traders. Zac is especially good when it comes to putting into place a hostile takeover, so Corman asks Zac to help him take over Albion. Zac also acts as a narrator of this play, filling in background information. Zac tries to stop Scilla from investigating Jake's death, but it is not clear if he is doing this for her sake, or for his.

THEMES

Greed

The strongest theme of this play is greed. The main point of the play is to demonstrate how greedy people in the investment business became during the 1980s after the deregulations that went into effect in London. It is not just that people wanted money, but that they were willing to do anything to get it. As the use of the word greed implies, the people never seem satisfied with what they have and they always want more.

There were different kinds of greed that had various effects on other people. Corman's plan to take over Albion exemplifies greed that is sated at any cost, whether it is legal or not. Corman demands that everyone give up their families for as long as it takes to get the job done. Corman has no concern for the employees of the company he is taking over. He thinks of Albion only in terms of how much profit he can make.

Both Nigel and Jacinta's greed affects their countries. They both take what riches they can find and invest their profits in other countries' economies. Jacinta, in particular, has no problems making money off of illegal drugs; she is not concerned about what effects the drugs have on the people who buy them.

Jake and Scilla's greed is based on wanting to buy things for themselves. Jake wants to retire from work by the time he is thirty, so he bends as many rules as he can to make this possible. Scilla is not as shrewd as Jake at first. However, while investigating his death and reading his diary, she learns that Jake was making a lot more money than she is. One of the driving forces in her investigation of his death was to find out where

TOPICS FOR FURTHER STUDY

- One of the first things that is usually noted about *Serious Money* is the rapid-fire delivery of the dialogue. Choose one of the scenes, paying special attention to the stage directions, that mark where one character's lines are interrupted by another, such as one of the scenes where the characters are on the floor of the stock market. Practice with three or four classmates so you can deliver these lines as fast as possible. Then present the scene to your class.

- Research the practice of hostile takeovers that occurred in the 1970s and 1980s. How did this practice come to an end? Could they happen again? Are there any government regulations set in place in the United States to stop this practice? Write a paper presenting your findings.

- Jake's death is never explained. Why do you think this is? Lead a discussion with your class about this. Include discussion of who the murderer might have been. Make sure that each suggestion cites examples from the test. Was Jake murdered or does the class think it was a suicide? What details help them come to this conclusion? What character has the best motive for killing Jake?

- Many of Churchill's plays are influenced by her feminist views. Although this play is more focused on greed, Churchill still includes a few references to sexism. Research feminism and reread the play. Write an essay on feminism and its appearance in Churchill's work.

he stashed all his money. By the end of the play, Scilla has changed. She is learning to play dirty, as Jake had once confessed that he had been.

Power

Power is another main theme in this play. It is represented in several ways. There is the power of the British parliament, with one member who stops the hostile takeover of Albion by threatening to kill Corman. Then, when the elections are over, the same member tells Corman he can continue with his illegal practices and parliament will look the other way. This is a corruption of power.

There is also the power of the D.T.I. that investigates Jake. The D.T.I. is set up to regulate the investment activities, but in the play, it is insinuated that the D.T.I. might have been responsible for Jake's death. It is unclear just how powerful the D.T.I. is, although the D.T.I. does cause the characters in the play a lot of concern.

The power of corporate executives is very evident in this play. Corman has the power to affect hundreds, if not thousands, of lives. He buys and sells companies without any thought given to the people who are involved. He tells everyone around him what to do and how to do it, even though it is illegal and very disruptive to their personal lives. Merrison, who holds a grudge against his former colleague (who becomes involved with Corman), searches for a small business owner whose company he can threaten to demolish if the small business owner does not do as Merrison tells him, which is to take over Corman's business. Merrison uses his power to seek revenge.

Jake has power because he knows a lot of people in the investment world and hears a lot of insider information. He uses this information as the tool to wield his power. Biddulph has power because she knows how to manipulate the media. She creates a do-gooder image for Duckett so the community will stop the hostile takeover of Duckett's company. There is also the power that comes with having a lot of money, which many of the characters in this play have. Power, as exemplified in this play, is not used to do good. It is used to help people become even more powerful.

Deceit

In this play, everyone appears to have his or her own agenda. To this end, the characters are willing to say anything to anyone to accomplish their goal, even if that person has no intention of following through on what he or she has promised. There are a lot of ambiguities in the play, so it is never clear who is telling the truth and who is not. For example, the audience never finds out what Nigel is up to. He takes a couple million pounds from Corman, who thinks Nigel is going

Margaret Thatcher (AP Images)

to use the money to buy stocks in Albion. Nigel confesses that he has no intention of doing this, although he is not clear about what his plans are. Nigel and Jacinta are scheming something, as Jacinta praises Nigel for pulling off a deception, but the audience is not in on the deal that Jacinta and Nigel have pre-arranged. Jacinta tells Corman that she will buy stocks, too, in order to help him out. However, as soon as she leaves his office, she goes straight to Albion and promises to help save that company. The play suggests that power and money come to these people because they are deceitful. The person who makes the biggest profit is not necessarily the most intelligent, but rather is the one who can lie and get away with it.

STYLE

Historical Opening Scene

The first scene in Churchill's play *Serious Money* comes from a Restoration era production, Thomas Chadwell's *The Volunteers*, first staged in 1692. By using this scene to open her play, Churchill informs her audience that her play is about the stock market, that it is a satirical comedy (which Restoration plays were known for being), and that the practices Churchill is about to expose have been going on for a long time. Chadwell's play is about the beginnings of the idea of investing in another person's business. As Chadwell presents it, the beginnings were not much more ethical than the dealings in the late twentieth-century markets, as Churchill presents them. So Chadwell's play is used as a reference and as a comparison. It deepens the meaning of Churchill's play because it shows a long-standing precedent. Churchill might present Chadwell's scene to make her audiences think. Maybe it is not just the insider trading that is wrong, but also the whole idea of stock markets that is a bit shaky.

Brechtian Tactics

Bertolt Brecht (1898–1956) revolutionized the form of drama. Brecht, a German playwright, believed drama should be created not to entertain but rather to educate his audiences. Churchill's dramas are almost always referred to by critics as having been influenced by Brecht. Some of these influences can be seen not just in Churchill's delivery of a message (such as the destructive effects of greed in this play) but also in the form of her play. Brecht did not want his audiences to come to the play for enjoyment. He did not want his plays to draw his audience in through their emotions. His plays were not intended as escapes from reality, so he did everything possible to continually remind his audiences that the play was not to be confused with reality. Churchill accomplishes this in several ways. First, by opening with the scene from someone else's play, she calls attention to the fact that her production is also a play. Although it is not apparent in reading the play, some productions of *Serious Money* include actors exchanging roles right in the middle of a scene. Also, in the hunt scene, actors play their roles as well as being their own horses. In addition, the songs at the ends of each act are similar to Brecht's use of a chorus, which sums up some of the action that has taken place in the play.

Dialogue in Rhyming Couplets

In formal writing, a couplet is a two-line stanza, with the last words in each line forming rhymes. Much of Churchill's play is written in two-line couplets. Often a character might read the first of the lines and another character will read the second line of the rhyming pair. There are a few

occasions when one character, like Merrison when he tells his story of the good old days in banking and trading, delivers a monologue that takes the form of a long unbroken stanza of multiple sets of couplets. Critics have noted that some of the rhyming schemes appear forced or silly, which might add to the comic nature of the play. Churchill's play may include rhymes, as many passages in Restoration comedies did. She might also have used rhymes to make the actor's lines appear otherworldly, thus keeping the audience from forgetting that what she is presenting on stage is not reality, according to Brecht's dramatic theories.

Flashback

The use of flashback, which is a scene that interrupts the chronological flow of a literary work, thus taking the reader or the audience back in time, is most often used to provide missing information or to fill out a scene. In traditional form, the flashback is prefaced, so the reader or audience knows the scene occurred at an earlier time. In Churchill's *Serious Money*, flashbacks happen spontaneously. For example, after Jake has died, he pops up in future scenes as if he were still alive. This forces the audience to bridge the gaps, keeping them consciously involved in the play. Churchill might have interjected these flashbacks without warning as another tactic to remind the audience that what they are seeing on stage is not to be confused with reality.

HISTORICAL CONTEXT

The Big Bang

On October 27, 1986, major operational changes occurred for the London Stock Exchange. A number of rules that had previously restricted competition were dramatically changed or abolished. Those changes included a new job position, called market maker, which combined the functions of a stockbroker and a stockjobber (trader). Stockbrokers, who used to do all transactions face to face, were allowed to make deals via the phone and a computer quotation system, which sped up the transactions. The deregulation meant that ownership of member firms by an outside corporation was now allowed. There were also no minimums on the commission that could be received on a sale.

COMPARE
&
CONTRAST

- **1980s:** After one of the greatest prolonged stock market booms, everything changes in October 1987. Referred to as Black Monday, October 19, 1987 saw one of the largest drops in stock prices in one day, a drop of 22.68 percent.

  Today: The Dow Jones Industrial Average, an indicator of how the U.S. stock market is doing, reaches 14,000 points in 2007 for the first time, an 88 percent rise just since 2002.

- **1980s:** Prime Minister Margaret Thatcher orders the merger of the Department of Trade with the Department of Industry to create the Department of Trade and Industry (D.T.I.), which regulates business practices in the United Kingdom as well as trade functions and radio frequencies.

  Today: The D.T.I., as of 2007, is now the Department for Business, Enterprise, and Regulatory Reform.

- **1980s:** With Margaret Thatcher in power as Britain's Prime Minister, Churchill writes *Serious Money*, a play that satirizes the consequences and changes that occur in London's stock market due to Thatcher's deregulations.

  Today: With Tony Blair having just completed nearly ten years in office as British Prime Minister, Churchill writes *Drunk Enough to Say I Love You?*, a play that satirizes Blair's collusions with U.S. President George W. Bush in the war on terror and the war in Iraq.

Margaret Thatcher, British Prime Minister from 1979 to 1990, wanted to improve and update Britain's role as a financial center, so she put these deregulations in place. As a result, London, which had previously focused on domestic trade, is now considered a global financial center.

London International Financial Futures Exchange (LIFFE)

In the play, Scilla works at the London International Financial Futures Exchange (LIFFE), one of London's stock exchanges through which futures are traded. A stock exchange is an organized marketplace where people gather to buy, sell, or trade stocks or other types of investment instruments. LIFFE specializes in a type of investment called Futures. Futures are contracts to buy or to sell specific quantities of a commodity (like wheat, corn, or sugar) or a financial instrument (such as the value of U.S. currency) at a predetermined price and by a specified date in the future.

Insider Trading

Insider training, though often referred to in relationship to crime, is both legal and illegal. The legal type of insider trading involves employees and officials of a company buying or selling stock in their own company. As long as they report these trades (if done in the United States) to the Securities and Exchange Commission (SEC), their actions are considered legal.

Examples of the illegal types of insider trading happen when the corporate employees and officials trade securities after they have learned of confidential information that the general public does not have access to. The same could apply to friends, business associates, and family members of the employees and officials if they buy or sell the securities after being tipped off by having been given this same confidential information that is still not general, public knowledge.

Ivan Boesky, who is mentioned in Churchill's play, was caught for illegal insider trading. His name is used as a warning about what happens if you are working on an illegal investment deal

Signage of the new London Stock Exchange is seen in London in 2004 after the exchange moved from the Old Broad Street site to its new location (Bruno Vincent | Getty Images)

and get caught. Ivan Boesky, an American citizen, was worth at least 200 million dollars in 1986 before the SEC caught him making illegal insider trades. Boesky worked his way up to become one of the more influential traders on Wall Street. His world collapsed on November 14, 1986, when he pleaded for a deal with the SEC. The commission fined him 100 million dollars and made him ineligible to work in securities for the rest of his life. In exchange, Boesky (who is now unflatteringly referred to as The Mouth) gave the SEC names of people involved in his illegal deals.

Guinness Four

The name Guinness is also used in Churchill's play as a warning. This time it is a reference to a British misdeed in the stock market world. This fraud involved arbitrarily inflating stock prices for the distillery Guinness to enable Guinness to go forward with a takeover bid of Distillers, a Scottish brewing company. The white-collar crime was one of the United Kingdom's biggest. Four of the country's most successful businessmen were charged with the crime. They were Ernest Saunders, Guinness chief executive, Gerald Ronson, an oil businessman, Jack Lyons, a financier, and Anthony Parnes, a stockbroker. Known as the Guinness Four, the men were

convicted, assigned jail terms, and heavily fined. The fraud was uncovered when Ivan Boesky gave names and details of the fraud in his plea bargaining with the SEC.

Thomas Shadwell (1642–1692)

Shadwell was a seventeenth-century British playwright and a poet who was writing in a period known as the English Restoration. The Restoration began in 1660 with the return of Charles II to the throne of England after the dissolution of the Commonwealth of Oliver Cromwell. The theaters in England had been officially closed while the Puritans were in power, thus the Restoration refers to the re-opening of the English theaters in addition to the restoration of the monarchy. Shadwell was known for his witty dialogue and realistic portrayals of London society in his comedies of manners, a type of play that makes fun of society and was very popular in the seventeenth and eighteenth century in England. Restoration comedy was a theatrical form that heavily influenced Churchill. Shadwell's play, which begins Churchill's play, is called *The Volunteers, or Stockjobbers* and was published in 1693. It was Shadwell's last play and was staged after his death. Other plays include *The Humorist* (1671), *Psyche* (1675), and *The Virtuoso* (1676). In 1688, Shadwell was named the poet laureate for Britain.

CRITICAL OVERVIEW

With scandals in the financial world in both the United States and in the United Kingdom, Churchill's *Serious Money* enjoyed a great deal of critical attention in both countries. The 1980s were renowned for corporate hostile takeovers, and Churchill's play capitalized on this topic. Indeed, the play was awarded an Obie for best new play of the year.

Lynn Homa, writing in *American Banker*, calls the play "a sort of combination horse race/spy flick/Marx Brothers routine of financial wheeling and dealing." Homa finds the play to be fast paced, very funny, and "politically cutting theater." Frank Rich, writing in the *New York Times*, continually praises Churchill in his review, despite a few flaws that he carefully points out. Overall, though, Rich finds the play to be intelligently written. Churchill proves, Rich writes, that though it is different from news reports and novels based on contemporary themes, the stage is as good a media for "dramatizing the big, immediate stories of our day." Rich states: "If *Serious Money* is an angry, leftist political work about ruthlessness and venality, about plundering and piggishness, it is also vivid entertainment."

Also writing in the *New York Times*, Leonard Silk describes Churchill's play as a "carnival of sinful freaks, caught in flagrante delecto, lying, cheating, screaming and, in the best bit, prancing like horses." Moira Hodgson, writing in the *Nation*, writes that *Serious Money* "is one of the most interesting of the season." Hodgson also describes the play as "a brutal satire." She goes on to write that "the language is harsh and savage, sometimes brilliant, sometimes puerile—and often startling."

Writing in the *Los Angeles Times*, Robert Koehler states that Churchill's play offers "entertaining complexity." Ted Hoover, writing in the *Pittsburgh City Paper*, calls Churchill "one of the greatest playwrights at work today; Horrifically intelligent, scathingly funny, woozily theatrical." Hoover continues, stating that Churchill, through her play, is "hurling so many non-stop staggering ideas at you, so many swirling theatrical styles and so much lush, giddy dialogue you don't really want to be anywhere else at that moment."

In an article that focuses on the playwright rather than the play, Sarah Lyall, writing in the *New York Times*, comments that Churchill, as a playwright, is all but held in awe, especially in London. Lyall writes that Churchill "is one of the most critically acclaimed playwrights in the English-speaking world." Churchill is so esteemed because of "her passion, curiosity, rigor, openness to collaboration." She is also uncommonly less predictable. To demonstrate her uniqueness, Lyall states that Churchill's plays feature "highly stylized conceits," such as "flashbacks, twisted chronologies, huge leaps of logic, elements of absurdity, overlapping dialogue, different actors playing the same character in different scenes, interjected songs and, in the case of *Serious Money*, dialogue written almost entirely in verse." Lyall adds that all playwrights are known for specific traits. Churchill's is that she is "a constant surprise."

CRITICISM

Joyce M. Hart

Hart has degrees in English and creative writing and is a freelance writer and published author. In this essay, she examines the primary characters in Serious Money.

The secondary characters in *Serious Money* help color the dramatic story, adding complications, turns and twists, as well as filling in gaps in the storyline, while the primary characters move the plot along. The secondary characters might only appear in one scene, such as Soat, the president of Missouri Gumballs, the man who is coerced into undermining Corman's business. Soat's action provides a fitting ending to the play. The results of Soat's actions are significant, but Soat's character is insignificant. He appears briefly toward the end of the play and recites very few lines. Like Soat, there are numerous other secondary characters of varying significance. Frosby is in two scenes and confesses to his role in turning Jake over to the D.T.I. Merrison is a disgruntled banker who pressures Soat into action. T.K., Marylou's personal assistant, does not do much more than answer the phone.

Amidst this large cast, it can be argued that there are three major characters in this play. Although Corman, Marylou, and Jacinta have a lot of money and power, they are not major characters. When they are not present, not much is said about them by the other characters. Although they represent the big wheelers and dealers in this fictional financial world, the play

WHAT DO I READ NEXT?

- There are two companion collections of Churchill's plays: *Churchill Plays 1* (1985) and *Churchill Plays 2* (1990). These provide a good overview of the playwright's work.

- Churchill's 2007 play, *Drunk Enough to Say I Love You?*, portrays an affair between two men to comment on the submissive role that Britain has played in supporting U.S. foreign policy in the twenty-first century. The two characters, Sam (as in Uncle Sam for the United States) and Jack (as in Union Jack, a nickname for England) discuss military diplomacy, regime changes in the world, and rigged elections, among other things.

- Tom Wolfe's *Bonfire of the Vanities* (1987) captures 1980s New York in all its glories and debasement. It depicts the greed of those working on Wall Street. Sherman McCoy, the protagonist, is a Wall Street investment banker who makes a wrong turn one night on his way home. The consequences of this act erupt into a story that shines a literary light on corruption in the legal system as well as on prejudice and greed.

- *The Predators's Ball: The Inside Story of Drexel Burnham and the Rise of the Junk Bond Raiders* (1989), by Connie Bruck, provides a factual overview of what went right and what went wrong during the boom and bust of Wall Street and its players at the height of 1980s greed. Reportedly, the people involved in this story tried to stop its publication.

- Sarah Ruhl is an award-winning American playwright with an intelligent sense of humor. In *The Clean House and Other Plays* (2006), Ruhl demonstrates a unique voice that takes common themes such as love and death and breathes new understanding into them.

does not stop and go on their presence. Rather, one would do best to examine Scilla, Zac, and Jake as the most significant roles in *Serious Money*.

> INDEED, SCILLA'S CHARACTER PATH IS NOT ONE THAT CAN BE LAUDED, UNLESS THE AUDIENCE CHEERS FOR A CHARACTER WHO VALUES POWER ABOVE ALL ELSE. NEVERTHELESS, HER ROLE DOES PRESENT THE ONLY CHARACTER ARC IN THE ENTIRE PLAY. FOR THIS REASON, SHE MUST BE CONSIDERED AS ONE OF THE MAJOR CHARACTERS."

Scilla is a primary character for several reasons. First, Scilla's determination to find her brother's killer drives a lot of the action. She also provides the suspense in this play. If this is a murder mystery, than Scilla is the detective. She moves the scenes along as she travels from meetings with Zac to talk about her brother's death, to confrontations with her father about Jake. Then she sneaks into Corman's meetings, showing up under disguise, pushing her way into scenes that otherwise have nothing to do with her. She has Jake's diary, which includes the names of many of the other characters. This gives Scilla the excuse to talk to or to investigate almost everyone in the play. Scilla is also the only character who is transformed over the course of the play. She starts out rather innocent, struggling with being a woman in a traditionally male profession. Her father hates that she is working as a trader; and it is through Scilla that the play demonstrates how male traders can belittle women, reducing them to mere body parts. When her brother dies, Scilla becomes a more vital character. She is driven to find out who is responsible for Jake's death and will not be deterred, even though Zac attempts to stop her. Scilla even accuses her father of being responsible. She is not afraid of anyone, even while she realizes that she too might be murdered.

Yet, the more Scilla investigates Jake's life to discover who might have had a strong enough motive to kill him, the more she learns how much money Jake has made. She is at first disappointed by the fact that Jake never confided in her. Then she is angered that he did not tell her the secrets to his success. Finally, she becomes obsessed by the power Jake once held, and she wants to achieve the same for herself. Scilla not only wants to find out how Jake accumulated his wealth but also where he hid it. By the end of the play, she no longer cares who murdered her brother. Indeed, Scilla's character path is not one that can be lauded, unless the audience cheers for a character who values power above all else. Nevertheless, her role does present the only character arc in the entire play. For this reason, she must be considered as one of the major characters.

Another major character is Zac. Throughout much of the play, Zac acts as a narrator. Through Zac, background information is presented as are details that connect one scene to the next. For example, Zac introduces the story about Durkfeld telling Merrison to retire early. Although this tidbit is not completely understood when it is first presented, it proves to be essential to the plot when Merrison retaliates against Durkfeld near the end of the play.

Like Scilla, Zac appears in nearly all of the scenes. He has a more subtle power than Corman or Marylou, but they are dependent on him. Zac is a major figure in the network of bankers, traders, stockbrokers, and corporate executives. He is level headed, sure of himself, and he attempts to keep everyone calm. He tries to calm Scilla so she will not cause more problems than Jake's death has already caused. He is the person who notifies everyone of Jake's death. He knows all the key characters, not from Jake's diary, like Scilla, but from his actual experience and relationships with them. He is at the heart of Corman's plans for a hostile takeover. Furthermore, Zac is an American, and Churchill uses the U.S. stock market as a model for greed. The British traders and markets take their lead from the Americans. Zac, therefore, serves as a figurative representative of U.S. financial dealings. There are other Americans, like Marylou, Merrison, and Durkfeld, but they are not as pivotal to the play as Zac is. He not only pushes the action forward, but he also slows it down. He tells Corman when to act. He flirts with Scilla and Jacinta. He knows when Marylou is lying. Indeed, in this fast-paced play, the audience comes to depend on Zac to explain what is happening.

Identifying Jake as a central character might appear troublesome. After all, Jake dies at the beginning of the play. However, the play is not strictly chronological and Jake appears in several scenes after his death has been announced. In his last encounter with his sister, Jake tells her

that he thinks someone might hurt him. Later in the play, as Zac is working with Corman, Jake suddenly appears again; this time in a bar with Zac. The two men talk about their dreams of making money. Jake reappears in the second act with Zac again, and Jake asks for Zac's advice. Jake knows the D.T.I. investigators will come to him, so he asks Zac what he should do. Then Jake introduces Jacinta to Zac so the Corman deal can go through. This scene demonstrates Jake's continued importance to the play's plot. He has the contacts that Zac needs. Later, Jake reappears in Corman's office and then with Marylou. Even in the scenes in which Jake is already dead, his ghost is felt throughout the entire play. Several characters are afraid that Jake might have mentioned their names to the D.T.I. before he died. Then there is the ever-present question of who killed Jake and why. Jake's death dictates Jake's memory. This also gives Scilla the courage to confront Marylou. Marylou had trusted Jake, and when she sees how determined Scilla is, she gives Scilla a job because of her past relationship with Jake.

Thusly, Jake, Scilla, and Zac represent the new market makers. Jake represents what can happen when things go wrong in this system. Scilla is the model for how to manipulate the system. Zac, who profits from the system, is the observer; he adapts to the system and makes the best of it.

Source: Joyce M. Hart, Critical Essay on *Serious Money*, in *Drama for Students*, Gale, Cengage Learning, 2008.

Frances Gray
In the following excerpt, Gray gives a critical analysis of Churchill's life and work.

Now established as one of the most important contemporary British playwrights, Caryl Churchill is often grouped with the dramatists of the late 1960s who revitalized and reshaped British theater, not only in terms of their political subject matter but also in terms of their chosen venues and company structures. While this connection is an accurate reflection of both her importance and her socialist perspective, the trajectory of her career is remarkably different from that of contemporaries such as Howard Brenton or David Hare. While the male dramatists of the period generally proceeded from university to the founding of a fringe theater company and thence to the major subsidized playhouses,

THE PLAY WAS, DISCONCERTINGLY, A HUGE SUCCESS WITH THE VERY COMMUNITY IT SATIRIZED, AND DURING THE WEST END TRANSFER, THE WYNDHAM WAS FILLED WITH CITY SPECULATORS. THE ACTION PRESENTS A SELF-CONTAINED WORLD, A CAPITALIST DYSTOPIA WITH ITS OWN LANGUAGE AND LOGIC."

Churchill's path was fragmented and complex, marked by several major shifts in direction.

Churchill was born in London on 3 September 1938. She was an only child; her mother was a model and actress, and her father, Robert Churchill, was a cartoonist. When she was ten the family moved to Montreal, Canada, where she was educated at the Trafalgar School. She returned to England to study at Lady Margaret Hall, Oxford, in 1957, and finished her degree in English in 1960, just as the first wave of British postwar playwrights was beginning to make its presence felt. While this development may have prompted her to write several pieces for the stage, which received student productions, her own dramaturgy was shaped more by radio than the theater, and her first professional radio production, *The Ants* (1962), originally envisaged for television, was submitted to the BBC Third Programme on the advice of her agent, Margaret "Peggy" Ramsay. *The Ants* was also included in the Penguin *New English Dramatists* volume covering radio drama in 1969. What made *The Ants* outstanding was not so much the youth of the author— Churchill was twenty-four—as a remarkable clarity of design that gives it an unusual authority. The story of a child who cannot articulate his feelings about either the war that occupies the headlines or the corrosive breakup of his parents, and who joins his grandfather in the destruction of an ants' nest he had formerly loved to watch, reflects preoccupations that recur throughout Churchill's work: the interrelation of the personal and the political; the ways in which the silenced struggle to find expression; and the idea of alternative worlds, both utopia and dystopia.

Churchill married the barrister David Harter in 1961, and between 1963 and 1969 they had three sons. She claimed in Catherine Itzin's *Stages in the Revolution* (1980) that the years she spent at home with the children "politicized" her. They were also instrumental in her early choice of medium. Radio has, from the outset, offered women opportunities to experiment and work. Its large output and relatively low profile mean that an author's gender is not emphasized. As plays are rehearsed and recorded at speed, the writer can work almost entirely from home; and, in a life filled with differing responsibilities, a play that is structured in small, often vividly contrasting, scenic units can be easier to build.

Because a radio play has no embodied form, it is also a medium in which the line between the abstract and the concrete can be blurred; ideas are colored by the voice that speaks them; and scenes of vigorous action derive their strength from the movement they create within characters rather than from spectacle. In Churchill's *Abortive* (1971), for example, a husband and wife reflect on her recent abortion; their thoughts seem to be drawn out of them by the carefully orchestrated sound effects of wind and rain. Gradually, the audience becomes aware that the couple read past events differently. The wife seems to have been raped by Billy, the father of her aborted child. Both she and her husband, however, hold Billy in affection, though their accounts of him do not tally. The husband, for instance, remembers a day on the river, "an English scene so remarkable for its pale green that it seemed even at the time like a memory," a moment made beautiful by Billy's vulnerability as he told their small daughter that he had never been in a boat and was tenderly encouraged by her to step in. The wife comments, "He was certainly lying because he told me he'd worked his passage to South America." There is no "true" version of the story, and the audience never hears Billy himself; what is important is the concrete effect his actions have had upon the relationship, on the ways the couple define themselves, their sexuality, their child, the possible lives that have now been closed to them, and those that remain.

Schreber's Nervous Illness (1972) enters the mind of the protagonist, a judge at the turn of the century and a patient of Sigmund Freud, to render concrete the images that afflict him. Schreber sees himself as assailed by "nerve rays" that speak to him in a variety of voices; in an arresting first speech he claims that "the Order of the World has been broken and God and I find ourselves in a situation that has never arisen before." As his illness progresses he sees himself as participating in "miracles" and as undergoing a transformation into a female state, his body becoming quick with new life. His monologues and the interruptions of the "rays" are intercut with statements from the Director of the Asylum, who never addresses the protagonist directly. As Elaine Aston has pointed out, this image parallels other plays in the 1970s, such as David Edgar's *Mary Barnes* (performed in 1978, published in 1979), that explore the "anti-psychiatry" of R. D. Laing. Churchill's use of radio puts the listener in the position of a Laingian psychiatrist: the audience hears, as Schreber does, the voices of the "rays" and of God himself—and with no visual dimension to suggest otherwise, their presence is not measurably different from that of the doctor. The audience has no choice, therefore, but to accept the validity of Schreber's experience— not to believe in the existence of the rays, but to acknowledge the significance of the psychological journey that he undergoes and the newly strengthened self with which he emerges. Churchill's interest in the ways the human subject can make and remake, articulate, and express itself is an abiding preoccupation.

What she has described as the second stage of her career, the period that marked a return to the theater, this time as a professional playwright, was inaugurated in 1972 with *Owners* at the Royal Court Theatre Upstairs. The darkly funny *Owners* tells with elegant symmetry the story of two couples: property owner Marion and her pushy capitalist husband, Clegg, and tenants Alec and Lisa. Written in three days as Churchill recovered from a miscarriage, *Owners* explores sexual and familial, as well as financial, ownership. Clegg likes to think of himself as owning Marion: "It's very like having a talking dog." His stereotypical chauvinism is so outrageous that the audience is set up to expect an uncomplicated enjoyment of Marion's refusal to conform; they are instantly challenged by her shameless adoption of the "dog" image. She converts it from Samuel Johnson's dismissive type of ineptitude ("A woman preaching is like a dog walking on its hind legs: it is not well done, but you are surprised to find it done at all") to that of the "capitalist running dog" of Mao Tse-tung: "I work like a dog. Most women are fleas but I'm the dog." Marion and Clegg both assume that

they have the right to own Lisa's child: Marion because she desires her former lover Alec, Clegg because he has slept with Lisa, and both because they can afford to exploit Lisa's poverty. In contrast, when Marion gets her go-between Worsely to set the house on fire, Alec not only saves his family but sacrifices his life to save a neighbor's baby. While he sees life as something that can be spent in a good cause, he is equally willing to assume the responsibility of taking life: when his elderly mother goes into a permanent coma, he releases her. In contrast, Worsely, who subscribes to the capitalist assumption that life is what one makes it, is always trying to commit suicide; his failures are a running gag, as is his ongoing debate with a Samaritan: "I told him I wanted to kill myself and could he help. He said in a very feeling voice he would certainly try. But does he hell. The bastard's always trying to stop me."

Like many of Churchill's plays, *Owners* became more topical with time: the right-wing government elected in 1979 increasingly preached individual responsibility for life. Margaret Thatcher characteristically invoked the story of the Good Samaritan who could afford to do good. The extent of this responsibility was explored in real-life events such as the "Baby Cotton" case in 1984, which raised questions about payment for surrogate parenthood, and the Hillsborough Stadium disaster in 1989 (when ninety-six football fans were crushed to death in the press of a badly managed crowd), which left one young victim in a permanent coma from which his parents struggled for the right to release him.

Churchill saw the mid 1970s as marking the beginning of a third phase in her work. As she became active in the women's movement she also moved from solitary to collaborative work, a process she described in Rob Ritchie's *The Joint Stock Book* (1987) as leaving her "as thrilled as a child at a pantomime." For many dramatists, collaborative writing, or "workshopping" material with a company, was a useful apprenticeship to be discarded as competence developed. Churchill had been a playwright for eighteen years when she encountered the feminist company Monstrous Regiment on an abortion march; the result was *Vinegar Tom* (performed in 1976, published in 1978), about the seventeenth-century witch trials. At the same time, she worked with the socialist company Joint Stock on a play about the same period, *Light Shining in Buckinghamshire* (performed in 1976, published in 1978). Working with companies from the outset gave her the support she needed to work on a broader canvas with larger casts and to make use of their personal experiences and stage skills.

Churchill's plays differ from those of most of her male contemporaries, even those of broadly leftist/feminist sympathy, whose works frequently track the career of a female hero, a romantic conscience for a corrupt world, leaving old assumptions about gender and personality unshaken. Churchill's dramaturgy reflects the collective process that engendered the play. To watch *Light Shining in Buckinghamshire*, for example, is to experience a disorienting shift of focus. The play presents the experiences of the ordinary people who made the English revolution in the seventeenth century. There are no heroes with whom to identify; characters are played by several different actors, so they may be seen to grow in terms of understanding their situation, but not in terms of "personality." This undercutting of audience identification made *Light Shining in Buckinghamshire*—along with *Vinegar Tom*, which broke up the seventeenth-century story with modern songs—Churchill's most Brechtian work to date.

Like much of Bertolt Brecht's work, the play is charged with an excitement that stems from its ability to catch a political process and make it human and concrete. In one key scene, two women are looking in a mirror. The conversation concentrates on the material aspects of their situation. One explains to the other that they can take what they need, blankets and cattle, from the manor house, and she claims their right to do so as Saxons dispossessed by Norman aristocrats, as workers on the land betrayed by those whose title lies only in paper: "We're burning his papers . . . that's like him burnt." Feminist critiques of Churchill identify this scene as a liminal moment embodying the idea that the act of becoming a subject, a political being, is open to all. Throughout the play characters take hold of the language that has constructed them and shape new selves: a woman claims the right to preach; a butcher refuses meat to the rich; a vagrant ceases to identify herself as "evil" and can allow herself to be touched, in a meeting charged with a sense that "you're God, you're God, no one's more God than you if you could know it yourself, you're lovely, you're perfect." Yet, even in this

scene it is clear that the revolution has been betrayed. Oliver Cromwell refuses the chance to set up a democracy and invests the government of the country in the propertied classes; the preacher who recruited for the New Model Army evicts his tenants while assuring himself he is doing it to provide corn for all. "Jesus Christ did come," one of the empowered women tells us, "and nobody noticed." The last lines of the play are spoken by men while the women keep silent.

Churchill's subsequent plays with Joint Stock and the Royal Court Theatre, especially *Cloud Nine* (performed and published in 1979), *Top Girls* (performed and published in 1982), and *Fen* (performed and published in 1983), brought her to much greater prominence. All three transferred to New York, where *Cloud Nine* and *Top Girls* won Obie Awards. *Fen* won the Susan Smith Blackburn Award in 1984, and Churchill's first collection of plays was published by Methuen in 1985. Since then all three works have been revived frequently by both amateur and professional companies. It was an extraordinary achievement, given the combination of political complexity and theatrical innovation in the plays. Their reception was prompted by the uprush of feminist consciousness in all aspects of life: novels, consciousness-raising groups, rape crisis centers, shelters for battered women, and an increasing body of feminist theory began to transform life at many levels, and Churchill's works took on the status of classics.

She continued to be active in the women's movement and in 1977 contributed to the Monstrous Regiment cabaret, *Floorshow*. The heady sense of new possibilities and the swift and stylized cabaret medium generated ideas that emerged in the bold imagery and cartoon-like tableaux of *Cloud Nine*, developed with Joint Stock in 1979 out of a series of workshops exploring sexuality and sexual politics. The title was taken from the term for orgasm used by the caretaker of the rehearsal room, who had been drawn into the discussions. In the middle of the second act the whole company unite to celebrate the varieties of love and sing "It'll be fine when you reach Cloud Nine." This scene is, however, a utopian moment that can only exist outside the narrative; within it, characters have to struggle and engage with the legacy of Victorian patriarchy. Churchill reveals the complexity of this legacy only gradually. The first act, which takes place circa 1879, is a wildly comic parody of the television series of the 1970s such as *Upstairs Downstairs*, which cast a nostalgic glow over the days of the British Empire; Churchill mocks the enforced sexual and social passivity of women and the insensitivity and colonizing greed of men:

> BETTY Do you think of me sometimes then?
>
> HARRY You have been thought of where no white woman has been thought of before.
>
> BETTY It's one way of having adventures. I suppose I will never go in person.

In this act Churchill continually subverts the idea that the bodies of women (or of any oppressed group) are to be looked at as powerless and unchanging objects by the white male hierarchy. Because Betty is solely defined by male desire, she is played by a man; her son, Edward, who likes dolls, has yet to be made a man, and is played by a woman; her daughter, Victoria, the most passive of all, is a doll; and the black servant Joshua, who sings English Christmas carols and flogs native rebels but eventually shoots Betty's husband, Clive, is played by a white actor in unconvincing makeup that reveals him as a construct of white culture. The pattern the actors weave onstage also echoes the trap in which women are caught. The sexually articulate Mrs. Saunders speaks of desire, but as Clive vanishes underneath her skirts, emerging moments later to disguise the damp patch on his trousers with champagne, she can only ponder her dislike of him; the lesbian governess Ellen is played by the actress playing Mrs. Saunders, thus simultaneously embodying the attraction and the impossibility of a union between them. Ellen is married off to Harry Bagley, neatly crushing her hopeless desire for Betty and his for Clive in a single miserable union.

While the cross-dressing and farce-like speed are outrageously comic, reflecting the enthusiasm Churchill found in the workshops, they have an underlying savagery that emerges fully in the second act. The action moves to 1979, but Betty, Edward, and Victoria have aged only twenty-five years, and they are played by actors of the appropriate gender. They may thus be understood to have "matured" or "grown up" and absorbed the experience of earlier generations, but their engagement with the sexual politics of the 1970s is still warped and distorted despite the distance they have traveled. Betty has left her painful marriage; so has Victoria, now a mother and tentatively exploring a relationship with another woman. Edward is gay and struggling to come to terms with his lover Gerry's promiscuity. While the action—apart from the wild energy of Victoria's daughter, Cathy, played by a man with no attempt to disguise the incongruity—is primarily naturalistic, it borders on surrealism. If the Victorian Age can now be viewed as comic caricature, Churchill implies, humans are still far from utopia; a better world can be glimpsed in the moments when characters are at their least rational—as when Edward, Victoria, and her lover Lin make a drunken and giggly attempt to evoke the Goddess. Their language suggests an ideal past, the "history we haven't had," and, through Victoria's socialist-feminist analysis, explains how this past is so rooted in a long-dead economic system that it can never be recovered. They raise not a goddess but evidence of patriarchal corruption: first, Victoria's husband, Martin, who is nostalgic for the 1960s, "when liberation just meant fucking"; and second, the ghost of Lin's brother Bill, a soldier in Northern Ireland, who sees brutal sex as an antidote to his rage as a victim of a still-operative colonialism.

The closing moments of the play measure the distance between what 1970s feminism has achieved and what still has to be overcome. Visited by the ghosts of her mother and Ellen, Betty narrates her attainment of selfhood through self-induced orgasm:

> I thought well there is somebody there. It felt very sweet.... Afterwards I thought I'd betrayed Clive. My mother would kill me. But I felt triumphant because I was a separate person from them. And I cried because I didn't want to be. But I don't cry about it any more. Sometimes I do it three times in one night and it really is great fun.

Betty can now begin to renegotiate her relationship with her children, acknowledging their sexuality and articulating, through an awkward attempt to pick up Gerry, the hope that she may have a sexual relationship herself. At this point, the last image in the play, it is possible for her to embrace the Betty of the previous act; it is an image of great tenderness and optimism, and also one that only exists in imagined as opposed to real space, implying that the reconciliation of past and present has still to occur. Its echo of the mirror scene in *Light Shining in Buckinghamshire*, however, implies that it is not impossible.

Top Girls and *Fen* mark a new phase in feminist political drama; as the 1970s gave way to the Thatcher era, images of women united in a struggle against a patriarchal legacy gave way to a more fragmented picture. In both plays Churchill turns to an examination of the position of women in contemporary capitalism. In the opening scene of *Top Girls*, the protagonist, Marlene, places herself in a continuum of "successful" women in history who gather to celebrate her promotion at a dinner: Isabella Bird, the Victorian explorer and traveler; Pope Joan, an apocryphal figure who allegedly served as the pontiff from 855 to 858; Lady Nijo, a thirteenth-century Japanese imperial court concubine and Buddhist nun; Patient Griselda, the "obedient wife" character from medieval and Renaissance sources such as Giovanni Boccaccio's *Decameron* and Geoffrey Chaucer's *Canterbury Tales;* and Dull Gret, the key figure in a painting by Pieter Brueghel the Elder. The scene itself is theatrically and politically uplifting, with an energy arising both from obstacles transcended and heroic failure, sometimes sharply juxtaposed: Joan, for instance, reduces the company to ribald and delighted laughter with an account of giving birth unexpectedly during a papal procession, a laughter she suddenly ruptures with the comment, "They took me by the feet and dragged me out of town and stoned me to death." Much of the vigor of the first scene derives from the way lines overlap, so that the rhythms of nineteenth-century reminiscence or Japanese haiku collide with those of the Latin Mass or the twitterings of Griselda. As virtually every critique of the play has since pointed out, this overlap dramatizes the point that these historical heroines could function only on the individual level; they lack the power to support one another or to offer help to their contemporaries—except, perhaps, for Gret, monosyllabic apart from one speech in which she describes organizing her neighbors to go and beat the devils in hell: "We'd had worse, you see, we'd had the Spanish. We'd all had family killed. Men on wheels. Babies on swords. I'd had enough, I was mad, I hate the bastards."

In the next act, the actress who plays Gret, powerful but unheard, becomes the equally marginalized figure of Angie, Marlene's slow-witted daughter. Churchill tracks their relationship backward; the audience first meets Angie in the country, announcing that she is going to run away to London to visit her aunt, Marlene, whom she believes to be her mother. When she arrives at Marlene's office, she sits ignored, sometimes asleep, through a series of interactions between Marlene and various colleagues that are notable not simply for their infectious ruthlessness (Angie gapes in admiration as Marlene tells a wife interceding for her failed husband to "piss off" and a would-be saleswoman intones like a mantra, "I'm not very nice") but also for their linguistic poverty. Marlene's role in sustaining the capitalist culture is more overtly argued out in the following section, which takes place one year earlier. She visits her sister Joyce and confirms that she is Angie's true mother. The sisters bicker, at first with affection, then corrosively as the row becomes political; Joyce hurls the epithet "Hitlerina," while Marlene, who has won over Angie with presents, is confronted with the personal implications of her beliefs:

> MARLENE . . . Anyone can do anything if they've got what it takes.
>
> JOYCE And if they haven't?
>
> MARLENE If they're stupid or lazy or frightened, I'm not going to help them get a job, why should I?
>
> JOYCE What about Angie?
>
> MARLENE What about her?
>
> JOYCE She's stupid, lazy and frightened, so what about her?

Angie closes the play with a single word born out of the nightmare she has been having offstage: "Frightening," a word that sums up both her own future and that of a country in which feminism can contemplate an alliance with capitalism.

Fen is also a state-of-the-nation play, but in this play the gulf between those who control the land and those who work it is so wide that not even the acrid dialogue of Joyce and Marlene is possible. Rather, the opening, in which a Japanese businessman gazes at the Fens and looks for someone to tell him "old tales" of the Fen Tigers' resistance to the draining of their land, serves to stress that the figures of power in the play, such as the landowner Tewson, are themselves at the mercy of the multinational corporations. The lives of the sixteen women in the play are shaped by these forces, whose impact on the most intimate parts of their lives was indicated by the set designed by Annie Smart. Domestic paraphernalia was surrealistically planted in the soil on which they worked, so that they were never wholly free of the land. Economic conditions were seen to dictate vicious and frustrated relationships like that between Angela and her stepdaughter Becky, and the doomed love affair of Val, shuttling between her lover Frank, who cannot afford to support her, and her husband and children, until she finally asks Frank to kill her.

The women speak the same debased language of the *Top Girls* clientele: when Val bids her daughter a last good-bye it is subtextual, beneath an exchange of elephant jokes; as she seeks for God, a woman testifies to finding Jesus in the words "More jam, mum." Men do not tell stories, as Churchill's doubling plot stresses; they are all played by a single actor, indicating a failure to negotiate, or unite, or provide any kind of community. (At one point, Frank considers the futility of asking for a raise, taking the part of his boss as well as himself, and finally hits himself in the face.) The women, however, speak together. Nell tells stories of the past and refutes the chants of "witch" by telling the village children that she is a princess; and the ghost of a woman whose child died starving continues to challenge the landowners, warning them that she watches television alongside them and sees both their greed and the suffering they cause. As Val herself becomes a ghost, she liberates the dream-lives of the women: Nell is a Fen Tiger on stilts; Shirley, the worker, is ironing the field, but recalls the days when workers fought back and killed the owners' cattle; her mother, who would never sing, now does so in a burst of glory that brings the play to its end. The dream-lives create a context for the documentary material of which Churchill makes extensive use, much of it derived from interviews in Mary Chamberlain's book *Fenwomen* (1975), which narrates the lives of women in an English village. They show that the most tightly circumscribed daily lives have still a capacity for energy and vision; they alert both characters and audience to utopian possibilities not yet dead.

Serious Money (performed and published in 1987), Churchill's second play to win a Susan Smith Blackburn Award and the third in what might be called her state-of-the-nation plays at the Royal Court Theatre, is far less optimistic. Set at the time of the "Big Bang" that transformed the stock exchange in the 1980s, it narrates the takeover of a company, significantly called Albion. It is also a murder story—except that no one actually cares about justice, and with the murder unsolved, the cast ends the play with an exuberant song welcoming in five more years of the Thatcher administration. The play was, disconcertingly, a huge success with the very

community it satirized, and during the West End transfer, the Wyndham was filled with city speculators. The action presents a self-contained world, a capitalist dystopia with its own language and logic. The theatrical pleasure is rooted in the energy of the presentation: the play bounds along in verse, deriving comedy from the sort of outrageous rhymes associated with Cole Porter's witty love lyrics rather than the language of finance.

The verse, however, offers more than just pantomime energy. Studies of Churchill's language point out how she habitually defamiliarizes words; in this play she concentrates on those once used to denote tangible commodities, such as copper and cocoa (and cocaine), on which the lives of Third World communities depend. In the face of the Big Bang they have assumed the status of paper money, with a fluctuating face value. This volatile status is as true for those in a position to save those communities as it is for the young Thatcherites who now dominate the city. Jacinta Condor, for example, does not see herself as in any way responsible for the workers in her copper mine or for the political destiny of her country; the pat rhythms betray her lack of real concern while the drop into prose indicates the area in which she is prepared to engage with complex ideas:

> I lose every quarter
>
> The cash goes like water
>
> Is better to close the mine.
>
> I choose very well
>
> The moment to sell,
>
> I benefit from the closures in Surinam because of guerrilla activity, and also I leak the news I am closing my mines, which puts the price up a little, so it is fine.

Everything, in this world, can be reduced to commodities, and there is no longer a vocabulary outside that of trading. In the last moments, the ghost of the murder victim appears, perfunctorily; unlike the long-dead woman in *Fen*, he cannot speak of what has happened to him. While in *Fen* the women have the power to see spirits and imagine other worlds, in *Serious Money* there is no apparent possibility of a considered and vigorous dissent—no words, no societies or actions that are not ultimately controlled and corroded by city values. *Serious Money* won a London *Evening Standard* award for best comedy and the Laurence Olivier/BBC Award for best new play, both in 1987.

Mad Forest (performed and published in 1990) is a work on an equally ambitious scale about the revolution in Romania. The project was suggested to Churchill by Mark Wing-Davey, the artistic director of the Central School of Speech and Drama, who knew Churchill from *Monstrous Regiment*, just weeks after the execution of overthrown Romanian president Nicolae Ceausescu and his wife on Christmas Day 1989. By April 1990, Churchill, Wing-Davey, ten students, and a team of designers were working with students from the Caragiale Institute of Theatre and Cinema in Bucharest. The techniques Churchill had developed in her Joint Stock work were used to explore the experience of the Romanian students and other Romanian people whom they interviewed. The result was a play that combined a sense of being still under construction, like a series of dispatches from a war zone, with great formal coherence. The play has three acts. Acts 1 and 3 center on two weddings involving the working-class Vladu family and the Antonescu family, members of the intelligentsia. The weddings take place before and after the revolution. The revolution is presented in Act 2 through a series of testimonies by ordinary Romanians—including students, doctors, and artists. The documentary quality of this act is reinforced by the use of the Romanian accent; elsewhere characters speak unaccented English or Romanian. The division is not between the personal and the political—politics permeates the lives of the fictional families, while the testimonies are as concerned with the feelings of parents and children as they are with the actions of the army—rather, it is between the fact of the revolution and its implications for a complex society. Churchill's structure refutes any suggestion that her exploration of these implications can be comprehensive: the action proceeds in a series of vignettes, each introduced with a short sentence in Romanian; the effect is of a phrase book, eclectic and sometimes surreal, each "lesson" defamiliarizing the one before.

The pressures of the Ceausescu regime are presented in a series of scenes linking material and linguistic deprivation. In Act 1 the Vladus have a row about Lucia's forthcoming marriage to an American. It is conducted in shouts masked by a loud radio, a strategy employed to avoid bugging. Meanwhile, a subtext about poverty

plays itself out as Lucia offers eggs and cigarettes. When her father smashes one of the eggs, her mother and sister carefully gather it up. As the play progresses it is clear that sexual life is similarly circumscribed: Lucia conducts a (bugged) conversation with a doctor who tells her "There is no abortion in Romania. I am shocked that you even think of it," while they exchange notes and a large wad of money. Even the spiritual is touched: a priest talks to his angel, hoping that his flock can still retreat into a "blue" of peace but realizing that while no words can be safely spoken there is no meaning in silence. "I try to keep clear of the political side," explains the angel blandly.

Churchill explains in her notes to the play that "the play goes from the difficulty of saying anything to everyone talking." The play rejects obvious theatrical opportunities—flags, shooting, heroics—to present the attempts of Romanian citizens to use their apparent newfound freedom of speech to analyze what has happened to them. For many, this freedom means speaking about confusion. This confusion is borne out by the final act, which centers on the wedding of Florina Vladu, who is marrying Radu Antonescu. It opens, not with one of the central characters, but with a scene between a vampire and a dog. The connotations the figure of the vampire bears in the West are complex: potent religion; forbidden sexuality; luxury and decadence; a specifically Eastern European culture; a near-feudal social structure; superstition; and, as a staple of the movies, capitalism itself. In vampire movies arcane knowledge has to be resurrected to make sense of the world, and everyone is under the threat of death. The image sets an agenda for the final part of the play.

Occasionally, briefly, there is a glimpse of utopia: Florina's old aunt seems to embody a new national awareness as she chants peasant wedding verses. But the overall picture is dark. In the hospital, Lucia's brother Gabriel is feted as a hero, but an unnamed patient asks again and again, "Who was shooting on the 22nd? . . . Did we have a revolution or a putsch?" Radu and Florina welcome Gabriel home with a bit of impromptu theater, acting out the execution of the Ceausescus; the scene is wildly funny but displays a disturbing level of mimic violence, which becomes real as Lucia (who married and dumped her American) is embraced by her lover Ianos and Gabriel lashes out with "Get your filthy Hungarian hands off her." No one is clear what they have been liberated to: their choices, their identity, their purchasing power, their rights. The play ends with everyone speaking at once, nobody listening, no new identity articulated except that of the vampire, whose speech cuts through the rest: "You begin to want blood, your limbs ache, your head burns, you have to keep moving faster and faster."

The confidence with which Churchill was able to engage with the two different student companies and with audiences in London and Bucharest is reflected in the experimentalism of much of her work since 1985, the year Joint Stock fell victim to Arts Council cuts. Her final work with them, *A Mouthful of Birds* (performed and published in 1986), on which she collaborated with David Lan and the choreographer Ian Spink, indicated the direction much of her later work took in making the stage a place of magical transformation. Churchill dates her interest in working with dance and song from seeing a production of Brecht's *Seven Deadly Sins* (1933) in 1979 and the politically resonant dance work of Pina Bausch in the 1980s at Sadlers Wells. However, while the images in *Fen* made the dreams of the characters concrete, and *Mad Forest* dredged up the vampire from the Romanian subconscious to articulate new political nightmares, *A Mouthful of Birds* was her first real attempt to use dance and speech in equal measure to explore extreme states of feeling.

Its starting point is Euripides' *Bacchae*, but while characters act out the story of Dionysus and Pentheus, the focus is different. *The Bacchae* tells the story of one man's opposition to the cult, which destroys him, and of the possession of a group of women who tear him to pieces in their ecstasy and then, horrified, resume their lives. Much of its fascination lies in its subversive images of authority brought down by its own rigidity, of women consumed by a violence that not only runs counter to all accepted forms of female behavior but that is in some degree holy. Churchill echoes the subversion of sexual stereotypes, exploring both female violence and male tenderness, but lays new emphasis on the variety of possibilities inherent in the idea of possession and the variety of characters who experience it. In workshops she explored different kinds of "being beside ourselves," as she explained in the published version of the play, including spiritualism, hypnotic regression, and living in the

open, and developed the idea of the "undefended day," in which seven characters would step out of their normal lives and explore extremes. Lena, for example, hears the voice of her husband droning on about everyday defeats in counterpoint to the insistence of a spirit that she kill her baby in order to exist. The act of killing is symbolized by the washing of a shawl; Churchill is concerned to explore the feeling of power generated by violence rather than to evoke horror. Paul, working in an office and dealing in statistics and reports, falls in love with a pig, and they dance with great tenderness. Derek is unemployed, and works out to avoid the sense of emasculation experienced by his father when out of work. His journey through the play is the most extraordinary, as he takes on the identity of Herculine Barbin, the hermaphrodite, and then becomes Pentheus as the other men become Dionysus and the women Bacchantes. He is torn to pieces, but in the final section, as the characters all decide how to lead their lives after the "undefended day," he is born into a female body in which he finds peace and happiness.

Churchill continued to develop her work with Spink and his company Second Stride, and with *Lives of the Great Poisoners* (performed in 1991, published in 1993), they also explored the use of song with the composer Orlando Gough. The company consisted of four dancers, four singers (one of whom acted), and an actor, and explored the idea of "poison"—mythological, with the story of Medea; historical, with the cases of Cora Crippen (a music-hall singer murdered by her husband in 1910) and Madame de Brinvilliers (beheaded in 1676 for poisoning her father and two brothers); and environmental, with the story of Thomas Midgley Jr., the American engineer and chemist who put lead into gasoline with benevolent intentions. Modes of expression and historical periods flow into one another: Cora Crippen does her lamentable music-hall turn, is sung to death by a Chorus of Poisons, and returns as Medea to take her revenge; Jason discusses his forthcoming marriage to Creusa with Midgley as she dances her death with the Poisons.

What is perhaps most important about both these plays with Spink is their attempt to explore political questions by using resources no longer normally associated with political theater; they turn back to the spectacle and excess of melodrama, a medium whose political dynamic is gradually being rediscovered. The play on which Churchill worked steadily throughout the whole period of her association with Gough, *The Skriker*, completed and staged at the National in 1994, made this political aspect more explicit through its choice of central characters. Josie and Lily are everything the Tory values of the 1990s reviled—unemployed single mothers. Josie is in a psychiatric hospital after killing her baby. Alongside their gray and deprived world is another, inhabited by spirits, grotesque folkloric figures who dance, silently, their own stories and interactions with humanity. The only one to engage in dialogue, however, is the Skriker, described by Churchill as "a shapeshifter and death portent, ancient and damaged." Dazzlingly portrayed by Katherine Hunter in the original production, the Skriker continually transforms herself into social victims such as mental patients and lost children, into pieces of furniture, into psychotic men, and—most signficantly, perhaps, in a play employing the persecuted young mothers of melodrama—into a pantomime fairy in pink tulle and glitter. She offers what otherworld spirits have always offered in folktales: wishes interpreted with dangerous literalmindedness, gifts that cause only pain—Josie and Lily find their mouths dropping toads and pound coins like Rose Red and Snow White—and visits to her own world that savagely skew the time frame in this one.

While folk stories tend to construct spirits as troublesome but nonetheless in overall harmony with the natural world, the Skriker's "damage" is a product of an environment wrecked by twentieth-century capitalism:

> Sunbeam sunburn in your eye socket to him. All good many come to the aids party. When I go uppety, follow a fellow on a dark road dank ride and jump thrump out and eat him how does he taste? toxic waste paper basket case, salmonelephantiasis, blue blood bad blood blad blodd blah blah blah. I remember dismember the sweet flesh in the panic, tearing limb from lamb chop you up and suck the tomorrowbones. Lovely lively lads and maiden England. . . .

Her language is breaking down, corrupted by a Nature abused by men. Toxic waste and the poisoning of the food chain break up the balance between the real and the supernatural. Lily, marginalized and despised, behaves as the heroine of a fairy-tale should and tries to save the world; but the twentieth century has destroyed the possibility of a fairy tale ending, and she

finds herself on a blasted Earth whose inhabitants bellow at her in blind hatred. *The Skriker* never shows a figure who might be held responsible for what happens. At one point the Skriker tries to understand how the earth has been poisoned, but Lily cannot explain it. The paradox of the play lies in the theatrical complexity and richness that is used to depict the deprivation imposed by capitalism—a deprivation not only material but also spiritual and linguistic.

Churchill's preoccupation with the relationships between politics, language, and excess continued with her translation of Seneca's *Thyestes* in 1994. After seeing Ariane Mnouchkine's landmark production of the Greek tragic cycle *The House of Atreus* two years previously, Churchill researched the beginnings of the story in Latin and became attracted to the possibilities of the language. While earlier translators had tended to equate Latin itself with the Latinate borrowings in English that make for grandiloquence, producing an overblown rhetoric to match the extremes of violence in the plays, Churchill was attracted to the speed and compression possible in an inflected language. Her verse translation was fast, rough, and plain. Seneca's focus upon drought and a damaged Earth, the hellish landscapes in which he sets the narratives of murder, revenge, and cannibalism, echo the imagery of *The Skriker*, and much of the text reads like a more rhythmic and immediate version of the descriptions of a polluted world in that play:

> Have we been chosen
>
> out of everyone
>
> somehow deserving
>
> to have the world smash up and fall on us? or have the last days come
>
> in our lifetime? It's
>
> a hard fate, whether we've lost the sun
>
> or driven it away.

Churchill's work of the late 1990s continued to experiment with language; her plays also took on a new intimacy, an intense preoccupation with the personal. This intimacy springs from the way Churchill deploys subtext. The double bill *Hotel* (performed and published in 1997) was once again worked out in collaboration with Second Stride, directed and choreographed by Spink with music by Gough. The first piece, *Eight Rooms*, is an opera rather than a play with song and dance; both Churchill and Gough were interested in the way language works at the high points in an opera when a whole ensemble is singing different words. In *Hotel*, Churchill developed a text of fragments, incomplete sentences that the audience might grasp at different points as repeats were sung. The scraps form a mosaic that offer glimpses into the lives of fourteen hotel guests, couples and singles, who occupy the same room-oblivious of one another. Their stories hint at pain and loss: one couple is silent; a woman having an affair cannot sleep because she is worried about her children; a gay couple fail to communicate; a drunken couple quarrel and wake everyone up. While the audience works to extrapolate stories from these fragments of private unhappiness, the onstage action is full of wit: Spink coordinated the everyday actions of the guests—brushing teeth, watching TV, making phone calls—into a complex choreography that culminate in a point at which fourteen people lie on the bed, moving in a weird synchronicity that still reflects their own characters. The effect of the whole is a Bergsonian comedy—in which the human figures become cogs in a machine—which nevertheless implies the existence of tragedy.

The companion piece, *Two Nights*, was a dance to what Gough called "a kind of song cycle" built out of scraps from a diary. The theme of these scraps is disappearance; phrases come from an account of a magician making a building vanish, a Greek spell, and a manifesto that posits disappearance, not confrontation, as the ultimate way of taking power. The subtext is dark and disturbing; one can infer the possibility of suicide in lines such as: "will I still have a shadow? / will I still have a mind?" Dancers appear and disappear through cracks in the walls of the room. It is for the audience, finally, to decode the room and its inhabitants, as with the projects of Sophie Calle in the 1990s. Calle worked as a chambermaid in a Venice hotel and photographed the rooms she cleaned, exposing the lives of the occupants through their intimate debris: underwear slung across a chair, scribbled notes, and casual purchases. Both Calle and Churchill push the audience to reflect on the fragility of identity in an urban society lacking the old certainties of community.

The same theme is echoed in *Blue Heart*, the paired plays *Heart's Desire* and *Blue Kettle* (performed and published in 1997), which marked a reunion for Churchill and Joint Stock, resurrected by Max Stafford-Clark as Out of Joint. The use of actors' games and exercises creates a surface playfulness, but the precision of the subtext has the darkness of *Hotel. Heart's Desire* uses a technique Churchill developed in her 1977 play *Traps*, in which the actors play out different versions of the same event, so that as the story advances the audience become aware of multiple possibilities. *Heart's Desire* shows a couple in their sixties, Brian and Alice, who with Brian's sister Maisie are waiting for their daughter Susy to arrive from Australia. The wait, and later the arrival, are played out many times in different ways: sometimes the action is replayed at double speed with the smallest of variations; sometimes there are radical differences in what occurs—a horde of small children stampedes onstage, or two gunmen burst in and kill everybody. Each time the scene is reset to the beginning. When the play reaches the ring at the door, Susy does arrive, but so, as the scene resets again and again, do an anonymous "official," a friend of Susy from Australia, and an enormous bird. The speed and surrealism give the play a wild comic edge; but what remains consistent is the undertone of bitterness between the couple ("I've thought for forty years that you were a stupid woman, now I know you're simply nasty," says Brian time and again as the scene continually resets), and what the narrative seems to aspire to—the articulation of Brian's love for his daughter—takes place only once, in the penultimate run. "You are my heart's desire," he tells her—and at once the whole scene begins again, this time cutting itself off as he begins to speak the line for the second time. The narrative structure dramatizes the fact that the expression of love is far rarer than the corrosive rows engendered by a family politics shaped by a society growing less free, as rare as Churchill's carnival bird, which appears only once.

Blue Kettle is also about family politics in a capitalist world—this time, specifically about the marketing of family values. Derek operates a scam: he tracks down women who gave up babies for adoption in their youth and pretends to be their long-lost son. He denies that he is interested in anything but their money; but his motives, and those of the "mothers" he meets, become more complex and opaque as the play progresses. This complexity is partly because language itself is undergoing a metamorphosis, with the words "blue" and "kettle" replacing words the audience comes to expect by their context. At first this substitution occurs only a few times in a scene, and it is always simple to guess the replaced word; it is as if Churchill is combining a naturalistic text with a party game. Later, however, more words are substituted, until the final scene is almost entirely languageless:

> MRS PLANT Tle hate k later k, k bl bl bl shocked.
>
> DEREK K, t see bl.
>
> MRS PLANT T b k k k k l?
>
> DEREK B.K.

This tactic makes for a radical shift in the relationship between actors and audience. The audience is neither passively accepting a naturalistic illusion, or judging a Brechtian *gestus;* rather, the process of decoding forces them to confront the values they normally bring to scenes dealing with mother-child relationships, to select for themselves a vocabulary that is adequate to both the emotional and economic aspects. "Mother," "son," "love," "money," all become fluid signs whose meaning is constantly being negotiated between the actors and the audience. It remains, though, a comic process, a party game in which the possibility of a wrong inflection can lead to a collapse like the fall of a house of cards.

Since the early 1990s Churchill has not been prolific, but the plays she has written continue to challenge actor, director, and audience alike. The short play *Far Away* (performed and published in 2000) shows a world at war. Its opening scenes between a girl, Joan, and her Aunt Harper set out the theme of complicity. Joan wakes in the night to see her uncle loading prisoners on a lorry; she is told that he is "part of a big movement now to make things better." Her willingness to accept the lie is pushed into a deeper complicity: the second section shows her in a workshop making elaborate, fantastic hats—their purpose to enliven processions of the condemned on their way to execution. The image of this parade—Churchill writes, "five is too few and twenty better than ten. A hundred?"—is horrifying. It tempts an audience to respond with delight in its own refined sensibility. It proves, however, to be only a preparation for a more searching analysis. A dialogue between Joan and her coworker Todd deconstructs that very response. They debate the nature of art and beauty—"It seems so sad to burn them [the hats] with the bodies. . . . No, that's the joy of it"—and determine to expose not the realities that horrified the younger Joan but the "corrupt financial basis of how the whole hat industry is run."

The debate pushes the audience further from the assurance that the events of the last century cannot repeat themselves. In fact, it is only logical that the evasions and betrayal implicit in the narrow liberalism of Todd and Joan lead to world war in the literal sense—not simply involving nations, but dragging all existence into destruction. Todd says, matter-of-factly, "I've shot cattle and children in Ethiopia. I've gassed mixed troops of Spanish, computer programmers and dogs. I've torn starlings apart with my bare hands." As the play ends, the audience is confronted with scores of these verbal images, as unstageable as they are disturbing. Joan's last question is "Who's going to mobilize darkness and silence?" The trajectory Churchill traces from a single act of unthinking and almost innocent collaboration to the destruction of a planet is accomplished with such apparent simplicity that its frightening implications only dawn on the audience after the power of the text has already done its work.

In *A Number* (performed and published in 2002), the setting is one of extreme simplicity: two men, "father" and "son," in a room. What makes it troubling is that although the same actors play every scene, each "son" proves to be different—an "original" and two clones, Bernard 1, Bernard 2, and Michael. All three—aware that "a number" of them exist, created by scientists without reference to their future needs or desires—are engaged in a struggle to discover and articulate an identity for themselves. It becomes increasingly apparent, however, that no language exists for their situation. Stories about origins shift. Salter, the "father," tells Bernard 2 that the "original" died in a car crash and that he wanted to replicate his perfection—immediately exposed as a lie as he confesses to Bernard 1 he abandoned him as delinquent in order to start afresh with "the same basic the same raw materials because they were perfect." Bernard 1 destroys Bernard 2 and then himself. Salter searches out the unauthorized clones, and the play closes as he struggles to connect with Michael, who is happy with his life for reasons that undermine all Salter's investment in the notions of individuality and parenthood: "We've got ninety-nine per cent the same genes as any other person. We've got ninety per cent the same as a chimpanzee. We've got thirty per cent the same as a lettuce. Does that cheer you up at all? I love about the lettuce. It makes me feel I belong."

Every mythology of Western selfhood that seems to bear on the story—Cain and Abel, Oedipus, nature and nurture, scientific progress, capitalism—proves inadequate. Salter, Bernard 1, and Bernard 2 all find themselves deprived of a language in which to describe their relationship, and their syntax flounders, as when Bernard 2 says:

> Maybe he shouldn't blame you, maybe it was a genetic, could you help drinking we don't know or drugs at the time philosophically as I understand it it wasn't viewed as not like now when our understanding's different and would a different person not have been so vulnerable because there could always be some genetic additive and then again someone with the same genetic exactly the same but at a different time a different cultural and of course all the personal. . . .

Michael, centered on other people and the world around him, speaking of concrete things such as lettuce and his wife's ears, is the only one at ease with language and himself. *A Number* won the 2002 London *Evening Standard* award for best play.

Caryl Churchill's name may be less well known than those of, say, Harold Pinter or Tom Stoppard, but this relative lack of visibility is a reflection of her continuing engagement with theater rather than with movies, her loyalty to the Royal Court Theatre rather than the larger subsidized theaters (the National Theatre has produced only two of her plays, the Royal Shakespeare Company only one), and her love of personal privacy. However, there is a considerable body of critical material about her, and the critical consensus places her as a major force in shaping the contemporary theatrical landscape. She not only has raised feminist concerns within the theater but also has provided a new theatrical vocabulary with which to investigate sexual politics. Her influence has been acknowledged by playwrights as diverse as Mark Ravenhill and Tony Kushner; it also reaches out to impact coming generations.

Source: Frances Gray, "Caryl Churchill," in *Dictionary of Literary Biography*, Vol. 310, *British and Irish Dramatists Since World War II, Fourth Series*, edited by John Bull, Gale, 2005, pp. 51–65.

Klaus Peter Muller

In the following excerpt, Muller discusses Serious Money *as a "City Comedy," a moralistic genre first established in the seventeenth century. Based*

> "IN CHURCHILL'S PLAY THERE IS NO SIGN OF HOPE AND POSSIBLE IMPROVEMENT. NOT ONLY DO THE TWO ACTS OF HER PLAY REVEAL THAT THE NEGATIVE ELEMENTS PORTRAYED ARE ALL-PERVASIVE, BUT THE SECOND ACT CLEARLY SHOWS THAT EVERYTHING IS IN FACT DETERIORATING."

on his comparisons, Muller concludes that Serious Money *is a satire and not a comedy.*

. . . The audiences' decision to see *Serious Money* either as comedy or satire may explain their different reactions towards the play. Seen as a satire, the play must provide, however indirectly, moral norms which help to formulate value-judgments on the characters and their actions. As "satire is militant irony," and as the "satirist commonly takes a high moral line," morality is obviously an important aspect for the difference between comedy and satire in contemporary definitions. It is also the distinctive feature in the differences of the present-day spectator responses. The "moral line" in *Serious Money* is not so easily detected, however, if it is not seen in connection with the genre, the City Comedy, and its history.

The City Comedy proper was established "by about 1605" with "such plays as Jonson's *Volpone*, Marston's *Dutch Courtezan* and Middleton's *Michaelmas Term*." Churchill's use of Shadwell makes it necessary to remember an English tradition that was already a century old in 1692. The link between the past and the present is consciously established in the modern play, when one of Shadwell's characters, at the end of Churchill's first scene which is taken completely from the end of Act Two in Shadwell's *The Volunteers*, leads the audience into the contemporary world: "Look ye Brethren, hye ye into the city and learn what ye can" (p. 14). The introductory scene in *Serious Money* thus reminds the audience of the tradition of the genre. It also refers to the long history of stockjobbing, which in 1692 was called "the modern Trade, or rather Game." A third effect of the first scene is that it introduces a significant leitmotiv, because one characteristic element of the society of stockjobbers is highlighted, namely that of making use of everything for only one end, "to turn the penny." It is not the utility value of a thing that matters, but only its trade value.

...The keen interest in the social achievements and follies of society that is noticeable in the City Comedy is also valid in *Serious Money*. The old form depicted only part of the society, its negative elements and distorted, dangerous aspects. There was still a chance to reform, though. However indirectly it may have been hinted at in the plays, the audience was quite aware of this possibility. Even when some of Jonson's and Middleton's plays showed that "aggressive individualism has become an accepted behavioral norm and reductive conceptions of human nature hold sway," the reality was regarded as being redeemable. There was still a chance of improvement in human life and history.

In Churchill's play there is no sign of hope and possible improvement. Not only do the two acts of her play reveal that the negative elements portrayed are all-pervasive, but the second act clearly shows that everything is in fact deteriorating. Humanity repeats its mistakes all over again, but on an even greater scale. Churchill uses the third-world-motif to make this evident at the beginning of Act Two. Jacinta Condor flies in to London to buy more Eurobonds and invest her country's money most profitably for herself. Zackerman sarcastically comments upon this and the third world's plight: "Pictures of starving babies are misleading and patronising. Because there's plenty of rich people in those countries, it's just the masses that's poor." The South American, Jacinta, is joined by an African, Nigel Ajibala, "a prince and exceedingly rich," educated at Eton, who expresses his basic education quite simply: "One thing one learned from one's colonial masters, / One makes money from other people's disasters." History thus repeats itself; the former colonies act in the same way as their masters did in the past (and have been doing ever since), or even worse, as they exploit their own people. Nobody is interested in learning from history how the lot of human beings as a whole could be improved; everyone is just madly trying to better his or her personal financial situation. Once again there is no distinction made between men and women.

Is this world only "depicted, not disturbed," as in the City Comedy? Dr. Johnson said about the playwrights of the 17th century that "they pleas'd their age, and did not aim to mend." The audience was seen as "ironically contemplating its viciousness," rather than "'joyfully contemplating its well-being.'" The same can be said about a great number of the spectators of *Serious Money*. Churchill clearly indulges them, by offering intriguing visual effects, music and rhyme. But she also obviously works with exaggerations. She increases the speed of change in our society. She makes clear that this change is for the worse. It is like cancer. She writes about it in verse, making her sentences rhythmical, seemingly light and funny. But what sounds and looks funny, good-humoured, and easy-going actually describes the loss of all human values and an attitude that brings about death. The frivolities of wit or repartee, the language that constitutes for some critics the "most conspicuous quality" of the City Comedy, are found in the modern play with a special destructive macabre twist and often an excessive aggressiveness. The motto in the coat of arms of the London Stock Exchange, *Dictum Meum Pactum* (My word is my bond), for instance, is changed into: "My word is my junk bond." Because of its offensiveness and violence, the glossy, seemingly light presentation does not distract from the cruel facts lurking behind the amusing performance. Whether Jake killed himself or was murdered, his death is inseparable from the world he lived in, from his job and aspirations. Like him, the society, industry, and human life in general will be destroyed. The characters in the play are indeed dancing on a volcano, for "five more glorious years," i.e., as long as the (Thatcher) Government and the people will support this way of life. It is a dance macabre, ingenuously choreographed by Caryl Churchill and intended to be disturbing.

Jake's death and its possible causes have become irrelevant by the end of the play. Corman's take-over deal has been postponed, as the undertaking is unpopular with the public and might damage the election chances of the Tory government. Both items are of minimal importance compared with the vital question of how the basis for the world portrayed can be secured. Its foundation is shown to be the Conservative government of Margaret Thatcher and the political atmosphere it provides. Caryl Churchill has written the portrait of a society, not a play about a murder case or a business transaction. Her topics are more or less the same as in the traditional City Comedies. "Moneymaking" is the most important one. It takes up so much of the characters' time that the "pursuit of women" is reduced to dirty language and greedy looks. "Self-interest" and "survival" are necessary aspects of a world that is thoroughly predatory.

Churchill uses the two-act structure in order to repeat and intensify the images, motifs, topics and themes in her play. The people unscrupulously making serious money continue in their endeavours to be successful. Money and jobs are turned over faster and faster. The speed will increase. The old generation is completely forgotten in the second act, and life is reduced to the amoral game of having a try at being personally successful. It is like a ride on a merry-go-round. But it is evident that the game will end in catastrophe, because it is based on a senseless, self-indulgent egoism destructive of all human values and long-term prospects of human life. The accelerated development towards destruction is vividly captured in the two acts of Churchill's play. Even those of the audience who do not think that the Thatcher government is responsible for such a development can identify with this phenomenon.

The play's theme is certainly not to "assert Eternal Providence, / And justify the ways of God to men," as in Milton's *Paradise Lost*. It is rather "to assert the eternal mechanism of making serious money, how this affects human life and how not to justify the ways of men to men." If the effect on human life is ignored, the play may be regarded as a light, funny city comedy, partly indulging in the mechanism of Bergson's laughter. As a "Serious" City Comedy, however, it encompasses much more than that. *Serious Money* seems to be a satire rather than a comedy. The situation at the end of the play has not improved but deteriorated, the society presented is death-bound. The play employs hunt and war imagery. Society is playing amoral games that destroy human life. It is the object of a satiric attack which takes its moral norm from the human life excluded from or annihilated in the absurd world of the play.

Why then is this moral norm not generally found in the play, and why do so many spectators not feel disturbed by the performance, but rather amused and exhilarated? It is the history of the modern age, the complexity of the contemporary situation, the human predicament of our time that make it particularly difficult to adopt a moral point of view. The situation

presented in the play will not essentially change by replacing a Tory government with a Labour cabinet. The greed disease has too firm a hold. Thus anyone seeing in the play just an attack on the Thatcher government may indeed simply laugh about it and brush it aside as a distortion of reality. The play has a far wider scope. The Conservatives are indeed criticized for supporting the ideology that dominates the play. But it is rather this state of mind as such that the play attacks, the materialistic egoism that destroys all human, life-enhancing values. Although the butt of the satire is shown, nothing is presented that could put an end to the destruction of human life. While the spectator of a traditional City Comedy and of satire was usually presented with, or aware of, a clear view of the remedial system and actual ways of making it real, the contemporary world is largely characterized by the lack of such a system. Neither does our time have anything similar to the concept of the seven deadly sins, i.e., a clear view of evil. Even when basic values are generally acknowledged, there is much disagreement about how to achieve them and what a "normal" and "good" society would actually be like.

Churchill reveals important shortcomings of contemporary (Western?) society, without offering easy solutions. She does not write from a simple feminist position either. By satirizing the seemingly easy-going, playful and amoral attitude of the play's characters, she also makes evident that the postmodern position of *laissez faire* is equally unsatisfactory. Her play requires a modern spectator who is quite conscious of the social and political alternatives at hand. For a self-indulgent yuppie, *Serious Money* can be pure fun. For anyone with a mind for history and moral concern, it is more than that. It is a satire in the traditional sense which has connected satire with morality. It is, at the same time, a comedy in the traditional sense which attributed three elements (and sub-genres) to comedy: humour, wit and satire. Churchill's satirical comedy combines the traditional elements with a typically modern perspective, insofar as her play does not refer to an implicit ideal and a generally accepted morality, but leaves it to the spectator to find ways of improving the present society. For this purpose, knowledge of the history of humanity is required, and knowledge of literary history is helpful.

The term "Serious City Comedy" thus points out the similarities with, and differences from, the traditional genre. The historical awareness needed for an evaluation of the play's effect also helps to place it within the literary tradition. Its place is founded in the history of the modern world, beginning in the Renaissance with its two-sided aspects that we are still wrestling with:

> "the Development of the Individual," "the Revival of Antiquity," "the Discovery of the World and of Man" [on the one hand, and, on the other hand] the thrust of capitalist enterprise, the rise of economic individualism, the development of an amoral "realism" in political thought and action. We are aware, above all, of a great reorientation of attitude that prepared the way not only for the scientific achievements of the seventeenth century and the rationalism of the Enlightenment, but for the materialism of industrial civilization, the spiritual bewilderment of the nineteenth century, and the urgent anxieties of our own time.

Churchill, evoking this past, is today concerned with humanity's future. For her, there has been no "Advancement of Learning" since Bacon, certainly not in our knowledge of "Natural" and "Civil History," nor in our "Moral Culture" or "Civil Knowledge," at least none that has made itself evident in improved living conditions. Humanity rather seems to be "bound / Upon a wheel of fire," with this wheel of human history spinning faster and faster. Churchill can no longer believe, like Hobbes, in a Common-Wealth secured by the authority of "the Civil Sovereign" and founded on "*Faith in Christ,* and *Obedience to Laws.*" To her, "civilization" is not a safeguard anymore, it is destroying itself and about to ruin life altogether.

Churchill has shown in her plays, especially in *Vinegar Tom, Light Shining in Buckinghamshire, Fen* and *Top Girls,* that this destructive course of human history has again and again been unconsciously chosen out of fear and greed, egoism and, above all, fatal ignorance. Many of her characters could say: "What's wrong with me / the way I am? / I know I'm sad. / I may be sick. / I may be bad. / Please cure me quick, / oh doctor." Most of them do not know that the cure is only within themselves. Many do not want to know, because it is painful knowledge demanding hard work. Ellen, burned as a witch in *Vinegar Tom,* understands something of this truth and urges people to "think out what [they] want," to become aware of themselves and their own position. Hoskins in *Light Shining...* wants people to see the "Light shining from us—." But they fail, and the world is still "fraught with tidings of the same clamour, strife and contention that abounded when [they] left it."

Lack of knowledge and concern are the dominant traits in Churchill's view of human history. There is, therefore, profound truth and dramatic irony in Pope Joan's statement in *Top Girls*: "Damnation only means ignorance of the truth." Joan is as ignorant of herself and the world in which she lived as all the other women in the play, those of the past as well as of the present. Ignorance is what they all "have in common" and what makes them "all so miserable." They are also great egoists, which often is a common consequence of ignorance. The least egoistic person, Joyce, is also the least ignorant, and the one most favourably presented in the play.

Only knowledge and humane behaviour could stop humanity's self-destructive progress. This is the history and value-judgment behind the funny, comical, satirical and musical elements of *Serious Money,* too. Under the surface of a light, though aggressive City Comedy there is the threat of death and complete extinction. That is why the play is serious about the need for an historical perspective, for a moral standard and for adequate human action. If these are not found, Churchill indicates, human history will deteriorate in an accelerating spiral of repetition leading to the ultimate annihilation of humankind.

Source: Klaus Peter Muller, "A Serious City Comedy: Fe-/Male History and Value Judgments in Caryl Churchill's *Serious Money,*" in *Modern Drama,* Vol. 33, No. 3, September 1990, 13 pp.

Robert Brustein

In the following review, Brustein classifies Serious Money *as a satire. Though Brustein feels that the plot is too "complicated" and that the characters lack humanity, he nevertheless claims that the themes in* Serious Money *are so important that the play transcends these shortcomings.*

Caryl Churchill writes hard-boiled, unpredictable, untidy plays, and with *Serious Money,* now playing at the Public Theater, she is at the top of her disheveled form. I was first exposed to the left hook of this unusual English dramatist when her early work *Owners* opened at a London fringe theater in 1972. It was a play about rackrenting in the East End, a terse treatment of social injustice in a style of episodic realism—ironic, cold, and detached enough to disguise a subterranean fury. The arresting thing about *Owners* was not its relatively conventional form so much as its disinterested radical posture. A product of a fiercely independent mind, it offered a negative Marxist critique unblemished by Marxist

> UNDERNEATH HER FEROCIOUS IRONY LIES
> AN UNDERSTANDING THAT THE WORST EXCESSES OF
> CAPITALISM CAN BE EXCITING AND ENGROSSING,
> WHICH IS WHY SO MANY INTELLIGENT, DYNAMIC
> PEOPLE TODAY ARE ATTRACTED TO BUSINESS. BUT
> SHE IS ALSO CONSCIOUS OF HOW DEBILITATING
> SUCH PRACTICES CAN BE TO THE BRAIN AND
> SPIRIT—OF HOW 'WHEN THE TRADING STOPS, YOU
> DON'T KNOW WHAT TO DO WITH YOUR MIND.'"

ideology. Since that time, in such plays as *Cloud Nine*, *Fen*, and *Top Girls*, Churchill has been experimenting with more fantastical techniques, but her remorseless inquest into the English social system continues unabated. *Serious Money* may be the most incisive autopsy she has yet attempted.

It is also an extremely difficult, sometimes even repellent play. *Serious Money* is a prodigiously researched examination of the workings of the world's money markets, where virtually all recognizable human feeling is subordinated to a passion for acquisition. American drama is often faulted for lacking public dimension. What's missing from *Serious Money* is any sign of private emotion other than covetousness. This, I gather, is precisely Churchill's point. In the world of money, all vestiges of softer virtues—love, loyalty, friendship, family feeling, the aesthetic sense—must be ruthlessly eliminated as obstacles in the path of profit; venality is the foundation stone of political and financial empire. In *Serious Money*, Plutus and Hobbes are reincarnated in the shape of Ivan Boesky (his spirit also informs the recently released movie *Wall Street*), whose much-quoted tribute to greed as the basis for the health and wealth of nations is the theme of the play.

The result is a dramatis personae of ruthless robots whose behavior seems as automated as the computer systems they use to conduct their corporate raids, mergers, takeovers, deals, and arbitrages. The setting for *Serious Money* might be a Pac-Man game: a maze of squeaking mouths devouring other mouths and getting gobbled up in turn. These hungry mouths are filled not only

with corporate corpses but with venal epigrams: "You don't make money out of land, you make money out of money." "Being in debt is the best way to be rich." "Anyone who can buy oranges for ten and sell at eleven in a souk or bazaar has the same human nature and can go equally far." One character would like to own "a big cube of sea, right down to the bottom, all the fish, weeds, the lot, there'd be takers for that." Another prefers a square meter of space "and a section of God at the top." Corporations are in business not to produce products but to produce money, and governments (also moneymaking machines) exist to facilitate the process through deregulation.

The play begins with a scene from Thomas Shadwell's Restoration comedy *The Volunteers* (subtitled *The Stockjobbers*) involving the disposition of stocks and patents in the City of London, as if to prove that the System hasn't changed a bit through the ages. Churchill then proceeds to compose a cacophonous opera, simultaneously conducted in three different dealing rooms, the performers being jobbers and brokers screaming numbers at each other. (Audaciously, she has written most of the work in rhymed couplets and overlapping dialogue, which accentuates the bedlam.) Gradually, a kind of plot emerges out of the Babel of buying and selling. A corporate raider named Billy Corman is preparing to take over an old-fashioned firm called Albion (England?), which commands the loyalty of its employees and the support of the local community. Jake Todd, an industrial spy, has died under suspicious circumstances, and Scilla, his stock-dealing sister, appears determined to discover the cause of his death.

But Scilla, cheerfully admitting she is "greedy and completely amoral," is really more interested in placing herself on the ladder of financial transaction. And, though Jake may actually be a suicide, she manages through bullying and blackmail to attain a profitable position of power from those implicated in his death. Churchill is a feminist, but one of her theatrical virtues (also displayed in *Top Girls*, is a capacity to create female characters as covetous and corruptible as her males. (She is equally democratic toward black American dealers and African plutocrats.) Perhaps the most cunning figure in the play is a Peruvian businesswoman named Jacinta Condor who, when not speculating on the London metal exchange, is selling cocaine and paying off the *contras*. And perhaps the most chilling scene concerns Jacinta's unsuccessful effort to make a date with a young American banker, when both are too busy arranging deals to find an hour for lunch or dinner.

The takeover of Albion is complicated by white knights and competitive bids and a government investigation, so Corman drops his interest' in the firm in return for knighthood. As "Lord" Corman, he must improve his public image. A p.r. consultant advises him to think of culture: "You need the National / Theatre for power, opera for decadence, / String quartets bearing your name for sensitivity and elegance, / And a fringe show with bad language for a thrill. " Corman becomes chairman of the board of the National Theatre. The cause of Jake's death is never determined. Jacinta starts dealing in China. Scilla becomes a rising star on Wall Street. Other characters become ambassadors or run for president of the United States or end up in jail. And the play ends with a rousing finale called "Five More Glorious Years," a tribute to the triumph of greed under Margaret Thatcher.

It is, as someone says, a dangerous system that could crash at any minute, but it is a source of incredible, if misguided, vitality, and it drives the play. None of Churchill's rapacious birds and beasts of prey has a recognizably human moment, but then neither do the cormorants of Ben Jonson's *Volpone* or Henri Becque's *The Vultures* or Bertolt Brecht's *Saint Joan of the Stockyards*, the satiric tradition to which *Serious Money* belongs. Like her mordant predecessors, Churchill seems to have a sneaking admiration for the foibles of cheats and charlatans. Underneath her ferocious irony lies an understanding that the worst excesses of capitalism can be exciting and engrossing, which is why so many intelligent, dynamic people today are attracted to business. But she is also conscious of how debilitating such practices can be to the brain and spirit—of how "when the trading stops, you don't know what to do with your mind."

Max Stafford-Clark's all-English production is serviceable, if not altogether satisfying. The setting is not sufficiently abstract to accommodate the almost cinematic scenic structure; and the doubling, trebling, and (in the case of Allan Corduner) even quadrupling of roles compounds the confusion of what is already a difficult-to-distinguish cast of characters. (In a company of 16, for some reason, eight actors play the 20 principal parts.) The production numbers have

a percussive punchiness, though they occasionally look like a varsity show, and the director usually navigates effectively through the verbose maze of the rhymed verse. But the absence of a human dimension in the writing prevents the acting from becoming truly distinguished, and the plot is too complicated to be absorbed in a single sitting. As a result, *Serious Money* is not a truly successful work of theater. But it is something considerably more important—a scathing social anatomy of the greedy scavengers feeding on the rotting economic flesh of the West.

Source: Robert Brustein, "Birds and Beasts of the West," in *New Republic*, Vol. 198. No. 3, January 18, 1988, pp. 27–28.

SOURCES

Bennetts, Leslie, "Frenetic Pace in *Serious Money*," in the *New York Times*, January 28, 1988, p. C21.

Churchill, Caryl, *Serious Money*, Methuen, 1987, pp. 21–22, 25, 28, 38–39, 60.

Hodgson, Moira, Review of *Serious Money*, in the *Nation*, January 16, 1988, p. 65.

Homa, Lynn, "*Serious Money* Portrays Recent Financial Foibles as Serious Fun," in *American Banker*, December 31, 1987, Vol. 152, No. 255, p. 12.

Hoover, Ted, Review of *Serious Money*, in the *Pittsburgh City Paper*, March 3, 2004, Vol. 14, No. 8, p. 36.

Koehler, Robert, "*Serious Money*: Wheeling and Dealing at Berkeley Rep," in the *Los Angeles Times*, July 11, 1989, p. 5.

Lyall, Sarah, "The Mysteries of Caryl Churchill," in the *New York Times*, December 5, 2004, p. 2.9.

Rich, Frank, "The Stage: *Serious Money*," in the *New York Times*, December 4, 1987, p. C3.

Silk, Leonard, "Is Wall Street as Bad as It's Painted?," in the *New York Times*, January 3, 1988, p. A20.

FURTHER READING

Geisst, Charles R., *Wall Street: A History: From Its Beginnings to the Fall of Enron*, Oxford University Press, 2004. Geisst provides a provocative history of Wall Street, from crash to boom. This is the first history of Wall Street and it provides a glimpse at the enormous influence that Wall Street has come to bear on national and world affairs.

Hall, Roger, *Writing Your First Play*, Focal Press, 1998. Hall teaches dramatic arts at James Madison University, and his book guides students in writing a play. In this book, Hall explains dramatic form and discusses fundamentals such as developing a voice and how to choose a point of view.

Komporaly, Jozefina, *Staging Motherhood: British Women Playwrights, 1956 to the Present*, Palgrave Macmillan, 2007.

Komporaly explores the changing role of female playwrights in the United Kingdom from the 1950s through the twenty-first century. She addresses the impact of personal life on female playwrights as seen through their

dramatic works and the transformations of women's position in society as reflected in the playwrights's staged productions.

Stewart, James B., *Den of Thieves*, Simon & Schuster, 1992.

This bestselling book about some of the biggest and best-known crooks on Wall Street will fill in details about such characters as Ivan Boesky, Michael Milken, Martin Siegel, and Dennis Levine, best remembered for their insider trading violations in the 1980s.

Stanley

PAM GEMS

1996

Stanley, by British playwright Pam Gems, is about the life of Sir Stanley Spencer (1891–1959), one of the most renowned British artists of the twentieth century. The play, which was first produced in London in 1996, is available and still in print in an edition published by Nick Hern Books that same year. The play covers about thirty-five years in Spencer's life, from the early days of his initially happy marriage to fellow artist Hilda Carline, to his last days spent in a solitary pursuit of his art. The focus of the play is on Spencer's tortured relationships with Hilda and another artist, Patricia Preece. Spencer became infatuated with Preece and divorced Hilda in order to marry her; the triangular emotional involvement proved disastrous for all concerned. In her play, Gems presents Spencer as a visionary artist who loves to share his ideas about God, art, creativity, and sex, but who is also selfish, childish, and egotistical—a man who is willing to damage other people's lives in order to fulfill his own needs and desires. The play was nominated for an Antoinette Perry (Tony) award in 1997.

AUTHOR BIOGRAPHY

English dramatist and novelist Pam Gems was born August 1, 1925, in Bransgore, Hampshire, England; the daughter of Jim and Elsie Mabel (Annetts) Price. After attending Brockenhurst County Grammar School, she served in the

Pam Gems *(© Lebrecht Music and Arts Photo Library / Alamy)*

WRENS (Women's Royal Naval Service) during World War II. After the war, Gems attended the University of Manchester, and she graduated with a Bachelor of Arts degree in 1949. In the same year, she married Peter Gems, and the couple had four children.

Gems worked at a variety of jobs in the early part of her life, including as a charwoman, chambermaid, street vendor, antique dealer, clerk-typist, mannequin and furniture designer, sheetmetal worker, shop assistant, hatcheck girl, cashier, and factory worker. From 1950 to 1953, she was a research assistant for the British Broadcasting Corporation (BBC).

Gems did not start writing plays until she was in her forties and had raised her children. Her earliest plays were written for a feminist collective, Almost Free Theatre, in London. In 1976, she first reached a wider audience when her play *Dead Fish*, about four girls who share a London apartment, was produced at the Edinburgh Festival.

The play, retitled *Dusa, Fish, Stas, and Vi*, then had a successful run in London. The following year, Gems's play, *Queen Christina*, about a seventeenth century Swedish queen, was produced by the Royal Shakespeare Company.

Since then Gems has written many successful plays, many of which focus on feminist themes such as the need for women to discover their own authentic place in a male-dominated society. Some of her best known plays include *Piaf* (1978), based on the life of the singer Edith Piaf, *Loving Women* (1976), *Aunt Mary* (1982), *The Danton Affair* (1986), *Deborah's Daughter* (1994), *Stanley* (1996), which won the 1997 Laurence Olivier Award for Best Play, and *Marlene* (1996), which was based on the life of the movie star Marlene Dietrich. Gems's most recent play is *The Snow Palace*; it was produced in Chicago in 2000.

Gems has also written two novels, *Mrs. Frampton* (1989) and its sequel, *Bon Voyage, Mrs. Frampton* (1990).

PLOT SUMMARY

Act 1, Scenes 1–3

The first scene of *Stanley* begins in the studio of English artist Stanley Spencer, where he is working on a painting. The music of Bach plays on a gramophone. The date is the mid-1920s. Hilda, Stanley's wife, enters and tries to talk to Stanley, but he is absorbed in his work. She gets him to talk about his ideas about painting, and he says its purpose is to reveal the world through love. He also recalls some of the horrors of World War I, in which he fought. After they recall when they first met and the attraction they felt toward each other, Stanley says he expects the painting he is working on to silence his critics, and Hilda assures him he is brilliant.

In scene 2, at a London studio, Hilda and Stanley sit around talking and drinking with Dudley (Stanley's agent), and their artist friends, Gwen and Henry. They are soon joined by the artist Augustus John, Dorothy Hepworth, and her friend, Patricia Preece. John and Stanley indulge in some horseplay, and then the conversation turns to art. Stanley expresses his theories about painting from the heart not the head, and mentions his painting, "The Apple Gatherers," which took him a year to finish. He shares some childhood memories of growing up in a happy home. As everyone starts to leave, Patricia, who is a lesbian and lives with Dorothy, gazes at Stanley, sizing him up and expressing her interest.

Scene 3 takes place in Stanley's bedroom. Hilda undresses and gets into bed with Stanley, assuring him that nothing will ever come between them, but Stanley says she does not deserve his complete love and devotion. He reveals his attraction towards Patricia and criticizes Hilda, accusing her of not liking his ideas about art.

Stanley goes to nearby Moor Thatch, where Patricia and Dorothy live. Patricia poses for Stanley, who sketches her. She says that she and Dorothy are both painters but are unable to sell their work. Stanley makes a sexual advance to her. After he leaves, Dorothy and Patricia quarrel. Patricia throws things at her and they fight, with Dorothy pinning Patricia's arm. After they are reconciled, Dorothy tells her not to flirt with Stanley; Patricia reveals that she has contempt for him but plans to use him to her advantage.

Act 1, Scenes 4–6

Hilda enters scene 4 with a baby in a pram, but Stanley does not take much notice. He also reveals that he took the violets Hilda gave him to Patricia. They quarrel.

Across on the other side of the stage, Patricia reveals her dislike of Hilda to Dorothy, because Hilda told Augustus John she thought Patricia was a narcissist. She undresses in readiness for Stanley, who is coming to paint her.

Hilda feeds the baby, but Stanley says he cannot work with the baby in the room. He feels neglected by Hilda.

Stanley crosses to Patricia's side of the stage and paints her, saying he will buy her gifts. He is infatuated with her. Back with Hilda, he continues to complain that she is neglecting him. He feels he has a right to her attention. As Elsie the maid and Hilda admire the baby, Stanley escapes.

Scene 5 takes place at a party at Stanley's newly bought house, Lindworth, in the village of Cookham. Patricia is dressed as Narcissus, Dorothy as Oscar Wilde, Stanley as Hilda and Hilda as Stanley. Stanley puts up some paintings for display. He explains one painting to Patricia, who shows no interest, but eventually says, as the others praise his work, that it is a work of genius. She is insincere, but Stanley is pleased by her compliment.

Patricia confronts Dudley, who has been unable to mount a show for her. She says he had better do so, or she will have to marry Stanley, although she speaks of him in derogatory terms. After the guests have left, Stanley goes to see Patricia, looking at her through a window. He tells Hilda he must paint Patricia, and adds that he thinks she is pursuing him, and that he is pursuing her. He and Hilda look at each other, alarmed.

In scene 6, Patricia complains to Dorothy that she does not have enough money to buy the clothes she needs. She says that Stanley can be useful to her because he knows so many people and has influence. She plans to marry him.

Act 1, Scenes 7–9

In scene 7, Patricia accompanies Stanley to a shop, where he buys her expensive silk lingerie and black stockings. He then gives her a necklace.

In scene 8, Hilda poses for Stanley and warns him that he is making a fool of himself over Patricia and that she may not be what she seems. He says he can feel spiritually close to more than one woman, and Hilda gives him permission to go to London with Patricia.

In scene 9, Stanley and Patricia are in a field on a hillside. Stanley is sketching and talks about how he loves the spring. She suggests that he put his house in her name. It appears that they have agreed to marry, although Patricia does not welcome his sexual advances.

With a distressed Hilda on one side of the stage and Patricia on the other, Stanley crosses back and forth between them. Stanley accuses Hilda of deserting him, but she points out that it is the other way round. She is lonely without him. He replies that he deserves to have Patricia; he paints himself and Patricia nude. Hilda protests at how little money he is offering her, but he tells her he wants no further connection with her.

After Stanley and Patricia marry, she says she will get him all the women he wants; she and Dorothy will go to St. Ives, Cornwall, while he remains at home and can see Hilda, who still loves him. Patricia and Dorothy set off for Cornwall, leaving Stanley bewildered.

Act 2, Scenes 1–3

Arriving at Stanley's house in scene 1, Hilda is surprised to find that Stanley is still there and Patricia is in Cornwall with Dorothy. Stanley shows her portraits of himself and Patricia nude, saying that Dudley thinks they will not sell. He and Hilda say they have missed each other, and they make love.

Scene 2 takes place on the beach at St. Ives, where Patricia and Dorothy are painting seascapes. Patricia talks of her plan to get more income by renting out Stanley's house, which is now in her name. She talks of taking a foreign vacation, but Dorothy is uncomfortable with the idea of living off Stanley. Patricia says the money is hers and she is doing it to help Dorothy. She reveals that she has not allowed Stanley to touch her; all she does is sit for him.

In scene 3, Hilda and Stanley eat in the garden and speculate over whether their lovemaking constitutes adultery. Hilda says even if it does, she does not care. Stanley leads her to believe that they can be together again; she does not understand the full situation, thinking that Stanley and Patricia have split up. Then Stanley explains that Patricia will allow him to have two women. Hilda is angry at being invited back as a mistress.

Act 2, Scenes 4–6

At Augustus John's studio in scene 4, Stanley says he should be allowed to have two women. John humors him, and then Stanley criticizes him for doing portrait-painting just because it brings in money. He adds that he misses Hilda.

Scene 5 takes place at Hilda's family home in Hampstead, London. Hilda's mother, Mrs. Carline, reproaches Stanley for divorcing Hilda. She tells him that the present situation involving two women cannot go on, and that he should say goodbye to Hilda and their two daughters for good. Mrs. Carline invites them to join her in silent prayer, after which she leaves. Stanley asks Hilda to return to live with him and accept the fact that he needs more than one woman. He says he has never not wanted her; she softens but is still not reconciled to the situation.

In scene 6, Stanley arrives at Gwen's house. He is worried about money, since Dudley cannot sell his work because it is too erotic and shocks people. Stanley says that Patricia has rented his house out and only allows him in the studio. Dudley and Henry enter. Stanley tries to justify himself, but Henry criticizes him, and Stanley lunges at him. But then Henry makes it clear he admires Stanley's work, at which Stanley breaks down and cries.

Act 2, Scenes 7–9

Hilda visits Dorothy at the cottage in Cornwall in scene 7, but Patricia interrupts them. She asks Hilda if she will come back to Cookham. Hilda says she will if Patricia divorces Stanley. Patricia refuses, and also says she will not give the house back to Hilda. Patricia asks again if Hilda will come back, since the situation puts her, Patricia, in a bad light. No one in the village will speak to her. Hilda says that Patricia is using Stanley as a means of paying her debts. Hilda leaves, her silence an indication that she is refusing Patricia's terms.

In scene 8, Hilda is in a mental institution. Dudley visits, and she inquires after Stanley's health. She is worried about him because of his debts. She writes a check to Stanley for five thousand pounds and signs it Mrs. Perkins. Dudley is baffled.

In scene 9, Stanley visits Hilda in the hospital. It is now after World War II, and Stanley has been working in Glasgow. Stanley wants her to come and live with him. He plans to get a divorce from Patricia and remarry Hilda. Hilda says she needs to get better before she can make a decision.

Act 2, Scenes 10–12

In scene 10, Stanley paints while Hilda observes. She complains that Patricia stole Stanley from her; he says he misses her, but she replies that it is too late for them to be together. She says she will have nothing to do with Patricia and cannot bear the idea of Stanley's divorce from her, since that would imply that he she had been a wife to him.

Stanley visits Patricia in scene 11, but Dorothy says she will not see him. Stanley has come seeking her agreement to an annulment of their marriage, but Dorothy says Patricia will not agree to it. Patricia enters and she and Stanley have a fierce argument in which they both finally say in highly uncomplimentary terms what they think of each other. She spits at him and hands him some of the bills she has incurred for her work and tells him he must pay them. After Stanley leaves, Patricia cries and Dorothy comforts her.

In scene 12, Hilda is in the hospital with breast cancer, awaiting surgery. Stanley says it will be all right and that he will be there.

Act 2, Scenes 13–14

In scene 13, which is wordless, Stanley sits at Hilda's bedside. They smile at each other and he holds her hand.

Scene 14 begins on the streets of Cookham, where local people congratulate Stanley on his knighthood. He is now Sir Stanley Spencer. A reporter interviews Patricia, who says that Stanley's work is either vulgar or deranged. Dorothy, on the other hand, gives the reporter a positive evaluation of Stanley's work. The play ends with a monologue by Stanley, alone on stage as he works. He talks appreciatively to Hilda, who has been dead for some years. He tells her she is the only person he can really talk to and that she is there in his imagination. He talks about his work, saying that an artist is a mediator between God and man.

CHARACTERS

Mrs. Carline

Mrs. Carline is Hilda's mother. She is a very religious woman who tries to resolve the awkward situation between Hilda and Stanley. Stanley is not impressed by her conventional religious beliefs, which differ from his own views about religion.

Elsie

Elsie is maid to the Spencers. Stanley finds her sexually attractive and likes to watch her as she works.

Gwen

Gwen is an artist. She is very supportive of Stanley and his work. She is based on the artist Gwen Raverat, formerly Gwen Darwin, the granddaughter of the naturalist, Charles Darwin.

Henry

Henry is an artist friend of Stanley's. He is a spirited character who is always ready for an argument about art. He admires Stanley's work. Henry is based on the real-life artist, Henry Lamb.

Dorothy Hepworth

Dorothy Hepworth is a painter who has had little success in selling her paintings. She is a lesbian and lives with Patricia Preece, with whom she has a stormy relationship. Dorothy is a more reasonable and likeable woman than Patricia. She shows some friendliness to Hilda and feels uncomfortable about Patricia's plan for the two of them to live off Stanley's money. Dorothy is based on a real-life artist of the same name, who lived from 1898 to 1978. Hepworth met Patricia Preece in 1917 when they were both students at the Slade School of Art in London.

Augustus John

Augustus John is a painter and friend of Stanley's. He calls Stanley "Cookham," a reference to Stanley's attachment to the village in which he lives, and they have some good-natured arguments. John has a reputation for lechery; he befriends Patricia and tries to seduce her. Augustus John was a renowned British painter who lived from 1878 to 1961.

Patricia Preece

Patricia Preece is an upper-class woman who aspires to be a successful painter. She is a lesbian and lives with fellow artist Dorothy Hepworth. Patricia is a vain, superficial, manipulative, narcissistic woman. She cynically plays on Stanley's desire for her while using him as a means of paying her bills and advancing her career. She has no interest in his art and urges him to paint landscapes, which he does not like to do, simply because it is an easy way for him to make money, which she thinks will be of benefit to her. When she and Stanley marry, she immediately goes off to live with Dorothy, and she never allows Stanley to make love to her. She tricks him into putting his house in her name and then evicts him. She also refuses him a divorce. In real life, Patricia Preece (1900–1971) met Dorothy when they were art students in London. Patricia's art received some attention between the two world wars, although much of it may have been Dorothy's work sold under Patricia's name.

Hilda Spencer

Hilda Spencer is Stanley's wife. She is completely in love with Stanley and remains loyal to him. In the first scene of the play, it is clear that she knows how to get along with Stanley. She shows interest in him, asking him questions about himself, and listening to what he says. As a fellow artist, she understands and appreciates his work. She also understands him personally more than anyone else does, and she tolerates his weaknesses, even making excuses for his bad behavior. She seems willing to take a subordinate role in their relationship and is quite self-sacrificial. It is as if she feels she does not deserve to have happiness with Stanley, or that she has no rights in the relationship. At one point, she even says that Stanley must go with Patricia if that is what he wants to do. But later in their marriage, she is pushed to her limit by Stanley's rejection of her and his involvement with Patricia, which hurts her deeply. She also seems to acquire a determination that she lacked before, telling Stanley (in act 1, scene 8), that he has no right to push her out of the way. After the divorce, Hilda goes into a decline. Her health deteriorates; she does not have enough money to live on, and she feels that the world is a cold, lonely place. She tells Stanley that what he is doing is murder. Eventually Hilda's health breaks down and she is admitted to a mental hospital with delusions. When Stanley tries to be reconciled with her, she refuses to return to live with him unless he has nothing to do with Patricia. Only when she is ill with breast cancer do she and Stanley fully reconcile, but by then it is almost too late, since she dies shortly after. In reality, Stanley Spencer met Hilda Carline in 1919, when she was an art student. They married in 1925, and she bore him two children.

Stanley Spencer

Stanley Spencer is an artist known for the religious content of his paintings and also for their eroticism. He believes that art must be motivated by love and passion, and that the erotic is the key to understanding religion. He also has a deep, child-like appreciation of nature. However, although he is an immensely gifted artist, Stanley is an egotistical, self-centered man who is unable to maintain mature, happy relationships with the women in his life. He feels that other people are there to serve his own needs, and he is particularly hard on his devoted wife, Hilda. He expects constant support and encouragement from her, thinking it is her job to inspire him and listen to him as he explains his ideas about art. But he reserves the right to criticize her, complaining that since she gave birth to children, she is no longer attractive to him. He also resents the attention she gives the children, which he feels should be given to him instead. In fact, he takes very little notice of his own children, so wrapped up is he in his artistic visions. Because Stanley is frustrated by the deterioration in his relationship with Hilda, he becomes infatuated with Patricia, whom he finds sexually attractive. But he turns out to be a poor judge of character, and is unable to see that Patricia is manipulating him and is interested only in cheating him out of his money and his house. Even while he is involved with Patricia, Stanley wants to continue sexual

relations with Hilda, on the grounds that whatever he wants, he should be allowed to have because it will feed his artistic genius. After he finally has an acrimonious split with Patricia, he is reconciled to Hilda and wants to remarry her, but she refuses. Stanley lives on for nine years after Hilda's death in 1950. These are years in which the quality of his art is finally recognized by the public, and he receives a knighthood. He retains his deep attachment to Hilda, carrying on imaginary conversations with her. In the final scene, he is alone, talking to Hilda about his work. He seems happy, despite the failure of his closest relationships. He claims not to be lonely or to feel sorrow. It is his art that is the most important thing for him, and he tells Hilda about his belief that the artist is the mediator between God and man.

Dudley Tooth

Dudley Tooth is Stanley's art dealer. He reports that he has difficulty in selling Stanley's controversial erotic work. He also agrees to help Patricia's career, but she complains that he has not come through on his promise.

THEMES

God, Sex, and the Creative Imagination

Stanley has a very high-minded approach to his art. He has a strongly developed religious sense, and he believes that the artist is a mediator between God and man. He sees his art as being produced for the glory of God. At several points in the play, he reflects on the nature of his art and the source of his creative imagination. He places great store on the innocent purity of perception he associates with childhood, and he also sees love as playing an essential role in art. The painter must be able "to reveal the nature of the world. Through love," he tells Hilda in act 1 scene 1. He also insists several times that art should come from the heart, even though that may be more difficult than painting from the mind. He means he does not have an intellectual approach to his work; he prefers to cultivate feeling and passion. For Stanley, creative imagination is God speaking and creating through him; he seems almost to regard the paintings as a cooperative venture between himself and God. Stanley also sees no division between the spiritual and the sensual aspects of life. He states bluntly that he is "convinced that the erotic is

TOPICS FOR FURTHER STUDY

- Find some reproductions of paintings by Stanley Spencer. Print them out from the Internet or make copies from books, and use your printouts in a class presentation about the painter's work. Describe your own response to these paintings. Do you like them? Why, or why not? Which paintings do you prefer? What was the artist trying to convey in the paintings?

- Research the topic of narcissism. How did the condition get its name? How would you recognize a narcissistic personality? How is the condition defined and how is it treated? Write an essay in which you discuss your findings.

- Many artists and poets, including Spencer, William Blake (*Songs of Innocence and of Experience*), William Wordsworth ("Ode: Intimations of Immortality") and Dylan Thomas ("Fern Hill") have idealized childhood. Write an essay in which you examine these paintings and poems and explain why such creative artists value childhood so highly. Why do they look back so nostalgically at childhood? Is the child's way of seeing the world something to be emulated or outgrown? In what sense is this so? What is lost in the transition to adulthood?

- In the play, Stanley speaks frequently about the sources of his creativity. Investigate creativity in art, literature and science. What have other writers, artists and composers said about their own creative process? How do great works get written? What conditions favor creativity? What is the secret of it? What is the difference between, say, the creativity of Mozart and that of Vincent van Gogh? Does suffering help or hinder creativity? Conduct a class presentation on the topic.

the essence of religion." He believes he can access the spiritual through the physical, and this accounts for his interest in painting nude women and his need to satisfy his sexual desires with more than one woman. He regards sexual fulfillment as necessary for his creativity to flourish, since it makes him feel more fully alive. Just as he acknowledges no distinction between the spiritual and the sexual, he sees no division between the divine and the mundane realms. It is this religious vision that enables him to create paintings in which Biblical figures such as Christ and the Apostles appear in the village of Cookham, as when the apostles are presented watching some local boys playing hopscotch. This suggests that the divine can be found anywhere, even in the most mundane of settings.

Selfishness and Narcissism versus Self-Sacrificial Love

Stanley is a self-centered individual. He puts his own needs above those of others; he has convinced himself that because he is a prominent artist, he deserves to have others cater to his needs so that he can continue to produce the best art he is capable of. Many examples can be cited from the play. In act 1, scene 4, when he is feeling frustrated with Hilda because he thinks she is giving too much attention to the babies and not enough to him, he says, "If I'm to work I have to feel right, and people have to see to it that I'm all right and not feeling riled or fed up." Stanley can rarely see beyond his own desires. When he complains that he does not want to pay alimony to Hilda, like a child he exclaims, "You're stopping me from doing what I want!" an attitude he repeats in act 2, scene 3, when he insists to Hilda that he needs to have two women: "This is what I want, it's what I need."

Patricia, the woman Stanley become infatuated with, is even more narcissistic. (Narcissism refers to an excessive concern with one's self and a belief in one's own importance.) She is thoroughly vain and feels she has a right to have everything she wants, even if it means cynically manipulating Stanley. Attention is brought to her narcissism when she reports to Dorothy the visit she paid to Sigmund Freud in London. Freud appears to have diagnosed her as a narcissistic personality and given her a book to read about the condition. Patricia describes the symptoms to Dorothy, which include manipulating others, but she does not take the diagnosis seriously. She cannot see her own faults because she is too full of her own sense of entitlement.

Set against the two narcissistic personalities, Stanley and Patricia, are the long-suffering Hilda, and, to a lesser extent, Dorothy. Hilda genuinely loves Stanley and is self-sacrificial in her attitudes. She is willing to put up with Stanley's bad behavior, and she never withdraws her love. Readers may feel, however, that just as Stanley and Patricia are too selfish, Hilda is too selfless. She is unable to stand up for herself and so allows her narcissistic husband to be emotionally abusive.

Dorothy, who appears to be a down-to-earth woman with some common sense, also seems willing to put up with Patricia's selfishness, even though she finds her partner's behavior confusing and upsetting. Indeed, none of these four major characters is able to find a balance in his or her personality that would enable them to forge successful, fulfilling relationships.

STYLE

Staging

The play's dynamic revolves around Stanley's relationships with two women, each of whom represents something different to him. This is represented on stage by the split scenes in which Hilda is on one side of the stage and Patricia is on the other. Stanley crosses from one to the other, showing by his physical movement the restlessness of his personality, drawn to one woman for the ways in which she meets his needs and then to another to supply the needs the first woman cannot fulfill.

This first happens in act 1, scenes 3 and 4. In the latter, there is a contrast between what the two women are doing: Hilda pays attention to the baby and ignores Stanley, and he immediately crosses the stage, where Patricia lies naked and Stanley sketches her. After Patricia invites him to give her gifts, speaking of diamonds and sapphires, Stanley crosses the stage once more back to Hilda, where the two quarrel as Hilda holds "a battered enamel pisspot"; the contrast between the alluring glamour of Patricia and the domesticity represented by Hilda is sharp.

The same contrast is apparent in act 1, scene 9, in which Hilda sits at the side of the stage, in hat and coat, with her handbag, while Stanley makes a sexual advance to Patricia. Then just after Hilda speaks, on the other side of the stage Patricia undresses slowly in preparation for Stanley to sketch her. This alternation between

Patricia and Hilda continues throughout the scene, as Hilda pleads for Stanley to return while Patricia continues her heartless manipulation of the painter. The split in Stanley's personality, his attempt to create a kind of psychic wholeness by having intimate relationships with two women, is therefore visually represented in the positioning of the three characters within single scenes.

Wordlessness and Monologue

The play includes one unusual device: an entirely wordless scene (act 2, scene 13), that makes its point by gesture and symbolism. Hilda is in her hospital bed and Stanley sits by her side. He holds her hand and after a long moment in which they are motionless, she turns her head slowly towards him and smiles at him. This demonstrates without words that Hilda, for all that she has had to endure at Stanley's hands, retains her love for him. She seems endlessly forgiving, almost to the point of becoming a martyr. He smiles at her, indicating how he still values and needs her, despite his appalling behavior toward her. When the lights change, Stanley is in a black overcoat, a suitably somber attire, as if he is at a funeral. Indeed, this is the last time he sees Hilda, who is in fact on her death bed. The bed is then taken away, and Stanley gets his pram and sets up his outdoor easel. The pram is a poignant symbol. Stanley never took much interest in his children, preferring to pursue his vision as an artist, so the fact that the pram contains his working tools is appropriate to the character. The pram also conveys the idea that Stanley remains a child at heart, unable to establish rewarding adult relationships. It is fitting that the play ends with his long monologue, in which he talks to the dead Hilda. Since Stanley is a narcissistic personality, the subject of his conversation is always himself, so it is appropriate that the dramatist shows him at the end, essentially talking to himself, and apparently quite happy to do so.

HISTORICAL CONTEXT

Life of Stanley Spencer

The British painter Stanley Spencer was born in the village of Cookham-on-Thames in 1891. Growing up in a large family, he had a happy childhood, as the several references to childhood in Stanley confirm. His father was an organist

COMPARE
&
CONTRAST

- **1920s:** Britain is still recovering from World War I, in which nearly a million of its citizens died. Veterans must deal with the psychological trauma suffered on the battlefield. Such stress is referred to as shell shock. Some recover quickly; others still feel the effects many years later.

  1950s: World War II veterans are dealing with shell shock, which is now referred to as battle fatigue or combat fatigue. Britain recovers from World War II; rationing ends and a prosperous consumer society emerges.

  Today: Britain fights wars in Afghanistan and Iraq. Veterans receive more support in dealing with the mental trauma that follows exposure to combat. The condition is now referred to as post-traumatic stress disorder.

- **1920s:** Divorce in Britain is based on fault; one person must be declared the guilty party. Grounds for divorce include adultery.

  1950s: A Royal Commission is set up in 1951 to propose possible changes in the Matrimonial Causes Act of 1937. Changing social attitudes lead to demands that divorce should be permitted if the marriage has broken down, regardless of whether there has been adultery or cruelty. However, the Commission, mindful of marriage as a cornerstone of social

stability, does not recommend any radical change in divorce laws.

  Today: The divorce rate is much higher than it was in the 1950s, Divorce is now granted if the marriage is declared to have broken down irretrievably. Some social scientists, as well as politicians, regard the high divorce rate as part of a crisis in society, since divorce destabilizes families.

- **1920s:** Censorship for reasons of obscenity is still governed by the Obscene Publications Act of 1857. D. H. Lawrence's novel *Lady Chatterley's Lover* (1928) is banned for obscenity.

  1950s: The British public remains conservative regarding matters of censorship. Spencer is threatened with prosecution for obscenity. However, attitudes are gradually changing; in 1960, after a famous trial, publication of *Lady Chatterley's Lover* is allowed. Because of the controversy, it soon tops the bestseller lists.

  Today: The Obscene Publications Act determines what materials may be published in Britain. Because of this, there is concern over the availability of pornography, especially child pornography, on the Internet. However, courts have shown little interest in legislation that would restrict access to the Internet.

---

and music teacher. Spencer attended the Slade School of Art from 1908 to 1912, where he acquired the nickname "Cookham" because of his love for his home village. (In the play, Augustus John refers to Stanley as "Cookham.") During World War I he served as a medical orderly at a war hospital near Bristol, England, and later in an infantry battalion in the Balkans.

Spencer married fellow artist Hilda Carline in 1925, and they had two daughters, Shirin and Unity. During the 1920s, Spencer painted murals based on his wartime experiences and had his

first one-man exhibition. In 1927, he finished one of his most famous works, "The Resurrection," set in Cookham churchyard. Figures are shown rising from their tombs, God the Father and Christ are represented, as are Spencer himself and Hilda. (This is the painting Stanley discusses with Hilda in act 1, scene 1 of the play, saying that he will put her in the painting, sniffing a daisy—which he did.) It was paintings such as this that established Spencer as an original painter of genius, whose religious vision expressed itself through the ordinary sights of Cookham village.

Stanley Spencer (AP Images)

The erotic nature of some of Spencer's art, including paintings such as "Nude, Patricia Preece" (he married Preece in 1937, just four days after divorcing Hilda) aroused controversy, In the 1940s, his work fell out of favor, and he was forced to paint landscapes to make a living. In 1950, Spencer was threatened with prosecution for obscenity after some of his private drawings found their way into the hands of Sir Alfred Munnings, a former president of the Royal Academy. Alarmed, Spencer destroyed some of his works and wrapped up one painting, "Leg of Mutton Nude," which showed himself and Patricia nude alongside a leg of mutton, and placed it under his bed. That same year, his former wife Hilda died after a three-year battle with breast cancer.

In the 1950s Spencer's reputation recovered, and in 1955, London's Tate Gallery mounted a retrospective exhibition of his work. In June 1959, he was knighted, henceforth to be known as Sir Stanley Spencer. He died in December of the same year.

For some years after his death, Spencer was regarded as a rather solitary figure, outside the mainstream of art history. In 1964, for example, William Gaunt in *A Concise History of English Painting*, described him in this way: "As a religious painter and mural decorator he is like no one else, a visionary as much on his own as Blake with whom in some respects he may be compared." However, in the 1970s and 1980s, there was a reevaluation of Spencer's work. Major exhibitions were held in Britain, and Spencer's paintings became known in the United States and Europe. Instead of being regarded as an outsider, he was discussed in the same category as international artists such as Max Beckmann, Otto Dix, and Marc Chagall. In 1997, a year after *Stanley* was written, there was an exhibition of sixty of Spencer's works at the Hirschhorn Museum in Washington, DC.

Britain's Female Playwrights

When she wrote *Stanley* in 1996, Gems was working in a cultural environment that was much more supportive of female playwrights than it had been at the beginning of her career. Until the late 1950s there were almost no female playwrights working in the British theater. It was not until the late 1960s, when the feminist movement gathered momentum, that opportunities for women playwrights emerged. At first these feminist writers were associated with fringe theater companies such as Portable Theatre, The Brighton Combination, and later, Monstrous Regiment. Gems was part of this first wave of feminist theater, writing plays such as *The Amiable Courtship of Miz Venus and Wild Bill* and *After Birthday*, both of which were produced by the feminist collective, Almost Free, in 1973.

Feminist playwrights of the 1970s attempted to create a new kind of theatrical experience, rejecting much of traditional theatrical forms which they claimed represented only the male experience of life. They wrote for female actors in a style and on topics that were relevant for women's lives. Some feminist groups, such as The Women's Theatre Group, refused to have any men in the cast.

By the 1990s, when Gems wrote *Stanley*—not an explicitly feminist play but one that does focus on the lives of two rather different women in the mid-twentieth century—there were many more women active in the theater in many different capacities as writers, directors, and designers. Women writers were also successful in television. Feminist playwrights showed a concern for social issues such as AIDS-awareness and domestic violence.

A notable trend in the 1990s, due in part to generous and flexible funding by the British Arts Council, was for a new wave of feminist playwrights to pursue experimental work, including dance, mime, and multi-media, that did not rely on the traditional written script. Representative companies included The Hairy Marys, a physical theater and dance company in London, and Anna O, a feminist group that explored issues such as gender and power in interdisciplinary forms. At the same time, more work by women was produced in mainstream theater, including Churchill's *The Skriker* (1994).

CRITICAL OVERVIEW

Stanley received appreciative reviews when it was first produced in England by the National Theatre in February 1996. In the *Spectator*, Sheridan Morley calls it a "gem of a play . . . endlessly fascinating." He praises the production and remarks upon "the conflations of sacred and profane that inform all of Stanley's self-justificatory speeches." However, John Simon, writing in *New York*, and reviewing the play when it was presented at New York's Circle in the Square in 1997, notes reservations about the play itself, questioning why it won awards in Britain since, in his view, it does not rise above the "boulevard level." This lack of enthusiasm about the play itself is echoed by David Sheward in *Back Stage*, who calls *Stanley* "muddy and overlong. . . . the play does not give us a reason to care about Stanley, his work, or his sordid triangular relationships." A more positive view is taken by Nancy Franklin in the *New Yorker*. Franklin praises the portrayal of Spencer as "emotionally agile," which encourages the audience to "accept his feelings as real . . . Ridiculous (and destructive) as he is, you can't help thinking that he's on to something vital and important." According to Franklin, the play shows that the childlike quality of the character is a vital part of his creativity, suggesting that "genius does have something to do with never fully growing up."

WHAT DO I READ NEXT?

- Gems's *Piaf* (1978) presents incidents from the life of the famous singer Edith Piaf, as well as renditions of some of her most popular songs. The play undermines the glamorous public image of Piaf in favor of a more sordid reality in which prostitution, violence, and drugs dominate. Piaf is shown as unable to cope with the contradiction between her public and private self. The play can be found in *Three Plays: Piaf, Camille, and Loving Women*, published by Penguin (revised ed., 1986).

- Like Gems, much of British playwright Caryl Churchill's work emphasizes feminist themes. Her play *Cloud Nine*, first performed in 1979, puts the spotlight on colonial and gender oppression. Set partly in Africa in the nineteenth century and partly in London a hundred years later, the play presents themes including women's liberation, gay liberation, and the sexual revolution. The play can be found in *Churchill: Plays One* (1985).

- *Vincent in Brixton* (2003), by Nicholas Wright, won the Olivier Award for Best Play and had a successful run in London's West End and on Broadway. The play is a dramatization of the time that Vincent Van Gogh spent in Brixton, London, in the 1870s, a period before he became a painter. Vincent develops a rapport with a widow twice his age, which blossoms into a full-blown love affair, only to be cur-

tailed by the arrival of his young sister, a fierce puritan.

- *Clever as Paint: The Rossettis in Love* (1998), by Kim Morrissey, is a play about the pre-Raphaelite painting circle of Dante Gabriel Rossetti, his wife Lizzie Siddal, and his protégé William Morris. After Siddal's suicide, Rossetti buried his love poems in her coffin. Seven years later he dug them up again, publishing them to please his new lover and model, Janey Morris (wife of William Morris). This witty play offers insight into art, grief, inspiration, and despair.

- *Proof* (2001), a play by David Auburn, won the Pulitzer Prize in 2001. Set in Chicago, it explores the link between madness and genius as revealed in the life of a recently deceased mathematician. The story is in part based on the life of John Forbes Nash Jr., a gifted mathematician who suffered from schizophrenia and was the subject of the popular film *A Beautiful Mind* (1998).

- *The Spiritual in Twentieth-Century Art* (2007), by Roger Lipsey, focuses on the works of painters such as Pablo Picasso, Marcel Duchamp, and Henri Matisse, among others. Letters, diaries, and interviews provide insights into the artists' views, and show how these artists differed from Spencer in their conception of the spiritual in art.

CRITICISM

Bryan Aubrey

Aubrey holds a Ph.D. in English. In this essay, he discusses Gems's play Stanley *and the title character's need to uphold his religious vision and recapture his boyhood feelings about Cookham. Aubrey also explores how these needs led in part to Stanley's involvement with Patricia Preece.*

The artistic genius, be he painter, poet, or composer, is rarely the best of men or the most reasonable of men. Such individuals are revered not because they are paragons of virtue or embodiments of bourgeois moral values but because they have extraordinary gifts. Obsessed by their artistic calling, to which all other aspects of life must be subordinated, they are not always easy people for others to know or get along with. So it is with the

> IT MUST HAVE SEEMED TO SPENCER LIKE A CONVENIENT AND WELCOME BONUS THAT HE ALSO FOUND PREECE EXTREMELY SEXUALLY ALLURING. SHE PROVIDED FUEL FOR HIS EROTIC IMAGINATION, AND HE WOULD ENCOURAGE HER TO WEAR FLIMSY UNDERWEAR AND OTHER SEXY ATTIRE."

artist Stanley Spencer in Pam Gems's play, *Stanley*. Stanley is presented as self-centered, egotistical, selfish, narcissistic, and childish—a man who thinks that he should be allowed to have whatever he wants simply because he wants it. But the tendency to judge or condemn Stanley for his obvious inadequacies is withheld because he is clearly a man inspired by a vision. This is apparent not only in the text of the play but also in stage productions, such as the one at New York's Circle in the Square in 1997, in which reproductions of Spencer's paintings are incorporated into the set.

The playwright wastes no time in introducing the audience to the spiritual underpinnings of Stanley's work. In act 1, scene 1, Stanley tells Hilda about an experience he had on the battlefield during World War I. As he was making a difficult march up to the front—a reference to the historical Spencer's service in the British infantry in Macedonia—he heard someone moaning, and just when he was thinking that he could not bear any more of the chaos of war, suddenly everything changed for him: "it was as if the stars turned warm. As if the snow had little flames, licking up round me, so I felt . . . it's all right . . . everything is as it should be!" This description has many of the hallmarks of the visions or experiences reported by mystics and others throughout history who have received sudden, unexpected moments of spiritual illumination. In such elevated moments, in spite of all the suffering of humanity and the apparent chaos and injustice of life, everything seems perfect. There is an order to life that underlies and permeates the apparent chaos. There is nothing to strive for, nothing to achieve, and somehow the whole world seems glorified. Stanley says as he continues the description that "it was as if I was in a great big church of the world . . . like lights streaming down from clerestory windows . . . on me . . . I was in the middle of it . . . I was it."

Trying to maintain or recapture that spiritual vision of life is at the heart of Stanley's artistic enterprise. His recipe for fulfillment in life is to "Carry that blinding moment of worship inside you like the ark of the covenant." He also knows that such moments may be few and far between, and he looks to two very different aspects of his life to help nourish his spiritual aspirations. First, his memories of his happy childhood in Cookham, when he felt deeply connected to his surroundings. He alludes to this several times in the play, taking pleasure in recalling for Gwen the serene family life he knew when he was a boy and the sensual delight he remembers in such ordinary day-to-day moments: "Oh, the feel of everything . . . wet ivy by the door, cold lino, the iron latch on the privy in winter . . . and the smells! Our old dog coming in with a wet coat . . . barley soup." Like William Blake, another artist to whom he is often compared, Stanley has a deep reverence for the innocent perception of the child. As he explains to Hilda, "How it was . . . before sex. Just that clear child's eye. I miss that." The second aspect of life to which Stanley looks for creativity and spiritual fulfillment is sex. Whether it is making suggestive remarks to the maid Elsie or lewd proposals to Patricia or talking to Hilda, Stanley has an almost obsessive, if high-minded, interest in sex. As he says to Hilda, "The whole of my life in art has been a slow realization of the mystery of sex! It's the key to everything!" For Stanley, it is sex, the erotic imagination, that seems to deeply satisfy his need to fuse the spiritual and the sensual, to find the divine in human flesh.

It is these two things together, the serene feelings he associated with childhood and youth in Cookham, and the persistent desire for erotic intensity, that help to explain the extraordinary tangle Stanley gets into with the two women in his life—Hilda, his first wife and Patricia, his second. In her dramatization of this unhappy situation, the playwright presents quite an accurate portrait of the historical figure of Stanley Spencer and the turbulence of his intimate relationships. He first met Hilda Carline in 1919, and his letters to her over the next few years made his feelings plain: "You are the most secret & greatest joy of my life, you are like redemption to me," he wrote in the spring of 1923. After they married in 1925, they were initially happy, as the first scene of *Stanley* shows. But within a few years, Spencer began to get irritated with his wife and complain that she was not interested in his art or his ideas. Sometimes, when he was expounding his views on some matter of great importance to him, Hilda's attention would wander and she would even fall asleep while he was talking. Spencer was also annoyed that Hilda, who was herself an artist of some talent, had given up painting and taken up gardening instead, an activity in which he had no interest.

Spencer's dissatisfaction with his wife was accentuated after he became infatuated with Patricia Preece. He had meet Preece at a café in Cookham in 1929, and when the Spencers moved back to Cookham from Hampshire in 1932, Spencer began to see Preece frequently, a fact he did not hide from his wife. Spencer saw in Preece everything he found lacking in Hilda. She was attractive, charming, sophisticated, stylish, and sexy. It appeared at first that she was enthusiastic about his art. In addition, Preece aroused in Spencer the same kind of feelings that he associated with his youth and early manhood in Cookham, and which he regarded as vitally important for his artistic vision. Preece therefore appeared to offer him the chance to regain his sense of purpose regarding his art, and for a while he was ecstatic about the prospect. His feelings in this regard are suggested in act 1, scene 9 of *Stanley*, in which Stanley and Patricia are in a field of marguerites on a hillside in Cookham. Stanley tells her, "I wanted to bring you here. Among the marguerites. They're the first things I remember. I remember touching them. The petals. The foxy smell . . . ooooh!" His 1935 painting, "Patricia at Cockmarsh Hill," shows Preece sitting among the wildflowers on the hill, and he later wrote about how he regarded Preece as "exquisitely the thing. She was the exact incarnation of the infant memory of those flowers. It was a thing I never believed could have happened" (quoted in Kenneth Pople's *Stanley Spencer: A Biography*). It must have seemed to Spencer like a convenient and welcome bonus that he also found Preece extremely sexually alluring. She provided fuel for his erotic imagination, and he would encourage her to wear flimsy underwear and other sexy attire. His intense desire for her and fascination with her physical form is captured in the remark Stanley makes in the play: "I'd like to be an ant crawling all over you." The stage direction that follows his remark is significant: Stanley "shudders with excitement" while Patricia laughs. Whatever Spencer might have wished, Patricia Preece neither understood his art nor had any deep feelings

for him personally, either romantic or sexual. As the play accurately shows, she would tease him and manipulate him while planning to take advantage of him materially. Preece and her lover Dorothy Hepworth—who was the more accomplished artist of the two—were struggling financially, and Preece feared that they might sink into poverty. She saw in Spencer an opportunity to improve her financial situation and also advance her own artistic career by getting him to use his influence to help her and Dorothy sell more of their work.

Spencer's attempt to maintain sexual relationships with both Hilda and Preece was doomed to failure. Although he divorced Hilda and married Preece in 1937, it is unlikely that the second marriage was ever consummated. Preece had no objection to Spencer continuing a sexual relationship with Hilda, but Hilda, understandably, was not so enthusiastic about such an arrangement. Within a couple of years, Spencer had decided that divorcing Hilda had been a mistake, and he spent many years trying to be reconciled with her, even suggesting in 1942 that they remarry. But Hilda could not contemplate such a move; the stress brought on by the divorce had worn her down, and later that year she was admitted to a mental hospital suffering from delusions. She remained in the hospital for nine months. Long since disillusioned with Preece, Spencer continued to seek a reunion with Hilda until her death in 1950.

Although the Stanley of the play does not reflect on how his own behavior helped to bring such chaos to his close relationships, Spencer in real life appears to have done so. As his biographer Pople describes it, in later life Spencer "questioned whether he had been capable of a committed love in the everyday sense. Unable to yield to those compromises which make normal relationships supportable, he felt that despite his natural wishes he had been compelled to betray many who were close and dear to him."

This is a harsh verdict for someone to make about his or her own life, but anyone who reads or sees *Stanley* will feel that there is some truth to it, especially in regard to his behavior toward Hilda. Stanley's compulsive need to consume everything and everyone into himself may have been a key to his artistic genius, but it did not make for happiness in personal relationships.

Source: Bryan Aubrey, Critical Essay on *Stanley*, in *Drama for Students*, Gale, Cengage Learning, 2008.

> SPENCER WAS A VISIONARY ARTIST WHO SAW HIS NATIVE ENGLISH VILLAGE AS AN EARTHLY PARADISE, AND USED IT AS A SETTING FOR SCENES FROM THE LIFE OF CHRIST."

Gale

In the following excerpt, the critic gives a critical analysis of Gem's work.

Pam Gems is, according to Janet E. Gardner in *Feminist Writers*, "one of the handful of British feminist dramatists who has been successful in the mainstream theater." In such plays as *Dusa, Fish, Stas, and Vi*, *Queen Christina*, *Piaf*, and *Marlene*, Gems has written works with feminist themes and wide audience appeal. Rodelle Weintraub in the *Dictionary of Literary Biography* writes: "Gems has produced a considerable canon which examines the human condition, especially the plight of women in western society. For a theater which has traditionally had few roles for women and even fewer roles for realistic women rather than stereotypes derived from male fears and fantasies, Gems has produced a great many nonstereotypic roles.... She has forcefully examined the roles western society has imposed not only upon actresses but upon all women and, in the tradition of Bernard Shaw, has done so with humor, understanding, extraordinary insight, and her own razor-sharp scalpel."

Gems only began her career as a playwright after raising four children. In her forties, she became involved with England's fringe theater movement, writing plays for the feminist collective, Almost Free. These early plays were produced by the collective at lunchtime performances. In 1976 Gems's play *Dead Fish* won her attention at the Edinburgh Festival. The play was soon moved to London, where it enjoyed a long and successful run under the title *Dusa, Fish, Stas, and Vi*. The story focuses on four women brought together by economic pressures and mistreatment by the men in their lives. Gardner believes that *Dusa, Fish, Stas, and Vi* "is ultimately about solidarity and the strength women find in their friendships."

The following year, Gems's *Queen Christina* was produced by the Royal Shakespeare Company.

With a cast of thirty-two actors and a complex, episodic plot, *Queen Christina* tells the story of a seventeenth-century Swedish monarch. "Raised as a boy to prepare her for leadership of her country," Gardner explained, "the boisterous and frankly sexual Christina grows up to find herself discontented with the limitations of women's roles." Christina alternates between male and female roles in an attempt to find a sense of self. When she is offered the kingdom of Naples, she takes up masculine values again, but when this leads to her having to kill her lover, she "rejects the whole male ethos, setting herself against domination in all its forms, master/servant as well as man/woman," reported a writer for *Contemporary Dramatists*. "Finally, when she is too old to bear children, she discovers the value of maternal instincts and affirms her biological nature." The *Contemporary Dramatists* writer noted that *Queen Christina* "struck a new note" for Gems and "established her central themes."

One of Gems's greatest successes has been her dramatization of the sensational and tragic life of Edith Piaf, the Parisian chanteuse known as the "little sparrow." *Piaf* recounts the singer's rise from brothel-born cabaret artist to international star, and her subsequent physical decline and early death. According to Richard Christiansen of the *Chicago Tribune*, "the play's brief segments . . . do not attempt to deal with Piaf's childhood as a rickety street urchin. But they do cover the course of her sensation-filled adult life." Those events include "her early involvement with thieves and murderers," friendships and love affairs with celebrities, a disastrous marriage, and then a happy marriage to Theo Sarapo, "who adored her and cared for her in her last enfeebling illness."

Reviewing *Piaf* for *Newsweek*, Jack Kroll said that "Gems's writing has power and velocity; 'Piaf' leaps at us right from the gutter. . . . Like tabloid sheets roaring out of a press, the scenes snapshoot Piaf's chaotic and feverish life." Christiansen, too, admired the strength of Gems's work, noting that "the vitality in Gems' writing" makes the play's familiar ingredients of tragedy "work so effectively."

Some other critics voiced reservations about Gems's play. After crediting Gems with capturing the "central, perhaps inexplicable mystery of Piaf's magic," Frank Rich of the *New York Times* argued that "instead of raising substantive issues about Piaf, the evening's cartoonish archetypes call the playwright's craft into question." Rich also termed *Piaf* a "rather frail play," and *New Yorker*'s Brendan Gill labelled it "rudimentary" and "inept." Another *New York Times* critic, Mel Gussow, saw "serious defects" in *Piaf*. Reviewing the London Warehouse Theatre production, which played an extended engagement before capacity crowds, Gussow noted that "the script often stumbles, plunging into bathos." Despite her frailties, Piaf was a strong, independent person, and Gems has remarked, according to Christensen, that she views "her play partly as a feminist document celebrating an extraordinary woman."

Gems offered theatergoers new versions of two stories, *The Blue Angel* and *Camille*, both of which had previously been made into classic films starring Marlene Dietrich. Perhaps that led to her play *Marlene*, based on the star's life. In *Marlene*, the aging actress is in Paris, waiting to go on stage for a performance in what will be her final tour. Her dialogue and actions reveal her life story and complex psyche. A celebrity of immense fame, she complains and browbeats her servants, yet also spreads her mink on the floor, kneels on it, and starts to scrub her dressing room. References to concentration camps and Hitler—including a servant made mute by the horrors of the Dachau death camp—give *Marlene* a dark quality. Finally, in the show's last half-hour, the Dietrich character sings seven of the songs that made the actress famous. Much like *Piaf*, Gem's *Marlene* "makes Dietrich into a metaphor for the chasm between on stage illusion and backstage reality," commented reviewer David A. Rosenberg in *Back Stage*.

Gems offered another slice of biography in her play *Stanley*, based on the life and work of British painter Sir Stanley Spencer. Spencer was a visionary artist who saw his native English village as an earthly paradise, and used it as a setting for scenes from the life of Christ. "Gems empathetically shows Spencer as an emotionally infantile genius," reported Jack Kroll in *Newsweek*. Spencer left his down-to-earth wife to pursue a doomed love for a narcissistic lesbian painter. Spencer saw himself as a mouthpiece for God and accordingly considered himself to be outside the norms of society. From this story, "three major themes gradually emerge and intertwine: God, art and love," stated Joseph J. Feeney in *America*. And yet, "this is not an esoteric tale of religious fervor, or a somber concert or art lecture disguised as a play," assured Elyse Sommer in

CurtainUp.com. Rather, the drama "focuses on the messy and complicated love life of the man Stanley Spencer who happened to be a gifted painter but a wacky, immature loser in his personal relationships."

"Although involved in and helped by the feminist movement," Weintraub reflected, "Gems rejects some of the movement's hostility toward men. She feels that women, despite the damage they suffer and their sexual oppression, need men, and children need two parents. While recognizing the need for feminist theater, she insists that 'an all-woman theatre wouldn't work. It would be chauvinistic and boring.'"

Source: Gale, "(Iris) Pam(ela) Gems," in *Contemporary Authors Online*, The Gale Group, 2002.

Joseph J. Feeney

In the following review of a 1996 Royal National Theatre production of Stanley *(performed in London), Feeney discusses the play's intertwined themes of God, art, and love, as well as the relationships between men and women and the artist's need to work constantly. He comments that the play is also a celebration of the physicality of art.*

Sir Stanley Spencer: painter of genius, visionary of angels, willful child. He saw God in the villagers of his native Cookhamon-Thames and divorced his wife to marry a money-grubber. He painted a 17-foot "Christ Preaching at Cookham Regatta" and painted erotic nudes with himself as onlooker. He was almost prosecuted for obscenity in 1950 and knighted in 1958. He makes a lively subject for Pam Gems's new play, *Stanley*.

Stanley Spencer (1891–1959) seems a curious hero, especially for a feminist play-wright. Yet Pain (for Pamela) Gems, born in 1925 and known for her poignant *Piaf* (London 1978, New York 1981), was drawn by "admiration and a wish to celebrate" Spencer's "English genius" as expressed in his warm light and color, misshapen forms, Christian iconography and shocking nudes. She also enjoyed the challenge of using biographical data as both "springboard" and "lure." The challenge was well met: *Stanley*, which opened on Feb. 1 at the Royal National Theatre, was by summer one of London's rarest tickets and manifestly the best new play of 1996.

It begins as Spencer, brilliantly played by Antony Sher, works on an enormous canvas while listening to Bach. His wife enters—Hilda Carline, artist and mother of their children—and they discourse on light, love and the Great War. Scenes change quickly—there are 23—and Stanley meets the painters Patricia Preece and her lover, Dorothy Hepworth. Self-centered as usual, Stanley finds Patricia appealing; she thinks him useful for her career. He gives her daisies (picked by Hilda!), paints her nude, abandons Hilda for her and finds that Patricia still prefers Dorothy to him. Never quite seeing what went wrong, Stanley escapes to his painting. Scene by scene runs his life: he returns to Hilda, Patricia refuses a divorce, Hilda dies, Stanley is knighted. Three major themes gradually emerge and intertwine: God, art and love.

The weave of God and art is sometimes touching, sometimes ludicrous. At his best, Spencer sees God-on-earth in the Cookham villagers, and his "Visitation" portrays a milkmaid and a butcher's daughter. His Christ has "His body flung onto the grass...holding the grass in rapture." Art's very purpose is to "fill space for the glory of God." While painting, though, Stanley thinks "God's at his elbow, telling him what to rub out" and wants—like Michelangelo—to decorate a whole church and make "every wall, every space...a cathedral of me." And so he does—a chapel in Burghclere, Hampshire. But his egotism is also disarming. In a closing monologue he tells his dead Hilda:

"It makes me feel closer to Heaven with you there. Specially after work, when I'm tired. I see this great picture of God and all His angels sitting on these beautiful three-dimensional clouds and on His left hand sits Bach and on His right hand Stanley! I'm only joking, of course."

Stanley also weaves together God and love. Hilda tells Stanley, "We're married. One flesh... It's sacred, and we're sacred." Stanley finds Hilda "the most wonderful gift from heaven" and wants "to paint an altar-piece" of her. Infatuated with Patricia Preece, he thinks "it's perfectly possible for me to have a strong spiritual closeness to more than one woman." But he finally admits marrying Patricia for "social vanity," without any "spiritual relationship."

Art, finally, is interwoven with love. He finds Hilda attractive because she is a painter, with Patricia, he paints "the land-scapes of your legs." His is paintings-angular, muted in color, looking (said The Times in 1927) "as if a Pre-Raphaelite had shaken hands with a Cubist"—are often rapturous studies of women. And all art is about "love" and "passion," designed to reveal the nature of the world. Through love."

As a play, Stanley is far more than this serio-comic weave of art, God and love. It is about the relationships of men and women, about grasping for money, about an artist's need to work constantly. And it celebrates the physicality of art and the artist, as when Spencer describes an English spring: "the first hints, shallots poking through, broad beans showing knobby fists, snow-drops, pussy willow, crocus, then the daffs, the first bluebell, blackbirds starting up five o'clock in the bloody morning...and then...oh then...chick-weed, scarlet pimpernel, dandelion, flags, campion, clover, ragged robin, cow parsley."

But above all, *Stanley* about the person of Stanley Spencer. The Sunday Times called it the "haunting portrayal of a difficult, childishly selfish man," the Independent, "the potty, painful comedy of his complicated marital arrangements." Stanley, as seen by Pam Gems, is genius and child, visionary and sensualist, innocent and egoist, pure artist and sexual gymnast, a man of painterly clarity and human confusion. But his art finally prevails, eloquently celebrated by Dorothy Hepworth: "Rightly acclaimed as one of England's greatest painters," he is "uniquely gifted... There is a sort of unique human clumsiness about his work—it's deliberate of course. He paints people trapped, as it were, in their own flesh, pinned down to this earth, and yet they seek to soar and he makes that seem so very possible... Everything is celebrated and revered with a balance that speaks of the most tender spiritual equality...I particularly draw your attention to Sir Stanley's colours...without the shout of a colourist, they nonetheless show the most infinite variety of subtlety and tone. Very English."

At play's end, after talking to his dear, dead Hilda about God and art and love, Stanley slowly shuffles offstage wheeling his canvas and paint on the chassis of an old pram. The image catches him well: chastened adult, still a child, always a painter. As he leaves, the theater walls—covered with his paintings—shine with light. And the music of Bach swells.

Source: Joseph J. Feeney, "*Stanley*," in *America*, Vol. 175, No. 15, November 16, 1996, p. 16.

SOURCES

Franklin, Nancy, "Stars over Russia: Three Bored Sisters, and One Bumptious Artist," in the *New Yorker*, Vol. LXXIII, No. 3, March 10, 1997, p. 97.

Gaunt, William, *A Concise History of English Painting*, Frederick A. Praeger, 1964, p. 210.

Gems, Pam, *Stanley*, Nick Hern Books, 1996.

Glew, Adrian, ed., *Stanley Spencer: Letters and Writings*, Tate Publishing, 2001, p. 121.

Morley, Sheridan, "Morally Bankrupt," in the *Spectator*, Vol. 276, No. 8743, February 10, 1996, p. 43.

Pople, Kenneth, *Stanley Spencer: A Biography*, Collins, 1991, pp. 329, 461.

Sheward, David, Review of *Stanley*, in *Back Stage*, Vol. 38, No. 9, February 28, 1997, p. 60.

Simon, John, "Wild at Art," in *New York*, Vol. 30, No. 8, March 3, 1997, p. 55.

FURTHER READING

Godiwala, Dimple, *Queer Mythologies: The Original Stage Plays of Pam Gems*, Intellect Books, 2006, pp. 91–95.
Godiwala discusses *Stanley* in terms of a crisis in masculinity; Patricia, because of her independence, represents a more masculine figure; her cold rationality contrasts with Stanley's feminine feeling and passion. Patricia possesses the power and exposes Stanley's effeminacy.

Goodman, Lizbeth, *Feminist Stages: Interviews with Women in Contemporary British Theatre*, Routledge, 1996, pp. 24–31.
Gems discusses why gender matters in the theater, how the position of women in the theater has changed over her lifetime, and her personal definition of feminism. She also makes some comments about *Stanley*.

Hauser, Kitty, *Stanley Spencer*, Princeton University Press, 2001.
This is a concise guide to Spencer's life and art. Hauser shows how Spencer's artistic imagination was rooted in specific places and people, and how he transformed his experiences in the process of creating his paintings.

Innes, Christopher, *Modern British Drama: The Twentieth Century*, Cambridge University Press, 2002, pp. 239–49.
Innes discusses nine of Gems's most important plays, including *Stanley*. He argues that, although art and creativity are important themes, the focus is really on women and how they are portrayed.

Wandor, Michelene, *Carry on Understudies: Theatre and Sexual Politics*, Routledge & Kegan Paul, 1986, pp. 161–66.
!This is a discussion of the plays Gems wrote during the 1970s and 1980s; Wandor explores how Gems depicts women, and the different forms of feminism she made use of in these plays.

Glossary of Literary Terms

A

Abstract: Used as a noun, the term refers to a short summary or outline of a longer work. As an adjective applied to writing or literary works, abstract refers to words or phrases that name things not knowable through the five senses. Examples of abstracts include the *Cliffs Notes* summaries of major literary works. Examples of abstract terms or concepts include "idea," "guilt" "honesty," and "loyalty."

Absurd, Theater of the: See *Theater of the Absurd*

Absurdism: See *Theater of the Absurd*

Act: A major section of a play. Acts are divided into varying numbers of shorter scenes. From ancient times to the nineteenth century plays were generally constructed of five acts, but modern works typically consist of one, two, or three acts. Examples of five-act plays include the works of Sophocles and Shakespeare, while the plays of Arthur Miller commonly have a three-act structure.

Acto: A one-act Chicano theater piece developed out of collective improvisation. *Actos* were performed by members of Luis Valdez's Teatro Campesino in California during the mid-1960s.

Aestheticism: A literary and artistic movement of the nineteenth century. Followers of the movement believed that art should not be mixed with social, political, or moral teaching. The statement "art for art's sake" is a good summary of aestheticism. The movement had its roots in France, but it gained widespread importance in England in the last half of the nineteenth century, where it helped change the Victorian practice of including moral lessons in literature. Oscar Wilde is one of the best-known "aesthetes" of the late nineteenth century.

Age of Johnson: The period in English literature between 1750 and 1798, named after the most prominent literary figure of the age, Samuel Johnson. Works written during this time are noted for their emphasis on "sensibility," or emotional quality. These works formed a transition between the rational works of the Age of Reason, or Neoclassical period, and the emphasis on individual feelings and responses of the Romantic period. Significant writers during the Age of Johnson included the novelists Ann Radcliffe and Henry Mackenzie, dramatists Richard Sheridan and Oliver Goldsmith, and poets William Collins and Thomas Gray. Also known as Age of Sensibility

Age of Reason: See *Neoclassicism*

Age of Sensibility: See *Age of Johnson*

Alexandrine Meter: See *Meter*

Allegory: A narrative technique in which characters representing things or abstract ideas are used to convey a message or teach a lesson.

Allegory is typically used to teach moral, ethical, or religious lessons but is sometimes used for satiric or political purposes. Examples of allegorical works include Edmund Spenser's *The Faerie Queene* and John Bunyan's *The Pilgrim's Progress.*

Allusion: A reference to a familiar literary or historical person or event, used to make an idea more easily understood. For example, describing someone as a "Romeo" makes an allusion to William Shakespeare's famous young lover in *Romeo and Juliet.*

Amerind Literature: The writing and oral traditions of Native Americans. Native American literature was originally passed on by word of mouth, so it consisted largely of stories and events that were easily memorized. Amerind prose is often rhythmic like poetry because it was recited to the beat of a ceremonial drum. Examples of Amerind literature include the autobiographical *Black Elk Speaks,* the works of N. Scott Momaday, James Welch, and Craig Lee Strete, and the poetry of Luci Tapahonso.

Analogy: A comparison of two things made to explain something unfamiliar through its similarities to something familiar, or to prove one point based on the acceptedness of another. Similes and metaphors are types of analogies. Analogies often take the form of an extended simile, as in William Blake's aphorism: "As the caterpillar chooses the fairest leaves to lay her eggs on, so the priest lays his curse on the fairest joys."

Angry Young Men: A group of British writers of the 1950s whose work expressed bitterness and disillusionment with society. Common to their work is an anti-hero who rebels against a corrupt social order and strives for personal integrity. The term has been used to describe Kingsley Amis, John Osborne, Colin Wilson, John Wain, and others.

Antagonist: The major character in a narrative or drama who works against the hero or protagonist. An example of an evil antagonist is Richard Lovelace in Samuel Richardson's *Clarissa,* while a virtuous antagonist is Macduff in William Shakespeare's *Macbeth.*

Anthropomorphism: The presentation of animals or objects in human shape or with human characteristics. The term is derived from the Greek word for "human form." The fables

of Aesop, the animated films of Walt Disney, and Richard Adams's *Watership Down* feature anthropomorphic characters.

Anti-hero: A central character in a work of literature who lacks traditional heroic qualities such as courage, physical prowess, and fortitude. Anti-heros typically distrust conventional values and are unable to commit themselves to any ideals. They generally feel helpless in a world over which they have no control. Anti-heroes usually accept, and often celebrate, their positions as social outcasts. A well-known anti-hero is Yossarian in Joseph Heller's novel *Catch-22.*

Antimasque: See *Masque*

Antithesis: The antithesis of something is its direct opposite. In literature, the use of antithesis as a figure of speech results in two statements that show a contrast through the balancing of two opposite ideas. Technically, it is the second portion of the statement that is defined as the "antithesis"; the first portion is the "thesis." An example of antithesis is found in the following portion of Abraham Lincoln's "Gettysburg Address"; notice the opposition between the verbs "remember" and "forget" and the phrases "what we say" and "what they did": "The world will little note nor long remember what we say here, but it can never forget what they did here."

Apocrypha: Writings tentatively attributed to an author but not proven or universally accepted to be their works. The term was originally applied to certain books of the Bible that were not considered inspired and so were not included in the "sacred canon." Geoffrey Chaucer, William Shakespeare, Thomas Kyd, Thomas Middleton, and John Marston all have apocrypha. Apocryphal books of the Bible include the Old Testament's Book of Enoch and New Testament's Gospel of Peter.

Apollonian and Dionysian: The two impulses believed to guide authors of dramatic tragedy. The Apollonian impulse is named after Apollo, the Greek god of light and beauty and the symbol of intellectual order. The Dionysian impulse is named after Dionysus, the Greek god of wine and the symbol of the unrestrained forces of nature. The Apollonian impulse is to create a rational, harmonious world, while the Dionysian is to express the irrational forces of personality. Friedrich Nietzche uses these terms in *The*

Birth of Tragedy to designate contrasting elements in Greek tragedy.

Apostrophe: A statement, question, or request addressed to an inanimate object or concept or to a nonexistent or absent person. Requests for inspiration from the muses in poetry are examples of apostrophe, as is Marc Antony's address to Caesar's corpse in William Shakespeare's *Julius Caesar*: "O, pardon me, thou bleeding piece of earth, That I am meek and gentle with these butchers!... Woe to the hand that shed this costly blood!..."

Archetype: The word archetype is commonly used to describe an original pattern or model from which all other things of the same kind are made. This term was introduced to literary criticism from the psychology of Carl Jung. It expresses Jung's theory that behind every person's "unconscious," or repressed memories of the past, lies the "collective unconscious" of the human race: memories of the countless typical experiences of our ancestors. These memories are said to prompt illogical associations that trigger powerful emotions in the reader. Often, the emotional process is primitive, even primordial. Archetypes are the literary images that grow out of the "collective unconscious." They appear in literature as incidents and plots that repeat basic patterns of life. They may also appear as stereotyped characters. Examples of literary archetypes include themes such as birth and death and characters such as the Earth Mother.

Argument: The argument of a work is the author's subject matter or principal idea. Examples of defined "argument" portions of works include John Milton's *Arguments* to each of the books of *Paradise Lost* and the "Argument" to Robert Herrick's *Hesperides*.

Aristotelian Criticism: Specifically, the method of evaluating and analyzing tragedy formulated by the Greek philosopher Aristotle in his *Poetics*. More generally, the term indicates any form of criticism that follows Aristotle's views. Aristotelian criticism focuses on the form and logical structure of a work, apart from its historical or social context, in contrast to "Platonic Criticism," which stresses the usefulness of art. Adherents of New Criticism including John Crowe Ransom and Cleanth Brooks utilize and value the basic ideas of Aristotelian criticism for textual analysis.

Art for Art's Sake: See *Aestheticism*

Aside: A comment made by a stage performer that is intended to be heard by the audience but supposedly not by other characters. Eugene O'Neill's *Strange Interlude* is an extended use of the aside in modern theater.

Audience: The people for whom a piece of literature is written. Authors usually write with a certain audience in mind, for example, children, members of a religious or ethnic group, or colleagues in a professional field. The term "audience" also applies to the people who gather to see or hear any performance, including plays, poetry readings, speeches, and concerts. Jane Austen's parody of the gothic novel, *Northanger Abbey,* was originally intended for (and also pokes fun at) an audience of young and avid female gothic novel readers.

Avant-garde: A French term meaning "vanguard." It is used in literary criticism to describe new writing that rejects traditional approaches to literature in favor of innovations in style or content. Twentieth-century examples of the literary *avant-garde* include the Black Mountain School of poets, the Bloomsbury Group, and the Beat Movement.

B

Ballad: A short poem that tells a simple story and has a repeated refrain. Ballads were originally intended to be sung. Early ballads, known as folk ballads, were passed down through generations, so their authors are often unknown. Later ballads composed by known authors are called literary ballads. An example of an anonymous folk ballad is "Edward," which dates from the Middle Ages. Samuel Taylor Coleridge's "The Rime of the Ancient Mariner" and John Keats's "La Belle Dame sans Merci" are examples of literary ballads.

Baroque: A term used in literary criticism to describe literature that is complex or ornate in style or diction. Baroque works typically express tension, anxiety, and violent emotion. The term "Baroque Age" designates a period in Western European literature beginning in the late sixteenth century and ending about one hundred years later. Works of this period often mirror the qualities of works more generally associated with the label "baroque" and sometimes feature elaborate conceits. Examples of Baroque works include John Lyly's *Euphues: The Anatomy of Wit,* Luis de Gongora's *Soledads,* and William Shakespeare's *As You Like It.*

Baroque Age: See *Baroque*

Baroque Period: See *Baroque*

Beat Generation: See *Beat Movement*

Beat Movement: A period featuring a group of American poets and novelists of the 1950s and 1960s—including Jack Kerouac, Allen Ginsberg, Gregory Corso, William S. Burroughs, and Lawrence Ferlinghetti—who rejected established social and literary values. Using such techniques as stream of consciousness writing and jazz-influenced free verse and focusing on unusual or abnormal states of mind—generated by religious ecstasy or the use of drugs—the Beat writers aimed to create works that were unconventional in both form and subject matter. Kerouac's *On the Road* is perhaps the best-known example of a Beat Generation novel, and Ginsberg's *Howl* is a famous collection of Beat poetry.

Black Aesthetic Movement: A period of artistic and literary development among African Americans in the 1960s and early 1970s. This was the first major African-American artistic movement since the Harlem Renaissance and was closely paralleled by the civil rights and black power movements. The black aesthetic writers attempted to produce works of art that would be meaningful to the black masses. Key figures in black aesthetics included one of its founders, poet and playwright Amiri Baraka, formerly known as LeRoi Jones; poet and essayist Haki R. Madhubuti, formerly Don L. Lee; poet and playwright Sonia Sanchez; and dramatist Ed Bullins. Works representative of the Black Aesthetic Movement include Amiri Baraka's play *Dutchman,* a 1964 Obie award-winner; *Black Fire: An Anthology of Afro-American Writing,* edited by Baraka and playwright Larry Neal and published in 1968; and Sonia Sanchez's poetry collection *We a BaddDDD People,* published in 1970. Also known as Black Arts Movement.

Black Arts Movement: See *Black Aesthetic Movement*

Black Comedy: See *Black Humor*

Black Humor: Writing that places grotesque elements side by side with humorous ones in an attempt to shock the reader, forcing him or her to laugh at the horrifying reality of a disordered world. Joseph Heller's novel *Catch-22* is considered a superb example of the use of black humor. Other well-known authors who use black humor include Kurt Vonnegut, Edward Albee, Eugene Ionesco, and Harold Pinter. Also known as Black Comedy.

Blank Verse: Loosely, any unrhymed poetry, but more generally, unrhymed iambic pentameter verse (composed of lines of five two-syllable feet with the first syllable accented, the second unaccented). Blank verse has been used by poets since the Renaissance for its flexibility and its graceful, dignified tone. John Milton's *Paradise Lost* is in blank verse, as are most of William Shakespeare's plays.

Bloomsbury Group: A group of English writers, artists, and intellectuals who held informal artistic and philosophical discussions in Bloomsbury, a district of London, from around 1907 to the early 1930s. The Bloomsbury Group held no uniform philosophical beliefs but did commonly express an aversion to moral prudery and a desire for greater social tolerance. At various times the circle included Virginia Woolf, E. M. Forster, Clive Bell, Lytton Strachey, and John Maynard Keynes.

Bon Mot: A French term meaning "good word." A *bon mot* is a witty remark or clever observation. Charles Lamb and Oscar Wilde are celebrated for their witty *bon mots.* Two examples by Oscar Wilde stand out: (1) "All women become their mothers. That is their tragedy. No man does. That's his." (2) "A man cannot be too careful in the choice of his enemies."

Breath Verse: See *Projective Verse*

Burlesque: Any literary work that uses exaggeration to make its subject appear ridiculous, either by treating a trivial subject with profound seriousness or by treating a dignified subject frivolously. The word "burlesque" may also be used as an adjective, as in "burlesque show," to mean "striptease act." Examples of literary burlesque include the comedies of Aristophanes, Miguel de Cervantes's *Don Quixote,,* Samuel Butler's poem "Hudibras," and John Gay's play *The Beggar's Opera.*

C

Cadence: The natural rhythm of language caused by the alternation of accented and unaccented syllables. Much modern poetry—notably free verse—deliberately manipulates cadence to create complex rhythmic effects. James Macpherson's "Ossian poems" are richly cadenced, as is the poetry of the Symbolists, Walt Whitman, and Amy Lowell.

Caesura: A pause in a line of poetry, usually occurring near the middle. It typically corresponds to a break in the natural rhythm or sense of the line but is sometimes shifted to create special meanings or rhythmic effects. The opening line of Edgar Allan Poe's "The Raven" contains a caesura following "dreary": "Once upon a midnight dreary, while I pondered weak and weary . . . ."

Canzone: A short Italian or Provencal lyric poem, commonly about love and often set to music. The *canzone* has no set form but typically contains five or six stanzas made up of seven to twenty lines of eleven syllables each. A shorter, five- to ten-line "envoy," or concluding stanza, completes the poem. Masters of the *canzone* form include Petrarch, Dante Alighieri, Torquato Tasso, and Guido Cavalcanti.

Carpe Diem: A Latin term meaning "seize the day." This is a traditional theme of poetry, especially lyrics. A *carpe diem* poem advises the reader or the person it addresses to live for today and enjoy the pleasures of the moment. Two celebrated *carpe diem* poems are Andrew Marvell's "To His Coy Mistress" and Robert Herrick's poem beginning "Gather ye rosebuds while ye may . . . ."

Catharsis: The release or purging of unwanted emotions— specifically fear and pity— brought about by exposure to art. The term was first used by the Greek philosopher Aristotle in his *Poetics* to refer to the desired effect of tragedy on spectators. A famous example of catharsis is realized in Sophocles' *Oedipus Rex,* when Oedipus discovers that his wife, Jacosta, is his own mother and that the stranger he killed on the road was his own father.

Celtic Renaissance: A period of Irish literary and cultural history at the end of the nineteenth century. Followers of the movement aimed to create a romantic vision of Celtic myth and legend. The most significant works of the Celtic Renaissance typically present a dreamy, unreal world, usually in reaction against the reality of contemporary problems. William Butler Yeats's *The Wanderings of Oisin* is among the most significant works of the Celtic Renaissance. Also known as Celtic Twilight.

Celtic Twilight: See *Celtic Renaissance*

Character: Broadly speaking, a person in a literary work. The actions of characters are what constitute the plot of a story, novel, or poem. There are numerous types of characters, ranging from simple, stereotypical figures to intricate, multifaceted ones. In the techniques of anthropomorphism and personification, animals—and even places or things—can assume aspects of character. "Characterization" is the process by which an author creates vivid, believable characters in a work of art. This may be done in a variety of ways, including (1) direct description of the character by the narrator; (2) the direct presentation of the speech, thoughts, or actions of the character; and (3) the responses of other characters to the character. The term "character" also refers to a form originated by the ancient Greek writer Theophrastus that later became popular in the seventeenth and eighteenth centuries. It is a short essay or sketch of a person who prominently displays a specific attribute or quality, such as miserliness or ambition. Notable characters in literature include Oedipus Rex, Don Quixote de la Mancha, Macbeth, Candide, Hester Prynne, Ebenezer Scrooge, Huckleberry Finn, Jay Gatsby, Scarlett O'Hara, James Bond, and Kunta Kinte.

Characterization: See *Character*

Chorus: In ancient Greek drama, a group of actors who commented on and interpreted the unfolding action on the stage. Initially the chorus was a major component of the presentation, but over time it became less significant, with its numbers reduced and its role eventually limited to commentary between acts. By the sixteenth century the chorus—if employed at all—was typically a single person who provided a prologue and an epilogue and occasionally appeared between acts to introduce or underscore an important event. The chorus in William Shakespeare's *Henry V* functions in this way. Modern dramas rarely feature a chorus, but T. S. Eliot's *Murder in* *the Cathedral* and Arthur Miller's *A View from the Bridge* are notable exceptions. The Stage Manager in Thornton Wilder's *Our Town* performs a role similar to that of the chorus.

Chronicle: A record of events presented in chronological order. Although the scope and level of detail provided varies greatly among the chronicles surviving from ancient times, some, such as the *Anglo-Saxon Chronicle,* feature vivid descriptions and a lively recounting of events. During the Elizabethan Age, many dramas— appropriately called "chronicle plays"—were based on material from chronicles. Many of William Shakespeare's dramas of English history as well as Christopher Marlowe's *Edward II* are based in part on Raphael Holinshead's *Chronicles of England, Scotland, and Ireland.*

Classical: In its strictest definition in literary criticism, classicism refers to works of ancient Greek or Roman literature. The term may also be used to describe a literary work of recognized importance (a "classic") from any time period or literature that exhibits the traits of classicism. Classical authors from ancient Greek and Roman times include Juvenal and Homer. Examples of later works and authors now described as classical include French literature of the seventeenth century, Western novels of the nineteenth century, and American fiction of the mid-nineteenth century such as that written by James Fenimore Cooper and Mark Twain.

Classicism: A term used in literary criticism to describe critical doctrines that have their roots in ancient Greek and Roman literature, philosophy, and art. Works associated with classicism typically exhibit restraint on the part of the author, unity of design and purpose, clarity, simplicity, logical organization, and respect for tradition. Examples of literary classicism include Cicero's prose, the dramas of Pierre Corneille and Jean Racine, the poetry of John Dryden and Alexander Pope, and the writings of J. W. von Goethe, G. E. Lessing, and T. S. Eliot.

Climax: The turning point in a narrative, the moment when the conflict is at its most intense. Typically, the structure of stories, novels, and plays is one of rising action, in which tension builds to the climax, followed by falling action, in which tension lessens as the story moves to its conclusion. The climax in James Fenimore Cooper's *The Last of the Mohicans* occurs when Magua and his captive Cora are pursued to the edge of a cliff by Uncas. Magua kills Uncas but is subsequently killed by Hawkeye.

Colloquialism: A word, phrase, or form of pronunciation that is acceptable in casual conversation but not in formal, written communication. It is considered more acceptable than slang. An example of colloquialism can be found in Rudyard Kipling's *Barrack-room Ballads:* When 'Omer smote 'is bloomin' lyre He'd 'eard men sing by land and sea; An' what he thought 'e might require 'E went an' took—the same as me!

Comedy: One of two major types of drama, the other being tragedy. Its aim is to amuse, and it typically ends happily. Comedy assumes many forms, such as farce and burlesque, and uses a variety of techniques, from parody to satire. In a restricted sense the term comedy refers only to dramatic presentations, but in general usage it is commonly applied to nondramatic works as well. Examples of comedies range from the plays of Aristophanes, Terrence, and Plautus, Dante Alighieri's *The Divine Comedy,* Francois Rabelais's *Pantagruel* and *Gargantua,* and some of Geoffrey Chaucer's tales and William Shakespeare's plays to Noel Coward's play *Private Lives* and James Thurber's short story "The Secret Life of Walter Mitty."

Comedy of Manners: A play about the manners and conventions of an aristocratic, highly sophisticated society. The characters are usually types rather than individualized personalities, and plot is less important than atmosphere. Such plays were an important aspect of late seventeenth-century English comedy. The comedy of manners was revived in the eighteenth century by Oliver Goldsmith and Richard Brinsley Sheridan, enjoyed a second revival in the late nineteenth century, and has endured into the twentieth century. Examples of comedies of manners include William Congreve's *The Way of the World* in the late seventeenth century, Oliver Goldsmith's *She Stoops to Conquer* and Richard Brinsley Sheridan's *The School for Scandal* in the eighteenth century, Oscar Wilde's *The Importance of*

Being Earnest in the nineteenth century, and W. Somerset Maugham's *The Circle* in the twentieth century.

Comic Relief: The use of humor to lighten the mood of a serious or tragic story, especially in plays. The technique is very common in Elizabethan works, and can be an integral part of the plot or simply a brief event designed to break the tension of the scene. The Gravediggers' scene in William Shakespeare's *Hamlet* is a frequently cited example of comic relief.

Commedia dell'arte: An Italian term meaning "the comedy of guilds" or "the comedy of professional actors." This form of dramatic comedy was popular in Italy during the sixteenth century. Actors were assigned stock roles (such as Pulcinella, the stupid servant, or Pantalone, the old merchant) and given a basic plot to follow, but all dialogue was improvised. The roles were rigidly typed and the plots were formulaic, usually revolving around young lovers who thwarted their elders and attained wealth and happiness. A rigid convention of the *commedia dell'arte* is the periodic intrusion of Harlequin, who interrupts the play with low buffoonery. Peppino de Filippo's *Metamorphoses of a Wandering Minstrel* gave modern audiences an idea of what *commedia dell'arte* may have been like. Various scenarios for *commedia dell'arte* were compiled in Petraccone's *La commedia dell'arte, storia, technica, scenari,* published in 1927.

Complaint: A lyric poem, popular in the Renaissance, in which the speaker expresses sorrow about his or her condition. Typically, the speaker's sadness is caused by an unresponsive lover, but some complaints cite other sources of unhappiness, such as poverty or fate. A commonly cited example is "A Complaint by Night of the Lover Not Beloved" by Henry Howard, Earl of Surrey. Thomas Sackville's "Complaint of Henry, Duke of Buckingham" traces the duke's unhappiness to his ruthless ambition.

Conceit: A clever and fanciful metaphor, usually expressed through elaborate and extended comparison, that presents a striking parallel between two seemingly dissimilar things— for example, elaborately comparing a beautiful woman to an object like a garden or the sun. The conceit was a popular device throughout the Elizabethan Age and Baroque Age and was the principal technique of the seventeenth-century English metaphysical poets. This usage of the word conceit is unrelated to the best-known definition of conceit as an arrogant attitude or behavior. The conceit figures prominently in the works of John Donne, Emily Dickinson, and T. S. Eliot.

Concrete: Concrete is the opposite of abstract, and refers to a thing that actually exists or a description that allows the reader to experience an object or concept with the senses. Henry David Thoreau's *Walden* contains much concrete description of nature and wildlife.

Concrete Poetry: Poetry in which visual elements play a large part in the poetic effect. Punctuation marks, letters, or words are arranged on a page to form a visual design: a cross, for example, or a bumblebee. Max Bill and Eugene Gomringer were among the early practitioners of concrete poetry; Haroldo de Campos and Augusto de Campos are among contemporary authors of concrete poetry.

Confessional Poetry: A form of poetry in which the poet reveals very personal, intimate, sometimes shocking information about himself or herself. Anne Sexton, Sylvia Plath, Robert Lowell, and John Berryman wrote poetry in the confessional vein.

Conflict: The conflict in a work of fiction is the issue to be resolved in the story. It usually occurs between two characters, the protagonist and the antagonist, or between the protagonist and society or the protagonist and himself or herself. Conflict in Theodore Dreiser's novel *Sister Carrie* comes as a result of urban society, while Jack London's short story "To Build a Fire" concerns the protagonist's battle against the cold and himself.

Connotation: The impression that a word gives beyond its defined meaning. Connotations may be universally understood or may be significant only to a certain group. Both "horse" and "steed" denote the same animal, but "steed" has a different connotation, deriving from the chivalrous or romantic narratives in which the word was once often used.

Consonance: Consonance occurs in poetry when words appearing at the ends of two or more verses have similar final consonant sounds but have final vowel sounds that differ, as with "stuff" and "off." Consonance is found in "The curfew tolls the knells of parting day" from Thomas Grey's "An Elegy Written in a Country Church Yard." Also known as Half Rhyme or Slant Rhyme.

Convention: Any widely accepted literary device, style, or form. A soliloquy, in which a character reveals to the audience his or her private thoughts, is an example of a dramatic convention.

Corrido: A Mexican ballad. Examples of *corridos* include "Muerte del afamado Bilito," "La voz de mi conciencia," "Lucio Perez," "La juida," and "Los presos."

Couplet: Two lines of poetry with the same rhyme and meter, often expressing a complete and self-contained thought. The following couplet is from Alexander Pope's "Elegy to the Memory of an Unfortunate Lady": 'Tis Use alone that sanctifies Expense, And Splendour borrows all her rays from Sense.

Criticism: The systematic study and evaluation of literary works, usually based on a specific method or set of principles. An important part of literary studies since ancient times, the practice of criticism has given rise to numerous theories, methods, and "schools," sometimes producing conflicting, even contradictory, interpretations of literature in general as well as of individual works. Even such basic issues as what constitutes a poem or a novel have been the subject of much criticism over the centuries. Seminal texts of literary criticism include Plato's *Republic,* Aristotle's *Poetics,* Sir Philip Sidney's *The Defence of Poesie,* John Dryden's *Of Dramatic Poesie,* and William Wordsworth's "Preface" to the second edition of his *Lyrical Ballads.* Contemporary schools of criticism include deconstruction, feminist, psychoanalytic, poststructuralist, new historicist, postcolonialist, and reader- response.

D

Dactyl: See *Foot*

Dadaism: A protest movement in art and literature founded by Tristan Tzara in 1916. Followers of the movement expressed their outrage at the destruction brought about by World War I by revolting against numerous forms of social convention. The Dadaists presented works marked by calculated madness and flamboyant nonsense. They stressed total freedom of expression, commonly through primitive displays of emotion and illogical, often senseless, poetry. The movement ended shortly after the war, when it was replaced by surrealism. Proponents of Dadaism include Andre Breton, Louis Aragon, Philippe Soupault, and Paul Eluard.

Decadent: See *Decadents*

Decadents: The followers of a nineteenth-century literary movement that had its beginnings in French aestheticism. Decadent literature displays a fascination with perverse and morbid states; a search for novelty and sensation—the "new thrill"; a preoccupation with mysticism; and a belief in the senselessness of human existence. The movement is closely associated with the doctrine Art for Art's Sake. The term "decadence" is sometimes used to denote a decline in the quality of art or literature following a period of greatness. Major French decadents are Charles Baudelaire and Arthur Rimbaud. English decadents include Oscar Wilde, Ernest Dowson, and Frank Harris.

Deconstruction: A method of literary criticism developed by Jacques Derrida and characterized by multiple conflicting interpretations of a given work. Deconstructionists consider the impact of the language of a work and suggest that the true meaning of the work is not necessarily the meaning that the author intended. Jacques Derrida's *De la grammatologie* is the seminal text on deconstructive strategies; among American practitioners of this method of criticism are Paul de Man and J. Hillis Miller.

Deduction: The process of reaching a conclusion through reasoning from general premises to a specific premise. An example of deduction is present in the following syllogism: Premise: All mammals are animals. Premise: All whales are mammals. Conclusion: Therefore, all whales are animals.

Denotation: The definition of a word, apart from the impressions or feelings it creates in the reader. The word "apartheid" denotes a political and economic policy of segregation by race, but its connotations— oppression, slavery, inequality—are numerous.

Denouement: A French word meaning "the unknotting." In literary criticism, it denotes the resolution of conflict in fiction or drama. The *denouement* follows the climax and provides an outcome to the primary plot situation as well as an explanation of secondary plot complications. The *denouement* often involves a character's recognition of his or her state of mind or moral condition. A well-known example of *denouement* is the last scene of the play *As You Like It* by William Shakespeare, in which couples are married, an evildoer repents, the identities of two disguised characters are revealed, and a ruler is restored to power. Also known as Falling Action.

Description: Descriptive writing is intended to allow a reader to picture the scene or setting in which the action of a story takes place. The form this description takes often evokes an intended emotional response—a dark, spooky graveyard will evoke fear, and a peaceful, sunny meadow will evoke calmness. An example of a descriptive story is Edgar Allan Poe's *Landor's Cottage,* which offers a detailed depiction of a New York country estate.

Detective Story: A narrative about the solution of a mystery or the identification of a criminal. The conventions of the detective story include the detective's scrupulous use of logic in solving the mystery; incompetent or ineffectual police; a suspect who appears guilty at first but is later proved innocent; and the detective's friend or confidant— often the narrator—whose slowness in interpreting clues emphasizes by contrast the detective's brilliance. Edgar Allan Poe's "Murders in the Rue Morgue" is commonly regarded as the earliest example of this type of story. With this work, Poe established many of the conventions of the detective story genre, which are still in practice. Other practitioners of this vast and extremely popular genre include Arthur Conan Doyle, Dashiell Hammett, and Agatha Christie.

Deus ex machina: A Latin term meaning "god out of a machine." In Greek drama, a god was often lowered onto the stage by a mechanism of some kind to rescue the hero or untangle the plot. By extension, the term refers to any artificial device or coincidence used to bring about a convenient and simple solution to a plot. This is a common device in melodramas and includes such fortunate circumstances as the sudden receipt of a legacy to save the family farm or a last-minute stay of execution. The *deus ex machina* invariably rewards the virtuous and punishes evildoers. Examples of *deus ex machina* include King Louis XIV in Jean-Baptiste Moliere's *Tartuffe* and Queen Victoria in *The Pirates of Penzance* by William Gilbert and Arthur Sullivan. Bertolt Brecht parodies the abuse of such devices in the conclusion of his *Threepenny Opera.*

Dialogue: In its widest sense, dialogue is simply conversation between people in a literary work; in its most restricted sense, it refers specifically to the speech of characters in a drama. As a specific literary genre, a "dialogue" is a composition in which characters debate an issue or idea. The Greek philosopher Plato frequently expounded his theories in the form of dialogues.

Diction: The selection and arrangement of words in a literary work. Either or both may vary depending on the desired effect. There are four general types of diction: "formal," used in scholarly or lofty writing; "informal," used in relaxed but educated conversation; "colloquial," used in everyday speech; and "slang," containing newly coined words and other terms not accepted in formal usage.

Didactic: A term used to describe works of literature that aim to teach some moral, religious, political, or practical lesson. Although didactic elements are often found in artistically pleasing works, the term "didactic" usually refers to literature in which the message is more important than the form. The term may also be used to criticize a work that the critic finds "overly didactic," that is, heavy-handed in its delivery of a lesson. Examples of didactic literature include John Bunyan's *Pilgrim's Progress,* Alexander Pope's *Essay on Criticism,* Jean-Jacques Rousseau's *Emile,* and Elizabeth Inchbald's *Simple Story.*

Dimeter: See *Meter*

Dionysian: See *Apollonian and Dionysian*

Discordia concours: A Latin phrase meaning "discord in harmony." The term was coined by the eighteenth-century English writer

Samuel Johnson to describe "a combination of dissimilar images or discovery of occult resemblances in things apparently unlike." Johnson created the expression by reversing a phrase by the Latin poet Horace. The metaphysical poetry of John Donne, Richard Crashaw, Abraham Cowley, George Herbert, and Edward Taylor among others, contains many examples of *discordia concours.* In Donne's "A Valediction: Forbidding Mourning," the poet compares the union of himself with his lover to a draftsman's compass: If they be two, they are two so, As stiff twin compasses are two: Thy soul, the fixed foot, makes no show To move, but doth, if the other do; And though it in the center sit, Yet when the other far doth roam, It leans, and hearkens after it, And grows erect, as that comes home.

Dissonance: A combination of harsh or jarring sounds, especially in poetry. Although such combinations may be accidental, poets sometimes intentionally make them to achieve particular effects. Dissonance is also sometimes used to refer to close but not identical rhymes. When this is the case, the word functions as a synonym for consonance. Robert Browning, Gerard Manley Hopkins, and many other poets have made deliberate use of dissonance.

Doppelganger: A literary technique by which a character is duplicated (usually in the form of an alter ego, though sometimes as a ghostly counterpart) or divided into two distinct, usually opposite personalities. The use of this character device is widespread in nineteenth- and twentieth- century literature, and indicates a growing awareness among authors that the "self" is really a composite of many "selves." A well-known story containing a *doppelganger* character is Robert Louis Stevenson's *Dr. Jekyll and Mr. Hyde,* which dramatizes an internal struggle between good and evil. Also known as The Double.

Double Entendre: A corruption of a French phrase meaning "double meaning." The term is used to indicate a word or phrase that is deliberately ambiguous, especially when one of the meanings is risque or improper. An example of a *double entendre* is the Elizabethan usage of the verb "die," which refers both to death and to orgasm.

Double, The: See *Doppelganger*

Draft: Any preliminary version of a written work. An author may write dozens of drafts which are revised to form the final work, or he or she may write only one, with few or no revisions. Dorothy Parker's observation that "I can't write five words but that I change seven" humorously indicates the purpose of the draft.

Drama: In its widest sense, a drama is any work designed to be presented by actors on a stage. Similarly, "drama" denotes a broad literary genre that includes a variety of forms, from pageant and spectacle to tragedy and comedy, as well as countless types and subtypes. More commonly in modern usage, however, a drama is a work that treats serious subjects and themes but does not aim at the grandeur of tragedy. This use of the term originated with the eighteenth-century French writer Denis Diderot, who used the word *drame* to designate his plays about middle- class life; thus "drama" typically features characters of a less exalted stature than those of tragedy. Examples of classical dramas include Menander's comedy *Dyscolus* and Sophocles' tragedy *Oedipus Rex.* Contemporary dramas include Eugene O'Neill's *The Iceman Cometh,* Lillian Hellman's *Little Foxes,* and August Wilson's *Ma Rainey's Black Bottom.*

Dramatic Irony: Occurs when the audience of a play or the reader of a work of literature knows something that a character in the work itself does not know. The irony is in the contrast between the intended meaning of the statements or actions of a character and the additional information understood by the audience. A celebrated example of dramatic irony is in Act V of William Shakespeare's *Romeo and Juliet,* where two young lovers meet their end as a result of a tragic misunderstanding. Here, the audience has full knowledge that Juliet's apparent "death" is merely temporary; she will regain her senses when the mysterious "sleeping potion" she has taken wears off. But Romeo, mistaking Juliet's drug-induced trance for true death, kills himself in grief. Upon awakening, Juliet discovers Romeo's corpse and, in despair, slays herself.

Dramatic Monologue: See *Monologue*

Dramatic Poetry: Any lyric work that employs elements of drama such as dialogue, conflict, or characterization, but excluding works that are intended for stage presentation. A monologue is a form of dramatic poetry.

Dramatis Personae: The characters in a work of literature, particularly a drama. The list of characters printed before the main text of a play or in the program is the *dramatis personae*.

Dream Allegory: See *Dream Vision*

Dream Vision: A literary convention, chiefly of the Middle Ages. In a dream vision a story is presented as a literal dream of the narrator. This device was commonly used to teach moral and religious lessons. Important works of this type are *The Divine Comedy* by Dante Alighieri, *Piers Plowman* by William Langland, and *The Pilgrim's Progress* by John Bunyan. Also known as Dream Allegory.

Dystopia: An imaginary place in a work of fiction where the characters lead dehumanized, fearful lives. Jack London's *The Iron Heel,* Yevgeny Zamyatin's *My,* Aldous Huxley's *Brave New World,* George Orwell's *Nineteen Eighty-four,* and Margaret Atwood's *Handmaid's Tale* portray versions of dystopia.

E

Eclogue: In classical literature, a poem featuring rural themes and structured as a dialogue among shepherds. Eclogues often took specific poetic forms, such as elegies or love poems. Some were written as the soliloquy of a shepherd. In later centuries, "eclogue" came to refer to any poem that was in the pastoral tradition or that had a dialogue or monologue structure. A classical example of an eclogue is Virgil's *Eclogues,* also known as *Bucolics.* Giovanni Boccaccio, Edmund Spenser, Andrew Marvell, Jonathan Swift, and Louis MacNeice also wrote eclogues.

Edwardian: Describes cultural conventions identified with the period of the reign of Edward VII of England (1901-1910). Writers of the Edwardian Age typically displayed a strong reaction against the propriety and conservatism of the Victorian Age. Their work often exhibits distrust of authority in religion, politics, and art and expresses strong doubts about the soundness of conventional values. Writers of this era include George Bernard Shaw, H. G. Wells, and Joseph Conrad.

Edwardian Age: See *Edwardian*

Electra Complex: A daughter's amorous obsession with her father. The term Electra complex comes from the plays of Euripides and Sophocles entitled *Electra,* in which the character Electra drives her brother Orestes to kill their mother and her lover in revenge for the murder of their father.

Elegy: A lyric poem that laments the death of a person or the eventual death of all people. In a conventional elegy, set in a classical world, the poet and subject are spoken of as shepherds. In modern criticism, the word elegy is often used to refer to a poem that is melancholy or mournfully contemplative. John Milton's "Lycidas" and Percy Bysshe Shelley's "Adonais" are two examples of this form.

Elizabethan Age: A period of great economic growth, religious controversy, and nationalism closely associated with the reign of Elizabeth I of England (1558-1603). The Elizabethan Age is considered a part of the general renaissance—that is, the flowering of arts and literature—that took place in Europe during the fourteenth through sixteenth centuries. The era is considered the golden age of English literature. The most important dramas in English and a great deal of lyric poetry were produced during this period, and modern English criticism began around this time. The notable authors of the period—Philip Sidney, Edmund Spenser, Christopher Marlowe, William Shakespeare, Ben Jonson, Francis Bacon, and John Donne—are among the best in all of English literature.

Elizabethan Drama: English comic and tragic plays produced during the Renaissance, or more narrowly, those plays written during the last years of and few years after Queen Elizabeth's reign. William Shakespeare is considered an Elizabethan dramatist in the broader sense, although most of his work was produced during the reign of James I. Examples of Elizabethan comedies include John Lyly's *The Woman in the Moone,* Thomas Dekker's *The Roaring Girl, or, Moll Cut Purse,* and William Shakespeare's *Twelfth Night.* Examples of Elizabethan tragedies include William Shakespeare's *Antony and Cleopatra,* Thomas Kyd's *The Spanish Tragedy,* and John Webster's *The Tragedy of the Duchess of Malfi.*

Empathy: A sense of shared experience, including emotional and physical feelings, with someone or something other than oneself. Empathy is often used to describe the response of a reader to a literary character. An example of an empathic passage is William Shakespeare's description in his narrative poem *Venus and Adonis* of: the snail, whose tender horns being hit, Shrinks backward in his shelly cave with pain. Readers of Gerard Manley Hopkins's *The Windhover* may experience some of the physical sensations evoked in the description of the movement of the falcon.

English Sonnet: See *Sonnet*

Enjambment: The running over of the sense and structure of a line of verse or a couplet into the following verse or couplet. Andrew Marvell's "To His Coy Mistress" is structured as a series of enjambments, as in lines 11-12: "My vegetable love should grow/Vaster than empires and more slow."

Enlightenment, The: An eighteenth-century philosophical movement. It began in France but had a wide impact throughout Europe and America. Thinkers of the Enlightenment valued reason and believed that both the individual and society could achieve a state of perfection. Corresponding to this essentially humanist vision was a resistance to religious authority. Important figures of the Enlightenment were Denis Diderot and Voltaire in France, Edward Gibbon and David Hume in England, and Thomas Paine and Thomas Jefferson in the United States.

Epic: A long narrative poem about the adventures of a hero of great historic or legendary importance. The setting is vast and the action is often given cosmic significance through the intervention of supernatural forces such as gods, angels, or demons. Epics are typically written in a classical style of grand simplicity with elaborate metaphors and allusions that enhance the symbolic importance of a hero's adventures. Some well-known epics are Homer's *Iliad* and *Odyssey*, Virgil's *Aeneid,* and John Milton's *Paradise Lost.*

Epic Simile: See *Homeric Simile*

Epic Theater: A theory of theatrical presentation developed by twentieth-century German playwright Bertolt Brecht. Brecht created a type of drama that the audience could view with complete detachment. He used what he termed "alienation effects" to create an emotional distance between the audience and the action on stage. Among these effects are: short, self-contained scenes that keep the play from building to a cathartic climax; songs that comment on the action; and techniques of acting that prevent the actor from developing an emotional identity with his role. Besides the plays of Bertolt Brecht, other plays that utilize epic theater conventions include those of Georg Buchner, Frank Wedekind, Erwin Piscator, and Leopold Jessner.

Epigram: A saying that makes the speaker's point quickly and concisely. Samuel Taylor Coleridge wrote an epigram that neatly sums up the form: What is an Epigram? A Dwarfish whole, Its body brevity, and wit its soul.

Epilogue: A concluding statement or section of a literary work. In dramas, particularly those of the seventeenth and eighteenth centuries, the epilogue is a closing speech, often in verse, delivered by an actor at the end of a play and spoken directly to the audience. A famous epilogue is Puck's speech at the end of William Shakespeare's *A Midsummer Night's Dream.*

Epiphany: A sudden revelation of truth inspired by a seemingly trivial incident. The term was widely used by James Joyce in his critical writings, and the stories in Joyce's *Dubliners* are commonly called "epiphanies."

Episode: An incident that forms part of a story and is significantly related to it. Episodes may be either self- contained narratives or events that depend on a larger context for their sense and importance. Examples of episodes include the founding of Wilmington, Delaware in Charles Reade's *The Disinherited Heir* and the individual events comprising the picaresque novels and medieval romances.

Episodic Plot: See *Plot*

Epitaph: An inscription on a tomb or tombstone, or a verse written on the occasion of a person's death. Epitaphs may be serious or humorous. Dorothy Parker's epitaph reads, "I told you I was sick."

Epithalamion: A song or poem written to honor and commemorate a marriage ceremony. Famous examples include Edmund Spenser's "Epithalamion" and e. e. cummings's "Epithalamion." Also spelled Epithalamium.

Epithalamium: See *Epithalamion*

Epithet: A word or phrase, often disparaging or abusive, that expresses a character trait of someone or something. "The Napoleon of crime" is an epithet applied to Professor Moriarty, arch-rival of Sherlock Holmes in Arthur Conan Doyle's series of detective stories.

Exempla: See *Exemplum*

Exemplum: A tale with a moral message. This form of literary sermonizing flourished during the Middle Ages, when *exempla* appeared in collections known as "example-books." The works of Geoffrey Chaucer are full of *exempla*.

Existentialism: A predominantly twentieth-century philosophy concerned with the nature and perception of human existence. There are two major strains of existentialist thought: atheistic and Christian. Followers of atheistic existentialism believe that the individual is alone in a godless universe and that the basic human condition is one of suffering and loneliness. Nevertheless, because there are no fixed values, individuals can create their own characters—indeed, they can shape themselves—through the exercise of free will. The atheistic strain culminates in and is popularly associated with the works of Jean-Paul Sartre. The Christian existentialists, on the other hand, believe that only in God may people find freedom from life's anguish. The two strains hold certain beliefs in common: that existence cannot be fully understood or described through empirical effort; that anguish is a universal element of life; that individuals must bear responsibility for their actions; and that there is no common standard of behavior or perception for religious and ethical matters. Existentialist thought figures prominently in the works of such authors as Eugene Ionesco, Franz Kafka, Fyodor Dostoyevsky, Simone de Beauvoir, Samuel Beckett, and Albert Camus.

Expatriates: See *Expatriatism*

Expatriatism: The practice of leaving one's country to live for an extended period in another country. Literary expatriates include English poets Percy Bysshe Shelley and John Keats in Italy, Polish novelist Joseph Conrad in England, American writers Richard Wright, James Baldwin, Gertrude Stein, and Ernest Hemingway in France, and Trinidadian author Neil Bissondath in Canada.

Exposition: Writing intended to explain the nature of an idea, thing, or theme. Expository writing is often combined with description, narration, or argument. In dramatic writing, the exposition is the introductory material which presents the characters, setting, and tone of the play. An example of dramatic exposition occurs in many nineteenth-century drawing-room comedies in which the butler and the maid open the play with relevant talk about their master and mistress; in composition, exposition relays factual information, as in encyclopedia entries.

Expressionism: An indistinct literary term, originally used to describe an early twentieth-century school of German painting. The term applies to almost any mode of unconventional, highly subjective writing that distorts reality in some way. Advocates of Expressionism include dramatists George Kaiser, Ernst Toller, Luigi Pirandello, Federico Garcia Lorca, Eugene O'Neill, and Elmer Rice; poets George Heym, Ernst Stadler, August Stramm, Gottfried Benn, and Georg Trakl; and novelists Franz Kafka and James Joyce.

Extended Monologue: See *Monologue*

F

Fable: A prose or verse narrative intended to convey a moral. Animals or inanimate objects with human characteristics often serve as characters in fables. A famous fable is Aesop's "The Tortoise and the Hare."

Fairy Tales: Short narratives featuring mythical beings such as fairies, elves, and sprites. These tales originally belonged to the folklore of a particular nation or region, such as those collected in Germany by Jacob and Wilhelm Grimm. Two other celebrated writers of fairy tales are Hans Christian Andersen and Rudyard Kipling.

Falling Action: See *Denouement*

Fantasy: A literary form related to mythology and folklore. Fantasy literature is typically set in non-existent realms and features supernatural beings. Notable examples of fantasy literature are *The Lord of the Rings* by J. R. R. Tolkien and the Gormenghast trilogy by Mervyn Peake.

Farce: A type of comedy characterized by broad humor, outlandish incidents, and often vulgar subject matter. Much of the "comedy" in film and television could more accurately be described as farce.

Feet: See *Foot*

Feminine Rhyme: See *Rhyme*

Femme fatale: A French phrase with the literal translation "fatal woman." A *femme fatale* is a sensuous, alluring woman who often leads men into danger or trouble. A classic example of the *femme fatale* is the nameless character in Billy Wilder's *The Seven Year Itch,* portrayed by Marilyn Monroe in the film adaptation.

Fiction: Any story that is the product of imagination rather than a documentation of fact. characters and events in such narratives may be based in real life but their ultimate form and configuration is a creation of the author. Geoffrey Chaucer's *The Canterbury Tales,* Laurence Sterne's *Tristram Shandy,* and Margaret Mitchell's *Gone with the Wind* are examples of fiction.

Figurative Language: A technique in writing in which the author temporarily interrupts the order, construction, or meaning of the writing for a particular effect. This interruption takes the form of one or more figures of speech such as hyperbole, irony, or simile. Figurative language is the opposite of literal language, in which every word is truthful, accurate, and free of exaggeration or embellishment. Examples of figurative language are tropes such as metaphor and rhetorical figures such as apostrophe.

Figures of Speech: Writing that differs from customary conventions for construction, meaning, order, or significance for the purpose of a special meaning or effect. There are two major types of figures of speech: rhetorical figures, which do not make changes in the meaning of the words, and tropes, which do. Types of figures of speech include simile, hyperbole, alliteration, and pun, among many others.

Fin de siecle: A French term meaning "end of the century." The term is used to denote the last decade of the nineteenth century, a transition period when writers and other artists abandoned old conventions and looked for new techniques and objectives. Two writers commonly associated with the *fin de siecle* mindset are Oscar Wilde and George Bernard Shaw.

First Person: See *Point of View*

Flashback: A device used in literature to present action that occurred before the beginning of the story. Flashbacks are often introduced as the dreams or recollections of one or more characters. Flashback techniques are often used in films, where they are typically set off by a gradual changing of one picture to another.

Foil: A character in a work of literature whose physical or psychological qualities contrast strongly with, and therefore highlight, the corresponding qualities of another character. In his Sherlock Holmes stories, Arthur Conan Doyle portrayed Dr. Watson as a man of normal habits and intelligence, making him a foil for the eccentric and wonderfully perceptive Sherlock Holmes.

Folk Ballad: See *Ballad*

Folklore: Traditions and myths preserved in a culture or group of people. Typically, these are passed on by word of mouth in various forms—such as legends, songs, and proverbs— or preserved in customs and ceremonies. This term was first used by W. J. Thoms in 1846. Sir James Frazer's *The Golden Bough* is the record of English folklore; myths about the frontier and the Old South exemplify American folklore.

Folktale: A story originating in oral tradition. Folktales fall into a variety of categories, including legends, ghost stories, fairy tales, fables, and anecdotes based on historical figures and events. Examples of folktales include Giambattista Basile's *The Pentamerone,* which contains the tales of Puss in Boots, Rapunzel, Cinderella, and Beauty and the Beast, and Joel Chandler Harris's Uncle Remus stories, which represent transplanted African folktales and American tales about the characters Mike Fink, Johnny Appleseed, Paul Bunyan, and Pecos Bill.

Foot: The smallest unit of rhythm in a line of poetry. In English-language poetry, a foot is typically one accented syllable combined with one or two unaccented syllables. There are many different types of feet. When the accent is on the second syllable of a two syllable word (con- *tort*), the foot is an "iamb"; the reverse accentual pattern (*tor* -ture) is a "tro-chee." Other feet that commonly occur in poetry in English are "anapest", two unaccented syllables followed by an accented syllable as in in-ter-*cept*, and "dactyl", an accented syllable followed by two unaccented syllables as in *su*-i- cide.

Foreshadowing: A device used in literature to create expectation or to set up an explanation of later developments. In Charles Dickens's *Great Expectations,* the graveyard encounter at the beginning of the novel between Pip and the escaped convict Magwitch foreshadows the baleful atmosphere and events that comprise much of the narrative.

Form: The pattern or construction of a work which identifies its genre and distinguishes it from other genres. Examples of forms include the different genres, such as the lyric form or the short story form, and various patterns for poetry, such as the verse form or the stanza form.

Formalism: In literary criticism, the belief that literature should follow prescribed rules of construction, such as those that govern the sonnet form. Examples of formalism are found in the work of the New Critics and structuralists.

Fourteener Meter: See *Meter*

Free Verse: Poetry that lacks regular metrical and rhyme patterns but that tries to capture the cadences of everyday speech. The form allows a poet to exploit a variety of rhythmical effects within a single poem. Free-verse techniques have been widely used in the twentieth century by such writers as Ezra Pound, T. S. Eliot, Carl Sandburg, and William Carlos Williams. Also known as *Vers libre.*

Futurism: A flamboyant literary and artistic movement that developed in France, Italy, and Russia from 1908 through the 1920s. Futurist theater and poetry abandoned traditional literary forms. In their place, followers of the movement attempted to achieve total freedom of expression through bizarre imagery and deformed or newly invented words. The Futurists were self-consciously modern artists who attempted to incorporate the appearances and sounds of modern life into their work. Futurist writers include Filippo Tommaso Marinetti, Wyndham Lewis, Guillaume Apollinaire, Velimir Khlebnikov, and Vladimir Mayakovsky.

G

Genre: A category of literary work. In critical theory, genre may refer to both the content of a given work—tragedy, comedy, pastoral—and to its form, such as poetry, novel, or drama. This term also refers to types of popular literature, as in the genres of science fiction or the detective story.

Genteel Tradition: A term coined by critic George Santayana to describe the literary practice of certain late nineteenth-century American writers, especially New Englanders. Followers of the Genteel Tradition emphasized conventionality in social, religious, moral, and literary standards. Some of the best-known writers of the Genteel Tradition are R. H. Stoddard and Bayard Taylor.

Gilded Age: A period in American history during the 1870s characterized by political corruption and materialism. A number of important novels of social and political criticism were written during this time. Examples of Gilded Age literature include Henry Adams's *Democracy* and F. Marion Crawford's *An American Politician.*

Gothic: See *Gothicism*

Gothicism: In literary criticism, works characterized by a taste for the medieval or morbidly attractive. A gothic novel prominently features elements of horror, the supernatural, gloom, and violence: clanking chains, terror, charnel houses, ghosts, medieval castles, and mysteriously slamming doors. The term "gothic novel" is also applied to novels that lack elements of the traditional Gothic setting but that create a similar atmosphere of terror or dread. Mary Shelley's *Frankenstein* is perhaps the best-known English work of this kind.

Gothic Novel: See *Gothicism*

Great Chain of Being: The belief that all things and creatures in nature are organized in a hierarchy from inanimate objects at the bottom to God at the top. This system of belief was popular in the seventeenth and eighteenth centuries. A summary of the concept of the great chain of being can be found in the first epistle of Alexander Pope's *An Essay on Man,* and more recently in Arthur O. Lovejoy's *The Great Chain of Being: A Study of the History of an Idea.*

Grotesque: In literary criticism, the subject matter of a work or a style of expression characterized by exaggeration, deformity, freakishness, and disorder. The grotesque often includes an element of comic absurdity. Early examples of literary grotesque include Francois Rabelais's *Pantagruel* and *Gargantua* and Thomas Nashe's *The Unfortunate Traveller,* while more recent examples can be found in the works of Edgar Allan Poe, Evelyn Waugh, Eudora Welty, Flannery O'Connor, Eugene Ionesco, Gunter Grass, Thomas Mann, Mervyn Peake, and Joseph Heller, among many others.

H

Haiku: The shortest form of Japanese poetry, constructed in three lines of five, seven, and five syllables respectively. The message of a *haiku* poem usually centers on some aspect of spirituality and provokes an emotional response in the reader. Early masters of *haiku* include Basho, Buson, Kobayashi Issa, and Masaoka Shiki. English writers of *haiku* include the Imagists, notably Ezra Pound, H. D., Amy Lowell, Carl Sandburg, and William Carlos Williams. Also known as *Hokku.*

Half Rhyme: See *Consonance*

Hamartia: In tragedy, the event or act that leads to the hero's or heroine's downfall. This term is often incorrectly used as a synonym for tragic flaw. In Richard Wright's *Native Son,* the act that seals Bigger Thomas's fate is his first impulsive murder.

Harlem Renaissance: The Harlem Renaissance of the 1920s is generally considered the first significant movement of black writers and artists in the United States. During this period, new and established black writers published more fiction and poetry than ever before, the first influential black literary journals were established, and black authors and artists received their first widespread recognition and serious critical appraisal. Among

the major writers associated with this period are Claude McKay, Jean Toomer, Countee Cullen, Langston Hughes, Arna Bontemps, Nella Larsen, and Zora Neale Hurston. Works representative of the Harlem Renaissance include Arna Bontemps's poems "The Return" and "Golgotha Is a Mountain," Claude McKay's novel *Home to Harlem,* Nella Larsen's novel *Passing,* Langston Hughes's poem "The Negro Speaks of Rivers," and the journals *Crisis* and *Opportunity,* both founded during this period. Also known as Negro Renaissance and New Negro Movement.

Harlequin: A stock character of the *commedia dell'arte* who occasionally interrupted the action with silly antics. Harlequin first appeared on the English stage in John Day's *The Travailes of the Three English Brothers.* The San Francisco Mime Troupe is one of the few modern groups to adapt Harlequin to the needs of contemporary satire.

Hellenism: Imitation of ancient Greek thought or styles. Also, an approach to life that focuses on the growth and development of the intellect. "Hellenism" is sometimes used to refer to the belief that reason can be applied to examine all human experience. A cogent discussion of Hellenism can be found in Matthew Arnold's *Culture and Anarchy.*

Heptameter: See *Meter*

Hero/Heroine: The principal sympathetic character (male or female) in a literary work. Heroes and heroines typically exhibit admirable traits: idealism, courage, and integrity, for example. Famous heroes and heroines include Pip in Charles Dickens's *Great Expectations,* the anonymous narrator in Ralph Ellison's *Invisible Man,* and Sethe in Toni Morrison's *Beloved.*

Heroic Couplet: A rhyming couplet written in iambic pentameter (a verse with five iambic feet). The following lines by Alexander Pope are an example: "Truth guards the Poet, sanctifies the line,/ And makes Immortal, Verse as mean as mine."

Heroic Line: The meter and length of a line of verse in epic or heroic poetry. This varies by language and time period. For example, in English poetry, the heroic line is iambic pentameter (a verse with five iambic feet); in

French, the alexandrine (a verse with six iambic feet); in classical literature, dactylic hexameter (a verse with six dactylic feet).

Heroine: See *Hero/Heroine*

Hexameter: See *Meter*

Historical Criticism: The study of a work based on its impact on the world of the time period in which it was written. Examples of post-modern historical criticism can be found in the work of Michel Foucault, Hayden White, Stephen Greenblatt, and Jonathan Goldberg.

Hokku: See *Haiku*

Holocaust: See *Holocaust Literature*

Holocaust Literature: Literature influenced by or written about the Holocaust of World War II. Such literature includes true stories of survival in concentration camps, escape, and life after the war, as well as fictional works and poetry. Representative works of Holocaust literature include Saul Bellow's *Mr. Sammler's Planet*, Anne Frank's *The Diary of a Young Girl*, Jerzy Kosinski's *The Painted Bird*, Arthur Miller's *Incident at Vichy*, Czeslaw Milosz's *Collected Poems*, William Styron's *Sophie's Choice*, and Art Spiegelman's *Maus*.

Homeric Simile: An elaborate, detailed comparison written as a simile many lines in length. An example of an epic simile from John Milton's *Paradise Lost* follows: Angel Forms, who lay entranced Thick as autumnal leaves that strow the brooks In Vallombrosa, where the Etrurian shades High over-arched embower; or scattered sedge Afloat, when with fierce winds Orion armed Hath vexed the Red-Sea coast, whose waves o'erthrew Busiris and his Memphian chivalry, While with perfidious hatred they pursued The sojourners of Goshen, who beheld From the safe shore their floating carcasses And broken chariot-wheels. Also known as Epic Simile.

Horatian Satire: See *Satire*

Humanism: A philosophy that places faith in the dignity of humankind and rejects the medieval perception of the individual as a weak, fallen creature. "Humanists" typically believe in the perfectibility of human nature and view reason and education as the means to that end. Humanist thought is represented in the works of Marsilio Ficino, Ludovico

Castelvetro, Edmund Spenser, John Milton, Dean John Colet, Desiderius Erasmus, John Dryden, Alexander Pope, Matthew Arnold, and Irving Babbitt.

Humors: Mentions of the humors refer to the ancient Greek theory that a person's health and personality were determined by the balance of four basic fluids in the body: blood, phlegm, yellow bile, and black bile. A dominance of any fluid would cause extremes in behavior. An excess of blood created a sanguine person who was joyful, aggressive, and passionate; a phlegmatic person was shy, fearful, and sluggish; too much yellow bile led to a choleric temperament characterized by impatience, anger, bitterness, and stubbornness; and excessive black bile created melancholy, a state of laziness, gluttony, and lack of motivation. Literary treatment of the humors is exemplified by several characters in Ben Jonson's plays *Every Man in His Humour* and *Every Man out of His Humour*. Also spelled Humours.

Humours: See *Humors*

Hyperbole: In literary criticism, deliberate exaggeration used to achieve an effect. In William Shakespeare's *Macbeth*, Lady Macbeth hyperbolizes when she says, "All the perfumes of Arabia could not sweeten this little hand."

I

Iamb: See *Foot*

Idiom: A word construction or verbal expression closely associated with a given language. For example, in colloquial English the construction "how come" can be used instead of "why" to introduce a question. Similarly, "a piece of cake" is sometimes used to describe a task that is easily done.

Image: A concrete representation of an object or sensory experience. Typically, such a representation helps evoke the feelings associated with the object or experience itself. Images are either "literal" or "figurative." Literal images are especially concrete and involve little or no extension of the obvious meaning of the words used to express them. Figurative images do not follow the literal meaning of the words exactly. Images in literature are usually visual, but the term "image" can also refer to the representation of any sensory experience. In his poem "The Shepherd's Hour," Paul Verlaine presents the following image: "The Moon is red through horizon's fog;/ In a dancing mist the hazy meadow sleeps." The first line is broadly literal, while the second line involves turns of meaning associated with dancing and sleeping.

Imagery: The array of images in a literary work. Also, figurative language. William Butler Yeats's "The Second Coming" offers a powerful image of encroaching anarchy: Turning and turning in the widening gyre The falcon cannot hear the falconer; Things fall apart . . . .

Imagism: An English and American poetry movement that flourished between 1908 and 1917. The Imagists used precise, clearly presented images in their works. They also used common, everyday speech and aimed for conciseness, concrete imagery, and the creation of new rhythms. Participants in the Imagist movement included Ezra Pound, H. D. (Hilda Doolittle), and Amy Lowell, among others.

In medias res: A Latin term meaning "in the middle of things." It refers to the technique of beginning a story at its midpoint and then using various flashback devices to reveal previous action. This technique originated in such epics as Virgil's *Aeneid.*

Induction: The process of reaching a conclusion by reasoning from specific premises to form a general premise. Also, an introductory portion of a work of literature, especially a play. Geoffrey Chaucer's "Prologue" to the *Canterbury Tales,* Thomas Sackville's "Induction" to *The Mirror of Magistrates,* and the opening scene in William Shakespeare's *The Taming of the Shrew* are examples of inductions to literary works.

Intentional Fallacy: The belief that judgments of a literary work based solely on an author's stated or implied intentions are false and misleading. Critics who believe in the concept of the intentional fallacy typically argue that the work itself is sufficient matter for interpretation, even though they may concede that an author's statement of purpose can be useful. Analysis of William Wordsworth's *Lyrical Ballads* based on the observations about poetry he makes in his "Preface" to the second edition of that work is an example of the intentional fallacy.

Interior Monologue: A narrative technique in which characters' thoughts are revealed in a way that appears to be uncontrolled by the author. The interior monologue typically aims to reveal the inner self of a character. It portrays emotional experiences as they occur at both a conscious and unconscious level. images are often used to represent sensations or emotions. One of the best-known interior monologues in English is the Molly Bloom section at the close of James Joyce's *Ulysses.* The interior monologue is also common in the works of Virginia Woolf.

Internal Rhyme: Rhyme that occurs within a single line of verse. An example is in the opening line of Edgar Allan Poe's "The Raven": "Once upon a midnight dreary, while I pondered weak and weary." Here, "dreary" and "weary" make an internal rhyme.

Irish Literary Renaissance: A late nineteenth- and early twentieth-century movement in Irish literature. Members of the movement aimed to reduce the influence of British culture in Ireland and create an Irish national literature. William Butler Yeats, George Moore, and Sean O'Casey are three of the best-known figures of the movement.

Irony: In literary criticism, the effect of language in which the intended meaning is the opposite of what is stated. The title of Jonathan Swift's "A Modest Proposal" is ironic because what Swift proposes in this essay is cannibalism—hardly "modest."

Italian Sonnet: See *Sonnet*

J

Jacobean Age: The period of the reign of James I of England (1603-1625). The early literature of this period reflected the worldview of the Elizabethan Age, but a darker, more cynical attitude steadily grew in the art and literature of the Jacobean Age. This was an important time for English drama and poetry. Milestones include William Shakespeare's tragedies, tragi-comedies, and sonnets; Ben Jonson's various dramas; and John Donne's metaphysical poetry.

Jargon: Language that is used or understood only by a select group of people. Jargon may refer to terminology used in a certain profession, such as computer jargon, or it may refer to any nonsensical language that is not understood by most people. Literary examples of jargon are Francois Villon's *Ballades en jargon,* which is composed in the secret language of the *coquillards,* and Anthony Burgess's *A Clockwork Orange,* narrated in the fictional characters' language of "Nadsat."

Juvenalian Satire: See *Satire*

K

Knickerbocker Group: A somewhat indistinct group of New York writers of the first half of the nineteenth century. Members of the group were linked only by location and a common theme: New York life. Two famous members of the Knickerbocker Group were Washington Irving and William Cullen Bryant. The group's name derives from Irving's *Knickerbocker's History of New York.*

L

Lais: See *Lay*

Lay: A song or simple narrative poem. The form originated in medieval France. Early French *lais* were often based on the Celtic legends and other tales sung by Breton minstrels— thus the name of the "Breton lay." In fourteenth-century England, the term "lay" was used to describe short narratives written in imitation of the Breton lays. The most notable of these is Geoffrey Chaucer's "The Minstrel's Tale."

Leitmotiv: See *Motif*

Literal Language: An author uses literal language when he or she writes without exaggerating or embellishing the subject matter and without any tools of figurative language. To say "He ran very quickly down the street" is to use literal language, whereas to say "He ran like a hare down the street" would be using figurative language.

Literary Ballad: See *Ballad*

Literature: Literature is broadly defined as any written or spoken material, but the term most often refers to creative works. Literature includes poetry, drama, fiction, and many kinds of nonfiction writing, as well as oral, dramatic, and broadcast compositions not necessarily preserved in a written format, such as films and television programs.

Lost Generation: A term first used by Gertrude Stein to describe the post-World War I generation of American writers: men and women haunted by a sense of betrayal and emptiness brought about by the destructiveness of the war. The term is commonly applied to Hart Crane, Ernest Hemingway, F. Scott Fitzgerald, and others.

Lyric Poetry: A poem expressing the subjective feelings and personal emotions of the poet. Such poetry is melodic, since it was originally accompanied by a lyre in recitals. Most Western poetry in the twentieth century may be classified as lyrical. Examples of lyric poetry include A. E. Housman's elegy "To an Athlete Dying Young," the odes of Pindar and Horace, Thomas Gray and William Collins, the sonnets of Sir Thomas Wyatt and Sir Philip Sidney, Elizabeth Barrett Browning and Rainer Maria Rilke, and a host of other forms in the poetry of William Blake and Christina Rossetti, among many others.

M

Mannerism: Exaggerated, artificial adherence to a literary manner or style. Also, a popular style of the visual arts of late sixteenth-century Europe that was marked by elongation of the human form and by intentional spatial distortion. Literary works that are self-consciously high-toned and artistic are often said to be "mannered." Authors of such works include Henry James and Gertrude Stein.

Masculine Rhyme: See *Rhyme*

Masque: A lavish and elaborate form of entertainment, often performed in royal courts, that emphasizes song, dance, and costumery. The Renaissance form of the masque grew out of the spectacles of masked figures common in medieval England and Europe. The masque reached its peak of popularity and development in seventeenth-century England, during the reigns of James I and, especially, of Charles I. Ben Jonson, the most significant masque writer, also created the "antimasque," which incorporates elements of humor and the grotesque into the traditional masque and achieved greater dramatic quality. Masque-like interludes appear in Edmund Spenser's *The Faerie Queene* and in William Shakespeare's *The Tempest.* One of the best-known English masques is John Milton's *Comus.*

Measure: The foot, verse, or time sequence used in a literary work, especially a poem. Measure is often used somewhat incorrectly as a synonym for meter.

Melodrama: A play in which the typical plot is a conflict between characters who personify extreme good and evil. Melodramas usually end happily and emphasize sensationalism. Other literary forms that use the same techniques are often labeled "melodramatic." The term was formerly used to describe a combination of drama and music; as such, it was synonymous with "opera." Augustin Daly's *Under the Gaslight* and Dion Boucicault's *The Octoroon, The Colleen Bawn,* and *The Poor of New York* are examples of melodramas. The most popular media for twentieth-century melodramas are motion pictures and television.

Metaphor: A figure of speech that expresses an idea through the image of another object. Metaphors suggest the essence of the first object by identifying it with certain qualities of the second object. An example is "But soft, what light through yonder window breaks?/ It is the east, and Juliet is the sun" in William Shakespeare's *Romeo and Juliet.* Here, Juliet, the first object, is identified with qualities of the second object, the sun.

Metaphysical Conceit: See *Conceit*

Metaphysical Poetry: The body of poetry produced by a group of seventeenth-century English writers called the "Metaphysical Poets." The group includes John Donne and Andrew Marvell. The Metaphysical Poets made use of everyday speech, intellectual analysis, and unique imagery. They aimed to portray the ordinary conflicts and contradictions of life. Their poems often took the form of an argument, and many of them emphasize physical and religious love as well as the fleeting nature of life. Elaborate conceits are typical in metaphysical poetry. Marvell's "To His Coy Mistress" is a well-known example of a metaphysical poem.

Metaphysical Poets: See *Metaphysical Poetry*

Meter: In literary criticism, the repetition of sound patterns that creates a rhythm in

poetry. The patterns are based on the number of syllables and the presence and absence of accents. The unit of rhythm in a line is called a foot. Types of meter are classified according to the number of feet in a line. These are the standard English lines: Monometer, one foot; Dimeter, two feet; Trimeter, three feet; Tetrameter, four feet; Pentameter, five feet; Hexameter, six feet (also called the Alexandrine); Heptameter, seven feet (also called the "Fourteener" when the feet are iambic). The most common English meter is the iambic pentameter, in which each line contains ten syllables, or five iambic feet, which individually are composed of an unstressed syllable followed by an accented syllable. Both of the following lines from Alfred, Lord Tennyson's "Ulysses" are written in iambic pentameter: Made weak by time and fate, but strong in will To strive, to seek, to find, and not to yield.

Mise en scene: The costumes, scenery, and other properties of a drama. Herbert Beerbohm Tree was renowned for the elaborate *mises en scene* of his lavish Shakespearean productions at His Majesty's Theatre between 1897 and 1915.

Modernism: Modern literary practices. Also, the principles of a literary school that lasted from roughly the beginning of the twentieth century until the end of World War II. Modernism is defined by its rejection of the literary conventions of the nineteenth century and by its opposition to conventional morality, taste, traditions, and economic values. Many writers are associated with the concepts of Modernism, including Albert Camus, Marcel Proust, D. H. Lawrence, W. H. Auden, Ernest Hemingway, William Faulkner, William Butler Yeats, Thomas Mann, Tennessee Williams, Eugene O'Neill, and James Joyce.

Monologue: A composition, written or oral, by a single individual. More specifically, a speech given by a single individual in a drama or other public entertainment. It has no set length, although it is usually several or more lines long. An example of an "extended monologue"—that is, a monologue of great length and seriousness—occurs in the one-act, one-character play *The Stronger* by August Strindberg.

Monometer: See *Meter*

Mood: The prevailing emotions of a work or of the author in his or her creation of the work. The mood of a work is not always what might be expected based on its subject matter. The poem "Dover Beach" by Matthew Arnold offers examples of two different moods originating from the same experience: watching the ocean at night. The mood of the first three lines—The sea is calm tonight The tide is full, the moon lies fair Upon the straights . . . . is in sharp contrast to the mood of the last three lines— And we are here as on a darkling plain Swept with confused alarms of struggle and flight, Where ignorant armies clash by night.

Motif: A theme, character type, image, metaphor, or other verbal element that recurs throughout a single work of literature or occurs in a number of different works over a period of time. For example, the various manifestations of the color white in Herman Melville's *Moby Dick* is a "specific" *motif,* while the trials of star-crossed lovers is a "conventional" *motif* from the literature of all periods. Also known as *Motiv* or *Leitmotiv.*

Motiv: See *Motif*

Muckrakers: An early twentieth-century group of American writers. Typically, their works exposed the wrongdoings of big business and government in the United States. Upton Sinclair's *The Jungle* exemplifies the muckraking novel.

Muses: Nine Greek mythological goddesses, the daughters of Zeus and Mnemosyne (Memory). Each muse patronized a specific area of the liberal arts and sciences. Calliope presided over epic poetry, Clio over history, Erato over love poetry, Euterpe over music or lyric poetry, Melpomene over tragedy, Polyhymnia over hymns to the gods, Terpsichore over dance, Thalia over comedy, and Urania over astronomy. Poets and writers traditionally made appeals to the Muses for inspiration in their work. John Milton invokes the aid of a muse at the beginning of the first book of his *Paradise Lost: Of Man's First disobedience, and the Fruit of the Forbidden Tree, whose mortal taste Brought Death into the World, and all our woe, With loss of Eden, till one greater Man Restore us, and regain the blissful Seat, Sing Heav'nly Muse, that on the secret top of Oreb, or of Sinai, didst inspire That Shepherd, who first taught the chosen Seed, In the Beginning how the Heav'ns and Earth Rose out of Chaos . . . .*

Mystery: See *Suspense*

Myth: An anonymous tale emerging from the traditional beliefs of a culture or social unit. Myths use supernatural explanations for natural phenomena. They may also explain cosmic issues like creation and death. Collections of myths, known as mythologies, are common to all cultures and nations, but the best-known myths belong to the Norse, Roman, and Greek mythologies. A famous myth is the story of Arachne, an arrogant young girl who challenged a goddess, Athena, to a weaving contest; when the girl won, Athena was enraged and turned Arachne into a spider, thus explaining the existence of spiders.

N

Narration: The telling of a series of events, real or invented. A narration may be either a simple narrative, in which the events are recounted chronologically, or a narrative with a plot, in which the account is given in a style reflecting the author's artistic concept of the story. Narration is sometimes used as a synonym for "storyline." The recounting of scary stories around a campfire is a form of narration.

Narrative: A verse or prose accounting of an event or sequence of events, real or invented. The term is also used as an adjective in the sense "method of narration." For example, in literary criticism, the expression "narrative technique" usually refers to the way the author structures and presents his or her story. Narratives range from the shortest accounts of events, as in Julius Caesar's remark, "I came, I saw, I conquered," to the longest historical or biographical works, as in Edward Gibbon's *The Decline and Fall of the Roman Empire,* as well as diaries, travelogues, novels, ballads, epics, short stories, and other fictional forms.

Narrative Poetry: A nondramatic poem in which the author tells a story. Such poems may be of any length or level of complexity. Epics such as *Beowulf* and ballads are forms of narrative poetry.

Narrator: The teller of a story. The narrator may be the author or a character in the story through whom the author speaks. Huckleberry Finn is the narrator of Mark Twain's *The Adventures of Huckleberry Finn.*

Naturalism: A literary movement of the late nineteenth and early twentieth centuries. The movement's major theorist, French novelist Emile Zola, envisioned a type of fiction that would examine human life with the objectivity of scientific inquiry. The Naturalists typically viewed human beings as either the products of "biological determinism," ruled by hereditary instincts and engaged in an endless struggle for survival, or as the products of "socioeconomic determinism," ruled by social and economic forces beyond their control. In their works, the Naturalists generally ignored the highest levels of society and focused on degradation: poverty, alcoholism, prostitution, insanity, and disease. Naturalism influenced authors throughout the world, including Henrik Ibsen and Thomas Hardy. In the United States, in particular, Naturalism had a profound impact. Among the authors who embraced its principles are Theodore Dreiser, Eugene O'Neill, Stephen Crane, Jack London, and Frank Norris.

Negritude: A literary movement based on the concept of a shared cultural bond on the part of black Africans, wherever they may be in the world. It traces its origins to the former French colonies of Africa and the Caribbean. Negritude poets, novelists, and essayists generally stress four points in their writings: One, black alienation from traditional African culture can lead to feelings of inferiority. Two, European colonialism and Western education should be resisted. Three, black Africans should seek to affirm and define their own identity. Four, African culture can and should be reclaimed. Many Negritude writers also claim that blacks can make unique contributions to the world, based on a heightened appreciation of nature, rhythm, and human emotions—aspects of life they say are not so highly valued in the materialistic and rationalistic West. Examples of Negritude literature include the poetry of both Senegalese Leopold Senghor in *Hosties noires* and

Martiniquais Aime-Fernand Cesaire in *Return to My Native Land.*

Negro Renaissance: See *Harlem Renaissance*

Neoclassical Period: See *Neoclassicism*

Neoclassicism: In literary criticism, this term refers to the revival of the attitudes and styles of expression of classical literature. It is generally used to describe a period in European history beginning in the late seventeenth century and lasting until about 1800. In its purest form, Neoclassicism marked a return to order, proportion, restraint, logic, accuracy, and decorum. In England, where Neoclassicism perhaps was most popular, it reflected the influence of seventeenth- century French writers, especially dramatists. Neoclassical writers typically reacted against the intensity and enthusiasm of the Renaissance period. They wrote works that appealed to the intellect, using elevated language and classical literary forms such as satire and the ode. Neoclassical works were often governed by the classical goal of instruction. English neoclassicists included Alexander Pope, Jonathan Swift, Joseph Addison, Sir Richard Steele, John Gay, and Matthew Prior; French neoclassicists included Pierre Corneille and Jean-Baptiste Moliere. Also known as Age of Reason.

Neoclassicists: See *Neoclassicism*

New Criticism: A movement in literary criticism, dating from the late 1920s, that stressed close textual analysis in the interpretation of works of literature. The New Critics saw little merit in historical and biographical analysis. Rather, they aimed to examine the text alone, free from the question of how external events—biographical or otherwise—may have helped shape it. This predominantly American school was named "New Criticism" by one of its practitioners, John Crowe Ransom. Other important New Critics included Allen Tate, R. P. Blackmur, Robert Penn Warren, and Cleanth Brooks.

New Negro Movement: See *Harlem Renaissance*

Noble Savage: The idea that primitive man is noble and good but becomes evil and corrupted as he becomes civilized. The concept of the noble savage originated in the Renaissance period but is more closely identified with such later writers as Jean-Jacques

Rousseau and Aphra Behn. First described in John Dryden's play *The Conquest of Granada,* the noble savage is portrayed by the various Native Americans in James Fenimore Cooper's "Leatherstocking Tales," by Queequeg, Daggoo, and Tashtego in Herman Melville's *Moby Dick,* and by John the Savage in Aldous Huxley's *Brave New World.*

O

Objective Correlative: An outward set of objects, a situation, or a chain of events corresponding to an inward experience and evoking this experience in the reader. The term frequently appears in modern criticism in discussions of authors' intended effects on the emotional responses of readers. This term was originally used by T. S. Eliot in his 1919 essay "Hamlet."

Objectivity: A quality in writing characterized by the absence of the author's opinion or feeling about the subject matter. Objectivity is an important factor in criticism. The novels of Henry James and, to a certain extent, the poems of John Larkin demonstrate objectivity, and it is central to John Keats's concept of "negative capability." Critical and journalistic writing usually are or attempt to be objective.

Occasional Verse: poetry written on the occasion of a significant historical or personal event. *Vers de societe* is sometimes called occasional verse although it is of a less serious nature. Famous examples of occasional verse include Andrew Marvell's "Horatian Ode upon Cromwell's Return from England," Walt Whitman's "When Lilacs Last in the Dooryard Bloom'd"— written upon the death of Abraham Lincoln—and Edmund Spenser's commemoration of his wedding, "Epithalamion."

Octave: A poem or stanza composed of eight lines. The term octave most often represents the first eight lines of a Petrarchan sonnet. An example of an octave is taken from a translation of a Petrarchan sonnet by Sir Thomas Wyatt: The pillar persht is whereto I leant, The strongest stay of mine unquiet mind; The like of it no man again can find, From East to West Still seeking though he went. To mind unhap! for hap away hath rent Of all my joy the very bark and rind;

And I, alas, by chance am thus assigned Daily to mourn till death do it relent.

Ode: Name given to an extended lyric poem characterized by exalted emotion and dignified style. An ode usually concerns a single, serious theme. Most odes, but not all, are addressed to an object or individual. Odes are distinguished from other lyric poetic forms by their complex rhythmic and stanzaic patterns. An example of this form is John Keats's "Ode to a Nightingale."

Oedipus Complex: A son's amorous obsession with his mother. The phrase is derived from the story of the ancient Theban hero Oedipus, who unknowingly killed his father and married his mother. Literary occurrences of the Oedipus complex include Andre Gide's *Oedipe* and Jean Cocteau's *La Machine infernale,* as well as the most famous, Sophocles' *Oedipus Rex.*

Omniscience: See *Point of View*

Onomatopoeia: The use of words whose sounds express or suggest their meaning. In its simplest sense, onomatopoeia may be represented by words that mimic the sounds they denote such as "hiss" or "meow." At a more subtle level, the pattern and rhythm of sounds and rhymes of a line or poem may be onomatopoeic. A celebrated example of onomatopoeia is the repetition of the word "bells" in Edgar Allan Poe's poem "The Bells."

Opera: A type of stage performance, usually a drama, in which the dialogue is sung. Classic examples of opera include Giuseppi Verdi's *La traviata,* Giacomo Puccini's *La Boheme,* and Richard Wagner's *Tristan und Isolde.* Major twentieth- century contributors to the form include Richard Strauss and Alban Berg.

Operetta: A usually romantic comic opera. John Gay's *The Beggar's Opera,* Richard Sheridan's *The Duenna,* and numerous works by William Gilbert and Arthur Sullivan are examples of operettas.

Oral Tradition: See *Oral Transmission*

Oral Transmission: A process by which songs, ballads, folklore, and other material are transmitted by word of mouth. The tradition of oral transmission predates the written record systems of literate society. Oral transmission preserves material sometimes over generations, although often with variations. Memory plays a large part in the recitation and preservation of orally transmitted material. Breton lays, French *fabliaux,* national epics (including the Anglo- Saxon *Beowulf,* the Spanish *El Cid,* and the Finnish *Kalevala*), Native American myths and legends, and African folktales told by plantation slaves are examples of orally transmitted literature.

Oration: Formal speaking intended to motivate the listeners to some action or feeling. Such public speaking was much more common before the development of timely printed communication such as newspapers. Famous examples of oration include Abraham Lincoln's "Gettysburg Address" and Dr. Martin Luther King Jr.'s "I Have a Dream" speech.

Ottava Rima: An eight-line stanza of poetry composed in iambic pentameter (a five-foot line in which each foot consists of an unaccented syllable followed by an accented syllable), following the abababcc rhyme scheme. This form has been prominently used by such important English writers as Lord Byron, Henry Wadsworth Longfellow, and W. B. Yeats.

Oxymoron: A phrase combining two contradictory terms. Oxymorons may be intentional or unintentional. The following speech from William Shakespeare's *Romeo and Juliet* uses several oxymorons: Why, then, O brawling love! O loving hate! O anything, of nothing first create! O heavy lightness! serious vanity! Mis-shapen chaos of well-seeming forms! Feather of lead, bright smoke, cold fire, sick health! This love feel I, that feel no love in this.

P

Pantheism: The idea that all things are both a manifestation or revelation of God and a part of God at the same time. Pantheism was a common attitude in the early societies of Egypt, India, and Greece—the term derives from the Greek *pan* meaning "all" and *theos* meaning "deity." It later became a significant part of the Christian faith. William Wordsworth and Ralph Waldo Emerson are among the many writers who have expressed the pantheistic attitude in their works.

Parable: A story intended to teach a moral lesson or answer an ethical question. In the West, the best examples of parables are those of Jesus Christ in the New Testament, notably "The Prodigal Son," but parables also are used in Sufism, rabbinic literature, Hasidism, and Zen Buddhism.

Paradox: A statement that appears illogical or contradictory at first, but may actually point to an underlying truth. "Less is more" is an example of a paradox. Literary examples include Francis Bacon's statement, "The most corrected copies are commonly the least correct," and "All animals are equal, but some animals are more equal than others" from George Orwell's *Animal Farm.*

Parallelism: A method of comparison of two ideas in which each is developed in the same grammatical structure. Ralph Waldo Emerson's "Civilization" contains this example of parallelism: Raphael paints wisdom; Handel sings it, Phidias carves it, Shakespeare writes it, Wren builds it, Columbus sails it, Luther preaches it, Washington arms it, Watt mechanizes it.

Parnassianism: A mid nineteenth-century movement in French literature. Followers of the movement stressed adherence to well-defined artistic forms as a reaction against the often chaotic expression of the artist's ego that dominated the work of the Romantics. The Parnassians also rejected the moral, ethical, and social themes exhibited in the works of French Romantics such as Victor Hugo. The aesthetic doctrines of the Parnassians strongly influenced the later symbolist and decadent movements. Members of the Parnassian school include Leconte de Lisle, Sully Prudhomme, Albert Glatigny, Francois Coppee, and Theodore de Banville.

Parody: In literary criticism, this term refers to an imitation of a serious literary work or the signature style of a particular author in a ridiculous manner. A typical parody adopts the style of the original and applies it to an inappropriate subject for humorous effect. Parody is a form of satire and could be considered the literary equivalent of a caricature or cartoon. Henry Fielding's *Shamela* is a parody of Samuel Richardson's *Pamela.*

Pastoral: A term derived from the Latin word "pastor," meaning shepherd. A pastoral is a literary composition on a rural theme. The conventions of the pastoral were originated by the third-century Greek poet Theocritus, who wrote about the experiences, love affairs, and pastimes of Sicilian shepherds. In a pastoral, characters and language of a courtly nature are often placed in a simple setting. The term pastoral is also used to classify dramas, elegies, and lyrics that exhibit the use of country settings and shepherd characters. Percy Bysshe Shelley's "Adonais" and John Milton's "Lycidas" are two famous examples of pastorals.

Pastorela: The Spanish name for the shepherds play, a folk drama reenacted during the Christmas season. Examples of *pastorelas* include Gomez Manrique's *Representacion del nacimiento* and the dramas of Lucas Fernandez and Juan del Encina.

Pathetic Fallacy: A term coined by English critic John Ruskin to identify writing that falsely endows nonhuman things with human intentions and feelings, such as "angry clouds" and "sad trees." The pathetic fallacy is a required convention in the classical poetic form of the pastoral elegy, and it is used in the modern poetry of T. S. Eliot, Ezra Pound, and the Imagists. Also known as Poetic Fallacy.

Pelado: Literally the "skinned one" or shirtless one, he was the stock underdog, sharp-witted picaresque character of Mexican vaudeville and tent shows. The *pelado* is found in such works as Don Catarino's *Los effectos de la crisis* and *Regreso a mi tierra*.

Pen Name: See *Pseudonym*

Pentameter: See *Meter*

Persona: A Latin term meaning "mask." *Personae* are the characters in a fictional work of literature. The *persona* generally functions as a mask through which the author tells a story in a voice other than his or her own. A *persona* is usually either a character in a story who acts as a narrator or an "implied author," a voice created by the author to act as the narrator for himself or herself. *Personae* include the narrator of Geoffrey Chaucer's *Canterbury Tales* and Marlow in Joseph Conrad's *Heart of Darkness*.

Personae: See *Persona*

Personal Point of View: See *Point of View*

Personification: A figure of speech that gives human qualities to abstract ideas, animals, and inanimate objects. William Shakespeare used personification in *Romeo and Juliet* in the lines "Arise, fair sun, and kill the envious moon,/ Who is already sick and pale with grief." Here, the moon is portrayed as being envious, sick, and pale with grief—all markedly human qualities. Also known as *Prosopopoeia*.

Petrarchan Sonnet: See *Sonnet*

Phenomenology: A method of literary criticism based on the belief that things have no existence outside of human consciousness or awareness. Proponents of this theory believe that art is a process that takes place in the mind of the observer as he or she contemplates an object rather than a quality of the object itself. Among phenomenological critics are Edmund Husserl, George Poulet, Marcel Raymond, and Roman Ingarden.

Picaresque Novel: Episodic fiction depicting the adventures of a roguish central character ("picaro" is Spanish for "rogue"). The picaresque hero is commonly a low-born but clever individual who wanders into and out of various affairs of love, danger, and farcical intrigue. These involvements may take place at all social levels and typically present a humorous and wide-ranging satire of a given society. Prominent examples of the picaresque novel are *Don Quixote* by Miguel de Cervantes, *Tom Jones* by Henry Fielding, and *Moll Flanders* by Daniel Defoe.

Plagiarism: Claiming another person's written material as one's own. Plagiarism can take the form of direct, word-for-word copying or the theft of the substance or idea of the work. A student who copies an encyclopedia entry and turns it in as a report for school is guilty of plagiarism.

Platonic Criticism: A form of criticism that stresses an artistic work's usefulness as an agent of social engineering rather than any quality or value of the work itself. Platonic criticism takes as its starting point the ancient Greek philosopher Plato's comments on art in his *Republic*.

Platonism: The embracing of the doctrines of the philosopher Plato, popular among the poets of the Renaissance and the Romantic period. Platonism is more flexible than Aristotelian

Criticism and places more emphasis on the supernatural and unknown aspects of life. Platonism is expressed in the love poetry of the Renaissance, the fourth book of Baldassare Castiglione's *The Book of the Courtier,* and the poetry of William Blake, William Wordsworth, Percy Bysshe Shelley, Friedrich Holderlin, William Butler Yeats, and Wallace Stevens.

Play: See *Drama*

Plot: In literary criticism, this term refers to the pattern of events in a narrative or drama. In its simplest sense, the plot guides the author in composing the work and helps the reader follow the work. Typically, plots exhibit causality and unity and have a beginning, a middle, and an end. Sometimes, however, a plot may consist of a series of disconnected events, in which case it is known as an "episodic plot." In his *Aspects of the Novel,* E. M. Forster distinguishes between a story, defined as a "narrative of events arranged in their time- sequence," and plot, which organizes the events to a "sense of causality." This definition closely mirrors Aristotle's discussion of plot in his *Poetics.*

Poem: In its broadest sense, a composition utilizing rhyme, meter, concrete detail, and expressive language to create a literary experience with emotional and aesthetic appeal. Typical poems include sonnets, odes, elegies, *haiku,* ballads, and free verse.

Poet: An author who writes poetry or verse. The term is also used to refer to an artist or writer who has an exceptional gift for expression, imagination, and energy in the making of art in any form. Well-known poets include Horace, Basho, Sir Philip Sidney, Sir Edmund Spenser, John Donne, Andrew Marvell, Alexander Pope, Jonathan Swift, George Gordon, Lord Byron, John Keats, Christina Rossetti, W. H. Auden, Stevie Smith, and Sylvia Plath.

Poetic Fallacy: See *Pathetic Fallacy*

Poetic Justice: An outcome in a literary work, not necessarily a poem, in which the good are rewarded and the evil are punished, especially in ways that particularly fit their virtues or crimes. For example, a murderer may himself be murdered, or a thief will find himself penniless.

Poetic License: Distortions of fact and literary convention made by a writer—not always a poet—for the sake of the effect gained. Poetic license is closely related to the concept of "artistic freedom." An author exercises poetic license by saying that a pile of money "reaches as high as a mountain" when the pile is actually only a foot or two high.

Poetics: This term has two closely related meanings. It denotes (1) an aesthetic theory in literary criticism about the essence of poetry or (2) rules prescribing the proper methods, content, style, or diction of poetry. The term poetics may also refer to theories about literature in general, not just poetry.

Poetry: In its broadest sense, writing that aims to present ideas and evoke an emotional experience in the reader through the use of meter, imagery, connotative and concrete words, and a carefully constructed structure based on rhythmic patterns. Poetry typically relies on words and expressions that have several layers of meaning. It also makes use of the effects of regular rhythm on the ear and may make a strong appeal to the senses through the use of imagery. Edgar Allan Poe's "Annabel Lee" and Walt Whitman's *Leaves of Grass* are famous examples of poetry.

Point of View: The narrative perspective from which a literary work is presented to the reader. There are four traditional points of view. The "third person omniscient" gives the reader a "godlike" perspective, unrestricted by time or place, from which to see actions and look into the minds of characters. This allows the author to comment openly on characters and events in the work. The "third person" point of view presents the events of the story from outside of any single character's perception, much like the omniscient point of view, but the reader must understand the action as it takes place and without any special insight into characters' minds or motivations. The "first person" or "personal" point of view relates events as they are perceived by a single character. The main character "tells" the story and may offer opinions about the action and characters which differ from those of the author. Much less common than omniscient, third person, and first person is the "second person" point of view, wherein the author tells the story as if it is happening to the reader. James Thurber employs the omniscient point of view in his short story "The Secret Life of Walter Mitty." Ernest Hemingway's "A Clean, Well-Lighted Place" is a short story told from the third person point of view. Mark Twain's novel *Huck Finn* is presented from the first person viewpoint. Jay McInerney's *Bright Lights, Big City* is an example of a novel which uses the second person point of view.

Polemic: A work in which the author takes a stand on a controversial subject, such as abortion or religion. Such works are often extremely argumentative or provocative. Classic examples of polemics include John Milton's *Aeropagitica* and Thomas Paine's *The American Crisis.*

Pornography: Writing intended to provoke feelings of lust in the reader. Such works are often condemned by critics and teachers, but those which can be shown to have literary value are viewed less harshly. Literary works that have been described as pornographic include Ovid's *The Art of Love,* Margaret of Angouleme's *Heptameron,* John Cleland's *Memoirs of a Woman of Pleasure; or, the Life of Fanny Hill,* the anonymous *My Secret Life,* D. H. Lawrence's *Lady Chatterley's Lover,* and Vladimir Nabokov's *Lolita.*

Post-Aesthetic Movement: An artistic response made by African Americans to the black aesthetic movement of the 1960s and early '70s. Writers since that time have adopted a somewhat different tone in their work, with less emphasis placed on the disparity between black and white in the United States. In the words of post-aesthetic authors such as Toni Morrison, John Edgar Wideman, and Kristin Hunter, African Americans are portrayed as looking inward for answers to their own questions, rather than always looking to the outside world. Two well-known examples of works produced as part of the post-aesthetic movement are the Pulitzer Prize-winning novels *The Color Purple* by Alice Walker and *Beloved* by Toni Morrison.

Postmodernism: Writing from the 1960s forward characterized by experimentation and continuing to apply some of the fundamentals of modernism, which included existentialism and alienation. Postmodernists have gone a step further in the rejection of tradition begun with the modernists by also rejecting traditional forms, preferring the anti-novel over the novel and the anti-hero over the hero. Postmodern writers include Alain Robbe-Grillet, Thomas Pynchon, Margaret Drabble, John Fowles, Adolfo Bioy-Casares, and Gabriel Garcia Marquez.

Pre-Raphaelites: A circle of writers and artists in mid nineteenth-century England. Valuing the pre-Renaissance artistic qualities of religious symbolism, lavish pictorialism, and natural sensuousness, the Pre-Raphaelites cultivated a sense of mystery and melancholy that influenced later writers associated with the Symbolist and Decadent movements. The major members of the group include Dante Gabriel Rossetti, Christina Rossetti, Algernon Swinburne, and Walter Pater.

Primitivism: The belief that primitive peoples were nobler and less flawed than civilized peoples because they had not been subjected to the tainting influence of society. Examples of literature espousing primitivism include Aphra Behn's *Oroonoko: Or, The History of the Royal Slave,* Jean-Jacques Rousseau's *Julie ou la Nouvelle Heloise,* Oliver Goldsmith's *The Deserted Village,* the poems of Robert Burns, Herman Melville's stories *Typee, Omoo,* and *Mardi,* many poems of William Butler Yeats and Robert Frost, and William Golding's novel *Lord of the Flies.*

Projective Verse: A form of free verse in which the poet's breathing pattern determines the lines of the poem. Poets who advocate projective verse are against all formal structures in writing, including meter and form. Besides its creators, Robert Creeley, Robert Duncan, and Charles Olson, two other well-known projective verse poets are Denise Levertov and LeRoi Jones (Amiri Baraka). Also known as Breath Verse.

Prologue: An introductory section of a literary work. It often contains information establishing the situation of the characters or presents information about the setting, time period, or action. In drama, the prologue is spoken by a chorus or by one of the principal characters. In the "General Prologue" of *The Canterbury Tales,* Geoffrey Chaucer describes the main characters and establishes the setting and purpose of the work.

Prose: A literary medium that attempts to mirror the language of everyday speech. It is distinguished from poetry by its use of unmetered, unrhymed language consisting of logically related sentences. Prose is usually grouped into paragraphs that form a cohesive whole such as an essay or a novel. Recognized masters of English prose writing include Sir Thomas Malory, William Caxton, Raphael Holinshed, Joseph Addison, Mark Twain, and Ernest Hemingway.

Prosopopoeia: See *Personification*

Protagonist: The central character of a story who serves as a focus for its themes and incidents and as the principal rationale for its development. The protagonist is sometimes referred to in discussions of modern literature as the hero or anti-hero. Well-known protagonists are Hamlet in William Shakespeare's *Hamlet* and Jay Gatsby in F. Scott Fitzgerald's *The Great Gatsby*.

Protest Fiction: Protest fiction has as its primary purpose the protesting of some social injustice, such as racism or discrimination. One example of protest fiction is a series of five novels by Chester Himes, beginning in 1945 with *If He Hollers Let Him Go* and ending in 1955 with *The Primitive*. These works depict the destructive effects of race and gender stereotyping in the context of interracial relationships. Another African American author whose works often revolve around themes of social protest is John Oliver Killens. James Baldwin's essay "Everybody's Protest Novel" generated controversy by attacking the authors of protest fiction.

Proverb: A brief, sage saying that expresses a truth about life in a striking manner. "They are not all cooks who carry long knives" is an example of a proverb.

Pseudonym: A name assumed by a writer, most often intended to prevent his or her identification as the author of a work. Two or more authors may work together under one pseudonym, or an author may use a different name for each genre he or she publishes in. Some publishing companies maintain "house pseudonyms," under which any number of authors may write installations in a series. Some authors also choose a pseudonym over their real names the way an actor may use a stage name. Examples of pseudonyms (with the author's real name in parentheses) include

Voltaire (Francois-Marie Arouet), Novalis (Friedrich von Hardenberg), Currer Bell (Charlotte Bronte), Ellis Bell (Emily Bronte), George Eliot (Maryann Evans), Honorio Bustos Donmecq (Adolfo Bioy-Casares and Jorge Luis Borges), and Richard Bachman (Stephen King).

Pun: A play on words that have similar sounds but different meanings. A serious example of the pun is from John Donne's "A Hymne to God the Father": Sweare by thyself, that at my death thy sonne Shall shine as he shines now, and hereto fore; And, having done that, Thou haste done; I fear no more.

Pure Poetry: poetry written without instructional intent or moral purpose that aims only to please a reader by its imagery or musical flow. The term pure poetry is used as the antonym of the term "didacticism." The poetry of Edgar Allan Poe, Stephane Mallarme, Paul Verlaine, Paul Valery, Juan Ramoz Jimenez, and Jorge Guillen offer examples of pure poetry.

Q

Quatrain: A four-line stanza of a poem or an entire poem consisting of four lines. The following quatrain is from Robert Herrick's "To Live Merrily, and to Trust to Good Verses": Round, round, the root do's run; And being ravisht thus, Come, I will drink a Tun To my *Propertius*.

R

Raisonneur: A character in a drama who functions as a spokesperson for the dramatist's views. The *raisonneur* typically observes the play without becoming central to its action. *Raisonneurs* were very common in plays of the nineteenth century.

Realism: A nineteenth-century European literary movement that sought to portray familiar characters, situations, and settings in a realistic manner. This was done primarily by using an objective narrative point of view and through the buildup of accurate detail. The standard for success of any realistic work depends on how faithfully it transfers common experience into fictional forms. The realistic method may be altered or extended, as in stream of consciousness writing, to record highly subjective experience. Seminal authors in the tradition of Realism include

Honore de Balzac, Gustave Flaubert, and Henry James.

Refrain: A phrase repeated at intervals throughout a poem. A refrain may appear at the end of each stanza or at less regular intervals. It may be altered slightly at each appearance. Some refrains are nonsense expressions—as with "Nevermore" in Edgar Allan Poe's "The Raven"—that seem to take on a different significance with each use.

Renaissance: The period in European history that marked the end of the Middle Ages. It began in Italy in the late fourteenth century. In broad terms, it is usually seen as spanning the fourteenth, fifteenth, and sixteenth centuries, although it did not reach Great Britain, for example, until the 1480s or so. The Renaissance saw an awakening in almost every sphere of human activity, especially science, philosophy, and the arts. The period is best defined by the emergence of a general philosophy that emphasized the importance of the intellect, the individual, and world affairs. It contrasts strongly with the medieval worldview, characterized by the dominant concerns of faith, the social collective, and spiritual salvation. Prominent writers during the Renaissance include Niccolo Machiavelli and Baldassare Castiglione in Italy, Miguel de Cervantes and Lope de Vega in Spain, Jean Froissart and Francois Rabelais in France, Sir Thomas More and Sir Philip Sidney in England, and Desiderius Erasmus in Holland.

Repartee: Conversation featuring snappy retorts and witticisms. Masters of *repartee* include Sydney Smith, Charles Lamb, and Oscar Wilde. An example is recorded in the meeting of "Beau" Nash and John Wesley: Nash said, "I never make way for a fool," to which Wesley responded, "Don't you? I always do," and stepped aside.

Resolution: The portion of a story following the climax, in which the conflict is resolved. The resolution of Jane Austen's *Northanger Abbey* is neatly summed up in the following sentence: "Henry and Catherine were married, the bells rang and every body smiled."

Restoration: See *Restoration Age*

Restoration Age: A period in English literature beginning with the crowning of Charles II in 1660 and running to about 1700. The era, which was characterized by a reaction against Puritanism, was the first great age of the comedy of manners. The finest literature of the era is typically witty and urbane, and often lewd. Prominent Restoration Age writers include William Congreve, Samuel Pepys, John Dryden, and John Milton.

Revenge Tragedy: A dramatic form popular during the Elizabethan Age, in which the protagonist, directed by the ghost of his murdered father or son, inflicts retaliation upon a powerful villain. Notable features of the revenge tragedy include violence, bizarre criminal acts, intrigue, insanity, a hesitant protagonist, and the use of soliloquy. Thomas Kyd's *Spanish Tragedy* is the first example of revenge tragedy in English, and William Shakespeare's *Hamlet* is perhaps the best. Extreme examples of revenge tragedy, such as John Webster's *The Duchess of Malfi,* are labeled "tragedies of blood." Also known as Tragedy of Blood.

Revista: The Spanish term for a vaudeville musical revue. Examples of *revistas* include Antonio Guzman Aguilera's *Mexico para los mexicanos,* Daniel Vanegas's *Maldito jazz,* and Don Catarino's *Whiskey, morfina y marihuana* and *El desterrado.*

Rhetoric: In literary criticism, this term denotes the art of ethical persuasion. In its strictest sense, rhetoric adheres to various principles developed since classical times for arranging facts and ideas in a clear, persuasive, appealing manner. The term is also used to refer to effective prose in general and theories of or methods for composing effective prose. Classical examples of rhetorics include *The Rhetoric of Aristotle,* Quintillian's *Institutio Oratoria,* and Cicero's *Ad Herennium.*

Rhetorical Question: A question intended to provoke thought, but not an expressed answer, in the reader. It is most commonly used in oratory and other persuasive genres. The following lines from Thomas Gray's "Elegy Written in a Country Churchyard" ask rhetorical questions: Can storied urn or animated bust Back to its mansion call the fleeting breath? Can Honour's voice provoke the silent dust, Or Flattery soothe the dull cold ear of Death?

Rhyme: When used as a noun in literary criticism, this term generally refers to a poem in which words sound identical or very similar and appear in parallel positions in two or more lines. Rhymes are classified into different types according to where they fall in a line or stanza or according to the degree of similarity they exhibit in their spellings and sounds. Some major types of rhyme are "masculine" rhyme, "feminine" rhyme, and "triple" rhyme. In a masculine rhyme, the rhyming sound falls in a single accented syllable, as with "heat" and "eat." Feminine rhyme is a rhyme of two syllables, one stressed and one unstressed, as with "merry" and "tarry." Triple rhyme matches the sound of the accented syllable and the two unaccented syllables that follow: "narrative" and "declarative." Robert Browning alternates feminine and masculine rhymes in his "Soliloquy of the Spanish Cloister": Gr-r-r—there go, my heart's abhorrence! Water your damned flower-pots, do! If hate killed men, Brother Lawrence, God's blood, would not mine kill you! What? Your myrtle-bush wants trimming? Oh, that rose has prior claims— Needs its leaden vase filled brimming? Hell dry you up with flames! Triple rhymes can be found in Thomas Hood's "Bridge of Sighs," George Gordon Byron's satirical verse, and Ogden Nash's comic poems.

Rhyme Royal: A stanza of seven lines composed in iambic pentameter and rhymed *ababbcc*. The name is said to be a tribute to King James I of Scotland, who made much use of the form in his poetry. Examples of rhyme royal include Geoffrey Chaucer's *The Parlement of Foules,* William Shakespeare's *The Rape of Lucrece,* William Morris's *The Early Paradise,* and John Masefield's *The Widow in the Bye Street.*

Rhyme Scheme: See *Rhyme*

Rhythm: A regular pattern of sound, time intervals, or events occurring in writing, most often and most discernably in poetry. Regular, reliable rhythm is known to be soothing to humans, while interrupted, unpredictable, or rapidly changing rhythm is disturbing. These effects are known to authors, who use them to produce a desired reaction in the reader. An example of a form of irregular rhythm is sprung rhythm poetry; quantitative verse, on the other hand, is very regular in its rhythm.

Rising Action: The part of a drama where the plot becomes increasingly complicated. Rising action leads up to the climax, or turning point, of a drama. The final "chase scene" of an action film is generally the rising action which culminates in the film's climax.

Rococo: A style of European architecture that flourished in the eighteenth century, especially in France. The most notable features of *rococo* are its extensive use of ornamentation and its themes of lightness, gaiety, and intimacy. In literary criticism, the term is often used disparagingly to refer to a decadent or over-ornamental style. Alexander Pope's "The Rape of the Lock" is an example of literary *rococo.*

Roman à clef: A French phrase meaning "novel with a key." It refers to a narrative in which real persons are portrayed under fictitious names. Jack Kerouac, for example, portrayed various real-life beat generation figures under fictitious names in his *On the Road.*

Romance: A broad term, usually denoting a narrative with exotic, exaggerated, often idealized characters, scenes, and themes. Nathaniel Hawthorne called his *The House of the Seven Gables* and *The Marble Faun* romances in order to distinguish them from clearly realistic works.

Romantic Age: See *Romanticism*

Romanticism: This term has two widely accepted meanings. In historical criticism, it refers to a European intellectual and artistic movement of the late eighteenth and early nineteenth centuries that sought greater freedom of personal expression than that allowed by the strict rules of literary form and logic of the eighteenth-century neoclassicists. The Romantics preferred emotional and imaginative expression to rational analysis. They considered the individual to be at the center of all experience and so placed him or her at the center of their art. The Romantics believed that the creative imagination reveals nobler truths—unique feelings and attitudes—than those that could be discovered by logic or by scientific examination. Both the natural world and the state of childhood were important sources for revelations of "eternal truths." "Romanticism" is also used as a general term to refer to a type of sensibility found in all periods of literary history and usually considered to be in opposition to the principles of classicism. In this sense, Romanticism signifies any work or philosophy in which the exotic or dreamlike figure strongly, or that is devoted to individualistic expression, self-analysis, or a pursuit of a higher realm of knowledge than can be discovered by human reason. Prominent Romantics include Jean-Jacques Rousseau, William Wordsworth, John Keats, Lord Byron, and Johann Wolfgang von Goethe.

Romantics: See *Romanticism*

Russian Symbolism: A Russian poetic movement, derived from French symbolism, that flourished between 1894 and 1910. While some Russian Symbolists continued in the French tradition, stressing aestheticism and the importance of suggestion above didactic intent, others saw their craft as a form of mystical worship, and themselves as mediators between the supernatural and the mundane. Russian symbolists include Aleksandr Blok, Vyacheslav Ivanovich Ivanov, Fyodor Sologub, Andrey Bely, Nikolay Gumilyov, and Vladimir Sergeyevich Solovyov.

S

Satire: A work that uses ridicule, humor, and wit to criticize and provoke change in human nature and institutions. There are two major types of satire: "formal" or "direct" satire speaks directly to the reader or to a character in the work; "indirect" satire relies upon the ridiculous behavior of its characters to make its point. Formal satire is further divided into two manners: the "Horatian," which ridicules gently, and the "Juvenalian," which derides its subjects harshly and bitterly. Voltaire's novella *Candide* is an indirect satire. Jonathan Swift's essay "A Modest Proposal" is a Juvenalian satire.

Scansion: The analysis or "scanning" of a poem to determine its meter and often its rhyme scheme. The most common system of scansion uses accents (slanted lines drawn above syllables) to show stressed syllables, breves (curved lines drawn above syllables) to show unstressed syllables, and vertical lines to separate each foot. In the first line of John Keats's *Endymion*, "A thing of beauty is a joy forever:" the word "thing," the first syllable of "beauty," the word "joy," and the second syllable of "forever" are stressed, while the words "A" and "of," the second

syllable of "beauty," the word "a," and the first and third syllables of "forever" are unstressed. In the second line: "Its loveliness increases; it will never" a pair of vertical lines separate the foot ending with "increases" and the one beginning with "it."

Scene: A subdivision of an act of a drama, consisting of continuous action taking place at a single time and in a single location. The beginnings and endings of scenes may be indicated by clearing the stage of actors and props or by the entrances and exits of important characters. The first act of William Shakespeare's *Winter's Tale* is comprised of two scenes.

Science Fiction: A type of narrative about or based upon real or imagined scientific theories and technology. Science fiction is often peopled with alien creatures and set on other planets or in different dimensions. Karel Capek's *R.U.R.* is a major work of science fiction.

Second Person: See *Point of View*

Semiotics: The study of how literary forms and conventions affect the meaning of language. Semioticians include Ferdinand de Saussure, Charles Sanders Pierce, Claude Levi-Strauss, Jacques Lacan, Michel Foucault, Jacques Derrida, Roland Barthes, and Julia Kristeva.

Sestet: Any six-line poem or stanza. Examples of the sestet include the last six lines of the Petrarchan sonnet form, the stanza form of Robert Burns's "A Poet's Welcome to his love-begotten Daughter," and the sestina form in W. H. Auden's "Paysage Moralise."

Setting: The time, place, and culture in which the action of a narrative takes place. The elements of setting may include geographic location, characters' physical and mental environments, prevailing cultural attitudes, or the historical time in which the action takes place. Examples of settings include the romanticized Scotland in Sir Walter Scott's "Waverley" novels, the French provincial setting in Gustave Flaubert's *Madame Bovary*, the fictional Wessex country of Thomas Hardy's novels, and the small towns of southern Ontario in Alice Munro's short stories.

Shakespearean Sonnet: See *Sonnet*

Signifying Monkey: A popular trickster figure in black folklore, with hundreds of tales about this character documented since the 19th century. Henry Louis Gates Jr. examines the history of the signifying monkey in *The Signifying Monkey: Towards a Theory of Afro-American Literary Criticism,* published in 1988.

Simile: A comparison, usually using "like" or "as", of two essentially dissimilar things, as in "coffee as cold as ice" or "He sounded like a broken record." The title of Ernest Hemingway's "Hills Like White Elephants" contains a simile.

Slang: A type of informal verbal communication that is generally unacceptable for formal writing. Slang words and phrases are often colorful exaggerations used to emphasize the speaker's point; they may also be shortened versions of an often-used word or phrase. Examples of American slang from the 1990s include "yuppie" (an acronym for Young Urban Professional), "awesome" (for "excellent"), wired (for "nervous" or "excited"), and "chill out" (for relax).

Slant Rhyme: See *Consonance*

Slave Narrative: Autobiographical accounts of American slave life as told by escaped slaves. These works first appeared during the abolition movement of the 1830s through the 1850s. Olaudah Equiano's *The Interesting Narrative of Olaudah Equiano, or Gustavus Vassa, The African* and Harriet Ann Jacobs's *Incidents in the Life of a Slave Girl* are examples of the slave narrative.

Social Realism: See *Socialist Realism*

Socialist Realism: The Socialist Realism school of literary theory was proposed by Maxim Gorky and established as a dogma by the first Soviet Congress of Writers. It demanded adherence to a communist worldview in works of literature. Its doctrines required an objective viewpoint comprehensible to the working classes and themes of social struggle featuring strong proletarian heroes. A successful work of socialist realism is Nikolay Ostrovsky's *Kak zakalyalas stal* (*How the Steel Was Tempered*). Also known as Social Realism.

Soliloquy: A monologue in a drama used to give the audience information and to develop the speaker's character. It is typically a projection of the speaker's innermost thoughts. Usually delivered while the speaker is alone on stage, a soliloquy is intended to present an illusion of unspoken reflection. A celebrated soliloquy is Hamlet's "To be or not to be" speech in William Shakespeare's *Hamlet.*

Sonnet: A fourteen-line poem, usually composed in iambic pentameter, employing one of several rhyme schemes. There are three major types of sonnets, upon which all other variations of the form are based: the "Petrarchan" or "Italian" sonnet, the "Shakespearean" or "English" sonnet, and the "Spenserian" sonnet. A Petrarchan sonnet consists of an octave rhymed *abbaabba* and a "sestet" rhymed either *cdecde, cdccdc,* or *cdedce.* The octave poses a question or problem, relates a narrative, or puts forth a proposition; the sestet presents a solution to the problem, comments upon the narrative, or applies the proposition put forth in the octave. The Shakespearean sonnet is divided into three quatrains and a couplet rhymed *abab cdcd efef gg.* The couplet provides an epigrammatic comment on the narrative or problem put forth in the quatrains. The Spenserian sonnet uses three quatrains and a couplet like the Shakespearean, but links their three rhyme schemes in this way: *abab bcbc cdcd ee.* The Spenserian sonnet develops its theme in two parts like the Petrarchan, its final six lines resolving a problem, analyzing a narrative, or applying a proposition put forth in its first eight lines. Examples of sonnets can be found in Petrarch's *Canzoniere,* Edmund Spenser's *Amoretti,* Elizabeth Barrett Browning's *Sonnets from the Portuguese,* Rainer Maria Rilke's *Sonnets to Orpheus,* and Adrienne Rich's poem "The Insusceptibles."

Spenserian Sonnet: See *Sonnet*

Spenserian Stanza: A nine-line stanza having eight verses in iambic pentameter, its ninth verse in iambic hexameter, and the rhyme scheme ababbcbcc. This stanza form was first used by Edmund Spenser in his allegorical poem *The Faerie Queene.*

Spondee: In poetry meter, a foot consisting of two long or stressed syllables occurring together. This form is quite rare in English verse, and is usually composed of two monosyllabic words. The first foot in the following line from Robert Burns's "Green Grow the Rashes" is an example of a spondee: Green grow the rashes, O

Sprung Rhythm: Versification using a specific number of accented syllables per line but disregarding the number of unaccented syllables that fall in each line, producing an irregular rhythm in the poem. Gerard Manley Hopkins, who coined the term "sprung rhythm," is the most notable practitioner of this technique.

Stanza: A subdivision of a poem consisting of lines grouped together, often in recurring patterns of rhyme, line length, and meter. Stanzas may also serve as units of thought in a poem much like paragraphs in prose. Examples of stanza forms include the quatrain, *terza rima, ottava rima,* Spenserian, and the so-called *In Memoriam* stanza from Alfred, Lord Tennyson's poem by that title. The following is an example of the latter form: Love is and was my lord and king, And in his presence I attend To hear the tidings of my friend, Which every hour his couriers bring.

Stereotype: A stereotype was originally the name for a duplication made during the printing process; this led to its modern definition as a person or thing that is (or is assumed to be) the same as all others of its type. Common stereotypical characters include the absent-minded professor, the nagging wife, the troublemaking teenager, and the kindhearted grandmother.

Stream of Consciousness: A narrative technique for rendering the inward experience of a character. This technique is designed to give the impression of an ever-changing series of thoughts, emotions, images, and memories in the spontaneous and seemingly illogical order that they occur in life. The textbook example of stream of consciousness is the last section of James Joyce's *Ulysses.*

Structuralism: A twentieth-century movement in literary criticism that examines how literary texts arrive at their meanings, rather than the meanings themselves. There are two major types of structuralist analysis: one examines the way patterns of linguistic structures unify a specific text and emphasize certain elements of that text, and the other interprets the way literary forms and conventions affect the meaning of language itself. Prominent structuralists include Michel Foucault, Roman Jakobson, and Roland Barthes.

Structure: The form taken by a piece of literature. The structure may be made obvious for ease of understanding, as in nonfiction works, or may obscured for artistic purposes, as in some poetry or seemingly "unstructured" prose. Examples of common literary structures include the plot of a narrative, the acts and scenes of a drama, and such poetic forms as the Shakespearean sonnet and the Pindaric ode.

Sturm und Drang: A German term meaning "storm and stress." It refers to a German literary movement of the 1770s and 1780s that reacted against the order and rationalism of the enlightenment, focusing instead on the intense experience of extraordinary individuals. Highly romantic, works of this movement, such as Johann Wolfgang von Goethe's *Gotz von Berlichingen,* are typified by realism, rebelliousness, and intense emotionalism.

Style: A writer's distinctive manner of arranging words to suit his or her ideas and purpose in writing. The unique imprint of the author's personality upon his or her writing, style is the product of an author's way of arranging ideas and his or her use of diction, different sentence structures, rhythm, figures of speech, rhetorical principles, and other elements of composition. Styles may be classified according to period (Metaphysical, Augustan, Georgian), individual authors (Chaucerian, Miltonic, Jamesian), level (grand, middle, low, plain), or language (scientific, expository, poetic, journalistic).

Subject: The person, event, or theme at the center of a work of literature. A work may have one or more subjects of each type, with shorter works tending to have fewer and longer works tending to have more. The subjects of James Baldwin's novel *Go Tell It on the Mountain* include the themes of father-son relationships, religious conversion, black life, and sexuality. The subjects of Anne Frank's *Diary of a Young Girl* include Anne and her family members as well as World War II, the Holocaust, and the themes of war, isolation, injustice, and racism.

Subjectivity: Writing that expresses the author's personal feelings about his subject, and which may or may not include factual information about the subject. Subjectivity is demonstrated in James Joyce's *Portrait of the Artist as a Young Man,* Samuel Butler's *The Way of All Flesh,* and Thomas Wolfe's *Look Homeward, Angel.*

Subplot: A secondary story in a narrative. A subplot may serve as a motivating or complicating force for the main plot of the work, or it may provide emphasis for, or relief from, the main plot. The conflict between the Capulets and the Montagues in William Shakespeare's *Romeo and Juliet* is an example of a subplot.

Surrealism: A term introduced to criticism by Guillaume Apollinaire and later adopted by Andre Breton. It refers to a French literary and artistic movement founded in the 1920s. The Surrealists sought to express unconscious thoughts and feelings in their works. The best-known technique used for achieving this aim was automatic writing—transcriptions of spontaneous outpourings from the unconscious. The Surrealists proposed to unify the contrary levels of conscious and unconscious, dream and reality, objectivity and subjectivity into a new level of "super-realism." Surrealism can be found in the poetry of Paul Eluard, Pierre Reverdy, and Louis Aragon, among others.

Suspense: A literary device in which the author maintains the audience's attention through the buildup of events, the outcome of which will soon be revealed. Suspense in William Shakespeare's *Hamlet* is sustained throughout by the question of whether or not the Prince will achieve what he has been instructed to do and of what he intends to do.

Syllogism: A method of presenting a logical argument. In its most basic form, the syllogism consists of a major premise, a minor premise, and a conclusion. An example of a syllogism is: Major premise: When it snows, the streets get wet. Minor premise: It is snowing. Conclusion: The streets are wet.

Symbol: Something that suggests or stands for something else without losing its original identity. In literature, symbols combine their literal meaning with the suggestion of an abstract concept. Literary symbols are of two types: those that carry complex associations of meaning no matter what their contexts, and those that derive their suggestive meaning from their functions in specific literary works. Examples of symbols are sunshine suggesting happiness, rain suggesting sorrow, and storm clouds suggesting despair.

Symbolism: This term has two widely accepted meanings. In historical criticism, it denotes an early modernist literary movement initiated in France during the nineteenth century that reacted against the prevailing standards of realism. Writers in this movement aimed to evoke, indirectly and symbolically, an order of being beyond the material world of the five senses. Poetic expression of personal emotion figured strongly in the movement, typically by means of a private set of symbols uniquely identifiable with the individual poet. The principal aim of the Symbolists was to express in words the highly complex feelings that grew out of everyday contact with the world. In a broader sense, the term "symbolism" refers to the use of one object to represent another. Early members of the Symbolist movement included the French authors Charles Baudelaire and Arthur Rimbaud; William Butler Yeats, James Joyce, and T. S. Eliot were influenced as the movement moved to Ireland, England, and the United States. Examples of the concept of symbolism include a flag that stands for a nation or movement, or an empty cupboard used to suggest hopelessness, poverty, and despair.

Symbolist: See *Symbolism*

Symbolist Movement: See *Symbolism*

Sympathetic Fallacy: See *Affective Fallacy*

T

Tale: A story told by a narrator with a simple plot and little character development. Tales are usually relatively short and often carry a simple message. Examples of tales can be found in the work of Rudyard Kipling, Somerset Maugham, Saki, Anton Chekhov, Guy de Maupassant, and Armistead Maupin.

Tall Tale: A humorous tale told in a straightforward, credible tone but relating absolutely impossible events or feats of the characters. Such tales were commonly told of frontier adventures during the settlement of the west in the United States. Tall tales have been spun around such legendary heroes as

Mike Fink, Paul Bunyan, Davy Crockett, Johnny Appleseed, and Captain Stormalong as well as the real-life William F. Cody and Annie Oakley. Literary use of tall tales can be found in Washington Irving's *History of New York,* Mark Twain's *Life on the Mississippi,* and in the German R. F. Raspe's *Baron Munchausen's Narratives of His Marvellous Travels and Campaigns in Russia.*

Tanka: A form of Japanese poetry similar to *haiku.* A *tanka* is five lines long, with the lines containing five, seven, five, seven, and seven syllables respectively. Skilled *tanka* authors include Ishikawa Takuboku, Masaoka Shiki, Amy Lowell, and Adelaide Crapsey.

Teatro Grottesco: See *Theater of the Grotesque*

Terza Rima: A three-line stanza form in poetry in which the rhymes are made on the last word of each line in the following manner: the first and third lines of the first stanza, then the second line of the first stanza and the first and third lines of the second stanza, and so on with the middle line of any stanza rhyming with the first and third lines of the following stanza. An example of *terza rima* is Percy Bysshe Shelley's "The Triumph of Love": As in that trance of wondrous thought I lay This was the tenour of my waking dream. Methought I sate beside a public way Thick strewn with summer dust, and a great stream Of people there was hurrying to and fro Numerous as gnats upon the evening gleam, . . .

Tetrameter: See *Meter*

Textual Criticism: A branch of literary criticism that seeks to establish the authoritative text of a literary work. Textual critics typically compare all known manuscripts or printings of a single work in order to assess the meanings of differences and revisions. This procedure allows them to arrive at a definitive version that (supposedly) corresponds to the author's original intention. Textual criticism was applied during the Renaissance to salvage the classical texts of Greece and Rome, and modern works have been studied, for instance, to undo deliberate correction or censorship, as in the case of novels by Stephen Crane and Theodore Dreiser.

Theater of Cruelty: Term used to denote a group of theatrical techniques designed to eliminate the psychological and emotional distance between actors and audience. This concept, introduced in the 1930s in France, was intended to inspire a more intense theatrical experience than conventional theater allowed. The "cruelty" of this dramatic theory signified not sadism but heightened actor/audience involvement in the dramatic event. The theater of cruelty was theorized by Antonin Artaud in his *Le Theatre et son double* (*The Theatre and Its Double*), and also appears in the work of Jerzy Grotowski, Jean Genet, Jean Vilar, and Arthur Adamov, among others.

Theater of the Absurd: A post-World War II dramatic trend characterized by radical theatrical innovations. In works influenced by the Theater of the absurd, nontraditional, sometimes grotesque characterizations, plots, and stage sets reveal a meaningless universe in which human values are irrelevant. Existentialist themes of estrangement, absurdity, and futility link many of the works of this movement. The principal writers of the Theater of the Absurd are Samuel Beckett, Eugene Ionesco, Jean Genet, and Harold Pinter.

Theater of the Grotesque: An Italian theatrical movement characterized by plays written around the ironic and macabre aspects of daily life in the World War I era. Theater of the Grotesque was named after the play *The Mask and the Face* by Luigi Chiarelli, which was described as "a grotesque in three acts." The movement influenced the work of Italian dramatist Luigi Pirandello, author of *Right You Are, If You Think You Are.* Also known as *Teatro Grottesco.*

Theme: The main point of a work of literature. The term is used interchangeably with thesis. The theme of William Shakespeare's *Othello*—jealousy—is a common one.

Thesis: A thesis is both an essay and the point argued in the essay. Thesis novels and thesis plays share the quality of containing a thesis which is supported through the action of the story. A master's thesis and a doctoral dissertation are two theses required of graduate students.

Thesis Play: See *Thesis*

Three Unities: See *Unities*

Tone: The author's attitude toward his or her audience may be deduced from the tone of the work. A formal tone may create distance or convey politeness, while an informal tone may encourage a friendly, intimate, or intrusive feeling in the reader. The author's attitude toward his or her subject matter may also be deduced from the tone of the words he or she uses in discussing it. The tone of John F. Kennedy's speech which included the appeal to "ask not what your country can do for you" was intended to instill feelings of camaraderie and national pride in listeners.

Tragedy: A drama in prose or poetry about a noble, courageous hero of excellent character who, because of some tragic character flaw or *hamartia*, brings ruin upon him- or herself. Tragedy treats its subjects in a dignified and serious manner, using poetic language to help evoke pity and fear and bring about catharsis, a purging of these emotions. The tragic form was practiced extensively by the ancient Greeks. In the Middle Ages, when classical works were virtually unknown, tragedy came to denote any works about the fall of persons from exalted to low conditions due to any reason: fate, vice, weakness, etc. According to the classical definition of tragedy, such works present the "pathetic"—that which evokes pity—rather than the tragic. The classical form of tragedy was revived in the sixteenth century; it flourished especially on the Elizabethan stage. In modern times, dramatists have attempted to adapt the form to the needs of modern society by drawing their heroes from the ranks of ordinary men and women and defining the nobility of these heroes in terms of spirit rather than exalted social standing. The greatest classical example of tragedy is Sophocles' *Oedipus Rex*. The "pathetic" derivation is exemplified in "The Monk's Tale" in Geoffrey Chaucer's *Canterbury Tales*. Notable works produced during the sixteenth century revival include William Shakespeare's *Hamlet, Othello,* and *King Lear*. Modern dramatists working in the tragic tradition include Henrik Ibsen, Arthur Miller, and Eugene O'Neill.

Tragedy of Blood: See *Revenge Tragedy*

Tragic Flaw: In a tragedy, the quality within the hero or heroine which leads to his or her downfall. Examples of the tragic flaw include Othello's jealousy and Hamlet's indecisiveness, although most great tragedies defy such simple interpretation.

Transcendentalism: An American philosophical and religious movement, based in New England from around 1835 until the Civil War. Transcendentalism was a form of American romanticism that had its roots abroad in the works of Thomas Carlyle, Samuel Coleridge, and Johann Wolfgang von Goethe. The Transcendentalists stressed the importance of intuition and subjective experience in communication with God. They rejected religious dogma and texts in favor of mysticism and scientific naturalism. They pursued truths that lie beyond the "colorless" realms perceived by reason and the senses and were active social reformers in public education, women's rights, and the abolition of slavery. Prominent members of the group include Ralph Waldo Emerson and Henry David Thoreau.

Trickster: A character or figure common in Native American and African literature who uses his ingenuity to defeat enemies and escape difficult situations. Tricksters are most often animals, such as the spider, hare, or coyote, although they may take the form of humans as well. Examples of trickster tales include Thomas King's *A Coyote Columbus Story,* Ashley F. Bryan's *The Dancing Granny* and Ishmael Reed's *The Last Days of Louisiana Red*.

Trimeter: See *Meter*

Triple Rhyme: See *Rhyme*

Trochee: See *Foot*

U

Understatement: See *Irony*

Unities: Strict rules of dramatic structure, formulated by Italian and French critics of the Renaissance and based loosely on the principles of drama discussed by Aristotle in his *Poetics*. Foremost among these rules were the three unities of action, time, and place that compelled a dramatist to: (1) construct a single plot with a beginning, middle, and end that details the causal relationships of action and character; (2) restrict the action to the events of a single day; and (3) limit the scene to a single place or city. The unities were observed faithfully by continental European writers until the Romantic Age, but they were never regularly observed in English drama. Modern dramatists are typically more concerned with a unity of impression or emotional effect than with any of the classical unities. The unities are observed in Pierre Corneille's tragedy *Polyeuctes* and Jean-Baptiste Racine's *Phedre.* Also known as Three Unities.

Urban Realism: A branch of realist writing that attempts to accurately reflect the often harsh facts of modern urban existence. Some works by Stephen Crane, Theodore Dreiser, Charles Dickens, Fyodor Dostoyevsky, Emile Zola, Abraham Cahan, and Henry Fuller feature urban realism. Modern examples include Claude Brown's *Manchild in the Promised Land* and Ron Milner's *What the Wine Sellers Buy.*

Utopia: A fictional perfect place, such as "paradise" or "heaven." Early literary utopias were included in Plato's *Republic* and Sir Thomas More's *Utopia,* while more modern utopias can be found in Samuel Butler's *Erewhon,* Theodor Herzka's *A Visit to Freeland,* and H. G. Wells' *A Modern Utopia.*

Utopian: See *Utopia*

Utopianism: See *Utopia*

V

Verisimilitude: Literally, the appearance of truth. In literary criticism, the term refers to aspects of a work of literature that seem true to the reader. Verisimilitude is achieved in the work of Honore de Balzac, Gustave Flaubert, and Henry James, among other late nineteenth-century realist writers.

Vers de societe: See *Occasional Verse*

Vers libre: See *Free Verse*

Verse: A line of metered language, a line of a poem, or any work written in verse. The following line of verse is from the epic poem *Don Juan* by Lord Byron: "My way is to begin with the beginning."

Versification: The writing of verse. Versification may also refer to the meter, rhyme, and other mechanical components of a poem. Composition of a "Roses are red, violets are blue" poem to suit an occasion is a common form of versification practiced by students.

Victorian: Refers broadly to the reign of Queen Victoria of England (1837-1901) and to anything with qualities typical of that era. For example, the qualities of smug narrowmindedness, bourgeois materialism, faith in social progress, and priggish morality are often considered Victorian. This stereotype is contradicted by such dramatic intellectual developments as the theories of Charles Darwin, Karl Marx, and Sigmund Freud (which stirred strong debates in England) and the critical attitudes of serious Victorian writers like Charles Dickens and George Eliot. In literature, the Victorian Period was the great age of the English novel, and the latter part of the era saw the rise of movements such as decadence and symbolism. Works of Victorian literature include the poetry of Robert Browning and Alfred, Lord Tennyson, the criticism of Matthew Arnold and John Ruskin, and the novels of Emily Bronte, William Makepeace Thackeray, and Thomas Hardy. Also known as Victorian Age and Victorian Period.

Victorian Age: See *Victorian*

Victorian Period: See *Victorian*

W

Weltanschauung: A German term referring to a person's worldview or philosophy. Examples of *weltanschauung* include Thomas Hardy's view of the human being as the victim of fate, destiny, or impersonal forces and circumstances, and the disillusioned and laconic cynicism expressed by such poets of the 1930s as W. H. Auden, Sir Stephen Spender, and Sir William Empson.

Weltschmerz: A German term meaning "world pain." It describes a sense of anguish about the nature of existence, usually associated with a melancholy, pessimistic attitude. *Weltschmerz* was expressed in England by George Gordon, Lord Byron in his *Manfred* and *Childe Harold's Pilgrimage,* in France by Viscount de Chateaubriand, Alfred de Vigny, and Alfred de Musset, in Russia by Aleksandr Pushkin and Mikhail Lermontov, in Poland by Juliusz Slowacki, and in America by Nathaniel Hawthorne.

Z

Zarzuela: A type of Spanish operetta. Writers of *zarzuelas* include Lope de Vega and Pedro Calderon.

Zeitgeist: A German term meaning "spirit of the time." It refers to the moral and intellectual trends of a given era. Examples of *zeitgeist* include the preoccupation with the more morbid aspects of dying and death in some Jacobean literature, especially in the works of dramatists Cyril Tourneur and John Webster, and the decadence of the French Symbolists.

Cumulative Author/Title Index

Cumulative
Nationality/Ethnicity Index

Hispanic

Cruz, Nilo
Anna in the Tropics: V21
Fornes, Maria Irene
Fefu and Her Friends: V25
Valdez, Luis
Zoot Suit: V5

Indochinese

Duras, Marguerite
India Song: V21

Irish

Beckett, Samuel
Endgame: V18
Krapp's Last Tape: V7
Waiting for Godot: V2
Behan, Brendan
The Hostage: V7
Friel, Brian
Dancing at Lughnasa: V11
Leonard, Hugh
The Au Pair Man: V24
Da: V13
O'Casey, Sean
Red Roses for Me: V19
Shaw, George Bernard
Arms and the Man: V22
Major Barbara: V3
Man and Superman: V6
Mrs. Warren's Profession: V19
Pygmalion: V1
Saint Joan: V11
Sheridan, Richard Brinsley
The Critic: V14
The Rivals: V15
School for Scandal: V4
Synge, J. M.
Playboy of the Western World:
V18
Wilde, Oscar
An Ideal Husband: V21
The Importance of Being Earnest:
V4
Lady Windermere's Fan: V9
Salome: V8

Italian

Fo, Dario
Accidental Death of an Anarchist:
V23
Ginzburg, Natalia
The Advertisement: V14
Pirandello, Luigi
*Right You Are, If You Think You
Are:* V9

*Six Characters in Search of an
Author:* V4

Japanese

Abe, Kobo
The Man Who Turned into a Stick:
V14
Iizuka, Naomi
36 Views: V21

Jewish

Gardner, Herb
A Thousand Clowns: V20
Mamet, David
Reunion: V15
Odets, Clifford
Rocket to the Moon: V20
Sherman, Martin
Bent: V20
Simon, Neil
Biloxi Blues: V12
Brighton Beach Memoirs: V6
Lost in Yonkers: V18
The Odd Couple: V2
The Prisoner of Second Avenue:
V24
Uhry, Alfred
Driving Miss Daisy: V11
The Last Night of Ballyhoo: V15

Mexican

Carballido, Emilio
I, Too, Speak of the Rose: V4

Native Canadian

Highway, Tomson
The Rez Sisters: V2

Nigerian

Clark, John Pepper
The Raft: V13
Soyinka, Wole
Death and the King's Horseman:
V10

Norwegian

Ibsen, Henrik
Brand: V16
A Doll's House: V1
An Enemy of the People: V25
Ghosts: V11
Hedda Gabler: V6
The Master Builder: V15
Peer Gynt: V8
The Wild Duck: V10

Romanian

Ionesco, Eugène
The Bald Soprano: V4
The Chairs: V9
Rhinoceros: V25

Russian

Chekhov, Anton
The Cherry Orchard: V1
The Seagull: V12
The Three Sisters: V10
Uncle Vanya: V5
Gogol, Nikolai
The Government Inspector: V12
Gorki, Maxim
The Lower Depths: V9
Turgenev, Ivan
A Month in the Country: V6

Scottish

Barrie, J(ames) M.
Peter Pan: V7

South African

Fugard, Athol
Boesman & Lena: V6
A Lesson from Aloes: V24
"Master Harold" . . . and the Boys:
V3
Sizwe Bansi is Dead: V10

Spanish

Buero Vallejo, Antonio
The Sleep of Reason: V11
Calderón de la Barca, Pedro
Life Is a Dream: V23
García Lorca, Federico
Blood Wedding: V10
The House of Bernarda Alba: V4

Swedish

Strindberg, August
The Ghost Sonata: V9
Miss Julie: V4

Swiss

Frisch, Max
The Firebugs: V25

Venezuelan

Kaufman, Moisés
The Laramie Project: V22

Subject/Theme Index

Politics
 Hippolytus: 158, 159
 Rhinoceros: 212
 Serious Money: 258, 263–264
Pollution
 An Enemy of the People: 43, 44
Positivism
 Into the Woods: 184, 185, 192
Post World War II era
 The American Dream: 8, 13–14
Postmodernism
 Rhinoceros: 214
 Into the Woods: 184–189
Power
 The Dumb Waiter: 36
 Fefu and Her Friends: 87–88, 97,
  98
 Rhinoceros: 201–202
 Serious Money: 248–249, 255
Power
 Serious Money: 248–249
Powerlessness
 The Dumb Waiter: 30
 Fefu and Her Friends: 85
 Into the Woods: 171
Preconceptions
 Fefu and Her Friends: 104
Professional women
 *Fabulation; or, The Re-Education
  of Undine:* 74–75
Prose plays
 An Enemy of the People: 53
Psychology of Suffering, The
 Hippolytus: 151–152
Purgatory
 The Dumb Waiter: 30
Purity
 Hippolytus: 153
Pursuit
 Into the Woods: 165, 178

R

Race
 The Dumb Waiter: 41
Rapid pace
 *Fabulation; or, The Re-Education
  of Undine:* 73
 Into the Woods: 165, 174
Rationalism
 Rhinoceros: 200, 202–203,
  208–209, 217
Rationalization
 Rhinoceros: 211
Realism
 The American Dream: 20, 21
 Fefu and Her Friends: 100
 The Second Shepherds' Play: 221
Recognition
 An Enemy of the People: 53–54
Relationships between Women
 Fefu and Her Friends: 86–87

Relativism
 Into the Woods: 189, 190
Religion
 The Second Shepherds' Play:
  226–228
 Stanley: 280, 282
Religious Belief
 The Second Shepherds' Play: 226
Remorse
 Frozen: 134, 135
Resignation
 The American Dream: 18
Resistance
 The Dumb Waiter: 31–32
Responsibility
 Rhinoceros: 203
 Into the Woods: 191
Restorative justice
 Frozen: 137
Revenge
 Frozen: 135, 141
 Hippolytus: 158, 161
 Into the Woods: 181
Revenge and Forgiveness
 Frozen: 135–136
Reversal of fortune
 An Enemy of the People: 53, 58
 Hippolytus: 154, 155
Rhetoric
 Hippolytus: 154
Rhyming couplets
 Serious Money: 250
Riches-to-rags story
 *Fabulation; or, The Re-Education
  of Undine:* 66

S

Sacred and profane
 The Second Shepherds' Play: 236
Sadism
 The American Dream: 14–15
Sarcasm
 The American Dream: 10
 The Firebugs: 120, 121–122
Satire
 The American Dream: 10
 *Fabulation; or, The Re-Education
  of Undine:* 76
 The Firebugs: 116, 119, 120
 Rhinoceros: 209
 Serious Money: 241, 261, 267,
  269
Satisfaction
 The American Dream: 1, 9, 14
Science
 An Enemy of the People: 54–55
Self-control
 Hippolytus: 162
Self-deception
 An Enemy of the People: 61
 The Firebugs: 112–113

Self-Deception
 The Firebugs: 112–113
Self-interest
 An Enemy of the People: 44, 52, 58
 Hippolytus: 157, 158
Self-Interest
 An Enemy of the People: 52
Self-justification
 The Firebugs: 120
Self-knowledge
 The American Dream: 17
 An Enemy of the People: 59
 *Fabulation; or, The Re-Education
  of Undine:* 70
Self-righteousness
 Hippolytus: 160
Selfishness
 The American Dream: 7
 Stanley: 280–281, 286, 290
 Into the Woods: 165
**Selfishness and Narcissism versus
  Self-Sacrificial Love**
 Stanley: 280–281
Selflessness
 Stanley: 278, 280–281
Set
 Rhinoceros: 209
Sex and sexuality
 Fefu and Her Friends: 81, 87–88
 Hippolytus: 154–155, 162–163
 Stanley: 279–280
Sexual politics
 Serious Money: 259
**Sexuality, Power, and Gender
  Roles**
 Fefu and Her Friends: 87–88
Shared experience
 *Fabulation; or, The Re-Education
  of Undine:* 74
Single motherhood
 *Fabulation; or, The Re-Education
  of Undine:* 74
Small town life
 An Enemy of the People: 54
Social commentary
 The American Dream: 1, 17
 An Enemy of the People: 56–58
 Fefu and Her Friends: 102
 Rhinoceros: 212
 The Second Shepherds' Play:
  231
 Serious Money: 241
Social realism
 An Enemy of the People: 60–61
Social responsibility
 The American Dream: 6
 An Enemy of the People: 52
Social Responsibility
 An Enemy of the People: 52
Soliloquy
 The Second Shepherds' Play:
  227

Subject / Theme Index

LONGWOOD PUBLIC LIBRARY
Middle Country Road
Middle Island, NY 11953
(631) 924-6400
LIBRARY HOURS

Monday-Friday	9:30 a.m. - 9:00 p.m.
Saturday	9:30 a.m. - 5:00 p.m.
Sunday (Sept-June)	1:00 p.m. - 5:00 p.m.